RISK MANAGEMENT AND INSURANCE

Etti Baranoff

Virginia Commonwealth University

www.wiley.com/college/baranoff

To Steve, Dalit, Liat, Aviva, Josh, Jeremy, and Timy, for their patience and support.

Acquisitions Editor   *Leslie Kraham*
Marketing Manager   *Charity Robey*
Production Manager   *Lari Bishop*
Designer   *Jennifer Fisher*
Illustration Editor   *Benjamin Reece*
Copy Editor   *Christy Goldfinch*
Indexer   *Jacqueline Brownstein*
Cover Design   *Shoshanna Turek*
Cover Image   *© PhotoDisc, Inc.*

This book was set in Minion and was printed and bound by R. R. Donnelly & Sons. The cover was printed by Lehigh Press.

ISBN 0-471-27087-3

Printed in the United States of America

10 9 8 7 6 5 4 3

BRIEF CONTENTS

CONTENTS

11 Managing Automobile Risks   238

PREFACE

INTRODUCTION AND BACKGROUND

This textbook, designed to reflect the dynamic nature of the field of risk management and insurance, serves as an introduction to the field. This is a comprehensive revision of the seventh edition of *Risk Management and Insurance,* by S. Travis Prichett, Joan T. Schmit, Helen I. Doerpinghaus, and the late James L. Athearn. It includes new pedagogical enhancements, as well as discussion of new products, laws, conditions, and technologies in the field.

In the first years of this century, the terrorist attacks on the World Trade Center and the Pentagon and the accounting scandals of Enron and WorldCom all highlighted the importance of risk management and insurance. Giving particular attention to the market's increased sense of vulnerability and the newest technologies, *Risk Management and Insurance* provides a clear introduction to the complexities of this field. With chapters including topics such as e-risks and enterprise risk, EGTRRA 2001, loss development triangles, the health insurance evolution, the newest property/casualty endorsements, and a focus on connecting each chapter to the bigger picture, the objective is to show students how the latest developments and the field's traditional approaches fit together into holistic risk management.

In both the areas of property/casualty and life/health, the newest products, laws, and applications are explained in simple terms to allow hands-on learning. To this end, sample policies, examples, and cases are provided.

The objective of this revision is to retain the strengths of the previous edition while enhancing the pedagogical methods with new and updated areas relevant to the field of risk and insurance today. The clarity and simplicity of the previous text with its operational emphasis is maintained.

TEXT ORGANIZATION

- **An emphasis on the big picture—the Connection section.** The insurance industry, operations, and markets have been brought to the front of the book to clarify the "big picture" for students. Risk and insurance can appear to be a complex puzzle composed of many pieces. In addition to the early overview of industry, operations, and markets, a "Connection" section begins each chapter to highlight the relationships between various concepts and components of risk and insurance, so that students know how the pieces fit together.

- **Chapter 3 presents current risk management practices, including enterprise risk management.** The chapter moves from traditional risk management through risk mapping to enterprise risk management, including the use of the capital markets and cat bonds. Chapter 3 can be used to introduce risk management or for advanced study. Out of the cases at the end of the text, two are particularly relevant to this chapter: Case 3 provides advanced risk management tools for a large corporation and Case 4 experiments with the financial risk management tools described in Chapter 3.

- **Chapter 4 contains a review of insurance company operations and loss development techniques.** The chapter includes an actuarial loss development triangle technique for loss reserves and rate calculations. Understanding this process of estimating future losses based on past losses is at the heart of insurance operations. Students who understand how insurance companies deal with losses will understand the underlying dynamic of the industry. Thus, the up-front study of the loss development technique in this chapter is part of a conceptual framework that will help students learn the details of insurance that are covered later in the text.

- **Chapter 5 contains a review of insurance markets, underwriting cycles, regulated and unregulated markets, and regulation.** The chapter is designed to furnish an understanding of the global operations of insurance markets, so students can appreciate the importance of market conditions (and the underwriting cycles) on risk management decisions. The types of insurance institutions and the U.S. insurance regulation today are discussed, including the most recent updates. The chapter incorporates the insurance implications of the Gramm-Leach-Bliley (GLBA) Financial Services Modernization Act of November 12, 1999.

- **E-commerce risk:** This emerging and evolving risk is covered in detail in Chapter 8, which is devoted to property risk in general, and Chapter 9, which is centered around liability risks.

- **Employee benefits and individual life/health products:** All new laws are incorporated, including EGTRRA 2001, along with case examples of a dental office for pensions, comparative matrices for group health insurance and group underwriting, and rate quotes and policy features for individual health policies (in Chapter 19). This area is supplemented with Case 2, an employee benefits portfolio for a hypothetical company.

- **Social Security:** The chapter is updated with the most recent year's data (2003). All data will be kept current on the text's Web site.

- **Case studies:** The book begins with an introductory case on the losses of September 11, 2001, and concludes with a section featuring comprehensive cases in risk management and insurance for personal needs and business needs. These cases help students recognize the relevancy and applications of the book's concepts in the real world.

  - **Introduction with cases:** The introduction provides an overview of all the elements of the textbook, using the huge losses of September 11 as a first glimpse into the field. Two victim's families are featured, and the insurance coverages discussed include the United States' social insurance programs, employer provided employee benefits, and private insurance. Also, one business that sustained losses during September 11 is featured, and this raises discussion of business interruption coverage.

  - **Conclusion with case studies:** To complete the "big picture" of holistic risk for a family with hand-on application, Case 1 features the hypothetical Smith family and their risk management portfolio. To complete the understanding of the employee benefits packages offered by employers, Case 2 is featured. Cases 3 and 4 are for more advanced risk management techniques to augment Chapter 3.

NEW FEATURES

- **Important Issues:** Each chapter is filled with current real-life examples to liven up the study for the student and to clearly show the application of concepts of risks in our everyday lives. Important Issues boxes include discussions on topics such as punitive damages, mortality improvements, recent laws affecting health care, auto rates, business interruption issues, mold, and more.

- **Explore the Internet:** At the conclusion of each "Important Issues" box, the reader is directed to use Web sites applicable to the chapter and the stories. Within each chapter there are many references to Internet sites the student can use for additional information and updates.

- **Ethical Dilemma:** Each chapter features an "Ethical Dilemma" that deals with current issues, such as the federal terrorism insurance bill, redlining, obesity and lawsuits, the conversion of traditional defined benefit plans to cash balance pension plans, and the tradeoff between health care cost and benefits. At the conclusion of each story, questions are provided to prompt related discussion.

- **The newest sample ISO property/casualty personal policies and commercial endorsements** for terrorism, e-commerce, and mold coverages are discussed in detail. Hands-on examples using the policies encourage students to truly understand the workings of these policies.

- **New sample life insurance policies from State Farm** are furnished, along with a thorough explanation to give a clear understanding of the coverages and life products available in the marketplace today.

- **Student-friendly:** A clear, readable writing style helps to keep a complicated subject from becoming overwhelming. In-chapter examples and the "Ethical Dilemmas" and "Important Issues" let students apply the concepts they're learning.

- **New Discussion Questions and Exercises at the end of each chapter:** Many new questions and case exercises were added to provide more challenging applications to the students and to encourage the use of the policies provided at the back of the text.

SUPPLEMENTS

Instructors' Resources

All teaching supplements will be available for instructors to download from the password-protected instructors' companion Web site, at www.wiley.com/college/baranoff.

Instructor's Manual

This guide for instructors begins with suggestions on how to use the textbook to teach different levels of students, from beginning to intermediate. Each chapter has an orientation, complete outline, and answers to all discussion questions and exercises. In providing answers, we have included matrices for the comparison questions and spreadsheets for the more quantitative exercises.

Test Bank

The test bank consists of thirty multiple choice questions and five or more short answer questions for each chapter. Key concepts are emphasized throughout, with questions offered at a range of difficulty levels.

PowerPoint Presentations

PowerPoint slides provided for each chapter present key exhibits and outlines of the critical topics in each chapter.

Student Resources

The students' Web site, also available at www.wiley.com/college/baranoff, will furnish current reading and exercises, including updates to the Important Issues and Ethical Dilemma boxes.

ACKNOWLEDGEMENTS

This book lists one author, but it is based on the 1996 edition of the text book *Risk Management and Insurance* (seventh edition) by S. Travis Prichett, Joan T. Schmit, Helen I. Doerpinghaus, and the late James L. Athearn. Their textbook is the foundation of this text. Without this foundation and their recommendation that I undertake the overhauling of their book, I would not have accepted this large project.

My publisher, Leyh Publishing, provided extensive and excellent support in completing this work. Rick Leyh's excellent suggestions and support have been critical to my work. Rick has provided superb leadership in this undertaking. In addition, Lari Bishop, Kris Pauls, and Camille McMorrow kept the production and development work on target. The Wiley team, including Susan Elbe, Publisher, Leslie Kraham, Acquisitions Editor, and Charity Robey, Senior Marketing Manager, was very supportive. Most important to me was the exceptional work of my copyeditor and author of the Important Issues and some of the Ethical Dilemma boxes, Christy Goldfinch. Christy has been more than a copyeditor. She studied each topic and provided excellent questions and suggestions while ensuring the simplicity and clarity of the text. Many thanks also to my daughter, Dalit Baranoff, for her fine work on the test bank and the Ethical Dilemma boxes for Chapters 10 through 19, as well as for her support and additional suggestions as I wrote each chapter.

I would like to give special tribute and acknowledgment to all my students in my Risk and Insurance and Employee Benefits classes at Virginia Commonwealth University for their excellent work on projects similar to those featured in Cases 1 and 2. Special recognition is given to Jessica Duke, a Spring 2002 student, who provided much of the research and support for the e-commerce risk sections and the updates to the Social Security chapter. Most important is the work of my graduate student Denise Togger, who wrote Case 4 as a special studies project and contributed large sections of Chapter 3.

In addition, important suggestions were made by a number of colleagues who took their time to offer detailed comments on the book before its final revision. These reviewers include: Joan Lamm-Tennant, GeneralCologne Re Capital Consultants; Dan Anderson, University of Wisconsin at Madison; Dalit Baranoff, Johns Hopkins University; Cassandra Cole, Florida State University; Lee Colquitt, Auburn University; Anne Costello, University of Hartford; Mark Cross, Miami University of Ohio; Alan D. Eastman, Indiana University of Pennsylvania; Karen Epermanis, University of Mississippi; George Flanigan, Illinois State University; Lisa A. Gardner, Bradley University; Michael J. McNamara, Washington State University; Phyllis Myers, Virginia Commonwealth University; Laureen Regan, Temple University; Jerry Todd, St. Mary's University

ABOUT THE AUTHOR

Dr. Etti G. Baranoff is an associate professor of insurance and finance at Virginia Commonwealth University in Richmond, Virginia. She teaches insurance, pensions, employee benefits, and finance topics to graduate and undergraduate classes. Prior to her academic career, Dr. Baranoff was a Texas insurance regulator for twelve years, with a specialty in rate regulation, solvency studies, and modeling and legislative issues. Her career also includes experience with a life insurer, a Texas public risk pool, and consulting. Dr. Baranoff has spoken in many insurance forums and has published in the *Journal of Risk and Insurance,* the *Journal of Banking and Finance,* the *Journal of Insurance Regulation,* and *Best's Review,* among others. Her research subjects include solvency detection models, capital and risk relationship, capital, risk, organization and distribution structures relationships, risk financing, impact of insurance regulation, and risk management information systems. She received her Ph.D. in finance with minors in insurance and statistics from the University of Texas at Austin in 1993. She lives in Austin and commutes to teach at VCU. Dr. Baranoff can be contacted at: ebaranof@vcu.edu.

INTRODUCTION

Risk and Insurance after September 11, 2001

This introduction will cover the following topics:

1. An overview of the effect of September 11 on insurance markets
2. An overview of estimated losses
3. Example of losses and coverages of two hypothetical families
4. Example of losses and coverage of a hypothetical business
5. How the coverages fit together

On the morning of September 11, 2001, life as Americans had known it was turned upside down. Ripple effects touched on every aspect of American life. The world of risk immediately expanded beyond the reach of conventional assessments and into the realm of popular fiction. Before September 11, insurers adjusted their rates to account for the risk of weather-related catastrophes such as hurricanes, but not for man-made ones. Previously, Hurricane Andrew in 1992 was the largest catastrophic loss ever, with $22.896 billion in adjusted losses.

During the horrific events of September 11, the insurance industry suffered a disaster all its own.[1] Two large insurance brokerage houses, Marsh & McLennan and Aon, lost hundreds of employees at the World Trade Center. While grieving, insurers expedited assistance to the victims and their families.

In addition to the losses in human lives and property, the global economy experienced dislocations after the attack on the United States, and insurance was no exception. The worldwide insurance industry was already in the grips of a slowdown, with profitability down, losses up, and premiums rising. The man-made catastrophes of September 11 intensified the slowdown dramatically and raised major terrorism-coverage issues. The industry's capacity, measured by policyholders' surplus (that is, net worth) was hit severely. The immediate results were rate hikes in every line of insurance, lower coverage limits, elimination of terrorism coverage, and tightness (lack of availability) in the reinsurance markets.[2] Reinsurers, who insure insurance companies against large losses, experienced their greatest losses ever. One severe example is Swiss Re.[3] Swiss Re, the world's second-largest reinsurer, posted a 165 million Swiss franc ($99.0 million) loss for 2001, the company's first loss since 1868. Worse yet is Lloyd's of London, a major reinsurer, which posted "a loss of £3.11 billion ($4.53 billion) for 2001, largely as a result of claims from the September 11 terrorist attacks."[4] The year 2001 was the most difficult year for the insurance industry in memory. In addition to the September 11 attack, the failure of Enron and the problems with mold in Texas[5] contributed to major losses. This level of losses usually is accompanied by very tight markets, called "hard" markets (explained in detail in Chapter 5).[6] As noted above, in addition to rate hikes, coverages became very limited.

Insurers asked businesses to retain greater levels of the risk (to self-insure greater amounts) and offered lower limits of coverage.

The most pronounced action was the exclusion of terrorism coverage in policies that previously covered such risk. The elimination of such coverage prompted President George W. Bush to sign the terrorism bill on November 26, 2002 (see "Ethical Dilemma: Who Should Insure Against Terrorism" in Chapter 2). The government becomes involved in order to ensure smooth economic activity when the private insurance industry cannot afford to provide catastrophic coverages.

Estimates of private insurance losses from September 11, 2001, have run from $30 billion to over $90 billion by some estimates. Table A.1 shows the estimates provided by the actuarial consulting firm of Tillinghast-Towers Perrin. As shown, the majority of the difference lies in the liability line of coverage, a "long-tail" line in which losses may not be settled for many years. After all claims are ultimately reported, liability losses may range between $5 billion and $20 billion. The wide range is the result of the inability to estimate the claims that have been incurred but not yet reported (IBNR).

Table A.1 includes payment of losses to families and business affected by the events. The following sections illustrate different types of insurance coverage through the hypothetical cases of two families and one business affected by September 11. These examples are designed to bring to life the importance of insurance and the need for risk mitigation.

Every term introduced here will be covered in detail in later chapters. At the conclusion of the course, you should be able to converse freely in the terminology of risk and insurance. With the examples, cases, and detailed analysis of coverages, you will be able to understand insurance-related materials and feel comfortable with risk management in your own life.

LOSSES PAID TO HYPOTHETICAL VICTIMS' FAMILIES

To understand the spectrum of personal losses to the families, we introduce two hypothetical families who were directly affected by the World Trade Center catastrophe. The families are those of Allen Zang, who worked as a bond trader in the south tower of the World Trade Center, and his high school friend Mike Shelling, a graduate student who visited Allen on the way to a job interview. Both Mike and Allen were 34 years old and married. Mike had a six-year-old boy and Allen had three little girls.

Unfortunately, both Allen and Mike were among the casualties of the attack on the World Trade Center. But their eligibility for benefits was considerably different, since Mike

TABLE A.1

Range of Estimated Losses from September 11, 2001

Insured Loss Amounts ($ billions)

Line of Insurance	Low	High
Workers' Compensation	$ 3.0	$ 5.0
Aviation	3.0	6.0
Commercial Property	10.0	12.0
Life, AD&D	4.5	6.0
Liability	5.0	20.0
Business Interruption	3.5	7.0
Other	1.0	2.0
Total	$ 30.0	$ 58.0

Source: Tillinghast-Towers Perrin estimates (from Aon)

was not employed at the time. In the analysis of the losses or benefits paid to each family, we will first evaluate the benefits available under the social insurance programs mandated in the United States and in New York State. Second, we will evaluate the benefits available under the group insurance programs and pensions provided by employers. Third, we will evaluate the private insurance programs purchased by the families (as shown in Figure A.1). We will also evaluate the ways the families might attempt to collect benefits from negligent parties who may have contributed to the losses.

Social insurance programs include Social Security, workers' compensation, and unemployment compensation insurance (and, in a few states, state-provided disability insurance). In the United States, these programs are intended to protect members of the work force. The best-known aspect of Social Security is the mandatory plan for retirement ("old age" benefits). But the program also includes disability benefits, survivors' benefits, and Medicare. To be fully eligible, a person must have paid into the system for 40 quarters. Younger workers may be eligible to receive disability benefits and death benefits for fewer quarters, as will be explained in Chapter 15.

Table A.2 shows the benefits available to each of the families. It is important to note that both Mike and Allen were employed for at least 10 years (40 quarters). Therefore, they were fully insured for Social Security benefits, and their families were eligible to receive survivors' benefits under Social Security. Each family received the allotted $255 burial benefit. Also, since both had young children, the families were eligible for a portion of the fathers' Primary Insurance Amount (PIA). (PIA is explained further in Chapter 15.) The Social Security Administration provided the benefits immediately without official death

FIGURE A.1

Insurance Coverage Structure

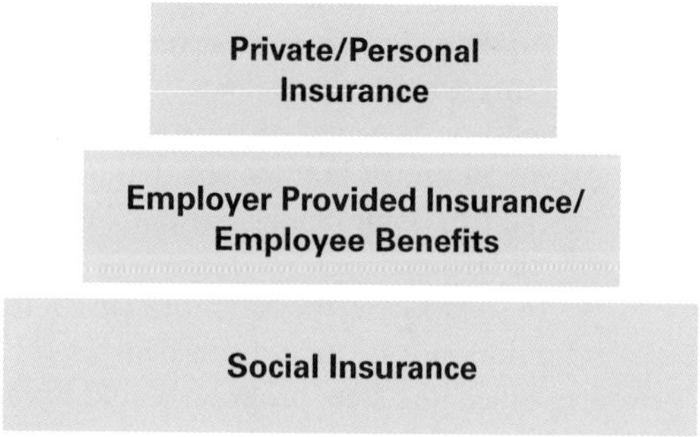

TABLE A.2

Benefits for Two Hypothetical Victims of the September 11 Attack

	Mike's Family	Allen's Family
Social insurance		
Death benefits (survivors' benefits) from Social Security	Yes	Yes
Worker's compensation	No	Yes
State disability benefits	No	No
Unemployment compensation	No	No
Employee benefits (group insurance)		
Group life	No	Yes
Group disability	No	Yes
Group medical	No	Yes (COBRA)
Pensions and 401(k)	Yes (former employers)	Yes
Personal insurance		
Individual life policy	Yes	No

certificates, as described by Commissioner Larry Massanari in his report to the House Committee on Ways and Means, Subcommittee on Social Security.[7]

Workers' compensation provides medical coverage, disability income, rehabilitation, and survivors' income (death benefits). Benefits are available only if the injury or death occurred on the job or as a result of the job. Since Allen was at the office at the time of his death, his family was eligible to receive survivors' benefits from the workers' compensation carrier of the employer. The Workers' Compensation Board of New York created a special Web site to help the families of the victims of September 11.[8]

The New York Workers' Compensation Statute states, "If the worker dies from a compensable injury, the surviving spouse and/or minor children, and lacking such, other dependents as defined by law, are entitled to weekly cash benefits. The amount is equal to two-thirds of the deceased worker's average weekly wage for the year before the accident. The weekly compensation may not exceed the weekly maximum, despite the number of dependents. If there are no surviving children, spouse, grandchildren, grandparents, brothers or sisters entitled to compensation, the surviving parents or the estate of the deceased worker may be entitled to payment of a sum of $50,000. Funeral expenses may also be paid, up to $6,000 in Metropolitan New York counties; up to $5,000 in all others."

The maximum benefit at the time of the catastrophe was $400 per week, less any Social Security benefits, for lifetime or until remarriage.[9] Thus, Allen's family received the workers' compensation benefits minus the Social Security amount. Under the workers' compensation system, the employee's family gives up the right to sue the employer. (This and other features of workers' compensation are explained in greater detail in Chapter 13.) Allen's family could not sue his employer, but Mike's family, not having received workers' compensation benefits, may believe that Allen's employer was negligent in not providing a safe place for a visitor and may sue under the employer's general liability coverage.

Victims' families can sue the parties involved in the attack. In April 2002, the husband of an investment manager who was working in the World Trade Center filed a $50 million wrongful-death suit against American Airlines, owner of the jets that were hijacked and used in the attack.[10] It may be that other victims' families will initiate or join in such lawsuits. At this point neither the families of Mike nor of Allen are contemplating taking part in such lawsuits.

In Mike's case, the New York Disability Benefits program did not apply, since the program does not include death benefits for "non-job injury." If Mike were disabled rather than killed, the state program would have paid him disability benefits. Of course, unemployment compensation does not apply here either. However, it would apply to all workers who lost their jobs involuntarily as a result of the September 11 catastrophe.

Since Allen was employed at the time, his family was also eligible to receive group benefits provided by his employer (See Chapters 16, 17, and 18 for detailed explanations.) Many employers offer group life and disability coverages, medical insurance, and some types of pension plans or 401(k) tax-free retirement investment accounts. Allen's employer gave twice the annual salary for basic group term life insurance and an additional twice the annual salary for accidental death and dismemberment (AD&D). The family received from the insurer death benefits in an amount equal to four times Allen's annual salary, free from income tax (see Chapters 14 and 19). Allen earned $100,000 annually, therefore, total death benefits were $400,000, tax-free.

Allen also elected to be covered by his employer's group short-term disability (STD) and long-term disability (LTD) plans. Those plans included supplemental provisions giving a small amount of death benefits. In Allen's case, the amount was $30,000. In addition, his employer provided a defined contribution plan and the accumulated account balance was available to his beneficiary. The accumulated amount in Allen's 401(k) account was also available to his beneficiary.

Mike's family could not take advantage of group benefits since he was not employed. Therefore, no group life or group STD and LTD were available to Mike's family. However, his pension accounts from former employers and any individual retirement accounts (IRAs) were available to his beneficiary.

Survivors' medical insurance was a major concern. Allen's wife did not work and the family had medical coverage from Allen's employer. Allen's wife decided to continue the health coverage the family had from her husband's employer under the COBRA law (Consolidated Omnibus Budget Reconciliation Act of 1986). The law provided for the continuation of health insurance up to thirty-six months for the widow at the whole cost of the coverage (both the employee and the employer's cost) plus two percent (see Chapter 17).

In the case of Mike's family, the situation was different since Mike was in graduate school. His wife covered the family under her employer's health coverage. She simply continued this coverage.

The third layer of available coverage is personal insurance programs. Here, the families' personal risk management comes into play. When Mike decided to return to school, he and his wife consulted with a reputable financial planner who helped them in their risk management and financial planning. Mike had made a series of successful career moves. In his last senior position at an Internet start-up company, he was able to cash in his stock options and create a sizable investment account for his family. Also, just before beginning graduate school, Mike purchased a $1 million life insurance policy on his life and $500,000 on his wife's life. They decided to purchase a 20-year level term life rather than a universal life policy (for details, see Chapter 14) because they wanted to invest some of their money in a new home and a vacation home on Fire Island, off Long Island.

The amount of insurance bought for his wife was lower because she already had sizable group life coverage under her employer's group life insurance package. Subsequent to Mike's death, his wife received the $1 million in death benefits within three weeks. Despite not having a death certificate, she was able to show evidence that her husband was at the World Trade Center at the time. She had a recording on her voice mail at work from Mike telling her that he was going to try to run down the stairs. The message was interrupted by the sound of the building collapsing. Thus, Mike's beneficiaries, his wife and son, received the $1 million life insurance and the Social Security benefits available. Since the family had sizable collateral resources (non-Federal Government sources), they were eligible for less than the maximum amount of the Federal Relief Fund created for the victims' families.

Allen's family had not undertaken the comprehensive financial planning that Mike and his family had. He did not have additional life insurance policies, despite planning to get to it "one of these days." His family's benefits were provided by his social insurance coverages and by his employer. The family was also eligible for the relief fund established by the federal government, less collateral resources.

LOSSES PAID TO A HYPOTHETICAL NEARBY BUSINESS

To see how the catastrophe affected nearby businesses, we will examine a hypothetical department store called Worlding. In our scenario, Worlding is a very popular discount store, specializing in name-brand clothing, housewares, cosmetics, and linens. Four stories tall, it is located in the heart of the New York financial district just across from the World Trade Center. At 9:00 AM on September 11, 2001, the store had just opened its doors. At any time, shoppers would have to fight crowds in the store to get to the bargains. The morning of September 11 was no different. When the first plane hit the first tower, a murmur spread throughout the store and the customers started to run outside to see what happened. As they were looking up, they saw the second plane hit the second tower. By the time the towers collapsed, all customers and employees had fled the store and the area. Dust and building materials engulfed and penetrated the building; the windows shattered, but the structure remained standing. Because Worlding leased rather than owned the building, its only property damage was to inventory and fixtures. But renovation work, neighborhood cleanup, and safety testing kept Worlding closed—and without income— for seven months.

The case of insurance coverage for Worlding's losses is straightforward since the owners had a business package policy that provided both commercial property coverage and general liability. Worlding bought the Causes of Loss – Special Form, which is an "open perils" or "all risk" coverage form (further explanation in Chapters 8 and 12). Instead of listing perils that are covered, the special form provides protection for all causes of loss not specifically excluded. Usually, most exclusions found in the special form relate to catastrophic potentials. The form did not include a "terrorism" exclusion at that time. Therefore, Worlding's inventory stock was covered in full. (For a full listing of the exclusions, refer to the example of a business package policy in Chapter 12.)

Worlding did not incur any liability losses to third parties, so all losses were covered by the commercial property coverage. Worlding provided regular inventory data to its insurer, who paid for the damages without any disputes. With its property damage and the closing of the neighborhood, Worlding had a nondisputable case of business interruption loss. Coverage for business interruption of businesses that did not have any property damage, such as tourist-dependent hotel chains and resort hotels,[11] depended on the exact wording in their policies. Some policies were more liberal than others.

Since Worlding was eligible for business income interruption coverage, the owners used adjusters to help them calculate the appropriate amount of lost income, plus expenses incurred while the business was not operational. (An example of such a detailed list is provided in Chapter 12.) The restoration of the building to Worlding's specifications was covered under the building owners' commercial property policy.

IMPORTANCE OF THE LOSS CASES AND SEPTEMBER 11

As these examples show, complete insurance is a complex maze of different coverages. This introduction is designed to provide a glimpse into the full scope of insurance that affects the reader as an individual or as a business operator. In our business case, if Worlding had not had business insurance, its employees would have been without a job to return to. Thus, the layer of the business coverage is as important in an introductory risk and insurance course as are all aspects of your personal and employment-related coverages.

In addition, emphasis is given to the structure of the insurance industry and its coverages and markets. As noted earlier in this introduction, the September 11 terror drastically affected the insurers of insurers—the reinsurers. This area is developed in this text, along with recent usages of the capital markets to mitigate risk. Emphasis is given to the new concept of considering all risks in an organization (enterprise risk management), not just those risks whose losses are traditionally covered by insurance (see Chapter 3 for more details).

The text is designed to show you, the student, the width and variety of the field of risk management and insurance. In this survey course, the pieces will be connected for you. Current events and their risk management outcomes will be clarified for you, whether the losses are to households or businesses. After you complete this course, you should have a tool set allowing you to comprehend complex risk and insurance stories in the media. Furthermore, you will have the basic tools to build efficient and holistic risk management portfolios for yourself, your family, and your business. If your business is complex, you will know where to gain the expertise to address your risk management needs. This level of expertise is usually the subject of more advanced risk and insurance courses.

The puzzle shown in Figure A.2 illustrates how separate types of coverage fit together. As you move along the text, this puzzle will become more familiar. Each chapter will show you how the pieces connect.

DISCUSSION QUESTIONS

1. What was the immediate impact of the horrific events of September 11 on the insurance markets?
2. Why is the federal government involved in providing terrorism coverage?
3. Why do estimates of the liability losses from September 11 have such a large range?
4. What are the main benefits under Social Security?
5. What are the main benefits under workers' compensation?
6. Why can a worker get group insurance, but not an unemployed person?
7. What types of group insurance were introduced in this section?
8. How can people who do not have group life insurance from an employer secure protection for their families?
9. What can a business do to ensure it will not become insolvent if its inventory is destroyed?
10. Can a business get business interruption income from its policy if it did not suffer direct loss?

FIGURE A.2

The Connection: The Puzzle of Risks We Face in Our Lives

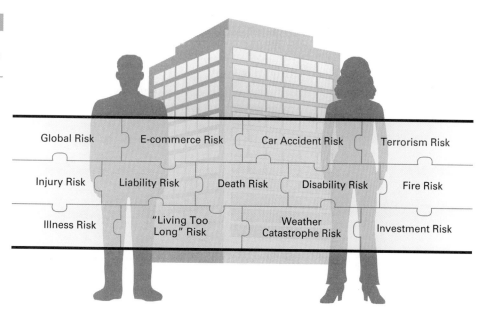

EXERCISES

A.1 Sheila Mollen was stocking the shelves at Dairlang Grocery Store in Richmond, Virginia, when a heavy shelf fell on her and killed her instantly. Mollen was married and had three children. Summarize what benefits are available to her family through every possible insurance coverage.

A.2 In the spring of 1992, Chicago experienced an unusual underground "flood," apparently caused by damage to a tunnel system. Many firms were required to shut down offices in the damaged area. Among them was a large toy store, Mr. Joys. No one was hurt, but all the inventory was damaged in the flood and the store was closed for four months. Describe, in general, what losses you think will be covered by insurance policies.

NOTES

1. Douglas McLeod, "Tragedy Touches Entire Market," *Business Insurance,* 17 September 2001, p. 1.
2. Michael Prince and Michael Bradford, "Fallout from Sept.11: Renewal Plans are Revised as Rates Firm Dramatically," *Business Insurance,* 22 October 2001, p. 1.
3. Carolyn Aldred, "Swiss Re records first loss since 1868," *Business Insurance,* 10 April 2002.
4. Sarah Veysey, "Lloyd's reports $4.5 billion loss for 2001," *Business Insurance,* 10 April 2002.
5. Judy Greenwald, "P/C insurers' combined ratio worsens in 2001" *Business Insurance,* 9 April 2002.
6. "Property market to remain tight for 2002: Marsh" *Business Insurance,* 9 April 2002.
7. "House Committee on Ways and Means, Subcommittee on Social Security (Shaw) on SSA's response to the terrorist attacks of September 11, Larry Massanari, Commissioner," a communication to Congress, can be found by searching the Social Security Administration's Web site at www.ssa.gov.
8. http://ww.wcb.state.ny.us/design/framework.emergencyinfo.htm.
9. Daniel Hays "Workers' Compensation Losses Might Top $1 Billion," *National Underwriter,* Property & Casualty/Risk & Benefits Management Edition, p. 10. Also see http://www.wcb.state.ny.us/content/main /onthejob/wc03005.htm.
10. Douglas McLeod, "American Airlines Faces $50 million WTC suit," *Business Insurance,* 9 April 2002.
11. John D. Dempsey and Lee M. Epstein, "Re-Examining Business Interruption Insurance" (part one of three), *Risk Management Magazine,* February 2002.

PART I

FUNDAMENTALS OF RISK MANAGEMENT AND INSURANCE

CHAPTER 1

Risk

Risk and how we manage it has been a critical aspect of our lives. How humans have conquered the fears of risk and used mathematics and statistics to manage it is the topic of the widely acclaimed book *Against the Gods: The Remarkable Story of Risk,* by Peter L. Bernstein (New York City: John Wiley & Sons, 1996). The ability to use mathematics and statistics to mitigate risk is truly the foundation of insurance. This text is devoted to the topics of risk and risk management, with emphasis on the use of insurance to manage risk. In this chapter, our objectives are to offer an understanding of risk, including a discussion of methods to measure it and convert it into a less intangible reality. While the concepts of risks are overshadowed in later chapters by practical issues of risk management and insurance, a good foundation in risk concepts will provide a much easier journey through the remainder of the text.

Chapter 1, therefore, includes the following topics:

1. The connection of all the risks in our lives
2. The nature of risk
3. How risk can be measured and evaluated
4. Standard deviation of risk
5. The law of large numbers as the basis of insurance
6. The concept of risk and categories of risk
7. The new risk paradigms and today's new risks

CONNECTION

When we look at **risk** from a personal standpoint, we see many aspects flowing through our lives from birth to death. We, or our parents, want to mitigate risk to maintain good quality of life. The risks of becoming ill, of being injured in an accident, or of losing one's home or job are genuine risks we face at various stages of our lives. They are an integral part of our journey through life. **Holistic risk** is the term used to discuss the entire spectrum of risk exposures. Holistic risk management encompasses all risks, not just bits and pieces. But there is no single method for mitigating the complete holistic risk picture. We do have separate solutions, some using insurance. For illness, we have health insurance. For injury in a car accident, we may have automobile medical coverage, or bodily injury coverage from a third party who was at fault. When our home is destroyed in a tornado, homeowners insurance provides the coverage to rebuild the house. When we become unemployed, we have coverage from unemployment insurance provided by the employers through unemployment taxes. The coverages are provided in bits and pieces to mitigate the various separate risks. Despite a holistic approach to risk, coverages are segmented.

In our "connection" section in each chapter, we will tie each coverage or risk management solution to you, the student, as the focal subject of holistic risk both on a personal level and in the business environment. If one could wave a magic wand to solve all risk problems in one single step, it would be a less complex issue. However, the solutions to solving the risk problems are a compilation, which completes a puzzle. Some of the personal and business risks we face are shown in the "connection" puzzle in Figure 1.1. As we progress through the text, each chapter will begin with the connection section to emphasize how the discussion in the chapter is connected to our holistic risk. Even in chapters discussing commercial insurance, the connection to you will be highlighted to show the interrelationships among the different risks. Today, risk management for personal and commercial risks requires coordination and management of all facets of the risk spectrum to deal with the total risk picture. The next section will define all types of risks more formally.

NATURE OF RISK

The Feelings Associated with Risk

Early in our lives, while protected by our parents, we enjoy the security they give us. But imagine yourself as your parents during the first years of your life. The "Risk Ball" game was created to illustrate the handling and transferring risk in a tangible way.[1] Some of the balls are shown in Figure 1.2. These balls represent risks such as dying prematurely, losing a home to fire, and losing the ability to earn an income because of injury. The risk balls are designed to bring the abstract notion of risk into a more tangible concept. You actually touch the risk, not just feel it emotionally with tightness in your stomach. If you held these balls, you would want to dispose of them as soon as you possibly could. One way to dispose of these risk balls is by transferring the risk to insurance companies. The benefits of these transfers and the factors involved in transferring the risks are important subjects of

FIGURE 1.1 The Connection: The Puzzle of Risks We Face in Our Lives

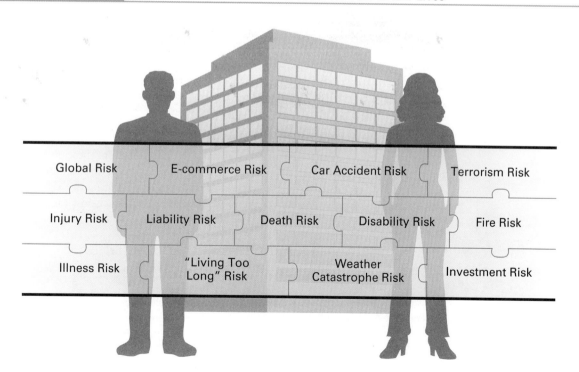

many of the chapters of this text. Right now, we focus on the risk itself. What do you actually feel when you hold the risk balls? Most likely, your answer would be "insecurity and uneasiness." Risks are associated with fears; a person who is **risk averse**—one who shies away from risk and prefers to have as much security and certainty as possible—would wish to lower the level of fear. Most of us are considered risk averse.

A person who is risk averse is often willing to pay in excess of the expected return in exchange for some certainty about the future. To pay an insurance premium, for example, is to forgo wealth in exchange for the insurer's promise that covered losses will be paid. Some people refer to this as an exchange of a certain loss (the premium) for an uncertain loss that causes us to not sleep at night. An important aspect of the exchange is that the premium is larger than the average or expected loss. A person willing to pay only the average loss as a premium would be considered **risk neutral.** Someone who accepts risk at less than the average loss, perhaps even paying to add risk such as through gambling, is a **risk seeker.**

Risk aversion is significant because it may result in lost opportunities. Many examples are possible. A vaccine manufacturer worried about potential liability lawsuits may choose not to introduce a promising treatment. A land developer concerned about erosion might decide not to build a convention center. The list could be quite long and even could become absurd—fear of being in an auto accident might keep us indoors indefinitely, for example. The point is that our negative reaction toward uncertain possible future losses leads us to want to manage the future, and thus to manage risk. By managing risk, we develop opportunities that might not otherwise be feasible.

Definition of Risk

More formally, we consider risk as the variability of future outcomes. Risk exists when outcomes may differ from expectations. For example, if we participate in a bike ride with our riding club, we expect to complete the ride and join the group for a picnic lunch. Deviation from expectation would be an accident that would send us to the hospital instead of to a fun outing. The possibility of lower-than-expected outcomes is critical to the definition of risk, because so-called "losses" produce the negative quality associated with not knowing the future, and managing the future is the essence of risk management. In this text, lower-than-expected outcomes are termed "losses," and higher-than-expected outcomes are termed "gains." While some situations involve the possibility of gain as well as loss (termed **speculative risks**), the risk management solution that involves insurance is concerned almost exclusively with situations in which no gain is possible (termed **pure risks**). While insurance is the risk-management tool for pure risk, pure and speculative risks often are closely linked. For example, a person buying life insurance for protection against the risk of premature death can choose from various types of policies. One of these policies is variable life insurance, which includes investments in the stock market through mutual funds. Thus, the pure risk of death may also be associated with the speculative risk of investments. Another example is saving for retirement. The protection against the pure risk of

FIGURE 1.2   Risk Balls

living too long can also be speculative should we decide to invest in the stock market and not only in safe instruments such as Treasury bills. Also, in the business environment, in evaluating the expected financial returns for a new product (speculative risk), issues concerning product liability, workplace accidents, and other potential losses, which would be categorized as pure risks, must also be considered. As illustrated in these examples, the pure and speculative risks are not separated. That is why the concepts of holistic risk and **enterprise risk,** as a firm's holistic risk is often termed, are so prevalent today. These risks will be further explained at the end of this chapter.

Pure risk has no meaning without **loss** being the outcome of concern, and most of the insurance discussions in this book will be about situations that involve potential for economic loss. This term implies that loss must be capable of being expressed in an easily measurable economic unit, such as dollars. Many losses, however, cannot be fully measured or described in economic terms. For example, the death of a family pet may be felt as a great loss, but the loss is not measurable entirely in economic terms. One may know the cost of buying another pet of the same kind, but this is not the only diminution in value.

Remember that for pure risk to exist, it must be possible for loss to occur. Our concern is with unfavorable, unpredictable deviations from expectations. Much of the job of **risk manager** (the person in charge of mitigating the risks of a firm), like our own personal risk assessment, involves estimating future outcomes (losses) and the variability of those future outcomes. Variability derives from deviations from expectations. The greater the size of deviations, the greater the variability, and the more difficult the task of planning. For example, think about the deviation from expectation that occurred on September 11, 2001: The catastrophe was the largest-ever loss and the greatest-ever deviation from expectation. It actually resulted in a lingering market turmoil. As a matter of fact, the September 11 losses were not part of any loss estimation for the future because they were beyond anyone's catastrophic scenarios.

MEASUREMENT OF RISK

Specific Measurement Techniques

To manage the future, we need to have some idea about possible outcomes and how likely each outcome is to occur. Estimates of the future typically are based primarily on historical and/or theoretical data. These data are used to develop probabilities, or likelihoods, of the future occurrence of each event. Representations of all possible outcomes along with their associated probabilities are called probability distributions. An example of a **probability distribution** is a normal distribution. When we know the pattern of the losses, we hope the same pattern will continue in the future and our predictions will be accurate. Missing the prediction is usually the result of inaccuracies in the ability to know the future distribution of losses. For example, when you read that polls predict that a candidate may win, you also read that the "margin of error" is 3 or 5 percent. The reason for such a margin is the fact that only a sample of voters is asked to provide an opinion. The sample may not be representative of the whole population or the future.

Average Value

Tables 1.1 and 1.2 show the probability distribution of two different samples of the number of claims for burnt homes during a five-year period in two locations. We are given the total number of claims per year and the amount of losses in dollars for these claims for each year.

TABLE 1.1 Insurer A Claims and Losses	Year	Number of Fire Claims	Fire Losses	Average Loss Per Claim
	1	11	$ 16,500.00	$ 1,500.00
	2	9	40,000.00	4,444.44
	3	7	30,000.00	4,285.71
	4	10	123,000.00	12,300.00
	5	14	105,000.00	7,500.00
	Total	51	$314,500.00	$ 6,166.67
	Mean	10.2	$ 62,900.00	$ 6,166.67

Frequency (average number of claims per year) = 10.2
Severity (average $ lass per claim per year) = $6,166.67

TABLE 1.2 Insurer B Claims and Losses	Year	Number of Fire Claims	Fire Losses	Average Loss Per Claim
	1	15	$ 16,500.00	$ 1,100.00
	2	5	40,000.00	8,000.00
	3	12	30,000.00	2,500.00
	4	10	123,000.00	12,300.00
	5	9	105,000.00	11,666.67
	Total	51	$314,500.00	$ 6,166.67
	Mean	10.2	$ 62,900.00	$ 6,166.67

Frequency (average number of claims per year) = 10.2
Severity (average $ loss per claim per year) = $6,166.67

We assume that each location has the same number of homes (1,000 homes). Each sample has a total of fifty-one claims for the five-year period, an average (or mean) of 10.2 claims per year. The average dollar amount of losses is also the same for each sample, $62,900 per year. The scientific notation of the average is in Appendix 1.1 of this chapter.

As shown in Tables 1.1 and 1.2, the total number of fire claims for Insurers A and B is the same, as is the total amount of losses shown. The average number of claims per year for the five-year period is a measure called **frequency.** The frequency of claims for Insurers A and B is 10.2 per year. The size of the loss in term of dollars lost per claim is called **severity.** The average dollars lost per claim per year in each sample is $1,166.67. The most important probabilities for risk managers are those associated with frequency and severity of losses during a specified period of time. Typically, the risk manager will relate the number of incidents to a base. For instance, to develop an average frequency, the number of injuries in the plant may be related to the average number of employees. In the examples in Tables 1.1 and 1.2, the severity is related to the number of claims in the five-year period. It is important to note that in these tables the distribution of the claims per year for Insurer A is different from that for Insurer B.

Variability

What is the difference between the claims for Insurers A and B? The difference is in the variability from year to year in the number of fire claims; that is, the distribution of claims. When you look at the tables, can you tell which one has greater variability? Probably you can, since it is clear that the range among the years is greater for Insurer

B. Insurer B shows a variability from five burnt homes per year to fifteen, while Insurer A shows from seven to fourteen. What other ways do you know to measure the variability? **Standard deviation** is the most common statistical measure of variability. In finance, the standard deviation is regarded as the measure of risk. Tables 1.3 and 1.4 show the measurement of the standard deviations of the two samples for the number of claims only.

To calculate the standard deviation you square the difference between the actual number of claims and the average number of claims each year. You add the squared amounts and divide by the number of years of observations. The division results in the variance. The square root of the variance is the standard deviation. As you can see, the standard deviation of the sample for insurer A is only 2.59 while the standard deviation of the sample of Insurer B is 3.70. The number of fire claims in Sample B is more spread out from year to year than those in Sample A. The standard deviation is the numeric representation of that spread. The scientific notation of the standard deviation is in Appendix 1.1 of this chapter.

To provide some meaningful measure of risk, economists often use the square root of the variance, the standard deviation, as a measure of risk. It provides a value comparable with the original expected outcomes. Remember that variance uses squared differences; therefore, taking the square root returns the measure to its initial unit of measurement.

TABLE 1.3

Standard Deviation of Fire Claims of Insurer A

Year	Number of Fire Claims	Difference From Mean	Difference Squared
1	11	−8.0	.64
2	9	−1.2	1.44
3	7	−3.2	10.24
4	10	−0.2	.04
5	14	3.8	14.44
Total	51		26.80

Mean = 10.2

Variance* = 6.70

Standard Deviation* = 2.59

* See Appendix 1.1 at the end of this chapter for the formulas for calculating variance and standard deviation.

TABLE 1.4

Standard Deviation of Fire Claims of Insurer B

Year	Number of Fire Claims	Difference From Mean	Difference Squared
1	15	4.8	23.04
2	5	−5.2	27.04
3	12	1.8	3.24
4	10	−0.2	.04
5	9	−1.2	1.44
Total	51		54.80

Mean = 10.2

Variance* = 13.70

Standard Deviation* = 3.70

* See Appendix 1.1 at the end of this chapter for the formulas for calculating variance and standard deviation.

If we compare one standard deviation with another distribution of equal mean but larger standard deviation—as when we compare Sample A with Sample B—we could say that the second distribution is riskier than the first. It is riskier because the observations are, on average, further away from the mean than the observations in the first distribution. Larger standard deviations, therefore, represent greater risk, everything else being the same.

Of course, distributions seldom have the same mean. What if we are comparing two distributions with different means? In this case, we would need to consider the **coefficient of variation,** which is the standard deviation of a distribution divided by its mean. The coefficient of variation gives us a relative value of risk when the means of the distributions are not equal.

Data Sources

Armed with these tools to measure variability, a risk manager is better able to make informed decisions. An important issue, however, is the general lack of data on which to develop probability distributions. Often the events under consideration are new or rare, making data collection difficult. A small organization, for example, may experience a specific type of loss no more than once every five years, on average. Unfortunately, three losses could occur in a single year, with none the next fifteen years. Even the most sophisticated data analysis techniques have trouble with these situations.

Law of Large Numbers

Availability of only small data sources (or sometimes none at all) is troublesome because most estimation techniques rely on numerous observations for accuracy. The benefit of many observations is well stated by the **law of large numbers,** an important statistical doctrine for the successful management of risk and the basic foundation for the existence of insurance in society.

The law of large numbers holds that as a sample of observations is increased in size, the relative variation about the mean declines. An example is given in Appendix 1.2. The important point is that with larger samples we feel more confident in our estimates.

If it were not for the law of large numbers, insurance would not exist. A risk manager (or insurance executive) uses the law of large numbers to estimate future outcomes for planning purposes. The larger the sample size, the lower the relative risk, everything else being equal. The ability to pool experience, therefore, is quite desirable and is discussed further in Chapter 2, where insurance operations are presented. The pooling of many exposures gives the insurer a better prediction of future losses. The insurer still has some risk or variability around the average. But the risk of an insurer with more exposures is relatively lower than that of an insurer with fewer exposures under the same expected distribution of losses, as presented in Appendix 1.2.

ELEMENTS OF PURE RISK

An important criterion for the law of large numbers to operate effectively is that the observations are generated from essentially the same type of conditions (that is, all observations are "homogeneous" or similar). Someone managing risk, therefore, needs to know the particular characteristics of the underlying potential losses. These can be described in terms of exposures, perils, and hazards.

Exposures and Risks

Although most insurance professionals describe risk as some form of variability, many continue to use the word "risk" to denote a property or a person exposed to losses. Most insurance-industry education and training materials, in contrast, use the term **exposure** to describe the property or person facing a condition in which loss or losses are possible. We also will use the term exposure this way.

The categorization of insurance "risks" often begins by putting them into broad types of exposures that are not mutually exclusive and may overlap. The pure risks that confront individuals, families, firms, and other organizations may, for example, cause personal, property, liability, catastrophic, or accidental loss exposures. Each of these categories receives extensive attention in future chapters and is introduced briefly below.

Personal Loss Exposures—Personal Risk

Because all losses are ultimately borne by people, it could be said that all exposures are personal. Some, however, have a more direct impact on people. Exposure to premature death, sickness, disability, unemployment, and dependent old age are examples of **personal loss exposures.** An organization may also experience loss from these events when such events affect employees. These events may be catastrophic, as was the case in September 11, 2001, or accidental, as would be the case of an employee falling off a ladder and breaking a leg.

Property Loss Exposures—Property Risk

Property owners face the possibility of both direct and consequential (indirect) losses. If a car is damaged in a collision, the direct loss is the cost of repairs. The **consequential losses** are the time and effort required to arrange for repairs, the loss of use of the car while repairs are being made, and the additional cost of renting another car while repairs are being made. **Property loss exposures** are associated with both "real" property such as buildings and "personal" property such as automobiles and the contents of a building. Again, the loss exposure may be due to accidental causes or catastrophic causes such as floods or hurricanes.

Liability Loss Exposures—Liability Risk

Under our legal system, one can be held responsible for causing damage to others. Thus, one is exposed to the possibility of **liability loss exposures** by having to defend against a lawsuit. In addition, the responsible party may become legally obligated to pay for injury to persons or damage to property. Liability risk may occur because of catastrophic loss exposure or because of accidental loss exposure.

Catastrophic Loss Exposure—Fundamental Risk   A loss that is catastrophic and includes large number of exposures in one location is considered a **fundamental risk.** Too many people or properties may be hurt or damaged in one location at once. Hurricanes in Florida and the eastern shores of the United States, floods in the midwestern states, and terrorism attacks are the types of loss exposures that are associated with fundamental risk. As will be explained in Chapter 2, such risk is hard to insure privately.

Accidental Loss Exposure—Particular Risk   Most pure risk relates to accidental losses, not man-made or intentional ones. Such losses are the best to provide the data for estimation of future losses. As will be seen in Chapter 2, these are the risks most commonly covered by the insurance industry. As opposed to fundamental losses, non-catastrophic accidental losses, such as fire, are considered **particular risks.**

Perils

Perils are the immediate causes of loss. People are surrounded by potential loss because the environment is filled with perils such as floods, theft, death, sickness, accidents, fires, tornadoes, and lightning. Table 1.5 is a list of some perils.

Although various efforts have been made to categorize perils, doing so is difficult. We could talk about **natural** and **human perils.** Natural perils are those over which people have little control, such as hurricanes, volcanoes, and lightning. Human perils, then, would be the causes of loss within the control of individuals, including suicide, war, and theft. Sometimes losses caused by recessions will be considered as caused by human perils, but they may be separated into a third category labeled **economic perils.** Employee strikes, arson for profit, and similar situations also are generally considered economic perils.

Another method of categorization is division into insurable and noninsurable perils. Typically, the noninsurable perils are those that might be considered catastrophic to an insurer or would encourage policyholders to cause loss. In both instances, the problem for the insurer is the security of its financial standing.

Hazards

Hazards are the conditions that lie behind the occurrence of losses, increasing the probability of losses, their severity, or both. Certain conditions are referred to as being "hazardous." For example, when summer humidity declines and temperature and wind velocity rise in heavily forested areas, the likelihood of fire increases. Conditions are such that a forest fire could start very easily and be difficult to contain. In this example, both the probability and the severity of loss are increased by low humidity. The more hazardous the conditions, the greater the probability and/or severity of loss. Two kinds of hazards—physical and intangible—affect the probability and severity of losses.

TABLE 1.5 Types of Perils		
Natural Perils		
Generally Insurable	**Generally Difficult to Insure**	
Windstorm	Flood	
Lightning	Earthquake	
Natural combustion	Epidemic	
Heart attacks	Volcanic eruption	
	Frost	
Human Perils		
Generally Insurable	**Generally Difficult to Insure**	
Theft	War	
Vandalism	Radioactive contamination	
Hunting accident	Civil unrest	
Negligence	Terrorism	
Fire and smoke		
Global		
E-commerce		
Mold		

Physical Hazards

Physical hazards are the tangible conditions of the environment that affect the frequency and/or severity of loss. Examples include slippery roads that increase the chance of an automobile accident, poorly lit stairwells that add to the likelihood of slips and falls, and old wiring that may increase the likelihood of a fire.

Location, construction, and use represent physical hazards that affect property. The location of a building affects its susceptibility to loss by fire, flood, earthquake, and other perils. If the building is located near a fire station and a good water supply, there is less chance that it will suffer a serious loss by fire than if it is in an isolated area with neither water nor firefighting service.

Construction affects the probability and severity of loss. While no building is fireproof, some types of construction are less susceptible to loss from fire than others. What is susceptible to one peril, however, is not necessarily susceptible to all. For example, a frame building is more apt to burn than a brick building, but it may suffer less damage from an earthquake.

Use or occupancy may also create physical hazards. A building will have a greater probability of loss by fire if it is used for a fireworks factory or a dry-cleaning establishment than if it is used as an office building. An automobile used for business purposes may be exposed to greater chance of loss than the typical family car if the business car is used more extensively and in more dangerous settings.

Similarly, people have physical characteristics that affect loss. Some of us have brittle bones, weak immune systems, or vitamin deficiencies. Any of these characteristics could increase the probability or severity of health expenses.

Intangible Hazards

Intangible hazards are attitudes and nonphysical cultural conditions that affect the probability and severity of loss. Their existence may lead to physical hazards. Traditionally, authors of insurance texts categorize these conditions as moral and morale hazards, which are important concepts but do not cover the full range of nonphysical hazards.[2] Even the distinction between moral and morale hazards is fuzzy.

Moral hazards involve dishonesty on the part of insureds. In the context of insurance, moral hazards are conditions that encourage insureds to cause losses intentionally. Generally, moral hazards exist when a person can gain from the occurrence of a loss. For example, an insured who will be reimbursed for the cost of a new stereo system following the loss of an old one has an incentive to cause loss. Such an incentive increases the probability of loss.

Morale hazards, in contrast, do not involve dishonesty. Rather, morale hazards are attitudes of carelessness and lack of concern that increase the chance a loss will occur or increase the size of losses that do occur. Poor housekeeping (for example, allowing trash to accumulate in the attic or basement) and careless cigarette smoking are examples of morale hazards that increase the probability of loss by fire. Often such lack of concern occurs because an insurer is available to pay for losses.

Many people unnecessarily and often unconsciously create morale hazards that can affect their health and life expectancy. These hazards include excessive use of tobacco, drugs, and other harmful substances; poor eating, sleeping, and exercise habits; unnecessary exposure to falls, poisoning, electrocution, radiation, venomous stings and bites, and air pollution; and other dangers to life and limb.

In addition to moral and morale hazards, legal and cultural conditions exist that increase loss frequency and/or severity. These **societal hazards** likely change over time, and yet can be quite significant. Many people today believe, for example, that business activities are more prone to litigation in the United States than anywhere else because of a greater "litigious attitude" in the country. Doing business in the United States is therefore considered hazardous. Outside of the U.S., a number of other societal hazards exist. More information is given later in this chapter and in upcoming chapters.

Hazards are critical characteristics because our ability to reduce their effects will reduce both overall costs and variability. Hazard management, therefore, can be a highly effective risk management tool. At this point, many corporations around the world have emphasized disaster control management in an attempt to reduce the impact of biological or terrorist attacks. Safety inspections in airports are one example of disaster control management that intensified after September 11. See "Ethical Dilemma: Is Airport Security Worth the Wait?" for a discussion of safety in airports.

Ethical Dilemma

Is Airport Security Worth the Wait?

Following the terrorist attacks of September 11, the Federal Aviation Administration wrestled with a large question: How could a dozen or more hijackers armed with knives slip through security checkpoints at two major airports? Sadly, it wasn't hard. Lawmakers and security experts had long complained about lax safety measures at airports, citing several studies over the years that had documented serious security lapses. "I think a major terrorist incident was bound to happen," Paul Bracken, a Yale University professor who teaches national security issues and international business, told *Wired* magazine a day after the attacks. "I think this incident exposed airport security for what any frequent traveler knows it is—a complete joke. It's effective in stopping people who may have a cigarette lighter or a metal belt buckle, but against people who want to hijack four planes simultaneously, it is a failure."

Two days after the attacks, air space was reopened under extremely tight security measures, including placing armed security guards on flights, ending curbside check-in, banning sharp objects (at first, even tweezers, nail clippers, and eyelash curlers were confiscated), restricting boarding areas to ticket-holding passengers, and conducting extensive searches of carry-on bags. Bottlenecks at security checkpoints caused such delays that passengers were asked to check in as much as four hours before their flight times. The long waits and frequent flight cancellations led some weary travelers to become violent, a phenomenon dubbed "air rage."

Frequent flier frustration continued as the Transportation Security Administration, created in the wake of the attacks and charged with improving airport security, proposed ever-more-invasive security measures. Identification systems known as "fusion biometrics" can scan the image, fingerprints, or irises of a person and compare the information with a database of known terrorists.

Already in place is a program known as the Computer Assisted Passenger Prescreening System, which checks passenger information such as name, address, and method of payment against terrorist patterns; the databases may soon be extended to include credit information and FBI and Secret Service records. These systems could tie in with a "trusted traveler" program, in which a frequent flier would undergo a one-time extensive background check in exchange for faster airport screening, and an airport would endure even more complaints from the "second class" passengers in the longer lines.

Next-generation scanning machines may reveal more than the passenger would like. The U.S. Customs department is now testing the Rapiscan Secure 1000, a full-body x-ray machine, in a few airports across the country. The machine shows every item a passenger is carrying; it shows everything else, too. That raises privacy concerns for Jay Stanley of the American Civil Liberties Union. "We think this is an extremely intrusive technology," he said on the television show *CyberCrime* in April 2002. "Passengers when they fly have a right to expect that they will not be seen naked."

Questions for Discussion

1. If your flying habits have changed since the September 11 attacks, are fear or frustration more to blame?

2. How long are you willing to stand in line for increased security? How much privacy are you willing to trade for feeling safe?

Sources: Dave Lenckus, "Airports Vulnerable Despite Higher Level of Security," *Business Insurance*, 6 May 2002; "U.S. Flyers Still at Risk," *National Underwriter* Property & Casualty/Risk & Benefits Management Edition, 1 April 2002; Stephen Power, "Background Checks Await Fliers," *The Wall Street Journal*, 7 June 2002; American Civil Liberties Union paper, "Airport Security: Increased Safety Need Not Come at the Expense of Civil Liberties," www.aclu.org.

Emerging and Growing Risks

In the post–September 11 era—encompassing the e-commerce revolution, the increased global economy, the collapse of corporate giants such as Enron, the accounting fraud of major corporations such as WorldCom,[3] and fears of terrorism, dirty bombs and biological or nuclear warfare—there is a heightened feeling of new and more frightening risks all around us. These risks are not only pure risks, but also speculative risks. Our world is not fragmented by pure and speculative risks. We think in terms of such separation only because many speculative risks do not have solutions that can be provided by private insurers.

The old model of isolated pure risk (of only loss and no gain) has given way to the paradigm of enterprise risk (which includes risks of gains as well as losses). Enterprise risks combine every aspect of risk the firm or individual is exposed to. In *Risk: The New Management Imperative in Finance* (Princeton: Bloomberg Press, 2000), James Gleason looks at two broad aspects of risk exposures of banks: financial risk, including market risk, credit risk, interest rate risk, and currency exchange rate risk; and nonfinancial risks, such as event risk, legal risk, regulatory risk, and operational risk. In his book, Gleason described the risks from the bank's point of view. But both financial risks and nonfinancial risks occupy every global and large business, as well as mom-and-pop operations and even families. Many of the nonfinancial risks can be insured. It is important to note that the traditional world of risk and insurance did not deal with the financial risks mentioned here. Today, there is a new breed of financial risk managers who deal solely with such risks. We will discuss their objectives and techniques in Chapter 3 as part of the evolution of risk management. It is important to note again that the emphasis of this text is on the risk and insurance aspects of the enterprise, or holistic risk, which is all aspects of risks within the firm or a household.

One of the risks with heightened sense of emergency that companies and individuals face is the electronic risk (e-risk) generated by the extensive use of computers, e-commerce, and the Internet. These risks are extensive and the exposures are not yet fully understood, as you can see in "Important Issues: The Growing Risks of E-exposures." (However, some of the exposure has become clearer, as will be noted in Chapters 8 and 9, in which insurance for such risks is explained along with risk management techniques.) The access of employers and regulatory bodies to employee e-mail is one such risk, as demonstrated by a recent government probe into Wall Street brokerage firms and their research analysts.[4]

Investigating Merrill Lynch & Co., Goldman Sachs, Morgan Stanley Dean Witter, and several other major firms on suspicion of touting questionable stocks in order to woo lucrative investment banking business, New York State Attorney General Eliot Spitzer subpoenaed company documents—including internal e-mails. Some of the analysts' e-mails revealed private opinions about stocks, particularly then-high-flying Internet stocks, that were quite different from their public recommendations. For instance, one top Merrill Lynch analyst wrote his colleagues that a firm called InfoSpace was "a piece of junk." Publicly, however, it got his highest rating.

When the e-mails were made public at a news conference, Merrill Lynch's own company stock lost close to 20 percent of its market value. Merrill Lynch ultimately agreed to a settlement of a $100 million fine and an apology for misleading investors. Private civil litigation, from investors who lost money on recommended stocks, will likely result in further liability.

Another relatively new—or newly discovered—risk is that of mold in buildings and, most recently, in automobiles. Mold is assumed to cause health hazards, and cleanup is extremely costly and time-consuming. It requires special handling by licensed professionals. While the home, school, or business is being cleaned, the occupants cannot enter the premises.

IMPORTANT ISSUES

The Growing Risks of E-exposures

Electronic risk, or e-risk, comes in many forms. Like any property, computers are vulnerable to theft and employee damage (accidental or malicious). Certain components are susceptible to harm from magnetic or electrical disturbance, or extremes of temperature and humidity. More important than replaceable hardware or software is the data they store: Theft of proprietary information cost *Fortune* 1000 companies almost $50 billion in 2001, with a nationwide tab estimated at more than $300 billion. Most data theft is perpetrated by employees, but "netspionage"—electronic espionage by rival companies—is on the rise.

Companies that use the Internet commercially—who create and post content, or sell services or merchandise—must follow the laws and regulations that traditional businesses do, and are exposed to the same risks. An online newsletter or e-zine can be sued for libel, defamation, invasion of privacy, or misappropriation (reproducing a photograph without permission, for example) under the same laws that apply to a print newspaper. Web site owners and companies conducting business over the Internet, known as "e-commerce," have three major exposures to protect: intellectual property (copyrights, patents, trade secrets), security (against viruses and hackers), and business continuity (in case of system crashes).

But all these losses are covered by insurance, right? Wrong. Some coverage is provided through commercial property and liability policies, but traditional insurance policies were not designed to include e-risks. In fact, standard policies specifically exclude digital risks. Commercial property policies cover physical damage to *tangible* assets—and computer data, software, programs, and networks are generally not counted as tangible property. (U.S. courts are still debating the issue.)

This coverage gap can be bridged either by buying a rider or supplemental coverage to the traditional policies or by purchasing special e-risk or e-commerce coverage. New e-risk property policies cover damages

to the insured's computer system or Web site, including lost income because of a computer crash. An increasing number of insurers are offering e-commerce liability policies that offer protection in case the insured is sued for spreading a computer virus, infringing on property or intellectual rights, invading privacy, and so forth. These policies go by such names as "Safety'Net Internet Liability" (Chubb), "CyberLiability Plus" (Gulf), and "Dot.Com Errors and Omissions Liability" (Great American). The U.K. specialty insurer Hiscox offers "Hacker Insurance," which covers the new crime of cyberextortion: According to its Web site (www.hiscox.com), "We will pay any ransom demands from hackers who threaten to publish or sell information they have stolen from you, such as credit card or private medical information."

Cybercrime is just one of the e-risk-related challenges facing today's risk managers, but many are not prepared for it. Nearly half of *Fortune* 500 risk managers have not quantified their electronic risk and do not know whether they have adequate insurance coverage for it, according to a 2001 survey by RM Access, a risk consulting and insurance brokerage firm. That figure is shocking: E-exposures cost U.S. companies on the order of billions of dollars each year, yet half of the largest companies do not have a plan to manage this risk. But they're working on it.

Explore the Internet

To find out how risk managers are learning to deal with these issues, use your school library's subscription to visit insurance-industry publications such as *National Underwriter, Business Insurance,* and *Best's Review* (www.nationalunderwriter.com, www.businessinsurance.com, and www.ambest.com). Search the archives for "e-exposure" and "cyber-exposure."

Sources: Harry Croydon, "Making Sense of Cyber-Exposures," *National Underwriter,* Property & Casualty/Risk & Benefits Management Edition, 17 June 2002; Joanne Wojcik, "Insurers Cut E-Risks from Policies," *Business Insurance,* 10 September 2001; Sam Friedman, "Many RMs Clueless About E-Exposures," *National Underwriter* Online News Service, 19 April 2002.

One of the leading weekly magazines for the insurance industry, *National Underwriter,* published more than 100 articles on mold between January 1997 and May 2002.[5] In one of the earliest articles, "Pervasive Indoor Air Hazards Are Called a 'Silent Crisis,'" the writer described mold as "the peril within … in a ventilation system, in the formaldehyde used in the backing of a rug or a piece of furniture."[6] The problem appears to be increasing in certain geographical areas, and lawsuits over mold are garnering large jury awards. This topic will be furthered discussed in Chapter 10.

Most frightening, of course, is the heightened risk of terrorism and biological warfare. Stories of "dirty bombs"—explosives packaged with radioactive materials—and nuclear terrorism appear in many media stories.[7] Because of their catastrophic nature, these kinds of risks may no longer be covered by private insurers. Today, they are considered fundamental risks. Therefore, President George W. Bush signed a Terrorism Insurance Bill on November 26, 2002[8] (see Ethical Dilemma: "Who Should Insure Against Terrorism" in Chapter 2). The insurance industry still participates in such risks with special policy endorsements or specialty writers, as will be described in Chapter 5.

The risk of losing your entire pension, as experienced by the employees of bankrupt Enron, is another scary risk that is not new but that has re-emerged in full strength. Furthermore, the ripple effect of Enron's collapse on the surety bond market could not be ignored.[9] Surety bonds pay out when a company under financial distress fails to finish a project, make a delivery, or meet a payment. Surety bonds are essential to the survival of companies since debt holders are assured that if the firm cannot pay its debt, the surety bond insurers will pay it. If a company could not obtain surety bonds, no one would lend money to that company. Using surety bonds in a fraudulent manner to secure non-deliverables has the potential to destroy the surety bond market. Companies then cannot give securities to their lenders. After the debacle of Enron and the problems it caused to the surety bond market, Kmart pointed out that one of the reasons for its bankruptcy was its inability to get surety protection.[10] When an insurance product like surety bond underwriting is not available, some solutions to safeguarding our security are provided through legislation and regulation, as is the case with the new accounting oversight procedures and pension laws being considered as we write this text.

In the next chapter, we will delve into understanding what insurance is as one solution to mitigating risk.

KEY TERMS

risk	frequency	particular risk
holistic risk	severity	peril
risk averse	standard deviation	natural peril
risk neutral	coefficient of variation	human peril
risk seeker	law of large numbers	economic peril
speculative risk	exposure	hazard
pure risk	personal loss exposure	physical hazard
enterprise risk	consequential loss	intangible hazard
loss	property loss exposure	moral hazard
risk manager	liability loss exposure	morale hazard
probability distribution	fundamental risk	societal hazard

DISCUSSION QUESTIONS

1. Explain why using squared differences from the mean is necessary in calculating variance. Try a numerical example.

2. The following is the experience of Insurer A for the last three years:

Year	Number of Exposures	Number of Collision Claims	Collision Losses
1	10,000	375	$350,000
2	10,000	330	250,000
3	10,000	420	400,000

   a. Calculate the mean of losses per year.
   b. Calculate the mean of losses per exposure.
   c. Calculate the mean of losses per claim.
   d. What is the frequency of the losses?
   e. What is the severity of the losses?
   f. What is the standard deviation of the losses?
   g. Calculate the coefficient of variation.

3. The following is the experience of Insurer B for the last three years:

Year	Number of Exposures	Number of Collision Claims	Collision Losses
1	20,000	975	$650,000
2	20,000	730	850,000
3	20,000	820	900,000

   a. Calculate the mean of losses per year.
   b. Calculate the mean of losses per exposure.
   c. Calculate the mean of losses per claim.
   d. What is the frequency of the losses?
   e. What is the severity of the losses?
   f. What is the standard deviation of the losses?
   g. Calculate the coefficient of variation.

4. Explain the law of large numbers. What is the importance of this law?

5. Compare the relative risk of Insurer A to Insurer B in the questions above.
   a. Which insurer carries more risk? Explain.
   b. Compare the severity and frequency of the insurers.

6. In a particular situation it may be difficult to distinguish between moral hazard and morale hazard. Why? Define both terms.

7. Some people with complete health insurance coverage visit doctors more often than required. Is this tendency a moral hazard, a morale hazard, or simple common sense? Explain.

8. Give examples of perils, exposures, and hazards for a university or college. Define each term.

9. Inflation causes both pure and speculative risks in our society. Can you give some examples of each?

10. Define holistic risk and enterprise risk and give examples of each.

11. Describe the new risks facing society today. Give example of risks in electronic commerce.

EXERCISES

1.1 Read the "Important Issues" in this chapter. Can you help the risk managers and identify all the risk exposures associated with e-commerce and the Internet?

1.2 Read the "Ethical Dilemma" in this chapter and respond to the discussion questions at the end. What additional risk exposures do you see that the article did not cover?

1.3 One medical practice that has been widely discussed in recent years involves "defensive medicine," in which a doctor orders more medical tests and x-rays than she or he might have in the past—not because of the complexity of the case, but because the doctor fears being sued by the patient for medical malpractice. The extra tests may establish that the doctor did everything reasonable and prudent to diagnose and treat the patient.

    a.   What does this tell you about the burden of risk?

    b.   What impact does this burden place on you and your family in your everyday life?

    c.   Is the doctor wrong to do this, or is it a necessary precaution?

    d.   Is there some way to change this situation?

1.4 Thompson's department store has a fleet of delivery trucks. The store also has a restaurant, a soda fountain, a babysitting service for parents shopping there, and an in-home appliance service program.

    a.   Name three perils associated with each of these operations.

    b.   For the pure-risk situations you noted in part 1 of this exercise, name three hazards that could be controlled by the employees of the department store.

    c.   If you were manager of the store, would you want all these operations? Which—if any—would you eliminate? Explain.

1.5 Omer Laskwood, the major income earner for a family of four, was overheard saying to his friend Vince, "I don't carry any life insurance because I'm young, and I know from statistics few people die at my age."

    a.   What are your feelings about this statement?

    b.   How does Omer perceive risk relative to his situation?

    c.   What characteristic in this situation is more important than the probability of loss?

    d.   Are there other risks Omer should consider?

1.6 The council members of Flatburg are very proud of the proposed new airport they are discussing at a council meeting. When it is completed, Flatburg will finally have regular commercial air service. Some type of fire protection is needed at the new airport, but a group of citizens is protesting that Flatburg cannot afford to purchase another fire engine. The airport could share the downtown fire station, or the firehouse could be moved to the airport, five miles away. Someone suggested a compromise—move the facilities halfway. As the council members left their meeting that evening, they had questions regarding this problem.

    a.   What questions would you raise?

    b.   How would you handle this problem using the information discussed in this chapter?

NOTES

1.   Etti G. Baranoff, "The Risk Balls Game: Transforming Risk and Insurance Into Tangible Concepts," *Risk Management & Insurance Review* 4, no. 2 (2001): 51–59

2. The author thanks Leroy L. Phaup for suggesting the intangible hazard.
3. See all newspapers around the country during the week of June 26, 2002.
4. "Wall Street Has Unlikely New Cop In New York State's Eliot Spitzer," *Wall Street Journal,* 25 April 2002.
5. See stories such as "On The Brink of Crisis: Lessons From Texas on Controlling Mold Exposure," *National Underwriter,* Property & Casualty/Risk & Benefits Management Edition, 14 January 2002. "Mold Claims Create Coverage Chaos," *National Underwriter,* Property & Casualty/Risk & Benefits Management Edition, 20 August 2001.
6. David M. Katz, "Pervasive Indoor Air Hazards Are Called a 'Silent Crisis,'" *National Underwriter,* Property & Casualty/Risk & Benefits Management Edition, 20 January 1997.
7. Joby Warrick, "Makings of a 'Dirty Bomb': Radioactive Devices Left by Soviets Could Attract Terrorists," *Washington Post,* 18 March 2002, sec. A, p. 1.
8. This topic has received widespread news coverage and is still being debated at the completion of writing of this text.
9. "Enron-Related Lawsuit Calls U.S. Surety Underwriting Practices into Question," Standard & Poor's press release, 21 March 2002.
10. Scott Bernard Nelson, "Enron's Fall Tripped Up Retailer: Damaged Insurers Couldn't Aid Chain; Enron Fall Sends Shocks Through Surety Sector," *The Boston Globe,* 23 January 2002, third edition.

Appendix 1.1

Average or Mean Value

Probability distributions allow us to measure expectations of the future, as well as the variability of those expectations. Our best guess of the future typically is measured as the mean or average. The sample mean is the sum of all observed outcomes divided by the number of observations. The mean in some situations can be defined as the sum of the products of each possible outcome multiplied by its probability. In equation form, the mean is:

$$\text{sample mean} = \sum_{i=1}^{n} X_i / N$$

$$\text{where } X_i = \text{ value of observation } i$$
$$n = \text{ number of observations}$$

Variability

The variability of outcomes, or "risk," can be measured in a number of ways. One measure is the range. The **range** is the difference between the largest value and the smallest value of possible outcomes. In Table 1.2 the range equals \$1,000 – 100, or \$900. Note that in most cases, zero will also be a possible outcome, although it is omitted in our example.

A more common measure of variability is the variance. The **variance** of a probability distribution is equal to the average squared difference of each outcome from the mean. In equation form, the sample variance is represented as:

$$\text{Variance} = \sum_{i=1}^{n} (X_i - \overline{X})^2 / (N-1)$$

$$\text{where } X_i = \text{ value of observation } i$$
$$\overline{X} = \text{ mean of the distribution}$$
$$n = \text{ number of observations where the last observation is N}$$

$$\text{Standard Deviation} = \sqrt{\text{Variance}}$$

Appendix 1.2

More Exposures, Less Risk

Assume that the riskiness of two groups is under consideration by an insurer. One group is comprised of 1,000 units and the other of 4,000 units. Each group anticipates incurring 10 percent losses within a specified period, such as a year. The first group, therefore, is expected to have 100 losses; the second group expects 400 losses. This example demonstrates a binomial distribution, one where only two possible outcomes exist, either loss or no loss. The average of a binomial equals the sample size times the probability of "success." Here we will define "success" as a loss claim and use the following symbols:

n = sample size
p = probability of "success"
q = probability of "failure" = $1 - p$
$n \times p$ = mean

For Group 1 in our sample, the mean is 100:
$$(1,000) \times (.10) = 100$$
For Group 2 the mean is 400:
$$(4,000) \times (.10) = 400$$
The standard deviation of a distribution is a measure of risk or dispersion. For a binomial distribution, the standard deviation is

$$\sqrt{n \times p \times q}$$

In our example, the standard deviations of Group 1 and Group 2 are 9.5 and 19 respectively.

$$\sqrt{(1000) \times (.1) \times (.9)} = 9.5$$
$$\sqrt{(4000) \times (.1) \times (.9)} = 19$$

Thus, while the mean, or expected number of losses, quadrupled with the quadrupling of the sample size, the standard deviation only doubled. Through this illustration you can see that the proportional deviation of actual from expected outcomes decreases with increased sample size. The relative dispersion has been reduced. The coefficient of variation (the standard deviation divided by the mean) is often used as a relative measure of risk. In the above example, Group 1 has a coefficient of variation of 9.5/100, or .095. Group 2 has a coefficient of variation of 19/400 = .0475, indicating the reduced risk.

Taking the extreme, consider an individual ($n = 1$) who attempts to retain the risk of loss. The person either will or will not incur a loss, and even though the probability of loss is only 10 percent, how does that person know whether he or she will be the unlucky one out of ten? Using the binomial distribution, that individual's standard deviation (risk) is $\sqrt{(1) \times (.1) \times (.9)} = .3$, a much higher measure of risk than that of the insurer. The individual's coefficient of variation is .3/.1 = 3, demonstrating this higher risk. More specifically, the risk is 63 times (3/.0475) that of the insurer, with 4,000 units exposed to loss.

CHAPTER 2

Insurance

In Chapter 1, we discussed the nature of risk. We defined risk, measured it, and tried to feel its impact. We showed the measurement of risk as the standard deviation and the fact that it decreases as the number of exposures[1] increases because of the law of large numbers. This law is critical to understanding the nature of insurance and how it works. Why we are willing to pay for insurance was graphically shown with the risk balls in Chapter 1. We purchase insurance because we want to lower our anxiety level and be able to sleep at night.

In this chapter, we will show how the transfer of risk to insurers also reduces the level of risk to society as a whole. In the transfer of risk to insurers, the risk of "loss" or "no loss" that we face changes. We pay premiums to get the security of the "no loss." When we transfer the risk, insurers do have some risk. But it is much lower. It is the risk of "missing the loss prediction." The insurer's risk is the standard deviation we calculated in Chapter 1. The larger the number of exposures, the lower the risk of missing the prediction of future losses. Thus, the transfer of risk to insurers also lowers the risk to society as a whole through the law of large numbers. Even further, insurance is one of the tools that keep our wealth and the value of firms intact. Every person and firm works to maximize value. One essential element in maximizing the value of our assets is preservation. Insurance, if purchased from a credible and well-rated insurance company, assures the preservation of assets and economic value. In this chapter, we will cover the following:

1. Connections
2. Definition of insurance
3. What insurance is and how it works
4. What types of losses are insurable and why
5. Types of insurance
6. Importance of insurer's good rating

CONNECTION

We, as the focal point of all risks (as was presented in the Connection section of Chapter 1), are also the focal point of making sure that the risks are being transferred or managed. The adverse, or negative, effects of most of the risks can be mitigated by transferring them to insurance companies. The challenge to the new traveler through the journey of risk mitigation is to ensure that the separate risks receive the appropriate treatment. In Figure 2.1, each of the silos, or puzzles, of the fragments of risks has its associated insurance solution or an indication of a non-insurance solution. Despite having all of the risks in one holistic figure, the insurance coverage solutions are not holistic. The coverages and policies are arranged as a puzzle that requires completion to ensure holistic risk management. Insurers sell separate policies that cover the separate risks. Each policy specifically excludes the coverage that another policy provides. For example, the auto policy excludes the coverages provided by the homeowners' policy. These exclusions are designed to prevent "double dipping," or double coverage. Every risk has its

FIGURE 2.1   Connections of Insurance Coverages to Risk Exposures

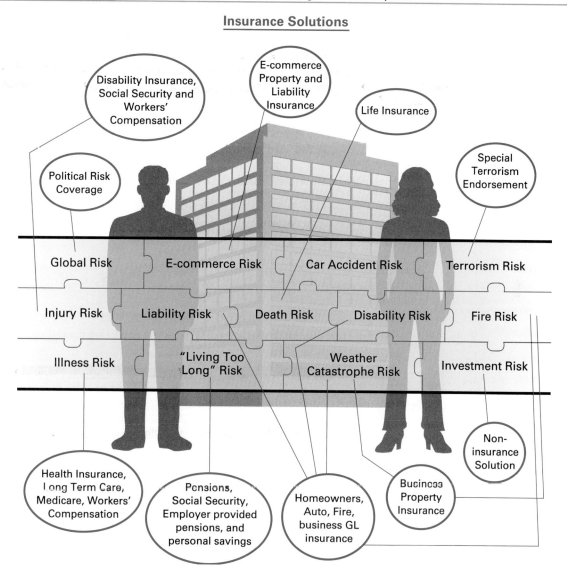

unique policy. For the risk of dying prematurely, we can purchase life insurance policies. For the risk of becoming ill and not being able to pay for medical care, we have health insurance. For the risk of losing our income because of injury, we have disability insurance, or workers' compensation if the injury occurred on the job. Throughout this text, you will learn about all the policies and how to create an entire portfolio to complete the puzzle shown here.

NATURE OF INSURANCE

A brief survey of insurance literature reveals differences of opinion among authors concerning how the term should be defined. Regardless of definition, however, the literature indicates that all authors are referring to the same thing when they say "insurance." The following is our definition:

Insurance is a social device in which a group of individuals (called "insureds") transfer risk to another party (called an "insurer") in order to combine loss experience, which permits statistical prediction of losses and provides for payment of losses from funds contributed (premiums) by all members who transferred risk.

Insurance (1) is a social device, in that people and organizations help themselves and each other by exchanging relatively small premiums for economic security against potentially large losses; (2) involves a large group of people or organizations who are exposed to similar risks; (3) allows each person or organization that becomes an insured to transfer risk to the whole group (pooling of risk), as evidenced by an insurance contract issued by an insurer; (4) involves the systematic accumulation of funds through the statistical prediction of losses and calculation of premiums; and (5) pays for losses in accordance with the terms of the insurance contract. An insurance contract is a legal document setting forth the agreement between the insured and the insurer.

HOW INSURANCE WORKS

Insurance works through the following:

- Transference of risk from the individual to a group (risk pooling) or insurance company
- Sharing and redistribution of losses on some equitable basis
- Discrimination via underwriting—the process of evaluating the risk and classifying it with similar risks

These characteristics lead to reduced risk in society and a sense of anxiety reduction. The risk an insurer faces is not simply the sum of risks transferred to it by individuals. An insurer can predict within narrow limits the amount of losses that will occur. (If the insurer could predict future losses with absolute precision, it would have no risk at all.) The accuracy of the insurer's prediction is based on the law of large numbers.

Risk Transfer (Assumption)

Insurance is created by an insurer that, as a professional risk-bearer, assumes the financial aspect of risks transferred to it by insureds. The insurer assumes risk in that it promises to pay whatever loss may occur as long as it fits the description given in the policy and is not larger than the amount of insurance sold. The loss may be zero, or it may be many thousands of dollars. In return for accepting this variability in outcomes (our definition of risk), the insurer receives a premium. Through the premium, the policyholder has paid a certain expense in order to transfer the risk of a possible large loss. The insurance contract stipulates what types of losses will be paid by the insurer.

Most insurance contracts are expressed in terms of money, although some compensate insureds by providing a service. A life insurance contract obligates the insurer to pay a specified sum of money upon the death of the person whose life is insured. A liability insurance policy requires the insurer not only to pay money on behalf of the insured to a third party but also to provide legal and investigative services needed when the event insured against occurs. The terms of some health insurance policies are fulfilled by providing medical and hospital services (for example, a semiprivate room and board, plus other hospital services) if the insured is ill or injured. Whether the insurer fulfills its obligations with money or with services, the burden it assumes is financial. The insurer does not guarantee that the event insured against will not happen. Moreover, it cannot replace sentimental value or bear the psychological cost of a loss. A home may be worth only $80,000 for insurance purposes, but have many times that value to the owner in terms of sentiment. The death of a loved one can cause almost unbearable mental suffering that is in no way relieved by receiving a sum of money from the insurer. Neither of these aspects of loss can be measured in terms of money; therefore, such risks cannot be transferred to an insurer. Because these noneconomic risks create uncertainty, it is apparent that insurance cannot completely eliminate uncertainty. Yet, insurance performs a great service by reducing the financial uncertainty created by risk.

Loss Sharing (Risk Distribution)

In general, the bulk of the premium required by the insurer to assume risk is used to compensate those who incur covered losses. Loss sharing is accomplished through premiums; therefore, group losses are shared by the group members. This is the essence of pooling.

Although premiums pay for losses incurred by members of the group, they are intended to reflect each insured's expected losses. For this purpose, actuaries, charged with determining appropriate rates (prices) for coverage, estimate the likelihood (probability) of loss and the corresponding size (severity) of loss. These estimates are made for a series of categories of insureds, with each category intended to group insureds that are similar with regard to their likelihood and size of loss. An underwriter then has the job of determining which category is appropriate for each insured (detailed discussion is available in Chapter 4). Actuaries combine the likelihood and size information to arrive at an average, or expected loss. Estimates generally are based on empirical (in this case, observed) data or theoretical relationships, making them objective estimates. When the actuary must rely on judgment rather than facts, the estimates are termed subjective. In most cases, both objective and subjective estimates are used in setting rates. For example, the actuary may begin with industry-determined rates based on past experience and adjust them to reflect the actuary's "feelings" about the insurer's own expected experience.

A life insurer may estimate that 250 of the 100,000 forty-year-old insureds it covers will die in the next year. If each insured carries a $1,000 policy, the insurer will pay out $250,000 in claims (250 × $1,000). To cover these claims, the insurer requires a premium of $2.50 from each insured ($250,000/100,000), which is the average or expected cost per policyholder. (An additional charge to cover expenses, profit, and the risk of actual losses exceeding expected losses would be included in the actual premium. A reduction of the premium would result from the insurer sharing its investment earnings with insureds.) In Chapter 4, we provide the loss development calculations that are performed by the actuary to determine the rates and calculate how much the insurer should keep on reserve to pay future expected claims. Chapter 4 also explains the relationship between rates and investment income of insurers. In this chapter we concentrate on the nature of the insurance device and how it works.

Predictions

The life insurer that estimates its claim payments at $250,000 is unlikely to be right on target. Actual claims may be more or less than expected; therefore, the insurer requires a buffer to protect itself against excessive losses. The relative size of this buffer reflects the insurer's ability to make reliable estimates for the pooled group. The larger the pooled group, the better the prediction capability.

The insurer is not required to predict which of the insureds will experience loss. Rather, the insurer needs to know only how many in the group will experience loss (assuming each carries a similar amount of coverage.) The large pool of exposures for which the insurer has assumed risk provides the insurer with a base upon which to make predictions. The larger that base, the more accurate the prediction. Thus, insurance not only provides certainty to insureds, it also reduces overall risk for society, permitting productive use of funds in medium and long-term investments rather than setting them aside in less productive liquid assets. As noted above, this statistical phenomenon through which the pooling of experience reduces risk is the law of large numbers (discussed in Chapter 1).

Pooling

The unique contribution of pooling to the insurer as a risk-bearer should now be apparent—it is a function of the law of large numbers. Insurer operations are affected by this law in two ways. First, if accurate estimates of the probability distribution are to be made prior to actually providing insurance, a large number of cases must be considered. If the statistical methods are used to determine, for example, the probability of death at age twenty-five, a large number of cases must be observed in order to define a reliable estimate.

Second, after an estimate of probability has been made, the law of large numbers can be used by an insurer as the basis for predicting future experience only when dealing with sufficiently large numbers.

As discussed previously, as far as an individual is concerned, knowing the probability of death during the coming year is of almost no help to the individual in predicting the future. Therefore, with respect to one individual's life, the insurer is in no better position to make predictions than is the individual. Given a large number of similar lives, however, the insurer can make rather accurate predictions of what will happen within the group.

Some scientists believe the law of large numbers applies to every natural occurrence in the universe. We are aware of how this law applies to human mortality, fires, auto accidents, and the like, because their probability is revealed in a relatively short time. For other events, such as earthquakes, tidal waves, and typhoons, it may take centuries for the law of large numbers to reveal a pattern.

The importance of the large number of exposures often prompts the question, "What can smaller insurers do to reduce the uncertainty in predicting losses?" Smaller insurers use the sharing of data that exists in the insurance industry. One such data collection and statistical analysis organization is the Insurance Services Office (ISO). In addition to being a statistical agent, this organization provides the uniform policy forms for the property/casualty industry (a small sample of these policies are in the Appendices at the end of the text). ISO is both a data collection agent and an advisory organization to the industry on matter of rates and policy forms. As you continue your study of this field, you will read about ISO in other chapters.

Discrimination: The Essence of Pooling

In order for the law of large numbers to work, the pooled exposures must have approximately the same probability of loss (that is, it must follow the same probability distribution, as demonstrated in Tables 1.3 and 1.4 in Chapter 1). In other words, the exposures need to be homogeneous (similar). Insurers, therefore, need to **discriminate** (classify) exposures according to expected loss. For this reason, twenty-year-old insureds with relatively low rates of mortality are charged lower rates for life insurance than are sixty-year-old insureds, holding factors other than age constant. The rates reflect each insured's expected loss, as is described in "Important Issues: Fitting into a Lower Risk-Exposure Pooling Group."

If the two groups of dissimilar risk exposures were charged the same rate, problems would arise. As previously stated, rates reflect average loss costs. Thus, a company charging the same rate to both twenty-year-old insureds and sixty-year-old insureds would charge the average of their expected losses. The pooling will be across ages, not by ages. Having a choice between a policy from this company and one from a company that charged different

IMPORTANT ISSUES

Fitting into a Lower Risk-Exposure Pooling Group

Your insurance company relies on the information you provide. Your obligation to the insurance company is not only to provide correct information but to provide complete information in order to be placed with your appropriate risk pooling group. The similar exposure in the pooling group is essential for the risk to be insurable as you saw in this chapter.

Since automobile insurance is an issue of great concern to most students, it is important to know how to handle the process of being placed in the appropriate risk pool group by an insurer. What do you need to tell the insurance agent when you purchase automobile insurance? The agent, usually the first person you talk to, will have routine questions: the make and model of the automobile, the year of manufacture, the location or "garage" of the car, and its usage (commuting to work, for example). The agent will also ask if you have had any accidents or traffic violations in the past three to five years.

You might be tempted to tell the agent that you keep the automobile at your parents' home, if rates there are cheaper. You may also be tempted to tell the agent that you have not had any traffic violations, when actually you have had three in the past year. Certainly your insurance premium will be lower if the agent thinks you have a clean record, but that premium savings will mean very little to you when the insurer notifies you of denial of coverage because of dishonesty. This occurs because you gave information that placed you in the wrong risk pool and you paid the wrong premiums for your characteristics.

Safe driving is key to maintaining reasonable auto insurance premiums by being placed in the less risky pool of drivers. The possibility of being placed in a high-risk pool and paying more premiums can be reduced in other ways, too:

- Avoiding traffic violations and accidents helps reduce the probability of loss to a level that promotes economic feasibility of premiums.
- Steering clear of sports and lavish cars that place you in a group of similar (homogeneous) insureds. Furthermore, a car that is easily damaged or expensive to repair will force up your physical damage premiums.
- Living outside the city limits ought to reduce insurance costs. Those costs can be reduced further if you use the car for pleasure only, instead of driving to and from work. Riding the bus or in a friend's car will lower the probability of an accident, making you a more desirable policyholder. Living outside the city limits has a similar effect.
- Passing driving courses, maintaining a B average, and not drinking earn discounts on premiums.

Explore the Internet

Would you trade in your Corvette for a Buick LeSabre to save on your auto insurance premium? Check out www.insure.com/auto/mostexpensive.html and www.insure.com/auto/leastexpensive.html for lists of the most and least expensive cars to insure. Other premium-reducing ideas for drivers under twenty-five years old—the highest risk group, and therefore the group that generally pays the most for insurance—are explained in "Auto Insurance for 20-Somethings," at Insurance.com, a division of Fidelity Investments. See auto.insurance.com/insurance_options/auto/auto_plan_twenties.asp.

rates based on age, the sixty-year-old insureds would choose this lower-cost, single-rate company while the young insureds would not. As a result, sixty-year-old policyholders would be over-represented in the group of insureds, making the average rate insufficient. The insureds know they represent higher risk, but want to enjoy lower rates.

This phenomenon of selecting an insurer that charges lower rates for a specific risk exposure is known as adverse selection because the insureds know they represent higher risk, but want to enjoy lower rates. **Adverse selection** occurs when insurance is purchased more often by people/organizations with higher than average expected losses than by people/organizations with average or lower than average expected losses. That is, insurance is of greater use to insureds whose losses are expected to be high (insureds "select" in a way that is "adverse" to the insurer). On this basis alone no problem would exist, because insurers could simply charge higher premiums to insureds with higher expected losses. Often, however, the insurer simply does not have enough information to be able to distinguish completely among insureds, except in cases of life insurance for younger versus older insureds. Furthermore, the insurer wants to aggregate in order to use the law of large numbers. Thus, some tension exists between limiting adverse selection and employing the law of large numbers.

Adverse selection, then, can result in greater losses than expected. Insurers try to prevent this by learning enough about applicants for insurance to identify such people so they can either be rejected or put in the appropriate rating class of similar insureds with similar loss probability. Many insurers, for example, require medical examinations for applicants for life insurance.

Some insurance policy provisions are designed to reduce adverse selection. The suicide clause in life insurance contracts, for example, excludes coverage if a policy holder takes his or her own life within a specified period, generally one or two years. The preexisting conditions provision in health insurance policies is designed to avoid paying benefits to people who buy insurance because they are aware, or should be aware, of an ailment that will require medical attention or disable them in the near future.[2]

IDEAL REQUISITES FOR INSURABILITY

Are all pure risks insurable by private (nongovernmental) insurers? No. The private insurance device is not suitable for all risks. Many risks are uninsurable. This section is devoted to a discussion of the requirements that must generally be met if a risk is to be insurable in the private market. As a practical matter, many risks that are insured privately meet these requirements only partially or, with reference to a particular requirement, not at all. Thus, in a sense, the requirements listed describe those which would be met by the ideal risk. Nevertheless, the bulk of the risks insured fulfill—at least approximately—most of the requirements. No private insurer can safely disregard them completely.[3]

A risk that was perfectly suited for insurance would meet the following requirements:

- The number of similar exposure units would be large.
- Losses that occurred would be accidental.
- A catastrophe could not occur.
- Losses would be definite.
- The probability distribution of losses would be determinable.
- **Coverage cost** would be economically feasible.

The sixth requirement influences the consumer demand for insurance and looks at what is economically feasible from the perspective of potential insureds. The other requirements influence the willingness of insurers to supply insurance.

Many Similar Exposure Units

As noted, an insurance organization prefers to have a large number of similar units when insuring a possible loss exposure. The concepts of mass and similarity are thus considered before an insurer accepts a loss exposure. Some insurance is sold on exposures that do not possess the requirements of mass and similarity, but such coverage is the exception, not the rule. An example is insurance on the fingers of a concert pianist, or on prize-winning racehorses. When there are no masses of exposures, the coverage is usually provided by specialty insurers. Lloyd's of London is known for insuring such "non-mass" exposures as Bruce Springsteen's voice. The types of insurers will be discussed in a later chapter.

Mass

A major requirement for insurability is **mass**; that is, there must be large numbers of exposure units involved. For automobile insurance, there must be a large number of automobiles to insure. For life insurance, there must be a large number of persons. An automobile insurance company cannot insure a dozen automobiles, and a life insurance company cannot insure the lives of a dozen persons. How large is a "large group"? For insurance purposes, the number of exposure units needed in a group depends upon the extent to which the insurer is willing to bear the risk of deviation from its expectations. Suppose the probability of damage to houses is 1/1,000. An insurer might assume this risk for 1,000 houses with the expectation that one claim would be made during the year. If no houses were damaged, there would be a 100 percent deviation from expectations, but such a deviation would create no burden for the insurer. On the other hand, if two houses were damaged, the claims to be paid would be twice the expected number. This could be a severe burden for the insurer, assuming average or higher loss severities. By increasing the number of similar houses insured to 10,000, the expected number of losses increases to ten but the stability of experience is increased. That is, there is a proportionately smaller deviation from expected losses than with a group of 1,000 houses. Similarly, if the group is increased to 100,000 houses, the variation between actual and expected losses would be likely to increase in absolute terms, but decline proportionately. Appendix 1.2 in Chapter 1 demonstrates the impact of larger number of exposures.

Similarity

The loss exposures to be insured and those observed for calculating the probability distributions must have **similarity**. The exposures assumed by insurers are not identical, no matter how carefully they may be selected. No two houses are identical, even though physically they may appear to be. They cannot have an identical location, and perhaps more importantly they are occupied by different families. Nevertheless, the units in a group must be reasonably similar in characteristics if predictions concerning them are to be accurate. For example, homes with brick sidings are similar for insurance purposes.

Moreover, probability distributions calculated on the basis of observed experience must also involve units similar to one another. Observing the occupational injuries and illnesses of a group of people whose age, health, and occupations were all different would not provide a basis for calculating workers' compensation insurance rates. For example, clerical work typically involves much lower probabilities of work-related loss than do occupations such as logging timber or climbing utility poles. Estimates based on experience require that the exposure units observed be similar to one another. Moreover, such estimates are useful only in predicting losses for comparable exposures.

Accidental Losses

The risks assumed by an insurer must involve only the possibility, not the certainty, of loss to the insured. Losses must be accidental or **fortuitous**; that is, they must be a matter of chance. Ideally, the insured should have no control or influence over the event to be insured. In fact, this situation prevails only with respect to limited situations. As mentioned in Chapter 1, intangible and physical hazards influence the probability of loss. Prediction of potential losses is based on a probability distribution that has been estimated by observing past experience. Presumably, the events observed were, for the most part, fortuitous occurrences. The use of such estimates for predicting future losses is based on the assumption that future losses will also be a matter of chance. If this is not the case, predictions cannot be accurate.

Small Possibility of Catastrophe

The possibility of **catastrophic loss** may make a loss exposure uninsurable. A catastrophic potential to an insurer is one that could imperil the insurer's solvency. When an insurer assumes a group of risks, it expects the group as a whole to experience some losses—but only a small percentage of the group members to suffer loss at any one time. Given this assumption, a relatively small contribution by each member of the group will be sufficient to pay for all losses. It is possible for a large percentage of all insureds to suffer a loss simultaneously, however, the "relatively small contributions" would not provide sufficient funds. Similarly, a single very large loss would also require large contributions. Thus, a requisite for insurability is that there must be no excessive possibility of **catastrophe** for the group as a whole. There must be limits that insurers can be reasonably sure their losses will not exceed. Insurers build up surpluses (net worth) and contingency reserves (funds for future claims) to take care of deviations of experience from the average, but such deviations must have practical limits. If losses cannot be predicted with reasonable accuracy and confidence, it is impossible to determine either insurance premium rates or the size of surpluses required. Chapter 4 explains surplus and reserves in more detail.

Catastrophic losses may occur in two circumstances. In the first, all or many units of the group are exposed to the same loss-causing event, such as war, flood, terrorist attack, or unemployment. For example, if one insurer had assumed the risk of damage by wind (hurricane) for all houses in the Miami, Florida, area, it would have suffered a catastrophic loss in 1992 when many structures were damaged simultaneously (and in fact several insurers were unable to withstand the losses). This is an example of dependent exposure units. Exposure units are **dependent** if loss to one affects the probability of loss to another. Thus, fire at one location increases the probability of fire at other homes in the area. Their experience is dependent. In the early days of insurance in the United States, many fire insurance companies concentrated their business in small areas near their headquarters. This worked in New York, for example, until a major fire devastated large sections of the city in 1835. Because of their concentrated exposures, several insurers suffered losses to a large percentage of their business. The insurers were unable to pay all claims and several went bankrupt.

A recent example of catastrophe exposure is the case of the mold described in Chapter 1. Mold has created a major availability and affordability issue in the homeowners and commercial property insurance arena. The *Wall Street Journal* article "Hit With Big Losses, Insurers Put Squeeze on Homeowner Policies" reported that "a slew of disasters [in 2001]—ranging from massive storms in the Midwest and a costly outbreak of mold in Texas to the September 11 terrorist attacks—has suddenly rocked insurers with big underwriting losses. Now the companies are trying to wring profits from homeowners policies, and growing numbers of the nation's 58.6 million homeowners are paying the price." [4] The article described massive exclusions of mold coverages because of the "avalanche of claims." (One of the appendices in the back of this textbook includes the ISO form "Fungi and Bacteria Exclusion.")

A second type of catastrophe exposure arises when a single large value may be exposed to loss. September 11, 2001, represents the ultimate catastrophic loss. Tremendous value was concentrated in the towers of the World Trade Center. The possibility of a man-made catastrophe of such magnitude was not anticipated. Private insurers stopped short of calling the terrorist attacks "acts of war"—which would have been excluded from coverage—and honored the policies covering the World Trade Center and the lives of the victims.

However, one consequence was the industry's action to immediately exclude terrorism coverage from new policies. The *National Underwriter* article "Check Rearview Mirror on Terrorism Risks" pointed out that one of the immediate reactions to mega-catastrophes has been retrenchment in the policies provisions provided by primary insurers and reinsurers.[5] When insurers and reinsurers (the insurers of the insurance companies) see the peril as having a far higher probability than previously perceived, they know that they can no longer accurately predict future losses, and their immediate reaction is to exclude the peril. However, because of regulation and oversight (explained in Chapter 5), the industry cannot make policy changes instantaneously.[6] (The ISO, which drafted the new policies on behalf of its member insurers, filed the policy modification. More will be discussed in future chapters.) When private insurers can no longer provide coverages, a solution is the creation of governmental pools, such as federal flood insurance. After September 11, many solutions using pools were proposed.[7] On November 26, 2002, President George W. Bush signed a Terrorism Insurance bill. The background and discussion is offered in the "Ethical Dilemma: Who Should Insure Against Terrorism?" in this chapter.[8] More on this topic and on reinsurance will be explained in more details in Chapters 4 and 5.

Definite Losses

Losses must be definite in time, place, and amount, because in many cases, insurers promise to pay in dollar amounts for losses if they occur during a particular time and in a particular geographical area. For example, the contract may cover loss by fire at a specified location. For this contract to be effective, it must be possible to determine when, where, and how much loss occurred. If this cannot be established, it is impossible to determine whether the loss is covered under the terms of the contract. The fact that "pain and suffering" is hard to measure in dollar terms increases the insurer's risk when calculating rates for liability insurance. One other reason the requirement of definiteness is essential is that it is necessary to accumulate data for future predictions. Unless such data can be accurate, they cannot provide the basis for useful predictions.

Determinable Probability Distribution

For an exposure to loss to be insurable, the expected loss must be calculable. Ideally, this means that there is a **determinable probability distribution** for losses within a reasonable degree of accuracy. Insurance premium rates are based on predictions of the future which are expressed quantitatively as expected losses. Calculation of expected losses requires the use of estimated probability distributions.

Probability distributions based on experience are useful for prediction, however, only when it is safe to assume that factors shaping events in the future will be similar to those of the past. For this reason, mortality (death) rates during times of peace are inappropriate for estimating the number of insured deaths during times of war. Similarly, the introduction of new technologies such as foam blanketing makes past experience of fire damage a poor indicator of future experience. Yet because the technology is new and no theory exists as to what the losses ought to be, the actuary has little information on which to base lower rates. The actuary must use subjective estimates as well as engineering information to develop proper rates.

When the probability distribution of losses for the exposure to be insured against cannot be calculated with reasonable accuracy, the risk is uninsurable. An example of purported uninsurability due to inability to predict losses is the nuclear power industry. Insurance experts convinced government officials in 1957 that the risk of loss caused by an incident at a nuclear power site was too uncertain (because of lack of experience and unknown

Ethical Dilemma

Who Should Insure Against Terrorism?

The terrorist attacks of September 11, 2001, caused the largest insurance losses ever recorded—more than twice as much as the runner-up, 1992's Hurricane Andrew, which destroyed 125,000 homes in Florida and Louisiana. As the insurance industry set about paying the estimated $50 billion in claims (with some claims from secondary effects still to be filed), it began reconsidering its ability to offer terrorism insurance, which until then was routinely included in commercial property policies.

Recall the functions of insurance: to predict losses based on experience, to pool risks, and to set premium prices accordingly. But no actuary can predict if or when another attack will occur, or whether it will cost $10,000 or $100 billion. Many insurers—as much as 80 percent, according to a survey conducted five months after the attacks—decided they couldn't afford to offer terrorism insurance at any price, and excluded it from their new and renewal business. Businesses that wanted terrorism coverage had to pay sky-high premiums to the few insurers that offered it.

Without complete insurance, builders and developers had difficulty getting financing for new projects—some banks were hesitant to lend millions of dollars against a building that just might be the next one to be blown up. Believing that the lack of terrorism coverage could put the economy at risk, the U.S. House and Senate each passed "terrorism backstop" bills. A version closer to the Senate bill was signed into law by President George W. Bush on November 26, 2002 after lengthy debate. Under the new law, the government could aid the industry on terrorism-related claims over a certain level of deductibles. The federal government would cover 90 percent over the deductibles. The program would be capped at $100 billion over three years, and no punitive damages will be included.

Consumer-advocacy groups much prefer the House's version. Under the house proposal the government would establish a loan fund that the insurers could use to pay terrorism-related claims, but the money would have to be repaid. In a joint statement, the Consumer Federation of America (CFA) and Consumers Union, the publisher of *Consumer Reports,* called the Senate bill a subsidy for the insurance industry. "It is shocking that Congress and the president accepted the wild claims made by insurance and real estate lobbyists at face value," said J. Robert Hunter, CFA's director of insurance. "The new law makes taxpayers liable for billions of dollars in losses that the insurance industry could easily afford." From a risk-management standpoint, some groups are concerned that government support could actually increase losses: Insurers with little to lose may be less likely to insist that their clients follow strict security policies and rehearse emergency procedures.

How can the needs of taxpayers, businesses, and the insurance industry all be met fairly?

Questions for Discussion

1. Since terrorism is a national problem, not controllable by insurers, shouldn't the government pay for terrorism-related damages?

2. Since insurance is the business of insurers, shouldn't they handle their problems without being subsidized by taxpayers?

Sources: Stephen Power and Christopher Oster, "U.S. Future as Insurer Is Unclear as Firms Disagree on Federal Role" *The Wall Street Journal,* 17 June 2002; Mark A. Hofmann, "Consumer Groups Oppose Terrorism Insurance Plan," *Business Insurance,* 28 May 2002;"RIMS Lobbies for Congress to Back Terrorism Reinsurance," *National Underwriter,* Property & Casualty/Risk & Benefits Management Edition, 18 February 2002; "Bush Signs Bill Limiting Insurers' Liability After an Attack" by The Associated Press, 26 November, 2002.

maximum severity) for commercial insurers to accept without some government intervention. As a result, the government limited the liability of owners of nuclear power plants for losses that would arise from such incidents.

Economic Feasibility

For insurance to be **economically feasible** for an insured, the size of the possible loss must be significant to the insured and the cost of insurance must be small compared with the potential loss. Otherwise, the purchase of insurance is not practical. If the possible loss is not significant to those exposed, insurance is inappropriate. Retention (bearing the financial loss by oneself) of many risks is almost automatic, because the loss would not be a burden. If all the people who own automobiles were wealthy, it is doubtful that much automobile collision insurance would be written, because such losses would not be significant to the wealthy owners. Insurance is feasible only when the possible loss is large enough to be of concern to the person who may bear the burden.

The possible loss must also be relatively large compared with the size of the premium. If the losses the insurer pays plus the cost of insurer operations are such that the premium must be very large in relation to the potential loss, insurance is not economically feasible. When the expected loss premium is high relative to the maximum possible loss, internal budgeting for the risk is preferable to insurance. The use of deductibles (a form of retention) to eliminate insurance reimbursement for frequent small losses helps make automobile collision premiums economically feasible.

The deductible eliminates claims for small losses. Small automobile collision losses have such high probability and the cost of settling them is so great that the premium for covering them would be very large compared with the size of actual losses. For example, if a policy with a $200 deductible costs $85 more than one with a $500 deductible, you may consider $85 too large a premium for $300 of insurance. Insurance is best suited for risks involving large potential losses with low probabilities, as will be described in Chapter 3. Large losses are key because insureds cannot bear them, and low probabilities for large losses make premiums relatively small compared with the possible losses. In other situations, insurance may not be economically feasible for the person or business facing risk.

SUMMARY OF INSURABLE RISKS

Table 2.1 provides an analysis of the insurability characteristics of a few common perils/risks. The first column lists the requirements for insurability that we have just discussed. Note that the risk of flooding is not considered insurable because of its potential for catastrophe: Many exposures can suffer losses in the same location. Thus flooding is covered by the federal government, not by private insurers. (Hurricanes, though similar to floods, are covered by private insurers, who obtain reinsurance to limit their exposure. After a catastrophe like Hurricane Andrew, however, many reinsurers became financially strapped or insolvent.)

The second example in Table 2.1 is the peril/risk of fire. Fire is an insurable risk, since it meets all the required elements. However, even this peril can be catastrophic if fires cannot be controlled and a large geographical area is damaged such as the large fires in Colorado and Arizona in 2002.[8] Disability is another type of peril that is considered insurable in most cases. The last example is terrorism risk. As noted above, it is no longer con-

TABLE 2.1

Examples of Insurable and Uninsurable Risks

	Flood	Fire	Disability	Terrorism
Large number of similar exposure units	Yes	Yes	Yes	No
Accidental, uncontrollable	Yes	Yes	Yes	No (Man-made, though not by the insured)
Potentially catastrophic	Yes	No	No	Yes
Definite losses	Yes	Yes	No	Yes
Determinable probability distribution of losses	Yes	Yes	Yes	No
Economically feasible	Depends	Depends	Depends	No
Insurable?	**No**	**Yes**	**Yes**	**No**

sidered an insurable risk due to the catastrophic element associated with this peril since the September 11, 2001, attack.

TYPES OF INSURANCE

Many types of insurance policies are available to families and organizations that do not wish to retain their own risks. The following questions may be raised about an insurance policy:

- Is it personal, group, or commercial?
- Is it life/health or property/casualty?
- Is it issued by a private insurer or a government agency?
- Is it purchased voluntarily or involuntarily?

Personal, Group, or Commercial

Personal insurance is purchased by individuals and families for their risk needs. Such insurance includes life, health, disability, auto, homeowner, and long-term care. **Group insurance** is provided by the employer for the benefit of employees. Group coverages include life, disability, health, and pension plans. **Commercial insurance** is property/casualty insurance for businesses and other organizations.

An insurance company is likely to have separate divisions within its **underwriting** department for personal lines, group lines, and commercial business. The criteria to assign insureds into their appropriate risk pool for rating purposes is different for each type of insurance. Staff in the personal lines division are trained to look for risk factors (for example, driving records and types of home construction) that influence the frequency and severity of claims among individuals and families; group underwriting looks at the characteristics and demographics, including prior experience, of the employee group; the commercial division has underwriting experts on risks faced by organizations. Personnel in other functional areas such as claims adjustment also may specialize in personal, group, or commercial lines. (More details are provided in Chapter 4.)

Life/Health or Property/Casualty

Life/health insurance covers exposures to the perils of death, medical expenses, disability, and old age. Private life insurance companies provide insurance for these perils, and individuals voluntarily decide whether or not to buy their products. Health insurance is provided primarily by life/health insurers but is also sold by some property/casualty insurers. All of these are available on an individual and a group basis.

The Social Security program provides substantial amounts of life/health insurance on an involuntary basis. This governmental program will be listed in Chapter 5 with further details in later chapters.

Property/casualty insurance covers property exposures such as direct and indirect losses of property caused by perils such as fire, windstorm, and theft. It also includes insurance to cover the possibility of being held legally liable to pay damages to another person. Before the passage of multiple-line underwriting laws in the late 1940s and early 1950s, property/casualty insurance had to be written by different insurers. Now they frequently are written in the same contract (for example, homeowners and commercial package policies, which will be discussed in later chapters).

A private insurer can be classified as either a life/health or a property/casualty insurer. Health insurance may be sold by either. Some insurers specialize in a particular type of insurance, such as property insurance. Others are affiliated insurers, in which several insurers (and sometimes non-insurance businesses) are controlled by a holding company; all or almost all types of insurance are offered by some company in the group.

Private or Government

Insurance is provided both by privately owned organizations and by state and federal agencies. Measured by premium income, the bulk of property/casualty insurance is provided by private insurers. Largely because of the magnitude of the Social Security program, however, government provides about one-third more personal insurance than the private sector. Our society has elected to provide certain levels of death, health, retirement, and unemployment insurance on an involuntary basis through governmental (federal and state) agencies. If we desire to supplement the benefit levels of social insurance or to buy property/casualty insurance, some of which is required, private insurers provide the protection.

Voluntary or Involuntary

Most private insurance is purchased voluntarily, although some types, such as automobile insurance or insurance on mortgages and car loans, are required by law or contracts. In many states, the purchase of automobile liability insurance is mandatory, and if the car is financed the lender requires property damage coverage. Automobile insurance and the requirements by laws are discussed in Chapter 11.

Government insurance is involuntary under certain conditions for certain people. Most people are required by law to participate in the Social Security program, which provides life, health, disability, and retirement coverage. Unemployment and workers' compensation insurance are also forms of involuntary social insurance provided by the government (discussed in Chapter 13). Some government insurance, however, is available to those who want it, but no one is required to buy it, such as flood insurance (discussed in Chapter 10).

SELECTING AN INSURER

As noted in the beginning of the chapter, the transfer of risk to a private insurer can be successful only if we use the appropriate insurer. We, therefore, add in this chapter ways to evaluate the financial quality of insurers.

Financial Strength

When buying insurance, one is buying a promise to be kept in the future. Will the insurer be able to keep its promises? Clearly, **financial strength** and stability are of prime importance to an insurance consumer. The study of an insurer's financial condition is critical. **Due diligence** is the process of determining the degree of financial strength that characterizes a financial services firm. Chapter 4 discusses the role of agents or brokers in the sale of insurance. Insurance sales people usually help in evaluating the financial strength of an insurer. The agents or brokers most likely would use the rating of some credible financial rating organization to learn about the quality of the insurers. Historically, the A. M. Best Company was the primary source of financial ratings for insurers. Now there are five rating organizations, Best's, Duff and Phelps, Moody's, Standard & Poor's, and Weiss. All these organizations provide specific guidelines to interpreting the insurer's rating. For example, Duff & Phelps, Moody's, and Standard & Poor's each have seven ratings that include the letter "A," which the general public tends to associate with excellence. Joseph M. Belth, professor emeritus of insurance at the University of Indiana and editor of *The Insurance Forum,* recommends that a conservative buyer select an insurer with a very high rating from at least two of the rating organizations.

For example, Best's A + + and A + may be considered very high ratings. Belth further recommends reading the reports provided by the rating organizations.[9] Any downward trend in financial ratings is a danger signal requiring exploration. The ratings of each insurer are available on the A. M. Best Web site, www.ambest.com. Best News also regularly publishes ratings changes. This source is available at most university libraries.

In the next chapter we will cover risk management. We will go through the processes of determining risk and the solutions to mitigating risk.

KEY TERMS

insurance	catastrophe	commercial insurance
law of large numbers	dependent	life/health insurance
discriminate	determinable probability	property/casualty
adverse selection	distribution	insurance
mass	economically feasible	financial strength
similarity	personal insurance	due diligence
fortuitous	group insurance	

DISCUSSION QUESTIONS

1. When you buy a service contract on your new refrigerator, are you buying insurance? Explain.
2. Your friend says, "I don't bother insuring against losses that probably won't happen. If the insurance company can be guided by probability, why can't I?" How would you respond to this statement?
3. How can small insurers survive without large number of exposures?
4. Professor Kulp said, "Insurance works well for some exposures, to some extent for many, and not at all for others." Do you agree? Why, or why not?
5. Insurance requires a transfer of risk. Risk is uncertain variability of future outcomes. Does life insurance meet the ideal requisites of insurance when the insurance company is aware that death is a certainty?
6. What are the benefits of insurance to individuals and to society?
7. What types of insurance exist? Describe the differences among them
8. How can we find out the quality of the insurance company we select?
9. Explain whether the following risks/perils are insurable by private insurer:
   a. a strike
   b. unemployment
   c. slipping in the grocery store
   d. falling off a ladder while cleaning the gutters
   e. a hail storm destroying your roof
   f. the life of an eighty-year-old man
   g. a flood
   h. mold

    i.   biological warfare

    j.   dirty bombs

EXERCISES

2.1 Hatch's furniture store has many perils that threaten its operation each day. Explain why each of the following perils may or may not be insurable. In each case, discuss possible exceptions to the general answer you have given.

    a.   The loss of merchandise because of theft when the thief is not caught and Hatch's cannot establish exactly when the loss occurred.

    b.   Injury to a customer when the store's delivery person backs the delivery truck into that customer while delivering a chair.

    c.   Injury to a customer when a sofa catches fire from internal combustion and burns the customer's living room. Discuss the fire damage to the customer's home, as well as the customer's bodily injury.

    d.   Injury to a customer's child who runs down an aisle in the store and falls.

    e.   Mental suffering of a customer whose merchandise is not delivered on schedule.

2.2 Jack and Jill decided they couldn't afford to buy auto insurance. Since they are in a class with 160 students, they came up with the idea of sharing the automobile risk with the rest of the students. Their professor loved the idea and asked them to explain in detail how it will work. Pretend you are Jack and Jill. Explain to the class the following:

    a.   If you expect to have only three losses per year on average (frequency) for a total of $10,000 each loss (severity), what will be the cost of sharing of these losses per student in the class?

    b.   Do you think you have enough exposures to predict only three losses a year? Explain.

NOTES

1.   Remember from Chapter 1 that an exposure is the property or person facing a condition in which loss is possible.

2.   Recent health care reforms (HIPAA, 1996) have limited the ability of insurers to reduce adverse selection through the use of preexisting condition limitations (see Chapter 17).

3.   Governmental insurance programs make greater deviations from the ideal requisites for insurability. They are able to accept greater risks because they often make their insurance compulsory and have it subsidized from tax revenues, while private insurers will operate only when a profit potential exists. The nature of government insurance programs will be outlined later in this chapter.

4.   Christopher Oster and Jeff D. Opdyke, "Hit With Big Losses, Insurers Put Squeeze on Homeowner Policies," *Wall Street Journal,* 14 May 2002.

5.   Sean F. Mooney, "Check Rearview Mirror on Terrorism Risks," *National Underwriter,* 25 February 2002.

6.   Insurance is regulated by the states. This will be covered in more detail in Chapter 5.

7.   "European airlines considering terrorism pool," BusinessInsurance.com, posted 5 May 2002; "French insurers form terrorism pool," *Business Insurance,* 17 December 2001; "Industry needs safety net," *Business Insurance,* 1 October 2001.

8.   Reported in all media sources during 2002. More details will be provided in the property risk exposure chapters later.

9.   Joseph M. Belth, "Financial Strength Ratings of 1,600 Life-Health Insurance Companies." *Insurance Forum,* Vol. 22, Nos. 3 & 4 (1995): pp 146–47.

CHAPTER 3

The Evolution of Risk Management

Traditionally, the **risk management** position in an organization was mostly responsible for buying insurance. Risk managers were charged with obtaining coverage for pure risks. When coverage became less available or more expensive because of large losses, risk managers became creative by using strategies of **risk retention** (keeping the risk in-house):

- Taking larger **deductibles** (not receiving first dollar of loss; losses are covered by insurance only after a certain amount is covered by the insured)
- Reducing coverage ceilings or limits
- Adopting loss control techniques

Such actions occurred when, for example, workers' compensation coverage—the coverage an employer is required to provide to its employees under most state laws in case of injury on the job—became prohibitively expensive. Risk managers retained large portions of the risk by self-insuring and buying "stop loss" insurance: coverage against large catastrophes such as for losses over one million dollars. (Other risk-retention strategies will be discussed in Chapters 4 and 5. Workers' compensation coverage is detailed in Chapter 13.)

Today, the evolution of information technology, globalization, and innovation in financial technologies have brought new solutions to old risks as well as to emerging ones such as espionage of intellectual property, terrorism, and biological warfare. Risk managers today find themselves stepping out of their traditional role. Many of them map the risks of their organizations, both pure and speculative. The risk management department of Microsoft created a system called **risk mapping** to identify all risks and their associated risk management solutions.[1] The risk managers found rather revealing surprises when they identified major risks that did not have insurance solutions. Most of these types of risk managers are also interested in more sophisticated insurance programs, such as those featured in Case 3 at the back of the textbook.

With the availability of **risk management information systems** (**RMIS**) and the heightened awareness of risks, today's complete picture of the risks in the organization is part of enterprise risk management. The risk management position post September 11, 2001, is no longer buried under the treasurer in the trenches of the business. Many risk managers are now called **chief risk officers** (**CROs**) and are members of the executive team charged with evaluating all aspects of risks. Managing speculative and pure risks now incorporates many financial technologies: derivative instruments like options and other financial market instruments, cash flow analysis, quantitative models such as the value at risk (VAR) technique, simulations, securitizations, and CAT bonds. We will discuss these complex non-insurance solutions briefly in this chapter and in Case 4 at the end of the textbook. Case 4 provides a glimpse into financial risk management and the new tools. If the risk manager is also a financial risk manager, the duties require a high level of sophistication beyond the traditional position of purchaser of insurance.

Financial risk management is introduced here as part of enterprise risk management. The brief explanations in this chapter are to show students how, in today's era of risk management and finance advances, the fields are integrated. Students interested in financial risk management are advised to take advanced finance courses.[2]

This chapter therefore includes the following:

1. Connections
2. The risk manager as a decision maker
3. The traditional risk management process
4. First expansion: Risk mapping and RMIS
5. Most recent expansion: Enterprise risk management and using the capital markets

CONNECTIONS

Insurance as an important component of risk management was the topic of Chapter 2. In this chapter, we follow the same connecting theme. Our holistic risk is the focus, and holistic risk management is connected to our complete package of risks as shown in Figure 3.1. In order to complete the connecting puzzle we have to identify all the risks and find risk management solutions to all of them. The risk management decision is dependent on the nature of the risk, the frequency and severity of losses, and external market conditions. Many pure risks have insurance solutions. Investment risks, on the other hand, do not have insurance solutions. For such risks, you, the student, are advised to take finance courses where you can study specific methods for reducing speculative risk. In this chapter you will be introduced to solutions to catastrophic risks via financial instruments. A way to mitigate potential stock market losses is the use of derivative instruments. Derivatives are financial instruments that are derived from a primary investment such as stocks. For example, options on stocks are a derivative instrument that was created to mitigate the risk of big fluctuations in stock prices. The options, as you will see later, act as an insurance policy against losses in stock.

In some cases, we may decide not to use insurance and instead avoid the risk altogether, self-insure it, or use safety provisions to reduce it. As this textbook focuses mostly on using insurance to manage risk, it is important to understand when it is most appropriate to use. Overall, in this connection section, shown in Figure 3.1, our puzzle become complete only when all the risks are mitigated in a smart risk management process. As individuals, we also care about the risk management of our own businesses or our employers'. Therefore, corporate risk management is paramount to our individual risk strategy.

In Figure 3.1, the focus is on how to manage pure risk, speculative risk, and external factors affecting the risk management decision. The basic matrix of the pure risk management decisions has traditionally used frequency and severity of losses as the paramount factors. However, it cannot stand alone without the external influences and the incorporation of financial management techniques.

THE RISK MANAGER'S FUNCTIONS

Traditionally, a risk manager had responsibility for specific risks and was charged with providing adequate coverage using insurance. The role's primary function was to reduce the costs of pure risks to a firm and initiate safety and disaster management. The typical processes employed by a risk manager of a large corporation that self-insures some of the exposures, such as workers' compensation, are as follows:

- Create a mission statement for risk management in the organization
- Communicate with every section of the business

- Develop risk management policy
- Identify and measure all exposures to loss
- Choose risk finance alternatives
- Set up risk management manual
- Allocate costs
- Develop risk management policy
- Negotiate insurance
- Adjust claims

FIGURE 3.1   The Connection among all Risks and the Risk Management Solutions

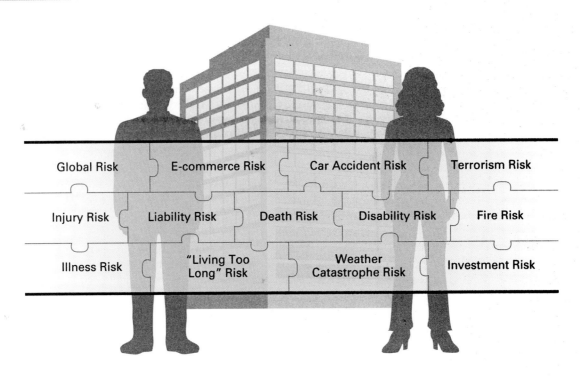

Risk Management Solutions

Pure Risk Solutions

	Low Frequency of Losses	High Frequency of Losses
Low Severity of Losses	Retention	Retention with Loss control
High Severity of Losses	Transfer—Insurance /reinsurance (New: Cat bonds and securitization for catastrophe risk)	Avoidance

Actions

Other Influences

- Financial Condition
- Nature of Risk
- External Market Conditions
- Size of the Firm

Solutions for Other Risks

- Cash Flow Management using Value at Risk (VAR)
- Using derivative instruments such as futures, swaps, and options

- Keep records
- Set up risk management manual
- Allocate costs
- Monitor and evaluate

The typical risk management position reports to the treasurer of the corporation, as shown in Figure 3.2 for the Navy Exchange Service Command (NEXCOM).[3] Since NEXCOM is a large corporation, the risk management department includes more than ten positions. As you will see, handling risk by self-insuring and paying claims in-house requires more personnel.[4] In a small company or sole proprietorship the owner usually performs the risk management function, establishing policy and making decisions. In fact, all of us are managers of our own risks, whether we have studied risk management or not. Every time we lock our house or car, check the wiring system for problems, or pay an insurance premium, we are performing the functions of a risk manager. So, while we will refer to risk managers in this text, keep in mind that many other people also manage risks.

Risk managers use the help of agents or brokers (see Chapter 4) to make smart insurance and risk management decisions. That traditional role has evolved. Corporations have begun to embrace enterprise risk management,[5] which is an evaluation of most risks—pure and speculative—in the organization. With this evolution, a new post called chief risk officer [6] has emerged. The role of CROs is to integrate their firm's "silos," or separate risks, into a holistic framework. Risks cannot be segregated; they interact and affect one another. Solutions are not limited to insurance, but rather include retaining risk; creating a **captive,** a separate insurance entity under the corporation mostly for the use of the firm (explained further in Chapter 5); using financial market instruments to hedge risk; even changing long standing business practices to mitigate potential risk. For example, a cereal manufacturer, dependent upon a steady supply of grain used in production, may decide to enter into "fixed-price" long-term contractual arrangements with its suppliers to avoid the risk of price fluctuations.

In larger organizations, the risk manager or CRO has differing authority depending upon the policy adopted by top management and adaptation to a culture of change. The dimensions of this authority are outlined in a policy statement. The risk manager may be authorized to make decisions in routine matters, but restricted to making only recommen-

FIGURE 3.2

Organization of a Risk Management Department

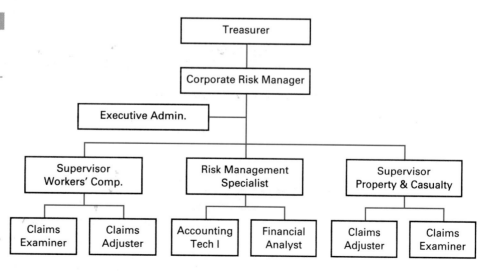

Source: Michael J. Lombardo, Corporate Risk Manager, Navy Exchange Service Command; presentation to Virginia Commonwealth University students, November 2001.

dations in others. For example, the risk manager may recommend that the costs of employee injuries be retained rather than insured, but a final decision of such magnitude would be made by top management.

THE TRADITIONAL RISK MANAGEMENT PROCESS

As described by the typical duties of the risk manager in a large corporation such as NEX-COM, risk management is the process of identifying, acknowledging, communicating, measuring, and monitoring key risks that are critical to the success or failure of the firm. We will review several vehicles used to aid the risk management process:

- communication tools
- identification tools and risk management decision tools
- on-going monitoring
- adjusting

From these cornerstone steps of the process, a framework can be developed that will enable a corporation to make appropriate risk management decisions. Risk managers begin the process by setting company objectives. From a traditional risk management viewpoint, those objectives will focus on the tradeoff between risk and return. Whatever objectives are chosen, success in meeting them depends somewhat on the ability to communicate them effectively.

Communication Tools

The primary tool used to communicate risk management objectives is a **risk management policy statement**. Risk management policy statements have had a place for many years in discussions of the risk management process. Other tools used to relay objectives may include company mission statements, a risk management manual (which provides specific guidelines for detailed risk management problems, such as how to deal with the death or disability of a key executive), and even the risk manager's job description. To be effective, risk management objectives must coincide with those of the organization generally, and both must be communicated consistently. Advertisements, employee training programs, and other public activities also can communicate an organization's philosophies and objectives.

Having set and communicated objectives, the next step in the process is to identify the many problems that could cause an organization to fail in meeting its objectives. The identification process includes the characteristics of the three categories discussed in Chapter 1: perils, exposures, and hazards.

Identification Tools and Risk Management Decision Tools: The Risk Management Matrix

Once identified, the risks are then evaluated with the intent of choosing appropriate mechanisms to reduce their adverse consequences. As discussed in Chapter 1, two important characteristics of potential losses must be measured to complete the evaluation phase of the risk management process. These are loss frequency and loss severity. Together, these characteristics help us understand the magnitude and riskiness of the problem under consideration.

The pure risk decision tool is frequently illustrated in a **risk management matrix**. On one axis, categories of relative frequency are listed; on the other, categories of relative severity. The simplest of these matrices is one with just four cells, as shown in the pure risk

FIGURE 3.3

The Traditional Risk
Management Matrix

Pure Risk Solutions

	Low Frequency of Losses	High Frequency of Losses
Low Severity of Losses	Retention—Self-insurance	Retention with Loss control—Risk reduction
High Severity of Losses	Transfer—Insurance	Avoidance

solutions in Figure 3.3. This matrix takes into account only two variables—frequency and severity. In reality, other variables—the financial condition of the firm, the size of the firm, and external market conditions, to name a few—are very important in the decision.[7]

Risk Avoidance

Starting with the lower right corner of the matrix in Figure 3.3, at the intersection of high frequency and high severity, we find **avoidance.** A situation falling in this category is best avoided, if possible. An example might be a firm that is considering construction of a building on the east coast of Florida. Flooding and hurricane risk would be high, with significant damage possibilities. Typically there are a dozen or more named tropical storms or hurricanes that occur during the June to November hurricane season.

Of course, we cannot always avoid risks. When Texas school districts were faced with high severity and frequency of losses in workers' compensation, schools could not close their doors to avoid the problem. Instead, the school districts opted to self-insure, that is, retain the risk up to a certain loss limit.

Not all avoidance necessarily results in "no loss." Avoidance of one loss potential may create another. Some people choose to travel by car instead of plane because of their fear of flying. While they have successfully avoided the possibility of being a passenger in an airplane accident, they have increased their probability of being in an automobile accident. Per mile traveled, automobile deaths are far more frequent than aircraft fatalities. By choosing cars over planes, these people actually raise their probability of injury.

Risk Assumption

The upper left corner of the matrix in Figure 3.3, representing both low frequency and low severity, shows **retention** of risk. When an organization uses a highly formalized method of retention on an insurable risk, it is said the organization has **self-insured** the risk. The company bears the risk without insurance and is willing to withstand the financial losses from claims, if any. It is important to note that the extent to which risk retention is feasible depends upon the accuracy of loss predictions and the arrangements made for loss payment. Because organizations are more likely to use the law of large numbers than is the typical individual, retention is especially attractive to large organizations.

When a company retains a risk, it usually employs a stop loss mechanism, which is insurance over a retention amount to safeguard against catastrophes. Stop loss in most cases is provided by reinsurers as a reinsurance coverage. **Reinsurance** is a system that reduces risk for an insurer. In effect, it is a method whereby an insurer transfers parts of the risk it obtained in order to diversify its exposure. The use of reinsurance expands risk sharing and makes the insurance transaction safer for the original consumer as well as the original insurer. Traditional reinsurance typically involves direct payment from a reinsurer to a primary insurer if a defined catastrophic event occurs. In some cases when a firm decides to self-insure, it buys reinsurance as a layer over the self-insurance amount to protect against catastrophes. In the example from NEXCOM, the company used layers of insurance over the self-insurance portion to protect against catastrophes, such as the major loss the company suffered in June 1991, with the volcanic eruption of Mt. Pinatubo in the Philippines. NEXCOM's property risks are protected though layers of insurance and reinsurance, but the first $2 million is self-insured. Thus, as you can see, retention or self-insurance is used for low frequency and severity of losses, but the fear of potential catastrophic loss such as volcanic eruption or a hurricane motivates the risk manager to undertake steps to protect the firm against catastrophes with insurance and reinsurance layers of stop loss coverage. These are done by purchasing layers of coverages over the retention level (explained further in Chapter 4). This concept is also illustrated in Case 3 at the back of the textbook.

Risk Reduction

Moving over to the upper right corner of the risk management matrix in Figure 3.3, the quadrant characterized by high frequency and low severity, we find retention with **loss control.** Where frequency is significant, efforts to prevent losses may be useful. If losses are of low value, they may be easily paid out of the organization's or individual's own funds. Highly frequent losses are predictable and are generally more cost-effectively financed through retention. An example might be losses due to wear and tear on equipment. Such losses are predictable and of a manageable, low annual value.

   Loss prevention efforts are aimed at reducing the probability of a loss occurring. **Loss reduction** efforts, on the other hand, are undertaken to lessen the severity of loss. If you want to ski in spite of the hazards involved, you may take instruction to improve your skills and reduce the likelihood of your falling down a hill or crashing into a tree. At the same time, you may engage in a physical fitness program to toughen your body to withstand spills without serious injury. Using both loss prevention and reduction techniques, you attempt to lower both the probability and severity of loss.

   The goal of loss prevention and reduction is to reduce losses to the minimum compatible with a reasonable level of human activity and expense. At any given time, economic constraints place limits on what may be done, although what is considered too costly at one time may be readily accepted at a later date. Thus, during one era, little effort may have been made to prevent injury to employees, because employees were regarded as expendable. The general notion today, however, is that such injuries are prevented because they have become too expensive. Change was made to adapt to the prevailing ideals concerning the value of human life and the social responsibility of business.

   When a risk manager makes the decision, each risk is evaluated separately. NEXCOM determined that its property risk was of sufficiently low frequency and severity to self-insure a portion of the loss with layers of coverage for catastrophes. Its workers' compensation losses, however, with low severity but high frequency, was a good candidate for retention with loss control. To prevent or control financial loss, NEXCOM adopted such techniques as instituting safety measures to reduce accidents and establishing return-to-work-programs for injured employees.

Risk Transfer

The lower left corner represents situations involving low frequency and high severity. Here we find **transfer of risk**—that is, insurance. A low-probability but high-valued event involves significant risk, which is most effectively managed when transferred, usually through the purchase of insurance. An example might be loss due to liability of the manufacture of a defective product, or loss caused by an interruption of business due to damage to a factory or terrorist attacks (as experienced on September 11). A common decision tool or process used by corporations when evaluating risky ventures is **cash flow analysis,** in which the actual flow of funds over the life of the project is estimated and valued. The proposed project must provide a sufficient risk/return tradeoff to meet the organization's goals. An example of cash flow analysis is given in Appendix 3.1 to this chapter.

To continue with our example, the corporate risk manager at NEXCOM transferred risk in two ways: by requiring its concessionaires and contractors to carry certain minimum levels of insurance, and by purchasing insurance itself. As explained before, in essence, risk transference is paying someone else to bear some or all of the risk of certain financial losses that cannot be avoided, assumed, or reduced to acceptable levels.

Some risks may be transferred through the formation of a corporation with limited liability for its stockholders. Others may be transferred by contractual arrangements, including insurance.

Corporations   The owner or owners of a firm face a serious potential loss in the responsibility for the payment of debts and other financial obligations when such liabilities exceed the firm's assets. If the firm is organized as a *sole proprietorship,* the proprietor faces this risk. His or her personal assets are not separable from those of the firm, because the firm is not a separate legal entity. The proprietor has unlimited liability for the firm's obligations. General partners in a *partnership* occupy a similar situation, each partner being liable without limit for the debts of the firm.

Because a corporation is a separate legal entity, investors who wish to limit possible losses connected with a particular venture may create a corporation and transfer such risks to it. This does not prevent losses from occurring, but the burden is transferred to the corporation. The owners suffer indirectly, of course, but their loss is limited to their investment in the corporation. A huge liability claim for damages may take all the assets of the corporation, but the stockholders' personal assets beyond their stock in this particular corporation are not exposed to loss. Such a method of risk transfer sometimes is used to compartmentalize the risks of a large venture by incorporating separate firms to handle various segments of the total operation. In this way, a large firm may transfer parts of its risks to separate smaller subsidiaries, thus placing limits on possible losses to the parent company owners. Courts, however, may not approve of this method of transferring the liability associated with dangerous business activities. For example, a large firm may be held legally liable for damages caused by a small subsidiary formed to manufacture a substance that proves dangerous to employees and/or the environment.

Contractual Arrangements   Some risks are transferred by a guarantee included in the contract of sale. A noteworthy example is the warranty provided the purchaser of an automobile. When automobiles were first manufactured, the purchaser bore the burden of all defects that developed during use. Somewhat later, automobile manufacturers agreed to replace defective parts at no cost, but the buyer was required to pay for any labor involved. Currently, manufacturers typically not only replace defective parts but also pay for labor, within certain constraints. The owner has, in effect, transferred a large part of the risk of purchasing a new automobile back to the manufacturer. The buyer, of course, is still subject to the inconvenience of having repairs made, but he or she does not have to pay for them.

Other types of contractual arrangements that transfer risk include leases and rental agreements, hold-harmless clauses,[8] and surety bonds.[9] Perhaps the most important arrangement for the transfer of risk important to our study is insurance.

Insurance is a common form of planned risk transfer as a financing technique for individuals and most organizations. The insurance industry has grown tremendously in industrialized countries, developing sophisticated products, employing millions of people, and investing billions of dollars. Because of its core importance in risk management, insurance is the centerpiece of this text. Various methods to improve the use of insurance in large corporations are explored in Case 3, "Non-Traditional Insurance Programs: The New Generation," at the back of this textbook. The case includes such programs as integrated risk and finite risk programs.

On-Going Monitoring

The process of risk management is continuous, requiring constant monitoring of the program to be certain that (1) the decisions implemented were correct and have been implemented appropriately; and that (2) the underlying problems have not changed so much as to require revised plans for managing them. When either of these conditions exists, the process returns to the step of identifying the risks and risk management tools and the cycle repeats. In this way, risk management can be considered a systems process, one in never-ending motion.

A summary of NEXCOM's risk management program for its various coverages is provided in Table 3.1. This data is pre-September 11, 2001. This is just an example of the magnitude of the work of a risk management department. The cost for this large corporation is staggering as shown in the pie chart of Figure 3.4. The cost is not adjusted to the post-September 11 extreme rate increases. In

	Coverage	Total Value Insured	Deductible	Layered Limit
TABLE 3.1 NEXCOM Risk Management Programs	Property—Catastrophic	$1.2 billion	$2.0 million (retention)	$100 million
	Property and Casualty	n.a.	$1.0 million	$25 million
	Group Life, Medical and Dental	self-insured	none	unlimited
	Fidelity & Fiduciary Liability	n.a.	$250K	$5 million
	Fiduciary Liability	n.a.	$10K	$10 million
	Workers' Compensation*	self-insured	none	unlimited
	Group Travel	n.a.	none	$100K

n.a.: not available.

*Governed by the U.S. Longshore and Harbor Workers' Compensation Act of 1927.

Source: Michael J. Lombardo, Corporate Risk Manager, Navy Exchange Service Command; presentation to Virginia Commonwealth University students, November 2001.

FIGURE 3.4

NEXCOM Risk Management Programs

Total Premium Costs: $2,001,000

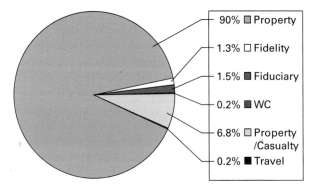

- 90% ◻ Property
- 1.3% ◻ Fidelity
- 1.5% ◼ Fiduciary
- 0.2% ◼ WC
- 6.8% ◻ Property /Casualty
- 0.2% ◼ Travel

Source: Michael J. Lombardo, Corporate Risk Manager, Navy Exchange Service Command; presentation to Virginia Commonwealth University students, November 2001.

all likelihood, a corporation such as NEXCOM would modify the risk management program dramatically to adjust to the changes in the insurance marketplace.

The mechanics of risk management is full of dynamics. As traditional pure risk solution methods became price prohibitive or less available, the risk management process became more creative. Technology aided the evolution of the process and added new risk to the enterprise spectrum. Additional quantitative techniques were required by risk managers to adapt to the change. A holistic risk management model was needed to understand the interrelations among the many risks, both old and new, that affected a corporation. Risk mapping is introduced as one of the new innovative techniques that are used to aid the ever-evolving risk management process.

FIRST EXPANSION OF THE RISK MANAGEMENT SCOPE: RISK MAPPING

Identification of risk management problems is difficult because there is so much to observe. The major steps involved in expanding upon identification tools used in the risk management process include:

- Risk profiling
- Risk mapping—creating the model
- Risk identification and loss estimates
- Plotting the risk map
- Comparing to current risk handling
- The effect of risk handling methods

Risk Profiling

The discovery process is critical to learning and understanding an organization's tolerance for risk. In addition, it is necessary to thoroughly review a firm's overall exposures. This process is known as **risk profiling.** Both the types of risk and the severity of risk can be vastly different among industries. Boeing, for example, has a tremendous wrongful-death exposure resulting from plane crashes. Intellectual property piracy and property rights issues could have a big impact upon the operations of an organization like Microsoft.[10]

Risk Mapping: Creating the Model

The results of risk profiling can be graphically displayed and developed into a model. One such model is risk mapping. Risk mapping involves consideration of the entire spectrum of risk, not individual risk "silos" from each separate business unit. It is useful both in identifying risks and in choosing approaches to mitigate them. Different facets of risk could include workers' compensation claims, earthquake or tornado exposure, credit risk, mold, terrorism, theft, intellectual property piracy, and a host of other concerns. Risks a company faces are put into a visual medium to see how risks are clustered and to understand the relationships among risks. Risk maps can be useful tools for explaining and communicating the various risks to management and employees. One map might be created to chart what risks are most significant to a particular company. This chart would be used to prioritize risk across the enterprise. Another map might show which risks are insured and which are not.[11] For comparative purposes, a risk map can be created to show frequency/severity risk plots before and after solutions are adopted. Figure 3.5 is a holistic risk map for an organization examining the dynamics of frequency and severity as they relate to each risk. By assigning the probability of occurrence against the estimate of current or future magnitude of possible loss, a risk manager forms a foundation on which a corporation can focus on risk areas in need of avoidance, loss control, or insurance (loss transfer) solutions.[12] Note that this risk map expands the traditional risk matrix by quantifying the measures of an X axis of frequency and a Y axis of severity and visually plotting their intersection points. Each point represents the relationship between the frequency of the exposure and the severity of the exposure for each risk measured.

Risk Identification and Loss Estimates

Strategies for risk mapping will vary from organization to organization. Just as in the traditional risk management process, company objectives must be determined in terms of risk and return. These objectives help determine the risk tolerance level of the organization. For most, the first step in mapping risk is to identify the firm's loss exposures and estimate the frequency and severity of each potential loss. Figure 3.5 displays for illustration purposes only the quantified estimates of the loss frequency and severity that are then used as inputs into the risk map for a hypothetical small import-export business, Notable Notions. The risk map graph is divided into the four quadrants of the classical risk management-matrix shown in Figure 3.3.

- Upper left quadrant: high severity and low frequency losses. This type of risk characteristics is best handled with insurance.

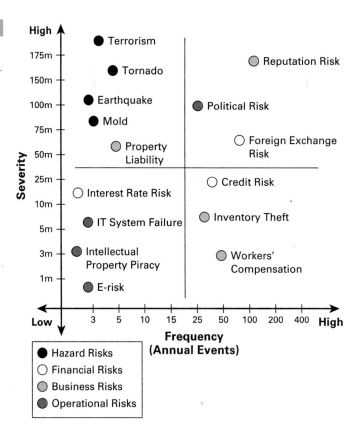

FIGURE 3.5

Notable Notions
Risk Map

- Upper right quadrant: high severity and high frequency losses. This type of risk is best to avoid. This is not always feasible, in which case loss control methods might be used to reduce frequency and severity. Another method is to create a captive, a dedicated insurance company for the business (explained in Chapter 5).

- Lower left quadrant: low frequency and low severity. These are risks usually retained (self-insured).

- Lower right quadrant: high frequency and low severity. Loss control techniques should be used to reduce the frequency of these losses.

Ethical Dilemma

What Does the Anthrax Scare Mean for Business Today?

The date staring up from the desk calendar reads June 1, 2002, so why is the Capitol Hill office executive assistant opening Christmas cards? It is because of a post-September 11, 2001, reality: Mail delivery is not what it used to be. For six weeks after an anthrax-contaminated letter was received in Senate Majority Leader Tom Daschle's office, all Capitol Hill mail delivery was stopped. As startling as that sounds, mail delivery is of small concern to the many public and private entities that suffered loss due to the terrorism-related issues of anthrax. The biological agent scare, both real and imagined, is generating unique issues for businesses and insurers alike.

Who is responsible for the clean-up costs related to bioterrorism? Who is liable for the exposure to humans within the contaminated facility? Who covers the cost of a shutdown of a business for decontamination? "Just a biological exposure to humans, without property damage, wouldn't be covered [under standard property insurance], said William C. Wilson, Jr., director of the Independent Insurance Agents of America's Virtual University. "A shutdown of a business for biochemical assessment, remediation, et cetera, could result in a large business income and extra expense loss that would be uninsured unless there has been direct damage." Sen. Charles Grassley (R-Iowa), member of the Senate Finance Committee, estimated that the cleanup project cost for the Hart Senate Office Building will exceed $23 million. Manhattan Eye, Ear, and Throat Hospital closed its doors in late October 2001 after a supply-room worker contracted and later died from pulmonary anthrax. The hospital, a small, thirty-bed facility, reopened November 6, 2001, announcing that the anthrax scare closure had cost the facility an estimated $700,000 in revenue.

These examples illustrate the necessity of holistic risk management and the effective use of risk mapping to identify *any* possible risk. Even if their companies are not likely to be directly targeted, risk managers must incorporate disaster management plans to deal with indirect atrocities that slow or abort the firms' operations. For example, an import-export business must protect against extended halts in overseas commercial air traffic. A mail-order-catalog retailer must protect against long-term mail delays. Evacuation of a workplace for employees due to mold infestation or biochemical exposure must now be added to disaster recovery plans. After a temporary closure, reopened facilities can still give cause for concern. Staffers at the Hart Senate Office Building were given the green light to return to work on January 22, 2002, after the anthrax remediation process was completed. Immediately staffers began reporting illnesses. By March, 255 of the building's employees had complained of symptoms that included headaches, rashes, and eye or throat irritation, possibly from the chemicals used to kill the anthrax. Was the decision to reopen the facility too hasty? Is Congressional credibility another victim of the anthrax scare?

Questions for Discussion

1. What factors would you have considered in deciding when to reopen the Manhattan Eye, Ear, and Throat Hospital and the Hart Senate Office Building?

2. How should management balance reputation with profitability goals in determining acceptable risk?

Sources: "US Lawmakers Complain About Old Mail After Anthrax Scare." Dow Jones Newswires, 8 May 2002; David Pilla, "Anthrax Scare Raises New Liability Issues for Insurers," A.M. Best Newswire, October 16, 2001; Sheila R. Cherry, "Health Questions Linger at Hart," *Insight on the News*, April 15, 2002, p.16; Cinda Becker, "N.Y. Hospital Reopens; Anthrax Scare Costs Facility $700,000," *Modern Healthcare*, 12 November 2001, p. 8; Sheila R. Cherry, "Health Questions Linger at Hart," *Insight on the News*, April 15, 2002, p. 16(2).

Plotting the Risk Map

Several sample risks are plotted in Notable Notions' holistic risk map.[13] This model can be used to help establish a risk-tolerance boundary and determine priority for risks facing the organization. Graphically, risk across the enterprise comes from four basic risk categories: hazard, financial, business, and operational.

Hazard risks are unforeseen events that arise outside of the normal operating environment. The risk map denotes that the probability of a hazard occurring is very low, but the potential severity is very high—in the event of a tornado, valued at approximately $160 million. This risk is similar to earthquake, mold exposure, and even terrorism, all of which also fall into the low frequency/high severity quadrant.[14] Post September 11, 2001, most corporations have reprioritized possible losses related to terrorism events. For example, more than 1,200 World Bank employees were sent home and barred from corporate headquarters for several days following an anthrax scare in the mailroom.[15] This possibility exposes firms to large potential losses associated with an unexpected interruption to normal business operations. See "Ethical Dilemma: What Does the Anthrax Scare Really Mean for Business Today?"

Financial risks arise from changing market conditions involving prices, volatility, liquidity, and credit risk. Variables such as interest rates and foreign exchange rates can affect the value of a firm's assets. Because of its global customer base, Notable Notions has a tremendous amount of exposure to exchange rate risk. Its risk map denotes the high number (frequency) of transactions in addition to the high dollar exposure (severity) associated with adverse foreign exchange rate movement. The frequent possibility for losses is predictable, however, and the risk manager uses this insight in evaluating possible alternative solutions. Exchange rate risk generally can be cost-effectively financed through a loss control technique. (In this case, foreign exchange futures contracts, explained later in this chapter, could be used to hedge or reduce exposure.)

One of the business risks is **reputation risk**, which is plotted in the high frequency/high severity quadrant. Reputation risk is one of the newest risks CROs are identifying in risk map models. Not only do manufacturers such as Coca-Cola rely on their high brand-name identification, so do smaller companies such as Notable Notions whose customers rely on stellar business practices. One hiccup in the distribution chain causing non-delivery or inconsistent quality in an order can damage a company's reputation and lead to cancelled contracts. The downside of reputation damage is potentially significant and has a long recovery period. Companies and their risk managers currently rate loss of good reputation as the greatest corporate threat to the success or failure of their organization.[16] A case in point is the impact on Martha Stewart's reputation after she was linked to an insider trading scandal involving the biotech firm ImClone.[17] The day after the story was reported in the *Wall Street Journal,* the stock price of Martha Stewart Living Omnimedia declined almost 20 percent, costing Stewart herself nearly $200 million.

Next we address an exposure in the operational risk category. **Operational risks** are those that relate to the ongoing day-to-day business activities of the organization. Here we reflect IT system failure exposure. This risk is plotted in the lower left quadrant, low severity and low frequency. Hard data shows that the down time related to IT system failure is low. (It is likely that this risk was originally more severe and has been reduced by back-up systems and disaster recovery plans.) In the case of a non-technology firm such as Notable Notions, electronic risk exposure and intellectual property risk are also plotted in the low frequency/low severity quadrant.

A pure risk like that of workers' compensation falls in the lower right quadrant for Notable Notions. The organization experiences a high frequency but low severity outcome for workers' compensation claims. Good internal record-keeping helps to track the experience data for Notable Notions. This allows for proper mitigation strategy.

The location of each of the remaining data points reflects a quantified actual or estimated severity and frequency exposure of Notable Notions' particular risks. Reviewing all these risks together allows the company to create a cohesive and consistent risk management strategy. Risk managers can also review a variety of effects that may not be apparent when operations are isolated. Small problems in one department may cause big ones in another, and small risks that have high frequency in each department can become severe in the aggregate.

Current Risk-Handling Method   At this point, the risk manager of Notable Notions can see the potential impact of its risks and its best risk management strategies. The next step in the risk mapping technique is the creation of separate graphs that show how the firm is currently handling each risk. Each of the risks in Figure 3.5 is now graphed according to whether the risk is uninsured, retained, partially insured or hedged, or insured. Figure 3.6 is the new risk map reflecting the current risk management handling.

When the two maps are overlaid, it can be clearly seen that some of the risk strategies suggested in Figure 3.5 differ from current risk handling as shown in Figure 3.6. For example, a broker convinced the risk manager to purchase an expensive policy for e-risk. The risk map shows that for Notable Notions, e-risk is low-severity and low-frequency, and thus should remain uninsured. By overlaying the two risk maps, the risk manager can see where current risk handling may not be appropriate.

The Effect of Risk Handling Methods

Another map can be created to show the effect of the risk management strategy of the maximum severity that the firm will end up having to handle after insurance. This occurs when insurance companies give only low limits of coverage. For example, if the potential

FIGURE 3.6

Notable Notions
Current Risk Handling

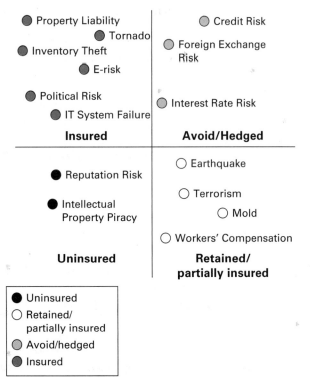

severity of Notable Notions' earthquake risk is $140 million, but coverage is offered only up to $100 million, the risk falls to a level of $40 million.

Using holistic risk mapping methodology presents a clear, easy-to-read presentation of a firm's overall risk spectrum or the level of risks that are still left after all risk mitigation strategies were put in place. It allows a firm to discern between those exposures that after all mitigation efforts are still (1) unbearable, (2) difficult to bear, and (3) relatively unimportant.

Risk mapping has five main objectives:

- To aid in the identification of risks and their interrelations
- To provide a mechanism to see clearly what risk management strategy would be the best to undertake
- To compare and evaluate the firm's current risk handling and to aid in selecting appropriate strategies
- To show the leftover risks after all risk mitigation strategies are put in place
- To easily communicate risk management strategy to both management and employees

Risk Management Information System

Data and analysis are the lifeblood of risk managers, permitting them to make informed decisions. A major task of the risk manager, therefore, is to quantify the organization's loss history, including types of losses, amounts, circumstances surrounding them, dates, and other relevant facts. Such a computerized quantification is called a **risk management information system,** or RMIS. An RMIS provides the risk manager with trends, such as a preponderance of workplace injuries in a particular plant, and increases or decreases in number and size of losses. The history may also permit establishment of probability distributions that can help the risk manager decide how best to manage risks. Those decisions must include consideration of financial concepts such as the time value of money. A number of computer programs (and models) have been developed to assist the risk manager in this task.

The key to good decision-making lies in the ability to analyze the large amounts of data collected. **Data warehousing** (a system of housing large sets of data for strategic analysis and operations) of risk data for a firm allows decision makers to evaluate multiple dimensions of risks as well as overall risk. Reporting techniques can be virtually unlimited in perspectives. For example, risk managers can sort data by location, by region, by division, and so forth. Because risk solutions are only as good as their underlying assumptions, RMIS allows for modeling data to assist in the risk exposure measurement process. Self-administered retained coverages have experienced explosive growth across all industries. The boom has meant that systems now include customized Web-based reporting capabilities.[18] Decision makers' ability to maximize a firm's risk reward tradeoff through data analysis is enhanced dramatically with the technological advances experienced in RMIS.

MOST RECENT EXPANSION: ENTERPRISE RISK MANAGEMENT

Enterprise risk management, or holistic risk management, recognizes that risk is an important part of any organization's operations, as noted in Chapter 1. It is the process of planning, leading, and controlling the activities of the organization to minimize the effects of risk on earnings and capital in order to maximize the value of the firm. It is the harvest of surveying the entire spectrum of all sources of loss and uncertainty, whether insurable or not, whether transferred or retained. This integrated approach is comprehensive in its coverage, and uses the technology of both insurance and non-insurance solutions to address the range of corporate risks. Earlier in the chapter, when creating a risk map model, we identified the broad range of corporate risks—hazard, financial, business, and operational. What each individual risk "silo" represents is of secondary importance. The contributions are not isolated; rather, they are considered in a comprehensive, aggregate manner to formulate a creative corporate strategy to treat risk.[19] Enterprise risk management has emerged from the following steps of maturation:

- Risk management using insurance
- Explosive growth in technology and communications
- Development of quantitative techniques and models to measure risk
- Evolution of the financial markets

These mechanisms combine to create a direct connection between the firm's overall appetite for risk, as set in company objectives, and making appropriate corporate-level choices for solutions in mitigating risks.

Risk Management Using Insurance: The First Step

A corporation begins by setting clear objectives in terms of risk and return. It sets "risk limits" and allows the risk management department to operate within those limits. Appropriate decisions can then be made as to how to meet those objectives. The evolution process began with the recognition that insurance was not the only possible risk management strategy. We introduced the methods for managing "pure risks" to include avoidance, loss control, and **loss financing** by retention. This expanded the role of the insurance manager to the broader role of risk manager.

Technology and Communications

We touched upon the technology role in the enterprise risk management process with the development of a risk management information system, or RMIS. Technology is necessary for managing the growing complexities of risk. Technologies have been evolving continually and have reached the point where data warehousing and data manipulation have become methods of risk decision support. Scenario analysis and simulations are examples of methodologies that has grown from technological advances. The business environment is subject to change, and scenario analysis allows companies to glimpse into the future by simulating or forecasting a range of outcome possibilities. Technology provides the ability to identify risk, to respond to changing conditions, to achieve greater significance in the measurement of risk, and to communicate that risk. Note that there is a "cost" associated with advancing technology. Today's CRO must incorporate e-risk and intellectual property risk associated with proprietary hardware and software systems development into the overall holistic risk spectrum.

Quantitative Techniques and Models: The Tools

The risk management process begins with identification of risks. Risk mapping uses a quantitative technique of modeling data critical to the risk identification process. The visual tool of a risk map allows risk managers to look at the spectrum of risks and their different effects to the enterprise as a whole. The risk manager can identify which risks have positive and negative correlation and take advantages of negatively correlated risks. For example. let's examine a hazard risk, such as fire. Naturally, this would be considered a possible risk exposure for Notable Notions; however, the risk manager must not stop there. A major fire at headquarters would cause not only property losses but also business interruptions and perhaps loss of life. The probabilities of loss in each of these separate risks are interdependent. On the other hands, the risk of directors and officers making major mistakes and creating liability risk would be uncorrelated with the risks caused by the fire but would be highly correlated with the firm's financial success or failure. Lawsuits are more likely when financial performance or stock price is declining. Therefore, there is a high correlation between its directors' and officers' liability risk and its business and financial market risk.[20] The complexity of enterprise risk management requires understanding the interrelationships of the spectrum of risks and being well prepared to address solutions using an integrated approach.[21] The approach of Integrated Risk and Finite Risk programs featured in Case 3 at the back of the textbook is one example of how the negative correlation among risks can be used in an integrated risk package to benefit the organization.

Value at Risk

Value at risk (VAR) modeling has become the standard tool for measuring an investment portfolio's exposure to financial market risk. Risk in this arena is not eligible for an insurance solution since it is in the category of speculative risk. Financial market instruments are one solution used to mitigate risk. But how does a company measure the success of the instruments chosen? VAR measures overall market risk taken across all markets and all instruments. A numeric example of how the values of assets or loans that are at risk are calculated is available at the end of the textbook in Case 4, "Financial Risk Management for Hometown Bank." J.P. Morgan Chase & Co., a financial holding company, can "instantly get a snapshot of its risk exposure to an individual instrument or instrument class in its investment portfolio by size, duration, desk and position across the firm. It can also indicate the risk impact on portfolios from changes in market prices."[22] Morgan usually runs VAR models across all the bank's investment positions at the end of each day to check that possible losses are within expected ranges. Most VAR calculations use simulation techniques and sophisticated statistical methodologies to determine the appropriate statistical distribution of losses such as credit losses. To help avoid any surprises from the extra market volatility during the two weeks following September 11, Morgan ran VAR models twice daily. VAR modeling has grown particularly in the banking industry since the Basel Accord, the framework of regulatory oversight for banks, agreed in 1998 to accept the methodology to evaluate market risk exposure.[23] The approval of the VAR methodology is for the minimum level of capital or equity required of banks based on the riskiness of their assets.[24] A simple example of VAR calculation is offered in Case 4 at the end of the text.

Evolution of the Financial Markets

The last two decades have been a period of rapid financial innovation. Capital markets soared and with the growth came the development of derivatives. **Derivatives** can be defined as financial securities whose value is derived from another "underlying" asset. Our discussion will incorporate three basic tools used: forwards/futures, swaps, and options. Derivatives are non-insurance instruments used to hedge, or protect, against adverse movements in prices (in stocks or in commodities such as rice and wheat) or rates (such as interest rates or foreign exchange rates). For example, breakfast cereal manufacturer Frosty O's must have wheat to produce its finished goods. As such, the firm is continually vulnerable to sudden increases in wheat prices. The company's risk management objective would be to protect against wheat price fluctuations. Using derivatives we will explore the different choices in how an enterprise risk manager might mitigate the unwanted price exposure.

Forward/Future Purchase

Forwards and *futures* are similar in that they are agreements that obligate the owner of the instrument to buy or sell an asset for a specified price at a specified time in the future. Forwards are traded in the over-the-counter market, and contract characteristics can be tailored to meet specific customer needs. Futures are exchange traded, with contract specifications standardized. Forwards and futures prices are derived from the spot, or cash market, which is "today's" price for a particular asset. An example of a spot contract would be an agreement by you to purchase a meal at a restaurant. The spot market is the quoted price on today's menu. A futures or forwards market would be the price you would have to pay if you wanted the same meal one year from today. Getting back to our cereal manufacturer, Frosty O's can either go to the spot market on an on-going basis or use the forwards/futures market to contract to buy wheat in the future at an agreed-upon price. Buying in the spot market creates exposure to later price fluctuation. Buying in the forwards/futures market allows the manufacturer to have guaranteed future delivery of the wheat at a locked-in price. Hence, this strategy is known as a "lock it in" defense.

Swaps

Swaps are agreements to exchange or transfer expected future variable-price purchases of wheat for a fixed contractual price today. In effect, Frosty O's is swapping its expected "floating" price exposure for wheat at different times in the future for a fixed rate cost. For example, if Frosty O's normal business practice is to buy its wheat on the first of each month, the company will have to pay whatever the spot price of wheat is on that day. Frosty O's is exposed to market price fluctuations for each of the twelve months over a year's time period. It can enter into a transaction to pay a fixed monthly rate over a year's time period instead of whatever the floating spot rate may be each month. The net effect of the swap transaction is to receive the necessary wheat allotment each month while paying a fixed predetermined rate. The swap rate quote would be fixed using the spot market and the one-year forward market for wheat. The adverse price exposure is eliminated by switching the "floating" price exposure for an agreed upon fixed price, as demonstrated in Case 4 at the back of the textbook. Swaps are used in the same manner to exchange floating interest rate liabilities for fixed interest rate liabilities. Hence, this strategy is known as a "switch out of it" defense.

Options

Agreements that give the right (but not the obligation) to buy or sell an underlying asset at a specified price at a specified time in the future are known as **options.** Frosty O's can purchase an option to buy the wheat it needs for production at a given strike price. The strike price (also called exercise price) is the specified price set in the option contract. In this fashion, Frosty O's can place a ceiling on the price it will pay for the needed wheat for production in future time periods. Until the maturity date of the option passes, the option holder can exercise his right to buy wheat at the strike price. If the future spot price of wheat rises above the strike price, Frosty O's will execute its option to purchase the wheat at the lower strike price. If the future price of wheat falls below the strike price, the company will not exercise its option and will instead purchase wheat directly in the spot market. This differentiates the option contract from the futures contract. An option is the *right* to buy (sell), whereas a futures/forward contract is an *obligation* to buy (sell). The cost of the option to buy wheat at the strike price is the option premium. A call option grants the right to buy at the strike price. A put option grants the right to sell at the strike price. A call option acts like insurance to provide an upper limit on the cost of wheat. A put option acts like insurance to protect a floor selling price for wheat. Hence, **option strategies** are known as "cap" and "floor" defenses.[25]

Individuals and companies alike use derivative instruments to hedge against their exposure to unpredictable loss due to fluctuations in prices. The increasing availability of different derivative products has armed enterprise risk managers with new risk management tool solutions. An importer of raw materials can hedge against changes in the exchange rate of the U.S. dollar to foreign currencies. An energy company can hedge using weather derivatives to protect against adverse or extreme weather conditions. And a bank can hedge its portfolio against interest rate risk. All of these risk exposures interrupt corporate cash flow and affect earnings, capital, and the bottom line, which is the value of the firm. These solutions, however, create new risk exposure. Over-the-counter market-traded derivatives, when there is no exchange acting as counterparty to the trade, expose a company to credit risk.

Risk Management Using Capital Markets

Securitization

Dramatic changes in the insurance industry in the past two decades, including a succession of catastrophic losses from hurricanes Hugo and Andrew and the Los Angeles earthquake, caused insurers and reinsurers to re-evaluate their risk analysis. The reassessment effort was made in full realization that these disasters, as horrible as they were, were by no means worst-case scenarios. Not only were individual, large-loss disasters a concern, but now the industry contemplated the issue of multiple *noncorrelated* catastrophic events occurring in a relatively short period of time. The affordability of coverage along with credit quality concerns of the risk transferred to reinsurers (who may have lost large chunks of capital and surplus or equity to those disasters) led to the first foray into using the capital markets as a reinsurance alternative.[26]

Packaging and transferring the insurance risks to the capital markets through the issuance of a financial security is termed securitization.[27] The aspects is that the underwriting risk is transferred into tradable securities whose returns are dependent on the underwriting experience of insurers. **Securitization** made a significant difference in the way insurance risk is traded—by making it a commodity and taking it to the capital markets instead of to the insurance/reinsurance market. Risks of various insurance companies for similar exposures in diversified locations are combined in one package that is sold to investors (who may also include insurers). Securitized catastrophe instruments can help in diversifying the risk exposure when reinsurance is not available. Because global capital markets are so vast, they offer a promising means of funding protection for even the largest potential catastrophes. Capital market solutions also allow the industry (insurers and reinsurers) to reduce credit risk exposure, also known as **counterparty risk**. This is the risk of loss from failure of a counterparty, or second party, in a derivatives contract to perform as agreed (contracted). Capital market solutions also diversify funding sources by spreading the risk across a broad spectrum of capital market investors. Securitization instruments, also called insurance-linked securities (ISLs), include catastrophe bonds, catastrophe risk exchange swaps, insurance related derivatives/options, catastrophe equity puts (Cat-E-Puts), contingent surplus notes, collateralized debt obligations (CDOs)and weather derivatives.

Catastrophe bonds, or CAT bonds, are designed to protect the insurance industry from catastrophic events. The bonds pay interest and return principal to investors the way other debt securities do—as long as the issuer does not experience losses above an agreed-upon limit. Insurers can come to the capital market to issue bonds that are tied to a single peril, or even to a portfolio or basket of risks. Embedded in each issue is a risk trigger that in the event of catastrophic loss allows for forgiveness of interest and/or principal repayment.

IMPORTANT ISSUES

The CAT Bond Story

Innovation is a key to the success stories on Wall Street. In November 1996, Morgan Stanley & Co. was about to make history as the first to underwrite an insurance-related issue offered to the public: catastrophe bonds. California Earthquake Authority (CEA), a state agency providing homeowners insurance, needed capital and had sought Wall Street's assistance. Morgan Stanley proposed a simple structure: bonds paying a robust 10 percent interest, but with a catastrophic loss trigger point of $7 billion. If CEA lost that much (or more) from any one earthquake, the investors would lose their principal.

The deal didn't happen, because Berkshire Hathaway's insurance division, National Indemnity Co., offered to underwrite CEA's earthquake risk. Many speculate that Berkshire was intent on foiling investment banking firms' attempt to steal away traditional reinsurance business.

The market didn't go away, however. In 1997, $900 million worth of CAT bonds were sold. In June of that year, USAA, a San Antonio-based insurer, floated an issue of $477 million in the capital markets with a one-year maturity. The loss threshold was $1 billion. As long as a hurricane didn't hit USAA for more than the $1 billion over the one-year time period, investors would enjoy a hefty coupon of 11 percent and would get their principal back. Reinsurer industry executives agreed upon only one thing: CAT bonds would radically change their business.

The number of major catastrophe losses between 1989 and 1995 was nearly double the total of the preceding two decades, a total of 19 major events. With ongoing property development in catastrophe-prone areas, the insurance industry's exposure to huge losses is only increasing, according to a Standard & Poor's study conducted in 1999. S&P calculates that the probability of a $1 billion loss

occurring in any given year is about 68 percent, while the probability of a $3 billion loss drops to about 31 percent. The chance of a $15 billion loss in a given year is about 4 percent.

CAT bonds have been hailed for the following reasons: They add capacity to the market, fill in coverage gaps, and give risk managers leverage when negotiating with insurers by creating a competitive alternative. As the insurance industry cycles, and the next wave of disasters depletes the capital and surplus of reinsurance companies, Wall Street will be poised to take advantage. During soft markets, CAT bonds are more expensive than traditional reinsurance. If reinsurance markets begin to harden, CAT bond issues are a practical alternative. However, there is some downside potential. What happens when you have a loss, and the bonds are used to pay for the exposure? Andrew Beazley, active underwriter of Beazley Syndicate 623 in London, said, "Once you have a loss, the bonds will pay, but you still have the exposure. The question is whether you'll be able to float another bond to cover it the next time something happens…. Reinsurers are expected to stick around and still write coverage after a loss, but can the same be said with CAT bond investors?"

Explore the Internet

One of the largest issuers of CAT bonds is the international reinsurance firm Swiss Re. To read its projection of the future of CAT bonds, "CAT Reinsurance: Meeting the Sustainable Level?" go to www.swissre.com and search for "CAT reinsurance."

Sources: Andrew Osterland, "The CATs Are out of the Bag," *BusinessWeek,* 26 January 1998; Douglas McLeod, "Cat Bonds to Grow: Increasing Frequency of Losses Will Contribute: S&P," *Business Insurance,* 12 July 1999, p2; Mike Hanley, "Cat Bond Market Almost There," *International Risk Management,* vol 8, no 1, Spring 2001; Sam Friedman, "There's More than One Way to Skin a Cat," *National Underwriter,* Property & Casualty/Risk & Benefits Management Edition, 8 May 2000.

An example of a CAT bond is the issue by Oriental Land Company Ltd., owner and operator of Tokyo Disneyland. Oriental Land used CAT bonds to finance one facility providing earthquake coverage and the other to provide stand-by financing to continue a $4 billion expansion of the theme park. Each facility raised $100 million via the bond market to cover property risk exposure and subsequent indirect business interruption loss in case of catastrophic loss from earthquake. The trigger event was for earthquake regardless of whether the event caused any direct physical damage to the park.[28] For more about how CAT bonds provide protection, see "Important Issues: The CAT Bond Story."

With **catastrophe equity puts (Cat-E-Puts)**, the insurer has the option to sell equity (e.g., preferred shares) at pre-determined prices, contingent upon the catastrophic event. **Contingent surplus notes** are options to borrow money in case of a specific event. **Collateralized debt obligations (CDOs)** are securities backed by a pool of diversified assets; these are referred to as collateralized bond obligations (CBOs) when the underlying assets are bonds and as collateralized loan obligations (CLOs) when the underlying assets are bank loans.[29] **Weather derivatives** are derivative contracts that pay based on weather-related events. All are examples of financial market instruments that have been used as risk transfer and risk financing vehicles.[30]

Advantages to investors in insurance-linked securities are diversification, as these instruments allow non-insurance investors to participate in insurance-related transactions, and above-average rates of return. Advantages to the issuers of such instruments are greater capacity and access to the capital markets. Insurance-linked securities provide issuers with more flexibility and less reliance on reinsurers. The presence of new instruments stabilizes the pricing of reinsurance and provides higher levels of risk transfer with cutting-edge understanding of both insurance and capital markets.[31]

We have shown that enterprise risk management for a corporation is complex. Full enterprise-wide risk management entails folding financial risk management into the CRO's department responsibilities. A chief risk officer's role is multi-faceted. Today risk managers develop goals to widen the understanding of risk management so that employees take into account risk considerations in their day-to-day operations. It is imperative to the overall health of the organization. Sound practices must incorporate the advancements on the technology front so that companies can compete in the global environment. Viewing all integrated segments of risk from across the enterprise in a holistic manner facilitates a global competitive advantage.

KEY TERMS

risk management	loss control	futures
risk mapping	loss prevention	swaps
risk management information systems (RMIS)	loss reduction	options
	transfer	securitization
chief risk officers (CROs)	cash flow analysis	counterparty risk
enterprise risk management	risk profiling	catastrophe bonds (CAT bonds)
	hazard risk	
deductibles	financial risk	catastrophe risk exchange swaps
risk retention	reputation risk	
captives	operational risk	insurance-related derivatives/options
risk management policy statement	enterprise risk management	
		catastrophe equity puts (Cat-E-Puts)
risk management matrix	data warehousing	
avoidance	loss financing	contingent surplus notes
retention	value at risk (VAR)	collateralized debt obligations (CDOs)
self-insured	derivatives	
reinsurance	forwards	weather derivatives

DISCUSSION QUESTIONS

1. What are the adverse consequences of risk? Give examples of each.
2. What is the traditional process of risk management?

3. How was the traditional process of risk management expanded?

4. The liability of those who own a corporation is limited to their investment, while proprietors and general partners have unlimited liability for the obligations of their business. Explain what relevance this has for risk management.

5. Using the basic risk management matrix, explain the following:
   a. When would you buy insurance?
   b. When would you avoid the risk?
   c. When would you retain the risk?
   d. When would you use loss control?

6. What are the three objectives of risk mapping? Explain one way a chief risk officer would use a risk map model.

7. Define the terms *loss prevention* and *loss reduction*. Provide examples of each.

8. What are the types of risks that are included in an enterprise risk analysis?

9. What has helped to expand risk management into enterprise risk management?

10. What financial instrument might a jeweler use to cap his price for gold, the main raw material used in jewelry production?

11. If an insurance company invests in the stock market, what type of instrument would the insurer use to mitigate the risk of stock price fluctuations?

12. What are the benefits of securitization in the insurance/reinsurance industry?

13. Some firms provide annual medical screening tests, weight control programs, exercise facilities, and other health-related programs for employees. Do you think this is just another form of compensation, or may there be other reasons for such programs?

14. It has been said that the most important thing in the world is to know what is most important now. What do you think is the most important risk for you now? What do you think will be the most important risk you will face twenty-five years from now?

15. Explain securitization and provide examples of insurance-linked securities.

EXERCISES

3.1 Brooks Trucking, which provides trucking services over a twelve-state area from its home base in Cincinnati, has never had a risk management program. Shawana Lee, Brooks Trucking's financial vice-president, has a philosophy that "lightning can't strike twice in the same place." Because of this, she does not believe in trying to practice loss prevention or loss reduction.
   a. If you were appointed its risk manager, how would you identify the pure-risk exposures facing Brooks?
   b. Do you agree or disagree with Shawana? Why?

3.2 Devin Davis is an independent oil driller in Oklahoma. He feels that the most important risk he has is small property damages to his drilling rig, because he constantly has small, minor damage to the rig while it is being operated or taken to new locations.
   a. Do you agree or disagree with Devin?
   b. Which is more important, frequency of loss or severity of loss? Explain.

3.3 Yu-Luen Pa does not believe that risk management can properly be used by a family. "After all," she argues, "my family is such a small group of people that I cannot predict when losses will happen. I can't manage risk—it's too uncertain." Explain why you agree or disagree with Yu-Luen.

3.4 Rinaldo's is a high-end jeweler with one retail location on Fifth Avenue in New York City. The majority of sales are sophisticated pieces that sell for $5,000 or more and are Rinaldo's own artistic creations using precious metals and stones. The raw materials are purchased primarily in Africa (gold, platinum, and diamonds) and South America (silver). Owing to a large amount of international marketing efforts, internet and catalog sales represent over 45 percent of the total $300 million in annual sales revenue. To accommodate his customers, Rinaldo will accept both the U.S. dollar and other foreign currencies as a form of payment. Acting as an enterprise risk manager consultant, create a risk map model to identify Rinaldo's risks across the four basic categories of business/strategic risk, operational risk, financial risk, and hazard risk.

3.5 As an agent for an independent insurance agency, you have been pondering a presentation you have to make to the Wompu Sports Car Club. Your task is to explain how a family moves through various growth stages, such as newly married, young children at home, children in high school and college, and finally the "empty nest" retirement years. The methods by which a family handles risk associated with these changes vary through the years. You want to give examples of how the risk varies and how it can be managed by the family over time.

a. Set up examples to explain these family changes and the changing risks associated with them.

b. Note the obstacles that could surface within a family through the years that would make it difficult for them to transfer various forms of risk.

NOTES

1. In conversations with Scott Lang, former risk manager of Microsoft. Also see: Phyllis S. Myers and Etti G. Baranoff, "Non-Traditional Insurance Programs: The New Generation," Academy of Insurance Education, Washington D.C. Instructional video with supplemental study guide. (Video produced by the Center for Video Education, 1997.)
2. This chapter incorporates material that is taught in advanced finance courses. The coverage here is only superficial with a case at the back of the textbook to demonstrate how some of these instruments work. It is not the intent of this chapter to teach the complete course of advance financial instruments. Students interested in in-depth study are invited to use advanced finance textbooks or take such courses at their universities..
3. "NEXCOM is a Nonappropriated Fund Instrumentality under the jurisdiction of the Department of the Navy that operates Navy Exchanges as a retail business. Money that would be considered profit in the private sector is given to the Department of the Navy Morale, Welfare and Recreation programs." It has 130 Exchanges (retail outlets) for the military and their families worldwide, 41 Navy Lodges (motels), 104 Navy Uniform Shops, and 190 Ship Stores. It has annual sales of $2.0 billion and employs over 18,000 people. NEXCOM also operates services operations such as gas stations, automotive service centers, mini-marts, video rentals, personalized services, and flower shops. It contracts operations with McDonald's, Applebee's, barbershops, beauty salons, dive shops, pet kennels, food courts, and more.
4. Our examples in this chapter are from a presentation given to Virginia Commonwealth University students in November 2001 by Michael J. Lombardo, Corporate Risk Manager, Navy Exchange Service Command. Mr. Lombardo was also president of the Virginia chapter of the Risk and Insurance Management Society (RIMS).
5. Anne E. Kleffner, Ryan B. Lee, and Bill McGannon, "The Effect of Corporate Governance on the Use of Enterprise Risk Management: Evidence from Canada" (working paper, University of Calgary, May 2002).
6. Joanne Wojcik, "Titles Vary, but Status of CRO on the Rise," *Enterprise Risk Management,* 18 February 2002.
7. Etti G. Baranoff, "Determinants in Risk-Financing Choices: The Case of Workers' Compensation for Public School Districts," *Journal of Risk and Insurance,* June 2000.
8. "A Hold Harmless Agreement is usually used where the Promisor's actions could lead to a claim or liability to the Promisee. For example, the buyer of land wants to inspect the property prior to close of escrow, and needs to conduct tests and studies on the property. In this case, the buyer would promise to indemnify the current property owner from any claims resulting from the buyer's inspection (i.e., injury to a third party because the buyer is drilling a hole; to pay for a mechanic's lien because the buyer hired a termite inspector, and so on). Another example is where

a property owner allows a caterer to use its property to cater an event. In this example the Catering Company (the "Promisor") agrees to indemnify the property owner for any claims arising from the Catering Company's use of the property." From Legaldocs, a division of USA Law Publications, Inc. www.legaldocs.com/docs/holdha_1.mv

9.   A surety bond is a three-party instrument between a surety, the contractor, and the project owner. The agreement binds the contractor to comply with the terms and conditions of a contract. If the contractor is unable to successfully perform the contract, the surety assumes the contractor's responsibilities and ensures that the project is completed. From the U.S. Small Business Administration, http://app1.sba.gov/faqs/faqindex.cfm?areaID=20.

10. See note 1 above.

11. Lee Ann Gjertsen, "'Risk Mapping' Helps RM's Chart Solutions," *National Underwriter*, Property & Casualty/Risk & Benefits Management Edition, 7 June 1999.

12. Michel Crohy, Dan Galai, and Robert Mark, *Risk Management* (McGraw-Hill, 2001), Chapter 16.

13. The exercise is abridged for demonstrative purposes. An actual holistic risk mapping model would include many more risk intersection points plotted along the frequency/severity X and Y axes.

14. Amanda Milligan, "Risk Mapping a New Path to Risk Financing Options," *Business Insurance*, 23 November 1998, p. 2.

15. Associated Press Newswire, May 22, 2002.

16. "Risk Whistle: Reputation Risk," Swiss Re publication, www.swissre.com.

17. Geeta Anand, Jerry Arkon, and Chris Adams, "ImClone's Ex-CEO Arrested, Charged with Insider Trading," *Wall Street Journal*, 13 June 2002, p. 1.

18. Joanne Wojcik, "Marsh RMIS Adds New Features," *Business Insurance: BI Daily News*, 27 March 2002.

19. Neil A. Doherty, *Integrated Risk Management: Techniques and Strategies for Reducing Risk* (McGraw-Hill, 2000): Chapter 1.

20. Ibid, p. 106.

21. Lee Ann Gjertsen, " 'Risk Mapping' Helps RMs Chart Solutions," *National Underwriter*, Property & Casualty/Risk & Benefits Management Edition, 7 June 1999.

22. Alison Rea, "Averting Future Liquidity Crises," case study of JP Morgan Chase, Risk, January 2002.

23. James T. Gleason, *The New Management Imperative in Finance Risk* (Princeton, New Jersey: Bloomberg Press, 2000), Chapter 12.

24. This is called risk-based capital. In Chapter 5 you will learn about risk-based capital requirements for insurance companies.

25. Gleason, *New Management Imperative*, Chapter 4.

26. Michael Himick et al., *Securitized Insurance Risk: Strategic Opportunities for Insurers and Investors* (Chicago: Glenlake Publishing Co. Ltd., 1998), p. 49–59.

27. "Risk Securitization 101, 2000 CAS Special Interest Seminar," by David Na, Deloitte & Touche, Bermuda. www.casact.org/coneduc/specsem/catastrophe/ 2000/handouts/na.ppt.

28. Sam Friedman, "There's More Than One Way to Skin a Cat," *National Underwriter*, Property & Casualty/Risk & Benefits, May 8, 2000.

29. Definition from *Investing in Collateralized Debt Obligations*, Frank J. Fabozzi, Laurie S. Goodman, eds (Wiley, 2001).

30. A comprehensive report by Guy Carpenter appears in "The Evolving Market for Catastrophic Event Risk," August 1998. www.guycarp.com/publications/white/evolving/evolv24.html.

31. See endnote 30.

Appendix 3.1

CASH FLOW ANALYSIS

Cash flow analysis is a decision rule by which the present value of cash inflows is compared with the present value of cash outflows for a given project. If the inflows exceed the outflows on this basis, the project meets the organization's profitability goals and may be implemented if other goals are also met (those goals may involve stability, liquidity, and social responsibility objectives).

Present value calculations allow decision makers to compare two or more cash streams that have unequal timing. That is, knowing the present value allows us to consider the investment opportunities of holding cash now (in the present) rather than later. Think about your preference for receiving a scholarship of $500 either now or one year from now. Generally, we prefer the cash now, because we are able to use it for productive purposes. Thus, we would even be willing to take something less than $500 in order to receive the funds now. How much less depends on other opportunities to use the money.

Generally, we calculate the present value as follows: $PV = (\$ \text{Funds Available in Future})$ $\times 1/(1+r)^t$ where r equals the opportunity cost of money (i.e., return available from other uses) and t equals the number of periods until the funds are available. If our opportunity cost for the scholarship is 5 percent, then the present value equals $(500)(1/(1+.05)^1) = \$476$. In other words, we would be willing to receive $476 or more today, versus $500 in one year.

A risk manager uses this concept of present value to make decisions about risk management options. Typically, these options will involve a stream of cash flows, which may be considered annuities. The calculation for the present value of an annuity is PV annuity = $(\$ \text{annual stream of funds}) \times [\{1 - 1/(1 + r)^t\} \div r]$.

The present value of four annual scholarships of $500 with an opportunity cost of 5 percent, then, equals $500 \times 3.54 = \$1,770$. Receiving $1,770 now is of equal value under these assumptions to four annual payments of $500 starting in one year.

For illustration, let's consider the decision of whether or not to add a sprinkler system to an existing building. Assume that the sprinkler would cost $20,000 to build. Further, assume that the expected loss distributions with and without the sprinkler are as shown in table A-1, that the expected life of the system is ten years, that the effective tax rate is .30, and that an annual inspection costs $100.

Note that the **net cash flow** is negative (see table A-2). The net cash flow is the comparison of the present value of cash inflows with the present value of cash outflows. If the net cash flow is negative, we know that the expected return of the project does not cover the expected costs. If the expected return were the only consideration, this project would be rejected. Reasons to accept would include objectives of safety and concern that estimated values are not precise. Estimating risk, however, can be incorporated into the analysis by employing a more conservative interest assumption.

A final observation on this analysis is that cash flow is the centerpiece. Thus, in calculating taxes, we consider the effect of depreciation (we used straight-line depreciation on the $20,000 sprinkler). In calculating cash flow, however, depreciation is otherwise irrelevant.

TABLE A-I	No Sprinkler			With Sprinkler		
Loss Distribution With and Without a Sprinkler	**Probability**	**Loss**	**E(Value)**	**Probability**	**Loss**	**E(Value)**
	.80	0	0	.80	0	0
	.10	1,000	100	.10	200	20
	.06	40,000	2,400	.06	25,000	1,500
	.03	75,000	2,250	.03	37,000	1,110
	.01	150,000	1,500	.01	62,000	620
			6,160			3,250

TABLE A-2

Cash Flow Analysis of a Sprinkler System

Change in Expected Losses	2,910
Change in Expected Costs (Inspection)	(100)
Before Tax Change in Cash Flow	2,810
Tax	
Change in Cash Flow	2,810
Change in Depreciation	(2,000)
Taxable Income	810
Change in Tax Requirements	
810 × .30	(243)
After Tax Cash Flow	2,567

$$PV_{\text{sprinkler}} = 2,567 \times \{[1 - 1/(1.05)^{10}] \div 05\}$$
$$= 2,567 \times 7.72 = 19,817.24$$
$$\text{Net Cash Flow} = PV_{\text{cash inflow}} - PV_{\text{cash outflow}}$$
$$= 19,817.24 - 20,000 = (\$182.76)$$

INSURANCE OPERATIONS, INSTITUTIONS, AND MARKETS

CHAPTER 4

Insurance Company Operations

The decision to seek coverage is only the first of many important choices you will have to make about insurance. Whether you are acting as your own personal risk manager or on behalf of your business, it will help you to know how insurance companies work. This chapter will explain the various departments that are involved in providing you with quality coverage by a quality insurer and will also introduce you to many possible insurance-related careers. This chapter will dispel the notion that insurance jobs are all sales positions. The marketing aspect of insurance operations is important, as it is for any business, but it is not the only aspect. The interesting and distinctive characteristic of insurance is that it is really a business with two separate parts, each equally important to the success of the operation. One part is the insurance underwriting business; the other, the investment of the funds paid by insureds. The insurance industry in fact, is one of the largest global financial industries, helping to propel the global economy. The money we pay into the insurance companies is used for mortgages, new startup industries, the building of schools and hospitals by government entities, and much more. Yet as important as they are, underwriting and investing are just two of insurers' activities. To provide you with the complete picture, this chapter covers the following:

1. Connection
2. Marketing
3. Underwriting
4. Administration
5. Actuarial analysis
6. Investments
7. Reinsurance
8. Legal and regulatory
9. Claims adjusting
10. Management

CONNECTION

As we have done in Chapters 1 through 3, before we begin describing the distinct functions in each insurance company, we first will connect this chapter to the complete picture of your holistic risk management. As consumers, it is our responsibility to know where our premium money is going and how it is being used. As noted in Chapter 1, risk is intangible. When we transfer it to the insurance company and pay the premium, we get an intangible product in return and a contract. But this contract is for future payments in case of losses.

Only when or if we have a loss will we actually see a return on our purchase of insurance. Therefore, it is imperative that the insurance company will be there when we need it.

The rating of insurance companies was explained in Chapter 2. Knowing that our insurer is financially sound is part of having "peace of mind." To complete the puzzle of assuring that our holistic risk management process is appropriate, we also need to understand how our insurance company operates. As the risks are not transferred to just one insurer, we must learn about the operations of a series of insurers—the reinsurers that insure the primary insurers. The descriptions provided in this chapter are typical to most insurers. But variations should be expected. To grasp how we relate to the operations of a typical insurer, look at Figure 4.1, which describes the fluid process of the operations within an insurer. Each function is closely linked to all the other functions, and none is performed in a vacuum. It is like a circular chain in which its link is as strong as the next link. Therefore, Figure 4.1 connects us, the focal point of risk, to the inner processes and functions of an insurance company to assure our holistic risk management process is complete.

FIGURE 4.1	Insurance Company Operations: A Fluid Linkage

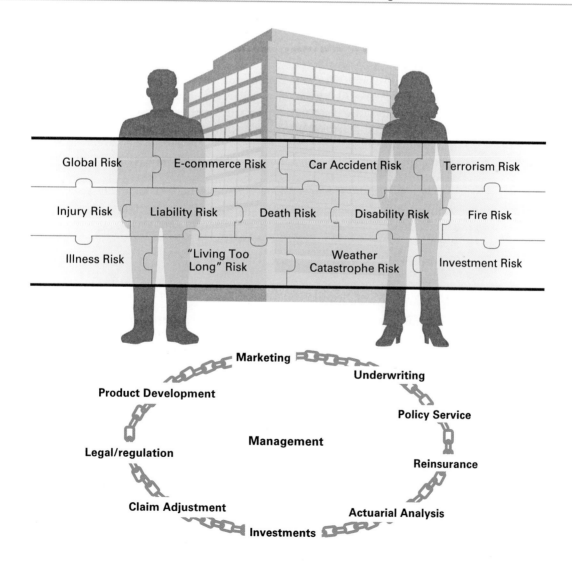

MARKETING

We begin with marketing despite the fact that it is not the first step in starting a business. But, from a consumer's point of view, it is the first glimpse into the operations of an insurer. Insurance may be bought through agents, brokers, or, in some cases, directly from the insurer (via personal contact or on the Internet). An agent legally represents the company, whereas a broker represents the buyer and in half of the states also the insurer because of state regulations.[1] Both agents and brokers are compensated by the insurer. In many states both agents and brokers are called **producers**. This new name is given to create some uniformity among the types of distribution systems.

Because life/health insurance and property/casualty insurance developed separately in the United States, somewhat different marketing systems evolved. We will therefore discuss these systems separately.

Life/Health Insurance Marketing

Most life/health insurance is sold through agents, brokers, or, the newest term, producers, who are compensated by commissions. These commissions are added to the price of the policy. Some insurance is sold directly to the public, without sales commissions. Fee-only financial planners often recommend such "no-load" insurance to their clients. Instead of paying an agent's commission, the client pays the planner a fee for advice and counseling and then buys directly from the no-load insurer. Unlike the agent, the planner has no incentive to recommend a high-commission product. Whether your total cost is lower depends on whether the savings on commissions offsets the planner's fee.

Some companies insist that their agents represent them exclusively, or at least that agents not submit applications to another insurer unless they themselves have refused to issue insurance at standard premium rates. Others permit their agents to sell for other companies, though these agents usually have a primary affiliation with one company and devote most of their efforts to selling its policies.

The two dominant types of life/health marketing systems are the general agency and the managerial (branch office). Both systems are commonly called career agency systems because money is invested by both general agents and insurers to hire and train new agents. In return, general agents and insurers hope that many of these people will make careers with their companies.

General Agency System

A **general agent** is an independent businessperson rather than an employee of the insurance company. The general agent's contract with the insurer authorizes him or her to sell insurance in a specified territory. Another major responsibility is the recruitment and training of subagents. Subagents usually are given the title of "agent" or "special agent." Typically, subagents are agents of the insurer rather than of the general agent. The insurer pays commissions (a percentage of premiums) to the agents on both new and renewal business. The general agent receives an override commission (a percentage of agents' commissions) on all business generated or serviced by the agency, pays most of it to the subagents, and keeps the balance for expenses and profit. Agent compensation agreements are normally determined by the insurer.

In most cases, the general agent has an exclusive franchise for his or her territory. The primary responsibilities of the general agent are to select, train, and supervise subagents. In addition, general agents provide office space and have administrative responsibilities for some customer service activities.

In recent decades, general agents have lost some of their independence from insurers; and because several insurers have recently been held legally liable for large damage awards to consumers claiming misrepresentations by agents, insurers are involved in controlling the market conduct of agents (as will be described in Chapter 6).

A large number of life/health insurers use **personal producing general agents.** Such agents seldom hire other agents; instead, they sell for one or more insurers, often with a higher-than-normal agent's commission. The extra commission helps cover office expenses. The trend is toward an agent representing several different insurers. This is desirable for consumers because no one insurer has the best products for all needs. To meet a client's insurance needs more completely, the agent needs to have the flexibility to serve as a broker or a personal producing general agent for the insurer with the most desirable policy.

Managerial (Branch Office) System

A branch office is an extension of the home office headed by a **branch manager.** The manager is a company employee who is compensated by a combination of salary, bonus, and commissions related to the productivity of the office to which he or she is assigned. The branch manager employs and trains agents for the company. The manager cannot employ an agent without the consent of the company, and compensation plans for agents are determined by the company.[2] All expenses of maintaining the office are paid by the company, which has complete control over the details of its operation.

Group and Supplemental Insurance Marketing

Group life, health, and retirement plans are sold to employers by agents in one of the systems described above, or by brokers. An agent may be assisted in this specialized field by a group sales representative. Large volumes of group business are also placed through direct negotiations between employers and insurers. A brokerage firm or an employee benefits consulting firm may be hired on a fee-only basis by the employer who wishes to negotiate directly with insurers, avoiding commissions to the agent/broker. In these direct negotiations, the insurer typically is represented by a salaried group sales representative.

Supplemental insurance plans that provide life, health, and other benefits to employees through employer sponsorship and payroll deduction have become common. These plans are marketed by agents, brokers, and exclusive agents. The latter usually work on commissions; some receive salaries plus bonuses.

Property/Casualty Insurance Marketing

Like life/health insurance, most property/casualty insurance is sold through agents or brokers who are compensated on a commission basis, but some is sold by salaried representatives or by direct methods. The independent agency system and the exclusive agency system account for the bulk of insurance sales.

Independent (American) Agency System

The distinguishing characteristics of the independent (American) agency system are the independence of the agent, the agent's bargaining position with the insurers he or she represents, and the fact that those who purchase insurance through the agent are considered by both insurers and agents to be the agent's customers rather than the insurer's. The **independent agent** usually represents several companies, pays all agency expenses, is compensated on a commission plus bonus basis, and makes all decisions concerning how the agency operates. Using insurer forms, the agent binds an insurer, sends underwriting information to the insurer, and later delivers a policy to the insured. The agent may or may not have the responsibility of collecting premiums. Legally, these agents represent the insurer, but as a practical matter they also represent the customer.

An independent agent "owns the **x-date**"; that is, has the right to contact the customer when a policy is due for renewal. This means that the insured goes with the agent if the agent no longer sells for the insurance company. This ownership right can be sold to another agent, and, when the independent agent decides to retire or leave the agency, the right to contact large numbers of customers creates a substantial market value for the agency. This marketing system is also known as the American Agency System. But it is best recognized for the "Big I" advertisements sponsored by the Independent Insurance Agents & Brokers of America. These advertisements usually emphasize the independent agent's ability to choose the best policy and insurer for you. (Formerly known as the Independent Insurance Agents of America, the 106-year-old association recently added the "& Brokers" to more accurately describe its membership.[3])

Direct Writers

Several companies, called **direct writers,**[4] market insurance through **exclusive agents** who are permitted to represent only their company or a company in affiliated group of insurance companies. A group is a number of separate companies operating under common ownership and management. This system is used by such companies as Allstate, Nationwide, and State Farm. These insurers compensate the agent through commissions that are lower than those paid to independent agents, partly because the insurer absorbs some expenses that are borne directly by independent agents. The insurer "owns the x-date." The customer is considered to be the insurer's rather than the agent's, and the agent does not have as much independence as do those who operate under the independent agency system. Average operating expenses and premiums for personal lines of insurance tend to be lower than those in the independent agency system.

Some direct writers place business through **salaried representatives,** who are employees of the company. Compensation for such employees may be a salary and/or a commission plus bonus related to the amount and quality of business they secure. Regardless of the compensation arrangement, they are employees rather than agents.

Brokers

A considerable amount of insurance and reinsurance is placed through brokers. A **broker** solicits business from the insured as does an agent, but the broker acts as the insured's legal agent when the business is placed with an insurer. In about half the states, brokers are required to be agents of the insurer. In the other states, brokers do not have ongoing contracts with insurers— their sole obligation is to the client. When it appears desirable, a broker may draft a specially worded policy for a client and then place the policy with an insurer. Some property/casualty brokers merely place insurance with an insurer and then rely on this company to provide whatever engineering and loss-prevention services are needed. Others have a staff of engineers to perform such services for clients. Modern brokerage firms provide a variety of related services, such as risk management surveys, information systems services related to risk management, complete administrative and claim services to self-insurers, and captive insurer management.

Brokers are a more significant part of the marketing mechanism in commercial property, liability, employee benefits, and marine insurance than in personal lines of insurance. Brokers are most active in metropolitan areas and among large insureds, where a broker's knowledge of specialized coverages and the market for them is important.

Some brokerage firms operate on a local or regional basis, whereas others are national or international in their operations.

With today's proliferation of lines and services, it is extremely difficult for brokers to completely understand all the products.[5] Brokers are always looking for unique product designs, but gaining access to innovative products and actually putting them into use are two different things. Generally, each broker selects about three favorite insurers. The broker's concern is the underwriting standards of their insurers. For example, a broker would like to be able to place a client who takes Prozac with an insurer that covers such clients.

Internet Marketing

With today's proliferation of **Internet marketing,** one can select an insurance product and compare price and coverage on the Internet. For example, someone interested in purchasing a life insurance policy can click on Insweb or another such Web site and fill out a questionnaire on financial needs and health status. The site will respond with quotes from insurers. The customer can then send contact information to selected insurers, who will begin the underwriting process to determine insurability. The sale is not finalized through the Internet, but the connection with the agent and underwriters is made. A search on any Internet search engine will lead to many such Web sites.[6]

Most insurance companies, like other businesses, set up their own Web sites to promote their products' features. They set up the sites to provide consumers with the tools to compare products and find the unique characteristics of the insurer. See "Important Issues: E-commerce and Insurance" for a description of the rating of insurers' Internet sites.

Mass Merchandising

Insurance is also sold on a **mass merchandising basis** by mail, telephone, television, or e-mail. Mass merchandising often involves a sponsoring organization such as an employer, trade association, university, or creditor; however, you are likely to be asked to respond directly to the insurer. Some mass merchandising mixes agents and direct response (mass mailing of information, for example, that includes a card the interested person can fill out return); an agent handles the initial mailing and subsequently contacts the responding members of the sponsoring organization.

In some cases, you can save money buying insurance by mass merchandising methods. Direct response insurers, however, cannot provide the counseling you may receive from a good agent or financial planner.

Financial Planners

A **financial planner** facilitates some insurance sales by serving as a consultant on financial matters, primarily to high-income clients. An analysis of risk exposures and recommendations on appropriate risk management techniques, including insurance, are major parts of the financial planning process. A fee-only financial planner, knowledgeable in insurance, may direct you to good-quality, no-load insurance products when they are priced lower than comparable products sold through agents. You are already paying a fee for advice from the financial planner. Why also pay a commission to an insurance agent or broker?

In many instances, it is appropriate for the financial planner to send you to an insurance agent. Products available through agents may have a better value than the still limited supply of no-load products. Also, your financial planner is likely to be a generalist with respect to insurance, and you may need advice from a knowledgeable agent. In any event, financial planners are now part of the insurance distribution system.

IMPORTANT ISSUES

E-commerce and Insurance

True to its name, Progressive was the first large insurer to begin selling insurance coverage via the Internet, in the late 1990s. Other big names like Allstate and Hartford quickly followed suit. So-called "aggregator" sites like Insure.com, Quotesmith.com, and InsWeb.com joined in, offering one-stop shopping for a variety of products. To tap the potential of e-commerce, insurers have had to overcome one big challenge: how to sell complex products without confusing and driving away the customer.

An insurance application can be frustrating even when an agent is sitting across the desk explaining everything, but most people don't walk out in the middle of filling out a form. On the Internet, however, about half of those filling out a quote request quit because it is too complicated or time-consuming. Most of those who do finish are "just looking," comparing prices and services. Twenty-seven million shoppers priced insurance online in 2001, according to a recent study by the Independent Insurance Agents of America and twenty-six insurers, but less than 5 percent closed the deal electronically.

This low figure is actually fine with most insurers, who don't want to cut their own agents out of the loop. While aggregator and matchmaker sites target "price-focused" purchasers—those whose top priority is getting the most coverage for the lowest premium—individual company sites cater to "relationship-focused" consumers, those who seek service and the security of a brand name. Most company Web sites now offer all the product information a consumer could want, including quoting programs and financial calculators, and then help the serious purchaser locate a nearby agent. Matchmaker sites such as 4BestQuotes.com perform a similar function.

The top five company sites as of June 2002, according to Gómez Internet Quality Measurement (www.gomez.com), were Progressive, Allstate, Nationwide, Geico, and Safeco. Gómez's ranking is based on on-site resources, ease of use, relationship services and customer confidence. The Canadian research firm Dalbar Inc., which ranks the brokerage, life insurance, and banking industries, had a completely different top five in its June 2001 survey of life insurance sites. Prudential Insurance Company of America, Fidelity Investments and TIAA-CREF earned "excellent" ratings, meaning they scored 80 out of a possible 100 points for usability, functions available, currency of content, and consistency of presentation.

Explore the Internet

State Farm (www.statefarm.com), which ranked sixth overall in Gómez's June 2002 quarterly scorecard, was first in on-site resources. With a third of major U.S. insurers still not offering such basic online customer-service capabilities as changing address or viewing a policy, State Farm is rapidly expanding its online functions. It has a site for Canadian policyholders and a Spanish-language site; more than sixty financial calculators covering auto purchases, budgeting, mortgages, and retirement planning; instant online quote for a range of products; and e-billing and payment.

Is its information-packed Web site helping State Farm keep its lead as the largest auto and home insurer in the United States? That's difficult to calculate. But considering that the company also scored top marks in Gómez's "one-stop shopping" category, it seems State Farm's customers and visitors are happy. And like a good neighbor, State Farm's Web site is always there.

Sources: Lynna Goch, "What Works Online: Some Insurers Have Found the Key to Unlocking Online Sales," *Best's Review,* May 2002; Ron Panko, "IdentityWeb: Linking Agents and Customers," *Best's Review,* May 2002; Trevor Thomas, "Carriers Web Sites For Agents Continue To Improve, Dalbar Says," *National Underwriter Life & Health/Financial Services Edition,* 13 August 2001.

Professionalism in Marketing

Ideally, an agent has several years of experience before giving advice on complicated insurance matters. You will be interested in the agent's experience and educational qualifications, which should cover an extensive study of insurance, finance, and related subjects. A major route for life/health agents to gain this background is by meeting all requirements for the Chartered Life Underwriter (**CLU**) designation or the Chartered Financial Consultant (**ChFC**) designation from The American College (for information see www.amercoll.edu/). Property/casualty agents gain a good background by earning the Chartered Property and Casualty Underwriter (**CPCU**) designation granted by the

American Institute for Property and Liability Underwriters (see www.aicpcu.org/). Another designation is Certified Financial Planner (**CFP**), awarded by the Certified Financial Planner Board of Standards (see www.cfp-board.org/).

UNDERWRITING

As noted in Chapter 2, **underwriting** is the process of classifying the potential insureds into the appropriate risk classification in order to charge the appropriate rate. An **underwriter** decides whether or not to insure exposures on which applications for insurance are submitted. There are separate procedures for group underwriting and individual underwriting. For group underwriting, the group characteristics, demographics, and past losses are judged. Because individual insurability is not examined, even very sick people such as AIDS patients can obtain life insurance through a group policy. For individual underwriting, the insured has to provide evidence of insurability in areas of life and health insurance or specific details about the property and automobiles in for property/casualty lines of business. An individual applicant for life insurance must be approved by the life insurance company underwriter, a process that is sometimes very lengthy.[7] It is not uncommon for the application to include a questionnaire about lifestyle, smoking habits, medical status, and the medical status of close family members. For large amounts of life insurance, the applicant is usually required to undergo a medical examination.

Once the underwriter determines that insurance can be issued, the next decision is to apply the proper premium rate. Premium rates are determined for classes of insureds by the actuarial department. An underwriter's role is to decide which class is appropriate for each insured. The business of insurance inherently involves discrimination; otherwise, adverse selection would make insurance unavailable. Recall from Chapter 2 that adverse selection may occur when pricing categories are so broad that both good and poor "risks" are lumped together to pay the same price. Under these conditions, high-risk individuals and businesses enjoy lower rates than their risk pool would require and low-risk individuals and businesses are charged higher rates. Therefore, the low-risk people will choose not to participate, because they realize they are getting a bad deal. With only poor risks participating, insurance becomes prohibitively expensive. To prevent this market failure, insurers must charge low-risk insureds lower rates than high-risk insureds; i.e., they must price discriminate.

Some people believe that any characteristic over which we have no control, such as gender, race, and age (although in life and annuity contracts, consideration of age seems to be acceptable), ought to be excluded from insurance underwriting and rating practices. Their argument is that if insurance is intended in part to encourage safety, then its operation ought to be based on behavior, not on qualities with which we are born. Others argue that some of these factors are the best predictors of losses and expenses, and without them, insurance will function only extremely inefficiently. Additionally, some argument could be made that virtually no factor is truly voluntary or controllable. Is a poor resident of Chicago, for instance, able to move out of the inner city? A *National Underwriter* article provided an interesting suggestion for mitigating negative characteristics: enclosing a personalized letter with an application to explain special circumstances.[8] For example, according to the article, "If your client is overweight, and his family is overweight but living a long healthy life, note both details on the record. This will give the underwriters more to go on." The article continues, "Sending letters with applications is long overdue. They will often shorten the underwriting cycle and get special risks—many of whom have been given a clean bill of health by their doctor or are well on their way to recovery—the coverage they need and deserve."

Over the years, insurers have used a variety of factors in their underwriting decisions. A number of these have become taboo from a public policy standpoint. Their use may be considered unfair discrimination. In automobile insurance, for instance, factors such as marital status and living arrangements have played a significant underwriting role, with divorced applicants considered "less stable" than never-married applicants. In property insurance, concern over **redlining** receives public attention periodically. Redlining occurs when an insurer designates a geographical area in which it chooses not to provide insurance, or to provide it only at substantially higher prices. These decisions are made without individually considering insurance applicants. Most often the redlining is in poor urban areas, placing low-income inner-city dwellers at great disadvantage. See "Ethical Dilemma: Redlining—Urban Discrimination Myth or Reality?" in Chapter 10.

A new controversy in the underwriting field is the use of genetic testing. In Great Britain, insurers use genetic testing to screen for Huntington's disease,[9] but U.S. companies are not yet using such tests. As genetic testing continues to improve, look for U.S. insurance companies to request access to that information as part of an applicant's medical history.

Two major areas of underwriting controversies are discussed in "Important Issues: Insurance and Your Privacy—Who Knows?" in Chapter 5 and "Ethical Dilemma: Keeping Score—Is It Fair to Use Credit Rating in Underwriting?" in this chapter. The need for information is a balancing act between underwriting requirements and preserving the privacy of insureds. The tug-of-war between more and less information is a regulatory matter featured in Chapter 5. The use of credit ratings in setting premiums illustrates a company's need to place insureds in the appropriate risk classification—a process that preserves the fundamental rules of insurance operations, as discussed in Chapter 2. We will explore underwriting further in other chapters as we look at types of policies.

ADMINISTRATION

After insurance is sold and approved by the underwriter, records must be established, premiums collected, customer inquiries answered, and many other administrative jobs performed. Administration is defined broadly here to include accounting, information systems, office administration, customer service, and personnel management.

Service

Insurance is a business in which the quality of the product depends on **service** and claims payments in addition to the financial strength of the insurer. An agent's or broker's advice and an insurer's claim practices are the primary services that the typical individual or business needs. In addition, prompt, courteous responses to inquiries concerning changes in the policy, the availability of other types of insurance, changes of address, and other routine matters are needed.

Another service that some insurers offer, primarily to commercial clients, is **engineering and loss control.** The prevention and reduction of loss whenever the efforts required are economically feasible are, therefore, of major significance. Much of the engineering and loss control activity may be carried on by the insurer or under its direction. The facilities the insurer has to devote to such efforts and the degree to which such efforts are successful is an important element to consider in selecting an insurer. Part of the risk manager's success depends upon this element. Engineering and loss control services are particularly applicable to workers' compensation and boiler and machinery exposures. With respect to the health insurance part of an employee benefits program, loss control is called cost containment and may be achieved primarily through managed care and wellness techniques.

ACTUARIAL ANALYSIS

Actuarial analysis is a highly specialized mathematic analysis that deals with the financial and risk aspects of insurance. The actuarial analysis takes past losses and project them to the future to determine the reserves an insurers needs to keep and the rates to charge. An **actuary** determines proper rates and reserves, certifies financial statements, participates in product development, and assists in overall management planning.

Actuaries are expected to demonstrate technical expertise by passing the examinations required for admission into either the Society of Actuaries, for life/health actuaries, or the Casualty Actuarial Society, for property/casualty actuaries. Passing the examinations requires a high level of mathematical knowledge and skill.

Prices and Reserves

Property/Casualty Lines—Loss Development

The rates or premiums for insurance are based first and foremost on the past experience of losses. Actuaries calculate the rates using various procedures and techniques. A hypothetical example of one loss reserving technique is featured here in Tables 4.1 through 4.5. The technique used in these tables is known as a "triangular method of **loss development** to the ultimate."[10] The example is for illustration only. Loss development is the calculation of how the losses are developed over time. Since the claims are paid progressively over time, like medical bills for an injury, the actuarial analysis has to project how losses will be developed into the future based on their past development.

With property/casualty lines such as product liability, the insurer's losses can continue for many years after the initial occurrence of the accident. For example, someone who took certain weight-loss medications in 1994 (the "accident year") might develop heart trouble six years later. Health problems from asbestos contact or tobacco use can occur decades after the accident actually occurred.

Table 4.1 describes an insurance company's **incurred losses** (paid plus known but not yet paid) for product liability from 1994 to 2000. Look at accident year 1996: Over the first 12 months after those accidents, the company posted losses of $38.901 million related to those accidents. Over the next 12 months—as more injuries came to light, or belated claims were filed, or lawsuits were settled—the insurer incurred almost $15 million, so that the cumulative losses after 24 developed months comes to $53.679 million. Each year brought more losses relating to accidents in 1996, so that by the end of the 60-month development period, the company had accumulated $70.934 million in incurred losses for

TABLE 4.1		Accident Year						
Incurred Losses for Accident Years by Development Periods (in $millions)	**Developed Months**	**1994**	**1995**	**1996**	**1997**	**1998**	**1999**	**2000**
	12	$37.654	$38.781	$38.901	$36.980	$37.684	$39.087	$37.680
	24	53.901	53.789	53.679	47.854	47.091	47.890	
	36	66.781	61.236	62.904	56.781	58.976		
	48	75.901	69.021	67.832	60.907			
	60	79.023	73.210	70.934				
	72	81.905	79.087					
	84	83.215						

incidents from accident year 1996. The table ends there, but the incurred losses continue; the ultimate total is not yet known.

To calculate how much money must be kept in reserve for losses, actuaries must estimate the ultimate incurred loss for each accident year. They can do so by calculating the rate of growth of the losses for each year, and then extending that rate to predict future losses. First we calculate the rate for each development period. In accident year 1996, the

Ethical Dilemma

Keeping Score—Is It Fair to Use Credit Rating in Underwriting?

Body-mass index, cholesterol level, SAT score, IQ: Americans are accustomed to being judged by the numbers. One important number that you may not be as familiar with is your credit score. Determined by the financial firm Fair, Isaac, and Co., a credit score (also known as a FICO score) is calculated from an individual's credit history, taking into account payment history, number of creditors, amounts currently owed, and similar factors.

Like your grade point average, your credit score is one simple number that sums up years of hard work (or years of goofing off). But while your GPA is unlikely to be important five years from now, your credit score will affect your major financial decisions for the rest of your life. This number determines whether you're eligible for "incentive" (low rate) financing on new cars, how many credit card offers get stuffed in your mailbox each month, and what your mortgage rate will be. In 2002, a home buyer with a "perfect" score of 850 could find a mortgage interest rate of less than 6 percent; someone with a score of 550, if he or she could get a loan at all, would pay at least 9.5 percent. Depending on the length and amount of the mortgage, the difference could amount to tens of thousands of dollars.

Your credit score may also affect how much you'll pay for insurance. About half of the companies that write personal auto or homeowners insurance now use credit data in underwriting or in setting premiums, and the "bad credit" penalty can be 20 percent or more. But it's not because they're worried that poor credit risks won't pay their insurance premiums. Rather, it's the strong relationship between credit scores and the likelihood of filing a claim, as study after study has borne out. Someone who spends money recklessly is also likely to drive recklessly, insurers will point out; someone who is lazy about making credit card payments is apt to be lazy about trimming a tree before it causes roof damage. Often a credit record is the best available predictor of future losses. Insurers vary on how much they rely on credit scoring—most consider it as one factor of many in setting premiums,

while a few flat-out refuse to insure anyone whose credit score is below a certain number—but almost all see it as a valuable underwriting tool. It's only fair, insurers say, for low-risk customers to pay lower premiums rather than subsidizing those more likely to file claims.

Consumer advocates disagree. Using credit scores in this manner is discriminatory and inflexible, they say, and some state insurance commissioners agree. Consumer advocate and former Texas insurance commissioner Robert Hunter finds credit scoring ludicrous. "If I have a poor credit score because I was laid off as a result of terrorism, what does that have to do with my ability to drive?" he asked at a meeting of the National Association of Insurance Commissioners in December 2001. Jim Bernstein, appointed Minnesota's chief insurance regulator in 2000, feels scoring is "manifestly unfair." He's concerned for his state's substantial immigrant population, many of whom are first-generation and, having not yet learned the American way of running up credit card debt, prefer to make large purchases only when they can afford to pay in full. Indeed, many decisions that seem fiscally sound, such as opening new credit card accounts in order to transfer balances from higher-rate cards, can actually hurt one's credit score—the formula deducts points for "card-hopping" and gives preference to longstanding accounts. For this reason, younger people generally have lower credit scores than those who have been American Express members since 1974. (You can track your credit score for a small fee at Fair, Isaac [www.myfico.com] and similar Web sites.)

The debate over the use of credit scoring has spread across the country. Dozens of states are considering regulations or legislation to curb its use by insurers. Some states have recently passed laws to prohibit carriers from refusing coverage or charging higher premiums based on credit history (Idaho, Utah) or to limit the premium surcharge for bad credit (Washington). Minnesota now requires insurers who use scoring to justify their methodology and rationale. Maryland has all but banned the practice.

Should credit scores count?

(Continued)

Ethical Dilemma (Continued)

Questions for Discussion

1. Mr. Smith and Mr. Jones, both twenty-eight, have the same educational and income levels. Mr. Smith has one speeding ticket and a credit score of 600. Mr. Jones has a clean driving record and a credit score of 750. Who should pay more for automobile insurance?

2. Upon investigation, you discover that Mr. Smith's credit score is low because his wife recently died after a long illness and he has fallen behind in paying her medical bills. Mr. Jones's driving record is clean because he hired a lawyer to have his many speeding tickets reduced to nonmoving violations. Who should pay more for auto insurance?

3. Considering the clear correlation between credit scores and losses, is credit scoring discriminatory?

Sources: Barbara Bowers, "Giving Credit Its Due: Insurers, Agents, Legislators, Regulators and Consumers Battle To Define The Role Of Insurance Scoring" and "Insurers Address Flurry of Insurance-Scoring Legislative Initiatives," *Best's Review,* May 2002; Caroline Saucer, "Minnesota Regulator Goes to the Mat Against Credit-Based Insurance Scores," *BestWire,* 11 June 2002; E.E. Mazier, "NAIC Struggles With Bevy of Issues in Philly," *National Underwriter Online News Service,* 13 June 2002.

$38.901 loss in the first development period increased to $53.679 in the second development period. The loss development factor for the 12-to-24-month period is therefore 1.380 (53.679/38.901), meaning that the loss increased, or developed, by a factor of 1.380 (or 38 percent). The factor for 24 to 36 months is 1.172 (62.904/53.679). The method to calculate all the factors follows the same pattern: second period divided by first period. Table 4.2 shows the factors for each development period from Table 4.1

After we complete the computation of all the factors in Table 4.2, we transpose the table in order to compute the averages for each development period. The transposed Table 4.2 is in Table 4.3. The averages of the development factors are at the bottom of the table. You see, for example, that the average of factors for the 36-to-48-month development period of all accident years is 1.104. This means that on average, losses increased by a factor of 1.104 (or 10.4 percent, if you prefer) in that period. That average is an ordinary mean. In order to exclude anomalies, however, actuaries often exclude the highest and lowest factors in each period, and average the remainders. The last line in Table 4.3 is the average excluding high and low, and it is this average that is used in Table 4 to complete the triangle.

In Table 4.4 we complete the incurred loss factors for the whole period of development. The information in the shaded triangle is from Table 4.2. The unshaded triangle of the development factors is added for the later periods when incurred loss data are not yet available. These are the predictions of future losses. Thus for accident year 1997, the shaded part shows the factors from Table 4.2, which were derived from the actual incurred loss information in Table 4.1. We see from Table 4.3 that we can expect losses to increase in any 48-to-60-month period by a factor of 1.046; in a 60–72 period, by 1.058; and in a

TABLE 4.2		Accident Year					
Loss Factors for Accident Years by Development Periods	**Developed Months**	**1994**	**1995**	**1996**	**1997**	**1998**	**1999**
	12–24	1.431	1.387	1.380	1.294	1.250	1.225
	24–36	1.239	1.138	1.172	1.187	1.252	
	36–48	1.137	1.127	1.078	1.073		
	48–60	1.041	1.061	1.046			
	60–72	1.036	1.080				
	72–84	1.016					
	84–ultimate						

TABLE 4.3		Developed Months					
Averages of the Incurred Loss Factors for Each Accident Year	**Accident Year**	**12–24**	**24–36**	**36–48**	**48–60**	**60–72**	**72–84**
	1994	1.431	1.239	1.137	1.041	1.036	1.016
	1995	1.387	1.138	1.127	1.061	1.080	
	1996	1.380	1.172	1.078	1.046		
	1997	1.294	1.187	1.073			
	1998	1.250	1.252				
	1999	1.225					
		12–24	**24–36**	**36–48**	**48–60**	**60–72**	**72–84**
	Average	1.328	1.198	1.104	1.049	1.058	1.016
	Average of last three years	1.256	1.204	1.093	1.049	1.058	1.016
	Average of last four years	1.287	1.187	1.104	1.049	1.058	1.016
	Average excluding high and low	1.328	1.199	1.103	1.046	1.058	1.016

TABLE 4.4		Accident Year						
Development of the Triangles of Incurred Loss Factors to Ultimate for Each Accident Year	**Developed Months**	**1994**	**1995**	**1996**	**1997**	**1998**	**1999**	**2000**
	12–24	1.431	1.387	1.380	1.294	1.250	1.225	1.328
	24–36	1.239	1.138	1.172	1.187	1.252	1.199	1.199
	36–48	1.137	1.127	1.078	1.073	1.103	1.103	1.103
	48–60	1.041	1.061	1.046	1.046	1.046	1.046	1.046
	60–72	1.036	1.080	1.058	1.058	1.058	1.058	1.058
	72–84	1.016	1.016	1.016	1.016	1.016	1.016	1.016
	84–ultimate*	1.020	1.020	1.020	1.020	1.020	1.020	1.020
	Development to Ultimate[†]	1.020	1.036	1.096	1.147	1.265	1.517	2.014

* Actuaries use their experience and other information to determine the factor that will be used from 84 months to ultimate. This factor is not available to them from the original triangle of losses.

[†] For example, the development to ultimate for 1997 is $1.046 \times 1.058 \times 1.016 \times 1.02 = 1.147$.

72–84 period, by 1.016. The "development to ultimate" factor is the product of all estimated factors: for 1997, it is $1.046 \times 1.058 \times 1.016 \times 1.02 = 1.147$. Actuaries will adjust the development-to-ultimate factor based on their experience and other information.[11]

To determine ultimate losses, these factors can be applied to the dollar amounts in Table 4.1. Table 4.5 provides the incurred loss estimates to ultimate payout for each accident year for this book of business. To illustrate how the computation is done, we estimate total incurred loss for accident year 1999. The most recent known incurred loss for accident year 1999 is as of 24 months: $47.890 million. To estimate the incurred losses at 36 months, we multiply by the development factor 1.199 and arrive at $57.426 million. That $57.426 million is multiplied by the applicable factors to produce a level of $63.326 million after 48 months, and $66.239 million after 60 months. Ultimately, the total payout for accident year 1999 is predicted to be $72.625 million. Since $47.890 million has already been paid out, the actuary will recommend keeping a reserve of $24.735 million to pay future claims. It is important to note that the ultimate level of incurred loss in this process includes **incurred but not reported losses (IBNR)**. This is usually an estimate that is hard to accurately project and is the reason the final projections of September 11 losses are still in question.

TABLE 4.5		Development of the Triangle of Incurred Losses to Ultimate (in $million)						

| | | | | Accident Year | | | | |
Developed Months	1994	1995	1996	1997	1998	1999	2000	Total
12	$37.654	$38.781	$38.901	$36.980	$37.684	$39.087	$37.680	
24	53.901	53.789	53.679	47.854	47.091	47.890	50.039	
36	66.781	61.236	62.904	56.781	58.976	57.426	60.003	
48	75.901	69.021	67.832	60.907	65.035	63.326	66.167	
60	79.023	73.210	70.934	63.709	68.027	66.239	69.211	
72	81.905	79.087	75.048	67.404	71.972	70.080	73.225	
84	83.215	80.352	76.249	68.482	73.123	71.201	74.396	
Ultimate	84.879	81.959	77.773	69.852	74.586	72.625	75.884	**537.559**
Pd. to date	83.215	79.087	70.934	60.907	58.976	47.890	37.680	**438.689**
Reserve	1.664	2.872	6.839	8.945	15.610	24.735	38.204	**98.870**

The process of loss development shown in the example of Tables 4.1 through 4.5 is used also for **rate calculations,** since the actuaries need to know the ultimate losses each book of business will incur. Once the ultimate level of loss is known, future rates are computed to meet the expected profits of the insurer. Taxes, expenses, and returns on investments as shown in Table 4.6 are also added to the loss development to determine the rates.

Life and Annuity Lines

For life insurance, actuaries use **mortality tables,** which predict the percentage of people in each age group who are expected to die each year. This percentage is used to estimate the required reserves and to compute life insurance rates. Life insurance, like other forms of insurance, is based on three concepts: pooling many exposures into a group, accumulating a fund by contributions (premiums) from the members of the group, and paying from this fund for the losses of those who die each year. That is, life insurance involves the group sharing of individual losses. To set premium rates, the insurer must be able to calculate the probability of death at various ages among its insureds, based on pooling. Life insurers must collect enough premiums to cover mortality costs (the cost of claims). In addition to covering mortality costs, a life insurance premium, like a property/casualty premium, must reflect several adjustments as noted in Table 4.6. First, the premium is reduced because the insurer expects to earn **investment income** on premiums paid in advance. Investment is a very important aspect of the other side of the insurance business. Insurers invest the premiums they receive from insureds until losses need to be paid. Income from the investments is an offset in the premium calculations. By reducing the rates, most of an insurer's investment income benefits consumers. Second, the premium is increased to cover the insurer's marketing and administrative expenses as described above. Taxes are the third component; those that are levied on the insurer also must be recovered. Fourth, in calculating premiums, an actuary usually increases the premium to cover the insurer's risk of not predicting future losses accurately (as explained in Chapter 2). The fifth element is the profits that the insurer should be aiming to get since insurers are not "not for profit" organizations. The actual prediction of deaths and the estimation of other premium elements are complicated actuarial processes.

TABLE 4.6

Term Premium Elements

Mortality cost
– **Investment income**
+ **Expense charge**
+ **Taxes**
+ **Risk change**
+ **Profit**

= **Gross premium charge**

The prediction of deaths is based on past observations. The mortality table in current use dates back to 1980. The 2001 Commissioners Standard Ordinary Mortality Table is awaiting approval from the National Association of Insurance Commissioners, and will likely be adopted by most states effective January 1, 2004.[12] See "Important Issues: New Mortality Tables" in Chapter 14. The new table reflects improvements in the mortality rate since 1980. The mortality rate has two important characteristics that greatly influence insurer practices and the nature of life insurance contracts. First, yearly probabilities of death rise with age. Second, for practical reasons, actuaries set at 1.0 the probability of death at an advanced age, such as ninety-nine. That is, death during that year is considered a certainty, even though some people survive. The characteristics are illustrated with the mortality curve.

Mortality Curve

If we plot the probability of death for males by age, as in Figure 4.2, we have a **mortality curve** that illustrates the relationship between age and the probability of death. This curve shows that the mortality rate for males is relatively high at birth but declines until age ten. It then rises to age twenty-one and declines between ages twenty-two and twenty-nine. This decline apparently reflects many accidental deaths among males in their teens and early twenties, followed by a subsequent decrease. The rise is continuous for females above age ten and for males after age twenty-nine. The rise is rather slow until middle age, at which point it begins to accelerate. At the more advanced ages, it rises very rapidly. The curve in Figure 4.2 is based on the Commissioners 1980 Mortality Table.

INVESTMENTS

As noted above, insurance companies are in "two" businesses; the insurance and investment businesses. The insurance side is the underwriting and reserving, while the investment side is the area of securing the best rate of return on the assets entrusted to the

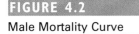

Male Mortality Curve

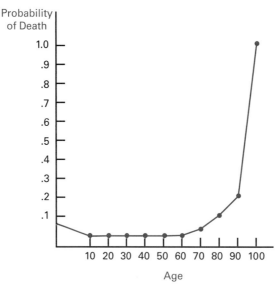

Source: Commissioners Standard Ordinary Mortality Table, 1980.

insurer by the policyholders seeking the security. Investment income is a significant part of total income in most insurance companies. Liability accounts in the form of reserves are maintained on balance sheets to cover future claims and other obligations. Assets must be maintained to cover the reserves and still leave the insurer with an adequate net worth in the form of **capital and surplus.** Capital and surplus are the equivalent of equity on the balance sheet of any firm. It is the net worth of the firm, the asset minus liabilities. For students who have taken a basic accounting course, the balance sheet of a firm will be very familiar. Figure 4.3 provides the two sides of the balance sheet of any company: assets and liabilities. Investments of insurers are part of the asset side of the balance sheet.

When reviewing the **asset portfolio,** also referred to as the **investment portfolio** or **asset allocation** of an insurer, we see the characteristics of the assets needed to support the payment of claims of the specific insurer. Asset allocation is the mix of assets held by an insurer. A property or health insurer needs a quick movement of funds and cannot invest in long-term investments. On the other hand, insurers that sell mostly life insurance or liability coverages know that the funds will be available for longer-term investment as the claims may not arrive until years into the future.

In light of these differences, asset allocation tables are provided separately for the life/health insurance industry in the aggregate and for the property/casualty insurance industry. The breakdown of the asset allocation of the property/casualty industry in the year 2000 is provided in Table 4.7 and for the life/health insurance industry is in Table 4.8. Standing out is the difference in the percent of mortgages in the asset allocation mix. The life/health insurance segment, which can hold longer-term investments, held 7.4 percent of its assets in mortgages while the property/casualty industry held only 0.18 percent of its assets in mortgages. Security analysts and investment managers are employed to attain the highest possible investment income, subject to the constraints imposed by state insurance laws and prudent management principles. Investment department employees are typically expected to have majored in finance. Many insurers require an MBA degree with a specialization in finance. For the student who is interested in this part of the insurer's operations, taking investment classes will be beneficial.

Many conglomerate insurance corporations own their own investment firms and provide mutual funds. In this area, insurers, like other financial institutions, are subject

FIGURE 4.3

Balance Sheet Main Items

Assets	Liabilities
Portfolio of invested assets	Liabilities including reserves
Premiums, reinsurance, and other assets	Capital and surplus

TABLE 4.7

Asset Allocation of the Property/Casualty Insurance Industry in the Year 2000

	Amount ($ million)	Allocation (%)
Bonds	505,119	55.39
Stocks	194,017	21.27
Mortgages	1,634	0.18
Real Estate	7,545	0.83
Cash	41,886	4.59
Other*	161,807	17.74
Total	912,009	100.00

* The main items in the "Other" include premiums and agents' balances and reinsurance recoverables.

Source: A.M. Best. Used with permission.

TABLE 4.8	Amount ($ million)	Allocation (%)
Bonds	$1,603,246	50.32
Stocks	992,278	31.15
Mortgages	236,614	7.43
Real Estate	35,906	1.13
Policy Loans	101,963	3.20
Misc.	215,937	6.78
Total	3,185,944	100.00

Asset Allocation of the Life/Health Insurance Industry in the Year 2000

Source: Life Insurers Fact Book 2001, American Council of Life Insurers.

to regulation by the states and by the Securities and Exchange Commission. A recent example of such regulation is the Patriot Act, which mandates that all financial services businesses, including those owned by insurance companies, have anti-money laundering programs in place.[13]

REINSURANCE

Reinsurance is an arrangement by which an insurance company transfers all or a portion of its risk under a contract (or contracts) of insurance to another company. The company transferring risk is called the **ceding insurer,** and the company taking over the risk is the **assuming reinsurer.** In effect, the insurance company that issued the policies is seeking protection from another insurer, the assuming reinsurer. Typically, the reinsurer assumes responsibility for part of the losses under an insurance contract; however, in some instances the reinsurer assumes full responsibility for the original insurance contract. As with insurance, reinsurance involves risk transfer, risk distribution, risk **diversification** across more insurance companies, and coverage against "insurance risk." Risk diversification is the spreading of the risk to other insurers to reduce the exposure of the primary insurer, the one that deals with the final consumer.

How Reinsurance Works

Reinsurance may be divided into three types: (1) treaty, (2) facultative, and (3) a combination of these two. Each of these types may be further classified as proportional or nonproportional. The original or primary insurer (the ceding company) may have a treaty with a reinsurer. Under a **treaty** arrangement, the original insurer is obligated to automatically reinsure any new underlying insurance contract that meets the terms of the prearranged treaty, and the reinsurer is obligated to accept certain responsibilities for the specified insurance. Thus, the reinsurance coverage is provided automatically for many policies. In a **facultative** arrangement, both the primary insurer and the reinsurer retain full decision-making powers with respect to each insurance contract. As each insurance contract is issued, the primary insurer decides whether or not to seek reinsurance and the reinsurer retains the flexibility to accept or reject each application for reinsurance on a case-by-case basis. The combination approach may require the primary insurer to offer to reinsure specified contracts (like the treaty approach) while leaving the reinsurer free to decide whether to accept or reject reinsurance on each contract (like the facultative approach). Alternatively, the combination approach can give the option to the primary insurer and automatically require acceptance by the reinsurer on all contracts offered for reinsurance. In any event, a contract between the ceding company and the reinsurer spells out the agreement between the two parties.

When the reinsurance agreement calls for **proportional** (or pro rata) **reinsurance,** the reinsurer assumes a prespecified percentage of both premiums and losses. Expenses are also shared in accord with this prespecified percentage. Because the ceding company has incurred operating expenses associated with the marketing, evaluation, and delivery of coverage, the reinsurer often pays a **ceding commission** to the original insurer. Such a commission may make reinsurance profitable to the ceding company, in addition to offering protection against catastrophe and improved predictability.

Nonproportional reinsurance obligates the reinsurer to pay losses when they exceed a designated threshold. **Excess-loss reinsurance,** for instance, requires the reinsurer to accept amounts of insurance that exceed the ceding insurer's retention limit. As an example, a small insurer might reinsure all property insurance above $25,000 per contract. The excess policy could be written per contract or per occurrence. Both proportional and nonproportional reinsurance may be either treaty or facultative. The excess-loss arrangement is depicted in Table 4.9. A proportional agreement is shown in Table 4.10.

In addition to specifying the situations under which a reinsurer has financial responsibility, the reinsurance agreement places a limit on the amount of reinsurance the reinsurer must accept. For example, the SSS Reinsurance Company may limit its liability per contract to four times the ceding insurer's retention limit, which in this case would yield total coverage of $125,000 ($25,000 retention plus $100,000 in reinsurance on any one property). When the ceding company issues a policy for an amount that exceeds the sum of its retention limit and SSS's reinsurance limit, it would need still another reinsurer, perhaps TTT Reinsurance Company, to accept a second layer of reinsurance. An example is available in Case 3 at the back of the textbook.

Benefits of Reinsurance

A ceding company (the primary insurer) uses reinsurance mainly to protect itself against losses in individual cases beyond a specified sum (i.e., its retention limit), but competition and the demands of its sales force may require issuance of policies of greater amounts. A company that issued policies no larger than its retention would severely limit its opportunities in the market. Many insureds do not want to place their insurance with several companies, preferring to have one policy with one company for each loss exposure. Furthermore, agents find it inconvenient to place multiple policies every time they insure a large risk.

In addition to its concern with individual cases, a primary insurer must protect itself from catastrophic losses of a particular type (such as a windstorm), in a particular area

TABLE 4.9
An Example of Excess-Loss Reinsurance

Original policy limit of $200,000 layered as multiples of primary retention

$75,000	Second reinsurer's coverage (equal to the remainder of the $200,000 contract)
100,000	First reinsurer's limit (four times the retention)
25,000	Original insurer's retention

TABLE 4.10
An Example of Proportional Reinsurance

Assume 30-70 split, premiums of $10,000, expense of $2,000, and a loss of $150,000. Ignore any ceding commission.

	Total Exposure	Premium	Expenses	Net Premium*	Loss
Reinsurer	70%	7,000	1,400	5,600	105,000
Ceding Insurer	30%	3,000	600	2,400	45,000
Total	100	10,00	2,000	8,000	150,000

*Net premium = Premium – Expenses

(such as a city or a block in a city), or during a specified period of operations (such as a calendar year). An **aggregate reinsurance** policy can be purchased for these potential situations. Sometimes they are considered excess policies, as described above, when the excess retention is per occurrence. An example of how an excess per occurrence policy works can be seen from the damage caused by Hurricane Andrew in 1992. Insurers who sell property insurance in hurricane-prone areas probably choose to reinsure their exposures not just on a property-by-property basis, but also above some chosen level for any specific event. Andrew was considered one event and caused billions of dollars of damage in Florida alone. A Florida insurer may have set limits, perhaps $100 million, for its own exposure to a given hurricane. For its insurance in force above $100 million, the insurer can purchase excess or aggregate reinsurance.

Other benefits of reinsurance can be derived when a company offering a particular line of insurance for the first time wants to protect itself from excessive losses and also take advantage of the reinsurer's knowledge concerning the proper rates to be charged and underwriting practices to be followed. In other cases, a rapidly expanding company may have to shift some of its liabilities to a reinsurer to avoid impairing its capital. Reinsurance often also increases the amount of insurance the underlying insurer can sell. This is referred to as "increasing capacity."

Reinsurance is significant to the buyer of insurance for a number of reasons. First, reinsurance increases the financial stability of insurers by spreading risk. This increases the likelihood that the original insurer will be able to pay its claims. Second, reinsurance facilitates placing large or unusual exposures with one company, thus reducing the time spent seeking insurance and eliminating the need for numerous policies to cover one exposure. This reduces transaction costs for both buyer and seller. Third, reinsurance helps small insurance companies stay in business, thus increasing competition in the industry. Without reinsurance, small companies would find it much more difficult to compete with larger ones.

Individual policyholders, however, rarely know about any reinsurance that may apply to their coverage. Even for those who are aware of the reinsurance, whether it be on a business or individual contract, most insurance policies prohibit direct access from the original insured to the reinsurer. The prohibition exists because the reinsurance agreement is a separate contract from the primary (original) insurance contract, and thus the original insured is not a party to the reinsurance Reinsurance became an urgent issue after the immense losses of September 11. Since reinsurance is part of the global insurance industry, globalization is also at center stage. More on the reinsurance industry and the offshore market will be discussed in Chapter 5.

LEGAL AND REGULATORY

In reality, the only tangible product we receive from the insurance company when we transfer the risk and pay the premium is a legal contract, in the form of a policy. Thus, the nature of insurance is very legal.[14] The wordings of the contracts are regularly challenged. Thus, law pervades insurance industry operations. Lawyers help draft insurance contracts, interpret contract provisions when claims are presented, defend the insurer in lawsuits, communicate with legislators and regulators, and help with various other aspects of operating an insurance business.

CLAIMS ADJUSTING

Claims adjusting is the process of paying insureds after they sustain losses. The **claims adjuster** is the person who represents the insurer when the policyholder presents a claim for payment. Relatively small property losses, up to $500 or so, may be adjusted by the sales agent. Larger claims will be handled by either a **company adjuster** (an employee of the insurer) or an independent adjuster. The **independent adjuster** is an employee of an adjusting firm that works for several different insurers and receives a fee for each claim handled.

A claims adjuster job includes (1) investigating the circumstances surrounding a loss, (2) determining whether the loss is covered or excluded under the terms of the contract, (3) deciding how much should be paid if the loss is covered, (4) paying valid claims promptly, and (5) resisting invalid claims. The varying situations give the claims adjuster opportunities to use knowledge of insurance contracts, investigative abilities, knowledge of law, skills of negotiation, and tactful communication. Most of the adjuster's work is done outside the office or at a drive-in automobile claims facility. Satisfactory settlement of claims is the ultimate test of an insurance company's value to its insureds and to society. Like underwriting, claims adjusting requires substantial knowledge of insurance.

Claim Practices

It is unreasonable to expect an insurer to be overly generous in paying claims or to honor claims that should not be paid at all, but it is advisable to avoid a company that makes a practice of resisting reasonable claims. This may signal financial trouble.

Information is available about insurer's claims practices. Each state's insurance department compiles complaints data; an insurer that has more than an average level of complaints level is best avoided.

MANAGEMENT

As in other organizations, an insurer needs competent managers to plan, organize, direct, control, and lead. The insurance management team functions best when it knows the nature of insurance and the environment in which insurers conduct business. Although some top management people are hired without backgrounds in the insurance business, the typical top management team for an insurer consists of people who learned about the business by working in one or more functional areas of insurance. If you choose an insurance career, you will probably begin in one of the functional areas discussed above.

KEY TERMS

producer	mass merchandising basis	actuary
general agent	financial planner	loss development
personal producing general agent	CLU	incurred losses
	ChFC	incurred but not reported losses (IBNR)
branch manager	CPCU	
independent agent	CFP	rate calculation
x-date	underwriting	mortality table
direct writer	underwriter	investment income
exclusive agent	redlining	premium elements
salaried representative	service	mortality curve
broker	engineering and loss control	capital and surplus
Internet marketing	actuarial analysis	asset portfolio

investment portfolio
asset allocation
reinsurance
ceding insurer
assuming reinsurer
diversification

treaty
facultative
proportional reinsurance
ceding commission
nonproportional
  reinsurance

excess-loss reinsurance
aggregate reinsurance
claims adjusting
claims adjuster
company adjuster
independent adjuster

DISCUSSION QUESTIONS

1. How do agents and brokers differ?
2. Would you rather shop for insurance on the Internet, or call an agent?
3. Advertising by the Independent Insurance Agents & Brokers of America extols the unique features of the American Agency System and the Independent Agent, whose logo is the "Big I." Does this advertising influence your choice of an agent? Do you prefer one type of agent to others? If so, why?
4. Upon hearing the advice that "It is usually best to buy life insurance from a person who has been in the business at least five years," a life insurance company general agent became upset and said rather vehemently, "How do you think we could recruit an agency force if everybody took your advice?" How would you have answered that question?
5. What does an underwriter do? Why is the underwriting function in an insurance company so important?
6. What is the relationship between the following functions within an insurance company?
    a. Marketing and underwriting
    b. Underwriting and actuarial
    c. Actuarial and investment
    d. Legal and underwriting
    e. Claims and marketing
    f. Claims adjusting and actuarial
7. In the fluidity of an insurance company operation, which function appears to you to be most important? Which appears to be least important?
8. Explain the process an actuary goes through for calculating reserves using the loss development triangle.
9. When do you think an actuary need to use judgment in adjusting the loss development factors?
10. What factors are used to calculate the rates for both life/health and property/casualty lines of insurance?
11. Compare the investment (asset) portfolio of the life/health insurance industry to that of the property/casualty insurance industry. Why do you think there are differences?
12. Distinguish between the different types of reinsurance and give an example of each. What are the advantages of reinsuring?
13. Occasionally, Insurer X will reinsure part of Insurer Y's risks, and Insurer Y will reinsure part of Insurer X's risks. Doesn't this seem like merely trading dollars? Explain.
14. List several approaches to negotiating with an insurer who does not seem to be settling your claim properly.

EXERCISES

4.1 Your acquaintance, Nancy Barns, recently commented to you that she and her husband wanted to reevaluate their homeowners insurance. Nancy said that it seemed the only time they ever had any contact with their present insurance agency was when a premium was due. Nancy asked if you knew of a good agency.

   a. Help Nancy set up standards to evaluate and choose a "good" agent.

   b. Review with her the standards of education and experience required of an agent, including the CPCU designation.

4.2 You are reading the Sunday newspaper when you notice a health insurance advertisement that offers the first month's coverage for one dollar. The insurance seems to be a real bargain.

   a. Are there any problems you should be aware of when buying insurance through the mail? List them, and explain how you could cope with them if you did purchase coverage in this manner.

4.3 The following are the incurred losses of the Maruri insurance company for its liability line.

Developed Months	Accident Year						
	1994	1995	1996	1997	1998	1999	2000
12	$27,634	$28,781	$28,901	$26,980	$27,684	$29,087	$27,680
24	$43,901	$43,777	$43,653	$37,854	$37,091	$37,890	
36	$56,799	$51,236	$52,904	$46,777	$48,923		
48	$65,901	$59,021	$57,832	$50,907			
60	$69,023	$63,210	$60,934				
72	$71,905	$69,087					
84	$73,215						

Using the example in this chapter as a guide:

   a. Create the loss development factors for this book of business.

   b. Calculate the ultimate reserves needed for this book of business. Make assumptions as needed.

4.4 Read the Ethical Dilemma box of this chapter regarding credit scoring and its usage by insurers. Respond to the discussion questions and reply to the following questions:

   a. Why are insurers using credit scoring in their underwriting?

   b. In what areas is it possible to misjudge a potential insured when using credit scoring?

   c. What other underwriting criteria would you suggest to replace the credit scoring criteria?

NOTES

1. See Etti G. Baranoff, Dalit Baranoff, and Tom Sager, "Nonuniform Regulatory Treatment of Broker Distribution Systems: An Impact Analysis for Life Insurers," Journal of Insurance Regulations, September 2000.
2. You may notice that this is essentially the same arrangement as described above for general agents who have lost some of their independence.
3. Sally Roberts, "Big I Changes Name to Reflect Membership Changes," Business Insurance, 6 May 2002.

4. The term "direct writer" is frequently used to refer to all property insurers that do not use the Independent Agency System of distribution, but some observers think there are differences among such companies. Two types are discussed in this and the next section.

5. Barry Higgins, "Brokerage Channel Challenges," National Underwriter, Life & Health/Financial Services Edition, 6 May 2002.

6. Our search using www.google.com turned up www.4autoquotes.com, www.getmequote.com, www.insure-com.com, and www.4insurance.com, among many others.

7. "Consultant Calls For Quicker Underwriting," National Underwriter Online News Service, 7 March 2002.

8. Paul P. Aniskovich, "Letters With Apps Can Make The Difference," National Underwriter, Life & Health/Financial Services Edition, 12 November 2001.

9. Catherine Arnold, "Britain Backs Insurers Use of Genetic Testing," National Underwriter, Life & Health/Financial Services Edition, 27 November 2000.

10. Wiser, R.F., "Loss Reserving," chap. 5 in Foundations of Casualty Actuarial Science, 3rd ed. (Arlington, VA: Casualty Actuarial Society, 1996).

11. In this example, we do not introduce actuarial adjustments to the factors. Such adjustments are usually based on management, technology, marketing, and other known functional changes within the company. The book of business is assumed to be stable without any extreme changes that may require adjustments.

12. Nancy M. Kenneally, "2001 CSO Table Could Pose Multiple Challenges For VUL Market," National Underwriter, Life & Health/Financial Services Edition, 8 April 2002.

13. Jim Connolly, "Insurers' Patriot Act Regs Imminent," National Underwriter, Life & Health/Financial Services Edition, 29 April 2002

14. See Etti G. Baranoff and Tom Sager, "The Relationship between Asset Risk, Product Risk, and Capital in the Life Insurance Industry," Journal of Banking and Finance, issue 26/6 (June 2002): 1181–97.

CHAPTER 5

Insurance Institutions, Markets, and Regulation

In 2000, world insurance premiums totaled $2.4 trillion, including property/casualty and life/health premiums. The United States led the world in total insurance premiums, as shown in Table 5.1. The U.S. insurance industry (including property/casualty and life/health companies and agents, brokers, and service personnel for all sectors) employed 2.3 million people in 2000. The transaction value of insurance-related mergers and acquisitions totaled $56 billion that year. U.S. catastrophe losses dropped to $4.3 billion in 2000 from $8.3 billion in 1999.[1] Total insured losses from the September 11, 2001, terrorist attack on the World Trade Center in New York City and all other insureds affected by all the attacks are expected to be between $40 billion to $60 billion.

The large size of the global insurance markets is demonstrated by the written premiums shown in Table 5.1. What institutions make these markets? What is the regulatory oversight of these institutions and the changing conditions of the market place? This chapter will answer these questions. In this chapter we will cover the following:

1. Connection
2. Markets conditions: underwriting cycles; availability and affordability; insurance markets post September 11, 2001; reinsurance markets
3. Regulation of insurance
4. Private insurance institutions and markets including captives, risk retention groups and governmental pools
5. Governmental insurance

CONNECTION

As we have done in the prior chapters, we begin with connecting the importance of this chapter to the complete picture of holistic risk management. We will become savvy consumers only when we understand the insurance marketplace and the conditions under which insurance institutions operate. When we make the selection of an insurer, we need to understand not only the organizational structure of that insurance organization, we also need to be able to benefit from the regulatory safety net available to protect us. Also important is our clear understanding of insurance market conditions affecting the products and their pricing. Major rate increases for coverages do not happen in a vacuum. As you saw in Chapter 4, past losses are most important in setting rates. Market conditions and availability and affordability of products are very important factors in the risk management decision, as you saw in Chapter 3. In Chapter 2 you learned that an insurable risk has to have the characteristic of being affordable. Because of **underwriting cycles,** the

TABLE 5.1		Direct premiums written, U.S. $billions			
The World's Leading Insurance Countries, 2000	**Country**	**Nonlife premiums***	**Life premiums**	**Total premiums**	**% of total world premiums**
	United States	$423.0	$442.4	$865.4	35.41%
	Japan†	102.5	401.5	504.0	20.62
	United Kingdom	57.2	179.7	236.9	9.70
	Germany	67.5	56.3	123.8	5.06
	France	37.1	84.8	121.9	4.99
	Italy	26.4	36.7	63.1	2.58
	South Korea	14.1	44.2	58.3	2.39
	Canada‡	23.3	23.3	46.6	1.91
	Spain	15.7	21.9	37.6	1.54
	The Netherlands	14.9	21.6	36.5	1.49

* Includes accident and health insurance.

† April 1, 2000–March 31, 2001.

‡ Life business expressed in net premiums.

Source: The Fact Book 2002, Insurance Information Institute (I.I.I.)

movement of insurance prices through time (explained next in this chapter), insurance rates are considered dynamic. In a **hard market,** when rates are high and **insurance capacity** (the quantity of coverage that is available in terms of limits of coverage) is low, we may choose to self-insure. Insurance capacity relates to the level of insurers' capital (net worth). If capital levels are low, insurers cannot provide a lot of coverage. In a **soft market,** when insurance capacity is high, we may select to insure for the same level of severity and frequency of losses. So, our decisions are truly related to external market conditions as denoted in Chapter 3.

The regulatory oversight over insurers is another important issue in our strategy. If we care to have a safety net of **guarantee funds,** which act as deposit insurance in case of insolvency of an insurer, we will select to work with a regulated insurer. In case of insolvency, a portion of the claims will be paid by the guarantee funds. We also need to understand the benefits of selecting a regulated entity as opposed to non-regulated one for other consumer protection actions such as complaints resolution. If we are unhappy with the claim settlement process of our insurer, the regulator in our state may help us resolve disputes if the entity is under the regulatory jurisdiction.

Thus, as you can see, understanding insurance institutions, markets, and insurance regulation are critical to our ability to complete the picture of our holistic risk management. Figure 5.1 provides the line of connection between our holistic risk picture (or a business holistic risk) and the big picture of the insurance industry and markets. As you can see, Figure 5.1 separates the industry's institutions into those that are government-regulated and those that are non- or semi-regulated. But, regardless of regulation, insurers are subject to market conditions and are structured along the same lines of corporate structure. However, some insurance structures such as governmental risk pools or Lloyd's of London do have specialized organization structure.

MARKET CONDITIONS

At any point in time, insurance markets may be in "hard" or "soft" conditions because of the "underwriting cycle." Soft conditions occur when insurance losses are low and prices

The Connection between Our Complete Holistic Picture and the Big Picture of the Insurance Industry and Markets by Regulatory Status

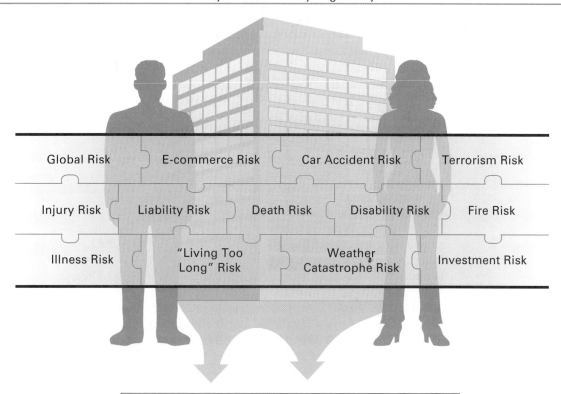

are very competitive. Hard conditions occur when insurance losses are above expectation (see loss development in Chapter 4) and reserves no longer are able to cover all losses. Insurers or reinsurers have to tap into their capital. Under these conditions, capacity (measured by capital level relative to premiums) is lowered and prices escalate. A presentation of the underwriting cycle of the property/casualty insurance industry from 1956 to 2000 is featured in Figure 5.2. The cycle is shown in terms of the industry's **combined ratio,** which is a measure of the relationship between premiums taken in and expenditures

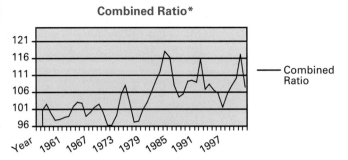

FIGURE 5.2

Underwriting Cycles of the U.S. Property/Casualty Insurance Industry, 1956–2000 (Peaks are "hard" markets, valleys are "soft" markets)

* Combined ratio after dividends.
Source: Aggregates and Averages for the Property/Casualty Industry, A. M. Best, 2001.
Estimates for 2001 and 2002 reprinted with permission from Best Preview/Review.

for claims and expenses. In other words, the combined ratio is the loss ratio (losses divided by premiums) plus the expense ratio (expenses divided by premiums). A combined ratio above 100 means that for every premium dollar taken in, more than a dollar was spent on losses and expenses. The ratio does not include income from investments, so a high number does not necessarily mean that a company is unprofitable. Because of investment income, an insurer may be profitable even if the combined ratio is over 100 percent. Each line of business has its own break-even point since each line of business has different loss payment time horizon with different length of time for the investment of the premiums. The breakeven point is determined on the basis of how much investment income is available in each line of insurance. If a line has a longer tail of losses, there is a longer period of time for investment to accumulate.

As you can see in Figure 5.2, the ups and downs are very visible for the whole industry for all lines of business. When the combined ratio is low, the industry lowers its underwriting standards in order to get more cash in that can be invested. This strategy is known as **cash flow underwriting.** The industry is regarded as "competing itself to the ground" and underwriting standards are loose. The last soft market, until the late 1990s, lasted about fifteen years. From 1986 to 1999, the combined ratio stayed in the range of 101.6 in 1997 to 109.6 in 1990 with only one jump in 1992 to a combined ratio of 115.7. Since the breakeven point of the industry combined ratio is 107, the industry was doing rather well during that long period. It caused new decision-makers (those without experience in underwriting cycles) to be less careful. In addition, computerized pricing models gave a false sense of security in making risk-selection and pricing decisions. Actual losses ended up causing rate increases and the soft market changed into a true hard market.[2]

During the 1990s, the soft markets conditions lasted longer than usual because the industry had large capacity. There were speculations that the introduction of capital markets as an alternative to reinsurance (see Chapter 3) kept rates down. But even before September 11, the industry began experiencing reduction in capacity and rates started to escalate as the market hardened. The U.S. property/casualty industry in 2001 racked up a loss of $7.9 billion, its first-ever net loss. While net income after taxes was a positive $20.6 billion in 2000, it turned negative in 2001 as a result of the horrific events of September 11, 2001, mold claims, and poor investment earnings on the industry's assets as the economy slowed down and the stock market maintained its decline.

Industry capacity (capital and surplus) also fell below $300 billion for the first time since 1996. While net written premiums increased from $299.7 billion in 2000 to $324 billion in 2001 (a small increase of 8.1 percent), incurred loss and loss adjustment expenses increased from $238 billion in 2000 to $276.1 billion in 2001. The increase in underwriting losses was accompanied by a decrease in net investment income from $56.9 billion in 2000 to $43.9 billion in 2001. The increase in underwriting losses by 16 percent along with the decrease in investment income by 22.8 percent represented significant worsening in underwriting results and deteriorating investments results. With both sides of the industry's income potential—the underwriting side and the investments side—being on the decline, and with the various catastrophic events, 2001 became a decisive year in solidifying the insurance market hard condition. With these levels of losses, mutual insurers had to lower the amount of dividends paid to their policyholders (as will be explained later in this chapter). Policyholders' dividends were reduced from $3.9 billion in 2000 to $2.3 billion in 2001, representing a reduction of 41 percent.[3] This reduction is, in essence, a rate increase to most policyholders who regard the dividends as a return on their premiums. Thus, not only did premiums begin to shoot up because of the poor results, many policyholders actually saw retroactive rate increases as the level of their dividends declined considerably.

The hardening of the market was exemplified with the contraction of the capacity in the market represented by the consolidated surplus of the property/casualty insurance industry. The surplus, as noted above, deteriorated from $356.5 billion in 2000 to $289.6 billion in 2001, an 18.8 percent reduction. The industry combined ratio for 2001 was 117, the third-worst on record. Combined ratios are also shown in Table 5.2 for each line of insurance separately.

Table 5.2, prepared in early 2002, projects improvements for that year over 2001, although commercial lines—the lines mostly affected by the September 11 attack—were not expected to break even. The year 2001 saw other major causes of losses, including mold claims and Enron's financial debacles. *National Underwriter* explained how the losses affected one company: "Since mold claims began to 'rear their ugly heads' in 2001 after a $32 million settlement, one Texas company—State Farm Lloyds—ended the year having lost all of its $700 million in capital [before replenishment by State Farm]…[leading to speculation that] mold could add three points to the national home-owners combined ratio in 2001."[4]

In the liability lines, the collapse of Enron contributed to soaring premiums. A 2001 study by the financial consulting firm Tillinghast-Towers Perrin pointed to high-profile

TABLE 5.2	A.M. Best Combined Ratio Estimates		
Estimated Combined Ratios by Product Line for the Property/Casualty Industry	Line of Business	2001	2002	Breakeven
	Homeowners	126.0	117.5	103
	Personal Auto	107.0	106.3	105
	Fire and Allied Lines	130.5	105.0	102
	Commercial Package	132.0	116.5	107
	Commercial Auto	114.5	110.0	107
	General and Product Liability	135.5	117.0	113
	Workers' Comp	129.0	107.8	112
	Medical Malpractice	143.0	122.0	115
	Inland Marine	102.5	95.0	107
	All Lines Other	109.5	95.0	106
	Total All Lines	117.0	107.5	107

* NPW = Net Premium Written

Source: A.M. Best Review/Preview. Used with permission.

bankruptcies like Enron's, improper corporate accounting procedures, and increasing litigation costs as some of the causes behind rising premiums for directors and officers liability insurance.[5]

Thus, in 2001, because of terror, mold, and corporate malfeasance, the hardening of the property/casualty market was solidified. Additional causes for the hard market and the prediction of its lingering are rising jury awards, reserve deficiencies, rising loss costs/expenses, and the downturn in the economy. Not only have primary rates been rising, the reinsurance market—which was responsible for paying about 60 percent of the insured losses for the September 11 terrorist attacks—has also suffered reduction in capacity and major rate increases. The life/health insurance markets conditions also deteriorated after September 11, except for the life insurance line.[6] In the area of variable life and annuity products (products associated with investments in the stock market), there was a decline in sales. The bearish stock market after the spectacular bubble in prices in the late 1990s has been the major contributor to this decline. More will be discussed in the life/health section of this text.[7]

The market most hurt was the health insurance market. Despite the managed-care revolution of the 1990s, healthcare costs continued to increase with no relief in sight.[8] According to *National Underwriter*, "Between 1965 and the early 1990s, the U.S. health insurance industry went through a clear-cut underwriting cycle, with high profit peaks in the good years and big losses and cost-cutting in the bad years. Since the early 1990s, the cycle has flattened out."[9] (For more discussion on these markets, see Chapters 17 and 19.)

Reinsurance Organizations and the Marketplace

As noted above, reinsurers were responsible for paying about 60 percent of the insured losses for the September 11 terrorist attacks. This fact requires better understanding of not only the reinsurance operations described in Chapter 4 but also the global reinsurance markets and the players.

The top ten reinsurance companies by gross premiums written for 2000 are provided in Table 5.3. Reinsurance, by its nature, is international. The worldwide growth of "jumbo" exposures, such as fleets of wide-bodied jets, super tankers, and offshore drilling platforms, creates the potential for hundreds of millions of dollars in losses from one event. No single insurer wants this kind of loss to its income statement and balance sheet. One mechanism for spreading these mammoth risks among insurers is the international reinsurance market.

As you can see in Table 5.3, most of the largest reinsurers are based in Europe. A description of Lloyd's of London (the sixth largest in 2000) as a unique insurance institution is provided later in this chapter. An emerging large growth is the reinsurance market in Bermuda. *Best's Review* reports, "Nearly 1,600 insurers are domiciled in Bermuda, a group of islands in the Atlantic Ocean some 570 miles east of North Carolina. More than 1,300 of those are captive insurance companies [explained later in this chapter]. The Bermuda insurance industry held $146 billion in total assets in 2000, according to the Bermuda Registrar of Companies." Insurers flock to Bermuda because it is a "tax haven" with no taxes on income, withholding, capital gains, premiums, or profits. It also has a friendly regulatory environment, industry talent, and many other reinsurers. After September 11, a new wave of reinsurers started in Bermuda as existing reinsurers lost their capacity.[10] As of writing of this chapter it appears that availability of reinsurance is improving.[11]

The reinsurance market conditions after September 11 propelled the passing of the Terrorism Insurance Bill discussed in Chapter 2, as well as that chapter's "Ethical Dilemma: Who Should Insure Against Terrorism?"

TABLE 5.3	Company	Country	Gross premiums written ($millions)*
Top Ten Global Reinsurance Companies by Gross Premiums Written, 2000	Munich Re: Segment Reinsurance	Germany	$17,269
	Swiss Re	Switzerland	16,176
	GE Global Insurance Holdings	U.S.	10,149
	Berkshire Hathaway	U.S.	9,270
	Hannover Re Group	Germany	7,841
	Lloyd's of London	U.K.	6,398
	Zurich Financial	Switzerland	5,107
	Gerling Global Reinsurance Group	Germany	4,897
	SCOR	France	3,259
	London Reinsurance Group	Canada	2,167

* Direct premiums plus assumed premiums; data include pro forma consolidations.

Source: The Fact Book 2002, Insurance Information Institute.

INSURANCE REGULATION

Insurance delivers only future payment in case of a loss. Therefore, it has long been actively regulated. The nature of the product requires strong regulation to ensure the solvency of insurers when claims are filed. This is the big picture of regulation of insurance in a nutshell. However, within this important overall objective, there are many areas and issues that are regulated as interim steps to achieve the main objective of availability of funds to pay claims. Most of the regulation has been at the state level for many years, although the possibility of federal involvement has also been raised, especially since the passage of the Gramm-Leach-Bliley Financial Services Modernization Act (GLBA) in 1999, and the subsequent activities including the optional federal charter of insurers discussed in "Important Issues: The State of State Insurance Regulation—Optional Federal Chartering" in this chapter.

Under state insurance regulation, state legislatures pass insurance laws that form the basis for insurance regulation. Common forms of insurance regulatory laws are listed in Figure 5.3. To ensure the smooth operation of insurance markets and the solvency of insurers, insurance laws are concerned not only with the operations and investments of insurers, but also with licensing requirements for insurers, agents, brokers, and claim adjusters and with rates and policy forms and consumer protection. The laws provide standards of financial solvency, including methods of establishing reserves and the types of investments permitted. Provisions are made in the states' laws for the liquidation or rehabilitation of any insurance company in severe financial difficulty. Since solvency is considered to be affected by product pricing (setting rates), rate regulation is an important part of insurance regulation. Trade practices, including marketing and claims adjustment, are also part of the law. Legislation further creates methods to make certain types of insurance readily available at affordable (that is, subsidized) prices. The taxation of insurers, at the state level, is also spelled out in the insurance code for each state.

FIGURE 5.3

Common Types of Insurance Regulatory Laws

- licensing requirements
- solvency standards
- liquidation/rehabilitation provisions
- rating (pricing) restrictions
- trade practice requirements
- subsidy programs
- taxation

Every state has an insurance department to administer insurance laws. In some states, the **commissioner of insurance** is also another official of the state government, such as state treasurer, state auditor, or director of banking. In most states, however, acting as commissioner of insurance is the person's sole responsibility. In some states the commissioner is appointed, in others she or he is elected. Most insurance departments have relatively few staff employees, but several are large such as in Texas, California, Illinois, Florida, and New York. The small departments are generally ill equipped to provide effective regulation of such a powerful industry.

As indicated above, the most important part of regulation is to assure solvency of insurers. Assisting this objective are the regulatory efforts in the area of consumer protection in terms of rates and policy forms. Of course, regulators protect insureds from fraud, unscrupulous agents, and white-collar crime. Regulators also make efforts to make coverage available at affordable prices while safeguarding the solvency of insurers. Regulation is a balancing act and it is not an easy one. Since insurance is regulated by the states, lack of uniformity in the laws and regulation is of great concern. Therefore, the **National Association of Insurance Commissioners (NAIC)** deals with the creation of model laws for adoption by the states to encourage uniformity. Despite the major effort to create uniformity, interest groups in each state are able to modify the NAIC model laws and those that are finally adopted may not be uniform across the states. The resulting maze of regulations is considered a barrier to the entry of new insurers. Since this is an introductory text, insurance regulation will be discussed only briefly here. For the interested student, the NAIC Web site (www.naic.org) is a great place to explore the current status of insurance regulation. Each state's insurance department has its own Web site as well.

The state insurance commissioner is empowered to:

- Grant, deny, or suspend licenses of both insurer and insurance agents
- Require an annual report from insurers (financial statements)
- Examine insurers' business operations
- Act as a liquidator or rehabilitator of insolvent insurers
- Investigate complaints
- Originate investigations
- Decide whether to grant all, part, or none of an insurer's request for higher rates
- Propose new legislation to the legislature
- Approve or reject an insurer's proposed new or amended insurance contract
- Promulgate regulations that interpret insurance laws

Licensing Requirements

An insurer must have a license from each state in which it conducts business. This requirement is for the purpose of exercising control. Companies chartered in a state are known as **domestic insurers. Foreign insurers** are those formed in another state; **alien insurers** are those organized in another country. The commissioner has more control over domestic companies than over foreign and alien ones. He or she has generally less control over insurers not licensed in the state.

An insurer obtains licenses in its state of domicile and each additional state where it plans to conduct insurance business. Holding a license implies that the insurer meets specified regulatory requirements designed to protect the consumer. It also implies that the insurer has greater business opportunities than nonlicensed insurers. A foreign insurer can conduct business by direct mail in a state without a license from that state. The insurer is considered nonadmitted and is not subject to regulation. Nonadmitted or nonlicensed insurers are also called **excess and surplus lines insurers.** They provide coverages that are not available from licensed insurers. That is, nonlicensed insurers are permitted to sell insurance only if no licensed company is willing to provide the coverage. There is access to nonadmitted insurers through persons who hold special "licenses" as **surplus lines agents** or brokers.

A license may be denied under certain circumstances. If the management is incompetent or unethical, or lacking in managerial skill, the insurance commissioner is prohibited from issuing a license. Because unscrupulous financiers have found insurers fruitful prospects for stock manipulation and the milking of assets, some state laws prohibit the licensing of any company that has been in any way associated with a person whose business activities the insurance commissioner believes are characterized by bad faith. The Equity Funding case, in which millions of dollars in fictitious life insurance were created and sold to reinsurers, for example, shows how an insurer can be a vehicle for fraud on a gigantic scale.[12] A more recent example is the story of Martin Frankel, who embezzled more than $200 million in the 1990s from small insurance companies in Arkansas, Mississippi, Missouri, Oklahoma, and Tennessee. Three insurance executives in Arkansas were charged in connection with the case. [13]

Financial Requirements

In order to qualify for a license, an insurer must fulfill certain financial requirements. Stock insurers must have a specified amount of capital and surplus (that is, net worth), and mutual insurers must have a minimum amount of surplus (mutual companies, in which the policyholders are the owners, have no stock and therefore do not show "capital" on their balance sheets). The amounts depend upon the line of insurance and the state law. Typically, a multiple-line insurer must have more capital (and/or surplus) than a company offering only one line of insurance.[14] Insurers must also maintain certain levels of capital and surplus to hold their license. Historically, these requirements have been set in simple dollar values. During the 1990s, requirements for risk-based capital were implemented by the states.

Solvency Regulations

Regulating insurers is most important in the area of safeguarding future payment of losses. Solvency regulation may help, but, in spite of the best efforts of insurance executives and regulators, some insurers fail. When an insurer becomes insolvent, it may be placed either in rehabilitation or liquidation. In either case, policyholders who have claims against the company for losses covered by their policies or for a refund of **unearned premiums**—premiums collected in advance of the policy period—may have to wait a long time while the wheels of legal processes turn. Even after a long wait, insurer assets may cover only a fraction of the amount owed to policyowners. In the aggregate, this problem is not large; only about 1 percent of insurers become insolvent each year. In 2001 and in 2000, there were thirty property/casualty insolvencies in each year. The number was much lower in 1999 with seven insolvencies and eighteen in 1998. The recent insolvencies were caused mostly by deficient loss reserves.[15] The prediction is for the trend to stabilize with more insolvencies in commercial lines than in personal lines. This is a result of the September 11 impact on commercial lines.

Investment Requirements

The solvency of an insurer depends partly on the amount and quality of its assets, and how the assets' liquidity matches the needs of liquidity to pay losses. Because poor investment policy caused the failure of many companies in the past, investments are carefully regulated. The states' insurance codes spell out in considerable detail which investments are permitted and which are prohibited. Life insurers have more stringent investment regulations than property/causality insurers, because some of the contracts made by life insurers cover a longer period of time, even a lifetime or more.

Risk-Based Capital

For **solvency regulation,** the states' insurance departments and the NAIC are looking into the investment and reserving of insurers. During the 1990s, requirements for **risk-based capital** were implemented by the states. Remember that capital reflects the excess value a firm holds in assets over liabilities. It represents a financial cushion against hard times. Some assets discussed in Chapter 4, such as common stocks, may have values that vary widely over time; that is, they involve more risk than do certain other assets. To account for variations in risks among different assets, commissioners of insurance, through their state legislators, have begun requiring firms to hold capital sufficient to produce a level that is acceptable relative to the risk profile of the asset mix of the insurer.[16] The requirements are a very important part of solvency regulation. The NAIC and many states also established an early warning system to detect potential insolvencies. Detection of potential insolvencies is a fruitful area of research. The interested student is invited to read the *Journal of Insurance Regulation* and *The Journal of Risk and Insurance* for articles in this area.[17]

Reserve Requirements

The investment requirements discussed above concern the nature and quality of insurer assets. The value of assets an insurer must hold is influenced by capital and surplus requirements and the regulation of reserves. Reserves are insurer liabilities that represent future financial obligations to policyholders. Reserves constitute the bulk of insurance company liabilities. See more about how to calculate reserves in Chapter 4.

Guaranty Funds Associations

All states have **state guaranty fund associations** for both property/casualty and life/health insurance to assure that the insured does not bear the entire burden of losses when an insurer becomes insolvent. Instead, unpaid claims and return premiums owed to insureds or claimants of a defunct company are paid through a guaranty fund. The guaranty funds are funded by involuntary contributions from solvent insurers doing business in the state. The guaranty association assesses each company on the basis of the percentage of its premium volume to cover the obligations to policyholders, as discussed later in this chapter.[18] Most guaranty associations limit the maximum they will reimburse any single insured, and most also provide coverage only to residents of the state.

Policy and Rate Regulation

In light of the new terrorism exclusion and mold coverage exclusions of 2001 and 2002, it is important that the students understand the extent of the state commissioners' power and the role they play in approving policy forms and controlling the rates for insurance. **Policy form and rate regulation** is part of the regulatory activity and it is a topic for open debate. As of the writing of this textbook, both California and New York insurance commissioners denied the industry's application to exclude terrorism risk from the all-risk commercial policy.

Most states consider property/casualty rates not adequately regulated by market forces. Therefore, rates are regulated for auto, property and liability coverages, and workers' compensation. Minimum rates for individual life insurance and annuity contracts are regulated indirectly through limits imposed on assumptions used in establishing reserves. Competitive forces are the only determinants of maximum rates for individual life, individual annuity, and group life/health insurance. Rates for individual health insurance are regulated in some states. Individual disability and accident rates are controlled in some states by their refusal to approve policy forms in which at least a target level of premiums is not expected to be returned to the policyholder as benefits.

One type of property/casualty rate regulation is the **prior approval** approach. In states that use this method, an insurer or its rating bureau (such as ISO discussed earlier) must file its new rates and have them approved by the commissioner before using them. Another approach called **file-and-use** allows an insurer to begin using a new rate as soon as it is filed with the commissioner. The commissioner can disapprove the new rate if it is determined to be undesirable within a specified period, generally thirty days. A few states have adopted **open competition** rating laws. This approach requires no rate filings by an insurer. The underlying assumption is that market competition is a sufficient regulator of rates. Although results are mixed, studies of the effects of different types of rate regulation generally find no significant differences in the prices paid by consumers under different systems for the same service.

Control of Agent's Activities

Insurance laws also prohibit certain activities on the part of agents and brokers, such as twisting, rebating, unfair practices, and misappropriation of funds belonging to insurers or insureds. **Twisting** (also called **churning**) is inducing a policyholder to cancel one contract and buy another by misrepresenting the facts or providing incomplete policy comparisons. An unfair or misleading comparison of two contracts can be a disservice if it causes the insured to drop a policy he or she had for some time in order to buy another that is no better, or perhaps not as good. On the other hand, sometimes changing policies is in the best interest of the policyholder, and justified replacements are legal. Twisting regulations, therefore, may include the requirement that the resulting policy change be detrimental to the policyholder.

Rebating is providing (substantial) value as an inducement to purchase insurance; for example the agent or broker shares his or her commission with the insured. Rebating is prohibited because:

- It is considered unfair competition among agents.
- Some knowledgeable consumers would buy a new policy each year when first year commissions are larger than renewal commissions; higher lapse rates increase long-run cost.
- More sophisticated consumers could negotiate larger rebates than the less informed, and this would be unfair.[19]
- Agents may be encouraged to engage in unethical behavior by selling new policies over renewal policies, due to the larger first-year commissions.

Some insurers adjust to rebating laws by offering their agents and brokers two or more series of contracts with the same provisions but with rates that reflect different levels of commissions. A particular insurer's "personal series," for example, may include a normal level of commissions. Its "executive series," however, may pay the agent or broker a lower commission and offer a lower rate to potential insureds. In competitive situations, the agent or broker is likely to propose the "executive series" in order to gain a price advantage. The Florida Supreme Court decided in 1986 that the antirebate law was unconstitutional. This decision had the potential to increase pressure on other states to reconsider the practice, but very little activity on the subject has occurred since then. California's Proposition 103 (passed in 1988), however, includes a provision to abandon the state's antirebate laws. In the settlement to resolve their Proposition 103 rollback obligations with the California state insurance department, insurers paid rebates to their 1989 customers.[20]

Unfair Practices

Unfair practice is a catchall term that can be applied to many undesirable activities of agents, claim adjusters, and insurers (including misleading advertisements). Unfair practices may lead to fines, removal of licenses, and, in extreme cases, to punitive damage awards by the courts. **Misappropriation of funds** refers to situations in which the agent keeps funds (primarily premiums) belonging to the company, the policyholder, or a beneficiary. For example, an insured was killed by accident; his $1,000 life insurance policy had a double indemnity rider. In order to impress the beneficiary with the value of this rider, the insurer mailed two checks in the amount of $1,000 each to the agent for delivery. The agent gave one check to the beneficiary and then induced the beneficiary to endorse the second check to the agent, claiming that its issuance was in error and so it had to be cashed and the money returned to the insurer. The insurance department recovered the $1,000, paid it to the beneficiary, and revoked the agent's license.

Control of Claims Adjusting

Every insured has contact with an insurer's marketing system, most often through an agent. Regulation of agents, therefore, has significant impact on most insureds. Only those who make claims on their policies, however, have contact with claims adjusters. This is the time when an insured may be vulnerable and in need of regulatory attention.

Insurance commissioners control claims adjusting practices primarily through policyholder complaints. Any insured who believes that the insurer improperly handled or denied a claim can contact the insurance commissioner's office with details of the transaction. The commissioner's office will investigate the complaint. Unfortunately for the insured, the commissioner's office cannot require an insurer to pay a claim, although a letter from the commissioner's office that the insured is "in the right" may be persuasive. The most common form of "punishment" for wrongdoing is either a reprimand or fine against the insurer. Some commissioner's offices keep track of the number of complaints lodged against insurers operating in the state and publish this information on a standardized basis (for example, per $100,000 of premium volume).

Control of Underwriting Practices

We have discussed the ways in which insurer pricing practices are regulated. Closely tied to ratemaking is an insurer's underwriting function. Over the years, insurers have used a variety of factors in their underwriting decisions. A number of these have become taboo from a public policy standpoint. Their use may be considered unfair discrimination. Insurance commissioner's office has some authority to regulate against inappropriate underwriting practices. See "Ethical Dilemma: Insurance and Your Privacy—Who Knows?" for a discussion of the conflict between the underwriting needs and privacy. Also, the issue of the use of credit scoring in underwriting was discussed in the "Ethical Dilemma: Keeping Score—Is It Fair to Use Credit Rating in Underwriting" of Chapter 4. The discussions in the boxes are only examples of the vast array of underwriting issues under regulatory oversight. For more issues, visit again the NAIC web site at www.NAIC.org.

Impact of the Gramm-Leach-Bliley Act on Insurance Regulation

Since the passage of the **Gramm-Leach-Bliley (GLBA) Financial Services Modernization Act** on November 12, 1999, insurance regulators have been working to maintain state regulation while complying with the new requirements under the Act. One of the outcomes is the current debate regarding optional Federal insurers' chartering debate (see "Important Issues: The State of State Insurance Regulation—Optional Federal Chartering"). Insurers on both sides—the life and the property/casualty—have lobbied for different ways to create federally chartered insurance companies.[21] Many insurers today are global players. The regional mindset of state regulation appears to not fit the needs of international players. Therefore, these insurers are pushing for federal charters.

After the enactment of the GLBA, which included some sweeping changes for insurance as part of the financial modernization act, the NAIC issued a Statement of Intent to assure the preservation of state regulation within the GLBA prerequisites. In this statement, the commissioners pointed out that "Fueled by enhanced technology and globalization, the world financial markets are undergoing rapid changes. In order to protect and serve more sophisticated but also more exposed insurance consumers of the future, insurance regulators are committed to modernize insurance regulation to meet the realities of an increasingly dynamic, and internationally competitive financial services marketplace" (see www.naic.org). Among the NAIC's commitments to change are:

- Amending state laws to include anti-affiliation statutes, licensure laws, demutualization statutes (discussed later in this chapter), and various essential consumer protections, including sales and privacy provisions.

- Streamlining and standardizing the licensing procedure for producers. One of the provisions of Gramm-Leach-Bliley requires U.S. jurisdictions to adopt uniform or reciprocal agent- and broker-licensing laws by November 2002 (three years after the enactment of the law). If this requirement is not met, a National Association of Registered Agents and Brokers will be created.[22] By leveraging work already done on the Producer Database and the Producer Information Network and by using IRIN (Insurance Regulatory Information Network), the NAIC has already succeeded in meeting the requirements by having enough state legislatures pass bills permitting reciprocity among the states.

- Building on initiatives already underway concerning national companies, such as review of financial reporting, financial analysis and examination, refining risk-based approach to examining the insurance operations of financial holding companies.

- Implementing functional regulation and sharing regulatory information to encourage the execution of information sharing agreements between the individual states and each of the key federal functional regulators.

In addition, the NAIC started to work on the **speed to market** concept of expediting the introduction of new insurance products into the marketplace (a process that had been too time-consuming). The idea is to develop state-based uniform standards for policy form and rate filings, without loss of flexibility. Other areas of improvements are **regulatory re-engineering,** which promotes uniformity, and **market conduct reform,** which creates a process to respond to changing market conditions, especially relating to e-commerce.

The debate regarding federal versus state insurance regulation has been heightened as a result of GLBA. As of January 2002, four proposals before Congress called for the creation of a federal insurance regulator position within the U.S. Treasury Department.[23] It is anticipated that the work on such changes will take years, but as insurance companies

Ethical Dilemma

Insurance and Your Privacy—Who Knows?

Your insurer knows things about you that your best friend probably doesn't. If you have homeowners, health, and auto coverage, your insurance provider knows how much money you make, whether you pay your bills on time, how much your assets are worth, what medications you're taking, and which embarrassing diseases you've contracted. Your personal identification numbers, such as Social Security and driver's license, are in those files as well. If you pay your premiums online, your insurance company has a record of your bank account number, too.

Insurance companies can't function without this personal information. Underwriters must know your history to determine your level of coverage, your risk pooling group, and your rate classification. Adjusters, particularly in workers' compensation and auto lines, need your identification numbers to gather information from outside providers so they can settle your claims promptly. And to stay competitive, insurers must be able to develop new products and market them to the people who might be interested—special "embarrassing diseases" coverage, perhaps.

But is this information safe? Many consumers who trust their insurance agents with personal information worry about it getting in the hands of the government, an identity thief or, worst of all, a telemarketer. Insurance companies worry about how to balance protecting their customers' privacy with maintaining enough openness to perform their day-to-day business operations for those same customers.

Two recent pieces of federal legislation address the issue. The Health Insurance Portability and Accountability Act (HIPAA) of 1996 authorized the Department of Health and Human Services to set minimum standards for protection of health information and gave states the right to impose tougher standards. The Financial Services Act of 1999, better known as the Gramm-Leach-Bliley Act (GLBA), gave consumers more control over the distribution of their personal financial information.

Insurance is a state-regulated business, so insurance-specific regulations fall within the authority of state insurance commissioners. Thus far, thirty-six states plus the District of Columbia are following a model developed by the National Association of Insurance Commissioners (see the model law and updates on state activity at http://www.naic.org/1privacy). An important component of NAIC's model is the "opt in" provision for health information, which regulators consider to be more sensitive than financial information. As opposed to GLBA's "opt out" provision, which gives insurers the right to share your financial information with outsiders unless you specifically tell them not to, NAIC's "opt in" provision means insurers can't share your health history unless you specifically permit them to do so.

But the system is far from airtight. Under GLBA provisions, insurers do not need your permission to share your data with its affiliates—and in these days of mega conglomerations, an insurance company can have lots of affiliates. Insurers are even permitted to disclose, without your permission, protected financial information to third parties with whom they have a marketing agreement.

For their part, insurers fear that further restrictions on sharing information would affect their ability to provide timely quotes and claims settlements. Another major concern is a broker's ability to "shop a policy around" to find the best rate and coverage for his or her client. And while consumers might complain about the paperwork involved in opting-out, insurance companies have had to develop and implement privacy policies, train all staff who handle personal information, and set up new departments to handle the opt-out wishes of tens of millions of customers. It's estimated that GBLA compliance could cost the insurance industry as much as $2 billion.

Any federal or state privacy legislation must protect consumers' right to control what happens to their personal data, but it also must preserve insurers' ability to operate their businesses. Where should the line be drawn?

Questions for Discussion

1. How concerned are you about privacy? Are you more protective about your health or your financial information?

2. When companies have to spend money to comply with the law, it's generally the consumer who winds up paying. Would you accept slightly higher premiums to cover the costs of keeping your personal information private?

3. Why would increased privacy provisions make it difficult for brokers to give their customers the best service?

Sources: National Association of Insurance Commissioners, "NAIC Privacy of Consumer Financial and Health Information," www.naic.org/1privacy; American Civil Liberties Union, "Defending Financial Privacy," http://www.aclu.org /Privacy/PrivacyMain.cfm; American Insurance Association, "Industry Issues: Privacy," www.aiadc.org/IndustryIssues/Privacy.asp; Steven Brostoff, "Stakes Are High in Battle over Health Data Privacy," *National Underwriter Property & Casualty/Risk & Benefits Management Edition*, 27 May 2002; Mark E. Ruquet, "Privacy Is Still A Hot Topic For Agents," *National Underwriter Property & Casualty/Risk & Benefits Management Edition*, 27 May 2002; Lori Chordas, "Secret Identity," *Best's Review*, June 2002.

IMPORTANT ISSUES

The State of State Insurance Regulation—Optional Federal Chartering

Did it surprise you to learn that insurance companies—many of them billion-dollar firms that conduct business across the nation and even around the globe—are regulated by states rather than by the federal government? The state-based regulatory system was established by Congress more than fifty years ago, when most insurers were local or regional—your "good neighbors." Each state's regulations grew more or less independently, based on its own mix of population, weather conditions, and industry, until they were finally quite different from one another. But for a long time it didn't matter: Florida agents rarely sold hurricane insurance to Nebraska farmers, so what difference did it make if the rules were different?

These days, however, a Florida-based insurance company might sell insurance policies and annuities to Nebraska farmers, Louisiana shrimpers, and California surfers. But it would have to file the policies for approval from each state involved, a complicated course that can take more than a year. Meanwhile, Huge National Bank goes through a single federal-approval process to sell its investment products, and voila: permission to market in all fifty states. The consumer, who doesn't have the opportunity to compare price and benefits, is the ultimate loser.

For life insurers in particular, many of the products sold are investment vehicles. That puts life insurers in direct competition with banks and securities firms, which, being federally chartered, can bring their products to market more quickly—and often at a competitive price, too, since they don't have to reformat to meet different requirements in different states.

Equitable market entry, faster review processes, and uniform rate regulation are the top goals for the many insurance groups who are calling for federal chartering as an option for insurance companies, as it has been for the banking industry for 140 years. In December 2001, Sen. Charles E. Schumer introduced a bill, the National Insurance Chartering and Supervision Act, that uses the banking industry's dual state-federal regulatory system as a model. Under this bill, insurance companies could choose between state and federal regulation. The following February, Rep. John J. LaFalce introduced the Insurance Industry Modernization and Consumer Protection Act, which also would create an optional federal charter for the companies but would keep the states in charge of overseeing insurance rates. (As of November 2002, neither bill had been scheduled for a vote.) And some insurance groups doubt the wisdom of federal chartering at all and urge a reform of the state system, arguing that state regulation is more attuned to the needs of the local consumer. Federal regulation, they contend, would merely add another layer of bureaucracy and cost that not only would hurt the consumer but also might drive small, specialty insurers out of business.

In the summer of 2002, a House Financial Services subcommittee began holding hearings on insurance regulation reform. Nearly every major insurance company and trade group has filed a report or proposal, and the industry is sharply divided. The chairman of Geico Corp. wants Congress to first give states the opportunity to improve their regulatory system. The American Insurance Association disagrees: Companies should be given the option of obtaining a single charter that will allow them to operate in all fifty states and be subject to uniformity in laws. The Independent Insurance Agents and Brokers of America supports using federal government tools to help modernize state insurance regulation, but opposes optional federal chartering. The American Council of Life Insurers strongly supports federally chartered insurers, who would "underwrite and sell in any state, any line of insurance for which they hold a federal license."

Members of Congress say that the issue will not be easily decided, and any reform will take years to accomplish. But all agree that some kind of change is needed. "No matter what side one takes in this long-standing debate, it has become clear to me that this is no longer a question of whether we should reform insurance regulation in the United States," said Rep. Paul Kanjorskiof, a member of the subcommittee. "Instead, it has become a question of how we should reform insurance regulation."

Exploring the Internet

Compare and contrast: The American Insurance Association, a trade group of more than 400 property and casualty insurers, strongly supports federal chartering. The National Association of Insurance Commissioners, an organization of state regulatory
(Continued)

are in national and global markets, they are at a disadvantage compared with federally regulated industries such as banking and securities. The need to obtain approval for products from fifty states costs the industry too much time. By contrast, securities firms bring new products to the market within 90 days, and banks almost immediately.[24] One proposal suggested that the federal government regulates insurers above a certain size or in certain business lines, while the states would retain responsibility for regulating the rest.[25] As noted above, the optional chartering proposals are featured in the Important Issues box of this chapter.

Now that you have some understanding of insurance markets and regulation, we will provide you with a brief description of the type of insurance institutions you may deal with as an insurance consumer or as a risk manager.

PRIVATE INSURING ORGANIZATIONS, THEIR MARKETS, AND THEIR REGULATION

As a risk manager for a family or organization, you will make better decisions when you know more about different types of insurers and their regulatory oversight. As you saw in Figure 5.1, the big picture of the insurance world includes both regulated and non-regulated insurers. Whether regulated by the states or not, insurance companies have different corporate structure characteristics. Next we will explore these organizational structures and trends that affect them.

Private insuring organizations are owned and controlled by private citizens, rather than by the government. They engage in risk bearing for a fee. In some cases, the objective is to make a profit. In other cases, it is to provide insurance at cost such as Blue Cross and Blue Shield (BCBS). This health plans were originally structured as not-for-profit entities.[26] Organizational structures are discussed next as follows: (1) stock insurers, (2) mutual companies and demutualization, (3) Lloyd's of London, (4) bank and insurance, and (5) captives, risk retention groups and alternative markets. Other forms of insurance organizations are featured in Appendix 5.1.

Stock Insurers

Stock insurers are organized in the same way as other privately owned corporations created for the purpose of making a profit and maximizing the value of the organization for the benefit of the owners. Individuals provide the operating capital for the company. Stock companies can be publicly traded in the stock markets or privately held. Stockholders receive dividends when the company is profitable.

Mutual Insurers

Mutual insurers are owned and controlled, in theory if not in practice, by their policy-owners. They have no stockholders and issue no capital stock. People become owners by purchasing an insurance policy from the mutual insurer. Profits are shared with owners as policyowners' **dividends.** Company officers are appointed by a board of directors that is, at least theoretically, elected by policyowners. The stated purpose of the organization is to provide low-cost insurance rather than to make a profit for stockholders.

Research shows that mutual and stock insurers are highly competitive in the sense that neither seems to outperform the other. There are high-quality, low-cost insurers of both types. A wise consumer will want to analyze both before buying insurance.[27]

Many mutuals in both the life/health and property/casualty fields are of great size and operate over large areas of the country. These large mutuals do a general business in the life/health and property/casualty insurance fields, rather than confining their efforts to a small geographic area or a particular type of insured. The largest property/casualty mutual insurer in the United States is State Farm, which was established in 1922 by George J. Mecherle, an Illinois farmer who turned to insurance sales. State Farm grew to be the leading auto and homeowners insurer in the United States, with twenty-five regional offices, more than 79,000 employees and nearly seventy million policies in force.[28] Because of the mutual status, State Farm is overcapitalized (holding relatively more surplus than its peer group or stock companies). It is interesting to compare the break-even point of the combined ratio of mutuals and stock companies. State Farm as a mutual company needs to achieve a combined ratio of about 105, on average, to break even, while stock companies need to aim for a combined ratio of 100. This difference is based on the need to satisfy stockholders who own the stock companies. This implies that mutual companies can take on larger loss and expense ratios than stock companies to be in a position of breaking even. It appears that stock companies such as Allstate and Progressive are able to reach this objective.[29]

Demutualization

When top managers of a mutual company decide they need to raise capital, they may go through a process of demutualization. In the last decade there was an escalated move to **demutualize** and become stock companies. Policyholders, who were owners of the mutual company, receive shares in the stock company. Part of the motive was to provide top management with an additional avenue of income in the form of stock options in the company. The demutualization wave in the life insurance industry reached its peak in December 2001, when the large mutual insurer, Prudential, converted to a stock company.[30]

While it is anticipated that the trend will continue, some large mutuals have kept their mutual status, such as Northwestern Mutual, Massachusetts Mutual, New York Life, and Guardian Life. During the International Insurance Society meeting in Vancouver in 2000, the chairman of New York Life advocated for continuing the mutual status. Those in favor of keeping the mutual form advocate that mutual insurers should not be forced to change their long-term strategy and survival.[31] Thus, it appears that there are forces for and against demutualization. The movement added $55.3 billion of capitalization to the life/health industry through the conversion of four big mutuals—MONY ($1.9 billion), John Hancock ($11.9 billion), MetLife ($24.1 billion), and Prudential ($17.4 billion).[32]

Lloyd's of London: A Global Insurance Exchange

Lloyd's of London—the oldest insurance organization in existence, which started in a coffee house in London—conducts a worldwide business primarily from England; it is also licensed in Illinois and Kentucky. It maintains a trust fund in the United States for the protection of insureds in this country. In states where Lloyd's is not licensed, it is considered a "nonadmitted" insurer. States primarily allow such nonadmitted insurers to sell only coverage that is unavailable from their licensed (admitted) insurers. This generally unavailable coverage is known as excess and surplus lines insurance, and it is Lloyd's primary U.S. business.[33]

Lloyd's does not assume risks in the manner of other insurers. Instead, individual members of Lloyd's, called **Names,** accept insurance risks by providing capital to an underwriting syndicate. Each syndicate is made up of many Names and accepts risks through one or more brokers. Surplus lines agents—those who sell for excess and surplus lines insurers—direct business to brokers at one or more syndicates. Syndicates, rather than Names, make the underwriting decisions of which risks to accept. Various activities of Lloyd's are supervised by two governing committees—one for market management and another for regulation of financial matters. The syndicates are known to accept exotic risks and reinsure much of the asbestos and catastrophic risk in the United States. They also insure aviation.

The arrangement of Lloyd's of London is similar to that of an organized stock exchange in which physical facilities are owned by the exchange but business is transacted by the members. The personal liability of individual Names has been unlimited; they have been legally liable for their underwriting losses under Lloyd's policies to the full extent of their personal and business assets. This point is sometimes emphasized by telling new male members that they are liable "down to their cufflinks," and for female members "down to their earrings." In addition to Names being required to make deposits of capital with the governing committee for financial matters, each Name is required to put premiums into a trust fund that makes them exclusively encumbered to the Name's underwriting liabilities until the obligations under the policies for which the premiums were paid have been fulfilled. Underwriting accounts are audited annually to ensure that assets and liabilities are correctly valued and that assets are sufficient to meet underwriting liabilities. Normally, profits are distributed annually. Following losses, Names may be asked to make additional contributions. A trust fund covers the losses of bankrupt Names. A supervisory committee has authority to suspend or expel members.

Seldom does one syndicate assume all of one large exposure; it assumes part. Thus, an individual Name typically becomes liable for a small fraction of 1 percent of the total liability assumed in one policy. Historically, syndicates also reinsured with each other to provide more risk sharing. The practice of sharing risk through reinsurance within the Lloyd's organization magnified the impact of heavy losses incurred by Lloyd's members for 1988 through 1992. Losses for these five years reached the unprecedented level of $14.2 billion. Reinsurance losses on U.S. business were a major contributor to losses due to asbestos and pollution, Hurricanes Hugo and Andrew, the 1989 San Francisco earthquake, the Exxon Valdez oil spill, product liabilities, and other **long-tail liability claims,** so called because the claims do not close for many years.

The massive losses wiped out the fortunes of many Names. In 1953 Lloyd's consisted of 3,400 Names, most of whom were wealthy citizens of the British Commonwealth. By 1989, many less wealthy, upper-middle-class people had been enticed to become Names with unlimited liability, pushing the total number of Names to an all-time-high of 34,000 in 400 syndicates. By mid-1994, only about 17,500 Names and 178 underwriting syndicates (with just ninety-six accepting new business) remained. As a result of the mammoth total losses (and bankruptcy or rehabilitation for many individual members), Lloyd's had reduced underwriting capacity and was experiencing difficulty in attracting new capital. What started in a coffeehouse was getting close to the inside of the percolator.

Among Lloyd's reforms was the acceptance of corporate capital. By mid-1994, 15 percent of its capital was from twenty-five corporations that, unlike individual Names, have their liability limited to the amount of invested capital. Another reform consisted of a new system of compulsory stop loss insurance designed to help members reduce exposure to large losses. Reinsurance among syndicates has ceased.[34]

For fiscal year 2000 Lloyd's reported losses of $1.7 billion, a slight improvement over their performance in the early 1990s. The following year, however, included claims resulting from September 11, and Lloyd's posted a loss of $4.5 billion for 2001. With a combined ratio of 140 for 2001, Lloyds predicted that they would have to raise premium rates in all their lines. Then-chairman Sax Riley proposed radical modernization, including ending the unlimited liability membership by 2005 and replacing existing regulatory and market boards and committees with a single "franchise" board. With these changes he hoped to steer Lloyd's toward franchise management, concentrating on planning and managing agencies to improve underwriting performance. The proposals were to be voted on by the end of 2002.[35]

Other forms of insurance entities that are in less use are featured in Appendix 5.1 of this chapter.

Banks and Insurance

For decades, savings banks in Massachusetts, New York, and Connecticut have sold life insurance in one of two ways: by establishing life insurance departments or by acting as agents for other savings banks with insurance departments. Savings banks sell the usual types of individual life insurance policies and annuities, as well as group life insurance. Business is transacted on an over-the-counter basis or by mail. No agents are employed to sell the insurance; however, advertising is used extensively for marketing. Insurance is provided at a relatively low cost.

Many savings and loan associations have been selling personal property/casualty insurance (and some life insurance) through nonbanking subsidiaries. Commercial banks have lobbied hard for permission to both underwrite (issue contracts and accept risks as an insurer) and sell all types of insurance. Approximately two thirds of the states have granted state-chartered banks this permission. At this time, national banks have not been granted such power.[36]

In November 1999, State Farm Mutual Automobile Insurance Company opened State Farm Bank. At the time of this writing, State Farm has banking services in eleven states— Alabama, Arizona, Colorado, Illinois, Indiana, Mississippi, Missouri, New Mexico, Nevada, Utah, and Wyoming—and plans to expand to all fifty states. The banking division benefits from State Farm's 16,000 agents, who can market a full range of banking products.[37]

The U.S. Supreme Court approved (with a 9–0 vote) the sale of fixed-dollar and variable annuities (explained in Chapter 19) by national banks, reasoning that annuities are investments rather than insurance. Banks are strong in annuities sales. Life and health insurance sales by banks were also on a rise with a growth to $422 million in 2000.[38] Banks make small profits on sales of life insurance, though.[39]

Since the passage of GLBA, only a few banks acquired insurance companies.[40] During the debate over the GLBA, there was a rush by insurers to apply for banking charters. Many thought that there would be more of the Citigroup type of deals (combining Citicorp and Travelers Insurance), but that did not materialize. A 2002 report by the American Bankers Insurance Association revealed that only a quarter of the banks it studied targeted the mass market.[41]

Captives, Risk Retention Groups, and Alternative Markets

Risk retention groups and captives are forms of self-insurance. Broadly defined, a **captive insurance company** is one that provides insurance coverage to its parent company and other affiliated organizations. The captive is controlled by its policyholder-parent. Some captives sell coverage to nonaffiliated organizations. Others are comprised of members of industry associations, resulting in captives that closely resemble the early mutual insurers.

Forming a captive insurer is an expensive undertaking. Capital must be contributed in order to develop a net worth sufficient to meet regulatory (and financial stability) requirements. Start-up costs for licensing, chartering, and managing the captive are also incurred. And of course, the captive needs constant managing, requiring that effort be expended by the firm's risk management department and/or that a management company be hired.

To justify these costs, the parent company considers various factors. One is the availability of insurance in the commercial insurance market. During the liability insurance crisis of the 1980s, for example, pollution liability coverage became virtually nonexistent. Chemical and other firms formed captives to fill the void. Today there is a big push for captives after the losses of September 11. Another factor considered in deciding upon a captive is the opportunity cost of money. If the parent can use funds more productively (that is, can earn a higher after-tax return on investment) than the insurer can, the formation of a captive may be wise. The risk manager must assess the importance of the insurer's claims adjusting and other services (including underwriting) when evaluating whether to create a captive. Insurers' services are very important considerations. One reason to create a captive is to have access to the reinsurance market for stop loss catastrophic coverage for the captive. One currently popular use of captives is to coordinate the insurance programs of a firm's foreign operations. An added advantage of captives in this setting is the ability to manage exchange rate risks as well as the pure risks more common to traditional risk managers. Perhaps of primary significance is that captives give their parents access to the reinsurance market.

As noted above, as of the writing of this text, the insurance industry is in a hard market condition. Captive managers in Bermuda received many inquiries after September 11 as U.S. insurance buyers searched for lower rates. The level of reinsurance capacity is always a concern for captive owners since reinsurers provide the catastrophic layer of protection as explained in Chapter 4. In the past, reinsurance was rather inexpensive for captives.[42] But, the picture has changed. The year 2001 saw a large number of new captive formations in Bermuda—a growth from fifty new licensed captives in 2000 to 108 in 2001. In 2001, there were 1,136 licensed captives in the United States.[43]

An interesting example of new group captives, known as a **risk retention group,**[44] is the one formed recently by the airline industry, which suffered disproportional losses as a result of September 11. A risk retention group designed to cover passenger and third-party war-risk liability for airlines gained regulatory approval in Vermont.[45] The risk retention group for airline is named Equitime. It was formed by the Air Transport Association (ATA), a Washington, D.C.-based trade group, and Marsh Inc. (one of the largest brokerage firms worldwide). The risk retention group, Equitime, offers as much as $1.5 billion in combined limits for passenger and third-party war-risk liability. The plan is for Equitime to retain $300 million of the limit and reinsure the balance with the federal government. The capitalization of this risk retention group is through a private placement of stock from twenty-four airlines belonging to the ATA and about fifty members of the Regional Airline Association.[46]

It is also reported that about half of the U.S. commercial market will be placed in **alternative markets** by 2003.[47] Alternative markets are the markets of all self-insurance programs. Captives and group captives will see steady growth in membership. In addition there are the **governmental risk pools** formed for governmental entities such as the Texas Association of School Boards (TASB); municipals risk pools; and other taxing-authorities pools. TASB, for example, offers to the Texas school districts pooling arrangement for workers' compensation and property, liability, and health insurance. Public Risk Pools has a large association, the Public Risk Management Association (PRIMA), that provides support and education to public risk pools.[48] During hard market conditions, alternative markets flourish. During hard markets, excess and surplus line insurers also flourish since they provide coverage where the regulated companies do not have the capacity. Surplus lines brokers were swamped with business even before September 11.[49] The problem with surplus lines writers and all alternative markets is that they are not part of the states' insurance regulatory system that protects consumers.

GOVERNMENT INSURING ORGANIZATIONS

Federal and state government agencies account for nearly half of the insurance activity in the United States. Primarily, they fill a gap where private insurers have not provided coverage (in most cases, because the exposure does not adequately meet the ideal requisites for private insurance). However, some governmental programs (examples include the Maryland automobile fund, state workers' compensation, insurance plans, crop insurance, and a Wisconsin life plan) exist for political reasons. Government insurers created for political goals usually compete with private firms. This section briefly summarizes state and federal government insurance activities.

State Insuring Organizations

- All states administer unemployment compensation insurance programs.
- All states also have **guaranty funds** (as discussed above) to ensure that insurance company failure will not be borne solely by certain policyowners. Covered lines of insurance and maximum liability per policyowner vary by state. Financing is provided on a post-loss assessment basis (except for pre-loss assessments in New York) by involuntary contributions from all insurance companies licensed in the state. An insurer's contributions to a particular state are proportionate to its volume of business in the state. No benefits are paid to stockholders of defunct insurers. The funds are responsible for obligations of insolvent companies to their policyowners.
- Eighteen states have funds to insure workers' compensation benefits; some are monopolistic, while others compete with private insurers.
- Several states provide temporary nonoccupational disability insurance, title insurance, or medical malpractice insurance. Many states provide medical malpractice insurance (discussed in upcoming chapters) through **joint underwriting associations** (JUA), which are created by state legislation. If the JUA experiences losses in excess of its expectations, it has the power to assess all insurers that write liability insurance in the state. However, rates are supposed to be set at a level adequate to avoid such assessments. Some states

have also created JUAs for lawyers and other groups that have had difficulties finding insurance in the private market.

- Seven states along the Atlantic and Gulf coasts assure the availability of property insurance, and indirect loss insurance in some states, to property owners of coastal areas exposed to hurricanes and other windstorms. Insurance is written through **beach and windstorm insurance plans.** Compliance with building codes is encouraged for loss reduction.

- The state of Maryland operates a fund to provide automobile liability insurance to Maryland motorists unable to buy it in the private market.

- The Wisconsin State Life Fund sells life insurance to residents of Wisconsin on an individual basis similar to that of private life insurers.

- In recent years, several states have created health insurance pools to give uninsurable individuals access to health insurance. Coverage may be limited and expensive.

Federal Insuring Organizations

- The Social Security Administration, which operates the Social Security program, collects more premiums (in the form of payroll taxes) and pays more claims than any other insurance organization in the United States. Detailed description is available in Chapter 15.

- The Federal Deposit Insurance Corporation insures depositors against loss caused by the failure of a bank. Credit union accounts are protected by the National Credit Union Administration. The Securities Investor Protection Corporation covers securities held by investment brokers and dealers.

- The Federal Crop Insurance Corporation provides open-perils insurance for farm crops. Policies are sold and serviced by the private market. The federal government provides subsidies and reinsurance.

- The Federal Crime Insurance Program covers losses due to burglary and robbery in both personal and commercial markets.

- Fair Access to Insurance Requirements (FAIR) plans have been established in a number of states under federal legislation. They are operated by private insurers as a pool to make property insurance available to applicants who cannot buy it in the regular market. Federal government reinsurance pays for excessive losses caused by riots and civil disorder.

- The National Flood Insurance Program provides flood insurance through private agents in communities that have met federal requirements designed to reduce flood losses. See description of the Federal flood insurance in Chapter 10.

- The Veterans Administration provides several programs for veterans.

- Several federal agencies insure mortgage loans made by private lenders against losses due to borrowers failing to make payments.

- The Pension Benefit Guaranty Corporation protects certain retirement plan benefits in the event the plan sponsor fails to fulfill its promises to participants. (For description, see Chapter 18.)

- The Overseas Private Investment Corporation (OPIC) protects against losses suffered by U.S. citizens through political risks in underdeveloped countries. (For discussion of political risk and OPIC, see Chapter 8.)

KEY TERMS

underwriting cycle
hard market
insurance capacity
soft market
guarantee funds
combined ratio
cash flow underwriting
commissioner (or
 superintendent) of
 insurance
National Association of
 Insurance Commissioners
 (NAIC)
solvency regulation
risk-based capital
domestic insurers
foreign insurers
alien insurers
excess and surplus lines
 insurers

surplus lines agents or
 brokers
stock insurers
unearned premiums
state guaranty associations
policy form and rate
 regulation
prior approval
file-and-use
open competition
twisting
churning
rebating
unfair practices
misappropriation of funds
Gramm-Leach-Bliley
 (GLBA) Financial Services
 Modernization Act
speed to market
regulatory re-engineering

market conduct reform
mutual insurers
dividends
demutualization
Lloyd's of London
Names
long-tail liability claims
captive insurance company
risk retention group
governmental risk pools
alternative markets
guaranty funds
joint underwriting
 associations
beach and windstorm
 insurance plans
reciprocals
interinsurance associations
Lloyds Associations
insurance exchanges

DISCUSSION QUESTIONS

1. Among the leading insurance markets in the world, which countries are the largest in life premiums and which are the largest in property/casualty premiums?
2. Explain the underwriting cycle. What causes the underwriting cycle? When would there be a hard market? Soft market?
3. What are the reasons for the high combined ratios of the commercial lines of property/casualty business in 2001?
4. Why did the world reinsurance market become hard in 2001?
5. Describe the emerging reinsurance markets. Why are they developing in Bermuda?
6. Describe the main activities of insurance regulators.
7. What methods are used to create uniformity in insurance regulation across the states?
8. What is the difference between:
   a. Admitted and non-admitted insurers?
   b. Regulated and non-regulated insurers?
   c. Surplus lines writers and regulated insurers?
   d. "File and use" and "prior approval" rate regulation?
   e. "Twisting" and "rebating"?
9. What is the function of the states' guarantee funds?
10. What are risk-based capital requirements, and what is their purpose?

11. Describe the efforts put forth by the National association of Insurance Commissioners to preserve state insurance regulation after the passage of the Gramm-Leach-Bliley Financial Services Modernization Act (GLBA) .

12. How do stock insurers differ from mutuals with respect to their ownership?

13. As a consumer, should you buy from a stock insurer chosen randomly or a mutual chosen randomly? Why, or why not?

14. Describe the organizational structure of Lloyd's of London. What changes took place? What are the current proposed changes?

15. a. What are captives? Describe the changes that occur during hard markets.
    b. What are risk retention groups and governmental risk pools? How are they affected by hard markets condition?

EXERCISES

5.1 The Happy Life Insurance Company is a stock insurer licensed in a large western state. Its loss reserves are estimated at $9.5 million and its unearned premium reserves at $1.7 million. Other liabilities are valued at $1.3 million. It is a mono-line insurer that has been operating in the state for over twenty years.

   a. What concern might the commissioner have if most of Happy's assets are stocks? How might regulation address this concern?

   b. If Happy fails to meet minimum capital and surplus requirements, what options are available to the commissioner of insurance? How would Happy's policyholders be affected? How would the policyholders of other life insurers in the state be affected?

5.2 "Insurance agents have been recognized as the group that brought the issue to the attention of regulators. "Credit can be valuable for underwriting, but it can't be misused or overutilized," Wes Bissett of the Independent Insurance Agents of America told the working group. Several independent studies have established an "undeniable correlation" between a person's credit score and the likelihood that he or she will file an auto or homeowners insurance claim, trade groups say. Members of the National Association of Independent Insurers report that using insurance scores enables them to charge lower premiums to customers with favorable scores, meaning those customers do not have to subsidize drivers who are likely to have more accidents. (*Source:* "Giving Credit Its Due: Insurers Address Flurry of Insurance-Scoring Legislative Initiatives" *Best's Review,* May 2002.)

   a. How is a person's credit rating related to insurance?

   b. Do you think agents were right to bring this issue to regulators?

   c. How do you think regulators can help? (See the "Important Issues" box in Chapter 4.)

5.3 Read the Ethical Dilemma of this chapter and respond to the following questions in addition to the questions that are in the box.

   a. What are privacy regulations?

   b. Why do you think state regulators have been working on adopting such regulation?

   c. What is your opinion about privacy regulation? What are the pros and cons of such regulation?

5.4 Harry is a risk manager of a global chain of clothing stores. The chain is very successful, with annual revenue of $1 billion in 2001. After September 11, his renewal of insurance coverages became a nightmare.

a. Why was the renewal so difficult?

b. Would you suggest to Harry to create a captive? Explain the pros and cons.

NOTES

1. *The Fact Book 2002*, Insurance Information Institute.
2. Joanne Wojcik, "Sept. 11, Enron push up rate hikes, Losses speed hardening of market: NAPSLO Midyear Meeting," *Business Insurance,* 11 March 2002.
3. Susanne Sclafane, "P-C Insurers Record First Net Loss Ever," *National Underwriter,* Property & Casualty/Risk & Benefits Management Edition, 22 April 2002.
4. Susanne Sclafane, "Old Problems Still Haunt P-C Industry," *National Underwriter,* Property & Casualty/Risk & Benefits Management Edition, 28 January 2002.
5. Michael Bradford, "D&O Premiums Soar: Survey," *Business Insurance,*17 June 2002; Roberto Ceniceros, "Big Losses Mean Tighter Market for Buyers," *Business Insurance,* 4 February 2002. Liability is discussed in various upcoming chapters.
6. Linda Koco, "UL Sales Soared, VL Plunged Last Year," *National Underwriter,* Life & Health/Financial Services Edition, 4 March 2002.
7. "Life After the Fall: In light of the drop in the stock market, scale will play an increasingly important role in the variable annuity market, and insurers will re-examine their overall approach to offering investment-oriented products." *Best's Review,* February 2002.
8. Ron Panko, "Healthy Selection: Less than a decade after the managed-care revolution began in earnest, new styles of health plans are on the market. Proponents see them as the next major trend in health insurance," *Best's Review,* June 2002.
9. Allison Bell, "Analyst Sees No Brakes On Health Rates" *National Underwriter* Online News Service, 6 May 2002.
10. David Hilgen, "Bermuda Bound—Bermuda: Insurance Oasis in the Atlantic," and "Bermuda Bound—The New Bermudians" *Best's Review,* March 2002.
11. Rodd Zolkos, "Terrorism reinsurance availability seen as improving," *Business Insurance,* 17 June 2002.
12. See Raymond L. Dirks and Leonard Gross, *The Great Wall Street Scandal* (New York: McGraw-Hill Book Company, 1974).
13. "Three Executives Charged in Frankel Case," *Best's Review,* February 2002.
14. The theory behind this requirement is that a company offering all lines of insurance may have greater variations of experience than a company engaged in only one or a few lines and, therefore, should have a greater cushion of protection for policyholders. It seems reasonable to believe, however, that the opposite may be the case; bad experience in one line may be offset by good experience in another line.
15. Rodd Zolkos, "Deficient Reserves Abetted 2001 Insolvencies: Best," *Business Insurance,* 19 June 2002.
16. See discussion of risk-based capital laws at www.naic.org. The requirement and formulas are continuously changing as the NAIC continues to study the changing environment. The basic formula prior to 1996, the Life RBC formula, comprised four components related to different categories of risk: asset risk (C-1), insurance risk (C-2), interest rate risk (C-3), and business risk (C-4). Each of the four categories of risk is a dollar figure representing a minimum amount of capital required to cover the corresponding risk. The final formula is: RBC Authorized Capital = (C-4) + Square Root of $[(C\text{--}1 + C\text{--}3)^2 + (C\text{--}2)^2]$
17. For some examples see Etti G. Baranoff, , Tom Sager, and Tom Shively, "Semiparametric Modeling as a Managerial Tool for Solvency," *Journal of Risk and Insurance,* September 2000; and Etti G. Baranoff, Tom Sager, and Bob Witt, "Industry Segmentation and Predictor Motifs for Solvency Analysis of the Life/Health Insurance Industry," *Journal of Risk and Insurance* March, 1999.
18. New York is the only state that funds the guaranty fund prior to losses from insolvent insurers.
19. John S. Moyse, "Legalized Rebating—A Marketing View," *Journal of the American Society of CLU,* vol. 40, no. 5 (1986): p. 57.
20. "Four More California Insurers Settle on Prop. 103 Rebates," *National Underwriter,* Property & Casualty/Risk & Benefits Management Edition, 18 March 1996. The article explains, "Prop. 103 rebates are determined by applying a formula contained in administrative regulation RH-291 into which a company's verifiable financial data is inserted. The purpose of the regulations is to determine rebate amounts so as not to conflict with the California Supreme Court's ruling in Calfarm v. Deukmejian that rebates may not deprive an insurer of a fair rate of return. After the California Supreme Court upheld the regulations in 1994, insurance companies appealed to the U.S. Supreme Court, which in February 1995 refused to review the case. Commissioner Quackenbush re-adopted the regulations in March, 1995."
21. Steven Brostoff, "Hearing Bares Insurers' Charter Split," *National Underwriter* Online News Service, 12 June 2002.

22. Irene Weber, "No Sale Despite Gramm-Leach-Bliley," *Best's Review,* May 2002.

23. E.E. Mazier, "Chartering Plans: They all Have Much in Common," *National Underwriter,* Property & Casualty/Risk & Benefits Management Edition, 28 January 2002

24. Steven Brostoff, "No Fast Action For Federal Charters," *National Underwriter* Online News Service, 5 June 2002.

25. For current information, search for "Federal Charter" at insurance publication Web sites such as www.nationalunderwriter.com and www.businessinsurance.com.

26. Sharon O'Brien, "Blues Review: Blue Cross & Blue Shield Plans Find Conversion to For-Profit Status Fraught With Red Tape," *Best's Review,* March 2002. The article explains, "The movement away from not-for-profit status is a direct response to the competitive changes in the health-care industry and the restrictions placed on the financial operations of not-for-profit health plans, including the inability to raise capital. The spectrum of health-plan corporate structures ranges from an independent not-for-profit plan with specific lines of business serving an exclusive geographic area to a publicly traded company offering multiple products in several geographical areas."

27. D. Mayers and C. Smith, "Ownership Structure and Control: The Mutualization of Stock Life Insurance Companies," *Journal of Financial Economics* 16 (1986): pp. 73–98; M. McNamara and G. Rhee, "Ownership Structure and Performance: The Demutualization of Life Insurance," *Journal of Risk and Insurance* 59 (1992): pp. 221–38.

28. Barbara Bowers, "State Farm: Behind the Veil," *Best's Review,* July 2001.

29. See note 4.

30. Robert W. Stein, "Riding the Demutualization Wave," *Best's Review,* June 2002.

31. Thomas Mulhare, "Insuring Against Demutualization," *Best's Review,* November 2001.

32. See endnote 9. Also see David Pilla ,"Meeting Life Today," *Best's Review,* September 2001.

33. In addition to large organizations like Lloyd's, nonadmitted insurers include many offshore captives (see more in this chapter on captives).

34. Parts of this discussion have been based on "Lloyd's Chairman to Address Annual Conference," *Coverage,* Vol. 2, No. 2 (February 1993): pp. 1–2; "David Rowland: Lloyd's of London One Year Later," *Coverage,* Vol. 3, No. 5 (July 1994): p. 5; "Lloyd's Lost £2.048 Billion in 1991," *National Underwriter,* Property & Casualty/Risk & Benefits Management Edition, No. 21 (23 May 1994): pp. 1 and 42; "The Deficit Millionaires," *The New Yorker* (September 1994): pp. 74–93; and "Lloyd's Lost £Billion in 1992," *National Underwriter,* Property & Casualty/Risk & Benefits Management Edition, 6 February 1995: p. 2.

35. Lisa S. Howard, "Lloyd's Loses £3.11 Billion In 2001," *National Underwriter* Online News Service, 10 April 10 2002; "Lloyd's Proposes Radical Modernization," *National Underwriter,* 21 January 2002, p.9, with follow-up coverage on 28 January, p.23, and 11 February, p. 23; Sarah Veysey, "Lloyd's Plans to Allow Nonmember Investors," *Business Insurance,* 24 May 2002; Lisa S. Howard, "Lloyd's Looks To Protect Reputation," *National Underwriter,* Property & Casualty/Risk & Benefits Management Edition, 11 March 2002.

36. An exception: National commercial banks in communities of less than 5,000 have for many years had the right to sell insurance.

37. Mark E. Ruquet, "Insurer-Bank Integration Stampede Unlikely," *National Underwriter,* Property & Casualty/Risk & Benefits Management Edition, 23 April 2001.

38. David Hilgen ,"Blending Banking and Insurance," *Best's Review,* September 2001.

39. Trevor Thomas, "For The Typical Bank, Profits From Life Insurance Sales Are Slim," *National Underwriter,* Life & Health/Financial Services Edition, 21 January 2002.

40. Irene Weber, "No Sale Despite Gramm-Leach-Bliley," *Best's Review,* May 2002.

41. Lorraine Gorski, "The New Producers: Insurers have a great opportunity to tap into banks' large customer bases, but they have to be willing to think like banks," *Best's Review,* May 2002.

42. Lisa S. Howard, "Tight Re Market Puts Heat On Fronts" *National Underwriter,* Property & Casualty/Risk & Benefits Management Edition, 4 March 2002. Abstract: "During the soft market of the past seven years, many companies that provided fronting for captives have been left with their fingers burned as a result of reinsurance recoverable problems and the general tightening in the reinsurance industry, according to a Bermuda captive manager."

43. Michael Bradford, "Hard Market Fuels Growth at Largest Captive Domicile," *Business Insurance,* 4 February 2002.

44. President Reagan signed into law the Liability Risk Retention Act in October 1986 (an amendment to the Product Liability Risk Retention Act of 1981). The Act permits formation of retention groups (a special form of captive) with fewer restrictions than existed before. The retention groups are similar to association captives. The Act permits formation of such groups in the U.S. under more favorable conditions than have existed generally for association captives. The Act may be particularly helpful to small businesses that could not feasibly self-insure on their own, but can do so within a designated group. How extensive will be the use of risk retention groups is yet to be seen. As of the writing of this text there are efforts to amend the Act.

45. "Vermont Licenses Industry-Backed Airline Insurer," *BestWire,* 11 June 2002.

46. Sue Johnson, "Airline Captive May Be Formed in Second Quarter," Best's Review, March 2002. Also see the document created by Marsh to explain the program along with other aviation protection programs (as of 8-14-2002) at: http://www.marsh.se/files/Third%20Party%20War%20Liability%20Comparison.pdf

47. "New Alternatives," *Best's Review,* June 2002.

48. For detailed information about PRIMA, search its Web site at: http://www.primacentral.org/default.php

49. Ross Zolkos and Roberto Ceniceros, "Surplus Lines Brokers Overloaded as Business Soars," *Business Insurance,* 10 September 2001.

Appendix 5.1

Reciprocal Insurers

Reciprocals are similar to mutuals in that both are formed to provide insurance at cost, rather than to make a profit for a third party. Each policyholder in a pure reciprocal, however, insures part of the risk of each of the other policyholders. If there were 100 insureds in the group, for example, and each had the same value at risk, each would, in effect, say to the other, "I will pay 1 percent of your losses if you will pay 1 percent of mine." The reciprocal itself is not liable to policyholders; instead, they are liable to each other. In a mutual, on the other hand, assets belong to the insurer, which is liable to policyholders. The reciprocal holds assets contributed by the policyholders as premiums, but the assets are pooled and each policyholder beneficially owns a proportionate share of that pool.

Whereas a mutual is incorporated, a reciprocal is unincorporated. Whereas a mutual is controlled by a board of directors, reciprocals are managed by an attorney-in-fact, whose powers are enumerated in a power of attorney granted by the policyholders. Part of the premium is paid to the attorney-in-fact for his or her services in soliciting business and managing the operations of the reciprocal, and the balance is credited to separate accounts maintained for each insured. When losses are paid, each insured's account is charged with his or her proportionate share of the loss. At the end of the year, funds remaining in each account may be left in the reciprocal or paid back to each insured as a dividend.

Reciprocals in their pure form are a minor, declining type of insurer. They are still strong in the western United States, especially as writers of personal automobile insurance. The bulk of reciprocal business is now written by **interinsurance associations,** which are more like mutuals than the pure reciprocals described in this section. They do not keep separate accounts for each member, and losses and expenses are not prorated among insureds. Furthermore, insureds do not have a claim to any portion of surplus funds. The United States Automobile Association (USAA) is of this type.

Lloyds Associations of the United States

There is no connection between Lloyds Associations of the United States and Lloyd's of London. **Lloyds Associations**—sometimes called "American Lloyds"—are corporations, partnerships, or associations made up of individuals who join together to offer insurance. Each individual assumes a specified portion of the liability under each policy and specifies a maximum amount of liability. The liability of each individual is limited. Rather than operating through syndicates like Lloyd's of London, Lloyds Associations are managed by an attorney-in-fact. Several have failed over the years. Lloyds in Texas are not rate-regulated, and became major providers of homeowners insurance during the mold crisis of 2001 and 2002. An example of such a company is Safeco Lloyds. A detailed explanation of homeowners insurance is the topic of Chapter 10.

Insurance Exchanges

Organizations similar in design to Lloyd's of London began business in Florida, Illinois, and New York during the early 1980s. The primary purpose of these **insurance exchanges** was to increase the financial ability of the United States insurance industry to handle reinsurance needs and insure unusual exposures without relying heavily on Lloyd's of London. Because of large losses, the Florida and New York exchanges closed in 1987. The Illinois exchange is still in operation, concentrating on large property/casualty exposures.

PART III

INSURANCE CONTRACTS

CHAPTER 6

Fundamental Doctrines Affecting Insurance Contracts

The insurance **contract** or **policy** we receive when we transfer the risk to the insurance company is the only physical product we receive at the time of the transaction. As described in the Risk Ball Game in Chapter 1, the contract makes the exchange tangible. Now that we have some understanding of the nature of risk and insurance, insurance company operations, markets, and regulation, it is time to move into understanding the contracts and the legal doctrines that influence insurance policies. Since contracts are subject to disputes, understanding their nature and complexities will make our risk management activities more efficient. Some contracts explicitly spell out every detail, while other contracts are considered incomplete and their interpretations are subject to arguments.[1] For example, in a health contract the insurer promises to pay for medicines. But as new drugs come to market every day, insurers can refuse to pay for an expensive new medication that was not on the market when the contact was signed. An example is Celebrex, exalted for being easier on the stomach than other anti-inflammatory drugs and a major favorite of the "young at heart" fifty-plus generation. Many insurers require pre-authorization to verify that the patient has no other choices of other, less expensive drugs.[2] The evolution of medical technology and court decisions makes the health policy highly **relational** to the changes and dynamics in the market place. The dynamic nature of the product that is covered by the health insurance policy makes the policy "incomplete" and open to disputes. The focus of Chapter 6 is on the insurance contract itself. We will explore the following:

1. Connection
2. Agency law, especially as applied to insurance
3. Basic contractual requirements
4. Important distinguishing characteristics of insurance contracts

CONNECTION

At this point in this text we are still focused on broad subject matters that connect us to our holistic risk and risk management puzzle. We are not yet drilling down into specific topics such as homeowners insurance or automobile insurance. We are still in the "big picture" of understanding the importance of clarity of insurance contracts and the legal doctrines that influence those contracts and the agents or brokers who deliver the contracts to us. If you think about the contracts as the layers of an onion that covers the core of the risk, you can apply your imagination to Figure 6.1.[3] We know now that each risk can be mitigated by various methods as discussed in prior chapters. The important point here is that each activity is associated with legal doctrines culminating in the contracts themselves. The field of risk and insurance is intertwined with law and legal implications. No wonder the legal field is so connected to the insurance field.

You, the student, will learn in this text that the field of insurance encompasses many roles and careers, including legal ones. As the nature of the contract, described above, becomes more incomplete (less clear or explicit), more legal battles are fought. These legal battles are not limited to disputes between insurers and insureds. In many cases, the agents or brokers are also involved. This point is emphasized in relations to the dispute over the final settlement regarding the World Trade Center (WTC) on September 11.[4] The case at hand is whether the collapse of the two towers should be counted as one insured event (because the damage was caused by a united group of terrorists) or two insured events (because the damage was caused by two separate planes some fifteen minutes apart). Why is this distinction important? Because Swiss Re, one of the principal reinsurers of the World Trade Center, is obligated to pay damages up to $3.5 billion – per insured event.

The root of the dispute involves explicit versus **incomplete contracts,** as described above. The leaseholder, Silverstein Properties, claims that the brokers, Willis Group Holdings, Ltd., promised a final contract that would interpret the attack as two events. The insurer, Swiss Re, maintains that it and Willis had agreed to a type of policy that would explicitly define the attack as one event. Willis was caught in the middle and, as you remember, brokers represent the insured. Therefore, a federal judge had to choose an appropriate way to handle the case. (See "Ethical Dilemma: One Event or Two?" in Chapter 12.) This story is only one of many illustrations of the complexities of relationships and the legal doctrines that are so important in insurance transactions. Additional examples will be featured in this chapter.

AGENCY LAW

Agents

Insurance is sold primarily by agents. The underlying contract, therefore, is affected significantly by the legal authority of the agent, which in turn is determined by well-established general legal rules regarding agency.

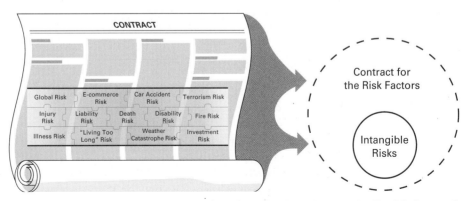

FIGURE 6.1

Connection between Each Risk and the Insurance Contract

Source: Etti G. Baranoff, "The Risk Balls Game: Transforming Risk and Insurance Into Tangible Concepts," *Risk Management & Insurance Review* 4, no. 2 (2001), pp. 51–59.

The **law of agency,** as stated in the standard work on the subject, "deals basically with the legal consequences of people acting on behalf of other people or organizations."[5] Agency involves three parties: the principal, the agent, and a third party. The **principal** (insurer) creates an agency relationship with a second party (the agent) by authorizing him or her to make contracts with third parties (policyholders) on the principal's behalf.[6] The source of the agent's authority is the principal. Such authority may be either expressed or implied. When an **agent** is appointed, the principal expressly indicates the extent of the agent's authority. The agent also has, by implication, whatever authority is needed to fulfill the purposes of the agency. By entering into the relationship, the principal implies that the agent has the authority to fulfill the principal's responsibilities. From the public point of view, the agent's authority is whatever it appears to be. This is sometimes referred to as **apparent authority.** If the principal treats a second party as if the person were an agent, then an agency is created. Agency law and the doctrines of waiver and estoppel have serious implications in the insurance business.

Binding Authority

The law of agency is significant to insurance in large part because the only direct interaction most buyers of insurance have with the insurance company is through an agent or a broker (also called a **producer;** see the National Association of Insurance Commissioners' Web site at www.naic.org and licensing reforms as part of the Gramm-Leach-Bliley Act prerequisites discussed in Chapter 5).[7] Laws regarding the authority and responsibility of an agent, therefore, affect the contractual relationship.

One of the most important of these agency characteristics is called the **binding authority.** In many situations an agent is able to secure ("bind") coverage for an insured without any additional input from the insurer. The agreement that exists before a contract is issued is called a **binder.** This arrangement, described in the offer and acceptance section presented later, is common in the property/casualty insurance areas. If you call a Geico agent in the middle of the night to obtain insurance for your new automobile, you are covered as of the time of your conversation with the agent. In life and health insurance, an agent's ability to secure coverage is generally more limited. Rather than issuing a general binder of coverage, some life insurance agents may be permitted to issue only a **conditional binder.** A conditional binder implies that coverage exists only if the underwriter ultimately accepts (or would have accepted) the application for insurance. Thus, if the applicant dies prior to the final policy issuance, payment is made if the applicant would have been acceptable to the insurer as an insured. The general binder, in contrast, provides coverage immediately, even if the applicant is later found to be an unacceptable policyholder and coverage is cancelled at that point.

Waiver and Estoppel

The agent's relationship between insured and insurer is greatly affected by doctrines of waiver and estoppel.

Waiver is the intentional relinquishment of a known right. In order to waive a right, a person must know he or she has the right, and must give it up intentionally. If an insurer considers a risk to be undesirable at the time the agent assumes it on behalf of the company, and the agent knows it, the principal (the insurer) will have waived the right to refuse coverage at a later date. This situation arises when an agent insures a risk the company has specifically prohibited.

Suppose, for example, that the agent knew an applicant's seventeen-year-old son was allowed to drive the covered automobile and also knew the company did not accept such risks. If the agent issues the policy, the company's right to refuse coverage on this basis later in the policy period has been waived.

In some policies, the insurer attempts to limit an agent's power to waive its provisions. A business property policy, for example, may provide that the terms of the policy shall not be waived, changed, or modified except by endorsement issued as part of the policy.

Unfortunately for the insurer, however, such stipulations may not prevent a waiver by its agent. For example, the business property policy provides that coverage on a building ceases after it has been vacant for over sixty days. In a case where the insured mentions to the agent that one of the buildings covered by the policy has been vacant sixty days, but also adds that the situation is only temporary, if the agent says, "Don't worry, you're covered," the right of the insurer to deny coverage in the event of a loss while the building is vacant is waived. The policy may provide that it cannot be orally waived, but that generally will not affect the validity of the agent's waiver. From the insured's point of view, the agent is the company and the insurer is responsible for the agent's actions.

This point came to a head in the mid 1990s when many life insurance companies were confronted by class action lawsuits that accused their agents of selling life insurance as a **"private pension"**[8]—that is, the agents elevated the investment portion or cash accumulation of the permanent life insurance policies to a position of a retirement account. There were also large numbers of complaints about misrepresentation of the interest rate accumulation in certain life insurance policies called universal life (discussed at length in Chapter 14).[9] The allegations were that insurers and their agents "furnished false and misleading illustrations to whole life insurance policyholders, failing to show that policies would need to be active over twenty years to achieve a 'comparable interest rate' on their premium dollars and used a 'software on-line computer program' and other misleading sales materials to do so."[10] These were dubbed **vanishing premiums** policies, because the policyholders were led to believe that after a certain period of time the policy would be paid in full, and they would no longer have to make premium payments.[11] Though no vanishing-premium case has been tried on the merits, litigation costs and settlement proceedings have cost companies hundreds of millions of dollars. Many large insurers such as Prudential, Met Life,[12] Money, Northwestern Life, Life of Virginia, and more were fined large fines by many states' insurance regulators and settled with their policyholders. Prudential's settlement with eight million policyholders will cost the company more than $3.5 billion.[13] Many of these companies created the new position of **compliance officer** to oversee all sales materials and to ensure compliance with regulations and ethics.[14] Meanwhile, states focused on modifying and strengthening market conduct regulations. See "Important Issues: Enforcing the Code—Ethics Officers" and "Ethical Dilemma: What would You Do?" for a review of insurers efforts regarding ethics and for ethical discussion questions. Ultimately, the insurer may hold the agent liable for such actions, but with respect to the insured, the insurer cannot deny its responsibilities. "The vexing problem of vanishing premiums has proven to be an expensive lesson for insurance companies on the doctrine of **respondeat superior**—a Latin phrase referring to the doctrine that the master is responsible for the actions taken by his or her servant during the course of duty."[15] Neither insurers nor regulators consider an agency relationship as an independent contractor relationship.

Estoppel occurs when the insurer or its agent has led the insured into believing that coverage exists. It means that the insurer cannot later claim that no coverage existed. For example, when an insured specifically requests a certain kind of coverage when applying for insurance and is not told it is not available, that coverage likely exists even if the policy wording states otherwise. This is because the agent implied such coverage at the time of sale, and the insurer is estopped from denying it.

IMPORTANT ISSUES

Enforcing the Code—Ethics Officers

In the minds of much of the public, insurance agents are up there with used-car dealers and politicians when it comes to ethical conduct. A May 2002 survey by Golin/Harris International, a public relations firm based in Chicago, ranked insurance second only to oil and gas companies as the least trustworthy industry in America. The factors that make an industry untrustworthy, Golin/Harris marketing director Ellen Ryan Mardiks told Insure.com, include perceptions that "these industries are distant or detached from their customers, are plagued by questionable ethics in their business practices, are difficult or confusing to deal with, or act primarily in self-interest."

That's how many people might describe insurance companies, as evidenced by the horror stories told on Web sites like screwedbyinsurance.com and badfaithinsurance.com. Of course, every industry has its detractors (and its detractors have Web sites), but insurance can be a particularly difficult sell. Think about it: In life, homeowners, property/casualty, and auto, the best-case scenario is the one in which you pay premiums for years and never get anything back.

Trust is important in a business of intangibles. The insurance industry's image of trustworthiness took big hit in the mid 1990s, when some of the biggest companies in the industry, including Prudential, Met Life, and New York Life, were charged with unethical sales practices. The class-action lawsuits were highly publicized, and consumer mistrust soared. The American Council of Life Insurers responded by creating the Insurance Marketplace Standards Association—not to placate the public, which remains mostly unaware of the program, but to set and enforce ethical standards and procedures for its members. IMSA's ethics are based on six principles:

- To conduct business according to high standards of honesty and fairness and to render that service to its customers which, in the same circumstances, it would apply to or demand for itself

- To provide competent and customer-focused sales and service

- To engage in active and fair competition

- To provide advertising and sales materials that are clear as to purpose and honest and fair as to content

- To provide for fair and expeditious handling of customer complaints and disputes

- To maintain a system of supervision and review that is reasonably designed to achieve compliance with these Principles of Ethical Market Conduct

IMSA members don't simply pledge allegiance to these words; they are audited by an independent assessor to make sure they are adhering to IMSA's principles and code. The members, who also must monitor themselves continually, found it more efficient to have one person or one division of the company in charge of overseeing these standards. Thus was born the ethics officer, sometimes called the compliance officer.

Actually, ethics officers have been around for some time, but their visibility, as well as the scope of their duties, has expanded greatly in recent years. Today, insurance companies have an ethics officer on staff. In large companies, this person might hold the title of vice president and oversee a staff that formulates policy for ethics and codes of conduct and is charged with educating employees. The ethics officer may also be responsible for creating and implementing privacy policies in accordance with the Gramm-Leach-Bliley Act. Ethics officers' mandate is to make sure that each employee in the company knows of and follows the company's ethical guidelines.

Exploring the Internet

The Insurance Marketplace Standards Association is a voluntary organization of life insurance companies whose charter is to promote high ethical standards in the sale of individual life insurance, long-term care insurance, and annuity products. Many other types of insurers have adopted its Principles and Code of Ethical Market Conduct. Read more about IMSA's code and the rigorous assessment process that insurers must pass to become members at www.imsaethics.org.

Sources: Vicki Lankarge, "Insurance companies are not to be trusted, say consumers," Insure.com, 30 May 2002. www.insure.com /gen/trust502.html; Insurance Marketplace Standards Association, www.imsaethics.org; Barbara Bowers, "Higher Profile: Compliance Officers Have Experienced Elevated Status Within Their Companies since the Emergence of the Insurance Marketplace Standards Association," *Best's Review,* October 2001; Lori Chordas, "Code of Ethics: More Insurers Are Hiring Ethics Officers to Set and Implement Corporate Mores," *Best's Review,* March 2001.

Ethical Dilemma

What Would You Do?

"No one will ever know." "If it's legal, it's ethical." "It's a big company—they'll never miss it." "Anybody dumb enough to fall for this deserves what he gets." "I don't get paid overtime, so I deserve these little 'perks.'"

These are common excuses for ethical breaches in the workplace. Interestingly, the biggest influence on employee ethics is the standards of their managers or the corporate culture; "peer pressure" is not just a high-school phenomenon. Yet simply having a corporate ethics program is not enough. In 2000, international financial-services firm KPMG found that although the vast majority of the companies surveyed had a formal ethics program, three out of four employees said they had observed illegal or unethical conduct on the job in the past year.

Business ethics is an increasingly prominent topic, particularly in the insurance field. "Massive changes in the insurance industry are encouraging enlightened leaders, particularly those in the compliance field, to become more ethically attuned to the needs of clients, agents, and other stakeholders," wrote ethicist Ronald Duska in the Journal of Insurance Regulation.

"An ethical perspective must overlay the compliance perspective, addressing three basic rules: fulfilling one's responsibilities, being fair, and doing no unnecessary harm," Duska said. How do your ethics fit with that description? How ethical are you?

Questions for Discussion

1. You are an agent who wishes to sell a $1 million life insurance policy. Your client thinks she can't afford a policy that large, so to reduce the price you tell her you will give her 50 percent of your commission. Is this legal or ethical?

2. To increase the market share of your business, you throw monthly country-dancing parties, including an open bar, for potential clients. Is this ethical?

3. A couple of years ago you filed a claim for water leakage in your home. Now, during the homeowner's coverage crisis, your insurer will not renew your policy with the same coverage and the same deductibles. You will have to pay higher premiums, and your deductible is larger. Is it ethical for the insurer to change your coverage so substantially?

4. When you bought your life insurance policy, your agent showed you a table of surrender values and said that upon surrender you would receive a specified amount of cash back. Three years later you surrendered the policy, but the amount you received was much less than promised. When you asked, your agent said that the difference was because interest rates had decreased. Was the agent's behavior ethical?

5. As the chief financial officer for a large insurance company, you receive a budget request from your ethics officer for $75,000 to be spent on ethics training for your employees. You can think of many other ways to spend this money that would directly increase sales or reduce expenses. With no tangible, bottom-line results, how do you measure whether ethics training is a good investment?

Sources: Ronald Duska, "Ethics and Compliance in the Business of Life Insurance: Reflections of an Ethicist," *Journal of Insurance Regulation* 18, No. 2 (Winter 1999): 246-257; KPMG Ethics Survey 2000.

http://www.kpmg.ca/english/services/docs/fas/ethicssurvey2000e.pdf; Catherine Valenti, "Ethical Culture."

"Is the Enron Saga a Sign that Ethics in the Workplace Are Disappearing?" ABCnews.com, 21 February 2002. http://abcnews.go .com/sections/business /DailyNews/corporate_ethics_020221.html.

Agency by Estoppel   An agency relationship may be created by estoppel when the conduct of the principal implies that an agency exists. In such a case, the principal will be estoped from denying the existence of the agency (recall the binding authority of some agents). This situation may arise when the company suspends an agent, but the agent retains possession of blank policies. People who are not agents of a company do not have blank policies in their possession. By leaving them with the former agent, the company is acting as if he or she is a current agent. If the former agent issues those policies, the company is estopped from denying the existence of an agency relationship and will be bound by the policy.

If an agent who has been suspended sends business to the company that is accepted, the agency relationship will be ratified by such action and the company will be estopped from denying the contract's existence. The company has the right to refuse such business when it is presented, but once the business is accepted the company waives the right to deny coverage on the basis of denial of acceptance.

REQUIREMENTS OF A CONTRACT

When an agent sells an insurance policy, he or she is selling a contract. A contract is an agreement enforceable by law. For any such agreement to be legally enforceable, it must meet the following minimum requirements:

- There must be an offer and an acceptance
- There must be consideration
- The parties to the contract must be competent
- Its purpose must be legal
- The contract must be in legal form

Offer and Acceptance

Offer and **acceptance** are essential elements to the creation of a contract. An agreement is reached when one party makes an offer and the other party accepts it. If the party to whom the offer was made requests a change in terms, a counteroffer is made, which releases the first offerer from the terms of the original offer. In the making of insurance contracts, usually the buyer offers to buy and the insurer accepts or rejects the offer. When you call an insurance agent for insurance on your new automobile and the agent provides coverage, there is an offer to buy and the agent has accepted the offer on behalf of his or her company. As stated previously, this acceptance is called a binder. The offer may be verbal, as in this case, or it may be in the form of a written application. This process differs for life and health insurance.

Consideration

A contract also requires the exchange of **consideration.** Consideration is the price each party demands for agreeing to carry out his or her part of the contract. The value of the consideration is usually unimportant, but lack of consideration will cause the contract to be regarded as a gift and therefore unenforceable. In many cases, insurance contracts stipulate that the consideration is both in the form of premium and certain conditions specified in the policy. Such conditions may include maintenance of a certain level of risk, timely notice of loss, and periodic reports to insurers of exposure values. Conditions will be explained in detail later in the text. Consideration, therefore, does not necessarily imply dollars.

Competent Parties

Another essential element for a contract is that the parties to the contract must be **competent parties.** Most people are competent to contract, but there are exceptions. Mentally ill or intoxicated persons are not competent. Minors may enter into contracts, but such contracts may be voided (or terminated). Upon reaching majority (age eighteen in some states, age twenty-one in others), the young person may ratify or reject the contract. If ratified, the contract would then have the same status as one originally entered into by competent parties.

A minor who enters into an insurance contract, therefore, may void it during infancy or when he or she reaches majority. Ratification of a policy at the age of majority can be accomplished (by oral or written communication) either explicitly or implicitly (by continuing the policy). Some states have laws giving minors the power to enter into binding life insurance contracts on their own lives as young as age fourteen.

Legal Purpose

A contract must have a **legal purpose.** If it does not, to enforce the contract would be contrary to public policy. A contract by a government employee to sell secret information to an agent of an enemy country, for example, would not have a legal purpose and would be unenforceable. For the same reason, a contract of insurance to cover losses caused by the insured's own arson would be illegal and contrary to public policy, and thus unenforceable.

Legal Form

Contracts may be either oral or written; they must, however, follow a specific **legal form,** which may vary from state to state. As noted, some insurance contracts are—at least initially—oral. Most states do not have laws directly prohibiting oral contracts of insurance. They do, however, require that some contract "forms" (the written version of standardized insurance policy provisions and attachments) be approved by the state before being offered for sale.

Moreover, the nature and general content of some policies are specified by law. Most states require that certain provisions be included in life and health insurance contracts. Thus, although some contracts may be oral, insurance contracts must—for the most part—be in writing, and must conform to the requirements of the states in which they are sold.

DISTINGUISHING CHARACTERISTICS OF INSURANCE CONTRACTS

In addition to the elements just discussed, insurance contracts have several characteristics that differentiate them from most other contracts. Risk managers must be familiar with these characteristics in order to understand the creation, execution, and interpretation of insurance policies. Insurance contracts are

- Based on utmost good faith
- Contracts of adhesion
- Contracts of indemnity
- Personal

Based on Utmost Good Faith

When an insurer considers accepting a risk, it must have accurate and complete information to make a reasonable decision. Should it assume the risk and, if so, under what terms and conditions? Because insurance involves a contract of **uberrimae fidei,** or utmost good faith, potential insureds are held to the highest standards of truthfulness and honesty in providing information for the underwriter. In the case of contracts other than for insurance, it is generally assumed that each party has equal knowledge and access to the facts, and thus each is subject to requirements of "good faith," not "utmost good faith." In contrast, eighteenth-century ocean marine insurance contracts were negotiated under circumstances that forced underwriters to rely on information provided by the insured, because they could not get it firsthand. A ship being insured, for example, might be unavailable for inspection because it was on the other side of the world. Was the ship seaworthy? The underwriter could not inspect it, so he (they were all men in those days) required the insured to warrant that it was. If the warranty was not strictly true, the contract was voidable. The penalty for departing from utmost good faith was having no coverage when a loss occurred. Today the concept of utmost good faith is implemented by the doctrines of (1), (2) concealment, and (3) warranties.[16]

Representations

When people are negotiating with insurers for coverage, they make statements concerning their exposures. These statements are called **representations.** They are made for the purpose of inducing insurers to enter into contracts, that is, provide insurance. If people misrepresent **material facts,** insurers can void their contracts and they will have no coverage, even though they do have insurance policies. In essence, the contracts never existed.

Note that "material" has been specified. If an insurer wants to void a contract it has issued to a person in reliance upon the information she provided, it must prove that what she misrepresented was material. That is, the insurer must prove that the information was so important that if the truth had been known, the underwriter would not have made the contract or would have done so only on different terms.

If, for example, you stated in an application for life insurance that you were born on March 2 when in fact you were born on March 12, such a misrepresentation would not be material. A correct statement would not alter the underwriter's decision made on the incorrect information. The policy is not voidable under these circumstances. On the other hand, suppose you apply for life insurance and state that you are in good health, even though you've just been diagnosed with a severe heart ailment. This fact likely would cause the insurer to charge a higher premium, or not to sell the coverage at all. The significance of this fact is that the insurer may contend that the policy never existed (it was void), and so loss by any cause (whether related to the misrepresentation or not) is not covered. Several exceptions to this rule apply, as presented in chapters discussing specific policies. In the case of life insurance the insurer can void the policy on grounds of material misrepresentation only for two years, as will be discussed in Chapter 14.

It is not uncommon for students to misrepresent to their auto insurers where their cars are garaged, particularly if premium rates at home are lower than they are where students attend college. Because location is a factor in determining premium rates, where a car is garaged is a material fact. Students who misrepresent this or other material facts take the chance of having no coverage at the time of a loss. The insurer may elect to void the contract.

Concealment

Telling the truth in response to explicit application questions may seem to be enough, but it is not. One must also reveal those material facts about the exposure that only he or she knows and that he or she should realize are relevant. Suppose, for example, that you have no insurance on your home because you "don't believe in insurance." Upon your arrival home one afternoon, you discover that the neighbor's house—only thirty feet from yours—is on fire. You promptly telephone the agency where you buy your auto insurance and apply for a homeowners policy, asking that it be put into effect immediately. You answer all the questions the agent asks, but fail to mention the fire next door. You have intentionally concealed a material fact you obviously realize is relevant. You are guilty of **concealment,** and the insurer has the right to void the contract.

If the insurance company requires the completion of a long, detailed application, an insured that fails to provide information the insurer neglected to ask about, cannot be proven guilty of concealment unless it is obvious that certain information should have been volunteered. Clearly, no insurance agent is going to ask you when you apply for insurance if the neighbor's house is on fire. The fact that the agent does not ask does not relieve you of the responsibility.

In both life and health insurance, most state insurance laws limit the period (usually one or two years) during which the insurer may void coverage for a concealment or misrepresentation. Other types of insurance contracts do not involve such time limits.

Contracts of Adhesion

Insurance policies are contracts of **adhesion.** Unlike contracts formulated by a process of bargaining, most insurance contracts are prepared by the insurer and then accepted or rejected by the buyer. The insured does not specify the terms of coverage, but rather accept the terms as stipulated. Thus, he or she "adheres" to the insurer's contract. That is for personal lines. In most business lines, insurers use policies prepared by the Insurance Services Office (ISO), but in some cases contracts are negotiated. These contracts are written by risk managers or brokers who then seek underwriters to accept them, whereas most individuals go to an agent to request coverage "as is".

The fact that buyers usually have no influence over the content or form of insurance policies has had a significant impact on the way courts interpret policies when there is a dispute.[17] When the terms of a policy are ambiguous, the courts favor the insured because it is assumed that the insurer that writes the contract should know what it wants to say and how to state it clearly. Further, the policy language generally is interpreted according to the insured's own level of expertise and situation, not that of an underwriter who is knowledgeable about insurance. When the terms are not ambiguous, however, the courts have been reluctant to change the contract in favor of the insured.

A violation of this general rule occurs, however, when the courts believe that reasonable insureds would expect coverage of a certain type. Under these conditions, regardless of the ambiguity of policy language (or lack thereof), the court may rule in favor of the insured. Courts are guided by the **expectations principle** (or reasonable expectations principle), which may be stated as follows:

> The objectively reasonable expectations of applicants and intended beneficiaries regarding the terms of insurance contracts will be honored even though painstaking study of the policy provisions would have negated those expectations.[18]

Thus, the current approach to the interpretation of contracts of adhesion is threefold: first, to favor the insured when terms of the contract drafted by the insurer are ambiguous; second, to read the contract as an insured would; third, to determine the coverage on the basis of reasonable expectations of the insured.

Indemnity Concept

Many insurance contracts are contracts of **indemnity.** This means the insurer agrees to pay no more (and no less) than the actual loss suffered by the insured. For example, suppose your house is insured for $100,000 at the time it is totally destroyed by fire. If its value at that time is only $80,000, that is the amount the insurance company will pay.[19] You cannot collect $100,000, because to do so would exceed the actual loss suffered. You would be better off after the loss than you were before. The purpose of the insurance contract is—or should be—to restore the insured to the same economic position as before the loss.

The indemnity principle has practical significance both for the insurer and for society. If insureds could gain by having an insured loss, some would deliberately cause losses. This would result in a decrease of resources for society, an economic burden for the insurance industry, and, ultimately, higher insurance premiums for all insureds. Moreover, if losses were caused intentionally rather than as a result of chance occurrence, the insurer likely would be unable to predict costs satisfactorily. An insurance contract that makes it possible for the insured to profit by an event insured against violates the principle of indemnity and may prove poor business to the insurer.

The doctrine of indemnity is implemented and supported by several legal principles and policy provisions, including the following:

- Insurable interest
- Subrogation
- Actual cash value provision
- Other insurance provisions

Insurable Interest

If a fire or auto collision causes loss to a person or firm, that person or firm has an **insurable interest.** A person not subject to loss does not have an insurable interest. Stated another way, someone who would be harmed by an economic loss has an insurable interest. The law concerning insurable interest is important to the buyer of insurance, because it determines whether the benefits from an insurance policy will be collectible. Thus, all insureds should be familiar with what constitutes an insurable interest, when it must exist, and the extent to which it may limit payment under an insurance policy.

Basis for Insurable Interest   Many situations constitute an insurable interest. The most common is ownership of property. An owner of a building will suffer financial loss if it is damaged or destroyed by fire or other peril. Thus, the owner has an insurable interest in the building.

A mortgage lender on a building has an insurable interest in the building. For the lender, loss to the security, such as the building being damaged or destroyed by fire, may reduce the value of the loan. On the other hand, an unsecured creditor generally does not have an insurable interest in the general assets of the debtor, because loss to such assets does not directly affect the value of the creditor's claim against the debtor.

If part or all of a building is leased to a tenant who makes improvements in the leased space, such improvements become the property of the building owner on termination of the lease. Nevertheless, the tenant has an insurable interest in the improvements, because he or she will suffer a loss if they are damaged or destroyed during the term of the lease. This commonly occurs when building space is rented on a "bare walls" basis. To make such space usable, the tenant must make improvements.

If a tenant has a long-term lease with terms more favorable than would be available in the current market, but which may be cancelled in the event that the building is damaged, the tenant has an insurable interest in the lease. A bailee who is responsible for the safekeeping of property belonging to others, and who must return it in good condition or pay for it, has an insurable interest. When you take your clothes to the local dry-cleaning establishment, for example, it acts as a bailee, responsible for returning your clothes in good condition.

A person has an insurable interest in his or her own life and may have such an interest in the life of another.[20] An insurable interest in the life of another person may be based on a close relationship by blood or marriage, such as a wife's insurable interest in her husband. It may also be based on love and affection, such as that of a parent for a child, or on financial considerations. A creditor, for example, may have an insurable interest in the life of a debtor, and an employer may have an insurable interest in the life of a key employee.

When Insurable Interest Must Exist   The time at which insurable interest must exist depends upon the type of insurance. In property insurance, the interest must exist at the time of the loss. As the owner of a house, one has an insurable interest in it. If the owner insures themself against loss to the house caused by fire or other peril, that person can collect on such insurance only if he or she still has an insurable interest in the house at the time the damage occurs. Thus, if one transfers unencumbered title to the house to another person before the house is damaged, he cannot collect from the insurer, even though the policy may still be in force. He or she no longer has an insurable interest. On the other hand, if the owner has a mortgage on the house that was sold, they will continue to have an insurable interest in the amount of the outstanding mortgage until the loan is paid.

As a result of the historical development of insurance practices, life insurance requires an insurable interest only at the inception of the contract. When the question of insurable interest in life insurance was being adjudicated in England, such policies provided no cash surrender values; the insurer made payment only if the person who was the subject[21] of insurance died while the policy was in force. An insured who was also the policyowner and unable to continue making premium payments simply sacrificed all interest in the policy.

This led to the practice of some policyowners/insureds selling their policies to speculators who, as the new owners, named themselves the beneficiaries and continued premium payments until the death of the insured. This practice is not new, but appears to have grown as reported in the Wall Street Journal.[22] In the past year or two, **life-settlement companies** emerged for seniors. These companies buy life insurance policies from senior citizens for a percent of the value of the death benefits. These companies pay the premiums and become the beneficiary when the insured passes away. This is similar to the **viatical-settlement companies** that bought life insurance policies of AIDS patients in the 1990s. An example of a life-settlement company is Stone Street Financial Inc. in Bethesda, Maryland, which bought the value of $500,000 of life insurance for $75,775 from an older person. The person felt he was making money on the deal since the policy surrender value was only $5,000. Viatical settlement companies ran into trouble after new drug regimens extended the lives of AIDS patients, and investors found themselves waiting years or decades, instead of weeks or months, for a return on their investments. The life-settlement companies contend that since there is no cure for old age, investors cannot lose in buying the policies from people over sixty-five years old with terminal illnesses such as cancer, amyotrophic lateral sclerosis (Lou Gehrig's disease), and liver disease.[23] These companies don't sell to individual investors, but rather package the policies they buy into portfolios for institutional investors. Discussion of viatical settlement and life settlement companies is available in "Important Issues: Do Viatical Settlements Have a Place in Today's Market?" in Chapter 16.

Because the legal concept of requiring an insurable interest only at the inception of the life insurance contract has continued, it is possible to collect on a policy in which such interest has ceased. For example, if the life of a key person in a firm is insured, in whose life the firm has an insurable interest because his or her death would cause a loss to the firm, the policy may be continued in force by the firm even after the person leaves its employ, and the proceeds may be collected when he or she dies. This point was brought to the lime light with the publication of the Wall Street Journal story "Big Banks Quietly Pile Up **'Janitors' Insurance**."[24] The article reports that banks and other large employers bought inexpensive life coverage (with group rates, as will be discussed in Chapter 16) on the lives of their employees. This practice did not require informing the employees or their families. Coverage was continued even after the employees left the company. Upon the death of the employees, the employer collected the proceeds and padded their bottom-line profits with tax-free death benefits. Many newspapers reported the story as a breach of ethical behavior. *The Charlotte* (North Carolina) *Observer* reported that employers were not required to notify workers of **COLI (corporate owned life insurance)** policies. However, the newspaper continued, "Some of the Charlotte area's biggest companies said they have notified all employees covered by the policies, but declined to say how they informed the workers. Use of COLI policies has raised outcries from human rights activists and prompted federal legislation calling for disclosure."[25] The NAIC formed a special working group to study these issues.

Extent to Which Insurable Interest Limits Payment In the case of property insurance, not only must an insurable interest exist at the time of the loss, but the amount the insured is able to collect is limited by the extent of such interest. For example, if you have a one-half interest in a building that is worth $100,000 at the time it is destroyed by fire, you cannot collect more than $50,000 from the insurance company no matter how much insurance you purchased. If you could collect more than the amount of your insurable interest, you would make a profit on the fire. This would violate the principle of indemnity. An exception exists in some states, where valued policy laws are in effect. These laws require insurers to pay the full amount of insurance sold if property is totally destroyed. The intent of the law is to discourage insurers from selling too much coverage.

In contrast to property insurance, life insurance payments are usually not limited by insurable interest. Most life insurance contracts are considered to be **valued policies.**[26] That is, they are contracts to pay a stated sum upon the occurrence of the event insured against, rather than to indemnify for loss sustained. For example, a life insurance contract provides that the insurer will pay a specified sum to the beneficiary upon receipt of proof of death of the person whose life is the subject of the insurance. The beneficiary does not have to prove that any loss has been suffered, because he or she is not required to have an insurable interest.

Some health insurance policies provide that the insurance company will pay a specified number of dollars per day while the insured is hospitalized. Such policies are not contracts of indemnity; they simply promise to make cash payments under specified circumstances. This makes such a contract "incomplete," as discussed in the introduction to this chapter. This also leads to more litigation, as there are no explicit payout amounts written into the contract while improvements in medical technology change the possible treatments daily.

Although an insurable interest must exist at the inception of a life insurance contract to make it enforceable, the amount of payment is usually not limited by the extent of such insurable interest. The amount of life insurance collectible at the death of an insured is limited only by the amount insurers are willing to issue and by the insured's premium-paying ability.[27] The life insurance amount of payout is expressed explicitly in the contract. Thus, in most cases, it is not subject to litigation and arguments over the coverage. The amount of the proceeds of a life insurance policy that may be collected by a creditor-beneficiary, however, is generally limited to the amount of the debt and the premiums paid by the creditor, plus interest.[28]

Subrogation

The principle of indemnity is also supported by the right of **subrogation.** This right gives the insurer whatever claim against third parties the insured may have as a result of the loss for which the insurer paid. For example, if your house is damaged because a neighbor burned leaves and negligently permitted the fire to get out of control, you have a right to collect damages from the neighbor, because a negligent wrongdoer is responsible to others for the damage or injury he or she causes. (Negligence liability will be discussed in later chapters.) If your house is insured against loss by fire, however, you cannot collect from both the insurance company and the negligent party who caused the damage. Your insurance company will pay for the damage and is then subrogated (that is, given) your right to collect damages. The insurer may then sue the negligent party and collect from him or her. This prevents you from making a profit by collecting twice for the same loss.

The right of subrogation is a common-law right the insurer has without a contractual agreement. It is specifically stated in the policy, however, so that the insured will be aware of it and refrain from releasing the party responsible for the loss. The standard personal auto policy, for example, provides that

> If we make a payment under this policy and the person to or for whom payment was made has a right to recover damages from another, that person shall subrogate that right to us. That person shall do whatever is necessary to enable us to exercise our rights and shall do nothing after loss to prejudice them.

> If we make a payment under this policy and the person to or for whom payment is made recovers damages from another, that person shall hold in trust for us the proceeds of the recovery and shall reimburse us to the extent of our payment.

Actual Cash Value

This clause is included in many property insurance policies. An insured generally does not receive an amount greater than the actual loss suffered, because the policy limits payment to actual cash value. A typical property insurance policy says, for example, that the company insures "to the extent of actual cash value ... but not exceeding the amount which it would cost to repair or replace ... and not in any event for more than the interest of the insured."

Actual cash value is not defined in the policy, but a generally accepted notion of it is the replacement cost at the time of the loss, less physical depreciation including obsolescence. For example, if the roof on your house has an expected life of twenty years, roughly half its value is gone at the end of ten years. If it is damaged by an insured peril at that time, the insurer will pay the cost of replacing the damaged portion, less depreciation. You must bear the burden of the balance. If the replacement cost of the damaged portion is $2,000 at the time of a loss, but the depreciation is $800, the insurer will pay $1,200 and you will bear an $800 expense.

Another definition of actual cash value is **fair market value,** which is the amount a willing buyer would pay a willing seller. For auto insurance, where thousands of units of virtually the same property exist, fair market value may be readily available. Retail value as listed in the NADA (National Automobile Dealers Association) guide or the Kelley Blue Book may be used. For other types of property, however, the definition may be deceptively simple. How do you determine what a willing buyer would be willing to pay a willing seller? The usual approach is to compare sales prices of similar property and adjust for differences. For example, if three houses similar to yours in your neighborhood have recently sold for $190,000, then that is probably the fair market value of your home. You may, of course, believe your house is worth far more because you think it has been better maintained than the other houses. Such a process for determining fair market value may be time-consuming and unsatisfactory, so it is seldom used for determining actual cash value. Such a process may, however, be used when obsolescence or neighborhood deterioration causes fair market value to be much less than replacement cost minus depreciation.

Property insurance is often written on a **replacement cost** basis, which means that there is no deduction for depreciation. With such coverage, the insurer would pay $2,000 for the roof loss mentioned above earlier and you would not pay anything. This coverage may or may not conflict with the principle of indemnity, depending upon whether you are better off after payment than you were before the loss.

If $2,000 provided your house with an entirely new roof, you have gained. You now have a roof that will last twenty years, rather than ten years. On the other hand, if the damaged portion that was repaired accounted for only 10 percent of the roof area, having it repaired would not increase the expected life of the entire roof. You are not really any better off after the loss and its repair than you were before the loss.

When an insured may gain, such as by having a loss paid for on a replacement cost basis, there is a potential moral or morale hazard. The insured may be motivated to be either dishonest or careless. For example, if your kitchen has not been redecorated for a very long time and looks shabby, you may not worry about leaving a kettle of grease unattended on the stove. The resulting grease fire will require extensive redecoration as well as cleaning of furniture and, perhaps, replacement of some clothing (assuming that the fire is extinguished before it gets entirely out of control).

Or, you may simply let your old house burn down. Insurers try to cope with these problems by providing in the policy that, when the cost to repair or replace damage to a building is more than some specified amount, the insurer will pay not more than the actual cash value of the damage until actual repair or replacement is completed. The insurer in this way discourages you from destroying the house in order to receive a monetary reward. Arson generally occurs with the intent of financial gain. Some insurers will insure personal property only on an actual cash value basis, because the opportunity to replace old with new may be too tempting to some insureds. Fraudulent claims on loss to personal property are easier to make than are fraudulent claims on loss to buildings. Even so, insurers find most insureds to be honest, permitting the availability of replacement cost coverage on most forms of property.

Other Insurance Provisions

The purpose of **other insurance provisions** in insurance contracts is to prevent insureds from making a profit by collecting from more than one insurance policy for the same loss. For example, if you have more than one policy protecting you against a particular loss, there is a possibility that by collecting on all policies you may profit from the loss. This would, of course, violate the principle of indemnity.

Most policies (other than life insurance) have some provision to prevent insureds from making a profit from a loss through ownership of more than one policy. The homeowners policy, for example, provides a clause about other insurance, or pro rata liability, that reads as follows:

> If a loss covered by this policy is also covered by other insurance, we will pay only the proportion of the loss that the limit of liability that applies under this policy bears to the total amount of insurance covering the loss.[29]

Suppose you have a $150,000 homeowners policy in Company A with $75,000 personal property coverage on your home in Montana, and a $100,000 homeowners policy in Company B with $50,000 personal property coverage on your home in Arizona. Both policies provide coverage of personal property anywhere in the world. If $5,000 worth of your personal property is stolen while you are traveling in Europe, because of the "other insurance" clause you cannot collect $5,000 from each insurer. Instead, each company will pay its pro rata share of the loss. Company A will pay its portion of the obligation ($75,000/$125,000=3/5) and company B will pay its portion ($50,000/$125,000=3/5). Company A will pay $3,000 and Company B will pay $2,000. You will not make a profit on this deal, but you will be indemnified for the loss you suffered. The proportions are determined as follows:

Amount of inusrance, Company A	$ 75,000
Amount of insurance, Company B	50,000
Total amount of insurance	$125,000
Company A pays $\frac{75,000}{125,000} \times 5,000 =$	$ 3,000
Company B pays $\frac{50,000}{125,000} \times 5,000 =$	$ 2,000
Total paid	$ 5,000

Personal

Insurance contracts are **personal.** They insure against loss to a person, not to the person's property. For example, you may say, "My car is insured." Actually, you are insured against financial loss caused by something happening to your car. If you sell the car, insurance does not automatically pass to the new owner. It may be assigned,[30] but only with the consent of the insurer. The personal auto policy, for example, provides that

> Your rights and duties under this policy may not be assigned without our written consent.

As you saw in "Ethical Dilemma: Keeping Score on Insurance Costs—The Credit Rating Story" in Chapter 4, underwriters are as concerned about who it is they are insuring as they are about the nature of the property involved, if not more so. For example, if you have an excellent driving record and are a desirable insured, the underwriter is willing to accept your application for insurance. If you sell your car to an eighteen-year-old male who has already wrecked two cars this year, however, the probability of loss increases markedly. Clearly, the insurer does not want to assume that kind of risk without proper compensation, so it protects itself by requiring written consent for assignment.

Unlike property insurance, life insurance policies are freely assignable. This is a result of the way life insurance practice developed before policies accumulated cash values. Whether or not change of ownership affects the probability of the insured's death is a matter for conjecture. In life insurance, the policyowner is not necessarily the recipient of the policy proceeds. As with an auto policy, the subject of the insurance (the life insured) is the same regardless of who owns the policy. Suppose you assign your life insurance policy (including the right to name a beneficiary) to your spouse while you are on good terms. Such an assignment may not affect the probability of your death. On the other hand, two years and two spouses later, the one to whom you assigned the policy may become impatient about the long prospective wait for death benefits. Changing life insurance policyowners may not change the risk as much as, say, changing auto owners, but it could (murder is quite different from stealing). Nevertheless, life insurance policies can be assigned without the insurer's consent.

Suppose you assign the rights to your life insurance policy to another person and then surrender it for the cash value before the insurance company knows of the assignment. Will the person to whom you assigned the policy rights also be able to collect the cash value? To avoid litigation and to eliminate the possibility of having to make double payment, life insurance policies provide that the company is not bound by an assignment until it has received written notice. The answer to this question, therefore, is generally no. The notice requirements, however, may be rather low. A prudent insurer may hesitate to pay off life insurance proceeds when even a slight indication of an assignment (or change in beneficiary) exists.

KEY TERMS

contract or policy
incomplete contracts
relational contracts
law of agency
principal
agent
apparent authority
producers
binding authority
binder
conditional binder
waiver
private pension
vanishing premium
compliance officer

respondeat superior
estoppel
offer
acceptance
consideration
competent parties
legal purpose
legal form
uberrimae fidei
representations
material fact
concealment
adhesion
expectations principle
indemnity

insurable interest
life-settlement companies
viatical settlement
  companies
janitors' insurance
COLI (corporate owned
  life insurance)
valued policies
subrogation
actual cash value
fair market value
replacement cost
other insurance provisions
personal

DISCUSSION QUESTIONS

1. What are the requirements of a contract? Provide an example.

2. Describe how agents can bring major liability suits from consumers against their insurers. Do you think insurers should really be liable for the actions of their agents?

3. Assuming you are a key employee, your employer can buy an insurance policy on your life and collect the proceeds even if you are no longer with the firm at the time of your death. Clearly, if you leave the firm, your employer no longer has an insurable interest in your life and would gain by your death. Would this situation make you uncomfortable? What if you learned that your former employer was in financial difficulty? Do you think the law should permit a situation of this kind? How is this potential problem typically solved? Relate your situation to the "janitors' insurance" stories described in this chapter. Explain.

4. Michelle Rawson recently moved to Chicago from a rural town. She does not tell her new auto insurance agent about the two speeding tickets she got in the past year. What problem might Michelle encounter? Explain.

5. You cannot assign your auto policy to a purchaser without the insurer's consent, but you can assign your life insurance policy without the insurer's approval. Is this difference really necessary? Why, or why not?

6. Explain how life-settlement companies work. What is the difference between these companies and viatical-settlement companies? Do you think these companies are ethical?

8. May the fact that an insurance policy is a contract of adhesion make it difficult for insurers to write it in simple, easy-to-understand terms? Explain.

9. Explain the concepts of waiver and estoppel and provide an example of each.

10. If your house is destroyed by fire because of your neighbor's negligence, your insurer may recover from your neighbor what it previously paid you under its right of subrogation. This prevents you from collecting twice for the same loss. But the insurer

collects premiums to pay losses and then recovers from negligent persons who cause them. Isn't that double recovery? Explain.

11. If you have a $100,000 insurance policy on your house but it is worth only $80,000 at the time it is destroyed by fire, your insurer will pay you only $80,000. You paid for $100,000 of insurance but you get only $80,000. Aren't you being cheated? Explain.

12. Who makes the offer in insurance transactions? Why is the answer to this question important?

EXERCISES

6.1 Henrietta Hefner lives in northern Minnesota. She uses a woodburning stove to heat her home. Although Henrietta has taken several steps to ensure the safety of her stove, she does not tell her insurance agent about it because she knows that most woodburning stoves represent uninsurable hazards.

Explain to Henrietta why she ought to tell her insurance agent about the stove.

6.2 Walter Brown owns a warehouse in Chicago. The building would cost $400,000 to replace at today's prices, and Walter wants to be sure he's properly insured. He feels he'll be better off to have two $250,000 replacement cost property insurance policies on the warehouse, because "then I'll know if one of the insurers is giving me the run-around. Anyhow, you have to get a few extra dollars to cover expenses if there's a fire—and I can't get that from one company."

a. If the building is totally destroyed by fire, how much may Walter collect without violating the concept of indemnity?

b. What is Walter's insurable interest? Does it exceed the value of the building?

6.3 During the application process for life insurance, Bill Boggs indicated that he had never had pneumonia, when the truth is that he did have the disease as a baby. He fully recovered, however, and with no permanent ill effects. Bill was unaware of having had pneumonia as a baby until, a few weeks after he completed the application, his mother told him about it. Bill was aware, however, that he regularly smoked three or four cigarettes a day when he answered a question on the application about smoking. He checked a block indicating that he was not a smoker, realizing that nonsmokers qualified for lower rates per $1,000 of life insurance. The insurer could have detected his smoking habit through blood and urine tests. Such tests were not conducted because Bill's application was for a relatively small amount of insurance compared to the insurer's average size policy. Instead, the insurer relied on Bill's answers being truthful.

Twenty months after the issuance of the policy on Bill's life, he died in an automobile accident. The applicable state insurance law makes life insurance policies contestable for two years. The insurer has a practice of investigating all claims that occur during the contestable period. In the investigation of the death claim on Bill Boggs, the facts about Bill's episode of pneumonia and his smoking are uncovered.

a. Will Bill's statements on the application be considered misrepresentations? Discuss what you know about misrepresentations as they could apply in this case.

b. Since the cause of Bill's death was unrelated to his smoking habit, his beneficiary will not accept the insurer's offer to return Bill's premiums plus interest. The beneficiary is insisting on pursuing this matter in court. What advise do you have for the beneficiary?

NOTES

1. The origin of the analysis of the type of contracts is founded in transaction cost economics (TCE) theory. TCE was first introduced by R.H. Coase in "The Nature of the Firm," *Economica,* November 1937: pp. 386–405, reprinted in Oliver E. Williamson, ed., *Industrial Organization* (Northampton, Mass: Edward Elgar Publishing, 1996); Oliver E. Williamson, *The Economic Institution of Capitalism* (New York: The Free Press, 1985); application to insurance contracts developed by Etti G. Baranoff and Thomas W. Sager, "The Relationship Among Asset Risk, Product Risk, and Capital in the Life Insurance Industry," *Journal of Banking and Finance,* June 2002.

2. Source: testimonials and author's personal experience.

3. The idea of using Risk Balls occurred to me while searching for ways to apply transaction costs economic theory to insurance products. I began thinking about the risk embedded in insurance products as an intangible item separate from the contract that completes the exchange of that risk. The abstract notion of risk became the intangible core and the contract became the tangible part that wraps itself around the core or risk.

4. Gavin Souter, "Willis Brokers Ordered to Testify in WTC Case," *Business Insurance,* 20 June 2002.

5. J. Dennis Hynes, *Agency and Partnership: Cases, Materials and Problems,* 2nd ed. (Charlottesville, Va.: The Michie Company, 1983), p. 4.

6. It is important to note the difference between an agent who represents the insurer and a broker who represents the insured. However, because of state insurance laws, in many states brokers are not allowed to operate unless they also obtain an agency appointment with an insurer. For details see Etti G. Baranoff, Dalit Baranoff, and Tom Sager, "Nonuniform Regulatory Treatment of Broker Distribution Systems: An Impact Analysis for Life Insurers," *Journal of Insurance Regulations,* September 2000.

7. Steven Brostoff, "Agent Groups Clash On License Reform," *National Underwriter* Online News Service, 20 June 2002. "Insurance producers agree on the need for agent and broker licensing reform, but disagree on how to achieve it. The differences were outlined this week during the third hearing by a House Financial Services Committee panel on insurance regulation and optional federal chartering.... While 46 states have enacted some type of reform since passage of GLB, there are some significant variations in the state laws, and the two largest states—New York and California—have not enacted legislation designed to meet the NARAB [National Association of Registered Agents and Brokers] threshold at all.... [T] He National Association of Insurance Commissioners will soon certify that a majority of states have met the NARAB threshold, thus averting creation of NARAB, even though there is still a lot of work to be done to reach true reciprocity and uniformity in all jurisdictions."

8. Donald F. Cady, "'Private Pension' Term Should Be Retired," *National Underwriter,* Life & Health/Financial Services Edition, 1 March 1999.

9. Allison Bell, "Met Settles Sales Practices Class Lawsuits," *National Underwriter,* Life & Health/Financial Services Edition, 23 August 1999.

10. Diane West, "Churning Suit Filed Against NW Mutual," *National Underwriter,* Life & Health/Financial Services Edition, 14 October 1996.

11. James Carroll, "Holding Down the Fort: Recent court rulings have shown life insurers that they can win so-called 'vanishing-premium' cases." *Best's Review,* September 2001.

12. Amy S. Friedman, "Met Life Under Investigation In Connecticut," *National Underwriter,* Life & Health/Financial Services Edition, 26 January 1998.

13. Lance A. Harke and Jeffrey A. Sudduth, "Declaration of Independents: Proper structuring of contracts with independent agents can reduce insurers' potential liability," *Best's Review,* February 2001.

14. Barbara Bowers, "Higher Profile: Compliance officers have experienced elevated status within their companies since the emergence of the Insurance Marketplace Standards Association," *Best's Review,* October 2001.

15. See endnote 13.

16. Warranties are stringent requirements that insureds must follow for coverage to exist. They were considered necessary in the early days of marine insurance because insurers were forced to rely on the truthfulness of policyholders in assessing risk (often the vessel was already at sea when coverage was procured, and thus inspection was not possible). Under modern conditions, however, insurers generally do not find themselves at such a disadvantage. As a result, courts rarely enforce insurance warranties, treating them instead as representations. Our discussion here, therefore, will omit presentation of warranties. See Kenneth S. Abraham, *Insurance Law and Regulation: Cases and Materials* (Westbury, NY: The Foundation Press, 1990) for a discussion.

17. Some policies are designed through mutual effort of insurer and insured. These "manuscript policies" might not place the same burden on the insurer regarding ambiguities.

18. See Robert E. Keeton, *Basic Text on Insurance Law* (St. Paul, Minn.: West Publishing Company, 1971), p. 351. While this reference is now more than 30 years old, it remains perhaps the most popular insurance text available

19. In some states, a valued policy law requires payment of the face amount of property insurance in the event of total loss, regardless of the value of the dwelling. Other policy provisions, such as deductibles and coinsurance, may also affect the insurer's effort to "indemnify" you.

20. Although a person who dies suffers a loss, he or she cannot be indemnified. Because the purpose of the principle of insurable interest is to implement the doctrine of indemnity, it has no application in the case of a person insuring his or her own life. Such a contract cannot be one of indemnity.

21. The person whose death requires the insurer to pay the proceeds of a life insurance policy is usually listed in the policy as the insured. He or she is also known as the cestuique vie or the subject. The beneficiary is the person (or other entity) entitled to the proceeds of the policy upon the death of the subject. The owner of the policy is the person (or other entity) who has the authority to exercise all the prematurity rights of the policy, such as designating the beneficiary, taking a policy loan, and so on. Often the insured is also the owner.

22. Lynn Asinof, "Is Selling Your Life Insurance Good Policy in the Long-Term?" *The Wall Street Journal,* 15 May 2002.

23. Ron Panko, "Is There Still Room for Viaticals?" *Best's Review,* April 2002.

24. Theo Francis and Ellen E. Schultz, "Big Banks Quietly Pile Up 'Janitors' Insurance,'" *The Wall Street Journal,* 2 May 2002.

25. Sarah Lunday, "Business Giants Could Profit from Life Insurance on Workers," *The Charlotte* (North Carolina) *Observer,* 12 May 2002. "Some of Charlotte's biggest companies—Bank of America Corp., Wachovia Corp. and Duke Energy Corp. included—stand to reap profits from life insurance policies purchased on current and former workers. In some cases, the policies may have been purchased without the workers or their families ever knowing."

26. Some property insurance policies are written on a valued basis, but precautions are taken to assure that values agreed upon are realistic, thus adhering to the principle of indemnity.

27. Life and health insurance companies have learned, however, that overinsurance may lead to poor underwriting experience. Because the loss caused by death or illness cannot be measured precisely, defining overinsurance is difficult. It may be said to exist when the amount of insurance is clearly in excess of the economic loss that may be suffered. Extreme cases, such as the individual whose earned income is $300 per week but who may receive $500 per week in disability insurance benefits from an insurance company while he or she is ill, are easy to identify. Life and health insurers engage in financial underwriting to detect overinsurance. The requested amount of insurance is related to the proposed insured's (beneficiary's) financial need for insurance and premium-paying ability.

28. This is an area in which it is difficult to generalize; the statement made in the text is approximately correct. The point is that the creditor-debtor relationship is an exception to the statement that an insurable interest need not exist at the time of the death of the insured and that the amount of payment is not limited to the insurable interest that existed at the inception of the contract. For further discussion, see Kenneth Black, Jr., and Harold Skipper, Jr., *Life Insurance,* 12th ed. (Englewood Cliffs, N.J.: Prentice-Hall, 1994), pp. 187–88.

29. See Appendix A-1, Section I: Conditions.

30. A complete assignment is the transfer of ownership or benefits of a policy; that is, to give someone else all rights of ownership in the policy

Structure and Analysis of Insurance Contracts

As discussed in Chapter 6, an insurance policy is a contractual agreement subject to rules governing contracts. Understanding those rules is necessary to comprehend an insurance policy. It is not, however, enough. We will be spending quite a bit of time in the following chapters discussing the specific provisions of various insurance contracts. These provisions add substance to the general rules of contracts already presented and should give you the skills needed to comprehend any policy.

In Chapter 7 we offer a general framework of **insurance contracts,** called policies. Because most policies are somewhat standardized, it is possible to present a framework applicable to almost all insurance contracts. As an analogy, think about grammar. In most cases, you can follow the rules almost implicitly, except when you have exceptions to the rules. Similarly, insurance policies follow comparable rules in most cases. Knowing the format and general content of insurance policies will help later in understanding the specific details of each coverage for each distinct risk. This chapter covers the following:

1. Connection
2. Entering into the contract: applications, binders, and conditional and binding receipts
3. The contract: declarations, insuring clauses, exclusions and exceptions, conditions, and endorsements and riders

CONNECTION

By now we assume you are accustomed to connecting the specific topics of each chapter to the big picture of your holistic risk. This chapter is wider in scope. We are not yet delving into the specifics of each risk and its insurance programs. However, compared with Chapter 6, we are drilling down a step further into the world of insurance legal documents. We focus on the "open peril" type of policy, which covers all risks. This means that everything is covered unless specifically excluded, as shown in Figure 7.1. Yet the open peril policy has many exclusions, and more are added as new risks appear on the horizon. For the student who is first introduced to this field, this unique element is an important one to understand. Most insurance contracts in use today do not list the risks that are covered; rather, the policy lets you know that everything is covered, even new unanticipated risks such as anthrax (described in Ethical Dilemma "What Does the Anthrax Scare Mean for Business Today?" in Chapter 3). When the industry realizes that a new peril is too catastrophic, it then exerts efforts to exclude such risks from the standardized, regulated policies. Such efforts are not easy and are met with resistance in many cases. A case at point that has been discussed already is terrorism exclusion after the September 11 attack. While the National Association of Insurance Commissioners (NAIC) endorsed the exclusion and most states approved it, California, Florida and New York did not.[1]

Another important element achieved by exclusions, in addition to excluding the uninsurable risk of catastrophes, is duplication of coverages. Each policy is designed to not overlap with another policy. Such duplication would violate the contract of indemnity principal of insurance contracts. The homeowners liability coverages exclude automobile liability, workers' compensation liability, and other such exposures that are nonstandard to home and personal activities. These specifics will be covered in later chapters, but for now, it is important to emphasize that exclusions are used to reduce the moral hazard of allowing insureds to be paid twice for the same loss.

Thus, while each insurance policy has the components outlined in Figure 7.1, the exclusions are the part that requires in-depth study. Exclusions within exclusions in some policies are like a maze. We not only must ensure we are covered for each risk in our holistic risk picture, we must also make sure no areas are left uncovered by exclusions. At this point, you should be beginning to appreciate the complexity of putting the risk management puzzle together to assure completeness.

ENTERING INTO THE CONTRACT

You may recall from Chapter 6 that every contract requires an offer and an acceptance. This is also true for insurance. The offer and acceptance occur through the application process.

Applications

Although much insurance is sold rather than bought, the insured is still required to make an **application,** which is an offer to buy. The function of the agent is to induce a potential insured to make an offer. As a practical matter, the agent also fills out the application and then asks for a signature after careful study of the application. The application identifies the insured in more or less detail, depending upon the type of insurance. It also provides information about the exposure involved.

For example, in an application for an automobile policy you would identify yourself, describe the automobile to be insured, indicate the use of the automobile, where it will be garaged, and who will drive it, and other facts that help the insurer assess the degree of risk you would represent as a policyholder. Some applications for automobile insurance also require considerable information about your driving and claim experience, as well as

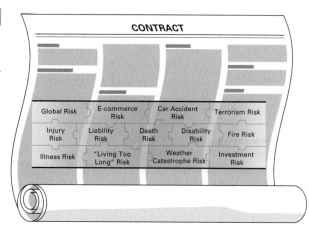

FIGURE 7.1

Connection between Each Risk and the Insurance Contract

Open (All) Risk Policy

Insurance policies are composed of five major parts:

- Declarations
- Insuring agreement
- Exclusions
- Conditions
- Endorsements and riders

information about others who may use the car. In many cases, such as life insurance, the written application becomes a part of the policy. Occasionally, before an oral or written property/casualty application is processed into a policy, a temporary contract, or binder, may be issued.

Binders

As discussed in Chapter 6, property/casualty insurance coverage may be provided while the application is being processed. This is done through the use of a **binder,** which is a temporary contract to provide coverage until the policy is issued by the agent or the company.

In property/casualty insurance, an agent who has binding authority can create a contract between the insurance company and the insured. Two factors influence the granting of such authority. First, some companies prefer to have underwriting decisions made by specialists in the underwriting department, so do not grant binding authority to the agent. Second, some policies are cancelable; others are not. The underwriting errors of an agent with binding authority may be corrected by cancellation if the policy is cancelable. Even with cancelable policies, the insurer is responsible under a binder for losses that occur prior to cancellation. If it is not cancelable, the insurer is obligated for the term of the contract.

The binder may be written or oral. For example, if you telephone an agent and ask to have your house insured, the agent will ask for the necessary information, give a brief statement about the contract—the coverage and the premium cost—and then probably say, "You are covered." At this point, you have made an oral application and the agent has accepted your offer by creating an oral binder. The agent may mail or e-mail a written binder to you to serve as evidence of the contract until the policy is received. The written binder shows who is insured, for what perils, the amount of the insurance, and the company in which coverage is placed.

In most states an oral binder is as legal as a written one, but in case of a dispute it may be difficult to prove its terms. Suppose your house burns after the oral binder has been made but before the policy has been issued, and the agent denies the existence of the contract. How can you prove there was a contract? Or, suppose the agent orally binds the coverage, a fire occurs, and the agent dies before the policy is issued. Unless there is evidence in writing, how can you prove the existence of a contract? Suppose the agent does not die and does not deny the existence of the contract, but has no evidence in writing. If the agent represents only one company, he or she may assert that the company was bound and the insured can collect for the loss. But what if the agent represents more than one company? Which one is bound? Typically, the courts will seek a method to allocate liability according to the agent's common method of distributing business. Or, if that is not determinable, relevant losses might be apportioned among the companies equally. Most agents, however, keep records of their communication with insureds, including who is to provide coverage.

Conditional and Binding Receipts

Conditional and binding receipts in life insurance are somewhat similar to the binders in property/casualty insurance but contain important differences. If you pay the first premium for a life insurance policy at the time you sign the application, the agent typically will give you either a **conditional receipt** or a binding receipt. The conditional receipt does not bind the coverage at the time it is issued, but it does put the coverage into effect retroactive to the time of application if you meet all the requirements for insurability as of the date of the application. A claim for benefits because of death prior to issuance of the policy generally will be honored, but only if you were insurable when you applied. Some conditional receipts, however, require the insured to be in good health when the policy is delivered.

In contrast, with a **binding receipt,** even if you are found not to be insurable but you die while your application is being processed, a claim for the death benefit will be paid. Thus, the binding receipt provides interim coverage while your application is being processed, whether or not you are insurable.[2] This circumstance parallels the protection provided by a binder in property/casualty insurance.

THE CONTRACT

Having completed the offer and the acceptance and met the other requirements for a contract, a contract now exists. What does it look like? Insurance policies are composed of five major parts:

- Declarations
- Insuring agreement
- Exclusions
- Conditions
- Endorsements and riders

These parts typically are identified in the policy by headings. (A section titled "definition" is also becoming common.) Sometimes, however, they are not so prominently displayed, and it is much more common to have explicit section designations in property/casualty contracts than it is in life/health contracts. Their general intent and nature, however, has the same effect.

Declarations

Generally, the declarations section is the first part of the insurance policy. Some policies, however, have a cover (or "jacket") ahead of the declarations. The cover identifies the insurer and the type of policy.

Declarations are statements that identify the person(s) or organization(s) covered by the contract, give information about the loss exposure, and provide the basis upon which the contract is issued and the premium determined. This information may be obtained orally or in a written application. The declarations section may also include the period of coverage and limitations of liability. (The latter may also appear in other parts of the contract.)

Period of Coverage

All insurance policies specify the **period of coverage** during which they apply. Life and health policies may cover for the entire life, a specified period of years, or to a specified age. Health policies and term life policies often cover for a year at a time. Most property insurance policies are for one year or less (although longer policies are available). Perpetual policies remain in force until cancelled by you or the insurer. Liability policies may be for a three-month or six-month period, but most are for a year. Some forms of automobile insurance may be written on a continuous basis, with premiums payable at specified intervals, such as every six months. Such policies remain in force as long as premiums are paid or until they are cancelled. Whatever the term during which any policy is to be in force, it will be carefully spelled out in the contract. During periods when insureds may expect a turn into hard markets in the underwriting cycles, they may want to fix the level of premiums for a longer period and will sign contracts for longer than one year, such as three years.

Limitations of Liability

All insurance policies have clauses that place **limitations of liability** (maximum amount payable) on the insurer. Life policies promise to pay the face amount of the policy. Health policies typically limit payment to a specified amount for total medical expenses during one's lifetime and have internal limits on the payment of specific services, such as a surgery. Property insurance policies specify as limits actual cash value or replacement value, insurable interest, cost to repair or replace, and the face amount of insurance. Limits exist in liability policies for the amount payable per claim, sometimes per injured claimant, sometimes per year, and sometimes per event. Remember the example in Chapter 6 of the dispute between the leaseholder and the insurer over the number of events in the collapse of the World Trade Center on September 11. The dispute was whether the attack on the WTC constituted two events or one. Defense services, provided in most liability policies, are limited only to the extent that litigation falls within coverage terms and the policy proceeds have not been exhausted in paying judgments or settlements. Because of the high cost of providing defense in recent years, however, attempts to limit insurer responsibility to some dollar amount have been made.

Retained Losses

In many situations, it is appropriate not to transfer all of an insured's financial interest in a potential loss. In Chapter 3, we provided the example of NEXCOM's risk management strategy of retention. As discussed, retention benefits the insured when losses are predictable and manageable. For the insurer, some losses are better left with the insured because of moral hazard concerns. Thus, an insured might retain a portion of covered losses through a variety of policy provisions. Some such provisions are deductibles, coinsurance in property insurance, copayments in health insurance, and waiting periods in disability insurance. Each is discussed at some length later in the textbook. For now, realize that the existence of such provisions typically is noted in the declarations section of the policy.

Insuring Clauses

The second major element of an insurance contract, the **insuring clause** or agreement, is a general statement of the promises the insurer makes to the insured. Insuring clauses may vary greatly from policy to policy. Most, however, specify the perils and exposures covered, or at least some indication of what they might be.

Variation in Insuring Clauses

Some policies have relatively simple insuring clauses, such as a life insurance policy, which could simply say, "The company agrees, subject to the terms and conditions of this policy, to pay the amount shown on page 2 to the beneficiary upon receipt at its Home Office of proof of the death of the insured." Package policies are likely to have several insuring clauses, one for each major type of coverage and each accompanied by definitions, exclusions, and conditions. An example of this type is the personal automobile policy, described in Chapter 11.

Some insuring clauses are designated as the "insuring agreement," while others are hidden among policy provisions. Somewhere in the policy, however, it states that the "insurer promises to pay...." This general description of the insurer's promises is the essence of an insuring clause.

Open-Perils versus Named-Perils

The insuring agreement provides a general description of the circumstances under which the policy becomes applicable. The "circumstances" include the covered loss-causing events, called **perils.** They may be specified in one of two ways.

A **named-perils** policy covers only losses caused by the perils listed. If a peril is not listed, loss resulting from it is not covered. For example, one form of the homeowners policy, HO–2, insures for direct loss to the dwelling, other structures, and personal property caused by eighteen different perils. Only losses caused by these perils are covered. Riot or civil commotion is listed, so a loss caused by either is covered. On the other hand, earthquake is not listed, so a loss caused by earthquake is not covered.

An **open-perils** (formerly called "all risk") policy covers losses caused by all perils except those excluded. This type of policy is most popular in property policies. It is important to understand the nature of such a policy since the insured has to look for what is not covered rather than what is covered. The exclusions in an open-perils policy are more definitive of coverage than in a named-perils policy. Generally, an open-perils policy provides broader coverage than a named-perils policy, although it is conceivable, if unlikely, that an open-perils policy would have such a long list of exclusions that the coverage would be narrower.

As noted in the Connection section, today many exclusions in property policies are in the limelight. After September 11, the terrorism exclusion was the first added exclusion to all commercial policies. The mold exclusion is another new exclusion of our age. This will be discussed further in Chapters 8, 9, 10 and 12. In the 1980s, pollution liability was excluded after major losses. As noted in Chapter 2, most catastrophes would be excluded since they are not considered insurable by private insurers. Thus it is no wonder that in the aftermath of September 11 the insurance industry pushed for terrorism exclusions. The Insurance Services Office has developed and filed exclusions for the property/casualty lines of insurance.[3] The NAIC endorsed terrorism exclusions for commercial lines, but rejected them for personal-lines policies and life/health individual and group policies.[4] As already noted, except for California, Florida, and New York, states adopted the exclusions for commercial lines.[5] More details about the exclusion for commercial lines will be in the upcoming chapters detailing the various lines of insurance.[6] A most common exclusion, as noted above, is war exclusion. The insurance industry decided not to trigger this exclusion in the aftermath of September 11. For a closer look, see "Important Issues: The Risk of War" in this chapter.

Policies written on a named-perils basis cannot cover all possible causes of loss because of "unknown peril." There is always the possibility of loss caused by a peril that was not known to exist and so was not listed in the policy. For this reason, open-perils policies cover many perils not covered by named-perils policies. This broader coverage usually requires a higher premium than a named-perils policy but is often preferable because it is less likely to leave gaps in coverage. The anthrax scare described in Chapter 3 is an example of an unknown peril that was covered by the insurance industry's policies.

Very few, if any, policies are "all risk" in the sense of covering every conceivable peril. Probably the closest approach to such a policy in the property insurance field is the comprehensive glass policy, which insures against all glass breakage except that caused by fire, war, or nuclear peril. Most life insurance policies cover all perils except for suicide during the first year or the first two years. Health insurance policies often are written on an open-perils basis, covering medical expenses from any cause not intentional. Some policies, however, are designed to cover specific perils such as cancer (discussed in Chapter 19). Limited-perils policies are popular, because many people fear the consequences of certain illnesses. Of course, the insured is well advised to be concerned with (protect against) the loss, regardless of the cause.

The Risk of War

"This means war!" was a frequent refrain among angry Americans in the days after September 11. Even President George W. Bush repeatedly referred to the terrorist attacks on the World Trade Center and the Pentagon as an "act of war." One politician who disagreed with that choice of words was Rep. Michael Oxley.

By definition and by U.S. law, "war" is an act of violent conflict between two nations. The hijackers, it was soon determined, were working not on behalf of any government but for the al-Qaeda network of terrorists. And thus a week after the attacks, Oxley, chairman of the Financial Services Committee of the U.S. House of Representatives, sent a letter to the National Association of Insurance Commissioners urging the insurance industry not to invoke war risk exclusions to deny September 11 claims.

Most insurers had already come to the same conclusion. Generally, auto, homeowners, commercial property, business interruption, and (in some states) workers compensation policies contain act-of-war exclusions,* meaning that insurance companies can refuse to pay claims arising from a war or a warlike act. Wars are not considered insurable events: They are unpredictable, intentional, and potentially catastrophic. (Recall the discussion in Chapter 2 on insurable and uninsurable risks.) The risks of war are simply too great for an insurance company to accept.

The war-exclusion clause has given rise to few lawsuits, but in each case the courts have supported its application "only in situations involving damage arising from a genuine warlike act between sovereign entities." *Pan American World Airways v Aetna Casualty and Surety Co.*, 505 F2d 989 (1974) involved coverage for the hijacking and destruction of a commercial aircraft. The Second Circuit Court of Appeals held that the hijackers, members of the Popular Front for the Liberation of Palestine, were not "representatives of a government," and thus the war exclusion did not apply. The insurers were liable for the loss. A war-exclusion claim denial was upheld in *TRT/FTC Communications,*

Inc. v. Insurance Company of the State of Pennsylvania, 847 F. Supp. 28 (Del. Dist. 1993), because the loss occurred in the context of a declared war between the United States and Panama—two sovereign nations.

With some $50 billion at stake from the September 11 attacks, it wouldn't have been surprising if some insurers considered taking a chance at invoking the war-exclusion clause. Instead, companies large and small were quick to announce that they planned to pay claims fairly and promptly. "We have decided that we will consider the events of September 11 to be 'acts of terrorism,' not 'acts of war,'" said Peter Bruce, senior executive vice president of Northwestern Mutual Life Insurance. The industry agreed.

Explore the Internet

The series "Attack on America: The Insurance Coverage Issues" provides comprehensive yet readable explanations of the challenges facing the insurance industry following September 11. The articles were written by analysts at the International Risk Management Institute, a research and publishing company focusing on risk management and insurance. Read Part I of the series, "War Risk Exclusions," at www.irmi.com/insights/articles/gibson008.asp

*The standard commercial property policy form provided by the Insurance Services Office contains these exclusions:

1. War, including undeclared or civil war;
2. Warlike action by a military force, including action in hindering or defending against an actual or expected attack, by any government, sovereign or other authority using military personnel or other agents; or
3. Insurrection, rebellion, revolution, usurped power, or action taken by governmental authority in hindering or defending against any of these.

Sources: "Insurers: WTC Attack Not Act of War," *Insurance-Letter,* 17 September 2001, www.cybersure.com/godoc/1872.htm; Jack P. Gibson et al., "Attack on America: The Insurance Coverage Issues," International Risk Management Institute Inc., September 2001, www.imri.com; Tim Reason, "Acts of God and Monsters No Longer Covered: Insurers Say Future Policies Will Definitely Exclude Terrorist Attacks," CFO.com, 19 November 2001, www.cfo.com/article/1,5309,5802%7C%7CA%7C736%7C8,00.html; Susan Massmann, "Legal Background Outlined For War Risk Exclusion," *National Underwriter Online News Service,* 18 September 2001; "Northwestern Mutual Won't Invoke War Exclusion on Claims," *The (Milwaukee) Business Journal,* 14 September 2001.

Exposures to Loss

Generally, the exposures to be covered are also defined (broadly speaking) in the insuring agreement. For example, the liability policy states that the insurer will pay "those sums the insured is legally obligated to pay for damages ..." In addition, "The Company shall have the right and duty to defend..." The exposures in this situation are legal defense costs and liability judgments or settlements against the insured.

In defining the exposures, important information such as the basis of valuation and types of losses covered is needed. Various valuation methods have already been discussed. Actual cash value and replacement cost are the most common means of valuing property loss. Payments required of defendants, either through mutually acceptable settlements or court judgments, define the value of liability losses. The face value (amount of coverage) of a life insurance policy represents the value paid upon the insured's death. Health insurance policies employ a number of valuation methods, including an amount per day in the hospital or per service provided, or, more likely, the lesser of the actual cost of the service or the customary and prevailing fee for this service. Health maintenance organizations promise the provision of services as such rather than a reimbursement of their cost.

The types of covered losses are also generally stated in the insuring agreement. Many property insurance policies, for example, cover only **direct loss.** Direct losses to property are the values physically destroyed or damaged, not the losses caused by inability to use the property. Other policies cover only the loss of use, called **consequential loss** or **indirect loss.** The Introduction to this text explained how important this coverage was to the businesses that suffered indirectly from the September 11 attacks. A report released by PricewaterhouseCoopers in New York City noted that **business interruption** claims came from a wide scope of industries, including financial services, communications, media, and travel industries, that were not in the attack zone.[7] Business interruption losses occur when an organization is unable to sell its goods or services, and/or unable to produce goods for sale. Generally, these losses will be due to some property damage. Such lost revenues typically translate into lost profits. The 1992 Chicago flood, for example, required that Marshall Fields' downtown store close its doors for several days while crews worked to clean up damage caused by the floodwaters.[8] When the loss is caused by property damage not owned by the business, it is considered a **contingent business interruption.** If Marshall Fields reduced its orders to suppliers of its goods, for instance, those suppliers may experience contingent business interruption loss caused by the water damage, even though their own property was not damaged.

Alternatively, some organizations choose to continue operating following property damage, but are able to do so only by incurring additional costs. These costs, which also reduce profits, are termed **extra expense** losses. Continuing with the 1992 Chicago flood example, consider the various accounting firms who could not use their offices the second week in April. With the upcoming tax deadline, these firms chose to rent additional space in other locations so they could meet their clients' needs. The additional rental expense (and other costs) resulted in reduced profits to the accounting firms. Yet a variety of service organizations, including accountants, insurance agents, and bankers, prefer to incur such expenses in order to maintain their reputation of reliability upon which long-term success and profits are dependent. Closing down, even temporarily, could badly hurt the organization.

Individuals and families too may experience costs associated with loss of use. For example, if your home is damaged, you may need to locate (and pay for) temporary housing. You may also incur abnormal expenses associated with the general privileges of home use, such as meals, entertainment, telephones, and similar conveniences. Likewise, if your car is unavailable following an accident, you must rent a car or spend time and money using other forms of transportation. Thus, while a family's loss of use tends to focus on extra expenses, its effect may be as severe as that of an organization.

Liability policies, on the other hand, may cover liability for property damage, bodily injury, personal injury, and/or punitive damages. Property damage liability includes responsibility both for the physical damage to property and the loss of use of property.

Ethical Dilemma

Are Punitive Damages Out of Control?

In 2002, a California state court judge called a $30 million award against grocery chain Kroger, where six employees had been verbally harassed by a store manager, "grossly excessive," and reduced it to a mere $8.25 million. A jury in Laredo, Texas, awarded $108 million to Mexican heiress Cristina Brittingham Sada de Ayala in a lawsuit against her stepmother for failing to repay a $34 million loan. A Utah jury ordered State Farm to pay a policyholder $145 million in punitive damages for handling a claim in bad faith and afflicting emotional distress. A Los Angeles jury ordered tobacco giant Philip Morris to pay Betty Bullock $28 *billion* in punitive damages.

The Bullock award of $28 billion (which was lowered to $28 billion and is still being appealed by Philip Morris) is by itself almost five times the combined amount of 2001's top ten largest jury awards to individuals and families. And the 2001 top-ten total, $5.7 billion, was more than double the previous year's. Though a Department of Justice study showed that only a small percentage of cases are awarded punitive damages, and that the majority of awards are under $40,000, the number and amounts of punitive awards have been geometrically increasing since 1959's high of $10,000.

Some people argue that a fine is the best way to punish a corporation for acting wrongly. For example, the 1994 case against McDonald's that won an elderly woman $2.7 million for spilling hot coffee in her lap is commonly seen as the beginning of our frivolous-lawsuit period. What the jury heard, but most people did not, was that McDonald's purposely kept its coffee at least forty degrees hotter than most restaurants did, as a cost-saving measure to extract more coffee from the beans; that more than 700 people had filed complaints of scalding coffee burns over the previous decade; that McDonald's knew their coffee was dangerously hot yet had no plans to turn the heat down or post warning signs. The woman in the case suffered third-degree burns to her groin, thighs, and buttocks that required skin grafts and a lengthy hospital stay. She filed suit against McDonald's only after the company refused to pay her medical bills. Even the famous multi-million-dollar award was reduced on appeal to $480,000.

The true problem, many say, is not the size of such awards but the method by which we determine them. Punitive damages are not truly "damages" in the sense of compensation for a loss or injury but rather a fine, levied as punishment. In determining the amount of a punitive award a jury is instructed to consider whether the defendant displayed reckless conduct, gross negligence, malice, or fraud—but in practice, a jury award often depends on how heart-tugging the plaintiff seems to be versus how heartless the big bad corporation appears.

Questions for Discussion

1. Were the facts behind the McDonald's lawsuit news to you? Do they change your opinion about this landmark case? What would you have done if you had been on the jury?

2. Betty Bullock, who has lung cancer, had been a regular smoker for forty years and blamed Philip Morris for failing to warn her about smoking risks. Do you think Philip Morris is responsible? Do you think learning more about the case might change your opinion?

3. Exxon was ordered to pay $125 million in criminal fines for the Valdez oil spill. In a separate trial, a civil jury hit Exxon with a $5 billion punitive award. Is it fair for a company to pay twice for the same crime?

4. Are juries—people who have no legal training, who know only about the case they are sitting on, who may be easily swayed by theatrical attorneys, and who are given only vague instructions—equipped to set punitive damage awards? Should punitive awards be regulated?

Sources: Theodore Olson, speech at the Manhattan Institute conference "Crime and Punishment in Business Law," 8 May 2002, reprinted at http://www.manhattan-institute.org/html/cjm_15.htm; "Surprise: Judges Hand Out Most Punitive Awards," *The Wall Street Journal*, 12 June 12 2000, p. 2b; Steven Brostoff, "Top Court To Review Punitive Damages," *National Underwriter Online News Service*, 27 June 2002; "McFacts about the McDonalds Coffee Lawsuit," *Legal News and Views*, Ohio Academy of Trial Lawyers, http://lawandhelp.com/q298-2.htm, Michael Bradford, "Phillip Morris to continue appeal of punitives award," *Business Insurance*, 19 December, 2002.

Bodily injury is the physical injury to a person, including the pain and suffering that may result. Personal injury is the nonphysical injury to a person, including damage caused by libel, slander, false imprisonment, and the like. Punitive damages are assessed against defendants for "gross negligence," supposedly for the purpose of punishment and to deter others from acting in a similar fashion. Examples of punitive damages in recent cases and their ethical implications are featured in "Ethical Dilemma: Are Punitive Damages Out of Control?"

Exclusions and Exceptions

Whether the policy is open-perils or named-perils, the coverage it provides cannot be ascertained without considering the **exclusions,** which represent the third major part of an insurance policy. Usually, an insured may not know what the policy covers until he or she finds out what it does not cover. Unfortunately, this is not always an easy task. In many policies, exclusions appear not only under the heading "exclusions" in one or more places, but also throughout the policy and in various forms. When we delve into homeowners policies in Chapter 10, you will be amazed at the many exclusions and exclusions to exclusions that you will encounter. The homeowners policy section I (which provides property coverage) has two lists of exclusions identified as such, plus others scattered throughout the policy. The last sentence in the description of loss of use coverage, for example, says, "We do not cover loss or expense due to cancellation of a lease or agreement." In other words, such loss is excluded. In "Perils Insured Against," the policy at one point says, "We insure for risks of physical loss to the property.... Except," followed by a list of losses or loss causes. Under the heading "Additional Coverages," several coverages are listed and then the following sentence appears: "We do not cover loss arising out of business pursuits...." Thus, such loss is excluded.

A policy may exclude specified locations, perils, property, or losses. Perhaps a discussion of the exclusions in some policies and the reasons for them will be helpful.

Reasons for Exclusions

Let us review the reasons for the existence of exclusions. As noted in Chapter 2, one reason exclusions exist is to avoid financial catastrophe for the insurer, which may result if many dependent exposures are insured or if a single, large-value exposure is insured. Because war would affect many exposures simultaneously, losses caused by war are excluded in most policies in order to avoid catastrophe. Exclusions also exist to limit coverage of nonfortuitous (that is, not accidental) events. Losses that are not accidental make prediction difficult, cause coverage to be expensive, and represent circumstances in which coverage would be contrary to public policy. As a result, losses caused intentionally (by the insured) are excluded. So too are naturally occurring losses that are expected. Wear and tear, for instance, is excluded from coverage. Adverse selection and moral hazard are limited by these exclusions.

Adverse selection is limited further by use of specialized policies and endorsements that standardize the risk. That is, limitations (exclusions) are placed in standard policies for exposures that are nonstandard. Those insureds who need coverage for such nonstandard exposures purchase it specifically. For example, homeowners policies limit theft coverage on jewelry and furs to a maximum amount ($2,500). Exposures in excess of the maximum are atypical, representing a higher probability (and severity) of loss than exists for the average homeowner. Insureds who own jewelry and furs with values in excess of the maximum must buy special coverage (if desired).

An important element is the point emphasized in the Connection section above. Some exclusions exist to avoid duplication of coverage with policies specifically intended to insure the exposure. As noted above, homeowners liability coverages exclude automobile liability, workers' compensation liability, and other such exposures that are nonstandard to home and personal activities. Other policies specifically designed to cover such exposures are available and commonly used. To duplicate coverage would diminish insurers' ability to discriminate among insureds and could result in moral hazard if insureds were paid twice for the same loss. A policy clause, termed an **other insurance clause** (discussed in Chapter 6), addresses the potential problem of duplicating coverage when two or more similar policies cover the same exposure. Through this type of provision, the insurer's financial responsibility is apportioned in such a way that payment in excess of the insured's loss is avoided.

These reasons for exclusions are manifested in limitations on:

- Locations
- Perils
- Property
- Losses

Following is a discussion of the purposes of limiting locations, perils, property, and losses.

Excluded Locations

Some coverages are location specific, such as to buildings. Other policies define the location of coverage. Automobile policies, for example, cover the United States and Canada. Mexico is not covered because of the very high auto risk there. In addition, some governmental entities in Mexico will not accept foreign insurance. Some property policies were written to cover movable property anywhere in the world except the eastern bloc countries, likely due to difficulty in adjusting claims. With the breakup of the communist bloc, these limitations are also being abandoned. Yet coverage may still be excluded where adjusting is difficult and/or the government of the location has rules against such foreign insurance. For a discussion of political risk—unanticipated political events that disrupt the earning or profit-making ability of an enterprise—see Chapter 8.

Excluded Perils

Some perils are excluded because they can be covered by other policies or because they are unusual or catastrophic. The earthquake peril, for example, requires separate rating and is excluded from homeowners policies. This peril can be insured under a separate policy or added by endorsement for an extra premium. Many insureds do not want to pay the premium required, either because they think their property is not exposed to the risk of loss caused by an earthquake or because they expect that federal disaster relief would cover losses. Given the choice of a homeowners policy that excluded the earthquake peril and one that included earthquake coverage but cost $50 more per year, they would choose the former. Thus, to keep the price of their homeowners policies competitive, insurers exclude the earthquake peril. It is excluded also because it is an extraordinary peril that cannot easily be included with the other perils covered by the policy. It must be rated separately.

As noted above, perils, such as those associated with war, are excluded because commercial insurers consider them uninsurable. Nuclear energy perils, such as radiation, are excluded from most policies because of the catastrophe exposure. Losses to homeowners caused by the nuclear meltdown at Three Mile Island in 1979, which forced homeowners to evacuate the damaged property in the area, were not covered by their homeowners insurance. Losses due to wear and tear are excluded because they are inevitable rather than accidental and thus not insurable. Similarly, inherent vice, which refers to losses caused by characteristics of the insured property, is excluded. For example, certain products, such as tires and various kinds of raw materials, deteriorate with time. Such losses are not accidental and are, therefore, uninsurable.

Excluded Property

Some property is excluded because it is insurable under other policies. Homeowners policies, as previously stated, exclude automobiles because they are better insured under automobile policies. Other property is excluded because the coverage is not needed by the average insured, who would, therefore, not want to pay for it.

Liability policies usually exclude damage to or loss of others' property in the care, custody, or control of the insured, because property insurance can provide protection for the owner against losses caused by fire or other perils. Other possible losses, such as damage to clothing being dry-cleaned, are viewed as a business risk involving the skill of the dry cleaner. Insurers do not want to assume the risk of losses caused by poor workmanship or poor management.

Excluded Losses

Losses resulting from ordinance or law—such as those regulating construction or repair—are excluded from most property insurance contracts. Policies that cover only direct physical damage exclude loss of use or income resulting from such damage. Likewise, policies covering only loss of use exclude direct losses. Health insurance policies often exclude losses (expenses) considered by the insurer to be unnecessary, such as the added cost of a private room or the cost of elective surgery.

Conditions

The fourth major part of an insurance contract is the conditions section. **Conditions** enumerate the duties of the parties to the contract and, in some cases, define the terms used. Some policies list them under the heading "Conditions," while others do not identify them as such. Wherever the conditions are stated, you must be aware of them. You cannot expect the insurer to fulfill its part of the contract unless you fulfill the conditions. Remember that acceptance of these conditions is part of the consideration given by the insured at the inception of an insurance contract. Failure to accept conditions may release the insurer from its obligations. Many conditions found in insurance contracts are common to all. Others are characteristic of only certain types of contracts. Some examples follow.

Notice and Proof of Loss

All policies require that the insurer be notified when the event, accident, or loss insured against occurs. The time within which notice must be filed and the manner of making it vary. The homeowners policy, for example, lists as one of the insured's duties after loss to "give immediate notice to us or our agent" and to file proof of loss within sixty days. A typical life insurance policy says that payment will be made "upon receipt ... of proof of death of the insured." A health policy requires that "written proof of loss must be furnished to the Company within twelve months of the date the expense was incurred." The personal auto policy says, "We must be notified promptly of how, when, and where the accident or loss happened."

In some cases, if notice is not made within a reasonable time after the loss or accident, the insurer is relieved of all liability under the contract. A beneficiary who filed for benefits under an accidental death policy more than two years after the insured's death was held in one case to have violated the notice requirement of the policy.[9] The insurer is entitled to such timely notice so it can investigate the facts of the case. Insureds who fail to fulfill this condition may find themselves without protection when they need it most—after a loss.

Suspension of Coverage

Because there are some risks or hazardous situations insurers want to avoid, many policies specify acts, conditions, or circumstances that will cause the **suspension of coverage** or, in other words, that will release the insurer from liability. The effect is the same as if the policy were cancelled or voided, but when a policy is suspended, the effect is only temporary. When a **voidance of coverage** is incurred in an insurance contract, coverage is terminated. Protection resumes only by agreement of the insured and insurer. Suspension, in contrast, negates coverage as long as some condition exists. Once the condition is eliminated, protection immediately reverts without the need for a new agreement between the parties.

Some life and health policies have special clauses that suspend coverage for those in military service during wartime. When the war is over or the insured is no longer in military service, the suspension is terminated and coverage is restored. See "Important Issues: Individual Coverage Rights When Called to Military Duty" in Chapter 19. The personal auto policy has an exclusion that is essentially a suspension of coverage for damage to your auto. It provides that the insurer will not pay for loss to your covered auto "while it is used to carry persons or property for a fee," except for use in a share-the-expense car pool. The homeowners policy (form 3) suspends coverage for vandalism and malicious mischief losses if the house has been vacant for more than thirty consecutive days. A property insurance policy may suspend coverage while there is "a substantial increase in hazard."

You can easily overlook or misunderstand suspensions of coverage or releases from liability when you try to determine coverage provided by a policy. They may appear as either conditions or exclusions. Because their effect is much broader and less apparent than the exclusion of specified locations, perils, property, or losses, it is easy to underestimate their significance.

Cooperation of the Insured

All policies require your cooperation, in the sense that you must fulfill certain conditions before the insurer will pay for losses. Because the investigation of an accident and defense of a suit against the insured are very difficult unless he or she will cooperate, liability policies have a specific provision requiring cooperation after a loss. The businessowners policy, for example, says that, "The insured shall cooperate with the Company, and upon the Company's request, assist in ... making of settlements; conducting of suits...."

It is not unusual for the insured to be somewhat sympathetic toward the claimant in a liability case, especially if the claimant is a friend. There have been situations in which the insured was so anxious for the claimant to get a large settlement from the insurer that the duty to cooperate was forgotten. If you do not meet this condition and the insurer can prove it, you may end up paying for the loss yourself.

This is illustrated by the case of a mother who was a passenger in her son's automobile when it was involved in an accident in which she was injured. He encouraged and aided her in bringing suit against him. The insurer was released from its obligations under the liability policy, on the grounds that the cooperation clause was breached.[10] The purpose of the cooperation clause is to force insureds to perform the way they would if they did not have insurance.

Protection of Property After Loss

Most property insurance policies contain provisions requiring the insured to protect the property after a loss in order to reduce the loss as much as possible. An insured who wrecks his or her automobile, for example, has the responsibility for having it towed to a garage for safekeeping. In the case of a fire loss, the insured is expected to protect undamaged property from the weather and other perils in order to reduce the loss. You cannot be careless and irresponsible just because you have insurance. Yet, the requirement is only that the insured be reasonable. You are not required to put yourself in danger or to take extraordinary steps. Of course, views of what is "extraordinary" may differ.

Examination

A provision peculiar to some disability income policies gives the insurer the right to have its physician examine the insured periodically during the time he or she receives benefits under the policy. This right cannot be used to harass the claimant, but the insurer is entitled to check occasionally to see if he or she should continue to receive benefits. Property insurance policies have a provision that requires the claimant to submit to examination under oath, as well as make records and property available for examination by representatives of the insurance company.

Endorsements and Riders

Sometimes (maybe often), but not always, an insurance policy will include a fifth major part: the attachment of endorsements or riders. Riders and endorsements are two terms with the same meaning. **Riders** are used with life/health policies, whereas **endorsements** are used with property/casualty policies. A rider or endorsement makes a change in the contract to which it is attached. It may increase or decrease the coverage, change the premium, correct a statement, or make any number of other changes.

The endorsement guaranteeing home replacement cost, for example, provides replacement cost coverage for a dwelling insured by a homeowners policy, regardless of the limit of liability shown in the declarations. This keeps the amount of insurance on the dwelling up-to-date during the term of the policy. A waiver of premium rider increases the benefits of a life insurance policy by providing for continued coverage without continued payment of premiums if the insured becomes totally disabled. Endorsements and riders are not easier to read than the policies to which they are attached. Actually, the way some of them are glued or stapled to the policy may discourage you from looking at them. Nevertheless, they are an integral part of the contract you have with the insurer and cannot be ignored. When their wording conflicts with that in exclusions or other parts of the contract, the rider or endorsement takes precedent, negating the conflict.

Insurers continually add and change endorsements and riders to the policies as market conditions change and the needs are altered. For example, the commercial insurance units of Travelers Indemnity and Aetna Casualty and Surety provided an endorsement to protect contractors against third-party bodily injury and property damage claims arising out of accidental releases of pollutants they bring to job sites.[11] Some features included were no time limits, full policy limits, and defense cost in addition to the basic full limits. Another example is a mold exclusion endorsement, approved by twenty states, that would provide a limited level of coverage for mold losses.[12]

An example of a rider to life insurance policies is the estate-tax repeal rider. This rider, which exemplifies the need to modify policies as tax laws change, was created in response to the Economic Growth and Tax Relief Reconciliation Act of 2001 (EGTRAA 2001). Under this act, the federal estate tax will be phased out completely by 2010 but would return in 2011 unless Congress votes to eliminate it. If Congress eliminates the tax, the rider would let holders of the affected policies surrender the policies without paying surrender charges.[13]

Another example of a rider relates to long-term care (LTC) insurance (discussed later in the text in Chapters 17 and 19). Most long-term care policies include a rider offering some sort of inflation protection, generally five percent annually.[14] The final example brings us back to the hot topic of exclusion after September 11—the terrorism exclusions. As more states adopted the exclusions, the need for endorsements arose.[15] A series of endorsements were created by the ISO as shown in the NAIC bulletin.[16]

KEY TERMS

insurance contracts	named-perils	bodily injury
application	open-perils	personal injury
binder	direct loss	punitive damages
conditional receipt	consequential loss or	exclusions
binding receipt	indirect loss	other insurance clause
declarations	business interruption	conditions
period of coverage	contingent business	suspension of coverage
limitations of liability	interruption	voidance of coverage
insuring clause	extra expense	riders
perils	property damage	endorsements

DISCUSSION QUESTIONS

1. What is the difference between a conditional and a binding receipt?
2. What are the main reasons for exclusions and endorsements and riders in insurance policies?
3. Describe a few exclusions and endorsements and riders.
4. What is the significance of an open-perils policy? In deciding between a named-perils and open-perils policy, what factors would you consider? Define both terms and explain your answer.
5. Dave was just at his insurance agent's office applying for health insurance. On his way home from the agent's office, Dave had a serious accident that kept him hospitalized for two weeks. Would the health insurance policy Dave just applied for provide coverage for this hospital expense?
6. Lightning struck a tree in the Gibsons' yard, causing it to fall over and smash the bay window in their living room. The Gibsons were so distraught by the damage that they decided to go out for dinner to calm themselves. After dinner, the Gibsons decided to take in a movie. When they returned home, they discovered that someone had walked through their broken bay window and stolen many of their valuable possessions. The Gibsons have a homeowners policy that covers both physical damage and theft. As the Gibsons' insurer, do you cover all their incurred losses? Why, or why not?
7. In the chapter on automobile insurance, you will find that portable stereos and tape decks are excluded from coverage. What do you think the insurance company's rationale is for such an exclusion? What are other reasons for insurance policy exclusions? Give examples of each.
8. Joe Phelps is a chemistry aficionado. For his twenty-ninth birthday last month, Joe's wife bought him an elaborate chemistry set to use in their attached garage. The set includes dangerous (flammable) substances, yet Joe does not notify his homeowners insurer. What problem might Joe encounter?

9. Joe has another insurance problem. He had an automobile accident last month in which he negligently hit another motorist while turning right on red. The damage was minor, so Joe just paid the other motorist for the repairs. Fearing the increase in his auto insurance premiums, Joe did not notify his insurer of the accident. Now the other motorist is suing for whiplash. What is Joe's problem, and why?

10. What are the shortcomings of limited peril health insurance policies, such as coverage for loss caused solely by cancer, from a personal risk management point of view?

11. When you apply for a life insurance policy, agent Dawn Gale says, "If you will give me your check for the first month's premium now, the policy will cover you now if you are insurable." Is this a correct statement, or is Dawn just in a hurry to get her commission for selling you the policy? Explain.

12. Your careless driving results in serious injury to Linda Helsing, a close personal friend. Because she knows you have liability insurance and the insurer will pay for damages on your behalf, she files suit against you. Wouldn't it be unreasonable for your insurer to expect you not to help Linda pursue maximum recovery in every conceivable way? Explain.

EXERCISES

7.1 "States approving terrorism exclusions for commercial property insurance are a help to the insurance industry, but two critical exposures aren't excluded from terrorism—workers' compensation and fire following a terrorist event." ("Even With Exclusions, Insurers Still Exposed to Workers' Comp, Fire Losses," *Best's Insurance News*, 10 January 2002.)

   a. What can be the impact on insurers' bottom line when such exclusions are not adopted?

7.2 "A Federal Reserve Board survey showing that banks are still making commercial real estate loans for "high profile" properties does not tell the whole story of the impact of problems in the terrorism insurance market, insurance industry officials contend." (Steven Brostoff, "Loans Still Coming Despite Terror Risks," *National Underwriter*, Property & Casualty/Risk & Benefits Management Edition, 3 June 2002.)

   a. Relate this story to the terrorism exclusion information you found in this chapter.

   b. What is the actual problem here?

7.3 Kevin Kaiser just replaced his old car with a new one and is ready to drive the new car off the lot. He did not have collision insurance on the old car, but he wants some on the new one.

   He calls his friend Dana Goldman, who is an insurance agent. "Give me the works, Dana. I want the best collision coverage you have." Soon after he drives the car away, he is struck by an eighteen-wheeler and the new car is totaled.

   Kevin then discovers that he has collision insurance with a $500 deductible which he must pay. He is upset, because to him "the works" meant full insurance for all losses he might have due to collision. Dana had thought that he wanted a more cost-efficient coverage, and had used the deductible to lower the premium. The applicable state law and insurer underwriting practices allow deductibles as low as $250, although they can be much higher.

   a. Kevin wants to take Dana to court to collect the full value of the auto. What would you advise him?

b.   What does this tell you about oral contracts?

7.4 A.J. Jackson was very pleased to hear the agent say that she was covered the moment she finished completing the application and paid the agent the first month's premium. A.J. had had some health problems previously and really didn't expect to be "covered" until after she had taken her physical and received notice from the company. The agent said that the conditional binder was critical for immediate coverage. "Of course," said the agent, "this coverage may be limited until the company either accepts or rejects your application." The agent congratulated A.J. again for her decision. A.J. began to wonder the next morning exactly what kind of coverage, if any, she had.

a.   What kind of coverage did A.J. have?

b.   Did her submission to the agent of the first month's premium have any impact on her coverage? Why?

c.   If you were the agent, how would you have explained this coverage to A.J.?

7.5 LeRoy Leetch had a heck of a year. He suffered all the following losses. Based on what you know about insurance, which would you expect to be insurable, and why?

a.   LeRoy's beloved puppy, Winchester, was killed when struck by a school bus. He has losses of burial expenses, the price of another puppy, and his grief due to Winchester's death.

b.   LeRoy has an expensive collection of rare clocks. Most are kept in his spare bedroom and were damaged when a fire ignited due to faulty wiring. The loss is valued at $15,000.

c.   Heavy snowfall and a rapid thaw caused flooding in LeRoy's town. Damage to his basement was valued at $2,200.

d.   Weather was hard on the exterior of LeRoy's house as well. Dry rot led to major damage to the first story hardwood floors. Replacement will cost $6,500.

NOTES

1.   Meg Fletcher, "More policy changes needed to limit terrorism losses: ISO," *Business Insurance,* 11 February 2002. "ISO [Insurance Services Office] filed two types of terrorism exclusions, depending on whether the state had a standard fire policy law. Regulators in nearly all jurisdictions subsequently approved insurers' use of those forms, except for California, Florida and New York."

2.   In a few states, the conditional receipt is construed to be the same as the binding receipt. See William F. Meyer, *Life and Health Insurance Law: A Summary,* 2nd ed. (Cincinnati: International Claim Association, 1990), pp. 196–217.

3.   Frank J. Coyne, "Trial by fire: Terrorism and nuclear exclusions are limited in states that adhere to the Standard Fire Policy," *Best's Review,* 1 April 2002.

4.   Susan Massmann, "Terrorism Exclusion Wording Unclear," *National Underwriter,* Property & Casualty/Risk & Benefits Management Edition; "Members Come to Agreement on Terrorism Exclusions: Say Exclusions Not Necessary for Individual and Group Life, Accident and Health Lines," NAIC press release, 17 March 2002.

5.   The NAIC endorsement is evident, because it created the model for the states that wish to adopt the exclusion. See the NAIC's Terrorism Bulletin at www.naic.org/general.htm.

6.   The most important part of the exclusion reads, "Exclusion for acts of terrorism only apply if the acts of terrorism result in industry-wide insured losses that exceed $25,000,000 for related incidents that occur within a 72 hour period." From the NAIC Terrorism Bulletin and as noted in "California, New York Take Big Risks on Terrorism Policies" (Editorial Comment), *National Underwriter,* Property & Casualty/Risk & Benefits Management Edition, 21 January 2002.

7.   "9/11 Business Interruption Claims Analysis," *National Underwriter* Online News Service, 20 February 2002.

8.   In April 1992, part of Chicago's underground tunnel system was flooded when the river pushed back a wall far enough to cause a rapid flow of water into the tunnels. Water levels rose high enough to damage stored

property, force electrical supplies to be shut off, and cause concern about the stability of structures built above the tunnels.

9. Thomas v. Transamerica Occidental Life Ins. Co., 761 F. Supp. 709 (1991).

10. *Beauregard v. Beauregard,* 56 Ohio App. 158, 10 N.E.2d 227 (1937).

11. "Travelers Construction Offers New Pollution Endorsements," *National Underwriter,* Property & Casualty/Risk & Benefits Management Edition, 10 March 1997.

12. E.E. Mazier, "Alabama OKs ISO Mold Endorsement," *National Underwriter* Online News Service, 26 February 2002.

13. "Hartford Introduces Estate-Tax Repeal Rider," *National Underwriter* Online News Service, 1 April 2002.

14. Jack Crawford, "Inflation Protection: Is The LTC Industry on the Right Path?" *National Underwriter,* Life & Health/Financial Services Edition, 21 January 2002.

15. Susan Massmann, "Terrorism Exclusion Wording Unclear," *National Underwriter,* Property & Casualty/Risk & Benefits Management Edition, 11 February 2002.

16. The bulletin was to all property & casualty insurers writing commercial lines insurance products regarding voluntary expedited filing procedures for exclusions related to acts of terrorism. For interested students, the endorsements list included in the Bulletin is as follows:

COMMERCIAL PROPERTY INTERLINE ENDORSEMENT: IL 09 41 01 02 (N/A to Standard Fire Policy States)

COMMERCIAL PROPERTY INTERLINE ENDORSEMENT: IL 09 40 01 02 (Applies in Standard Fire Policy States)

COMMERCIAL PROPERTY INTERLINE ENDORSEMENT: IL 09 42 01 02 (Applies in Standard Fire Policy States)

COMMERCIAL GENERAL LIABILITY ENDORSEMENT: CG 21 69 0102

COMMERCIAL GENERAL LIABILITY ENDORSEMENT: CG 31 42 01 02

COMMERCIAL GENERAL LIABILITY ENDORSEMENT: CG 31 43 01 02

COMMERCIAL LIABILITY UMBRELLA ENDORSEMENT: CU 21 29 01 02

BUSINESSOWNERS ENDORSEMENT: BP 05 11 01 02 (N/A to Standard Fire Policy States)

BUSINESSOWNERS ENDORSEMENT: BP 05 12 02 (Applies in Standard Fire Policy States)

BUSINESSOWNERS ENDORSEMENT: BP 05 13 01 02

FARM LIABILITY ENDORSEMENT: FL 10 30 01 02

PART IV

PROPERTY AND LIABILITY RISKS

CHAPTER 8

Property Risk, E-commerce Property Risk, and Global Risk

At this point you should feel somewhat comfortable with most of the overall picture of risk, but despite the many examples of risk management and coverages you have seen, the details of each coverage are not explicit yet. In this chapter we will elaborate on the property risk including that of electronic commerce, or **e-commerce risk** and **global risk** exposures. In Chapter 9 we will elaborate on liability risks overall and the particulars of e-commerce liability. Home coverage that includes both property and liability coverages will be discussed in detail in Chapter 10. Auto coverage will be discussed in Chapter 11. Chapters 10 and 11 focus on personal lines coverages. Chapters 12 and 13 take us into the world of commercial lines coverages and workers' compensation. In this part of the text you will be asked to relate sections of the actual policies provided in the Appendices (at the end of the textbook) to loss events. Our work will clarify many areas of property and liability of various risks, including the most recent e-commerce risk exposures and the fundamental global risk exposure. In this chapter we cover the following:

1. Connection
2. Property risks
3. E-commerce property risks
4. Global risks

CONNECTION

The most important part of property coverage is that you, as the **first party,** are eligible to receive benefits in the event you or your business suffers a loss. In contrast, liability coverage, discussed in Chapter 9, pays benefits to a **third party** if you cause a loss (or, if someone causes you to have a loss, his or her liability insurance would pay benefits to you). In this chapter we focus on the first type: coverage for you when your property gets damaged or lost.

In personal lines coverages such as homeowners and auto policies, the property coverage for losses you sustain, as the owner of the property, is only part of the policies. In commercial lines, you may use a packaged multi-lines policy that includes both commercial property and commercial general liability policies. In this chapter we focus only on the part of the policies relating to the property coverages for first party damages to you. As part of your holistic risk and risk management, it is important to have an appreciation of this part of the coverage.

As we develop the holistic risk management program, you now realize that you need a myriad of policies to cover all your property exposures, including that of e-commerce, and another myriad of policies to protect your liability exposures. In some cases property and liability coverages are packaged together such as in homeowners and auto policies, but what is actually covered under each? Our objective is to untangle it all and show how to achieve a complete risk management picture. To have a complete holistic risk management we have to put together a hierarchy of coverages for various exposures, perils, and hazards—each may appear in one or another policy—as shown in Figure 8.1 (see the elevated risks that indicate property or first party type risks applicable to this chapter). In addition to understanding this hierarchy we need to have a vision into the future. E-commerce risk, considered one of the emerging risks, is explored in this chapter. Hazards derived from global exposure are other important risks that receive special attention in this chapter.

PROPERTY RISKS

Property can be classified in a number of ways, including its mobility, use value, and ownership. Sometimes these varying characteristics will affect potential losses and, in turn, affect decisions about which risk management options work best. A discussion of these

FIGURE 8.1 Connection between Property Risks and Insurance Contracts

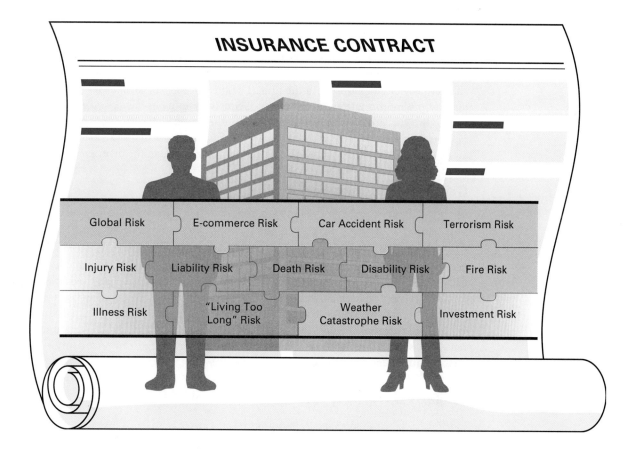

classifying characteristics, including consideration of the hot topic of electronic commerce (e-risk) exposures and global property exposures, follows.

Physical property generally is categorized as either real or personal. **Real property** represents permanent structures (realty) that if removed would alter the functioning of the property. Any building, therefore, is real property. In addition, built-in appliances, fences, and other such items typically are considered real property.

Physical property that is mobile (not permanently attached to something else) is considered **personal property.** Included in this category are motorized vehicles, furniture, business inventory, clothing, and similar items. Thus, a house is real property, while a stereo and a car are personal property. Some property, such as carpeting, is not easily categorized. The risk manager needs to consider the various factors discussed below in determining how best to manage such property.

Why is this distinction between real and personal property relevant? One reason is that dissimilar properties are exposed to perils with dissimilar likelihoods. When flood threatens a house, the opportunities to protect it are limited. Yet threatened flood damage to something mobile may be thwarted by movement of the item away from floodwaters. You may be able, for example, to drive your car out of the exposed area and to move your clothes to higher ground.

A second reason to distinguish between real and personal property is that appropriate valuation mechanisms may differ between the two. We will discuss later in this chapter the concepts of "actual cash value" and "replacement cost new." Because of moral hazard issues, an insurer may prefer to value personal property at actual cash value (a depreciated amount). The size of depreciation on real property, however, may outweigh concerns about moral hazard. Because of the distinction, valuation often varies between personal and real property.

When property is physically damaged or lost, the cost associated with being unable to use that property may go beyond the physical loss, as we saw from the many stories of the aftermath of the September 11 attacks. **Indirect loss** and **business interruption** losses discussed in "Important Issues: Business Interruption Without Direct Physical Loss" of this chapter provides a glimpse into the impact of this coverage on businesses and the importance of the appropriate wording in the policies. In many cases only loss of use of property that is directly damaged leads to coverage; in other cases, the loss of property itself is not a prerequisite to trigger loss of use coverage. You, as a student in this field, will become aware of the importance of the exact meaning of the words in the insurance policy.

General Property Coverage

The first **standard fire policy** (SFP) came into effect during the late 1800s. Two revisions of the SFP were made, in 1918 and 1943. Most recently, the SFP has been largely removed from circulation, replaced instead by homeowners policies for residential property owners, discussed in Chapter 10, and the **commercial package policy** (CPP), featured in Chapter 12. The SFP was simple and relatively clear. Most of its original provisions are still found in current policies, updated for the needs of today's insured. In light of the changes regarding terrorism exclusion that occurred after September 11 (discussed in Chapter 12), the topic of standard fire policies came under review. The issue at hand is that under current laws, standard fire policies cannot exclude fires resulting from terrorism or nuclear attacks without legislative intervention.[1]

Property Coverages and Determination of Payments

Once it is determined that a covered peril has caused a covered loss to covered property, several other policy provisions are invoked to calculate the covered amount of

IMPORTANT ISSUES

Business Interruption without Direct Physical Loss

In August 2002, the luxury hotel chain Wyndham International filed suit against half a dozen of its insurers and the brokerage firm Marsh & McLennan. Wyndham claimed that it had suffered $44 million in lost revenue following the terrorist acts of September 11, and that the insurers had acted in bad faith in failing to pay the corporation's business-interruption claims. The Wyndham properties that reported September 11-related losses included hotels in Chicago and Philadelphia and three Puerto Rico beach resorts. Wyndham owns no properties in downtown New York City.

Part of standard commercial property policies for more than a hundred years, business-interruption insurance coverage was intended to replace operating income only when *direct physical damage* prevented a company from conducting business as usual. In late 1999, companies alarmed about potential Y2K computer failures prepared to argue with their insurers over the definition of "physical damage"; but when the millennium clock struck without damage (physical or electronic), the issue snoozed for two more years.

September 11 was the wake-up call. It's estimated that some $10 billion in claims have been filed for business-interruption losses, much of them far away from Ground Zero. With the Federal Aviation Administration–ordered closing of airports nationwide, the travel industry bore major losses. Resort hotels like Wyndham's saw business fall dramatically. The two Chicago airports calculated that they lost $25 million in takeoff and landing fees, hotels and restaurant taxes, and parking-lot fees. Key3Media is claiming business-interruption losses of $61.5 million because its trade shows in Atlanta and Las Vegas had to be canceled.

Are losses recoverable if the business sustained no physical damage? It depends, of course, on the policy. Most small and midsize businesses have commercial policies based on standard forms developed by the

Insurance Services Office (ISO). The ISO's customary phrase is that the suspension of business to which the income loss relates must be caused by "direct physical loss of or damage to property at the premises described in the Declarations." Larger companies often have custom-written "manuscript" policies that may not be so restrictive. Whatever the wording is, it is likely to be debated in court.

Explore the Internet

Before September 11, the landmark lawsuit over business interruption without direct physical damage was *Archer Daniels Midland Company, et al., v. Hartford Fire Insurance Company.* ADM sought insurance reimbursement after tremendous floods in the upper Mississippi River basin disrupted shipping and railroad transport, which delayed shipments both into and out of its plants. However, no ADM property was damaged in the 1993 flooding, the largest in the U.S. history.

Find the March 2001 decision of the Seventh Circuit Court of Appeals by searching for Archer Daniels Midland or docket no. 98-1608 at www.Findlaw.com, and decide if you agree with the judges. (Legal language is surprisingly easy to understand. Example from Judge Evans Easterbrook: "Hartford and ADM agree that RHH [brokerage firm Rollins Hudig Hall] butchered the job. That's easy for them to say."*) You can also search Findlaw.com for updates on the Wyndham and Key3Media lawsuits.

* As part of this claim, ADM contended that Hartford was liable for damages because Rollins Hudig Hall erred in its role as Hartford's agent. Two years after filing this suit in Illinois, ADM sued Rollins Hudig Hall in Minnesota (*Archer Daniels Midland Co. v. Aon Risk Services, Inc.*, 187 F.R.D. 578 [D. Minn. 1999]), contending that RHH is liable for negligent execution of its duties as ADM's agent.

Sources: Sam Friedman, "9/11 Boosts Focus On Interruption Risks," *National Underwriter, Property & Casualty/Risk & Benefits Management Edition*, April 29, 2002; Joseph B. Treaster, "Insurers Reluctant to Pay Claims Far Afield From Ground Zero," *New York Times*, 12 September 2002; John Foster, "The Legal Aftermath of September 11: Handling Attrition and Cancellation in Uncertain Times," *Convene, the Journal of the Professional Convention Management Association*, December 2001.

compensation. As noted earlier, the topic of covered perils is very important. Catastrophes such as earthquakes are not considered covered perils for private insurance, but in many cases catastrophes such as hurricanes and other weather related catastrophes are covered. The "Ethical Dilemma: Should Insurance Pay for Natural Disasters?" of this chapter is designed to stimulate discussions about the payment of losses caused by catastrophes.

Ethical Dilemma

Who Should Pay for Natural Disasters?

No region of the United States is safe from environmental catastrophes. Floods and flash floods, the most common of all natural disasters, occur in every state. The Midwest's designated "Tornado Alley" ranges from Texas to the Dakotas, though twisters feel free to land just about anywhere. The Pacific Rim states of Hawaii, Alaska, Washington, Oregon, and California are hosts to volcanic activity, most famously the May 1980 eruption of Mount St. Helens in southwestern Washington, which took the lives of more than fifty-eight people. California is also home to the San Andreas Fault, which has birthed nine major earthquakes in the past 100 years; the January 1994 Northridge quake was the most costly in U.S. history, causing an estimated $20 billion in total property damage. (By comparison, the famous San Francisco earthquake of 1906 caused direct losses of $24 million, which would be about $10 billion in today's dollars.) Along the Gulf and Atlantic coasts, "natural disaster" means Hurricane Andrew, which battered Florida and Louisiana in September 1992 and caused fifty-eight deaths, $30 billion in damages—and 700,000 insurance claims.

Andrew cut a swath through Florida insurance companies, forcing seven into bankruptcy. California insurers paid out more in Northridge claims than they had collected in earthquake premiums over the previous thirty years; since California law requires insurers to make earthquake coverage available, many stopped writing homeowners policies altogether. In both states, insurers who wanted to stay in the market could do so only by reducing coverage and increasing premiums. Homeowners on both coasts saw their premiums skyrocket; new buyers had difficulty finding coverage at any price.

Fearing that the suffering housing, construction, and related industries would impair economic growth, state government stepped in. As part of the Hurricane Andrew clean-up, the Florida legislature created the Joint Underwriting Association, a state-sponsored pool to provide property and casualty insurance in coastal areas. The state-run California Earthquake Authority was established in 1996 to provide coverage to residential property owners in high-risk areas. Disaster insurance then went to the federal level: In March 2002, Rep. Dave Weldon of Florida offered to Congress the Homeowners Insurance

Availability Act (H.R. 4025), which would provide federal reinsurance for hurricane and earthquake coverage. The bill, co-sponsored by Reps. Chris John of Louisiana and Robert Matsui of California, is under review by the Subcommittee on Housing and Community Opportunity and the Financial Services Committee. Opponents of the bill argue that disaster reinsurance puts all taxpayers at danger for bailing out those who choose to live in high-risk areas.

Who should bear the financial burden of natural disasters?

Questions for Discussion

1. Lee is in favor of government-supported disaster reinsurance because it encourages economic growth and development. Chris believes that it encourages overgrowth and overdevelopment in environmentally fragile areas. Whose argument do you support?

2. The Gulf Coast town you live in has passed a building code requiring that new beachfront property be built on stilts. If your house is destroyed by a hurricane, rebuilding it on stilts will cost an extra $25,000. The standard homeowners' policy, HO-3, excludes costs caused by ordinance or laws regulating the construction of buildings. Is this fair? Who should pay the extra expense?

3. Jupiter Island, off the coast of south Florida, is the wealthiest town in the country. Its 620 year-round residents earn an average of just over $200,000 per year, per person — thus a typical household of two adults, two children, a housekeeper, a gardener/chauffeur, and a cook boasts an annual income of some $1.4 million. What is the reasoning for subsidizing their hurricane insurance?

Sources: Edwin Unsworth, "Natural disaster losses rise in 2001," *Crain's,* 2 January 2002; Mark E. Ruquet "Experts Say Hurricane Danger Ignored," *National Underwriter Online News Service,* 28 May 2002; Federal Emergency Management Agency, www.fema.gov; Jay Barnes, *Florida's Hurricane History* (University of North Carolina Press, 1998); Insurance Information Institute, "Earthquakes: Risk and Insurance Issues," May 2002, www.iii.org/media/hottopics/insurance/earthquake/; Jim Freer, "State to Help Those Seeking Property, Casualty Insurance," *The South Florida Business Journal,* 15 March 2002.

Important provisions in this calculation are the valuation clause, deductibles, coinsurance and other insurance clause.

Valuation Clause

The intent of insurance is to indemnify an insured. Payment on an **actual cash value** basis is most consistent with the indemnity principle, as discussed in Chapter 6. Yet the deduction of depreciation can be both severe and misunderstood. In response, property insurers often offer coverage on a **replacement cost new** (RCN) basis, which does not deduct depreciation in valuing the loss. Rather, RCN is the value of the lost or destroyed property if it were bought new or rebuilt on the day of the loss.

Deductibles

The cost of insurance to cover frequent losses (as experienced by many property exposures) is high. To alleviate the financial strain of frequent small losses, many insurance policies include a deductible.

A deductible requires the insured to bear some portion of a loss before the insurer is obligated to make any payment. The purpose of deductibles is to reduce costs for the insurer, thus making lower premiums possible. The insurer saves in three ways. First, the insurer is not responsible for the entire loss. Second, because most losses are small, the number of claims for loss payment is reduced, thereby reducing the claims processing costs. Third, the moral and morale hazards are lessened, because there is greater incentive to prevent loss when the insured bears part of the burden.[2]

The small, frequent losses associated with property exposures are good candidates for deductibles, because their frequency minimizes risk (the occurrence of a small loss is nearly certain) and their small magnitude makes retention affordable. The most common forms of deductibles in property insurance are:

1. Straight deductible
2. Franchise deductible
3. Disappearing deductible

A **straight deductible** requires payment for all losses less than a specified dollar amount. If, for example, you have a $200 deductible on the collision coverage part of your auto policy, you pay the total amount of any loss that does not exceed $200. In addition, you pay $200 of every loss in excess of that amount. If you have a loss of $800, therefore, you pay $200 and the insurer pays $600.

A **franchise deductible,** is similar to a straight deductible, except that once the amount of loss equals the deductible, the entire loss is paid in full. This type of deductible is common in ocean marine cargo insurance, although it is stated as a percentage of the value insured rather than a dollar amount. The franchise deductible is also used in crop hail insurance, which provides that losses less than, for example, 5 percent of the crop are not paid, but when a loss exceeds that percentage, the entire loss is paid.

The major disadvantage with the franchise deductible from the insurer's point of view is that the insured is encouraged to inflate a claim that falls just short of the amount of the deductible. If the claims adjuster says your crop loss is 4 percent, you may argue long and hard to get the estimate up to 5 percent. Because it invites moral hazard, a franchise deductible is appropriate only when the insured is unable to influence or control the amount of loss, such as in ocean marine cargo insurance.

The **disappearing deductible** is a modification of the franchise deductible. Instead of having one cut-off point beyond which losses are paid in full, a disappearing deductible decreases as the amount of the loss increases. If, for example, the deductible is $500 to begin with, as the loss increases, the deductible amount decreases, as illustrated in Table 8.1.

At one time, homeowners policies had a disappearing deductible. Unfortunately, it took only a few years for insureds to learn enough about its operation to recognize the benefit of inflating claims. As a result, it was replaced by the straight deductible.

The small, frequent nature of most direct property losses makes deductibles particularly important. Deductibles help maintain reasonable premiums because they eliminate administrative expenses of the low-value, common losses. In addition, the nature of property losses causes the cost of property insurance per dollar of coverage to decline with the increasing percentage of coverage on the property. That is, the first 10 percent value of the property insurance is more expensive than the second (and so on) percent value. The cost of property insurance follows this pattern because most property losses are small, and so the expected loss does not increase in the same proportion as the increased percent of the property value insured.

Coinsurance

A coinsurance provision first requires that you carry an amount of insurance equal to a specified percentage of the value of the property if you wish to be paid the amount of loss you incur. The provision (clause) further stipulates a proportional payment of loss for failure to carry sufficient insurance. It makes sense that if insurance coverage is less than the value of the property, losses will not be paid in full since the premiums charged are for lower values. For property insurance, as long as coverage is at least 80 percent of the value of the property, the property is considered fully covered under the coinsurance provision.

What happens when you fail to have the amount of insurance of at least 80 percent of the value of your building? Nothing happens until you have a partial loss. At that time, you are subject to a penalty. Suppose in January you bought an $80,000 policy for a building with an actual cash value of $100,000, and the policy has an 80 percent **coinsurance clause,** which requires an 80 percent of the value to be covered in order to receive the actual loss. By the time the building suffers a $10,000 loss in November, its actual cash value has increased to $120,000. The coinsurance limit is calculated as follows:

TABLE 8.1	**Amount of Loss**	**Loss Payment**	**Deductible**
How the Disappearing Deductible Disappears	$ 500.00	$ 0.00	$ 500.00
	1,000.00	555.00	445.00
	2,000.00	1,665.00	335.00
	4,000.00	3,885.00	115.00
	5,000.00	4,955.00	5.00
	5,045.00	5,045.00	0.00
	6,000.00	6,000.00	0.00

$$\frac{\text{Amount of insurance carried}}{\text{Amount you agreed to carry}} \times \text{Loss}$$

$$= \frac{\$80,000}{\$96,000 \ (80\% \ of \ \$120,000)} \times \$10,000 = \$8,333.33$$

The amount the insurer pays is $8,333.33. Who pays the other $1,666.67? You do. Your penalty for failing to carry at least 80 percent of the actual value is to bear a part of the loss. You will see in Chapter 10 that you should buy coverage for the value of the home and also include an inflation guard endorsement so that the value of coverage will keep up with inflation.

What if you have a total loss at the time the building is worth $120,000, and you have only $80,000 coverage? Applying the coinsurance formula would yield:

$$\frac{\$80,000}{\$96,000} \times \$120,000 = \$99,999.99$$

You would not receive $99,999.99, however, because the total amount of insurance is $80,000, which is the maximum amount the insurer is obligated to pay. When a loss equals or exceeds the amount of insurance required by the applicable percentage of coinsurance, the coinsurance penalty is not part of the calculation since the limit is the amount of coverage. The insurer is not obligated to pay more than the face amount of insurance in any event, because a typical policy specifies this amount as its maximum coverage responsibility.

You save money buying a policy with a coinsurance clause because the insurer charges a reduced premium rate, but you assume a significant obligation. The requirement is applicable to values only at the time of loss, and the insurer is not responsible for keeping you informed of value changes. That is your responsibility.

E-COMMERCE PROPERTY RISKS

This chapter, as noted above, introduces areas that are growing in importance in the world of insurance. Almost every home, family, and business has risk exposures because of use of computers, the Internet and the Web. Think about your own courses at the university. Each professor emphasizes his or her communication with you on the Web site for the course. You use the Internet as a research tool. Every time you log on, you are exposed to risks from the outside universe. Most familiar to you is the risk of viruses. But there are many additional risk exposures from electronic business, both to you as an individual and to businesses. Businesses with Web presence are those that offer professional services online and/or on-line purchasing. Some businesses are B to C (business to consumer) while others are B to B (business to business). As you saw in Chapter 4, some Web sites are created for promotions rather than for actual transactions.

Regardless of the nature of use of the Internet, cyberattacks have become more frequent and have resulted in large financial losses. According to the 2002 CSI/FBI Computer Crime and Security Survey, Internet-related losses increased from $100 million in 1997 to $456 million in 2002.[3] This study was based on responses from 503 computer security practitioners in U.S. corporations, governmental entities, universities, and other organizations, so the data does not reflect the actual total losses of all businesses, but the magnitude of growth in losses reflects the growing concerns with this risk. Businesses today are becoming aware of their e-commerce risk exposures. In every forum of insurers' meetings and in every insurance media, e-risk exposure is discussed as one of the major "less understood" risk exposures.[4] In this chapter we discuss the hazards and perils of e-commerce risk exposure to the business itself as the first party. In Chapter 9 we will discuss the liability side of the risk exposure of businesses due to the Internet and online connections. Next we discuss the hazards and perils of electronic business in general.

Causes of Loss in E-commerce

The 2002 CSI/FBI survey provided many categories of cause of losses in the computer/electronic systems area. The list included theft of proprietary information, sabotage of data networks, telecom eavesdropping (listening when not expected), system penetration by outsider, insider abuse of Net access, financial fraud, denial of service, spoofing (sending false information/deception), virus, unauthorized insider access, telecom fraud, active wiretapping, and laptop theft. The survey results revealed that most of the detected systems interruptions were virus attacks; second were insiders' abuse of Internet access; and third were thefts of laptops. Many of the respondents could not quantify the actual loss. The reported results showed that in dollar losses, theft of proprietary information had the largest level of loss for 2002, with $171 million; second was financial fraud, with $116 million; and third were viruses, with $50 million. Sixty percent of the respondents said they suffered unauthorized use of their computer systems in 2002. The points of attacks were from the Internet, remote dial, and internal systems. The likely sources of attack in 2002 were independent hackers, disgruntled employees, U.S. competitors, foreign corporations, and foreign governments. Global and political risk will be discussed next in this chapter

The 2002 CSI/FBI survey covered a wide spectrum of risk exposure in e-commerce, for both first party (property and business interruption) and third party (liability losses, covered in Chapter 9) losses. As you can see from this summary of the survey, the causes of **e-commerce property risks** are numerous. We can group these risks into four broad categories:

- Hardware and software thefts; information asset losses and corruption due to hackers, vandalism, and viruses
- Technological changes
- Regulatory and legal changes
- Trademarks infringements

Hardware and Software

Companies have rapidly become dependent on computers. When a company's computer system is down, regardless of the cause, the company risks losing weeks, months, possibly years of data. Businesses store the majority of their information on computers. Customer databases, contact information, supplier information, order forms, and virtually all documents a company uses to conduct business are stored on the computer system. Losses from theft of proprietary information, sabotage of data networks, or telecom eavesdropping can cause major losses to the infrastructure base of a business, whether it is done by outside hackers or inside disgruntled employees.

Hackers and crackers can cause expensive, if not fatal, damage to a company's computer systems. **Hackers** are virtual vandals who try to poke holes in a company's security network.[5] Hackers may be satisfied with defacing Web sites, while **crackers** are hackers who want to break in and steal proprietary information for personal gain. Potential terrorists are usually classified as crackers. Their objective is to hit specific companies in order to bring systems down, steal data, or modify data to destroy its integrity. A third group are

insiders who are upset with the company for some reason, perhaps because of a layoff or a failure to get an expected promotion. Inside access to the company computer network, and the knowledge of how to use it, gives this group the potential to cause the most damage to a business.

A **virus** is a program or code that replicates itself inside of a personal computer or a workstation with the intent to destroy an operating system or control program. When it replicates, it infects another program or document.[6]

Rapid Advances in Technology

Another risk companies face in the cyber world is the rapid advancement of technology. When a company updates its computer system, its software package, or the process for conducting business using the computer system, business is interrupted while employees learn how to conduct business using the new system. The result of this downtime is lost revenue.

Regulatory and Legal Risk

Almost as quickly as the Internet is growing, the government is adding and changing applicable e-commerce laws. In the past, there were few laws because the Internet was not fully explored nor fully understood, but now laws and regulations are mounting. Thus, companies engaged in e-commerce face legal risks arising from governmental involvement. An example of a law that is likely to change is the tax-free Internet sale. There is no sales tax imposed on merchants (and hence the consumer) on Internet sales between states, partly because the government has not yet determined how states should apportion the tax revenue. As the volume of online purchases increases, so do the consequences of lost sales tax revenue from e-commerce.

Lack of qualified lawyers to handle cases that arise out of e-commerce disputes is another new risk. There are many areas of e-law that lawyers are not yet specialized in. Not only are laws complex and tedious, they are also changing rapidly. As a result, it is difficult for lawyers to stay abreast of each law that governs and regulates cyberspace.

Trademarks

Domain name disputes are a serious concern for many businesses. In most cases, disputes over the rights to a domain name result from two specific events. **Domain name hijacking** occurs when an individual or a business reserves a domain name that uses the trademark of a competitor. The other event arises when a business or an individual reserves the well-recognized name or trademark of an unrelated company as a domain name with the intent of selling the domain name to the trademark holder. Seeking compensation for the domain name from the rightful trademark holder is known as **cybersquatting.**[7]

A recent case involving cybersquatting is *People for the Ethical Treatment of Animals vs. Doughney*. In August 2001, the Fourth Circuit Court of Appeals held that the defendant, Michael Doughney, was guilty of service mark infringement and unfair competition, and had violated the Anti-Cybersquatting Consumer Protection Act (ACPA). Doughney had created a web site at www.peta.org, which contained the registered service mark PETA. People for the Ethical Treatment of Animals (PETA) is an animal rights organization that opposes the exploitation of animals for food, clothing, entertainment, and vivisection. When users typed in www.peta.org, they expected to arrive at the site for People for the Ethical Treatment of Animals. Surprisingly, they arrived at People Eating Tasty Animals, a "resource for those who enjoy eating meat, wearing fur and leather, hunting, and the fruits of scientific research." The site contained links to a number of organizations that held views generally opposing those of PETA.[8] On two occasions, Doughney suggested that if PETA wanted one of his domains, or objected to his registration, it could "make me an offer" or "negotiate a settlement."

Web site hijacking occurs when a Web site operator knowingly deceives the user by redirecting the user to a site the user did not intend to view. A recent case, *Ford Motor Company vs. 2600 Enterprises, et al.,* caught attention in December 2001 when 2,600 Enterprises automatically redirected users from a Web site they operate at a domain name directing profanity at General Motors to the Web site operated by Ford at www.ford.com. The defendants redirected users by programming an embedded link, which utilized Ford's mark, into the code of the defendants' Web site.[9] Domain-name hijacking, cybersquatting, and Web site hijacking for the sake of parody or satire is protected by the First Amendment, but sometimes the pranksters' only purpose is to harass or extract profit from the trademark owner.[10]

Risk Management of E-commerce Exposures

Businesses can take loss control steps to reduce the e-commerce property and business interruption risks by using the following:

- Security products and processes
- System audits
- Antivirus protection
- Backup systems and redundancies
- Data protection and security
- Passwords
- Digital signatures
- Encryption
- Firewalls
- Virtual private network (VPN)

Businesses today buy electronic security systems and develop many steps to reduce the risk of data and hardware losses. Firms conduct regular system audits to test for breaches in network security. Auditors attempt to break into various components of the company computer system, including the operating systems, networks, databases, servers, Web servers, and business processes in general, to simulate attacks and discover weaknesses.[11] Managed security services provide an option for virus protection. They include both antivirus protection and firewall installation.

Regular system backup processes and off-site systems saved many businesses hurt by the September 11 attacks. One advantage of keeping back-up data files off site is having clean data in case of damage in the original files from viruses, hackers, and crackers. Since security may be breached from people within the company, Internet access is generally available only to authorized (via the use of passwords) internal and external users. E-mails are easy to intercept and read as they travel across the Internet. Attaching a digital signature allows the recipient to discern whether the document has been altered.[12] Another method to protect e-mails is **encryption.** It allows the sender of a file to scramble the contents of the document. Before the recipient can read the message, he or she needs to use a password for a private key. Encryption is used for confidential communications.

A **firewall** is another loss control solution that protects the local area network (LAN) or corporate network from unauthorized access. A firewall protects a network from intrusion by preventing access unless certain criteria are met. Another loss control technique is the **virtual private network** (VPN), which connects satellite offices with a central location.

VPNs allow remote users to gain secure access to a corporate network. VPNs provide endless opportunities for telecommuters, business travelers, and multiple independent offices of a bigger company.

E-commerce Property Insurance

Traditional property insurance covers physical damage to tangible property due to an insured peril. Electronic data can be considered property in most instances, but standard commercial insurance policies, discussed in Chapter 12, contain exclusions that "explicitly invalidate coverage for exposures in relation to the use of technology."[13] Some insurers now offer customized e-commerce insurance policies that expand the areas of coverage available for e-commerce property risk. Appendix C-1 (also discussed in Chapter 12) shows an ISO e-commerce endorsement that modifies insurance provided under commercial property coverage. Under this endorsement,

> insurers will pay for the cost to replace or restore electronic data which has suffered loss or damage by a Covered Cause of Loss ... including the cost of data entry, re-programming and computer consultation services.

The endorsement has four sections. Section I describes the electronic data coverage. Section II defines the period of coverage as well as the coverage of business income, extra expenses, and resumption of e-commerce activity. Section III classifies covered and excluded perils; exclusions include mechanical breakdown; downtime due to viruses, unless the computer is equipped with antivirus software; errors or omissions in programming or data processing; errors in design, maintenance, or repair; damage to one computer on the network caused by repair or modification of any other computer on the network; interruption as a result of insufficient capacity; and unexplained failure. Section IV of the endorsement is for other provisions as explained in Chapter 7.

In addition to this endorsement, a few insurers have created a variety of e-commerce policies. Some of the companies include ACE USA, Chubb, AIG, the Fidelity and Deposit Companies (members of Zurich Financial Services Group), Gulf Insurance Group, Legion Indemnity Company, and Lloyd's of London. This list is by no means all-inclusive.[14] These companies provide not only first-party e-commerce property and business interruption coverage, but also liability coverage for third-party liability risks. The liability coverage will be discussed in Chapter 9. Since e-commerce does not see boundaries, many policies provide worldwide e-commerce coverage.

GLOBAL PROPERTY EXPOSURES

As with the Internet, global exposure is rapidly growing for many companies. This forces management to think about the unique problems that arise when companies cross national borders. In a survey conducted by the insurance broker Aon[15] of *Fortune* 1000 companies in the United States, 26 percent of the respondents felt comfortable with their political risk exposure and 29 percent felt comfortable with their global financial or economic risk exposure. While most respondents felt comfortable with their property/casualty coverages, only a small percentage felt comfortable with their political risk protection. The survey was conducted during May 2001, before the September 11 attack.

Political risk can be defined as unanticipated political events that disrupt the earning or profit-making ability of an enterprise. In The Risk Report "Managing Political Risks," insurance expert Kevin M. Quinley describes some of the perils that can trip a global organization: nationalization, privatization, expropriation (taken away by the other nation according to its laws), civil unrest, revolution, foreign exchange restrictions, labor regulations, kidnapping, terrorism, seizure, and forfeiture. Some of the risks are considered political risks while others are economic risks. Table 8.2 explains some of these risks. In summary the main categories of global risk exposure are as follows:

- Destabilized international political environment, especially after September 11
- Terrorism risk that has been heightened by the September 11 attack
- Legal risk due to changes in local laws
- Lack-of-data risk
- Currency inconvertibility risk
- Cultural barriers risks

According to The Risk Report, the nature of the risks has changed. Twenty years ago the major risk was in the area of nationalization of capital assets, while the perils of today are more related to economic integration and the power of international financial market. It is the consensus that political risk looms larger after September 11. Following the September 11 attack, Marsh, one of the largest insurance brokers, began providing political risk assessment services to clients worldwide.[16] The consulting includes formulating and reviewing crisis management plans for events such as natural disasters, product recalls, and terrorism. The plans are comprehensive, and integrated throughout the enterprise. Integrated risk programs are featured in Case 3 at the back of the textbook.

Legal Risk

Often the decision to undertake operations in a particular country is made apart from any risk management considerations. Although the legal environment may have been carefully reviewed from the standpoint of firm operations, little information may have been obtained about insurance requirements and regulations. For example, in many countries social insurance is much broader than in the United States and there are few, if any, alternatives available to the risk manager. The risk manager may be forced by regulations to purchase local coverage that is inadequate in covered perils or limits of liability. Particularly in less developed countries, there simply may not be adequate insurance capacity to provide desirable amounts and types of coverage. The risk manager then must decide whether or not to ignore the regulations and use nonadmitted coverage.

Nonadmitted coverage involves contracts issued by a company not authorized to write insurance in the country where the exposure is located. **Admitted insurance** is written by companies so authorized. Nonadmitted contracts have advantages to some U.S. policyholders: They are written in English; use United States dollars for premiums and claims, thus avoiding exchange rate risk; utilize terms and conditions familiar to United States risk managers; and provide flexibility in underwriting. However, such contracts may be illegal in some countries, and the local subsidiary may be subject to penalties if their existence becomes known. Further, premium payment may not be tax deductible, even in countries where nonadmitted coverages are permitted. If nonadmitted insurance is purchased where it is prohibited, claim payments must be made to the parent corporation, which then has to find a way to transfer the funds to the local subsidiary.

Coverage is also affected by the codification of the legal system in the other countries. The Napoleonic code, for example, is used in France, Belgium, Egypt, Greece, Italy, Spain, and several other countries. Under this legal system, liability for negligence is not treated in the same way as liability is treated under the United States system of common law; any negligence not specifically mentioned in the code is dismissed. The common law system is based on legal precedent, and the judges play a much more significant role.

Data Risk

Another problem facing the international risk manager is the collection of adequate statistical information. Economic and statistical data commonly available in the United States may simply be nonexistent in other parts of the world. For example, census data providing an accurate reflection of mortality rates may not be available. Even in industrialized countries statistics may need careful scrutiny, because the method used to produce them may be vastly different from that typical to the risk manager. This is particularly true of rate-making data. Data may also be grossly distorted for political reasons. Officially stated inflation rates, for instance, are notoriously suspect in many countries.

Faced with this lack of reliable information, the risk manager has little choice but to proceed with caution until experience and internal data collection can supplement or confirm other data sources. Contacts with other firms in the same industry and with other foreign subsidiaries can provide invaluable sources of information.

Data collection and analysis are a problem not only in this broad sense. Communication between the corporate headquarters and foreign operations becomes difficult due to language barriers, cultural differences, and often a sense of antagonism about a noncitizen's authority to make decisions. Particularly difficult under these circumstances are the identification and evaluation of exposures and the implementation of risk management tools. Loss control, for instance, is much more advanced and accepted in the United States than in most other countries. Encouraging foreign operations to install sprinklers, implement safety programs, and undertake other loss control steps generally is quite difficult. Further, risk managers of United States–based multinational firms may have difficulty persuading foreign operations to accept retention levels as high as those used in the United States. Retention simply is not well accepted elsewhere. More on retentions is featured in Case 3 at the back of the textbook.

Currency Risk

Any multinational transaction, where payments are transferred from one currency to another, is subject to exchange rate risk. Under the current system of floating exchange rates, the rate of currency exchange between any two countries is not fixed and may vary substantially over time. Current exchange risk is in the area of liquidity and convertibility between currencies. The risk exposure is the inability of the global firm to exchange the currency and transfer out of hostile country. How this kind of risk can be mitigated is shown in Case 4 concerning Hometown bank. The swap idea can be used for foreign currency as well.

Cultural Differences Risk

As we are very acutely aware after the September 11 attack, cultural differences are at the root of much of the trouble around the world. But, this is not only in hostile events. When a business expands abroad, one of the first actions is the study of the local culture of doing business. If you ever were in the market in old Jerusalem you may have experienced the differences in shopping. You learn very quickly that a merchant never expects you to buy the item for the quoted price. The haggling may take a long time. You may leave and come back before you buy the item you liked for less than half the originally quoted price. This is the culture. You are expected to bargain and negotiate. Another cultural difference is the "connection" or "protection." Many business moves will never happen without the right connection with the right people in power.

Labor laws reflect another interesting cultural differences. In some countries, it is common to employ very young children—an act that is against the law in the U.S. The families in these countries depend heavily on the income of their children. But, an American business in such countries may be faced with an ethical dilemma: should it employ children, or adhere to the U.S. practices and labor laws?[17]

Global Risk Management

The steps in global risk management include processes to reduce risk and develop loss control policies along with obtaining the appropriate insurance. Table 8.2 lists ways to manage political risks. The steps include learning the culture of the country and becoming a good corporate citizen, learning about the reality of the country and finding ways to avoid political and legal traps. In the area of insurance, first the global firm looks for "public" insurance policies. The United States government established an insurance program administered through the Overseas Private Investment Corporation (OPIC) in 1948. Coverages available include expropriation, confiscation, war risks, civil strife, unfair calling of guarantees, contract repudiation, and currency inconvertibility. These are shown in Table 8.2. OPIC insurance is available only in limited amounts and only in certain developing countries that have signed bilateral trade agreements with the United States for projects intended to aid development. Some private insurers, however, also provide political risk insurance. Private insurers do not have the same restrictions as OPIC, but country limits do exist to avoid catastrophe (dependent exposure units). Additional coverages such as kidnap, ransom, and export license cancellation are also provided by private insurers. Poor experience in this line of insurance has made coverage more difficult and costly to obtain.

After September 11, some insurers pulled out of the political risk market while others took the opportunity to expand their global coverage offerings. A Canadian insurer reported that the demand for insurance for employee political risk and kidnap and ransom

TABLE 8.2	
Ten Ways to Tune Up Management of Political Risks	1. Look closely at foreign operations—current or planned—and identify all possible political risks
	2. Examine the locale of each foreign operation and stratify them along a risk continuum, according to susceptibility of political risks
	3. Explore "public" political risk insurance coverage through facilities such as MIGA and OPIC.
	4. Allow plenty of lead-time for procuring insurance for political risk coverage.
	5. Seek multiyear policies or coverage for as long a time frame as possible. Keep tight-lipped as to the existence of any political risk coverage you obtain.
	6. Engage an insurance broker who is specialized in procuring political risk coverage.
	7. Invest in infrastructure in host countries and cultivate a strong track record of being a good corporate citizen.
	8. Fine-tune security and anti-hijacking procedures to address the potential loss from kidnapping, ransom, extortion, or terrorism.
	9. Make sure that retention of any political risks is accompanied by realistic funding mechanisms.
	10. Strive to bring the same thoroughness to political risk management as the organization brings to more "mainstream" risks such as fire, flood, earthquake, and workers' compensation.

* Reproduced with permission of the publisher, International Risk Management Institute, Inc., Dallas, Texas, from The risk Report, copyright International Risk Management Institute, Inc., author Kevin Quinley CPCU, ARM. Further reproduction prohibited. For subscription information, phone 800-827-4242. Visit www.IRMI.com for practical and reliable risk and insurance information.

for a dozen global companies increased by 100 percent.[18] Zurich North America and Chubb expanded their political risk insurance offerings to the Asian market.[19] The private insurance market's ability to meet the demand has been strengthening each year since customers require a broader coverage with longer terms, up to ten years. Other companies expanding into the market are Bermuda's Sovereign Risk, AIG, and Reliance, among others.

Until recently, long-term political risk insurance was mostly available from international government agencies such as the Washington-based Multilateral Investment Guarantee Corp., (MIGA) a member of the World Bank Group; the U.S. Overseas Private Investment Corp (OPIC, mentioned above); the United Kingdom's Export Credit Guarantee Department and the French government's export credit agency, Coface. But now the private market has been competing in the longer-term coverages and has opened coverage to losses caused by war and currency inconvertibility. Capacity and limits increased as reinsurance became more available in this area of global risks. Lloyd's of London, for example, offered about $100 million in limits in 2002, a huge increase from the $10 million it could provide in 1992, according to Investment Insurance International, the specialist political risk division of Aon Group. AIG has increased its limits to $30 million per risk while the rest of the private market had about $55 million to work with.

Coverage is even available in Israel, where major concerns about security made investors and business people nervous. A political risk team at Lloyd's (MAP Underwriting) developed a policy to address those concerns.[20] The policy gives peace of mind to businesses that believe in the economic future of Israel by protecting the effects of "war and other political violence on their investments, property and personnel." This specific coverage includes acts of war.

As noted in Table 8.2, some global firms use captives for this exposure. Captives were discussed in Chapter 5.

KEY TERMS

e-commerce	straight deductible	Web site hijacking
global risk	franchise deductible	encryption
first party	disappearing deductible	firewall
third party	coinsurance clause	virtual private network
physical property	e-commerce property risks	political risk
real property	hackers	nonadmitted coverage
personal property	crackers	admitted insurance
standard fire policy	insiders	business interruption
commercial package policy	virus	indirect loss
actual cash value	domain name hijacking	
replacement cost new	cybersquatting	

DISCUSSION QUESTIONS

1. What is a deductible? Provide illustrative examples of straight, franchise, and disappearing deductibles.
2. What is the purpose of coinsurance? How does the policyholder become a "coinsurer"? Under what circumstances does this occur?
3. What is a standard policy? Why is a standard policy desirable (or undesirable)?
4. What are the risk exposures of e-commerce?
5. How should the property risk of e-commerce be managed?

6. Describe the parts of an e-commerce endorsement. Use the endorsement available in Appendix C-1

7. What is different about international property exposures as compared with U.S. property exposures?

8. Provide an example of a business interruption loss and of an extra expense loss in the e-commerce endorsement.

9. Describe the steps of political risk management.

EXERCISES

8.1 Assume you live on the Texas gulf coast, where hurricane damage can be extensive. Further assume that you own a two-story frame home valued at $120,000. You insured the house for $80,000, which was your purchase price four years ago. Respond to the following questions relating to co-insurance (assume 80 percent co-insurance is required):

a. If you had a total loss, what reimbursement would you receive from your insurer?

b. If you had a loss of $10,000, what reimbursement would you receive?

8.2 Erin Lavinsky works for the Pharmacy On-Line company in Austin, Texas. She uses her business computer for personal matters and has received a few infected documents. She was too lazy to update her Norton Utilities and did not realize that she was sending her infected material to her co-workers. Before long, the whole system collapsed and business was interrupted for a day until the back-up system was brought up. Respond to the following questions:

a. Describe the types of risk exposures Pharmacy On-Line is facing as a result of e-commerce.

b. If Pharmacy On-Line purchased the ISO endorsement in Appendix C-1, would it be covered for the lost day?

c. Describe what other risk exposures could interrupt the business of Pharmacy On-Line.

8.3 Marina Del Ro shipping company expanded its operations to the Middle East just before September 11. Respond to the following questions:

a. What are the global risk exposures of Marina Del Ro?

b. What should Marina Del Ro do to mitigate these risks in terms of non-insurance and insurance solutions?

NOTES

1. For more information, the student is invited to read the article "Standard Fire Policy Dates Back to 19th Century," by featured in *Best's Review,* April 2002.

2. For example, residents of a housing development had full coverage for windstorm losses (that is, no deductible). Their storm doors did not latch properly, so wind damage to such doors was common. The insurer paid an average of $100 for each loss. After doing so for about six months, it added a $50 deductible to the policies as they were renewed. Storm door losses declined markedly when insureds were required to pay for the first $50 of each loss.

3. Richard Power, "Computer Security Issues & Trends," Vol. VIII Mo I. The survey was conducted by the Computer Security Institute with the participation of the San Francisco Federal Bureau of Investigation's Computer Intrusion Squad. Established in 1974, CSI has thousands of members worldwide and provides a wide variety of information and education programs to assist in protecting the information assets of corporations and governmental organizations. For more information go to http://www.gocsi.com.

4. For example, see Lee McDonald, "Insurer Points Out Risks of E-Commerce," *Best's Review,* February 2000; Ron Lent, "Electronic Risk Gives Insurers Pause," *National Underwriter,* Property & Casualty/Risk & Benefits Management Edition, 7 May 2001; Caroline Saucer, "Technological Advances: Web Site Design Provides Clues to Underwriting Online Risks," *Best's Review,* December 2000.

5. George S. Sutcliffe, Esq. *E-Commerce and Insurance Risk Management,* (Boston: Standard Publishing Corp., 2001) p. 13.

6. Adapted from the online glossary of Symantec, a worldwide provider of Internet security solutions, at www.symantec.com/avcenter/refa.html.

7. See note 5.

8. *People for the Ethical Treatment of Animals v. Doughney,* No. 00-1918 (4th Cir2001); www.phillipsnizer.com/internetlib.htm

9. *Ford Motor Company v. 2600 Enterprises, et al.,* 177 F. Supp. 2d 661, 2001, U.S. District Court Lexis 21302 (E.D. Michigan2001); www.phillipsnizer.com/int-trademark.htm.

10. Monte Enbysk "Hackers and Vandals and Worms, Oh My!" Microsoft bCentral newsletter, www.bcentral.com.

11. Kevin Coleman, "How E-Tailers and Online Shoppers Can Protect Themselves," Web site of accounting firm KPMG, www.kpmg.com.

12. See note 5.

13. "New Policy Offered To Cover Tech Risks," *National Underwriter* Online News Service, 2 July 2002.

14. See note 5.

15. Mark E. Ruquet, "Big Firms Worry About Coverage For Political Risks Abroad," *National Underwriter* Online News Service, 9 August 2001. The Aon survey asked 122 risk managers, chief financial officers, and others in similar positions of responsibility to assess various aspects of their overseas risks. The surveys were done by telephone, and in some cases over the Internet.

16. "Marsh To Begin Crisis Consulting Led By Anti-Terror Expert" *National Underwriter* Online News Service, 12 October 2001.

17. Phyllis S. Myers and Etti G. Baranoff, "Ethics in Insurance," Academy of Insurance Education, Washington D.C., Instructional video with supplemental study guide. (Video produced by the Center for Video Education, 1997)

18. Daniel Hays, "Insurer Finds Good Market In Political Risk," National Underwriter Online News Service, 28 November 2001.

19. "Zurich North America Expands Political Risk Insurance to Asian Market," *National Underwriter* Online News Service, 6 April 2002; John Jennings, "Political Risk Cover Demand Surges: Insurers" *National Underwriter* Property & Casualty/Risk & Benefits Management Edition, 27 April 1998.

20. "Armed-Conflict Risks Covered," *National Underwriter,* Property & Casualty/Risk & Benefits Management Edition, 11 June 2001.

CHAPTER 9

The Liability Risk

As noted in Chapter 8, liability risk is the risk that we may hurt a third party and will be sued for bodily injury or other damages. Most of us have heard about auto liability, pollution liability, product liability, medical malpractice, and professional liability of lawyers, accountants, company directors and officers, and more. As of the writing of this text, the country is mired in the accounting scandals of Enron and WorldCom. While liability insurance is for unintentional actions, the fear of having to pay liability claims because of the errors and omissions of the accountants has caused insurance rates in these coverages to jump dramatically. The relationships between behavior and coverages will be strongly demonstrated in this chapter. The chapter will cover:

1. Connection
2. Nature of the liability exposure
3. Major sources of liability

CONNECTION

As discussed in the Connection section in Chapter 8, liability coverage is a coverage for a third party that may suffer a loss because of your actions. It also covers you in case you are hurt or your property is damaged because of someone else's actions, such as the actions of the accountants and executives of Enron and WorldCom. The harmed parties are investors and the employees of these companies. In personal lines coverages such as homeowners and auto policies, the liability of **property damage** or **bodily injury** you may inflict on others is covered up to a limit. In commercial lines, you may use a packaged multi-lines policy that also includes liability coverage. In this chapter we focus only on the liability sections of these policies.

As part of your holistic risk management program, you now realize that you need a myriad of policies to cover all your liability exposures. In many cases both the property and liability are in the same policies, but what liability coverage is actually included in each policy? As we delve further into insurance policies, we find many types of liability coverages. As you will see in this chapter, businesses have a vast number of liabilities: product, errors and omissions, professional, directors and officers, e-commerce, medical, employment, employee benefits, and more. The aftermath of September 11 revealed additional liabilities from terrorism. Liability risk exposure is scary for any individual or business, especially in such a litigious society as the United States. But it is important to have the recourse when someone has been wronged, as during the scandals of accounting irregularities and management fraud.

To better understand the complete holistic risk management process, it is imperative for us to understand all sections of the liability coverages in all the policies we hold. Figure 9.1 shows the connection among the coverages and the complete puzzle of risk. At this point we are drilling down into a massive type of risk exposure, which is covered by a myriad of policies. Our ability to connect them all allows us to complete the picture of our holistic risk.

FIGURE 9.1

Connection Between
Liability Risks and
Insurance Contracts

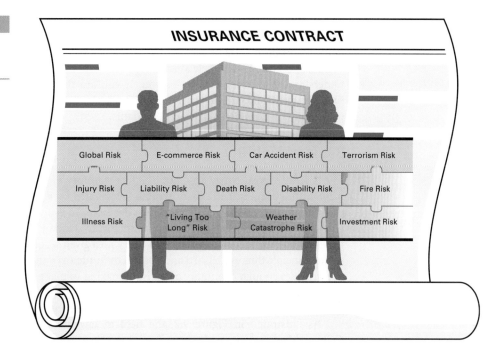

FIGURE 9.1

Connection Between
Liability Risks and
Insurance Contracts

NATURE OF THE LIABILITY EXPOSURE

Legal liability is the responsibility, based in law, to remedy some wrong done to another person or organization. Several aspects of this definition deserve further discussion. One involves the "remedy" of liability. A person who has been "wronged" or harmed in some way may ask the court to remedy or compensate him for the harm. Usually this will involve monetary compensation, but it could also involve some behavior on the part of the person who committed the wrong, the **tortfeasor.** For example, someone whose water supply has been contaminated by a polluting business may request an injunction against the business to force the cessation of pollution. A developer who is constructing a building in violation of code may be required to halt construction, based on a liability lawsuit.

When monetary compensation is sought, it can take one of several forms. **Special damages** compensate for those harms generally easily quantifiable into dollar measures. These include medical expenses, lost income, and repair costs of damaged property. Sometimes special damages are termed **economic damages.** Those harms that are not specifically quantifiable, but which are just as real, are called **general damages** or **non-economic damages.** Examples of non-economic or general damages include pain and suffering, mental anguish, and loss of consortium (companionship). The third type of monetary liability award is **punitive damages,** which was discussed in "Ethical Dilemma: Are Punitive Damages Out of Control?" in Chapter 7. In this chapter we will continue to discuss the controversy surrounds the use of punitive damages. Punitive damages are considered awards intended to punish a tortfeasor for exceptionally undesirable behavior. Punitive damages are intended not to compensate for actual harm incurred but rather to punish.

A second important aspect of the definition of liability is that it is "based in law." In this way, liability differs from other exposures because it is purely a creation of societal rules (laws), which reflect social norms. As a result, liability exposures will differ across societies (nations) over time. In the United States, liability is determined by the courts and by laws enacted by legislatures.

The risk of liability is twofold. Not only may you become liable to someone else and suffer loss, but someone else may become liable to you and have to pay you. You need to know about both sides of the coin, so to speak. Your financial well-being or that of your organization can be adversely affected by your responsibility to others or by your failure to understand their responsibility to you. If you are the party harmed, you would be the **plaintiff** in litigation. The party being sued is the **defendant.** In some circumstances the parties will be both plaintiffs and defendants.

Basis of Liability

The liability exposure may arise out of either statutory or common law, as shown in Figure 9.2. **Statutory law** is the body of written law created by legislatures. **Common law,** on the other hand, is based on custom and court decisions. In evolving common law, the courts are guided by the doctrine of **stare decisis** (Latin for "to stand by the decisions"). Under this doctrine, once a court decision is made in a case with a given set of facts, the courts tend to adhere to the principle thus established and apply it to future cases involving similar facts. This practice provides enough continuity of decision making so that many disputes can be settled out of court by referring to previous decisions. Some people believe that in recent years, as new forms of liability have emerged, continuity has not been as prevalent as in the past.

As illustrated in Figure 9.2, the field of law includes criminal law and civil law. **Criminal law** is concerned with acts that are contrary to public policy (crimes), such as murder or burglary. **Civil law,** in contrast, deals with acts that are not against society as a whole, but rather cause injury or loss to an individual or organization, such as carelessly running a car into the side of a building. A civil wrong may also be a crime. Murder, for instance, attacks both society and individuals. Civil law has two branches, one concerned with the law of contracts and the other with the law of torts explained in the next paragraph. Civil liability may stem from either contracts or torts.

FIGURE 9.2

Basis of Liability Risk

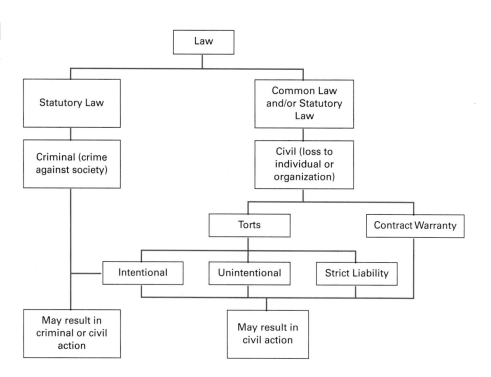

Contractual liability occurs in many settings. When you sign a rental agreement for tools, for example, the agreement may provide that the tools will be returned to the owner in good condition, ordinary wear and tear excepted. If they are stolen or damaged, you are liable for the loss. As another example, if you offer your car for sale and assure the buyer that it is in perfect condition, you have made a **warranty.** A warranty is simply a form of contract. If the car is not in perfect condition, you may be liable for damages because of a breach of warranty. This is why some sellers offer goods for sale on an "as is" basis; they want to be sure there is no warranty.

A **tort** is "a private or civil wrong or injury, other than breach of contract, for which the court will provide a remedy in the form of an action for damages."[1] That is, all civil wrongs, except breach of contract, are torts. A tort may be intentional, in that it is committed for the purpose of injuring another person or the person's property, or it may be unintentional. Examples of intentional torts include libel, slander, assault, and battery, as you will see in the contracts provided as appendices at the back of the text. While a risk manager may have occasion to be concerned about liability arising from intentional torts, the more frequent source of liability is the unintentional tort. By definition, unintentional torts involve **negligence.**

If someone suffers bodily injury or property damage as a result of your negligence, you may be liable for damages. Negligence refers to conduct or behavior. It may be a matter of doing something you should not do, or failing to do something you should. Negligence can be defined as a failure to act reasonably that causes harm to others. It is determined by proving the existence of four elements (sometimes people use three, combining the last two into one). These are:

- A duty to act (or not to act) in some way
- Breach of that duty
- Damage or injury to the one owed the duty
- A causal connection, called a **proximate cause,** between the breach and the injury

An example may be helpful. When a person operates an automobile, that person has a duty to obey traffic rules and to drive appropriately for the given conditions. A person who drives while drunk, passes in a no-passing zone, or drives too fast on an icy road (even if within set speed limits) has breached the duty to drive safely. If that person completes the journey without an incident, no negligence exists because no harm occurred. If, however, the driver causes an accident in which property damage or bodily injury results, all elements of negligence exist, and legal liability for the resulting harm likely will be placed on the driver.

A difficult aspect of proving negligence is showing that a breach of duty has occurred. Proof requires showing that a reasonable and prudent person would have acted otherwise. Courts use a variety of methods to assess "reasonableness." One is a cost-benefit approach, which holds behavior to be unreasonable if the discounted value of the harm is more than the cost to avoid the harm[2]—that is, if the present value of the possible loss is greater than the expense required to avoid the loss. In this way, courts use an efficiency argument to determine the appropriateness of behavior.

A second difficult aspect of proving negligence is to show a proximate cause between the breach of duty and resulting harm. Proximate cause has been referred to as an unbroken chain of events between the behavior and harm. The intent is to find the relevant cause through assessing liability. The law is written to encourage behavior with consideration of its consequences.

Liability will not be found in all the circumstances just described. The defendant has available a number of defenses, and the burden of proof may be modified under certain fact situations.

Defenses

A number of defenses against negligence exist, with varying degrees of acceptance. A list of defenses is shown in Table 9.1. One is **assumption of risk.** The doctrine of assumption of risk holds that if the plaintiff knew of the dangers involved in the act that resulted in harm, but chose to act in that fashion nonetheless, the defendant will not be held liable. An example would be a bungee cord jumper who is injured from the jump. One could argue that a reasonable person would know that such a jump is very dangerous. If applicable, the assumption of risk defense bars the plaintiff from a successful negligence suit. The doctrine was particularly important in the nineteenth century for lawsuits involving workplace injuries, where employers would defend against liability by claiming that workers knew of job dangers. With workers' compensation statutes in place today, the use of assumption of risk in this way is of little importance, as you will see in Chapter 13. Further, many states have abolished the assumption of risk doctrine in automobile liability cases, disallowing the defense that a passenger assumed the risk of loss if the driver was known to be dangerous or the car unsafe.

A second defense found in just a few states is the doctrine of **contributory negligence,** which disallows any recovery by the plaintiff if the plaintiff is shown to be negligent to any degree in not avoiding the relevant harm. Thus, the motorist who was only slightly at fault in causing an accident may recover nothing from the motorist who was primarily at fault. In practice, a judge or jury is unlikely to find a plaintiff slightly at fault where contributory negligence applies. Theoretically, however, the outcome is possible.

The trend today is away from use of contributory negligence. Instead, most states follow the doctrine of **comparative negligence.** As the name implies, the court compares the relative negligence of the parties and apportions recovery on that basis. At least two applications of the comparative negligence rule may be administered by the courts. Assume that in the automobile example both motorists experienced damages of $100,000, and that one motorist was one percent at fault, the other 99 percent at fault. Under the **partial comparative negligence** rule, only the motorist less than 50 percent at fault receives compensation. The compensation equals the damages multiplied by the percent not at fault, or $99,000 ($100,000 × .99) in our example. Under the **complete comparative negligence** rule, the damages would be shared by both parties. The motorist who was 1 percent at fault still receives $99,000, but must pay the other motorist $1000 ($100,000 × .01), resulting in a net compensation of $98,000. Because few instances exist when a party is completely free of negligence and our society appears to prefer that injured parties be compensated, comparative negligence has won favor over contributory negligence. An important question, though, is how the relative degrees of fault are determined. Generally, a jury is asked to make such an estimate, based on the testimony of various experts. Examples of the application of contributory and comparative negligence are shown in Table 9.2.

Last clear chance is a further defense to liability. Under the last clear chance doctrine, a plaintiff who assumed the risk or contributed to an accident through negligence is not barred from recovery if the defendant had the opportunity to avoid the accident but failed to do so. For instance, the motorist who could have avoided hitting a jaywalker, but did

TABLE 9.1

Defenses Against Liability

- Assumption of risk
- Contributory negligence
- Comparative negligence
- Last clear chance
- Sovereign, familial, and charitable immunity

TABLE 9.2

Contributory and
Comparative
Negligence

Assume that two drivers are involved in an automobile accident. Their respective losses and degrees of fault are as follows:

	Losses	Degree of Fault
Dan	$18,000	.60
Kim	22,000	.40

Their compensation would be determined as follows:

	Contributory	Partial Comparative *	Complete Comparative**
Dan	0	0	7,200
Kim	0	13,200	13,200

* Only when party is less at fault than the other is compensation available. Here Dan's fault exceeds Kim's.

** Complete comparative negligence forces an offset of payment. Kim would receive $6,000 from Dan ($13,200 – 7,200).

not, had the last clear chance to prevent the accident. The driver in this circumstance could not limit liability by claiming negligence on the part of the plaintiff. Today the doctrine has only minor application. It may, however, be used when the defendant employs the defense of contributory negligence against the plaintiff.

Last in this listing of defenses is **immunity.** Where immunity applies, the defendant has a complete defense against liability, merely because of its status as a protected entity, professional, or other party. For example, governmental entities in the United States were long protected under the doctrine of **sovereign immunity.** Sovereign immunity held that governments could do no wrong, and therefore could not be held liable. That doctrine has lost strength in most states, but still exists to some degree in certain circumstances. Other immunities extend to charitable organizations and family members. Like sovereign immunity, these too have lost most of their shield against liability.

Modifications

Doctrines of defense are used to prevent a successful negligence (and sometimes strict liability) lawsuit. Other legal doctrines modify the law to assist the plaintiff in a lawsuit. Some of these are discussed here and listed in Table 9.3.

Rules of negligence hold that an injured person has the burden of proof; that is, he or she must prove the defendant's negligence in order to receive compensation. Courts adhere to these rules unless reasons exist to modify them. In some situations, for example, the plaintiff cannot possibly prove negligence. The court may then apply the doctrine of **res ipsa loquitur** ("the thing speaks for itself"), which shifts the burden of proof to the defendant. The defendant must prove innocence. The doctrine may be used upon proof that the situation causing injury was in the defendant's exclusive control, and that the accident was one that ordinarily would not happen in the absence of negligence. Thus, the event "speaks for itself."

Illustrations of appropriate uses of res ipsa loquitur may be taken from medical or dental treatment. Consider the plaintiff who visited a dentist for the extraction of wisdom teeth and was given a general anesthetic for the operation. Any negligence that may have occurred during the extraction could not be proved by the plaintiff, who could not possibly have

TABLE 9.3

Modifications of
Negligence

- *Res Ipsa Loquitur*
- Strict liability
- Vicarious liability
- Joint and several liability

observed the negligent act. If, upon waking, the plaintiff has a broken jaw, res ipsa loquitur might be employed.

Doctrines with similar purposes to res ipsa loquitur may be available when a particular defendant cannot be identified. Someone may be able to prove by a preponderance of evidence, for example, that a certain drug caused an adverse reaction, but be unable to prove which company manufactured the particular bottle consumed. Courts may shift the burden of proof to the defendants in such a circumstance.[3]

Liability may also be "strict" (or, less often, absolute), rather than based on negligence. That is, if you have property or engage in an activity that is ultra-dangerous to others, you may become liable on the basis of **strict liability,** without regard to fault. In some states, for example, the law holds owners or operators of aircraft liable with respect to damage caused to persons or property on the ground, regardless of the reasonableness of the owner's or operator's actions. Similarly, if you dam a creek on your property to build a lake, you will be liable in most situations for injury or damage caused if the dam collapses and floods the area below. In product liability, discussed later in this chapter, a manufacturer may be liable for harm caused by use of its product, even if the manufacturer was reasonable in producing it. The manufacturer, thus, is strictly liable.

In some jurisdictions, the owner of a dangerous animal is liable by statute for any harm or damage caused by the animal. Such liability is a matter of law. If you own a pet lion, you may become liable for damages regardless of how careful you are. Similarly, the responsibility your employer has in the event you are injured or contract an occupational disease is based on the principle of liability without "fault."[4] Both situations involve strict liability.

In addition, liability may be vicarious. That is, the liability of one person may be based upon the tort of another. An employer, for example, may be liable for damages caused by the negligence of an employee who is on duty. Such an agency relationship may result in **vicarious liability** for the principal (employer) if the agent (employee) commits a tort while acting as an agent. The principal need not be negligent to be liable under vicarious liability. The employee who negligently fails to warn the public of slippery floors while waxing them, for instance, may cause his or her employer to be liable to anyone injured by falling. Vicarious liability will not, however, shield the wrongdoer from liability. It merely adds a second potentially liable party. The employer and employee in this case may both be liable. Recall the case of "vanishing premiums" described in Chapter 6. Insurers were found to have liability because of the actions of their agents.

A controversial modification to negligence is the use of the joint and several liability doctrine. **Joint and several liability** exists when the plaintiff is permitted to sue any of several defendants individually for the full harm incurred. Alternatively, the plaintiff may sue all or a portion of the group together. Under this application, a defendant may be only slightly at fault for the occurrence of the harm, but totally responsible to pay for it. The classic example comes from a case in which a Disney World patron was injured on a bumper car ride.[5] The plaintiff was found 14 percent contributory at fault; another park patron was found 85 percent at fault; and Disney was found 1 percent at fault. Because of the use of the joint and several liability doctrine, Disney was required to pay 86 percent of the damages (the percent the plaintiff was not at fault). Note that this case is an exceptional use of joint and several liability, not the common use of the doctrine.

MAJOR SOURCES OF LIABILITY

Individuals, families, firms, and other organizations are exposed to countless sources of liability. These may be related to the property they own or control, or to their activities (including using an automobile, providing professional services, manufacturing products, or being involved in e-commerce).

Property

You have a duty to the public not only with regard to your activities, but also in connection with real and personal property you own or for which you are responsible. The duty—the degree of care—varies with the circumstances. The owner or tenant of premises, for example, does not owe the same duty to each person who enters the property. The highest degree of care is owed to invitees, whereas the standard of care is less for licensees and lowest for trespassers.

A **trespasser** is a person who enters the premises of another without either express or implied permission from a person with the right to give such permission. Generally, the only duty owed to a trespasser is to refrain from taking steps to harm him or her. There are several exceptions to this, the most important concerning trespassing children. This exception is discussed in connection with the doctrine of "attractive nuisance."

A **licensee** is a person who enters premises with permission but (1) not for the benefit of the person in possession, or (2) without a reasonable expectation that the premises have been made safe. If your automobile breaks down and you ask the owners of the nearest house to use their telephone, the permission you receive to enter the house makes you a licensee. Because a licensee is the party who receives the benefit of entering the property, he or she is entitled to a minimum degree of care by the owner or tenant. An owner or tenant must avoid harm to licensees and must warn licensees of any dangerous activity or condition of the property. They need not, however, make the place safer than it is normally.

An **invitee** is a person who enters the premises with permission and for the benefit of the person in possession. The invitee is entitled to a higher degree of care than a licensee. Thus, a customer in a store is an invitee, whether or not he or she makes a purchase. The property owner is expected to maintain safe premises for invitees and to warn of dangers that cannot be corrected.

For the most part, it is a person's reasonable expectations that determine his or her status. If you reasonably expect that the premises have been made safe for you, you are an invitee. For example, if I invite you to a party at my home, you are an invitee. If you should reasonably expect to accept the premises as is without special effort on the part of the possessor, then you are a licensee. The distinction between a licensee and an invitee is not always clear, because it depends on reasonable expectations. Further, the courts have tended in recent years to place little weight on these distinctions. The question becomes, "What is reasonable of the property owner?" Generally, the owner has the responsibility to provide a reasonably safe environment.

In one case, a guest who fell on a slippery floor was awarded damages against the homeowner. In another case, a visitor fell down steps that were not properly lighted because a worker had failed to turn on a light. Although it was the worker who was negligent, the homeowner had to pay because the worker was his representative. Thus, the property owner's liability was vicarious; he was not negligent, but his employee was. In another case, a homeowner repaired a canopy and then hired a painter. When the painter crawled onto the canopy, the canopy collapsed. The homeowner was held liable for the injuries sustained.

Tenant's Liability to Public

If you are a tenant, you cannot assume that the owner alone will be liable for defects in the premises. In many cases, the injured party will sue both the owner and the tenant.

Furthermore, the owner may shift responsibility to the tenant by means of a **hold-harmless clause** in the lease. A hold harmless agreement is a contractual provision that transfers financial responsibility for liability from one party to another. This is particularly important to understand because many tenants who sign a lease do not realize they are assuming such liability by contract. A typical clause is as follows:

> ...That the lessor shall not be liable for any damage, either to person or property, sustained by the lessee or by any other person, due to the building or any part thereof, or any appurtenances thereof, becoming out of repair, or due to the happening of any accident in or about said building, or due to any act or neglect of any tenant or occupant of said building, or of any other person.

The gist of this clause is to transfer the financial aspects of the landlord's potential liability to the tenant.

Tenant's Liability to Owner

If your negligence results in damage to premises you lease, you may be liable to the owner. The fact that the owner has insurance to cover the damage does not mean you will not be required to pay for the loss. After the insurer pays the owner, the insurer receives subrogation of the owner's right to recover damages, meaning that the insurer is given legal recourse against you for any liability you may have to the owner.

Animals

Ownership of pets and other animals may also result in liability. Anyone owning an animal generally is responsible for damage or injury the animal may cause. In many jurisdictions, if the owner acted reasonably in controlling the animal, no liability will result. For example, in many places a pet dog that has been friendly and tame need not be leashed. Once that dog has bitten someone, however, more control is required. If the dog bites a second person, the owner is likely to be held liable for the harm. In this case, the owner had forewarning.

Likewise, anyone owning dangerous animals such as poisonous snakes or lions is held to a higher standard of care. In this case, strict liability may be applied. Knowledge of the potential danger already exists; thus, the owner must be given strong incentives to prevent harm. Pit bulls may be the most recent addition to this list of dangerous animals.

In a recent highly visible California case, a thirty-three-year-old woman was mauled to death by a 123-pound English mastiff/Presa Canary Island crossbreed. The owners were found guilty of second degree murder by the jury, but the judge, in a surprise move, changed the ruling.[6] This case illuminates statistics from the Center for Disease Control and Prevention in Atlanta, which reports ten to twenty deaths annually from dog bites. Lawmakers in various states enacted laws concerning dogs. The insurance industry also reacted to curtail the losses caused by dogs. In the ISO homeowners policy (see Appendix A-1 at the back of this textbook) there are "special provisions that excludes liability coverage for any insured for bodily injury arising out of the actions of a dangerous or vicious, and out of the insureds failure to keep the dangerous dog leashed or tethered or confined in a locked pen with a top or locked fenced yard. The owners are required to control the dogs and assure the safety of passersby."[7]

Attractive Nuisance

In some cases, small children are attracted by dangerous objects or property. In such circumstances, the owner has a special duty toward the children, especially if they are too young to be entirely responsible. This is called the doctrine of **attractive nuisance.** An attractive nuisance is anything that is (1) artificial, (2) attractive to small children, and (3) potentially harmful. People who own power lawn mowers, for example, must be especially watchful for small children who may be injured through their own curiosity. If you leave your mower running while you go in the house to answer the telephone and there are small children in the neighborhood who may be attracted to the mower, you may be held financially responsible for any harm they experience. The most common attractive nuisance is the swimming pool. Although some courts have held that those who own swimming pools are not necessarily baby-sitters for the community, it appears that pool owners do have the duty of keeping children out. There have been many cases in which children entered a neighbor's pool without permission and drowned. The result is a suit for damages and in many cases a verdict for the plaintiff.

Hazardous Waste

An increasingly important area of potential liability involving property derives from the possibility that land may be polluted, requiring cleanup and/or compensation to parties injured by the pollution. Because of significant legislation passed in the 1970s and 1980s, the cleanup issue may be of greater concern today than previously.

In 1980 the U.S. Congress passed the Comprehensive Environmental Response, Compensation, and Liability Act (known as either CERCLA or Superfund). This act places extensive responsibilities on organizations involved in the generation, transportation, storage, and disposal of hazardous waste. Responsibility generally involves cleaning or paying to clean polluted sites that are dangerous to the public. Estimates of total program costs run from $100 billion to $1 trillion, giving an indication of the potential severity of liability judgments. Any purchaser of realty (or creditor for that purchase) must be aware of these laws and take steps to minimize involvement in Superfund actions. A small amendment to the law was signed by President George W. Bush on January 11, 2002. Under the Small Business Liability Relief and Brownfields Revitalization Act, certain small contributors to Superfund sites were taken out of the liability system. The new law creates incentives for developers to purchase and restore abandoned urban sites known as "brownfields."[8] It is expected that 60 percent of Superfund sites will be cleaned by the end of 2003.

The area of pollution liability is very complex. Decisions have been made regularly in pollution cases. In a recent pollution case that went to the Ohio Supreme Court, Goodyear Tire & Rubber Co. sought to recover the cost of environmental cleanups at some of its sites from its insurers.[9] The insurers claimed that the coverage was excluded under the pollution exclusions provisions. However, the court sided with Goodyear, ordering that Goodyear be allowed to choose from the pool of triggered policies a single primary policy against which to make a claim.

Activities and Conduct

People also may be liable for damages caused by their own actions or those of someone else. In negligence suits, you will be judged on how a "reasonable" person in the same or similar circumstances with your training and ability would have acted. You will be judged according to different criteria for non-negligence suits.

Automobile Liability

Ownership and operation of an automobile is probably the most common source of liability any individual will encounter. Details about this liability will be given in Chapter 11.

As the driver of an automobile, you are responsible for its careful and safe operation. If you do not operate it in a reasonable and prudent fashion and someone is injured as a result of such lack of care, you may be held liable for damages. If, for example, you carelessly drive through a stop sign and run into another car, you may be liable for the damage done.

Through either direct or vicarious liability, the owner of an automobile may be responsible for the damage it causes when driven by another person. In some states, the **family purpose doctrine** makes the owner of the family car responsible for whatever damage it does, regardless of which member of the family may be operating the car at the time of the accident. The theory is that the vehicle is being used for a family purpose, and the owner as head of the family is therefore responsible.

Many parents assume responsibility for their children's automobile accidents without realizing they are doing so. In some states, minors between the ages of sixteen and eighteen are issued driver's licenses only if their application is signed by a parent or guardian. What many parents do not realize is that by signing the application they may assume responsibility for damage arising from the child's driving any automobile. Ordinarily, a child is responsible for his or her own torts, but the parent may become liable by contract.

Vicarious liability is possible in other settings as well. If you lend your car to a friend, Sid Smith, so he can go buy a case of liquor for a party you are having, he will be your agent during the trip and you may be held responsible if he is involved in an accident. Your liability in this case is vicarious; you are responsible for Smith's negligence. On the other hand, if Smith is not a competent driver, you may be held directly liable for putting a dangerous instrument in his hands. In such a case, it is your own negligence for which you are responsible.

A special problem for employers is the risk known as **nonownership liability.** If an employee offers to drop the mail at the post office as he or she drives home from work, the firm may be held liable if the employee is involved in an accident in the process. This possibility is easily overlooked, because the employer may not be aware that employees are using their cars for company business.

Professional Liability

Members of a profession claim to have met high standards of education and training, as well as of character and ethical conduct. They are expected to keep up with developments in their field and maintain the standards established for the profession. As a result, the duty a professional owes to the public is considerably greater than that owed by others. Along with this duty, of course, comes liability for damage caused by failure to fulfill it. People expect more from a professional, and when they do not get it, some sue for damages.

As noted above, at the time of the writing of this textbook, the nation is in the midst of a major scandal involving the accounting profession. With the accounting frauds perpetuated by WorldCom and Enron, and the destruction of documents by the accounting firm Arthur Andersen, it appears that this chapter will not be closed for a long time. The lack of trust of investors, small or large, in the accounting profession and corporate leadership in the United States is being featured daily in the news. Yet the accounting profession was in trouble even before these scandals, as a *National Underwriter* article pointed out amid the media uproar: "In part, the reason for the increases is a shaken faith in the ability of auditors to do the right thing…[it] can be traced back to the use of aggressive accounting by booming Internet companies, who used the now questionable practices to show positive earnings." The accounting practices of dot.com companies brought about an "onslaught of securities litigation, increasing claims for directors and officers and accountants' professional liability insurers."[10]

Errors and Omissions   Professionals' mistakes can result in professional liability claims. The insurance protection for this risk is **errors and omissions liability coverage** (E&O). In light of the Enron/Arthur Anderson debacle and the subsequent WorldCom fraud, it is no wonder that the price for E&O coverage is expected to skyrocket.[11]

Directors and Officers   The outcome of all these accounting irregularities and the pure fraud that is alleged is causing the rates of Directors and Officers liability coverage to soar.[12] Headlines such as "Insurers Likely to Balk at WorldCom D&O Coverage,"[13] "Lawsuits Send D&O Premiums Soaring,"[14] and "D&O Mkt. Could Face Catastrophic Year"[15] are just some examples of the reflection of the accounting, telecom and Enron scandals.

Medical Malpractice   The risks to which physicians and surgeons are exposed illustrates the position of a professional. In taking cases, doctors represent that they possess—and the law imposes upon them the duty of possessing—the degree of learning and skill ordinarily possessed by others in their profession. Doctors must use reasonable care and diligence and their best judgment in exercising their skill and applying their knowledge. If they fail to do so, they are guilty of malpractice.

Two cases illustrate the risk to which medical doctors are exposed. A plastic surgeon who made his patient look worse instead of better had to pay $115,000 for the damage. A court awarded $4.5 million to a girl suffering acute kidney failure as a result of malpractice.

The number of medical malpractice lawsuits has increased enormously over the past three decades, and the size of verdicts has multiplied several-fold. Hospitals and clinics also may be liable for damages. The growth in medical malpractice suits reflects the fact that plaintiffs' attorneys have found this field a lucrative one. With the growth of private health insurance and Medicare, far more people have access to health care and a greater proportion of a growing population is exposed to the possibility of malpractice.

Another factor contributing to the increase is a change in doctor-patient relationships. Unlike the days when a family had one doctor who took care of almost all health problems, the modern health care system is specialized; many patients are dealing primarily with doctors they do not know. Faith in and friendship with the family doctor have been displaced by impersonal, brief contact with a specialist who may be more efficient than friendly. Furthermore, publicity about fraud by some doctors under the Medicare and Medicaid programs and about the amount of unneeded medical procedures (often performed as a defense against lawsuits) has reduced the prestige of the medical profession. As a result, there has been a decrease in confidence and a rise in willingness to sue.

Some of the increase in lawsuits, however, has been caused by a combination of unrealistic expectations based on news about modern medical miracles and the belief by some that people are entitled to perfect care. When they do not get it, they feel entitled to compensation.

One result of the surge in medical malpractice suits has been a scarcity of professional liability insurance in the private market and a dramatic increase in the cost of protection for both doctors and hospitals. These costs, of course, are passed along by most doctors to the consumer. They represent one factor contributing to rising health care costs.

Another result is the rise of defensive medicine. Doctors and hospitals are guided not only by what is good for the patient but also by their own interests in preventing liability losses. The latter, of course, leads to practices that may not be medically necessary and that increase the size of the patient's bill. The total effect of defensive medicine on the cost of healthcare is difficult to determine, but it is likely significant.

Medical malpractice lawsuits continue to soar into the new millennium and availability of coverage is becoming very scarce in many states. Medical liability rates nearly doubled in some areas, and insurers left many states.[16] Unable to find liability coverage, many doctors in risky specialties such as obstetrics and neurosurgery simply left the business.[17]

For details see "Important Issues: The Medical Malpractice Crisis" Another area of major growth is employment practices liability, discussed in Chapter 12.

Operations

Many firms are exposed to liability from their operations. Contractors are particularly susceptible to **operations liability** because they perform most of their work away from their

---

IMPORTANT ISSUES

The Medical Malpractice Crisis

In December 2001, the nation's largest malpractice insurer, Minnesota-based St. Paul Co., pulled out of the insurance market after predicting a combined ratio of 271 for that book of business. (As you recall from Chapter 5's discussion of combined ratio, that figure means that for every $1 St. Paul received in premiums, it spent $2.71 in claims and expenses.) For St. Paul, that translated into a loss of $980 million in one year.

Other insurers did not rush in to fill St. Paul's 10 percent market share. These days, medical malpractice is not a healthy business for insurers: The industry-wide average combined ratio hovers around 130. With fewer insurers offering malpractice coverage, rates increased; in Nevada, where St. Paul once insured more than half the state's obstetricians, premiums doubled, tripled, even quintupled in 2002. As most doctors are locked into HMO or PPO plans and cannot pass premium increases along to their patients in the form of higher fees, these rate hikes—often as much as $100,000 per year—come out of the doctor's own pocket. In Las Vegas alone, nearly ninety obstetricians stopped delivering babies and focused their practice on lower-risk procedures. Others took the chance of going uninsured, moved to a less litigious state, or quit practicing medicine altogether.

Hospitals and other healthcare facilities were hit just as hard. A June 2002 survey by the American Hospital Association found that 20 percent of the association's 5,000 member hospitals had reduced services, and 6 percent had closed some units. Las Vegas's only trauma center shut down for two weeks in August 2002. In Florida, where three companies in addition to St. Paul have stopped underwriting malpractice, several nursing homes went out of business for lack of affordable insurance. "Our trauma system has basically fallen apart," Sam Cameron, the chief executive of the Mississippi Hospital Association, told *The New York Times* in August. "There is a so-called Golden Hour in which a patient with a serious head injury needs to see

a specialist like a neurosurgeon, and in some areas of our state that service is no longer available."

How did the situation get so bad? Doctors blame insurance companies for skyrocketing premiums. Insurers blame personal-injury attorneys who work on contingency. The American Medical Association blames jurors who award exorbitant punitive damages. In fact, much of the problem can be traced to ordinary business cycles and a bit of coincidence. The 1970s saw sweeping changes in both medicine and jurisprudence; broader liability rulings and rapid advances in medical technologies co-parented a rash of record-breaking lawsuits. Insurers raised premiums, and when lawsuits declined in the 1980s malpractice insurance again became a profit center for insurers, so much so that by the mid 1990s, the field became very competitive. The competition among insurers led to price wars, but lowering premiums depleted the insurers' reserves just as malpractice lawsuits began escalating again.

Medical liability insurance is not a luxury that can be put on hold in hard times. Medical malpractice is the eighth leading cause of death—higher than breast cancer or AIDS—with almost 100,000 Americans dying each year as a result of preventable medical errors, according to a report by the National Academy of Sciences. Certainly injured patients and their survivors have the right to seek compensation for their loss. But how much compensation? Even though doctors and hospitals win 60 percent of their cases, the median medical-malpractice award is roughly $1 million. In the high-risk areas of obstetrics and neurosurgery, $2 million is the norm.

Horror stories abound, of frivolous lawsuits on the plaintiff's side, appalling negligence on the defendant's, and exorbitant jury awards in the middle. As in the 1970s, many think the answer is in legislative reform. Twenty states now have medical-malpractice caps on jury awards. West Virginia is proposing a state-managed liability plan. Pennsylvania has banned "forum shopping," in which lawyers file their suits in

(Continued)

IMPORTANT ISSUES (CONTINUED)

jurisdictions where juries tend to awards huge damages; lawsuits now must be tried in the county where the malpractice took place. Mississippi, too, has recently instituted sweeping medical malpractice reform law, including a provision against forum shopping. President Bush and the American Medical Association are campaigning for a federal law modeled on California's, which capped malpractice punitive damage awards at $250,000 in 1975. Today California has a medical-malpractice combined ratio of less than 100, because losses in that state are relatively predictable. Perhaps these reforms will solve the medical malpractice crisis—at least until the 2030s.

Explore the Internet

Many Web sites relate to lawsuits. Some specific sites on the topic of medical malpractice can be searched at: http://www.fda.gov/ for stories such as "Make No Mistake: Medical Errors Can Be Deadly Serious."

Another suggested Web site is in the Journal of the American Medical Association at: http://jama.ama-assn.org/issues/ for "American Medical Malpractice Litigation in Historical Perspective" by James C. Mohr, PhD (Vol. 283 No. 13, April 5, 2000). Other sites with some political agenda are those of the American Medical Association at: http://www.ama-assn.org /ama/pub/ or American Tort Reform Association at: http://www.atra.org/ or the National Conference of Insurance Legislators at: http://www.ncoil.org/

Sources: Joseph B. Treaster, "Rise in Insurance Forces Hospitals to Shutter Wards," *New York Times,* 25 August 2002; Steven Brostoff, "Medical Malpractice Reform Bill Draws Praise From Insurers," *National Underwriter, Property & Casualty/Risk & Benefits Management Edition,* 7 October 2002; Rachel Zimmerman and Christopher Oster, "Insurers' Price Wars Contributed to Doctors Facing Soaring Costs," *Wall Street Journal,* 24 June 2002; Lori Chordas, "A Downward Spiral: Medical Malpractice Insurance Is Losing Its Place as a Top Performing Line of Business in the Property/Casualty Industry," *Best's Review,* August 2001.

premises. Their greatest liability exposure, therefore, is on the job, rather than arising from their own premises. Bystanders may be injured by equipment, excavations may damage the foundation of adjacent buildings, blasting operations may damage nearby property or injure someone. If harm is caused while performing the job, as opposed to a negligently completed job, the liability may be an operations one.

E-Commerce Liability

As was discussed in detail in Chapter 8, e-commerce poses not only property and interruption of business risks, but also third party liability arising from the following:[18]

- Invasion of privacy and identity theft
- Employee-related risks and harassment
- Intellectual property risks: copyright, trademark infringement, defamation, encryption, discovery
- Publishing and advertising risks
- Service denial risks: contractual risks
- Professional risks: errors and omissions risks

Online privacy issues continue to top headlines. According to the respondents of a survey conducted by the Yankee Group, a consulting firm focusing on global e-commerce and wireless markets, 83 percent of online consumers are somewhat or very concerned about their privacy on the Internet.[19] According to a Fox News/Opinion Dynamics Poll, 69 percent of those polled said they're "very concerned" about their ability to keep personal information, such as medical and financial records, confidential. While nearly two-thirds of Americans said they have access to the Internet at work, home, or school, only seven percent believe their most-personal information is secure from the prying eyes of hackers or bosses.[20] The reputation of the business is at stake if customers' information does not remain private and protected. Invasion of privacy is an issue of major public concern as noted in the "Ethical Dilemma: Insurance and Your Privacy: Who Knows?" in Chapter 5. Businesses often collect data about their customers or Website visitors by having them fill out an online form or by making the user register for permission to use the site. This information, if not protected, can create liability when the privacy of the customer is breached. When so much information is released on the Internet, there are many opportunities for committing public defamation and opening the door to lawsuits.

Another e-commerce liability risk is raised with encryption, that is, the coding of Internet messages so information cannot be read by an interceptor. Because the terrorists responsible for the September 11 attacks in New York City and Washington, D.C., presumably communicated via encrypted Internet messages, some lawmakers renewed calls for restricting the use of encryption and for giving law enforcement unrestricted access to codes, or "keys," for unlocking the encrypted text.

Employee privacy and the monitoring of employees' e-mail by employers are also key privacy issues. The courts appear to be on the employer's side by agreeing that employers have the right to monitor employee e-mails. In the case of *United States of America v. Eric Neil Angevine,* the Tenth Circuit Court of Appeals held that when the computer is provided to an employee (in this case a university professor) by the employer, the employee should not have privacy expectations.[21] Liability falls on the employer if an employee uses e-mail while at work to commit a federal crime or send a threat. The entire computer system can be subject to seizure (Federal Computer Seizure guidelines). A firm is liable for any e-mails sent by employees; the e-mails are written proof of what the employee promised. The company can also be held liable for any sexually harassing e-mails sent by employees.

Since a business derives much of its value from the uniqueness of its intellectual property, including trade secrets, copyrights, and trademarks, infringement of these properties opens the firm to liability lawsuits. There is increasing liability risk associated with statements posted on the Internet. Traditional publishing methods require many different people to proofread the document, checking for potentially harmful statements. None of this is required to place information online. This point is stressed by many professors when students are asked to write reports or do research. The validity of the material on the Internet is as good as the trust you have in the reputation of the source of the material. In the commercial world, advertising on the Internet brought both state and federal agencies into the act of protecting consumers from false advertisements on the Internet. Last year, the SEC sued to enjoin an illegal offer and sale of securities over America Online and the Internet without a prospectus, and the Department of Transportation fined Virgin Atlantic Airways for failing to disclose the full price of flights on its home page. The FDA is also looking into online advertisements for pharmaceuticals. The National Association of Attorneys General (NAAG) has formed a thirty-eight-state task force to develop enforcement guidelines for combating illegal activity on-line. The Federal Trade Commission (FTC) has been involved in cleaning up the Internet from false advertising by finding the perpetrators and fining them with large penalties. An example is the advertisers of "Super Nutrient Program" and "Fat Burner Pills," who had to pay $195,000 in penalties.[22]

"Denial of service" liability is caused when a third party cannot access a promised Web site. This may be a major contractual liability.[23] For example, if a hacker penetrated a company's Web site and caused a shut-down, customers and other businesses may file lawsuits contending that their inability to access the site caused them to suffer losses. These losses are different from the first party losses of the attacked company discussed in Chapter 8. The attacked company is covered under first party insurance of property and business interruption income or special e-commerce endorsement. Finally, the professional liability of errors and omissions may cause a third party to have a loss of income. This may occur when an Internet provider fails or security software fails to perform.

The possible liabilities outlined above are not a complete list. Many of the cause of losses described in Chapter 8 may be causes for liabilities as well. The important point is that e-commerce exposes businesses to liabilities not anticipated prior to the electronic age. These liabilities may not be available in the traditional commercial liability policy.

Risk Management of E-Commerce Liabilities   The first step in the risk management process of e-commerce liability is the development of privacy procedures. This is done to protect consumers and avoid personal injury of defamation of another person or entity.

The transfer of e-commerce liability risk is not commonly covered under the usual General Liability policy, discussed in Chapter 12. The Commercial General Liability policy provided in Appendix D does not cover all of the liabilities that result from loss of electronic information. Therefore, in the risk management process, the risk manager should look into separate e-commerce policies. An e-commerce liability policy generally will include, in Section I, the definitions of claims, defense costs, named insured, an Internet site that is noted on the Declaration page, policy period, and so forth. Section II usually includes the exclusions. As would be expected, bodily injury and property damage are excluded since they are usually covered under the general liability policy. Additional exclusions are fraud, anti-trust activities, breach of contract, employment practices, product liability, patent infringement, lotteries, loyalties, securities, governmental actions, prior claims, and prior pending litigation. Section III emphasizes that the coverage is the liability of only Internet-related activities. The limit of liability is set in the declaration page. The last sections of the policy include additional details relating to reporting of notice, and defense and settlement, other insurance and more.[24]

E-commerce liability policies are not standardized. Some provide more coverage while others are more limited. The interested student can find many examples on the Internet and in *E-Commerce Insurance and Risk Management* by George Sutcliffe (Boston: Standard Publishing Corp., 2001).

Product Manufacture

Products liability is one of the most widely debated sources of risk for a firm. The basis for such liability may be negligence, warranty, or strict liability in tort.

Products liability is a somewhat unusual aspect of common law, because its development has occurred primarily within the twentieth century. One explanation for this late development is the doctrine of **privity.** The privity doctrine required a direct contractual relationship between a plaintiff and defendant in a products suit. Thus, a consumer injured by a product had a cause of action only against the party from whom the product was purchased. The seller, however, likely had no control over the manufacture and design of the product, limiting potential liability. Consumers' only recourse was to claim a **breach of warranty** by the seller; this cause of action is still available.[25]

Once the privity doctrine was removed, **negligence** actions against manufacturers surfaced. Demonstrating a manufacturer's negligence, however, is difficult, because the manufacturer controls the production process. You may recall that the doctrine of res ipsa loquitur becomes relevant in such a circumstance, placing the burden of proof on the manufacturer.

By 1963, members of the judiciary for the United States seemed to have concluded that consumers deserved protection beyond res ipsa loquitur. Thus developed strict liability in products, as stated by Justice Traynor:

> A manufacturer is strictly liable in tort when an article he places on the market, knowing that it is to be used without inspection for defects, proves to have a defect that causes injury to a human being.[26]

These three doctrines of breach of warranty, negligence, and strict liability are available today as causes of action by a consumer in a products liability cases. Each is briefly described below.

Breach of Warranty

Many products are warranted suitable for a particular use, either expressly or by implication. The statement on a container of first-aid spray, "This product is safe when used as directed...," is an express warranty. If you use the product as directed and suffer injury as a result, the warranty has been breached and the manufacturer may be held liable for damages. On the other hand, if you use the product other than as directed and injury results, the warranty has not been breached. Directions on a container may create an implied warranty. A statement such as "apply sparingly to entire facial surface," for example, implies that the product is not harmful for such use, thus creating an implied warranty. If the product is harmful even when the directions are followed, the warranty has been breached.

Negligence

When a firm manufactures a product, sells a commodity, or acts in one of the other points in the marketing chain, it has a duty to act reasonably in protecting users of the commodity from harm. Failure to fulfill this duty constitutes negligence and may provide the basis of liability if harm results. According to Noel and Phillips, "negligence in products cases is most likely to involve a failure to warn or to warn adequately of foreseeable dangers, a failure to inspect fully or test, a failure in either design or production to comply with standards imposed by law or to live up to the customary standards of the industry." For example, failure to warn that the paint you sell may burn the skin unless removed immediately may result in injury to the buyer and a liability for the seller. The products liability exposure can extend over the life of a product, which may be a very long time in the case of durable goods. A number of proposals have been made both nationally and at the state level to limit the time period during which such responsibility exists.

Strict Liability

A firm may be held liable for damage caused by a product even though neither negligence nor breach of warranty is established. This is called strict liability.

The doctrine of strict liability has been applied primarily based on the description provided in 1965 by the American Law Institute in section 402 of the Second Restatement of Torts. It reads as follows:

1. One who sells any product in a defective condition unreasonably dangerous to the user or consumer or to his property is subject to liability for physical harm thereby caused to the ultimate user or consumer, or to his property, if
   a. the seller is engaged in the business of selling such a product, and
   b. it is expected to and does reach the user or consumer without substantial change in the condition in which it is sold.
2. The rule stated in Subsection (1) applies although
   a. the seller has exercised all possible care in the preparation and sale of his product, and

b.   the user or consumer has not bought the product from or entered into any contractual relation with the seller.

The important aspects of this description are that the product was sold in a defective condition, which makes it unreasonably dangerous, thereby causing physical harm to the ultimate user. Thus, the manufacturer and/or seller of the product may be held liable even if "all possible care in the preparation and sale" of the product was undertaken, and even if the injured party was not the buyer. Because of the extent of this liability, it is not surprising that manufacturers hope to eliminate or at least limit the use of strict liability.

As already discussed, product liability suits were rare prior to the 1960s, and awards were small by today's standards. Two legal changes altered the scope of the product liability system. First came the abolition of the privity rule. With the expansion of trade to include wholesalers and retailers, especially with respect to automobiles, the concept of privity seemed inappropriate. Then in 1963, strict liability was brought to the arena of products cases. With strict liability, an injured party could receive damages by showing that the product was inherently dangerous, and also defective. The result was a subtle shift from focus on the manufacturer's behavior to the product's characteristics.[27]

Since 1963, the United States has seen a rapid increase in product liability litigation. One of the most difficult and common forms of litigation today involves strict liability due to defective warnings. Another source of consternation is the "mass tort" area, in which thousands of people are injured by the same product or set of circumstances, such as the Dalkon Shield and asbestos products. Some users of the Dalkon Shield, an intrauterine contraceptive device (IUD), experienced severe medical problems allegedly due to the defective nature of the product. Another cause for "mass tort" is asbestos. Asbestos is an insulation material made of tiny fibers that when inhaled may cause respiratory ailments. Thousands of workers using asbestos in the 1930s and 1940s have been diagnosed with various forms of cancer.

The increase in product liability litigation and awards is believed to have been a major cause of the liability insurance "crisis" of the mid-1980s. The cost of insurance increased so much that some firms have gone out of business, while others have discontinued production of the items that seem to be causing the trouble.

In some circumstances, the discontinuance of a product line may not be very newsworthy. In others, however, the results could be quite detrimental. The threat of lawsuits, for instance, appears to have been the impetus for several vaccine manufacturers to leave the business. Merck & Co. is now the sole U.S. producer of the combined measles, mumps, and rubella (MMR) vaccine.

In other circumstances, companies have not only terminated the manufacture of products but have filed for bankruptcy. Johns Manville Corporation, an asbestos manufacturer, and A.H. Robbins, a producer of the Dalkon Shield IUD, are two examples of companies who filed for Chapter 11 bankruptcy to get out from under liability suits. In November 1991, over 100,000 asbestos bodily injury claimants were litigating with asbestos producers.[28] Estimates of the number of deaths in the next twenty years caused by exposure to asbestos range from 74,000 to 450,000. Keene Corporation estimates that it continues to pay defense attorneys $60 million per year to defend against asbestos liability.[29]

The largest-ever liability cases are the tobacco liability cases that started in the 1990s and are continuing with large awards given to the plaintiffs, who are victims of cancer and other illnesses caused by smoking cigarettes. Standing out is the case against R. J. Reynolds Tobacco Holdings Inc. where the Kansas judge, not the jury, levied a $15 million punitive damages awards to the amputee David Burton. The punitive damage awards were fifteen times larger than the $196,416 compensatory award.[30] Note also the major case against Philip Morris discussed in "Ethical Dilemma: Are Punitive Damages out of Control?" in Chapter 7.

The tobacco cases did not only end in courts. The states got into the action and brought lawsuits themselves. The states forced the industry to the negotiating table and the tobacco industry settled for $368 billion in 1997, four years after the battle began. Some of the stories of the hurt, loss, and misery caused by cigarette smoking and the lawsuits are described in *The People vs. Big Tobacco* by the Bloomberg News team of Carrick Mollenkamp, Adam Levy, Joseph Menn, and Jeffrey Rothfeder (Princeton, NJ: Bloomberg Press, 1998), and *Cornered: Big Tobacco at the Bar of Justice,* by Peter Pringle (New York: Henry Holt Co., 1998).

Now that the cases of illnesses from Tobacco has been unveiled and the courts provide large awards to plaintiffs, the next wave of law suits may be expected to target the food industry because of obesity. This topic is discussed in "Ethical Dilemma: Obesity and Insurance—Should Size Matter?" in this chapter.

Completed Operations

Closely related to products liability is liability stemming from activities of the firm in installing equipment or doing other jobs for hire off its own premises, called **completed operations.** Defective workmanship may cause serious injury or property damage for which the firm may be held liable.

Contingent Liability

Generally, a firm that hires an independent contractor is not liable for damage or injury caused by the contractor. There are, however, a number of exceptions to this general rule, resulting in **contingent liability.** In some situations, the firm may be liable for an independent contractor's negligence if the firm did not use reasonable care in selecting someone competent. If the activity to be performed by an independent contractor is inherently dangerous, the firm is strictly liable for damages and cannot shift its liability to the contractor. The fact that the contractor agrees to hold the firm harmless will not relieve it from liability. A firm that hires an independent contractor to do a job and then interferes in details of the work may also find itself liable for the contractor's negligence.

Liquor Liability

Many states have liquor laws—or **dramshop laws**—which impose special liability on anyone engaged in any way in the liquor business. Some apply not only to those who sell liquor but also to the owner of the premises on which it is sold. The laws are concerned with injury, loss of support, and damage to property suffered by third parties who have no direct connection with the store or tavern. If, for example, liquor is served to an intoxicated person or a minor and the person served causes injury or damage to a third party, the person or firm serving the liquor may be held liable. In some cases, liability has been extended to employers providing alcohol at employee parties.

Possible Solutions

A number of suggestions have been made to alleviate the problems of product liability and malpractice (professional) liability. Some would limit the right to use or improve the defendant's defenses; others would reduce the incentive to sue or provide an alternative to legal action.

In both areas, proposals would limit the compensation available to plaintiffs' attorneys. Most plaintiffs compensate their attorneys with a percentage (typically one third) of

Ethical Dilemma

Obesity and Insurance—Should Size Matter?

Houston, we have a big fat problem: For the second year in a row, the Texas metropolis took top honors in *Men's Fitness* magazine's "America's Fattest City" report. The magazine weighed such factors as number of fast-food restaurants; average commute time (the longer the drive, the larger the driver); levels of smoking, drinking, and television watching; quality of parks and recreational activities; and air and water quality. Houston may have scored the worst, but it's not alone.* The Centers for Disease Control estimates that 60 percent of Americans are overweight, defined as a body mass index score (a ratio of weight to height) of twenty-five or above. Forty million people are considered obese, with a BMI of thirty or more.†

Flab has become a national crisis. In December 2001, then-Surgeon General David Satcher predicted that obesity would soon surpass smoking as the leading cause of preventable deaths in the United States. Overweight people are ten times more likely to develop diabetes and six times more likely to have heart disease. Excess weight is linked to gallbladder disease, gout, respiratory problems, and certain types of cancer. Estimates of the annual healthcare costs of obesity run as high as $100 billion.

In this country, fat is cheap to come by and expensive to lose. Fast-food restaurants tout "value meals," in which 1,000 calories can be had for less than $2, while big-city gym memberships can run $80 a month—about the same as a thirty-day supply of one of the new weight-loss drugs. But even a modest drop in avoirdupois, as little as 5 or 10 percent, produces health benefits like lowering blood pressure and reducing cholesterol levels. In the long run, that alone could save billions in related healthcare costs.

The Internal Revenue Service has recently recognized obesity as a disease; expenses such as nutrition counseling and weight-management courses are tax-deductible if recommended by a physician. At the end of 2002, the Centers for Medicare and Medicaid Services, acknowledging "a growing body of literature that suggests that obesity may be considered a disease," were considering whether to cover the condition under Medicare. A few health plans, such as Kaiser Permanente, the largest non-profit HMO in the country, offer treatment for obese patients. Yet most insurers do not cover weight-loss programs and products, on the grounds that treating obesity would be so expensive

that everyone's premiums would have to be raised to cover the costs. Many individual (as opposed to group) plans won't underwrite obese people at all, noting that their increased risk for serious disease is simply too great.

And then there's the moral issue. Like mental-health illnesses and alcoholism, obesity is often seen as a simple failure of willpower. Lawsuits such as the one filed in summer 2002 by Caesar Barber (five foot eleven inches tall, weighing in at 270 pounds), who is blaming McDonald's, Wendy's, Burger King, and KFC for his two heart attacks, do not elicit much public sympathy. Perhaps despite their own experience, many people believe that maintaining a healthy weight is a simple matter of committing to a healthy diet and regular exercise, and that insurance companies cannot—and should not—compensate for personal irresponsibility. Mayo Clinic professor Michael Jensen, president of the North American Association for the Study of Obesity, supports coverage but says people also have to be realistic. "Let's face it," he told USA Today in early 2002. "We cannot afford to pay for doctors' visits for every overweight person in the United States. There's not enough money in the world for that."

Questions for Discussion

1. Is obesity a disease that needs medical intervention, in your opinion, or a lifestyle issue that calls for self-discipline? What factors influence your answer?

2. Should insurance companies treat obesity as an illness and cover related treatments? Should Medicare? Discuss both the ethical and the practical considerations.

* The heavyweight champs of 2001: Houston, Chicago, Detroit, Philadelphia, Dallas, Columbus, San Antonio, Fort Worth, St. Louis, and Indianapolis.

† Check your BMI, if you dare, with the CDC's Web calculator: www.cdc.gov/nccdphp/dnpa/bmi/calc-bmi.htm.

Sources: Karen Shideler, "Rising Cost of Obesity in America Hurts Us All," *The Wichita Eagle*, Oct. 27, 2002; "Weight Management and Health Insurance," American Obesity Association, www.obesity.org; "Overweight and Obesity," Centers for Disease Control, http://www.cdc.gov/nccdphp/dnpa/obesity/index.htm; Libby Copeland, "Snack Attack: After Taking On Big Tobacco, Social Reformer Jabs at a New Target—Big Fat," *Washington Post*, 3 November 2002, p. F01; Nanci Hellmich, "Weighing the Cost of Obesity," USA Today, 20 January 2002.

their award, called a **contingency fee.** The advantage of a contingency fee system is that low-income plaintiffs are not barred from litigation because of inability to pay legal fees. A disadvantage is that lawyers have incentives to seek very large awards, even in situations that may appear only marginally appropriate for litigation. Reduced contingency fee percentages and/or caps on lawyer compensation have been recommended as partial solutions to increases in the size of liability awards and the frequency of litigation itself. Similarly, shorter **statutes of limitation,** which determine the time frame within which a claim must be filed, have also been proposed as a means to reduce the number of liability suits.

Placing caps on the amount of damages available and eliminating the **collateral source rule** are recommendations that focus on the size of liability payments. Caps on damages typically limit recovery either for general damages or for punitive damages. Often, when actually awarded, general and punitive damages far exceed the special damages; thus, they dramatically increase the size of the award and can add significant uncertainty to the system.

The collateral source rule is a legal doctrine that prevents including information about a plaintiff's financial status and/or compensation of losses from other sources in the litigation. In a setting in which a plaintiff has available payments from workers' compensation or health insurance, for example, the jury is not made aware of these other payments when determining an appropriate liability award. The plaintiff may, therefore, receive double recovery.

Another prominent recommendation is to abolish or limit the use of joint and several liability. As previously described, joint and several liability has the potential to hold a slightly-at-fault party primarily responsible for a given loss. The extent of use of the doctrine, however, is disputed.

KEY TERMS

property damage	negligence	invitee
bodily injury	proximate cause	hold-harmless clause
legal liability	assumption of risk	attractive nuisance
tortfeasor	contributory negligence	family purpose doctrine
special damages	comparative negligence	errors and omissions
economic damages	partial comparative negli-	liability coverage
general damages	gence	nonownership liability
punitive damages	complete comparative	operations liability
plaintiff	negligence	products liability
defendant	last clear chance	privity
statutory law	immunity	breach of warranty
common law	sovereign immunity	negligence
stare decisis	res ipsa loquitur	completed operations
criminal law	strict liability	contingent liability
civil law	vicarious liability	dramshop laws
contractual liability	joint and several liability	contingency fee
warranty	trespasser	statutes of limitation
tort	licensee	collateral source rule

DISCUSSION QUESTIONS

1. Distinguish between criminal and civil law, and between strict liability and negligence-based liability.

2. Betsy Boomer does not own a car and she must rely on friends for transportation. Last month, Betsy asked Freda Farnsworth to drive her to the store. Freda is known to be a reckless driver, but Betsy is not in a position to be choosy. On the way to the store, Freda is distracted by Betsy and hits the median strip, forcing the car into a

telephone pole. The car, of course, is damaged, and Betsy is injured. Describe Freda's possible liability and the various defenses to or modifications of liability that her lawyer may try to employ in her defense.

3.   What is the impact of res ipsa loquitur on general doctrines of liability? What seems to be the rationale for permitting use of this modification?

4.   Ceci Willis sells books door-to-door. What responsibilities do you owe her when she visits your home? How would the circumstances change if you were the book seller and Ceci came to your home as a potential buyer? What if you owned several pet panthers?

5.   How might elimination of the "collateral source rule" and a shortened statute of limitations affect the availability and affordability of liability insurance?

6.   Your neighbor's small children run wild all day, every day, totally ignored by their parents. You have forcibly ejected them from your swimming pool several times but they return the next day. Your complaints to their parents have had no effect. Do you think it is fair to hold you responsible for the safety of these children simply because your swimming pool is an attractive nuisance? Aren't their parents being negligent? Can you use their negligence in your defense in the event one of the children drowns in your pool and they sue you for damages?

7.   Describe when strict liability applies in products. What is the practical effect of this doctrine?

8.   How does the contingency fee system work? How might it affect the frequency and severity of liability exposures?

9.   Considering the factors involved in establishing responsibility for damages based on negligence, what do you think is your best defense against such a suit?

10.   A physician or surgeon may become liable for damages on the basis of contract or negligence. Why is the latter more common than the former? Does your answer to this question tell you something about managing your liability risks? What?

EXERCISES

9.1   Your neighbor's English bulldog, Cedric, is very friendly, but you wouldn't know it by looking at him. Last Monday, a rather strange set of circumstances happened at the neighbor's home. The substitute mail carrier met Cedric as he was approaching the mailbox. Because the mail carrier is afraid of even small dogs, he collapsed from fright at the sight of Cedric approaching, fell to the ground, and broke his left arm. A motorist, who observed this situation while driving by, rammed the neighbor's parked car. The parked car then proceeded down the street through two fences, finally stopping in Mrs. Smith's living room.

   a.   Is there a case for litigation involving your neighbor?

   b.   Where does the motorist's liability fit into this picture?

9.2   In an interesting case in Arizona, *Vanguard Insurance Company v. Cantrell v. Allstate Insurance Company,* 1973 C.C.H. (automobile) 7684, an insurer was held liable for personal injuries inflicted on a storeowner when its insured robbed the store and fired a warning shot to scare the owner. The robber's aim was bad, and he hit the owner. Because he had not intended to harm the owner, the insured convinced the court that the exclusion under a homeowners policy of intentional injury should not apply.

   a.   What reasoning might the court have applied to reach this decision?

   b.   Do you agree with this decision? Why, or why not?

9.3 Most states have a vicarious liability law regarding the use of an automobile. For instance, California and New York hold the owner liable for injuries caused by the driver's negligence, whereas Pennsylvania and Utah make the person furnishing an automobile to a minor liable for that minor's negligence. Ohio, Indiana, Texas, Hawaii, and Rhode Island make the parent, guardian, or signer of the minor's application for a license liable for the minor's negligence.

    a.   Why do these states do this?

    b.   Do you agree with this approach? Why, or why not?

    c.   If you are a resident of a state that has no such vicarious liability statute, does this mean you are unaffected by these laws? Why or why not?

9.4 In *Steyer v. Westvaco Corporation,* 1979 C.C.H. (fire & casualty) 1229, and in *Grand River Lime Company v. Ohio Casualty Insurance Company* 1973 C.C.H. (fire & casualty) 383, industrial operators were held liable for damages caused by their discharge of pollutants over a period of years, even though they were not aware of the damage they were causing when discharging the pollutants.

    a.   How might this decision affect the public at large?

    b.   What impact will it have on liability insurance?

    c.   Since the discharge of pollutants was intentional, should it be insurable at all?

9.5 Erin Lavinsky (of Chapter 8) works for the Pharmacy On-Line company in Austin, Texas. She likes to work on private stuff on her business computer and has received a few infected documents. She was too lazy to update her Norton Utilities and did not realize that she was sending her infected material to her co-workers. Before long, the whole system collapsed and business was interrupted for a day until the back-up system was brought up.

    a.   Describe the types of liability risk exposures Pharmacy On-Line is facing as a result of her action.

    b.   If Pharmacy On-Line purchased the ISO e-commerce liability endorsement, would it be covered for the liability?

    c.   If Erin penetrated into the system and obtained information about the customers that she later sold to a competitor, what would be the liability ramifications? Is there insurance coverage for this breach of privacy issue?

NOTES

1. H.J. Black, *Black's Law Dictionary,* 5th ed. (St. Paul, Minn.: West Publishing Company, 1983), p. 774.
2. This was first stated explicitly by Judge Learned Hand in *U.S. v. Carroll Towing Co.,* 159 F. 2d 169 (1947).
3. Two such theories are called Enterprise Liability and Market Share Liability. Both rely on the plaintiff's inability to prove which of several possible companies manufactured the particular product causing injury when each company makes the same type of product. Under either theory, the plaintiff may successfully sue a "substantial" share of the market, without proving that any one of the defendants manufactured the actual product that caused the harm for which compensation is sought.
4. Workers' compensation is discussed in Chapter 13.
5. *Walt Disney World Co. v. Wood,* 489 So. 2d 61 (Fla. 4th Dist. Ct. Appl. 1986), upheld by the Florida Supreme Court (515 So. 2d 198, 1987).
6. Coverage of the story is available in all media stories in the beginning of June 2002.
7. Diane Richardson, "Bite Claims Can Dog Insurance Companies," *National Underwriter,* Property & Casualty/Risk & Benefits Management Edition, 14 May 2001; Daniel Hays, "Insurers Feel The Bite of Policyholders' Big Bad Dogs," *National Underwriter* Online News Service, 31 January 2001.
8. Steven Brostoff, "New Brownfields Law Falls Short of Sought-After Superfund Reforms," *National Underwriter* Property & Casualty/Risk & Benefits Management Edition, 25 March 2002.
9. Rodd Zolkos, "Ohio High Court Favors Policyholder in Pollution Case," *Business Insurance,* 27 June 2002.

10. Mark E. Ruquet, "Accountants Under Scrutiny Even Before Enron Failure," *National Underwriter,* Property & Casualty/Risk & Benefits Management Edition, 25 February 2002.

11. Mark E. Ruquet, "Accountants Paying More for E&O Coverage," *National Underwriter,* Property & Casualty/Risk & Benefits Management Edition, 25 February 2002.

12. The citations are too many to list, as the issues develop daily. To mention just a few, review information in *National Underwriter, Best's publications,* and *Business Insurance* to learn more. Some parts of these Web sites are open only to subscribers, students are encouraged to use their library's subscriptions to search these publications.

13. *Best Wire,* 1 July 2002.

14. *National Underwriter* Online News Service, 17 June 2002.

15. Lisa S. Howard, *National Underwriter,* Property & Casualty/Risk & Benefits Management Edition, 25 February 2002.

16. Steven Brostoff, "Malpractice Cover Worries Docs: AHA" *National Underwriter* Online News Service, 26 June 2002; Daniel Hays, "Another Malpractice Insurer Leaving Florida," *National Underwriter* Online News Service, 24 June 2002.

17. Rachel Zimmerman and Christopher Oster, "Insurers' Price Wars Contributed To Doctors Facing Soaring Costs; Lawsuits Alone Didn't Inflate Malpractice Premiums," *The Wall Street Journal,* 24 June 2002.

18. George Sutcliffe, *E-Commerce and Insurance Risk Management* (Boston: Standard Publishing Corp., 2001).

19. "Online Privacy Continues to Be a Major Concern for Consumers," research report, The Yankee Group, 27 July 2001.For its 2001 Interactive Consumer (IAC) report, the Yankee Group surveyed approximately 3,000 online consumers.

20. By Richard S. Dunham "Who's Worried about Online Privacy? Who Isn't?" *Business Week Online,* June 28, 2000 in http://www.businessweek.com/bwdaily/dnflash/june2000/nf00628c.htm?scriptFramed

21. Thomas Jackson, "Protecting Your Company Assets and Avoiding Risk in Cyberspace," article in online newsletter of legal firm Phillips Nizer Benjamin Krim & Ballon LLP, 16 July 1996.

22. See note 21 above.

23. See note 18 above.

24. This discussion is based on Safety'Net Internet Liability Policy by Chubb Group of Insurance Companies and Executive Risk Indemnity Inc.

25. See Dix W. Noel and Jerry J. Phillips, *Products Liability in a Nutshell* (St. Paul, Minn.: West Publishing Co., 1981).

26. *Greeman v. Yuba Power Products,* Inc., 377 P.2d 897 (Cal 1963)

27. Many people consider strict product liability to be anything but a subtle shift from negligence. For a discussion of the difference, however, see *Barrett v. Superior Court (Paul Hubbs),* 272 Cal. Rptr. 304 (1990).

28. Stacy Adler Gordon, "Asbestos Compensation Program Proposed," *Business Insurance,* 11 November 1991, p. 1.

29. Wade Lambert, "Keene's Asbestos Fight Spreads Beyond Courts, Onto Ad Pages," *Wall Street Journal,* 29 June 29 1992, p. 38.

30. Michael Bradford, "Tobacco firms facing string of legal defeats," Business Insurance, 1 July 2002.

CHAPTER 10

Managing Home Risks

In the summer of 2002, fires raged in large sections of Colorado and Arizona. The fires engulfed many homes and were officially declared as catastrophes by the Insurance Services Office.[1] ISO defines "catastrophe" as an event in which losses total at least $25 million. As you have learned, large losses lead to availability and affordability problems. The industry may even decide to pull out of a specific market and not renew policies; the state government, however, may prevent this action. In the case of the Colorado fires, the state senate passed a bill prohibiting insurers from refusing to issue fire insurance policies within wildfire disaster areas.[2] Regulatory protection appeared to be necessary. Another issue that has made homeowners coverage extremely expensive and brought it to the limelight is the issue of mold, which is discussed earlier in this textbook and in this chapter's "Important Issues: The Growing Problem of Mold."

If disaster struck your home, you, no doubt, would be devastated. Lesser risks, too, can be distressing. If a friend is hurt while visiting your home, who will pay her medical bills? As your invitee, she might be forced, through her health insurer, to sue you. These and many other pure risks associated with your home are very real. A partial listing of home risks is shown in Table 10.1. They need to be managed carefully. One of the most important risk management tools to finance such losses is the homeowners policy. We will discuss this coverage in detail. The policy includes both property and liability coverages.

The chapter includes discussion of the following:

1. Connection
2. Packaging coverages
3. Homeowners policy forms
4. The special form (HO-3)
5. Endorsements
6. Other risks: flood and title risks
7. Personal liability umbrella policies
8. Shopping for homeowners insurance

CONNECTION

At this point in our study we are drilling down into specific coverages. We first stay within the personal property/casualty line of the home coverage. The current policies combine both property and liability coverages in one package. In the next chapter we will drill down into the automobile policy, which too combines the liability and property coverages in a single packaged policy.

As part of our holistic risk management, we need to be assured that the place we call home is secure. Whether we buy our home or rent it, we care about its security and the

TABLE 10.1
Risks of Your Home

1. Liability
2. Damage to, or destruction of, the home
3. Loss of use of the home
4. Loss of, or damage to, personal property
5. Defective title

safety of our possessions. We also want to safeguard our possessions from lawsuits, by having some liability coverage within these policies. If we feel that the limits are not high enough, we can always obtain an **umbrella policy**—liability coverage for higher limits than is available in specific lines of insurance—which is discussed later in this chapter. How the risk management of our home fits into the big picture of a family holistic risk management portfolio is featured in Case 1 at the back of this textbook.

As you saw in Chapter 5, Table 5.2, as of the writing of this text, the industry's property/casualty combined ratio has been high, indicating hard market conditions and rising prices. The homeowners line combined ratio for 2001 was 126.0. It reflected the massive problems associated with mold. This extremely high combined ratio resulted in major price increases and lack of availability of mold coverage. This market condition may not affect each insured similarly. Your specific homeowner pricing factors such as the type of materials used for the sidings of the house, distance from fire station, age and location of the house are very critical. However, regardless of your home rating factors, you know by now that the external market conditions do affect the pricing of your coverage. Your risk management decision (as you saw in Chapter 3) will take external conditions into account and you may decide to use higher deductibles, lower limits, and fewer riders. How rating factors are used and the issue of **redlining**—the alleged practice of insurers charging higher premiums and providing less coverage for homeowners insurance in inner cities—is discussed in the "Ethical Dilemma: Redlining—Urban Discrimination Myth or Reality?" box of this chapter.

FIGURE 10.1	Connection Between Risks and Homeowners Insurance Policies

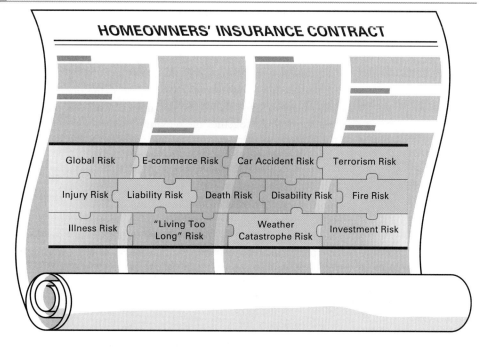

In addition to showing how market conditions affect our risk management decisions in the area of homeowner insurance, the concepts we studied thus far will help us quickly grasp the homeowners policy. As you learned in Chapter 7, most of the homeowners policies are "open peril": Everything that is not specifically excluded is covered. As you will see, the foremost topic of exclusion to our homeowners policies as of writing this text is the mold exclusion. Thus, the concepts you have learned up till now are coming together in one specific coverage. To better complete our holistic risk management puzzle, we need to understand how to read and interpret an open peril policy such as the Homeowners Special Form HO-3 discussed in this chapter.

PACKAGING COVERAGES

Homeowners policies are similar to automobile policies in that they combine several coverages into one policy. They are a combination of property and liability insurance, along with a little health insurance for guests and residence employees. The persons insured vary from coverage to coverage and place to place.

Homeowners policies are sometimes referred to as **package policies,** because they combine coverages that were previously provided by several policies and a number of endorsements. Before the availability of homeowners policies, someone trying to replicate coverage would have needed to buy a standard fire policy with a dwelling, building, and contents broad form; a personal property floater; and a comprehensive personal liability policy. In today's homeowners policies, packaging reduces cost and premiums by reducing administrative and marketing costs. It also provides broader protection and eliminates many gaps in coverage.

HOMEOWNERS POLICY FORMS

First we will look at the different kinds of homeowners policies shown in Table 10.2. Then we will examine the homeowners special form in some detail.

As shown in Figure 10.2, each policy consists of three parts: a **declarations page,** a homeowners policy jacket, and a policy form attached to the jacket. The declarations page identifies the specifics that are unique to the insured, such as the covered location, and also lists policy limits, period of coverage, the name of the insurer, and similar information. The policy jacket includes general, universal provisions, such as the title of the coverage, and acts to bind together the remaining policy parts. The policy form is the substance of the contract, spelling out the specific coverage provisions. Several types of forms are available from which the insured can choose.

Following the declarations page, the balance of each form is divided into two sections. Section I pertains to direct and indirect property losses related to the dwelling, other structures, personal property, and loss of use. A stated deductible ($250 in most states), which can be increased, applies to section I coverages. Section II includes personal liability coverages for you and medical payments to others. Each section lists the coverages provided, the perils insured against, and the exclusions and conditions applicable to that section.

TABLE 10.2 Homeowners Policy Forms*			
HO-1.	Basic form	HO-4.	Contents broad form
HO-2.	Broad form	HO-6.	Condominium unit owners form
HO-3.	Special form	HO-8.	Modified coverage

*The numbering and content vary in some states.

Finally, conditions applicable to both sections are listed. Table 10.3 outlines the coverages in section I, amounts of insurance for each coverage, and the perils included for the various forms.[3] Note that the limit for coverages B, C, and D is a specified percentage of the amount of insurance on the dwelling (coverage A) in forms 1, 2, and 3. Thus, when you decide upon the amount of insurance to have on your house, you have automatically selected the amount for other coverages. If additional amounts of coverage are needed, they are available with payment of additional premium. Forms 4 (for tenants) and 6 (for

Ethical Dilemma

Redlining—Urban Discrimination Myth or Reality?

The alleged practice of discrimination against inner-city residents by insurers, dubbed "redlining," has been a hot topic for two decades. During the 1990s, class-action lawsuits and allegations by consumer advocacy organizations plagued the insurance industry. Because redlining is a form of racial discrimination, these allegations have the potential to tarnish an insurer's reputation. As a result, most insurers have preferred to settle such cases out of court, not admitting to any wrongdoing.

Nationwide Mutual Insurance Company of Columbus, Ohio, has settled several such lawsuits in recent years. In 2000, Nationwide reached an agreement with Housing Opportunities Made Equal (HOME), a fair housing advocacy organization that had brought a lawsuit accusing the company of discriminating against black homeowners in urban neighborhoods in Richmond, Virginia. The insurer paid HOME $17.5 million to drop the suit and agreed to provide more services in underserved urban areas. Two years earlier, Nationwide had paid $3.5 million to settle a class action lawsuit alleging redlining in Toledo, Ohio. In a similar case, the same company paid almost $500,000 to homeowners in Lexington, KY. Nationwide admitted no wrongdoing in either case.

Do these settlements mean that redlining really occurs? The evidence is inconclusive. Studies conducted by the Ohio Insurance Department and the National Association of Insurance Commissioners, which looked at Ohio and Missouri homeowners, found little evidence that redlining existed. While the NAIC study found that average premiums were usually higher in high-minority urban neighborhoods in Missouri, it pointed out that "loss costs also appear to be higher in urban and minority areas and there is no indication that urban and minority homeowners pay higher premiums relative to the claim payments they receive." The Ohio Insurance Department also concluded that "it appears that companies in Ohio use the same underwriting standards throughout the state and do not unfairly discriminate."

A report by the Massachusetts Affordable Housing Alliance paints a less rosy picture. In 1996, Massachusetts passed an anti-redlining law, but in the four years after its passage, the state saw only modest improvement in availability of insurance in the state's most underserved zip codes, where, in 2000, 62 percent of homes were covered by the state-run insurer of last resort. Part of the problem, according to the report, was the predominance of flat-roofed triple-decker houses in these neighborhoods, which insurers said were more likely to suffer expensive water damage than pitched-roof houses.

Real or not, the redlining issue is not going away any time soon. Recently, it has entered the debate over federal chartering of insurance companies (see Chapter 5). Current proposed legislation would require national insurers to file annual reports identifying the communities in which they sell insurance policies and the types of policies sold in these communities. The law would bar them from refusing to insure a property because of its location.

Questions for Discussion

1. Do insurers have an ethical responsibility to minimize race, gender, age, and other discrimination, even if actuarially appropriate?

2. Does society benefit by limitation on insurer practices? Or is society negatively affected by higher insurance costs overall?

3. Could and should insurers be forced to find less socially significant factors for pricing and underwriting?

Sources: Amanda Levin, "Nationwide Settles Virginia Redlining Suit," *National Underwriter,* Property & Casualty/Risk & Benefits Management Edition, 1 May 2000; Tony Attrino, "Nationwide Settles Redlining Suit In Ohio," *National Underwriter,* Property & Casualty/Risk & Benefits Management Edition, 27 April 1998; L.H. Otis, "Ohio, Missouri Studies Fail To Confirm Redlining Fears," *National Underwriter,* Property & Casualty/Risk & Benefits Management Edition, 19 August 1996; John Hillman, "Study Says Mass. Homeowners Insurers Underserve Some Neighborhoods," *Best's Insurance News,* 8 November 2002; Steven Brostoff, "(A)Key Dem. Readies Federal Charter Bill," *National Underwriter* Online News Service, 6 February 2002.

condominium unit owners) do not cover a dwelling or other structures; the amount for coverage D is based on that selected for coverage C (personal property).

The basic amount for section II (coverages E and F) is the same for all forms but can be increased for additional premium. The insuring agreements, exclusions, and conditions for section II are the same for all forms. The basic differences among the forms are in the property coverages provided in section I. Forms 4 and 6 do not include insurance on the dwelling and other structures, because form 4 is for tenants and form 6 is for condominium owners. The latter have an interest in the building in which they live as well as related structures, but such property is insured on behalf of the owner and all occupants in a common separate policy. Limited coverage for permanent appliances is provided in Part A. Form 8 is for older homes that may involve special hazards. The valuation provision used in form 8 on the building is actual cash value, not replacement cost new. The perils covered represent another basic difference among the forms. Some are named perils while others are open perils. Note that form 8 has a much shorter list of covered perils than the others.

THE SPECIAL FORM (HO-3)

We will examine form HO-3 in some detail, because it is representative of the various forms and is the most popular homeowners policy. We will, in effect, take a guided tour through the policy using the most recent ISO HO-3 policy form in Appendix A-1. Our purpose is to

FIGURE 10.2

Homeowners Policy Structure

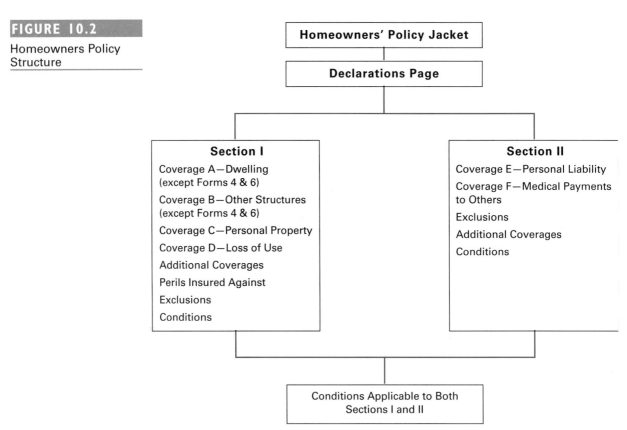

Source: A.M. Best. Used with permission.

familiarize you with its structure and content so you will know what to look for and how to find the coverages and exclusions in any homeowners policy. Your own policy may differ slightly from the one provided in the appendix due to state and company peculiarities. The basic coverage, however, is the same.

TABLE 10.3	Section 1: Homeowners Coverages				
Coverage	**Form HO-2**	**Form HO-3**	**Form HO-4**	**Form HO-6**	**Form HO-8**
A	15,000 minimum	15,000 minimum	Not included	$1,000 minimum	Varies by company
B	10% of A	10% of A	Not included	Not included	10% of A
C	50% of A	50% of A	$6,000 minimum	$6,000 minimum	50% of A
D	20% of A	20% of A	20% of C	40% of C	10% of A
Perils covered Under Section 1					
	Fire or lightening windstorm or hail Explosion Riot or civil commotion Aircraft Vehicles Smoke Vandalism or malicious mischief Theft Glass breakage Falling objects Weight of ice, snow , or sleet Collapse Accidental discharge of overflow of water or steam Rupture of heating or A-C system Freezing pluming and heating or A-C Artificially generated electricity Volcanic eruption	Open perils A, B, & D Contents same as HO-2	Contents same as HO-2 (except glass breakage)	Contents same as HO-2 Also covers improvements (e.g., carpet, wallpaper up to $1,000	Fire or lightening Windstorm or hail Explosion Riot or civil commotion Aircraft Vehicles Smoke Vandalism or malicious mischief Theft (limited) Volcanic eruption

Note: form HO-5 provided contents and real property coverage on an open perils basis. that coverage is now available through endorsement HO-15 to the HO-3 form, eliminating the need for HO-5. HO-1 provided a list of perils similar to that of HO-8 (i.e., shorter than

Insuring Agreement and Definitions

The insuring agreement and definitions parts of the policy follow the declarations page. They are the same in all homeowners forms. The insuring agreement says:

> We will provide the insurance described in this policy in return for the premium and compliance with all applicable provisions of this policy.

Two aspects of this agreement should be noted. First, the portion following the words "in return for" is the consideration that is vital to the contract. Unless you comply with the provisions of the policy, the consideration is incomplete. The insurer is saying, "If you comply with the provisions, we will provide the insurance described in the policy." Second, you must look further in the policy to find out what insurance is described.

Before you can determine this, you must know the meaning of the terms used in the policy. Words or phrases printed in bold letters are defined in detail under the heading "definitions." Because definitions are crucial to an understanding of the scope of coverage, these terms are listed separately in Table 10.4. Several other terms are defined in the body of the policy.

Armed with this terminology, you are prepared to examine the following parts of section I:

1. Coverages
2. Perils insured against
3. Exclusions
4. Conditions

Section I—Coverages

Coverage A—Dwelling

The dwelling on the **residence premises** (that is, your house) plus structures attached to the dwelling, such as an attached garage, are insured in coverage A. Also covered are materials and supplies on or adjacent to the residence premises for use in the construction, alteration, or repair of the dwelling or other structures. Land is not included.

Coverage B—Other Structures

The exposures insured in coverage B are structures on the residence premises that are separated from the dwelling, such as a detached garage. Coverage B does not apply to any structure used for business purposes or rented to any person not a tenant of the dwelling, unless used solely as a private garage. The location of this exclusion and the way it is stated illustrate two important points made in Chapter 5. First, exclusions are not always called exclusions. They may appear as "we do not cover," or following the word "except." Second, they may appear anywhere in the policy, not just under the heading "Exclusions."

TABLE 10.4
Essential Policy Terms

1. Bodily injury
2. Business
3. Insured
4. Insured location
5. Occurrence
6. Property damage
7. Residence employee
8. Residence premises

Coverage C—Personal Property

This part of the policy says:

> We cover personal property owned or used by any insured while it is anywhere in the world.

Note that this definition includes property you own as well as that belonging to others while you are using it.

If you borrow your neighbor's lawnmower, it is protected by your insurance as if it were yours.

If the insured requests, coverage C will apply to personal property owned by others while it is "on the part of the residence premises occupied by an insured," and to property of guests and residence employees while at any residence occupied by an insured. For example, if you store property of a friend at your residence premises, even though you are not using the property, you can cover the property under your policy. Or, if a guest at your vacation house (not the residence premises) has property damaged while visiting you there, that property too can be covered.

Property usually situated at an insured's residence other than the residence premises (such as the vacation house described above) is subject to a limit of 10 percent of coverage C or $1,000, whichever is greater. Coverage C, remember, is 50 percent of coverage A unless specifically amended to provide some other amount. Protection of $100,000 for coverage A, then, results in a $50,000 limit for coverage C. Ten percent of coverage C in this case is $5,000, which is greater than $1,000, and therefore is the limit on personal property usually kept at a residence other than the residence premises. If you, as a member of your parents' household, rent a room at school, the personal property normally kept in your school room is subject to this limit. Property brought there for a special occasion, perhaps when your sister drives up for a visit, is not subject to this limit.

Two provisions in coverage C merit careful attention. One is a **special limit of liability** and the other is **property not covered.** Under the first, dollar limits are placed on some property for loss caused by any peril, and on other property for loss caused by theft. These special limits should call your attention to any gaps in coverage if you have the kind of property listed. Note that for some items you can be reimbursed up to $2,500, while for others, such as money in any form (bank notes, coins, even value cards and smart cards) the limit is $200. You may want to cover the gaps with a scheduled personal property endorsement added to your policy. This endorsement is explained later in the chapter.

Most of the exclusions and limitations have the purpose of standardizing the risk, with coverage available by endorsement or in other policies. For example, much of the property not covered is related to conduct of a business and, therefore, not suited for homeowners coverage. A business-related policy or endorsement should be used to cover those items.

Some exclusions are of greater interest to a typical full-time college student than others. An example is the exclusion from coverage of compact discs and players when used in a motor vehicle. These items would be included in the automobile policy, sometimes under a special endorsement. As you know by now, if a certain item is covered by another policy, such as the automobile policy discussed in Chapter 11, it would be excluded from the homeowners policy to avoid duplication. Note also that if you rent your room in a private home, the landlord's homeowners policy does not cover your belonging. Your parents' homeowners policy may.

Coverage D—Loss of Use

Loss of use coverage protects you from losses sustained if the premises cannot be lived in as a result of a direct loss to either the premises or neighboring premises. **Additional living expense** is provided if a loss covered under section I makes the residence uninhabitable. An example is the large additional living expenses paid to homeowners whose homes where plagued with toxic mold and needed lengthy remediation. The growing problem of mold is discussed in the "Important Issues: The Growing Problem of Mold" box of this chapter. If a similar loss makes the part of the residence rented to others uninhabitable, the policy pays for its **fair rental value.** If a civil authority prohibits you from using the premises as a result of direct damage to neighboring premises by a peril insured against in this policy, both additional living expense and fair rental value loss will be paid for a period not exceeding two weeks. The two-week limit does not apply except for loss of use due to actions by a civil authority.

An important characteristic of coverage D is that it covers only additional expenses. A family forced out of its home for a week due to fire damage, therefore, will not receive payment for all expenses incurred during that week. Suppose that the family normally spent $250 a week on groceries, but had to pay $400 while away from the damaged premises. Only the difference, $150, plus other added expenses would be compensable.

Additional Coverages

At this juncture, you might think that every conceivable source of loss in connection with your home and personal property has been covered, modified, or excluded. Such is not the case.

Ten additional items of coverage are provided under the **additional coverages** section of the policy. First is debris removal, which provides payment for the cost of removing (1) debris of covered property damaged by a covered peril; (2) ash, dust, or particles from a volcanic eruption that has caused direct property loss; and (3) fallen trees that damage covered property. This additional protection is needed because other coverages provide only for the cost of repair or replacement of damaged property, not for the cost of hauling away the debris.

Several provisions in the additional coverages section of the policy are intended to encourage the insured to take steps that reduce the size of a loss after it has occurred. One is a reasonable repair, which provides payment for repairs made solely to protect property from further damage. For example, a temporary patch in the roof, following a covered loss, would be paid in order to prevent more extensive damages inside while awaiting permanent repairs. The conditions section further stipulates that if the insured fails to protect property in this way, some further damage might not be covered.

Similarly, property removed from premises endangered by a covered peril is covered while removed "against loss from any cause" for no more than thirty days. If this provision were not included, you might be better off to leave personal property in your house while it burned to the ground rather than remove it and risk having it damaged or destroyed by a peril other than those included in the policy.

The insurer also promises to pay fire department service charges incurred to save or protect covered property from a covered peril. Up to $500 per loss, without application of a deductible, is available.

Trees, shrubs, and other plants are also addressed in additional coverages. Loss to these items on the residence premises is covered if caused by one of several named perils. You should note that windstorm, ice, insects, and disease are not among the covered perils. No more than $500 per tree, shrub, or plant is available, with a total limit of 5 percent of coverage A.

Many of us have as many credit cards as we do trees, shrubs, or plants. The homeowners policy will pay up to $500 for such loss under the credit card, fund transfer card, forgery and counterfeit money coverage. The $500 limit is for loss caused by any single person, regardless of the number of cards or other instruments involved. No deductible applies to this coverage.

Many of us may also belong to an association of property owners (e.g., condominium projects). As members, we may be assessed charges for damage to association property. The loss assessment provision in the additional coverages section of the homeowners policy provides up to $1,000 to cover such charges. This provision has its greatest applicability in the condominium unit owners form (HO-6), but is included in all of the homeowners forms.

The additional coverages section also provides for direct physical loss to covered property due to two situations previously considered perils: collapse of a building, and loss caused to or by glass or safety glazing material. The definition and covered causes of collapse are outlined in this provision. Coverage is more narrowly defined for loss caused by collapse than had been the case when it was included under the open perils protection to real property. The glass coverage actually is slightly broader than that found in previous versions of the policy.

The tenth additional coverage found in the HO-3 is for landlord's furnishings. Up to $2,500 coverage is available to cover a landlord's appliances and other property located in an apartment on the residence premises that is usually available for rental. The same perils that are available for coverage C apply to this protection, except that theft is excluded.

Section I—Perils Insured Against

Coverages A and B—Dwelling and Other Structures

Under this heading, the policy says:

> We insure against risk of direct loss to property described in Coverages A and B.

The most important aspect of the agreement is that coverage is for open perils (sometimes also referred to as for "all risk"), but a close second is the limiting phrase "we do not insure, however, for loss." Three exceptions to coverage follow this phrase. Through these exceptions, the coverage, while it is for open perils, does not protect for all losses under all circumstances. The first exception is for collapse other than as provided in additional coverages noted above. The second exception lists six circumstances in which protection is not afforded under the policy. In general, these circumstances relate to especially hazardous situations or nonfortuitous events, such as theft in a dwelling under construction or loss due to wear and tear. One of these circumstances deals with losses arising from mold, fungus, and wet rot, which are covered only if hidden within walls or ceilings and caused from accidental discharge of water or steam. This coverage is available only for those states that did not adopt the ISO endorsement adding mold as a new exclusion (see Appendix A-1).[4] As of writing of this text, the following states adopted the ISO endorsement: Arizona, Colorado, Indiana, Iowa, Kentucky, Missouri, Montana, Nevada, Ohio, Pennsylvania, Tennessee and Utah.[5] For more information on the overwhelming problems with mold, see "Important Issues: The Growing Problem of Mold."

Coverage C—Personal Property

Unlike the open perils protection for the dwelling and other structures, personal property is covered against direct loss on a named perils basis, including the following:

- Fire or lightning
- Windstorm or hail
- Explosion
- Riot or civil commotion
- Aircraft
- Vehicles
- Smoke
- Vandalism or malicious mischief
- Theft
- Falling objects

IMPORTANT ISSUES

The Growing Problem of Mold

Erin Brockovich has a new crusade. The real-life legal activist, best known for being portrayed by Julia Roberts in a movie about toxic illness in a California town, nearly lost her California home to toxic mold infestation. The problem wasn't discovered until months after Brockovich and her family began to suffer flulike symptoms including runny nose and eyes, headaches, sinus congestion, cough, and fatigue. It cost her nearly $800,000 to have the house detoxified; Brockovich settled with her insurance company and is suing the builder of her house. The law firm representing her is handling more than a thousand mold cases in California.

Mold, a fungus in the same family as yeast and mushrooms, produces tiny spores that float through the air, indoors and out. Most of it is harmless, but certain strains can cause allergic reactions, respiratory distress, and even neurological problems. When mold spores find a nice, damp spot indoors, they can quickly grow. Such infestation is not new; in the mid-1980s, thousands of families in the Midwest became ill when their homes developed mold problems. But the issue hit national headlines—and brought an explosion of insurance claims—in 2001, when a Texas homeowner won a $32 million judgment against Farmers Insurance. Three years earlier, a pipe had burst in Melinda Ballard's twenty-two-room mansion just outside Austin. The break was quickly repaired, but damp-loving mold, encouraged by the warm, humid climate of central Texas, bloomed unnoticed behind the walls and spread throughout the house. It was the bad kind of mold: Soon Ballard and her family had a host of unexplained symptoms, including asthma, memory loss, and a persistent cough that produced chunks of blood. Experts said that her house could not simply be cleaned; it had to be destroyed. In her lawsuit, Ballard charged that Farmers had acted in bad faith by delaying her initial claims, which allowed the mold to spread out of control.

The standard homeowners policy considers mold, like rust, rot, and mildew, to be a maintenance issue for the property owner. Mold contamination is covered only if it is the result of a covered peril, such as Ballard's water damage from a burst pipe. But the sudden, drastic increase in mold-related claims meant insurers needed to limit their exposure or raise premiums. In 2000 and 2001, the 44,000 mold claims filed in Texas alone cost insurers just over $1 billion. Claims were rising dramatically in California, Florida, Arizona, Nevada, New York, Illinois, and Pennsylvania, too. In California, 200 insurers applied to the state commission for permission to restrict mold coverage. Farmers is negotiating with the Texas Department of Insurance over its attempts to withdraw from the homeowners market, and is being sued by the state attorney general's office for alleged unfair and deceptive business practices. State Farm announced a moratorium on new homeowners policies in both California and Texas. With fewer insurers willing to write policies, homeowners find themselves paying higher premiums for restricted coverage and less broad policy forms. Mold is covered for very low limits at an additional cost.

Rep. John Conyers Jr. of Michigan has introduced the U.S. Toxic Mold Safety and Protection Act, which would create a national insurance program to protect homeowners from catastrophic losses related to mold. The bill may be considered by Congress in 2003. In New York, Connecticut, Nevada, and other states, legislation is pending that would establish permissible mold limits, require that home sellers disclose to potential buyers any mold-related problems, and order insurers to make mold coverage available. The first such state bill to be signed into law was California's Toxic Mold Protection Act; Brockovich gave the bill much publicity by testifying before a California Senate committee and lobbying at a state assembly meeting. Is Julia Roberts available for *Erin Brockovich II?*

Exploring the Internet

Everything you always wanted to know about the fungus among us is explained at the U.S. Environmental Protection Agency's "Mold Resources" page at www.epa.gov/iaq/pubs/moldresources.html. The scientific yet entertaining Dr. Fungus site, www.doctorfungus.org, answers all mycological questions. For the full story on Melinda Ballard's mold woes in Texas, it's worth the $2.95 archive fee to call up the *New York Times Magazine* cover story at www.nytimes.com/2001/08/12/magazine/12MOLD.html.

Sources: Anastasia Hendrix, "Erin Brockovich Crusades Against Mold," *San Francisco Chronicle,* 8 March 2001; Deborah K. Dietsch, "Exorcizing A Mold Monster," *Washington Post,* 26 October 2002, p. H01; Daniel Hays, "Farmers Agrees To Delay Departing Texas," *National Underwriter* Online News Service, 11 November 2002; Christopher Oster and Jeff D. Opdyke, "Hit With Big Losses, Insurers Put Squeeze on Homeowner Policies, *Wall Street Journal,* 14 May 20; American Insurance Association, "Industry Issue: Mold," www.aiadc.org/IndustryIssues/MOLD.asp?Nav=1.33.44.

- Weight of ice, snow, or sleet
- Accidental discharge or overflow of water or steam
- Sudden and accidental tearing apart, cracking, burning, or bulging of a water heating or transporting appliance
- Freezing
- Sudden and accidental damage from artificially generated electrical current
- Volcanic eruption

Most of these perils are listed along with some explanation of what they involve, as well as specific exclusions. For example, damage by windstorm or hail to personal property in a building is not covered unless the opening is caused by wind or hail. Therefore, if hail broke a window and damaged property inside, the loss would be covered. If the window was left open, however, damage to property would not be covered. Similarly, furnishings, equipment, and other personal property are covered only if such property is inside a fully enclosed building. So, if your curtains are damaged by a windstorm while the window is left open, coverage C of HO-3 will not pay for the loss.

Smoke damage is covered if it is sudden and accidental, but not if it is caused by smoke from agricultural smudging or industrial operations. If, for example, your oil furnace malfunctions and spreads smoke throughout the house, the insurer will pay for redecorating and having smoky furniture and clothing cleaned. On the other hand, if you hang your clothing outside on the clothesline and it needs cleaning because of exposure to emissions from a coal-burning power plant, you will have to pay for any resulting loss.

Theft includes damages caused by attempted theft as well as loss of property from a known location when it is likely that the property has been stolen. If someone damages your bicycle in an attempt to steal it, such damage is covered. The second part of the theft definition is sometimes referred to as **mysterious disappearance.** Suppose, for example, you leave your camera at your table in McDonald's, go to the counter for another cup of coffee, return to your table, and find the camera gone. Was it stolen, or did it leave under its own power? It was probably stolen, so the loss is covered. Mysterious disappearance coverage requires that there be loss of property from a known place in such a fashion that theft is the likely cause.

Several exceptions to the theft coverage are enumerated in the policy. First, the HO-3 does not include loss caused by theft committed by any insured. This sounds absurd until you consider how many people are included in the definition of insured, which includes any resident relative and anyone under age twenty-one in the care of one of these resident relations.

Second, theft in or from a dwelling under construction or of materials and supplies for use in the construction is excluded because the risk is too great. Theft from any part of a residence rented by an insured to other than an insured is also excluded. If you rent a room to an outsider, for example, and he or she steals something from that room, the loss is not covered.

The third exception is one particularly important to typical college-age students. Unless an insured is residing there, theft from a residence owned by, rented by, rented to, or occupied by an insured, other than the residence premises, is excepted. Property of students kept at school, however, is covered as long as the student has been there within forty-five days. If you go home for winter break and your dorm room (or apartment) is broken into, your property is covered if you were not gone more than forty-five days at the time of the theft, subject of course to other policy exclusions and limitations.

Falling objects is the next listed peril. If a tree falls on your canoe, the damage is covered because the tree is a falling object. This peril does not, however, include loss to property contained in a building, unless the roof or an exterior wall of the building is first damaged by a falling object. If you drop a hammer on a piece of china, the loss is not covered. If the roof is damaged by a falling tree which, in turn, damages the china, the loss is covered. Similarly, damage to personal property caused by the weight of ice, snow, or sleet or the collapse of part or all of a building is covered.

Loss caused by accidental discharge or overflow of water or steam from a plumbing, heating, air conditioning, or automatic fire protective sprinkler system, or from a household appliance, is covered. Water could leak from a washing machine, for example, and cause damage to a painting hung on the wall of a room below. Sudden and accidental tearing, cracking, burning, or bulging of a steam or hot water heating system, an air conditioning or automatic fire protective sprinkler system, or a hot water heater could damage not only the premises but personal property. Such loss is covered.

Loss caused by freezing of a plumbing, heating, air conditioning, or automatic fire protective sprinkler system, or of a household appliance, is covered. This does not include loss on the residence premises while the dwelling is unoccupied, unless you arrange to maintain heat in the building or shut off the water supply and drain the system. If you leave your home during the winter for several weeks or months, losses caused by cold weather will not be covered unless you take the same precautions as would a prudent person who did not have insurance.

Damage to some property caused by a short circuit in your electrical system is covered. Excluded is loss to a tube, transistor, or similar electronic component. Thus, damage to your television or personal computer is not covered.

Section I—Exclusions

We have already noted so many exceptions and limitations that you would think an exclusion section is hardly worthwhile. Yet additional items are listed as general exclusions from section I coverages, nine exclusions under part A and three under Part B. These are listed in Table 10.5.

Some of these exclusions deserve comment. The law in your city, for example, may provide that a building that does not comply with the building code is permitted to stand, but if it is damaged by fire or other peril to the extent of 50 percent of its value, it must be demolished. The first exclusion listed in Table 10.5 says, in effect, "We will pay for the loss caused directly by an insured peril, but not one caused by an ordinance." If your garage does not meet building code requirements and is damaged by fire to such an extent that it must be razed, the insurer will pay only for the first damage. You will bear the rest of the loss.

If earth movement damages your house, the loss will not be paid. If, however, the damage is not total, and fire, explosion, or breakage of glass follows the earth movement, the additional loss caused by the following perils is covered. Of course, determining the property value following earth movement is not an easy task. Homeowners who want earthquake protection can purchase an endorsement for additional premium. This endorsement is discussed later in the chapter.

The water damage exclusion is not identical with the earth movement exclusion, but works in the same way. That is, it excludes loss caused by specified water damage and then says, "direct loss by fire, explosion, or theft resulting from water damage is covered." Specified exclusions are for flood, backup of sewers or drains, water seepage below the ground, and overflow of a sump.

Under the fourth exclusion listed in Table 10.5, loss caused by power failure off the residence premises is not covered. If the power failure results in the occurrence of a covered peril, however, loss caused by the covered peril is covered. Thus, if lightning strikes a

TABLE 10.5	A	B
Listed Exclusions	1. Ordinance or law	1. Weather
	2. Earth movement	2. Acts or decisions including groups, organizations or governmental body
	3. Water damage	
	4. Power failure	3. Faulty, inadequate or defective plans, design, material or maintenance
	5. Neglect	
	6. War	
	7. Nuclear hazard	
	8. Intentional loss	
	9. Governmental Action	

power station, cutting off electricity that heats your greenhouse, loss caused by frost to your plants is not covered. The freezing and bursting of your pipes, a covered peril, on the other hand, is covered.

The "neglect" exclusion can be confusing, especially because "neglect" is not defined in the policy. People often negligently cause damage to their homes, such as smokers who fall asleep with lit cigarettes in their hands. But negligence is not neglect, and these incidents are not excluded. Rather, the exclusion has the purpose of encouraging insureds to act at the time of loss to minimize the severity. You are not expected to run into a burning building to recover property. You are, however, expected to make temporary repairs to holes in the roof caused by wind damage in order to prevent further damage by rain before permanent repairs can be made.

The war and nuclear hazard exclusions require little explanation. Their purpose in the homeowners policy, of course, is to avoid the catastrophe potential.

Insurers have added the last exclusions under Part A and those in Part B in recent years because of several court decisions providing broader coverage than insurers intend. The intentional loss exclusion is directed toward court decisions that permitted insureds not guilty of any misrepresentation or concealment to collect for arson damage caused by another insured. The purpose is to discourage arson, or at least to avoid paying for it.

The remaining exclusions in the list in Table 10.5 are motivated by the doctrine of "concurrent causation." According to this doctrine, when a loss is caused simultaneously (concurrently) by two or more perils, at least one of which is not excluded, the loss is covered. The doctrine has been used most frequently in cases where earth movement, aggravated by negligent construction, engineering, or architecture of the building or weather conditions, was the cause of loss. Courts considered the negligence of third parties a concurrent peril, not excluded, resulting in coverage.[6] Insurers are responding to the concurrent causation doctrine by excluding weather conditions, act or decision of governmental body, and faulty, inadequate or defective planning, zoning, development, surveying, design, specifications, workmanship, repair, construction, renovation, remodeling, grading, compaction, and the like.

Section I—Conditions

As you have seen, there are several ways to place bounds around coverages provided by the policy, including:

- Special limits of liability, as in coverage C
- Listing property not covered, as in coverage C
- Listing losses not covered, as in additional coverages and perils insured against

Another place where coverages may be limited is the conditions section. Conditions outline your duties, the company's duties and options, what happens in the event of a dispute between you and the company about the amount of a loss, and the position of mortgagees and bailees.[7] Table 10.6 lists the conditions in section I of the policy.

Because the contract is conditional (meaning that your rights are dependent on fulfillment of certain duties), you must be familiar with the conditions. Your failure to fulfill one may result in a loss not being paid. This point is emphasized by condition G, which provides that you cannot bring legal action against the insurer unless you have complied with the policy provisions and the action is started within one year after the occurrence causing loss or damage.[8] Two other duties warrant further discussion: "duties after loss" and "loss settlement."

Duties After Loss

When a loss occurs, you must do the following:

1. Give immediate notice to the company or its agent.
2. Notify the police in case of theft.
3. Notify credit card companies, if applicable.
4. Protect the property from further damage, make reasonable and necessary repairs to protect it, and keep an accurate record of repair expenditures. If, for example, a falling tree makes a hole in the roof of your house, you should have temporary repairs made immediately to prevent water damage to the house and its contents in case of rain. The insurer will pay for such repairs, as noted in the additional coverages.
5. Cooperate with the insurer's investigations of the claim.
6. Prepare an inventory of damaged personal property showing the quantity, description, actual cash value, and amount of loss.
7. Exhibit the damaged property as often as required and submit to examination under oath.
8. Submit to the company, within sixty days of its request, a signed, sworn statement of loss that shows the time and cause of loss; your interest and that of all others in the property; all encumbrances on the property; other insurance that may cover the loss; and various other information spelled out in the policy.

Preparing an inventory (duty 6) after a loss is, for most people, a very difficult task. Generally, the loss adjuster for the insurance company will help you, but that does not assure a complete inventory. The only way to deal with this problem is before a loss. You should have an inventory not only before a loss but at the time you buy insurance so you will know how much insurance you need. Often insureds will use photographs or videotapes of their homes

TABLE 10.6 Section I—Conditions		
A. Insurable interest and limit of liability	K.	Mortgage clause
B. Duties after loss	L.	No benefit to bailee
C. Loss settlement	M.	Nuclear hazard clause
D. Loss to a pair or set	N.	Recovered property
E. Appraisal	O.	Volcanic eruption period
F. Other insurance or service agreement	P.	Policy period
G. Suit against us	Q.	Concealment or fraud
H. Our option	R.	Loss payable clause
I. Loss payment		
J. Abandonment of property		

and belongings to supplement an inventory. An up-to-date inventory of your household furnishings and personal belongings can help you do the following:

■ Determine the value of your belongings and your personal insurance needs

■ Establish the purchase dates and cost of major items in case of loss

■ Identify exactly what was lost (most people cannot recall items accumulated gradually)

■ Settle your insurance claim quickly and efficiently

■ Verify uninsured losses for income tax deductions

Loss Settlement

Personal property losses are paid on the basis of actual cash value at the time of loss, not exceeding the cost to repair or replace the property. Carpeting, domestic appliances, awnings, outdoor antennas, and outdoor equipment, whether or not attached to buildings, are paid on the same basis. Typically, anything permanently attached to a building is considered to be part of the building. You would expect such losses to be settled in the same way as buildings. But the phrase "whether or not attached to buildings," makes them coverage C (personal property) losses rather than coverage A or B (real property).

The provision for settling losses to buildings may be confusing, but it is similar to the co-insurance calculations shown in Chapter 8. Here is how it works: If the total amount of coverage equals at least 80 percent of the current replacement cost of your home (at least $100,000 on a $100,000 structure, for example), you are paid the full cost of replacing or repairing the damage up to the policy limits. There is no deduction for depreciation.

On the other hand, if the amount of coverage is less than 80 percent of the replacement cost, the insurer will pay the larger of (1) the actual cash value, which is replacement cost minus depreciation, or (2) that proportion of the cost to repair or replace, without deduction for depreciation, which the total amount of insurance on the building bears to 80 percent of its replacement cost. An example, similar to that provided in Chapter 8, may help clarify what the policy says.

Suppose that at the time of a $20,000 loss your home has a replacement value of $100,000. And suppose you have $70,000 worth of insurance on it. The loss could be settled as follows:

$$\frac{\text{Amount of insurance carried}}{80\% \text{ of replacement cost}} \times \text{loss} = \text{paymer}$$

$$\frac{\$70,000}{\$80,000} \times \$20,000 = \$17,500$$

If, however, the actual cash value of the loss—replacement cost minus depreciation—was greater than $17,500, you would be paid the larger amount. This example demonstrates that unless there is no depreciation, in most cases you would have to bear part of the loss if the coverage is less than 80 percent of the value of the building. On the other hand, if construction of the house was completed the day before the loss occurred, depreciation would be zero, actual cash value would equal replacement cost, and the loss would be paid in full. In most cases, of course, depreciation is greater than zero, so actual cash value is less than replacement cost.

Clearly, you are well advised to carry an amount of insurance equal to at least 80 percent of the replacement value of your house. But even if you do, what happens in the event of a total loss? If you have $80,000 insurance on your $100,000 house and it burns to the ground, you will lose $20,000. Remember that insurance works best against high value, low probability losses. It may be valuable to know also that replacement cost estimates do not include the value of foundations or land, which are not insured.

Furthermore, if you have $80,000 insurance at the beginning of this year, will that be 80 percent of the value of your house later in the year? If housing values in your area are increasing, you should (1) consider adding an **inflation guard endorsement** to your policy to increase the amount of insurance automatically every year, or (2) increase the amount of insurance to between 90 and 100 percent of replacement value and keep the amount up to date every time you pay the premium. That will assure being paid in full for partial losses and provide more complete protection against a total loss. Some insurers also offer a replacement cost guarantee endorsement whereby replacement cost is covered, even if it exceeds the limit of liability.

Determining Coverages

If you are like most people, the previous discussion has provided you with some new information. Yet the homeowners policy still remains a puzzle with pieces that do not seem to fit. How do you determine what coverage you have? Different people will find alternative methods of breaking a puzzle's code. We offer one method here that may help get you started. Figure 10.3 is a visual representation of the verbal path that follows.

To determine coverage once loss has occurred, ask yourself which type of property (real or personal) is involved in the loss. If both, consider each type separately.

If real property is involved, be certain it is covered by the policy (consult the declarations page to see if a premium was paid for coverage A). Next, check the exclusions listed under Section I—Perils Insured Against for coverages A and B, as well as those listed under Section I—Exclusions. If no exclusion applies, refer to the provisions of the loss settlement clause to determine how much of the loss will be compensated.

When the loss involves personal property, the process is slightly more complicated. First, make certain that the property is covered by referring to the special limits of liability and property not covered provisions of coverage C under Section I—Property Coverages. You hope the property is not listed here. Next, look to Section I—Perils Insured Against for coverage C for a listing of covered loss-causing events. If the loss was caused by a peril that is not listed, no coverage exists. If loss was caused by a covered peril, refer to Section I—Exclusions for limitations on protection. Last, apply the provisions of the loss settlement clause to determine how much you will be paid for the loss. An illustration of how a hypothetical family, the Smith family, determines the homeowners coverage needed and the rate comparison is provided in Case 1 at the back of the text.

Section II—Liability Coverages

As discussed in Chapter 9, many of our daily activities may result in our involvement in litigation. The liability exposures that are standard to homeowners are covered in the homeowners policy. The coverage includes defense costs. This liability protection is found in coverage E. Medical expenses incurred by others in circumstances that might result in litigation—or may not—are provided in coverage F.

Coverage E—Personal Liability

The insuring agreement for coverage E includes two promises by the insurer: to pay damages for which the insured is legally liable and to "provide a defense at our expense by counsel of our choice, even if the suit is groundless, false, or fraudulent." Both promises are of significant value, given the frequency of lawsuits, the size of awards, and the cost of defense. Note that the coverage is on an open perils basis; therefore, all events not excluded from coverage are included. One limitation is that damages must be either bodily injury or property damage, not

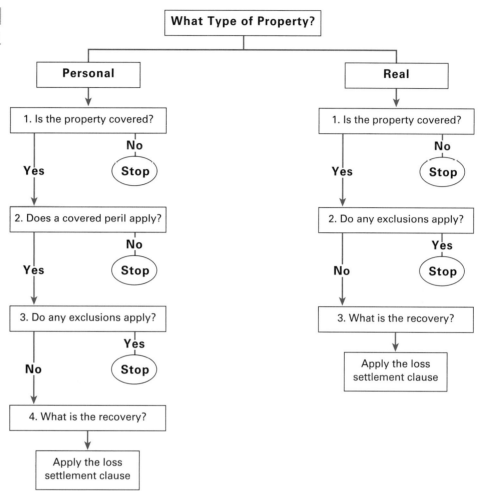

FIGURE 10.3

Determining Coverages

a non-physical personal injury such as libel. (Coverage for non-physical personal injuries is discussed later in the chapter.) Note the exact wording of the policy:

> A. Coverage E—Personal Liability
>
> If a claim is made or a suit is brought against an "insured" for damages because of "bodily injury" or "property damage" caused by an "occurrence" to which this coverage applies....

In addition, defense is provided only until the amount paid by the insurer for damages (court judgments or negotiated settlements) equals the limit of liability. Thereafter, the insured is responsible for defense. Deciding upon a sufficient amount for coverage E, therefore, is best done by considering both the exposure to liability and to extended litigation.

Coverage F—Medical Payments

You may at times be wise to pay for medical expenses of other people without requiring that they prove your fault. You may, for instance, feel morally obligated, or you may merely hope to avoid litigation by remaining on friendly terms with the injured person.

Coverage F of the homeowners policy provides funds for such events. Specifically, medical expenses will be paid if incurred within three years of an accident and arising out of one of five possible situations. This coverage differs from that found in your auto policy. In the auto policy, medical expense coverage is for you and your passengers. Here (in a homeowners policy), the coverage is for losses incurred by others. The covered situations are

    a.   To a person on the insured location with the permission of an insured

    b.   To a person off the insured location if the bodily injury

    c.   Arises out of a condition on the insured location

    d.   Is caused by the activities of an insured

    e.   Is caused by a residence employee in the course of employment by the insured

    f.   Is caused by an animal owned by or in the care of an insured

Expenses incurred by regular residents of the residence premises, except for residence employees, are not covered. The insured, spouse, and children living at the residence and others living there are excluded so that this policy does not become a first-party health insurance policy for them.

Section II—Exclusions

The exclusions to section II coverage in the homeowners policy are found in the following separate subsections:

    A.   Motor vehicle liability

    B.   Watercraft liability

    C.   Aircraft liability

    D.   Hovercraft liability

    E.   Further exclusions to both coverage E and coverage F

    F.   Exclusions to coverage E only

    G.   Exclusions to coverage F only

Section II exclusions E, F and G are listed in Table 10.7. All the exclusions fit the general purposes of exclusions discussed in Chapter 7.

Among the group of exclusions shared by coverages E and F, for instance, is the exclusion for acts that were not accidental. Also, war, as a catastrophic exposure, is excluded as well as communicable disease, sexual molestation, corporal punishment, and mental abuse. Substance abuse is also excluded. Premises that are owned by, rented to, or rented by an insured, but are not insured locations, are also excluded.

As you can see in Table 10.7, there are six more exclusions to coverage E. The first is exclusion of liability of losses charged against the insured as a member of an association or corporation. This is to omit coverage of most contractually assumed liabilities, which are nonfortuitous risks. Duplicate coverage is avoided in the fourth exclusion, where payments for bodily injury are available from various work-related laws. The last two exclude coverage for catastrophic nuclear exposure and coverage for bodily injury to the named insured.

Four exclusions apply to coverage F. The first is for medical payments to resident employees while away from the residence premises and arising out of events not related to employment duties. The second is where other available compensation exists. Third is the nuclear exclusion. The fourth exclusion clarifies the intention of omitting protection for the named insured and resident relatives, who are assumed to be covered by health insurance.

TABLE 10.7

Liability Exclusions For
ISO HO-3 Policy, 2000

E. Coverage E—Personal Liability And Coverage F—Medical Payments to Others
Coverages E and F do not apply to the following:
1. Expected or intended injury
2. "Business"
3. Professional services
4. "Insured's" premises not an "insured location"
5. War
6. Communicable disease
7. Sexual molestation, corporal punishment or physical or mental abuse
8. Controlled substance

F. Coverage E—Personal Liability
Coverage E does not apply to:
1. Liability for any loss assessment charged against you as a member of an association, corporation or community of property owners; under any contract or agreement entered into by an "insured".
2. "Property damage" to property owned by an "insured". This includes costs or expenses incurred by an "insured" or others to repair, replace, enhance, restore or maintain such property to prevent injury to a person or damage to property of others, whether on or away from an "insured location";
3. "Property damage" to property rented to, occupied or used by or in the care of an "insured".
4. "Bodily injury" to any person eligible to receive any benefits voluntarily provided or required to be provided by an "insured" under any workers compensation law; non-occupational disability law; or occupational disease law;
5. "Bodily injury" or "property damage" for which an "insured" under this policy is also an insured under a nuclear energy liability policy.
6. "Bodily injury" to you or an "insured" as defined under Definitions

G. Coverage F—Medical Payments to Others
Coverage F does not apply to "bodily injury":
1. To a "residence employee" if the "bodily injury" occurs off the "insured location"; and does not arise out of or in the course of the "residence employee's" employment by an "insured"
2. To any person eligible to receive benefits voluntarily provided or required to be provided under any: workers' compensation law; non-occupational dis-ability law; or occupational disease law
3. From any nuclear reaction; nuclear radiation; or radioactive contamination
4. To any person, other than a "residence employee" of an "insured", regularly residing on any part of the "insured location".

Section II—Additional Coverages

Section II of the homeowners policy provides four additional coverages. These are:

A. Claim expenses
B. First aid expenses
C. Damage to property of others
D. Loss assessment

The claim expenses and first aid expenses coverages stipulate what the insurer will pay. Claim expenses refer generally to costs associated with litigation, such as premiums on bonds and prejudgment interest assessed against the insured, other than the actual cost of defense. First aid expenses are those associated with bodily injury liability as covered under the policy, and therefore are not limited to the conditions required for medical payments to apply, but do require the possibility of an insured's liability. The coverage for damage to property of others is an added (small) benefit to cover others' property losses when you are not liable. You may at times feel a moral obligation to pay for someone's property damage even though you are not legally liable for such damage. This is similar to times when you feel a moral obligation to pay for someone's medical expenses (coverage F). When you are using someone else's property, coverage may exist in Section I, but what about the friend's coat that is damaged by your dog? You are not using the coat, and you'd rather not be sued for it. **Damage to property of others** provides up to $500 for such purposes. Of interest is that coverage applies even when loss is caused intentionally by an insured who is under thirteen years old, such as when a child throws a rock through a window. These types of intentional activity might be excluded under the liability coverage if the courts consider the child able to "intend" harm. The loss assessment provision is the same as that found in section I, except that it covers liability assessments instead of property assessments.

Section II—Conditions

Just as Section I contains a set of limiting conditions, Section II contains a set of conditions that limit and clarify coverage. Section II conditions are listed in Table 10.8.

"Limit of liability" clarifies that the maximum coverage available is the amount shown in the declarations. "Severability of insurance" provides coverage separately to each insured, although the total available for any one occurrence is the limit shown in the declarations. "Duties after loss" and "duties of an injured person" are similar to the duties stipulated in the Section I conditions, as is the "suit against us" condition. "Payment of claim, in regard to coverage F," merely emphasizes that payment is made without regard to fault. The "bankruptcy of an insured" condition requires the insurer be responsible for payment even if the insured has been relieved of his or her obligation due to bankruptcy. Finally, the "other insurance clause" makes coverage E "excess," meaning the policy pays only after another coverage is exhausted. However, if the other coverage has a similar provision, then the allocation is determined as discussed in Chapter 7. For example, if both policies provide the same level of coverage, each carrier will pay half of the loss.

Sections I and II—Conditions

Seven conditions apply to the entire contract. Three are discussed below. Refer to the ISO sample HO-3 policy in Appendix A-1 for the conditions not discussed here.

Cancellation

For various reasons, either the insured or the insurer may want to terminate the policy prior to the end of the policy period. You may cancel the policy at any time by giving the insurer written notice. State insurance regulations, however, have increasingly limited the cancellation privileges of insurers. As stated in the 2000 edition of the HO-3, four situations exist under which the insurer may cancel the policy.

First, nonpayment of premium is a justified reason for cancellation with ten-day written notice. Second, a new policy in effect less than sixty days may be cancelled for any reason with ten-day written notice. Third, a material misrepresentation or substantial change (increase) in risk will permit cancellation with thirty-day written notice. For example, an insured who began to store large

TABLE 10.8

Homeowners Section II Conditions

A. Limit of liability
B. Severability of insurance
C. Duties after "occurrence"
D. Duties of an injured person—coverage F. Medical payments to others
E. Payment of claim—coverage F—medical payments to others
F. Suit against us
G. Bankruptcy of an "insured"
H. Other insurance
I. Policy period
J. Concealment or fraud

amounts of flammables on the premises after purchasing the policy may cause the insurer to cancel the coverage when such use becomes known to the insurer. The policy may also be cancelled at renewal date for any reason with thirty-day written notice. Pre-paid premiums will be refunded. While this is the standard homeowners cancellation provision, some states may place restrictions on insurers that require different wording.

Assignment

Because of the personal nature of insurance, policy rights of ownership are not transferable (assignable) without the written permission of the insurer. As a result, when you sell your house, you cannot automatically transfer the insurance on it to the new owner.

Subrogation

Various provisions that limit over-indemnification were discussed in Chapter 6. One of these was subrogation, whereby the insured is required to transfer to the insurer any rights to recovery available from a third party. The transfer is made only to the extent of payment made by the insurer. For example, if part of an airplane detaches and falls on your house, the resulting damage is covered within the limits of your policy because it is a "falling object." Payment is limited by the loss settlement clause and deductible. If you did not have insurance, you likely would attempt to collect from the airline. The insurer, upon payment of your loss, has your right to sue the airline. Generally, the insured will be reimbursed for any out-of-pocket expenses not covered by insurance (such as deductibles and coinsurance) from any amount the insurer collects from the third party. If such collection exceeds the amount paid by the insurer to the insured, that too is the property of the insured. An additional point worth emphasizing is that the insured is precluded from interfering with the insurer's subrogation rights by, for example, settling with a negligent party without the insurer's consent.

ENDORSEMENTS

In addition to the inflation guard endorsement mentioned earlier, there are several other homeowners policy endorsements you should consider, including the following:

- Earthquake
- Personal property replacement cost
- Scheduled personal property
- Business pursuits
- Personal injury
- Mold (in states where the new ISO mold exclusion was approved; Appendix A-1)

Earthquake Endorsement

This endorsement can be added to your policy to cover losses such as those suffered by residents of the San Francisco Bay area when a 1994 earthquake caused damage of $20.30 billion. Unfortunately, only approximately 10 percent of the damage was covered by insurance, despite the frequency of earthquakes in California. The low reimbursement rate is due to several factors, including the failure of the majority of homeowners to purchase the endorsement and the effect of a deductible of 2 percent (in some states, 10 percent) of the insurance applicable separately to dwellings and other structures. A minimum deductible of $250 applies to any one loss. The endorsement covers damage caused by earth movement, including earthquakes, landslides, and volcanic eruptions.

Personal Property Replacement Cost Endorsement

Coverage C of HO-3 pays for loss on an actual cash-value basis, which means replacement cost minus depreciation. Except for something you bought very recently, you are underinsured from the replacement cost point of view. For example, your four-year-old large-screen television might cost $700 to replace today. If it has depreciated 10 percent per year, the insurer will pay you $420 in the event it is stolen or destroyed this year. You will have to find another $280 if you want to replace it. You can protect yourself from this unfavorable development by adding a personal property replacement cost endorsement to your homeowners policy. In the event of a loss, it will pay you the lowest of the following:

- The full cost of replacement (if replacement cost exceeds $500, actual replacement must occur)
- The cost incurred to repair or restore the item
- The limit of coverage C
- Any special limit stipulated in the policy
- Any limit separately endorsed to the policy

Scheduled Personal Property Endorsement

Some of the special limits that apply to personal property may be too low for you. Your jewelry or furs, for example, may be worth far more than the $1,000 limit. Such property can be listed and specifically insured to provide adequate coverage against all risks by adding the scheduled personal property endorsement. Another alternative is to pay extra premium to have the main policy's limit for a particular category of personal property, such as jewelry, watches, and furs, increased. (Note, however, that this leaves your coverage on a named-perils basis rather than changing it to open perils.) The insurer may require an appraisal at your expense before agreeing to a specified value.

Business Pursuits Endorsement

Personal liability coverage and medical payments to others coverage do not apply to bodily injury or property damage arising out of business pursuits of any insured, or out of rendering or failing to render professional services. The business pursuits exclusion, however, does not apply to activities that are ordinarily incident to nonbusiness pursuits. For example, your liability exposure in connection with an occasional garage sale would be covered. If you conduct garage sales regularly, however, such activity is a business pursuit and liability coverage does not apply. Liability stemming from rental operations, except for occasional rental of your residence or rental to no more than two people, is also excluded. Normal part-time employment, such as an after-school job, is not considered a business pursuit. But what about regular, full-time summer employment as a lifeguard? Such employment could be considered a business pursuit. The business pursuits endorsement eliminates these exclusions.

Personal Injury Endorsement

The liability coverage of your homeowners policy provides protection against losses caused by bodily injury or property damage for which you may be responsible. **Bodily injury** is defined as bodily harm, sickness, or disease. It does not include the following, which are considered to be **personal injury** and are added by the personal injury endorsement:

■ False arrest, detention, or imprisonment, or malicious prosecution

■ Libel, slander, defamation of character, or violation of the right of privacy

■ Invasion of right of private occupation, wrongful eviction, or wrongful entry

Could you become liable for personal injury? Suppose you write a letter to the editor of the local paper in which you make a defamatory statement about a person. You could be sued for libel. Or, suppose you make an oral defamatory statement about someone. You could be sued for slander.

Mold Endorsement

The new endorsements of 2002 relate to the **mold exclusions** adopted by many states to lower the cost of homeowners insurance, and particularly mold claims. The ISO "Limited Fungi, Wet or Dry Rot, or Bacteria Coverage" endorsement adds an exclusion to the HO-3 policy (see Appendix A-1). This endorsement specifies coverage limits per incidence of mold that are lower than the limits available under the HO-3. The endorsement specifies the following definitions:

> **SECTION I—PERILS INSURED AGAINST**
> In Form **HO 00 03:**
> **A. Coverage A—Dwelling And Coverage B—Other Structures**
> Paragraph **2.c.(5)** is deleted and replaced by the following:
> (5) Caused by constant or repeated seepage or leakage of water or the presence or condensation of humidity, moisture or vapor, over a period of weeks, months or years unless such seepage or leakage of water or the presence or condensation of humidity, moisture or vapor and the resulting damage is unknown to all "insureds" and is hidden within the walls or ceilings or beneath the floors or above the ceilings of a structure.
> Paragraph **2.c.(6)(c)** is deleted and replaced by the following:
> (c) Smog, rust or other corrosion;
> **B. Coverage C—Personal Property**
> **12. Accidental Discharge Or Overflow Of Water Or Steam**
> Paragraph **b.(4)** is deleted and replaced by the following:
> (4) Caused by constant or repeated seepage or leakage of water or the presence or condensation of humidity, moisture or vapor, over a period of weeks, months or years unless such seepage or leakage of water or the presence or condensation of humidity, moisture or vapor and the resulting damage is unknown to all "insureds" and is hidden within the walls or ceilings or beneath the floors or above the ceilings of a structure.

The following exclusion is added:

> **SECTION I—EXCLUSIONS**
> Exclusion **A.10.** is added.
> **10. "Fungi", Wet Or Dry Rot, Or Bacteria**
> "Fungi", Wet Or Dry Rot, Or Bacteria meaning the presence, growth, proliferation, spread or any activity of "fungi", wet or dry rot, or bacteria.
> This exclusion does not apply:

  a. When "fungi", wet or dry rot, or bacteria results from fire or lightning; or

  b. To the extent coverage is provided for in the "Fungi", Wet Or Dry Rot, Or Bacteria Additional Coverage under Section **I**—Property Coverages with respect to loss caused by a Peril Insured Against other than fire or lightning.

  Direct loss by a Peril Insured Against resulting from "fungi", wet or dry rot, or bacteria is covered.

The only coverage is what is provided under Addition Coverage as is bought by the insured and specified in the following Table:

These limits of liability apply to the total of all loss or costs payable under this endorsement, regardless of the number of "occurrences", the number of claims-made, or the number of locations insured under this endorsement and listed in this Schedule.		
1.	Section **I**—Property Coverage Limit Of Liability for the Additional Coverage "Fungi", Wet Or Dry Rot, Or Bacteria	$
2.	Section **II**—Coverage **E** Aggregate Sublimit of Liability for "Fungi", Wet Or Dry Rot, Or Bacteria	$

*Entries may be left blank if shown elsewhere in this policy for this coverage.

The delivery of section of the endorsement here is to provide the student with some explanation of how to read the endorsement in Appendix A-1.

OTHER RISKS

Two major risks that are too significant to be retained and cannot be avoided are the possibility of losses by flood or title defect.

Flood Risk

Homeowners policies exclude loss caused by flood because of the problem of adverse selection since only those living in flood-prone areas will buy the coverage. In some situations, this major gap in coverage can be filled by purchasing a flood insurance policy. Flood insurance is available through the National Flood Insurance Program, a federal program that provides flood insurance to individuals in flood-prone communities. Communities must apply to the program in order for citizens to become eligible to buy flood insurance policies. In addition, the communities must undertake certain required loss control activities under a program administered by the Federal Insurance Administration. Flood insurance is required by law in order to get secured financing to buy, build, or improve structures in areas that are designated Special Flood Hazard Areas (SFHAs).[9]

The policy covers losses that result directly from river and stream, coastal and lakeshore flooding. Structures that are covered by flood insurance include most types of walled and roofed buildings that are principally above ground and affixed to a permanent site. The contents of a fully enclosed building are also eligible for coverage; however, flood insurance policies do not automatically provide this coverage. It must be specifically requested. Commercial structures, multiple family dwellings, and single family residences are also eligible for coverage.

Flood insurance provides coverage for structures and (if covered) personal property or contents on an actual cash value basis. Flood policies do not offer replacement coverage for contents. If a single family residence is insured for 80 percent of its replacement cost, damage to the structure will be reimbursed on a replacement cost basis.

Two layers of coverage are available. The first is emergency coverage, available to residents of flood-prone communities as soon as the community enters the program. The rates are partially subsidized by the federal government.

Once a flood rate map is completed, a second, or "regular," layer of coverage is available at actual rather than subsidized rates. Insurance under the regular program is available only to communities that have passed required ordinances and have undergone studies by the Army Corps of Engineers.

In September 1994, Congress enacted the National Flood Insurance Reform Act.[10] One of the major provisions of the act was to provide for a substantial increase in the amount of flood insurance coverage available. An example of the limits and the costs are shown in Table 10.9.

The Reform Act also increased the waiting period from five to thirty days before a flood insurance policy is effective. This thirty-day waiting period begins the day after the application for flood insurance is made. This is a measure to reduce potential adverse selection from individuals who may be "downriver" from rising flood waters. The waiting period does not apply to the initial purchase of flood insurance coverage when the purchase is in connection with the making, increasing, extension, or renewal of a loan.

The Reform Act added an optional extension for mitigation insurance to help policyholders rebuild their substantially repetitively damaged homes and businesses according to the floodplain management code, including their community's flood proofing and mitigation regulations. This was previously unavailable under the flood insurance policy; however, substantially damaged structures were still required to be rebuilt according to floodplain management code.

Flood insurance may be required by law, such as under FHA, VA, and federally insured bank or savings and loan association mortgage agreements. Under a provision in the Reform Act of 1994, if a lender discovers at any time during the term of a loan that a building is located in a special flood hazard area, the lender must notify the borrower that flood insurance is required. If the borrower fails to respond, the lender must purchase coverage on behalf of the borrower.

Flood insurance can be purchased through any licensed property or casualty insurance agent or from some direct writing insurers. Some insurers actually issue the flood insurance policies, in partnership with the federal government, as a service and convenience for their policyholders. In those instances, the insurer handles the premium billing and collection, policy issuance, and loss adjustment on behalf of the federal government. These insurers are called Write Your Own (WYO) insurers. About 88 percent of all flood insurance policies in force are WYO policies. The remaining 12 percent of flood insurance policies are ordered directly from the federal government by agents not involved with a WYO program.

Another important result of the National Flood Insurance Reform Act of 1994 involves the availability of Federal Disaster Relief funds following a flood disaster. Individuals who

TABLE 10.9

National Flood Insurance Cost and Coverage (Data as of May 1, 2001)

Building Coverage/Regular Data

Occupancy Type	Coverage	Premium*
Single family	$125,000	$ 593
Two to four family	$150,000	$ 650
Other residential	$200,000	$1,840
Non-residential	$250,000	$2,700

Source: Federal Emergency Management Agency, www.fema.gov/nfip/avgcost.htm.

live in communities located in special flood hazard areas that participate in the National Flood Insurance Program and who do not buy flood insurance will no longer be eligible for automatic federal disaster aid for property losses suffered as a result of a flood.

Federal Disaster Assistance

Over the last five years, 61 percent of all property damage resulting from natural disasters has been due to floods. Therefore, it is advisable to obtain flood insurance. Figure 10.4 compares having insurance to using the Federal Disaster Funds (given to victims of floods for assistance in rebuilding their lives). The Federal Disaster Fund is usually activated when an area is declared a "disaster" by the President. The funds are provided to the victims at low interest rate. The example in Figure 10.4 was designed by the Federal Emergency Management Agency to educate residents of flood-prone areas about the value of obtaining flood insurance.

Title Risk

A **title defect** is a claim against property that has not been satisfied. One example of such a claim is a lien filed by an unpaid worker or materials supplier. Another example is a spouse whose signature does not appear on the deed signed by the other spouse when the property was sold. The claim is based on the spouse's community property interest in the couple's real property regardless of who originally paid for it.

If there is a defect in the title to your property, an informed buyer will insist that it be removed (cleared) before the title is acceptable, even though it may have originated many years ago. The clearing process can be time-consuming and expensive. A title insurance

---

FIGURE 10.4

A $50,000 Flood Damage Repair Cost Comparison

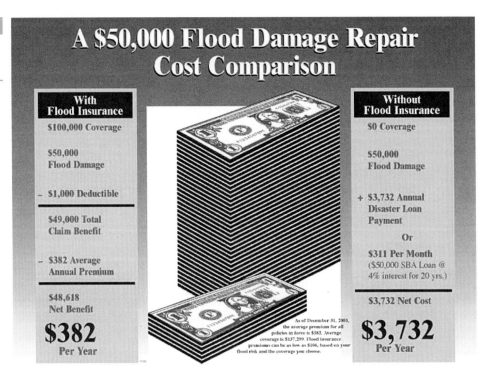

Source: Federal Emergency Management Agency, www.fema.gov/nfip/compar.htm.

policy protects the home buyer against loss caused by a defect in the title that existed at the time the policy was issued. It does not cover defects that come into existence after the policy is issued. The insurer says:

> If anything was wrong with the title to this property at the time this policy was issued, we will defend you and pay for the loss caused when it is discovered, within policy limits.

Before making this promise, the insurer attempts to determine if defects exist. If any are found, they are described in the policy and excluded from coverage, or a policy is not issued until they have been removed. A single premium is paid for the policy, and it remains in force indefinitely. As a general rule, it cannot be assigned. When title to the property is transferred, the purchaser must buy his or her own title insurance policy if protection is desired.

PERSONAL UMBRELLA LIABILITY POLICIES

Umbrella liability policies protect against catastrophic losses by providing high limits over underlying coverage. There are no standard umbrella policies, as there are in auto and home insurance. All do, however, have the following characteristics in common:

- They are excess over a basic coverage
- They are broader than most liability policies
- They require specified amounts and kinds of underlying coverage
- They have exclusions

Excess and Broad

Unlike other liability policies, umbrella policies do not provide first-dollar coverage. They pay only after the limits of underlying coverage, such as your auto or homeowners policies, have been exhausted. Furthermore, they cover some exposures not covered by underlying coverage. A typical umbrella policy covers personal injury liability, for example, whereas auto and homeowners policies do not. When there is no underlying coverage for a covered exposure, however, a deductible is applied. Some personal umbrella liability policies have deductibles (also called the "retained limit") as small as $250, but deductibles of $5,000 or $10,000 are not uncommon.

Minimum Underlying Coverage

Buyers of umbrella coverage are required to have specified minimum amounts of underlying coverage. If you buy a personal umbrella policy, for example, you may be required to have at least $100,000/$300,000/$50,000[11] (or a single limit of $300,000) auto liability coverage and $300,000 personal liability coverage (section II in your homeowners policy). If you have other specified exposures, such as aircraft or boats excluded by your homeowners policy, the insurer will require underlying coverage of specified minimum limits. Clearly, an umbrella liability policy is not a substitute for adequate basic coverage with reasonable limits.

Exclusions

Umbrella policies are broad, but they are not without limitations. Typically, they exclude the following:

- Obligations under workers' compensation, unemployment compensation, disability benefits, or similar laws
- Owned or rented aircraft, watercraft excluded by the homeowners policy, business pursuits and professional services, unless there is underlying coverage
- Property damage to any property in the care, custody, or control of the insured, or owned by the insured
- Any act committed by or at the direction of the insured with intent to cause personal injury or property damage
- Personal injury or property damage for which the insured is covered under a nuclear energy liability policy

SHOPPING FOR HOMEOWNERS INSURANCE

You can buy insurance for your home from many different sources, and premiums can vary greatly. As with any kind of purchase, price is not the sole consideration, but the possibility of saving 40 or 50 percent a year on your home insurance is worth some effort. The range of prices may not be as great where you live, but there is likely enough variation to justify shopping around. The startling difference between high and low prices clearly demonstrates that it pays to shop for home insurance.

There are three steps to shopping for homeowners' coverage:

- Figure out what you have
- Figure out what you want
- Collect your quotes and information about insurers before making your final decision

These steps are illustrated in Case 1 of the Smith family as noted above. You will need to inventory your possessions and organize all the information the insurer will need. Videotaping your property and keeping the tapes in a safe place away from your home is a good method of maintaining an inventory list. Figure 10. 5 shows the information about your property that you will need to provide your insurer, including such things as construction (brick, frame), access to fire hydrants, location, age, and security. The location of the property is important and may cause you to have to pay higher premiums. The issue of redlining—higher premiums for homes in inner cities—is discussed in the "Ethical Dilemma: Redlining—Urban Discrimination Myth or Reality?" of this chapter.

Next, you need to decide what insurance you want and the amounts of coverage. For example:

- Coverage A (dwelling) $100,000
- Coverage E (liability) $25,000
- Coverage F (medical payments), $500 per person

You will also need to choose your deductibles, such as $100, $250, and $500, and limits on coverages E and F, such as $100,000 or $300,000 on coverage E.

Finally, collect quotes from potential insurers. You might choose a couple of online or direct-mail insurers, some independent agents, and some exclusive-agency companies. Taking into account any differences in coverage, compare annual premiums and decide which company will provide what you want at the best price, as is demonstrated in Case 1 in the back of the text.

FIGURE 10.5	Homeowners' Insurance Quotation Worksheet

Applicant: _____

Address of property to be insured: _____

Number of losses in last 3 years if covered by insurance: _____

Dwelling:

Number of apartments or households in building: _____

Construction:

		Major Options	
(frame, brick, etc.) _____	Age of dwelling _____	Central air _____
Number of stories _____	Age of roof _____	Cen. vacuum _____
Number of rooms _____	Age/type of furnace _____	Cen. bur. al. _____
Total square feet _____		Smoke dec. _____
		Other _____

Owner occupant ☐ Yes ☐ No

Inside city limits ☐ Yes ☐ No

Outside city limits ☐ Yes ☐ No

Current Dwelling Replacement Cost	Current Market Value of Dwelling & Land	Purchase Price of Dwelling
Name of Fire Department	Distance from Hydrant/Station	

Cost of Your Insurance _____   Annual Premium _____

Property Coverage & Amount (% of replacement cost)		Company Name	Company Name
A. Dwelling	_____	$	$
B. Appurtenant structures	_____	$	$
C. Unscheduled personal property	_____	$	$
D. Additional living expense	_____	$	$
Liability Coverage & Amount			
E. Personal liability (bodily injury and property damage)	_____	$	$
F. Medical payments	_____	$	$
Deductible amount		$	$
Scheduled personal property		$	$
Other coverage(s)		$	$
Total Annual Premium		$	$
Installment charges		$	$
Total Annual Cost of Homeowners' Insurance		$	$

KEY TERMS

umbrella policy	additional living expense	mold exclusions
redlining	fair rental value	damage to property of
package policies	loss of use	others
declarations page	additional coverages	bodily injury
residence premises	mysterious disappearance	personal injury
special limit of liability	inflation guard	title defect
property not covered	endorsement	

DISCUSSION QUESTIONS

1. Name three exclusions in section I of the homeowners policy, and describe why each exclusion is appropriate.

2. Provide an example of a loss covered under section II of the homeowners policy.

3. Mrs. Gotcheaux's home in San Francisco was damaged by an earthquake. The earthquake caused a gas line to explode and a fire broke out, completely destroying the house. Mrs. Gotcheaux's homeowners policy explicitly excludes coverage for any damage caused by earth movement. Nevertheless, she files a claim with her insurer under her HO-3 policy. As Mrs. Gotcheaux's insurer, how would you handle her claim?

4. Why might auto policies exclude compact disks and players?

5. The Rupnicks' home was damaged in a fire, forcing them to stay at a nearby hotel for two weeks while repairs were being done. Due to the circumstances, the Rupnicks ate out every day, doubling the amount they would normally spend on food at home during a two-week period to $400. When the Rupnicks filed a claim for damages under their HO-3, they included the $400 cost of eating out as an expense resulting from the fire. How will the insurer respond to this claim for food? Explain.

6. Diane has her home and personal property insured under an HO-3 policy and is covering the actual value of the home. She has no endorsements. Indicate whether each of the following losses is covered and indicate what section of the HO-3 policy supports your answer.

    a. A fire damaged the home, destroying two of the end tables in the living room.

    b. The fire also destroyed Diane's fur coat valued at $100,000 and her three computers valued at $1,500 each.

    c. The house sustained smoke damage from a nearby industrial plant.

    d. A windstorm destroyed five trees in the large yard.

    e. A windstorm caused a tree to fall on the roof. The roof is a total loss.

    f. Diane's dog bit a neighbor's daughter.

    g. Diane hurt her teammate while playing soccer. The teammate was in the hospital for three days.

    h. During a skiing trip Diane left the fireplace burning in her cabin when she went out. The cabin was destroyed in the fire.

    i. Diane rented a snowmobile on the same trip and collided with a skier. He sued her for $50,000.

    j. Diane is a self-employed dietician who works as home. A client sued her for $30,000.

     k.   Diane entertained members of her bridge club and served a wonderful buffet lunch. Three guests become ill and sued Diane for damages. The court awarded each $15,000.

     l.   In light of all the losses sustained by Diane, she asked you to consult her about improving her coverage. What would you suggest that she should do? Think about everything that would improve her coverage using your newly acquired knowledge. Pretend she did not cover the actual value of her home. What would you suggest she should do?

     m.   Identify the major factors that determine the cost of a homeowners policy

7.   What is the mortgage clause in the HO-3 policy?

8.   Will the inflation guard endorsement alone assure that you have enough insurance on your home? Why, or why not? Discuss the application of the endorsement.

9.   What is the justification for the provision that damage to your home (coverages A and B) will be paid on a replacement basis up to the limits of your coverage if you have coverage equal to 80 percent of replacement cost, but on a less favorable basis if you have a smaller amount of insurance? Do you think this provision is reasonable?

10. What protection is provided by title insurance, and who receives that protection?

11. Under what conditions ought a homeowner to consider the purchase of a personal umbrella policy?

EXERCISES

10.1 Bill has a homeowners policy with form HO-3. His home has a replacement value of $80,000, and the contents are worth $45,000 at replacement cost or $35,000 at actual cash value. He has a detached greenhouse with heat and humidity control that houses his prized collection of exotic flowers. The flowers are valued at $11,000, and the greenhouse would cost $7,500 to replace at today's prices. His policy has the following coverages:

Dwellings	$60,000
Unscheduled personal property	$30,000
Personal liability, per occurrence	$25,000

A property coverage deductible of $250 per occurrence applies. Analyze each of the following situations in light of the above information. Determine all applicable coverage(s) and limit(s) and explain all factors that might affect the coverage provided by the policy.

     a.   A windstorm causes $20,000 in repair-cost damages to the house, and subsequent wind-blown rain causes damage to the contents of the house—$18,000 in replacement cost, or $11,000 at actual cash value. The greenhouse is a total loss, as are the exotic plants. Debris removal of the greenhouse to satisfy the city's health laws costs $350, and further debris removal to clear the way for repairs costs another $280. Two maple trees valued at $600 each are blown down, and their removal costs another $400. Bill must move his family to a nearby rental home for two months during repairs to the house. Rental costs are $600 per month, utilities at the rental house are $150 more per month, and his mortgage payments of $550 per month continue payable. It costs Bill another $80 per month to commute to work and to drive his children to their school. The telephone company charges him $50 to change his telephone to the rental unit and back to his home again.

    b.   After Bill and his family return to their home, faulty wiring (done during repair) causes a short and a small fire. All the family clothing has to be washed because of smoke damage, at a cost of $1200. Repair to the walls requires an additional $4,700. What might be the effect of subrogation in this case?

10.2 Brenda Joy is an accountant in a small Kansas town. She works out of her home, which has a replacement value of $125,000 and an actual cash value of $105,000. Brenda purchased an HO-3 with the following limits:

Coverage A: $110,000, $250 deductible
Coverage E: $300,000
Coverage F: $5,000

Discuss the application of Brenda's HO-3 to the following losses.

    a.   One of Brenda's clients sues her for negligent accounting advice. The suit alleges damages of $75,000.

    b.   A friend of Brenda's visits at Brenda's home and slips over a stack of books Brenda laid on the floor temporarily. Brenda takes the friend to the hospital, where treatment is received costing $645.

    c.   Brenda is the star pitcher for the local softball team. Unfortunately, Brenda's game was off last month and she beaned an opponent. The opponent's attorney filed a notice of claim against Brenda, asserting damages of $500,000.

    d.   Neighborhood children often run through Brenda's yard. Recently a group did just that, with one child falling over a rock hidden in the grass. The child needed stitches and an overnight stay in the hospital. It is not clear if the child's parents will sue.

10.3 As a newly graduated lawyer, Quinn Krueger was able to find a well-paying job and as a result a large enough mortgage to buy a nice house. The mortgage company required that Quinn also purchase a homeowners policy, and so Quinn obtained an HO-3 with $95,000 on coverage A (the replacement cost value), $60,000 for coverage C, $100,000 of coverage E, and $2,000 on coverage F. How would Quinn's insurer react to the following losses? Explain.

    a.   Coming home late one night, Quinn accidentally drives her car into the corner of her attached garage. Damage to the garage involves repairs of $2,300. The car needs repairs costing $3,200.

    b.   Quinn owns an electric guitar and likes to play it loudly. Neighbors sue Quinn for nuisance, claiming damages of $25,000 (the reduction in the value of their house).

    c.   Heavy snowfall, followed by rapid melting, results in high water levels. Quinn finds herself dealing with an overflow in her basement. It causes $2,700 in damage to personal property and requires repairs of $1,700 to the basement.

    d.   Thieves are not common in Quinn's neighborhood, but a group (police believe) of crafty criminals break into her house. The break-in damages the doorway, requiring $685 in repairs. The thieves take a Persian rug valued at $8,300, a television worth $500, jewelry assessed at $3,000, a CD player costing $450, and silverware worth $1,200.

NOTES

1. "Arizona Fires Declared a Catastrophe," *BestWire*, 1 July 2002.
2. Joanne Wojcik, "Colorado Bill Would Bar Nonrenewals in Wildfire Areas," *Business Insurance*, 11 July 2002.
3. The forms presented here are ISO forms used in most states.
4. ISO Homeowners policy form HO 04 27 04 02.
5. E.E. Mazier, "Alabama OKs ISO Mold Endorsement," *National Underwriter* Online News Service, 26 February 2002: "In terms of property coverage, Alabama homeowners will have a choice of three limits—$10,000, $25,000 or $50,000—on claims payouts within a policy year.... The limits for liability are $50,000 and $100,000.... Liability coverage would apply if, for example, a guest developed an illness due to exposure to mold in the host's home."
6. Safeco Insurance Co. of America v. Guyton, 692 F.2d 551 (1982), and *Premier Insurance Co. v. Welch*, 140 Cal.App.3d 420 (1983).
7. A mortgagee is the lending agency; when you borrow money to buy a home, you sign a note and a mortgage. You are the mortgagor who executes a mortgage in favor of the mortgagee. A bailee is a person who holds another person's property; the bailor is the person who leaves his or her property with the bailee
8. If the one-year time limit conflicts with state law, the law prevails. In South Carolina, for example, it is six years.
9. Federal Emergency Management Agency, www.fema.gov/nfip/nfip.htm.
10. Federal Insurance and Mitigation Administration (FIMA) is part of the Federal Emergency Management Agency (FEMA). The National Flood Insurance Program is under FEMA: www.fema.gov/nfip/laws.htm.
11. In Chapter 11, automobile limits are explained. These values represent $100,000 coverage per person for bodily injury liability and $300,000 total for all bodily injury liability per accident. Property damage liability coverage is $50,000 per accident.

Managing Automobile Risks

Automobiles are an essential part of American society. In 1999, there were more than 156.3 million cars, van, trucks, and sport utility vehicles insured in the United States. Private passenger automobile premiums for 2000 totaled $119.6 billion. In 1999, the highest average expense was in New Jersey, followed by the District of Columbia and New York. The trend of New Jersey leading the country in the cost of auto insurance continued in 2001, as is described in "Important Issues: Leaving the New Jersey Auto Insurance Market."

According to the U.S. Department of Transportation's National Highway Traffic Safety Administration, an auto accident death occurs, on average, every thirteen minutes and an injury every sixteen seconds. In the year 2000, there were 19.27 fatalities per 100,000 registered automobiles. In 41 percent of passenger cars involved in fatal accidents, the occupants were not wearing seat belts. Usage of seat belts across the nation in 2000 ranged from a low of 47.7 percent in North Dakota to a high of 88.9 percent in California. The seat-belt usage rate is higher in states with enforcement laws.

Drunk driving (driving while intoxicated, DWI, or driving under the influence, DUI) contributes dramatically to fatalities on the road. In 2000, 18,853 traffic deaths were related to drunk driving. Most states have DWI or DUI laws that include lower blood-alcohol level tolerances for drivers under 21. Because teenagers comprise 6.8 percent of drivers but account for 14.7 percent of fatal accidents, many states also have "young driver laws" that restrict night driving or numbers of passengers.[1]

To alleviate the economic risk of getting hurt or hurting someone else in an automobile accident, the law in most states requires automobile owners to buy automobile insurance. In this chapter we will learn about:

1. Connection to our holistic risk management
2. The fault system
3. Financial responsibility laws
4. Availability of auto insurance
5. The personal automobile policy (PAP)
6. Auto insurance premium rates
7. Types of automobile policies

CONNECTION

At this point in our study we are still in the realm of personal lines coverages. As with the homeowners policy, the automobile policy combines both property and liability coverage in one package. The liability part is now at the front of the policy rather than the property as in the homeowners policy.

As part of our holistic risk management, we need to be sure that when we are on the road we are covered. If we hurt anyone, we may be sued for every penny we and our parents ever earned. If we get hurt or damage our own car, we may not be able to get to work or be out of work for a long time. As you saw in the statistics above, car accidents do occur and no one is immune to them.

The personal auto line combined ratio, as you saw in Table 5.2 in Chapter 5, was above the break-even point for 2001 and estimated 2002, indicating hard market conditions. Of course, this overall trend may affect you more than another person depending on your specific pricing factors for private passenger automobile and your location, classification, car make, and so forth. Regardless of your individual rating factors, you know by now that external market conditions affect your risk management decision (as you saw in Chapter 3). When rates are high, for example, you may decide to use higher deductibles for your automobile coverage.

In addition to understanding how the market conditions affect our risk management decision in the area of automobile insurance, the concepts we studied thus far will be helpful in quickly capturing the essence of auto coverage and the particulars of the wording in the policy. Here, we need to know not only what coverage we have but also what is required by the various state laws. You will have the opportunity to delve into an actual policy (Appendix B) and complete your understanding of this important and costly risk. Figure 11.1 connects this topic to our holistic risk puzzle. An example of the automobile coverage of the Smith family mentioned in Chapter 10 is provided in Case 1 at the back of this text. The case shows how a family creates a complete risk management portfolio.

FIGURE 11.1   Connections between Risks and Auto Policies

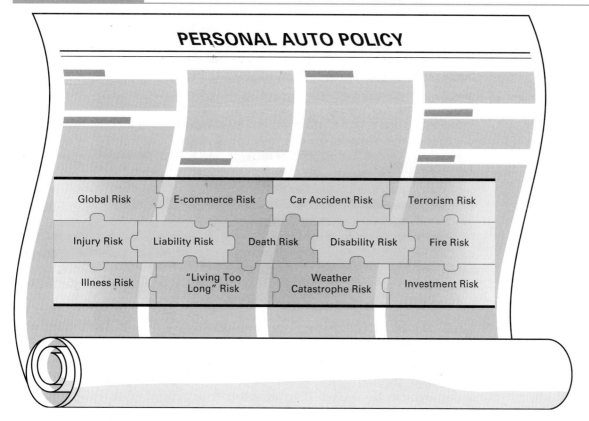

THE FAULT SYSTEM

An issue debated extensively over the past several decades is whether or not to maintain a fault-based compensation mechanism for automobile accidents. In response to the debate, over half the states have passed mandatory first-party benefits (also known as **no-fault**) laws. Subject to various limitations, such laws require that insurers compensate insureds for the insureds' medical expenses, lost wages, replacement service costs, and funeral expenses incurred as a result of an automobile accident. These benefits are provided without regard to who caused the accident and are usually termed **personal injury protection** (PIP).

Under the no-fault concept, first-party benefits such as PIP are provided without regard to fault, so as to negate legal battles. If you were involved in a multi-car accident where tort law applied, a suit between the parties likely would result. The suit would be an attempt to place "blame" for the accident, thereby also placing financial responsibility for the losses incurred. Under the no-fault concept, each injured party would receive compensation from his or her own insurance company. No need would exist to expend resources in determining "fault." Furthermore, the worry of being hit by someone who does not have automobile liability insurance would be eliminated. You already have a form of limited no-fault insurance in the coverages that compensate for damage to your car (discussed later in the chapter). The no-fault PIP benefits extend first-party coverage to expenses associated with bodily injury.

No-fault automobile laws are not uniform, yet they typically fall into three categories. Table 11.1 lists the laws in each state. **Pure no-fault** exists only theoretically. Such a plan would abolish completely the opportunity to litigate over automobile accidents. Only specific damages (economic losses, such as medical expenses and lost wages) would be available under pure no-fault, but these would be unlimited. Michigan's no-fault law is more like pure no-fault than are the laws of other no-fault states.

Michigan's plan, however, is an example of a **modified no-fault law.** Under a modified plan, rights to litigate are limited but not eliminated. Generally, suit can be brought against an automobile driver only when serious injury has resulted from the accident or special damages exceed a given dollar amount, called a threshold. For nonserious injuries and those resulting in losses below the threshold, only no-fault benefits are available. Serious injuries, or those resulting in losses in excess of the dollar-value threshold, permit the injured party to take legal action, including claims for general damages (such as pain and suffering).

In states that adopted modified no-fault laws as shown in Table 11.1, there are two types of modification: (1) the Verbal Threshold, which describes the types of injuries for which the party at fault is considered liable, as in Florida, Michigan, New Jersey, New York, and Pennsylvania, and (2) the Monetary Threshold, which has a monetary limit under which no fault is assigned. When the claim is over this amount (Massachusetts' threshold, for example, is $2,000), the at-fault system kicks in.

Some states do not limit rights to litigate but do require that insurers offer first-party coverage similar to what is available in no-fault states. An injured party can be compensated from his or her own insurer. The insurer in turn can sue the negligent driver. Because rights to litigate are not affected, these programs are called **add-on plans** or expanded first-party coverage.

No-Fault Appraised

Interest in no-fault grew from the belief that the tort system is slow, erratic in its results, and expensive considering the portion of the premium dollar used to compensate persons injured in automobile crashes.[2] If the tort system could be bypassed, all the expenses of the process—including costs of defense and plaintiff's counsel—could be eliminated. This

CHAPTER 11   MANAGING AUTOMOBILE RISKS   **241**

TABLE 11.1   State Auto Insurance Laws Governing Liability Coverage

"True" No-Fault	First-party benefits		Restrictions on lawsuits		Thresholds for lawsuits	
	Compulsory	Optional	Yes	No	Monetary	Verbal
Colorado	X		X		X	
Florida	X		X			X
Hawaii	X		X		X	
Kansas	X		X		X	
Kentucky	X		X	X	X	
Massachusetts	X		X		X	
Michigan	X		X			X
Minnesota	X		X		X	
New Jersey	X		X	X		X
New York	X		X			X
North Dakota	X		X		X	
Pennsylvania	X		X	X		X
Utah	X		X		X	
Puerto Rico	X		X		X	
Add-on						
Arkansas		X		X		
Delaware	X			X		
D.C.		X	X	X		
Maryland	X			X		
New Hampshire		X		X		
Oregon	X			X		
South Dakota		X		X		
Texas		X		X		
Virginia		X		X		
Washington		X		X		
Wisconsin		X		X		

"Choice" no-fault state. Policyholder can choose a policy on the no-fault system or traditional tort liability. Verbal threshold for the Basic Policy contains lower amounts of coverage. The District of Columbia is neither a true no-fault or add-on state. Drivers are offered the option of no-fault or fault-based coverage, but in the event of an accident, a driver who originally chose no-fault benefits has 60 days to decide whether to receive those benefits or file a claim against the other party.

Source: American Insurance Association as appeared in the *I.I.I. Insurance Fact Book,* 2002, p. 49.

would make more dollars available for compensation at no additional cost to insureds and, perhaps, even reduce the cost of insurance. Proponents of no-fault assert that enough money is spent on automobile insurance to compensate all crash victims but that the tort system wastes funds on the question of fault. Therefore, the concept of fault should be abandoned and the funds used more effectively. Furthermore, proponents argue that evidence is weak (if it exists at all) that insurance premiums actually reflect loss potentials and therefore work to deter unsafe driving.

Opponents of no-fault argue that it is simply compulsory health insurance with restrictions on tort action. They observe that workers' compensation was designed to reduce litigation by abandoning employers' liability, but that in recent times litigation in that field has been increasing. Opponents of no-fault assert that many people who favor no-fault do so primarily because they expect it will be cheaper than the present system when, in fact, it may cost more. This issue is featured in "Ethical Dilemma: Who Pays for Insurance Fraud?" It is argued that the no-fault system in New York is a major contributor to fraud, which, in turn, causes rate hikes in automobile insurance. They also point out that those who wish to cover their own life and health risks associated with the automobile on a voluntary basis may do so without giving up their right to sue the party at fault; such insurance is readily available and has been for a long time in the form of PIP and medical payments coverage (explained later).

FINANCIAL RESPONSIBILITY LAWS

Every state has some kind of **financial responsibility law** to induce motorists to buy auto liability insurance so victims of their negligence will receive compensation. A typical law requires evidence of financial responsibility when a driver is involved in an accident or convicted of a specified offense, such as driving while intoxicated. The simplest way to prove such responsibility is to have an auto liability insurance policy with specified limits that meet or exceed the minimum limits set by various state legislatures. The financial responsibility laws in the various states are shown in Table 11.2. Insurers and consumer

TABLE 11.2 Automobile Financial Responsibility/Compulsory Limits by State

State	Liability limits	State	Liability limits	State	Liability limits
Alabama	20/40/10	Kentucky	25/50/10	North Dakota	25/50/25
Alaska	50/100/25	Louisiana	10/20/10	Ohio	12.5/25/7.5
Arizona	15/30/10	Maine	50/100/25	Oklahoma	10/20/10
Arkansas	25/50/25	Maryland	20/40/15	Oregon	25/50/10
California[2]	15/30/5	Massachusetts	20/40/5	Pennsylvania	15/30/5
Colorado	25/50/15	Michigan	20/40/10	Rhode Island	25/50/25
Connecticut	20/40/10	Minnesota	30/60/10	South Carolina	15/30/10
Delaware	15/30/5	Mississippi	10/20/05	South Dakota	25/50/25
D.C.	25/50/10	Missouri	25/50/10	Tennessee[3]	25/50/10
Florida[4]	10/20/10	Montana	25/50/10	Texas	20/40/15
Georgia	25/50/25	Nebraska	25/50/25	Utah	25/50/15
Hawaii	20/40/10	Nevada	15/30/10	Vermont	25/50/10
Idaho	25/50/15	New Hampshire[6]	25/50/25	Virginia	25/50/20
Illinois	20/40/15	New Jersey[4]	15/30/5	Washington	25/50/10
Indiana	25/50/10	New Mexico	25/50/10	West Virginia	20/40/10
Iowa	20/40/15	New York[7]	25/50/10	Wisconsin[5]	25/50/10
Kansas	25/50/10	North Carolina	30/60/25	Wyoming	25/50/20

[1]The first two figures refer to bodily injury liability and the third figure to property damage liability. For example, 20/40/10 means coverage up to $40,000 for all persons injured in an accident, subject to a limit of $20,000 for one individual, and $10,000 coverage for property damage. [2]Low-cost policy limits for Los Angeles and San Francisco low-income drivers in the California Automobile Assigned Risk Plan are 10/20/3. This is a pilot program effective from July 1, 2000 until January 1, 2004. [3]Although legally defined as financial responsibility, Tennessee's law is similar to a compulsory law because drivers can be fined if stopped by police or after crashes if they cannot show proof of financial responsibility. [4]Only property damage liability is compulsory. [5]Liability insurance not compulsory; limits are for financial responsibility. [6]Drivers may choose a Standard or Basic Policy. Basic Policy limits are 10/10/5. [7]50/100 if injury results in death.

Source: Alliance of American Insurers; American Insurance Association; National Association of Independent Insurers; Insurance Information Institute, as featured in *The I.I.I. Insurance Fact Book,* 2002, p. 47.

advocacy groups recommend a minimum of $100,000 of bodily injury protection per person and $300,000 per accident to avoid paying from your pocket in case of liability.[3]

Several states also have **unsatisfied judgment funds** for situations when an injured motorist obtains a judgment against the party at fault but cannot collect because the party has neither insurance nor resources. The maximum amount the injured party may claim from the fund is usually the same as that established by the state's financial responsibility law. When the fund pays the judgment, the party at fault becomes indebted to the fund and his or her driving privilege is suspended until the fund is reimbursed.

Financial responsibility laws increased the percentage of drivers with auto liability insurance, but many drivers remained uninsured. Therefore, about half the states require evidence of insurance prior to licensing the driver or the vehicle. Unfortunately, in many such states only about 80 or 90 percent of the drivers maintain their insurance after licensing. Even a compulsory auto liability insurance law does not guarantee that you will not be injured by a financially irresponsible driver. A **compulsory auto liability insurance law** requires automobile registrants to have specified liability insurance in effect at all times; however, numerous drivers find ways to operate motor vehicles without insurance.

ASSURING AUTO INSURANCE AVAILABILITY

The assumption underlying laws requiring motorists to buy automobile liability insurance is that it is available. Unfortunately, some drivers cannot buy insurance through usual channels because, as a group, their losses are excessive. As a result, people injured by such drivers might not be able to collect anything for their losses. Presumably this problem could be solved by charging higher premium rates for such drivers, as is the case of insurers providing coverage to the so-called **substandard market,** in which some companies offer limited auto coverage to high-risk drivers at high premium rates. These insurers can do so because of the availability of computerized systems permitting them to calculate the rates for smaller groups of insureds.

The methods of creating a market for people who cannot buy auto insurance through the usual channels are listed in Figure 11.2. Known as the **residual market or shared market,** they are created by state law. The private passenger percent of cars that are insured by the shared market facilities was the largest in North Carolina in 1999 with 21.8 percent market share. This was followed by Massachusetts with 9.4 percent and South Carolina with 8.3 percent.[4]

Auto Insurance Plans

Auto insurance plans were formerly called **assigned risk plans** because they operate on an assignment basis. Drivers who cannot buy auto liability insurance through the usual channels can apply to such a plan. They are assigned to an insurer who must sell them coverage that meets the requirements of the financial responsibility law. Every company writing auto insurance in the state is a member of the plan and each must take its share of such business. If a company writes 10 percent of the auto insurance business in the state, it has to accept 10 percent of the qualified applicants. In spite of generally higher rates than in

FIGURE 11.2	Auto insurance plans	Joint underwriting associations
Auto Insurance Residual Market	Reinsurance facilities	Maryland state fund

the voluntary market, auto insurance plans have caused significant losses to the auto insurance industry.

Reinsurance Facilities

Where there is a **reinsurance facility**—Massachusetts, North Carolina, New Hampshire, and South Carolina—every auto insurer is required to issue auto insurance to any licensed driver who applies and can pay the premium. The insurer can transfer the burden of bad risks to the facility, a pool to which all auto insurers belong. As members of the pool, insurers share in both premiums and losses. The insured generally knows nothing about this arrangement; like all other insureds, he or she receives a policy issued by the company to which he or she applied. In some states, however, a specific insurer is designated to service the policy or pay for losses of a given insured; then the insured likely knows his or her status in the facility.

Joint Underwriting Associations

Where there is a **joint underwriting association**—Florida, Hawaii, and Missouri—all automobile insurers in the state are members and the association is, in effect, an insurance industry company. Several insurers are appointed as servicing carriers to act as agents for the association. An applicant for insurance who cannot meet underwriting requirements in the regular market is issued a policy by the servicing carrier on behalf of the association; so far as the policyholder is concerned, the association is his or her insurer. Premiums and losses are shared by all the auto insurers in the state, similar to the auto insurance plan. The JUA differs from an auto insurance plan in that only designated servicing carriers are able to issue coverage to participants.

Maryland State Fund

This government-operated residual market company provides coverage to drivers who cannot obtain insurance through the regular market. In spite of high premiums, however, it has suffered heavy losses. Originally, it was to bear such losses itself (through taxation), but the law now requires that the private insurance industry subsidize the fund.

PERSONAL AUTO POLICY

The **personal auto policy** (PAP) is the automobile insurance contract purchased by most individuals, whether to meet financial responsibility laws or just to protect against the costs associated with auto accidents. A copy of the Insurance Services Office's sample PAP is provided in Appendix B at the back of the text. It begins with a declarations page, general insuring agreement, and list of important definitions. These are followed by the policy's six major parts:

Part A—Liability coverage
Part B—Medical payments coverage
Part C—Uninsured motorists coverage
Part D—Coverage for damage to your auto
Part E—Duties after an accident or loss
Part F—General provisions

Each of the first four parts has its own insuring agreement, exclusions, and other insurance provisions, but most conditions are in parts E and F. In a sense, each of the first four parts is (almost) a separate policy and the PAP is a package that brings them all together. Each part is made effective by indicating in the declarations that the premium has been paid for that specific part and the coverage applies. When you receive your policy, check the declarations to be sure they show a premium for all the coverages you requested, and see that the information relating to your policy is correct.

Parts E and F apply to the entire policy. As we discuss each part, you will find reference to the specimen policy in Appendix B helpful.

Declarations

The declarations identify you by name and address and show the term of the policy, the premiums charged, the coverages provided, and the limits of liability of the coverages. You—and your spouse, if you are married—are the named insured(s). A description of the automobile(s) covered—by year, name, model, identification or serial number, and date of purchase—is included. The loss payee for physical damage to the automobile is listed to protect the lender who has financed the automobile's purchase, and the garaging address is shown. The latter is an important underwriting factor. Loss frequency and severity vary from one area (called territory by ratemakers) to another. For example, losses are generally greater in urban than in rural areas. Although many people drive all over the country, most driving is done within a rather short distance of the place the car is typically garaged. Thus, the place where it is garaged affects the premium.

Where is your car garaged if your home is in a rural area but you are attending a university in a large city or different state? It would be wise to talk to your agent about this question. He or she will—or should—know what the insurer's interpretation is about identifying the proper "garaging" location. You, of course, want to avoid misrepresenting a material fact, which could void the policy.

Definitions

Definitions are crucial elements of insurance policies, because the meaning of a term may determine in a particular instance whether or not you have coverage. Any term found in quotations in the policy is defined. Some are defined in the definitions section, others within the separate coverage sections.

Those found in the definitions section include the following. "You" and "your" refer to the "named insured" shown in the declarations, and the spouse if a resident of the same household. "We," "us," and "our" refer to the insurance company. A private passenger auto is deemed to be owned by a person if leased under a written agreement to that person for a continuous period of at least six months. If you refer to the PAP in Appendix B, you will see that the most recent ISO PAP is as of 1998. This PAP added to the definition of "you" and "your" the new limitation on spouses that leave the residence. These spouses are no longer covered.

> If the spouse ceased to be resident of the same household during the policy period or prior to the inception of this policy, the spouse will be considered "you" and "your" under this policy but only until the earlier of: (1) the end of 90 days following the spouse's change of residency,(2) the effective date of another policy listing the spouse as a named insured; or (3) the end of the policy period.

"Bodily injury" (page 1, section D) occurs when there is bodily harm, sickness, or disease, including resulting death. "Property damage" (in section H) involves physical damage to, destruction of, or loss of use of tangible property. A "business" includes trade, profession, or occupation. "Family member" (in section F) means a resident of your household related to you by blood, marriage, or adoption. This includes a ward or foster child. "Occupying" (in section G) means in, upon, getting in, on, out, or off. It may seem ridiculous to define a common word such as "occupying," but a reading of the exclusions for medical payments coverage shows how crucial the definition may be. A recent example provides helpful illustration. A woman walked to her car, and while unlocking the door was struck by another vehicle. The insurer included this scenario under the category of "occupying."

"Trailer" means a vehicle designed to be pulled by a private passenger auto or pickup, panel truck, or van. It also means a farm wagon or farm implement being towed by one of the vehicles listed.

"Your covered auto"(in section J) includes:

- Any vehicle shown in the declarations.
- A "newly acquired auto."
- Any "trailer" you own.
- Any auto or trailer you do not own while used as a temporary substitute for any other vehicle described in this definition that is out of normal use because of its breakdown, repair, servicing, loss, or destruction.

Section K defines "newly acquired auto" and the various provisions regarding such an auto.

Liability Coverage—Part A

In the PAP, the liability insuring agreement can be paraphrased as,

> We will pay damages for "bodily injury" or "property damage" for which any "insured" becomes legally responsible because of an auto accident. Damages include prejudgment interest awarded against the "insured." We will settle or defend, as we consider appropriate, any claim or suit asking for these damages. In addition to our limit of liability, we will pay all defense costs we incur…."

In the liability part of the PAP, the policy defines insured as:

1. You or any family member, for the ownership, maintenance, or use of any auto or trailer.
2. Any person using your covered auto.
3. For your covered auto, any person or organization, but only with respect to legal responsibility for acts or omissions of a person for whom coverage is afforded under this part.
4. For any auto or trailer other than your covered auto, any person or organization, but only with respect to legal responsibility for acts or omissions of you or any family member for whom coverage is afforded under this part. This provision applies only if the person or organization does not own or hire the auto or trailer.

In a situation where the owner of the car lends you the covered auto to take children to the church picnic, you become a covered person, according to definition 2. The policy will cover your liability in connection with an accident on the way to the picnic. It will also, according to definition 3, cover any liability the church may have in connection with the accident if the kids get hurt. If, on the other hand, I borrow the other person's car to take the children to the church picnic, I am a covered person according to definition 1, and the church's liability for any accident I might have is covered by definition 4. In both situations, coverage for the organization stems from the fact that the driver is a covered person. It is important to understand, that it does not matter who is driving the covered car; as long as the driver has permission to drive the car, he or she is covered under the policy. The coverage for the car is the first insurance company that pays for the accident. If the liability is larger, the other driver's policy picks up the rest of the liability.

Defense

Section A of Part A of the liability coverage quoted above indicates that legal defense is not part of the limits of liability. Defense costs often run into thousands of dollars, making this a significant benefit of liability insurance. If you are found liable, the insurer pays on your behalf to the plaintiff(s), up to the limit(s) of liability under the policy. The insurer's responsibility to defend ends when that limit is reached (is paid in award or settlement to third-party claimants).

The insurer retains the right to settle claims without the insured's approval if it finds this expedient. Such action keeps many cases out of court and reduces insurance claims expenses. It can, however, cause dissatisfaction if the insured did not expect to have to settle.

Exclusions

The wording of the insuring agreement of part A provides for open perils liability coverage. All events resulting in automobile liability, therefore, are covered unless specifically excluded. Some exclusions apply to unprotected persons and others to noncovered vehicles. The exclusions, listed in Table 11.3, can be discussed in terms of the purposes of exclusions presented in Chapter 6.

As in the homeowners policy, intentionally caused (nonfortuitous) harm is always excluded. As before, several exclusions exist to prevent duplicate coverage, which would result in over-indemnification. Property damage to owned or used property, for instance, ought to be covered under other property insurance contracts such as a homeowners policy and is, therefore, excluded in the PAP. As noted in the homeowners coverage, bodily injury to an employee of the covered person who is eligible for workers' compensation benefits is excluded. Anyone using a motor vehicle as a taxi, for example, represents greater risk than one who does not. Thus, persons using a vehicle as a "public livery or conveyance" are excluded from coverage. Because persons employed in the automobile business represent a significant risk while in their employment status, they too are excluded. You can understand that the insurer prefers not to provide coverage to the mechanic while he or she is test driving your car. The automobile business is expected to have its own automobile policy, with rates that reflect its unique hazards.

Certain other occupations require the use of vehicles that are hazardous regardless of who operates them. Large garbage trucks, for example, are difficult to control. Insurers do not provide liability protection while you operate such a vehicle. Insurers, however, do not exclude all business uses of motor vehicles. Specifically excepted from the exclusion are private passenger autos (for example, those of traveling salespeople); owned pickups, or vans; trailers used with any of these vehicles; and any vehicle used in a farming or ranching business.

Insurers also standardize the risk through exclusion of coverage while "using a vehicle without a reasonable belief that that person is entitled to do so." The insurance company rates the policy according to the insured's characteristics, which include who the insured allows to use the covered auto. A thief, or someone without permission to use the covered auto, does not reflect these characteristics. Questions sometimes arise when an insured's child allows a friend to use the covered car, despite parents' admonitions to the contrary. Court rulings are mixed on the application of the exclusion in such a setting. Generally, such persons represent greater risks. The use of a motor vehicle with less than four wheels also represents a greater risk than one with at least four wheels. It too is excluded.

To prevent catastrophic exposure, the PAP excludes persons covered under nuclear energy liability policies. This exclusion is a standard provision in all liability policies.

The final two exclusions are confusing. Their purpose is to prevent insureds from obtaining more coverage than was purchased. Thus, no coverage applies for accidents arising out of ownership, maintenance, or use of a motor vehicle "you" own or have available for regular use if it is not a declared auto in the declarations section of the policy. If such protection were available, you would need only to purchase coverage on one vehicle instead of on all your owned vehicles. The second exclusion is the same, except it applies to motor vehicles owned by or available for the regular use of "family members." This last exclusion does not apply to "you." Remember that "you" is the named insured and the named insured's spouse. Thus, if the named insured uses a noncovered vehicle owned by a family member (perhaps a son or daughter living at home), liability coverage exists. On the other hand, the family member who owns the noncovered vehicle is not protected while driving the undeclared auto.

Supplementary Payments

In addition to the limit for liability, the insurer will pay up to $250 for the cost of bail bonds required because of an accident, if the accident results in bodily injury or property damage covered by the policy. Note that this would not cover the cost of a bond for a traffic ticket you receive when there is no accident. Premiums on appeal bonds and bonds to release attachments are paid in any suit the insurer defends. Interest accruing after a judgment is entered and reasonable expenses incurred at the insurer's request are paid. Up to $200 a day for loss of earnings because of attendance at hearings or trials is also available.

Single or Split Limits

Although liability coverage under the PAP usually is subject to a single, aggregate limit (called a combined single limit, or CSL), it can be divided by use of an endorsement into two major subparts: bodily injury liability and property damage liability. Bodily injury liability applies when the use of your car results in the injury or death of pedestrians, passengers of other vehicles, or passengers of your automobile. Property damage liability coverage applies when your car damages property belonging to others. Although the first thing you probably think about under this coverage is the other person's car, and you are right, this coverage could also cover street signs, fences, bicycles, telephone poles, houses, and other types of property. Remember, however, that it does not apply to your house or to other property you own, because you cannot be legally liable to yourself.

If you choose a **single limit** of liability to cover all liability, including both property damage and bodily injury, then the insurer will pay on your behalf for all losses up to this limit for any single accident, whether they are property-related or injury-related. The only limit you are concerned with in this case is the single, or aggregate limit. Once all losses equal this limit, you will have to bear the burden of any further liability.

TABLE 11.3

Personal Auto Policy
Part A Exclusions as
listed in the ISO PAP,
1998

EXCLUSIONS

A.   We do not provide Liability Coverage for any "insured":

1.   Who intentionally causes "bodily injury" or "property damage".

2.   For "property damage" to property owned or being transported by that "insured".

3.   For "property damage" to property:

   a. Rented to;

   b. Used by; or

   c. In the care of;

   that "insured".

   This Exclusion **(A.3.)** does not apply to "property damage" to a residence or private garage.

4.   For "bodily injury" to an employee of that "insured" during the course of employment. This Exclusion **(A.4.)** does not apply to "bodily injury" to a domestic employee unless workers' compensation benefits are required or available for that domestic employee.

5.   For that "insured's" liability arising out of the ownership or operation of a vehicle while it is being used as a public or livery conveyance. This Exclusion **(A.5.)** does not apply to a share-the-expense car pool.

6.   While employed or otherwise engaged in the "business" of:

   a. Selling;

   b. Repairing;

   c. Servicing;

   d. Storing; or

   e. Parking;

   vehicles designed for use mainly on public highways. This includes road testing and delivery. This Exclusion **(A.6.)** does not apply to the ownership, maintenance or use of "your covered auto" by:

   a. You;

   b. Any "family member"; or

   c. Any partner, agent or employee of you or any "family member".

7.   Maintaining or using any vehicle while that "insured" is employed or otherwise engaged in any "business" (other than farming or ranching) not described in Exclusion **A.6.** This Exclusion **(A.7.)** does not apply to the maintenance or use of a:

   a. Private passenger auto;

   b. Pickup or van; or

   c. "Trailer" used with a vehicle described in **a.** or **b.** above.

(Continued)

If you choose a **split limit** of liability, a set of two limits will be specifically applied to bodily injury, and a single, aggregate limit applied to property damage. For the bodily injury limits, one limit applies per person, per accident, and a second limit is the total the insurer will pay for liability to all persons injured in an accident. The limit for property damage is shown separately. Thus, your limits are shown as, for example:

Bodily injury $150,000 each person, $300,000 each accident
Property damage $50,000 each accident

In insurance jargon, these limits would be described as 150/300/50. An example will help illustrate how the split limits work. If you caused an accident in which only one person was injured, the coverage is limited to $150,000 for that person. If the accident involved six people, each person is covered up to $150,000 but the total for all six injured people combined cannot exceed $300,000. So, if all are badly injured, the limit for the accident may not be sufficient. In this case and as discussed in Chapter 10, an umbrella policy with high limits—such as $1 million—may be very valuable.

Alternatively, a single limit, say $300,000, could be purchased to cover all liabilities from any one accident. Whether you have single or split limits, the need for adequate

8. Using a vehicle without a reasonable belief that that "insured" is entitled to do so. This Exclusion (**A.8.**) does not apply to a "family member" using "your covered auto" which is owned by you.
9. For "bodily injury" or "property damage" for which that "insured":
    a. Is an insured under a nuclear energy liability policy; or
    b. Would be an insured under a nuclear energy liability policy but for its termination upon exhaustion of its limit of liability.
    A nuclear energy liability policy is a policy issued by any of the following or their successors:
    a. Nuclear Energy Liability Insurance Association;
    b. Mutual Atomic Energy Liability Underwriters;
    or
    c. Nuclear Insurance Association of Canada.
B. We do not provide Liability Coverage for the ownership, maintenance or use of:
    1. Any vehicle which:
        a. Has fewer than four wheels; or
        b. Is designed mainly for use off public roads.
        This Exclusion (B.1.) does not apply:
        a. While such vehicle is being used by an "insured" in a medical emergency;
        b. To any "trailer"; or
        c. To any non-owned golf cart.
    2. Any vehicle, other than "your covered auto", which is:
        a. Owned by you; or
        b. Furnished or available for your regular use.
    3. Any vehicle, other than "your covered auto", which is:
        a. Owned by any "family member"; or
        b. Furnished or available for the regular use of any "family member".
        However, this Exclusion (B.3.) does not apply to you while you are maintaining or "occupying" any vehicle which is:
        a. Owned by a "family member"; or
        b. Furnished or available for the regular use of a "family member".
    4. Any vehicle, located inside a facility designed for racing, for the purpose of:
        a. Competing in; or
        b. Practicing or preparing for; any prearranged or organized racing or speed contest.

limits is imperative as noted above. Also note the clarifying language in "limit of liability," which states that the amount shown is the maximum payable, regardless of the number of covered persons, claims made, vehicles or premiums shown in the declarations, or vehicles involved in the auto accident. If two vehicles shown in the declarations are involved in the same accident, therefore, twice the limit of liability will not be available. At least, this is the intent of the insurer. Various state courts have interpreted the policy differently, permitting what is called **stacking**. Stacking may occur when a single policy covers two vehicles and the court interprets this situation to yield a limit of liability equal to double the amount shown in the declarations.

Out-of-State Coverage

Part A also has provisions for out-of-state coverage and other insurance. The out-of-state provision takes care of a situation in which your liability limits comply with the financial responsibility or compulsory insurance law in your state but are inadequate in another state. It provides that, under such circumstances, your policy will provide at least the minimum amounts and types of coverage required by the state in which you are driving. Suppose you have limits of 15/25/15 ($15,000/$25,000/$15,000), the minimum required in the state where your car is garaged. If you are driving in a state that requires 25/50/20 ($25,000/$50,000/$20,000) and are involved in an accident, your insurer will interpret your policy as if it had the higher limits. Thus, even though you have to meet only the requirements where you live, your policy will provide the limits you need in any state or province in which you may be driving.

Financial Responsibility

This one sentence states: "When this policy is certified as future proof of financial responsibility, this policy shall comply with the law to the extent required." The requirements in each state are shown in Table 11.2.

Other Insurance

The liability coverage of the PAP is excess with regard to a nonowned vehicle. In the event of a loss while you are driving a friend's car, your insurer will pay only the amount by which a claim (or judgment) exceeds the limits of your friend's auto insurance. In such a situation, your friend's insurance is **primary coverage** (it pays first) and your insurance is excess coverage. This means that coverage on the vehicle is always primary. If, however, two excess policies apply, then the "other insurance" provision calls for a pro rata distribution of liability. For example, if you were driving a friend's car whose insurance had expired and you were an insured under two policies (as, perhaps, a resident relative of two insureds who bought separate policies on their vehicles), these two policies would share in any liability attributable to you on a pro rata basis. This example, however, is quite unusual.

Medical Payments Coverage—Part B

Medical payments coverage, which is optional in some states and from some insurers, overlaps with family health insurance coverage. You may consider it unnecessary if you have excellent health insurance. Your own family health insurance does not cover nonfamily members riding in your vehicle, so it is narrower than is medical payments coverage. Yet, if you are liable, part A will provide coverage. If not, your passengers may have their own health insurance.

Insuring Agreement

Under part B, the insurer agrees to pay reasonable expenses incurred within three years from the date of an accident for necessary medical and funeral services because of bodily injury caused by an accident and sustained by a covered person. A covered person means you or any family member, while occupying, or as a pedestrian when struck by, a motor vehicle designed for use mainly on public roads, or a trailer of any type. It also includes any other person occupying your covered auto.

Note that you or a family member would be covered by your PAP medical payments protection while occupying a nonowned car, but not other passengers in the vehicle. No benefits are paid if you are struck by a machine not designed for use on the highway, such as a farm tractor.

Exclusions

Medical payments coverage is similar to liability coverage in that it is provided on an open perils basis within the category of automobile use. Seven of the exclusions to part A (liability) are nearly identical to exclusions found in part B (medical payments). These are:

- While occupying a motor vehicle with less than four wheels
- While occupying your covered auto when it is being used as a public livery or conveyance
- While occupying any vehicle located for use as a residence or premises
- During the course of employment if workers' compensation is available
- While occupying or when struck by any vehicle (other than your covered auto) which is: (a) owned by you, or (b) furnished or available for your regular use
- While occupying or when struck by any vehicle (other than your covered auto) which is: (a) owned by any family member; or (b) furnished or available for the regular use of any family member
- While occupying a vehicle without a reasonable belief that the insured is entitled to do so
- While occupying a vehicle when it is being used in the business or occupation of a covered person, unless the vehicle is a private passenger auto, pickup, or van owned by the insured, or trailer used with one of these means of transportation
- Caused by the consequence of nuclear weapon, war, civil war, insurrection, or rebellion or revolution
- Consequence of nuclear reaction to radiation or radioactive contamination
- While occupying any vehicle located inside a facility designed for racing, for the purpose of (a) competing in or (b) practicing or preparing for any prearranged or organized racing or speed contest

Limit of Liability

The limit of liability for medical payments is on a per person basis, such as $5,000 per person. This is the maximum limit of liability for each person injured in any one accident. If you have two autos insured with a medical payments limit for each shown on the declarations page, you cannot add all (stack) the limits together. It may appear that you have $10,000 in medical payments coverage because you have $5,000 on each vehicle, but such is not intended by the insurer.

When there is other applicable auto medical payments insurance, your policy will pay on a pro rata basis. With respect to nonowned automobiles, however, the PAP is excess. That is, it pays only after the limits of all other applicable insurance have been exhausted.

Other Insurance

Any amounts payable by this coverage are reduced by any amounts payable for the same expenses under part A (liability) or part C (uninsured motorists). Thus, a passenger in your car who is injured cannot recover under both liability and medical payments coverages for the same losses. Nor can you recover under both medical payments and the uninsured motorists coverages. Injured parties are entitled to indemnity, but not double payment.

Uninsured Motorists Coverage—Part C

Uninsured motorists coverage pays for bodily injuries (and property damage in some states) caused by an accident with another vehicle whose driver is negligent and either (1) has no liability insurance or less than that required by law, (2) was a hit-and-run driver, or (3) was a driver whose insurance company is insolvent. Covered persons include you or any family member, any other person occupying your covered auto, and any other person entitled to recovery because of bodily injury to a person in the first two categories. An example of "any other person entitled to recovery" is one who has suffered loss of companionship as a result of a spouse (who was in one of the first two categories) being injured in an accident.

Minimum coverage is the amount required to comply with your state's financial responsibility or compulsory insurance law. You can, however, purchase additional coverage up to the limit you purchased under part A. In addition, if you purchase increased amounts of uninsured motorists coverage, you are eligible to buy underinsured motorists coverage, which is discussed later in this chapter.

Uninsured Motor Vehicle

Because you can recover under part C of the PAP only if you are involved in an accident with a negligent driver of an uninsured motor vehicle, the definition of such a vehicle is crucial. The policy defines it as a land motor vehicle or trailer of any type, with the following specifications:

- One to which no bodily injury liability bond or policy applies at the time of the accident
- One to which there is a bodily injury liability bond or policy in force, but the limit of liability is less than that specified by the financial responsibility law in the state where your covered auto is garaged
- A hit-and-run vehicle whose operator/owner cannot be identified and that hits you or any family member, a vehicle you or any family member are occupying, or your covered auto
- One to which a bodily injury liability bond or policy applies at the time of the accident, but the company denies coverage or is insolvent

However, an uninsured motor vehicle does not include any vehicle or equipment:

- Owned by, furnished, or available for the regular use of you or any family member
- Owned or operated by a self-insurer under any applicable motor vehicle law, except a self-insurer which is or becomes insolvent
- Owned by any governmental unit or agency
- Operated on rails or crawler treads
- Designed mainly for use off public roads while not on public roads
- While located for use as a residence or premises

Exclusions

Perhaps because the definition of an uninsured motor vehicle is so limited, only four exclusions apply to part C. Like the prior two parts, uninsured motorist coverage excludes loss:

A. Involving an undeclared motor vehicle owned by you or any family member

B. While using a vehicle without reasonable belief of permission

C. When there is other coverage such as workers' compensation or disability benefits

D. Not applicable to punitive damages

In addition, exclusion B1 denies payment to a covered person "if that person or the legal representative settles the bodily injury claim without our consent." Just because a negligent driver is an uninsured motorist, he or she is not free from liability. The insurer, therefore, does not want its subrogation rights to be adversely affected by agreements between the insured and negligent driver, which could include collusive and fraudulent situations.

On the other hand, the auto insurer does not want to make uninsured motorists payments available through subrogation to a workers' compensation or disability benefits insurer. If the accident occurred during the course of employment, resulting in workers' compensation benefits, the compensation insurer might seek such subrogation. Exclusion C prevents this type of activity.

Last, the coverage is not intended to pay for punitive damages. These are excluded. Additionally, the insuring agreement is specific in promising to pay compensatory damages only. Punitive damages are not compensatory.

Other Provisions

The limit of liability provision for uninsured motorists coverage is virtually the same as for medical payments (although the actual limit is usually quite different). The other insurance provision is the same as that for parts A and B; namely, pro rata for your covered auto and excess for a nonowned auto. In the event of a dispute concerning the right to recover damages or their amount, either party—you or the insurer—can demand binding arbitration. Local rules as to procedure and evidence apply.

There are provisions for other insurance and for arbitration. The arbitration section specifies that if the insured and the insurer do not agree about the amounts of entitled recovery of damages, both parties can arbitrate. But both must agree to arbitration and may not be forced to arbitrate.

Underinsured motorists coverage fills in the coverage gap that arises when the negligent party meets the financial responsibility law of the state, but the auto accident victim has losses in excess of the negligent driver's liability limit. In such circumstances, when the negligent driver meets the legal insurance requirements but is legally responsible for additional amounts, the driver is not an uninsured motorist. The negligent driver may not have available other noninsurance resources to pay for the loss, leaving the injured party to bear the financial strain. Underinsured motorists coverage permits the insured to purchase coverage for this situation.

You may purchase underinsured motorists coverage in amounts up to the amount of liability (part A) protection you purchased. The same amount of uninsured motorists coverage must also be purchased. The underinsured motorists coverage will pay the difference between the at-fault driver's liability and the at-fault driver's limit of liability insurance, up to the amount of underinsured motorists coverage purchased. For example, assume you were hit by another motorist, incurring damages of $60,000. Further assume that the other driver is found liable for the full amount of your loss, but carries insurance of only $30,000, which meets the financial responsibility law requirement. An underinsured motorists coverage equal to your limit of liability coverage, say $100,000, would cover the remaining $30,000 of loss above the at-fault driver's insurance. Your total payment, however, could not exceed the underinsured motorists coverage limit of liability. If your loss were $115,000, therefore, you would receive $30,000 from the at-fault driver's insurer and $70,000 from your own insurer. The remaining $15,000 loss remains the responsibility of the at-fault driver, but you may have difficulty collecting it.

Coverage for Damage to Your Auto—Part D

Part D of the PAP is first-party property insurance. The insurer agrees to pay for direct and accidental loss to your covered auto and to any other nonowned auto used by you or a family member, subject to policy limitations and exclusions. Automobile equipment, generally meaning those items normally used in the auto and attached to or contained in it, is also covered. All of this is subject to a deductible.

You have the option of buying coverage for your automobile on an open perils basis by purchasing both **collision** and **other than collision** (also called **comprehensive**) coverage. You may instead opt to buy just collision (although it may be difficult to find a company to provide just collision coverage) or just other than collision, or neither. A premium for the coverage must be stated in the declarations for coverage to apply. The distinction between the two coverages may be important, because collision protection generally carries a higher deductible than other than collision coverage.

Collision means the upset (turning over) of the covered auto or "non-owned auto," or collision with another object. Every other type of loss-causing event is considered "other than collision." To help you identify certain ambiguous perils as either collision or other than collision, a list is provided in the policy. You might mistakenly take this list as one of exclusions. Rather, the perils shown in Table 11.4 are other than collision perils and are therefore covered along with other nonexcluded perils if other than collision coverage applies. For example, loss caused by an exploded bomb is neither collision nor among the events listed as examples of other than collision. Because breakage of glass may occur in a collision or by other means, the insurer will allow you to consider the glass breakage as part of the collision loss, negating dual deductibles.

In addition to the above, the insurer will pay up to $20 per day (to a maximum of $600) for transportation expenses in the event your covered auto is stolen. Transportation expenses would include car rental or the added cost of public transportation, taxis, and the like. You are entitled to expenses beginning forty-eight hours after the theft and ending when your covered auto is returned to you or its loss is paid. You must notify the police promptly if your covered auto is stolen.

Some insurers offer towing and labor coverage for additional premium. If your car breaks down, this coverage pays the cost of repairing it at the place where it became disabled or towing it to a garage. The limit of liability is $25 and a typical premium is $4 or $5. Considering the fact that you can get towing service and many other services for about the same cost from automobile associations, adding towing and labor to your policy may not be a bargain. Furthermore, if your car is disabled by collision or other than collision loss, the cost of towing it to the garage will be paid under those coverages.

TABLE 11.4 Other than Collision Losses		
1. Missiles and falling objects	6.	Hail, water, or flood
2. Fire	7.	Malicious mischief or vandalism
3. Theft or larceny	8.	Riot or civil commotion
4. Explosion or earthquake	9.	Contact with bird or animal
5. Windstorm	10.	Breakage of glass

Exclusions

Two of the exclusions found in part D (the first and third) have already been discussed. The remaining exclusions are dominated by limitations on the coverage for automobile equipment. Part D exclusions are listed in Table 11.5. One important exclusion reflects the high frequency of theft losses to certain equipment. Exclusion 4 omits coverage for electronic sound equipment unless permanently installed in the automobile. It also eliminates coverage on compact discs, tapes, and other equipment designed for the reproduction of sound, citizens band radios, two-way mobile radios, telephones, scanning monitor receivers, television monitor receivers, videocassette recorders, audiocassette recorders, or personal computers. Also excluded are personally installed telephones designed to be operated by use of the power from the auto's electrical system and any accessories used with the telephone. Overall, custom furnishings in pickups and vans and loss to awnings or cabanas and equipment designed to create additional living facilities are excluded. Such equipment represents nonstandard exposures for which insurance can be bought through endorsement.

Recall that trailers you own, whether declared or not, are defined as covered autos. To obtain property insurance on those trailers, they must be declared (permitting the insurer to charge a premium). Nonfortuitous losses are also excluded. Certain losses are expected or preventable, such as damage due to wear and tear, freezing, mechanical or electrical breakdown, and road damage to tires. Exclusion 7 denies coverage for loss or destruction because the government seized the vehicle. This exclusion follows the development of new laws associated with illegal drug trafficking and the handling of hazardous waste.

Prior to revisions in 1986, the PAP covered damage to nonowned autos (including temporary substitutes) for liability only. If you were driving a friend's car or a rental vehicle, the old policy would cover damage to that vehicle only if you were legally liable. The 1986 form provided property damage coverage for nonowned autos in part D, negating the requirement that you be liable. The 1989 form went one step further by including temporary substitutes (cars used because the declared vehicle is out of commission) in part D rather than part A.

The amount of coverage available for nonowned autos, however, is limited to the maximum available (actual cash value) on any declared auto. In addition, a deductible likely applies, and three exclusions relevant to nonowned autos have been added. First, a nonowned auto used without reasonable belief or permission to do so is not covered. Second, a nonowned vehicle damaged while being driven by someone performing operations associated with the automobile business (servicing, repairing, etc.) is not covered. Last, if the nonowned auto is driven by anyone in any business operation (other than a private passenger auto or trailer driven by "you" or any "family member"), the auto is not covered.

Other Provisions

The limit of liability is the lesser of the actual cash value of the stolen or damaged property or the amount necessary to repair or replace it. The insurer reserves the right to pay for the loss in money or repair or replace the damaged property. There are limits, however, as described in the policy: $500 for non-owned auto and $1,000 for equipment designed solely for the reproduction of sounds. For payment of loss, the insurer will repair or replace the damaged property. If the stolen property is returned damaged, the insurer will repair it.

TABLE 11.5

Personal Auto Policy Part D Exclusions as listed in the ISO PAP, 1998

EXCLUSIONS

We will not pay for:

1. Loss to "your covered auto" or any "non-owned auto" which occurs while it is being used as a public or livery conveyance. This Exclusion (**1.**) does not apply to a share-the-expense car pool.

2. Damage due and confined to:
   a. Wear and tear;
   b. Freezing;
   c. Mechanical or electrical breakdown or failure; or
   d. Road damage to tires.
   This Exclusion (**2.**) does not apply if the damage results from the total theft of "your covered auto" or any "non-owned auto".

3. Loss due to or as a consequence of:
   a. Radioactive contamination;
   b. Discharge of any nuclear weapon (even if accidental);
   c. War (declared or undeclared);
   d. Civil war;
   e. Insurrection; or
   f. Rebellion or revolution.

4. Loss to any electronic equipment designed for the reproduction of sound and any accessories used with such equipment. This includes but is not limited to:
   a. Radios and stereos;
   b. Tape decks; or
   c. Compact disc players.
   This Exclusion (**4.**) does not apply to equipment designed solely for the reproduction of sound and accessories used with such equipment, provided:
   a. The equipment is permanently installed in "your covered auto" or any "non-owned auto"; or
   b. The equipment is:
      (1) Removable from a housing unit which is permanently installed in the auto;
      (2) Designed to be solely operated by use of the power from the auto's electrical system; and
      (3) In or upon "your covered auto" or any "non-owned auto" at the time of loss.

5. Loss to any electronic equipment that receives or transmits audio, visual or data signals and any accessories used with such equipment. This includes but is not limited to:
   a. Citizens band radios;
   b. Telephones;
   c. Two-way mobile radios;
   d. Scanning monitor receivers;
   e. Television monitor receivers;
   f. Video cassette recorders;
   g. Audio cassette recorders; or
   h. Personal computers.
   This Exclusion (**5.**) does not apply to:
   a. Any electronic equipment that is necessary for the normal operation of the auto or the monitoring of the auto's operating systems; or
   b. A permanently installed telephone designed to be operated by use of the power from the auto's electrical system and any accessories used with the telephone.

(Continued)

The no benefit to bailee provision says, "This insurance shall not directly or indirectly benefit any carrier or other bailee for hire." If your car is damaged or stolen while in the custody of a parking lot or transportation company, your insurer will pay you and then have the right of subrogation against a negligent bailee. If other insurance covers a loss, your insurer will pay its share on a pro rata basis. If there is a dispute concerning the amount of loss, either you or the insurer may demand an appraisal, which is binding on

TABLE 11.5

Personal Auto Policy
Part D Exclusions as
listed in the ISO PAP,
1998 (Continued)

6. Loss to tapes, records, discs or other media used with equipment described in Exclusions **4.** and **5.**
7. A total loss to "your covered auto" or any "nonowned auto" due to destruction or confiscation by governmental or civil authorities.
This Exclusion **(7.)** does not apply to the interests of Loss Payees in "your covered auto".
8. Loss to:
   a. A "trailer", camper body, or motor home, which is not shown in the Declarations; or
   b. Facilities or equipment used with such "trailer", camper body or motor home. Facilities or equipment include but are not limited to:
      (1) Cooking, dining, plumbing or refrigeration facilities;
      (2) Awnings or cabanas; or
      (3) Any other facilities or equipment used with a "trailer", camper body, or motor home.
   This Exclusion **(8.)** does not apply to a:
   a. "Trailer", and its facilities or equipment, which you do not own; or
   b. "Trailer", camper body, or the facilities or equipment in or attached to the "trailer" or camper body, which you:
      (1) Acquire during the policy period; and
      (2) Ask us to insure within 14 days after you become the owner.
9. Loss to any "non-owned auto" when used by you or any "family member" without a reasonable belief that you or that "family member" are entitled to do so.
10. Loss to equipment designed or used for the detection or location of radar or laser.
11. Loss to any custom furnishings or equipment in or upon any pickup or van. Custom furnishings or equipment include but are not limited to:
    a. Special carpeting or insulation;
    b. Furniture or bars;
    c. Height-extending roofs; or
    d. Custom murals, paintings or other decals or graphics.
    This Exclusion **(11.)** does not apply to a cap, cover or bedliner in or upon any "your covered auto" which is a pickup.
12. Loss to any "non-owned auto" being maintained or used by any person while employed or otherwise engaged in the "business" of:
    a. Selling;
    b. Repairing;
    c. Servicing;
    d. Storing; or
    e. Parking;
    vehicles designed for use on public highways. This includes road testing and delivery.
13. Loss to "your covered auto" or any "non-owned auto", located inside a facility designed for racing, for the purpose of:
    a. Competing in; or
    b. Practicing or preparing for; any prearranged or organized racing or speed contest.
14. Loss to, or loss of use of, a "non-owned auto" rented by:
    a. You; or
    b. Any "family member";
    if a rental vehicle company is precluded from recovering such loss or loss of use, from you or that "family member", pursuant to the provisions of any applicable rental agreement or state law.

both parties. As a practical matter, appraisal is seldom used by an insured, because the cost is shared with the insurer.

The other insurance provision is pro rata except for nonowned autos, which is excess. In prior coverages, nonowned autos were included in the liability part, not part D. As in other parts of the policy, there is the appraisal section for evaluating the value of the loss.

Duties after an Accident or Loss—Part E

When an accident or loss occurs, you must notify the company promptly, indicating how, when, and where it happened. Notice should include the names and addresses of any injured persons and any witnesses. You can notify your agent or call the company. You must also comply with the following conditions:

- Cooperate with the insurer in the investigation, settlement, or defense of any claim or suit
- Promptly send the company copies of any notices or legal papers received in connection with the accident or loss
- Submit, as often as reasonably required and at the insurer's expense, to physical exams by physicians it selects, as well as examinations under oath
- Authorize the company to obtain medical reports and other pertinent records
- Submit a proof of loss when required by the insurer

A person seeking uninsured motorists coverage must also notify the police promptly if a hit-and-run driver is involved, and send copies of the legal papers if a suit is brought. The requirement that you notify the police concerning a hit-and-run driver is to discourage you from making such an allegation when, in fact, something else caused your accident. If, for example, you do not have coverage for damage to your auto but you do have uninsured motorists coverage, you may be tempted to use the latter after you fail to negotiate a sharp curve in the road. Having to report a hit-and-run driver to the police may deter you from making such an assertion.

If an accident causes damage to your car, or if it is stolen, you must also fulfill the following duties:

- Take reasonable steps after loss to protect the auto and its equipment from further loss (the company will pay for reasonable cost involved in complying with this requirement)
- Notify the police promptly if your car is stolen
- Permit the company to inspect and appraise the damaged property before its repair or disposal

The first duty listed means that you cannot just walk off and abandon your automobile after an accident. If you do, it may very well be stripped as an abandoned car. The second duty, prompt notification of the police in the event of theft, increases the probability that stolen property will be recovered. This requirement also reduces the moral hazard involved; people have been known to sell a car and then report it stolen. The third duty, permitting company appraisal, allows the insurer to inspect and appraise the loss before repairs are made in order to keep down costs. If you could simply take your damaged car to a repair shop, have the work done, and then send the bill to the insurance company, costs would increase immensely. The most common question you hear upon entering many (if not most) repair shops is, "Do you have insurance?"

General Provisions—Part F

Several general provisions apply to the whole contract. Following is a brief summary of each.

- Bankruptcy or insolvency of a covered person shall not relieve the insurer of any obligations under the policy. The fact that you are bankrupt does not relieve the insurance company of its obligation to pay a third-party claimant or you.

- Changes in the policy can be made only in writing, and may affect the premium charged. If the form is revised to provide more coverage without a premium increase, the policy you have will automatically provide it.

- The insurer does not provide any coverage for any insured who made fraudulent statements or engaged in fraudulent conduct in connection with any accident or loss for which coverage is sought under the policy.

- An insured cannot start legal proceedings against the insurer until there has been full compliance with all the terms of the policy.

- If a person who receives payment from the insurer has the right to recover damages from another, the insurer has the right to subrogation. Such a person must help the insurer to exercise its rights and do nothing after a loss to prejudice them. This would apply, for example, to a passenger in your car who is injured, receives payment under the medical payments coverage, and has the right to recover damages from a liable third party or a first-party health insurer. The company's subrogation right, however, does not apply under damage to your auto coverage against any person using your covered auto with a reasonable belief that he or she has the right to do so. If it were not for this provision, a person who borrowed your car with your permission and had a wreck would wind up paying for the damage if he or she was at fault.

- The policy's territorial limits are the United States, its territories and possessions, Puerto Rico, and Canada. Note that this does not include Mexico. If you are going to drive your car in Mexico, it is imperative that you buy Mexican insurance. You will have ample opportunity to do so in virtually any place you cross the border. Also, the coverage is limited to the policy period only.

- You can cancel the policy by returning it to the insurer or providing advance written notice of the date cancellation is to take effect.

- The insurer can cancel the policy at any time for nonpayment of premium. During the first sixty days the policy is in effect, the insurer can cancel upon ten days' notice for any reason, unless the policy is a renewal or continuation policy. After the first sixty days or if the policy is a renewal or continuation policy, the insurer can cancel only for nonpayment of premium or if your driver's license or that of any driver who lives with you or customarily uses your covered auto is suspended or revoked. In such instances, twenty days' notice must be given. If your state requires a longer notice period or special requirements concerning notice, or modifies any of the stated reasons for termination, the insurer will comply.

- Transfer of the interest in the policy may not be assigned without the insurer's written consent, except when the insured dies. The surviving spouse or the legal representative of the insured will have coverage until the end of the policy period.

- If you have another policy issued by the company and both apply to the same accident, the maximum limit under all the policies will not exceed the highest applicable limit of liability under any one policy. In other words, you cannot stack them. If this policy has a single limit for liability of $300,000 and another policy you have with the same company has a single limit of $200,000, your total coverage if both apply to the same accident is $300,000.

Insuring Other Vehicles

A miscellaneous type vehicle endorsement can be added to the PAP to insure motorcycles, mopeds, motorscooters, golf carts, motor homes, and other vehicles. The endorsement does not cover snowmobiles; they require a separate endorsement. The miscellaneous type vehicle endorsement can be used to provide all the coverages of the PAP, including liability, medical payments, uninsured motorists, and physical damage coverage. With a few exceptions, the PAP provisions and conditions applicable to these coverages are the same for the endorsement.

No-Fault Coverages

The liability coverage in the PAP protects you against loss if you are responsible to someone else for bodily injury or property damage because of an accident that was your fault. All the other coverages pay benefits without regard to fault. Thus, they could be referred to as no-fault coverages. This term, however, generally refers to legally required coverage added to the auto policy to compensate you and members of your family who are injured in an auto accident. This coverage, as discussed earlier, is called personal injury protection (PIP).

In some states, the PIP provides only medical payments, whereas in other states it will also replace part of your income if you are disabled in an auto accident. It may also include payments to replace uncompensated personal services, such as those of the parent who maintains the home. If you operate your vehicle in a no-fault state, your coverage will conform with the state law. Usually, there is an aggregate limit per person per accident for all benefits provided by the PIP.

AUTO INSURANCE PREMIUM RATES

Pricing factors of auto insurance include the make of the car, age of the car, whether the car is driven to and from work, age and gender of the driver, marital status, and location of the car. The location is critical since in some markets insurers are pulling out due to large losses. These factors are underwriting factors. Additionally, the driving record is an important factor in classifying a driver as a preferred driver or substandard risk. For description of the market condition in the most expensive New Jersey market, see "Important Issues: Leaving the New Jersey Auto Insurance Market." Fraudulent claims also affect rates; see "Ethical Dilemma: Who Pays for Insurance Fraud?" for a discussion.

Data show that younger drivers and male drivers cause more accidents. Figure 11.3 and Table 11.6 show that while drivers age 20 to 24 make up 8.5 percent of all drivers, they are responsible for 11.7 percent of accidents with fatalities and 10.2 percent of all accidents. For drivers under age 20, the ratios are alarming with 5.1 percent of the driving population responsible for 14 percent of the fatal accidents and 16.1 percent of all accidents. The data is from the National Safety Council for the year 2000. The national safety data estimated that there were 189.8 million licensed drivers in the year 2000; 50.3 percent of them male who accounted for about 73 percent of the miles driven each year. Since males drive more, they account for more accidents, as shown in Table 11.7.[5]

The general public perception is that auto insurance rating is unfair. California drivers decided to take matters into their own hands and in 1988 passed Proposition 103, legislation that set strict guidelines for insurance pricing activities. Proposition 103 also called for an elected insurance commissioner and provided that commissioner with expanded

Leaving the New Jersey Auto Insurance Market

Nationwide, in 2001 the annual average premium for combined liability, collision, and comprehensive coverage was $786. The cost of auto insurance varies widely from state to state. Iowa's is currently the lowest, with an average annual combined premium of $558. In New Jersey, the most expensive auto insurance state, the same coverage costs more than twice as much. The typical premium in 2001 was $1,146, and rates of $3,000 or more are not uncommon.

New Jersey auto insurers are no better off than their customers. In the past decade almost two dozen have left the state, and nineteen of the remaining sixty-seven—28 percent of the companies doing business in New Jersey—are on the verge of bankruptcy. Most of the large national companies are not currently writing business in New Jersey. The last remaining large insurer, State Farm, has stopped writing new policies and is dropping current policyholders at the rate of 4,000 a month.

The problem, most observers agree, is overregulation by the state's department of insurance. In New Jersey, insurers have little choice over drivers they can cover, what products they can offer, and how much they can charge.

- New Jersey is one of the few states with a "take all comers" law. Insurers are required to offer coverage to almost all applicants, no matter how high their risk. But because the state also caps premium amounts, very-high-risk drivers actually pay lower rates in New Jersey than they would in other states.

- New Jersey's form of no-fault insurance adds $100 to $200 each year to each policyholder's premium.

- Regulations like "prior rate approval" and "rate suppression" keep premiums artificially low for certain groups of policyholders. Rate increases must be approved by the state, and more than 90 percent of requests are denied.

- Withdrawal restrictions force auto insurance companies to keep selling their products until New Jersey regulators give permission to stop.

- If an insurance company shows a profit of more than 6 percent, New Jersey's "excess profit" law requires it to issue refunds to policyholders. And of course, the same restrictive regulations that are driving New Jersey insurers out of the market are also discouraging others from entering.

Coalitions of consumers, insurers, and state regulators are working together to find solutions to New Jersey's auto insurance problems. In March 2002 the New Jersey Department of Banking and Insurance formed a working group of consumer advocates, medical providers, attorneys, and insurance industry representatives to examine the system and propose improvements. Thus far one proposal has been implemented: allowing a few auto insurance companies to add surcharges of 10 percent to their premiums for new policyholders. State Assemblyman Lou Greenwald has introduced the New Jersey Auto Insurance Competition and Choice Act, which calls for eliminating the "take all comers" policy, simplifying withdrawal restrictions, allowing insurers to match rates to risk, and increasing the allowable profit margin to attract new insurers. Consumers and insurers are hoping that efforts like these will soon show results.

Exploring the Internet

Many states share some of New Jersey's problems. Read the New Jersey Coalition for Auto Insurance Competition's arguments for a competitive marketplace at www.njcaic.org, and consider whether proposed reforms might also benefit your state.

Sources: "No letup seen as New Jersey's State Farm customers abandon ship," Insure.com, 10 September 2002; New Jersey Department of Banking and Insurance, www.nj.gov/dobi/; Mark E. Ruquet, "N.J. Forms Insurance Improvement Group," National Underwriter Online News Service, 12 March 2002; Wayne T. Brough, "New Jersey Needs Auto Insurance Reform," Citizens for a Sound Economy, 11 November 2002, www.cse.org/informed/issues_template.php/1094.htm.

powers. A major selling point of this legislation to voters was the imposition of limitations on insurer use of geography as a rating factor. Specifically, Proposition 103 requires insurers to set prices primarily based on driving record, years of driving experience, and annual miles driven. Insurers are further restricted in their ability to incorporate age, gender, and zip code in their rating process.

Ethical Dilemma

Who Pays for Insurance Fraud?

Does your car have any dings or scratches on its exterior? Any car older than a few months probably has a few. Small scratches usually aren't worth getting fixed on their own, but what if you had a minor accident? Couldn't you just ask the body shop to include the cost of repairing the scratches in its repair estimates? The insurer is a big company; it won't even feel the effects of another couple of hundred dollars on your claim.

Many people feel justified in padding auto insurance claims. After all, they've been paying premiums for something! They might even make a deal with the body shop to charge the insurer more than the cost of the repairs and split the difference. These may be small-time claims, but collectively they exact a large price. Overall, insurance fraud costs Americans $80 billion dollars a year, or nearly $1,000 per family. The Insurance Services Office (ISO) estimates that as many as 10 percent of all U.S. auto claims are fraudulent. Fraud has contributed to automobile insurance rate increases in many states. Between 1996 and 1999, rates rose between 9 percent and 12 percent a year in Massachusetts. In 2002, Allstate Insurance Company, citing high levels of fraudulent claims, raised its auto insurance rates in New York by 10.5 percent.

In response to rate hikes, New York's insurance superintendent asked the legislature for an anti-fraud bill, a move the insurance industry also supported. The law, which provides for greater enforcement and stiffer penalties, is one way the industry and lawmakers are fighting back against fraud. Another is through high-tech systems to detect fraudulent claims.

Occupying an entire floor of a New Jersey skyscraper, ISO ClaimSearch, a sophisticated computer system, cross-references millions of claims every second. When a claim is entered, ClaimSearch automatically finds relevant public and insurance-related information about the claimant. In addition to flagging multiple claims, the system allows in-depth searches that help find links between claimants, doctors, and lawyers.

When ClaimSearch investigators believe they have found a fraud case, they turn their information over to law enforcement. In 2001, for example, the Hudson County, New Jersey prosecutor indicted 172 people for allegedly staging automobile accidents and filing false medical claims for more than $5 million. Nationwide, insurance fraud prosecutions and convictions are on the increase. According to the Washington, D.C.-based Coalition Against Insurance Fraud, state insurance fraud bureaus have doubled their criminal convictions of insurance scams since 1995.

More recently, Congress has gotten into the act. Proposed legislation would establish federal penalties for auto insurance fraud, with jail sentences ranging from five to fifteen years and fines up to $100,000.

While federal legislation offers some hope, some state laws may actually be making the situation worse. In New York, recent rate hikes have been blamed on that state's form of no-fault system. Under the current law, claimants have up to six months to submit a medical claim, but insurers have only thirty days to pay or deny, even if they suspect fraud. With vaguely worded billing guidelines and up to $50,000 in medical coverage for each insured, the system is ripe for corruption. According to the Insurance Information Institute, no-fault fraud costs New York drivers almost $2 million a day and adds $81 per car to the average annual cost of insurance, a figure that could rise to more than $300 by 2005.

Questions for Discussion

1. How far should the insurer go in its investigations of claims?
2. What should be the insurer's response when it finds out about overcharging for a claim?
3. What is the relationship between some of the forms of no-fault laws and fraud in auto insurance? Do you think reform would combat fraud?

Sources: Ron Panko, "Making a Dent in Auto Insurance Fraud: Computer Technology Drives Auto Insurers' Efforts to Stall Fraud Rings," Best's Review, October 2001; Steven Brostoff, "U.S. Insurance Fraud Bill Readied," National Underwriter Online News Service, April 9, 2002; "N.Y.'s No-Fault Auto Invites Criminals," National Underwriter Online News Service, Dec. 19, 2001.

It is important to note that there are also discounts for drivers, including ones for good student, nondrinkers, second car, driver training, and safety devices. Furthermore, having more than one car and not using it to drive to work, but as "pleasure use only" is cheaper than driving the car "to and from work."

As noted in Chapter 10 discussing homeowners policy, regulators in each state created well-designed booklets that inform consumers of the specific requirements in their states

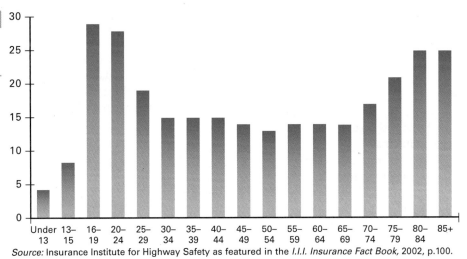

FIGURE 11.3

Motor Vehicle Deaths per 100,000 Persons by Age, 2000

Source: Insurance Institute for Highway Safety as featured in the *I.I.I. Insurance Fact Book,* 2002, p.100.

and the different rates for a typical automobile in many major locations. When purchasing auto insurance, it is advisable to read the booklet or explore the Internet for the best rates and the rating of insurers.

TYPES OF AUTOMOBILE POLICIES

There are two general types of auto insurance policies: commercial use (discussed as part of Chapter 12) and personal use, as discussed in this chapter. The Insurance Services Office has developed standard forms for each category.

Some insurers issue the standard policies; others issue policies that are similar but not identical. Variations result from competition that motivates insurers to try to differentiate their products. The PAP is the newest of the policies for personal use automobiles, having virtually displaced other personal use forms. You will probably buy a PAP or a policy similar to it, so we have discussed it in detail. (In Virginia, the Family Auto policy is still in use).

Bear in mind, however, that your policy may differ in some significant ways from the PAP. The major differences are in the perils covered, persons insured, exclusions and definitions, and the presence of personal injury protection (PIP) coverage or no-fault provisions that are required in some states. To understand your own coverage, therefore, be sure to read the specifics of your policy.

TABLE 11.6   Accidents by Age of Drivers, 2000

Age Group	Number of Drivers	% of Total	Drivers in Fatal Accidents	% of Total	Drivers in All Accidents	% of Total
Under 20	9,624,000	5.1%	8,600	14.0%	4,030,000	16.15%
20-24	16,081,000	8.5	7,200	11.7	2,560,000	10.2
25-34	35,915,000	18.9	11,600	18.9	5,540,000	22.1
35-44	41,815,000	22.0	12,200	19.9	5,240,000	20.9
45-54	36,573,000	19.3	9,300	15.1	3,690,000	14.7
55-64	22,778,000	12.0	5,000	8.1	1,960,000	7.8
65-74	15,741,000	8.3	3,700	6.0	1,190,000	4.7
Over 74	11,273,000	5.9	3,800	6.2	890,000	3.5
Total	**188,800,000**	**100.0**	**81,400**	**100.0**	**25,100,000**	**100.0**

Note: Percent of total columns may not add due to rounding.
Source: National Safety Council as featured in the *I.I.I. Insurance Fact Book,* 2002, p. 100.

TABLE 11.7   Sex of Drivers Involved in Accidents, 1975–2000

| | Drivers Involved in All Crashes | | | | | Drivers Involved in Fatal Crashes | | | |
| | Male | | Female | | | Male | | Female | |
Year	Number	Rate*	Number	Rate*		Number	Rate**	Number	Rate**
1975	19,100,000	212	8,400,000	195		46,500	52	9,600	22
1976	19,600,000	206	8,800,000	191		48,100	51	10,900	24
1977	20,600,000	209	9,300,000	193		51,900	53	11,800	25
1978	21,700,000	209	9,800,000	192		51,500	50	15,500	30
1979	20,600,000	202	9,100,000	180		52,700	52	12,500	25
1980	20,100,000	200	9,700,000	192		56,100	56	12,200	24
1981	20,500,000	200	9,500,000	183		53,200	52	11,800	23
1982	20,600,000	198	9,900,000	186		48,800	47	11,500	22
1983	20,400,000	187	10,300,000	184		46,300	43	11,700	21
1984	21,800,000	192	11,200,000	190		47,600	42	13,300	23
1985	21,400,000	185	11,600,000	191		46,800	40	12,700	21
1986	22,100,000	196	12,900,000	177		46,400	41	13,100	18
1987	20,700,000	192	12,300,000	148		45,500	42	13,500	16
1988	22,500,000	204	13,700,000	155		49,200	45	14,800	17
1989	14,100,000	95	8,700,000	143		47,000	32	14,800	24
1990	12,170,000	80	7,630,000	121		46,800	31	15,400	24
1991	12,070,000	86	7,430,000	97		43,600	31	14,200	19
1992	12,700,000	88	8,100,000	103		40,200	28	13,000	17
1993	12,900,000	87	8,200,000	101		40,400	27	13,500	17
1994	12,400,000	82	7,600,000	90		38,200	25	14,800	17
1995	10,600,000	69	7,000,000	80		37,500	24	13,000	15
1996	11,400,000	73	7,500,000	84		42,300	27	15,100	17
1997	14,300,000	90	9,600,000	103		43,600	27	16,100	17
1998	12,700,000	77	8,800,000	90		40,800	25	15,300	16
1999	10,600,000	83	7,400,000	74		30,400	18	11,800	12
2000	15,200,000	90	9,900,000	100		45,600	27	15,800	16

*Number of drivers in all accidents per 10 million miles driven.
**Number of drivers in fatal accidents per 1 billion miles driven.
Source: National Safety Council as featured in the *I.I.I. Insurance Fact Book,* 2002, p. 101.

KEY TERMS

no-fault
personal injury protection
pure no-fault
modified no-fault
add-on plans
financial responsibility law
unsatisfied judgment funds
compulsory auto liability
  insurance law
substandard market

residual market
shared market
auto insurance plans
assigned risk plans
reinsurance facilities
joint underwriting
  association
personal auto policy
single limit
split limit

stacking
primary coverage
uninsured motorists
  coverage
underinsured motorists
  coverage
collision coverage
other than collision coverage
  (comprehensive)

DISCUSSION QUESTIONS

1. Who is insured under the liability coverage of the PAP? Who gets paid in case of a loss?
2. What is considered a loss under the liability in the PAP?

3. What persons are insured for medical payment under the PAP? Who gets paid in case of a loss?

4. Explain the difference between a single limit for liability and split limits.

5. Do you think it is socially desirable to do away with age, gender, and marital status as classification factors for auto insurance premium rates? Why, or why not? What would be the implication if everyone paid the same rate?

6. Chris Malmud says, "Buying uninsured motorist coverage is an awkward substitute for life and health insurance. Besides that, it protects you only in certain situations. I'd rather spend my money on more and better life and health insurance." Do you agree? Why, or why not?

7. Automobile financial responsibility laws require you to have some minimum amount of auto liability insurance. If liability insurance is to protect you from loss caused by your negligence, why should the law force you to buy it? Don't you think this is a decision for you to make? Explain.

8. Morton C. Salt currently has a PAP with only bodily injury and property damage liability coverages. While hurrying home one evening, Mr. Salt smashed through his garage door. There was damage to his car and extensive damage to the garage and its contents. Will Morton be able to collect for these damages under his PAP? Explain.

9. The insuring agreement for part D of the PAP shown in Appendix B lists perils that are covered under other than collision coverage. Explain the meaning of this list and what protection is afforded under the policy for loss caused by one of the perils. Explain further the coverage for loss caused by a peril neither listed in the insuring agreement nor considered collision (such as lightning damage).

10. The deductible for other than collision is usually smaller than for collision coverage. Does this make sense to you? How do you account for it?

11. Discuss the forms of automobile no-fault laws presented in the text. What are their advantages and disadvantages?

12. Explain the difference between a monetary and a verbal threshold of no-fault laws.

13. If you permit a friend to drive your car, does he or she have protection under your policy? How will losses be shared if your friend has a PAP on his or her own auto and negligently causes an accident while driving your car?

EXERCISES

11.1 Joyce owns a Ford Explorer and her friend Sharon owns a Jeep. Joyce has coverage from State Farm and Sharon from ERIE. Both of them have exactly the same coverages and use the PAP. They have a single liability limit of $250,000 and the same limit for uninsured motorist. They have $250 deductible for collision and $100 deductible for other-than-collision. They have towing and labor and car rental reimbursement.

Please respond to the following questions:

a. Joyce borrowed Sharon's Jeep when her Explorer was in the shop to replace recalled tires. While driving the Jeep, she was seriously injured by an uninsured drunk driver. The Jeep is a total loss. How much will be paid by each policy if it is determined that Joyce has $370,000 of bodily injury loss? Explain the process of the payment. Whose insurance company pays first and whose insurance company pays second? What amount is covered by each insurer for all the damage in this case? Find the justification for the coverages (if possible) in the PAP.

b.   In this case the drunk driver destroyed his car. Would he get any reimbursement? Explain.

c.   Now that Sharon has no car and Joyce is in the hospital, Sharon is driving the Explorer. With her three children in the car, Sharon slid off an icy road and hit a tree. She was not injured, but the kids were taken to the emergency room for a few hours. The Explorer was damaged. What coverages will take care of these losses? Explain and find the justification in the PAP.

11.2   The Helsings (who have a PAP) are involved in an automobile accident (which was not their fault) on their way home from a dinner party. Although they are unharmed, their car is disabled. The police recommend that they leave the car by the side of the road and take a taxi home. When the Helsings return to the scene of the accident, they find that their car has been stripped down to the chassis. The Helsings submit a claim to their insurance agent for the entire loss. Are the Helsings covered under the PAP? Explain. What if the Helsings had not contacted the police, and leaving the car was their own idea?

11.3   Barney has a PAP with liability limits of 25/50/15 and collision coverage with a $200 deductible. While pulling his boat and trailer—which are not listed in the policy's declarations—to the lake, he passes a car, loses control, sideswipes the car he is passing with his trailer, then rams a tree with his car. The losses are as follows:

Barney (medical expenses)	$1,300
Barney's girlfriend (medical expenses)	$2,450
Driver of other car	
Lost income	10,000
Medical expenses	13,500
Mental anguish	20,000
	$43,500
Passenger of other car	
Lost income	5,500
Medical expenses	3,400
	$8,900
Barney's car	$4,000
Barney's boat	$800
Barney's trailer	$500
Farmer's tree	$300
Other driver's Mercedes	$29,800

Using the PAP in Appendix B, explain what will and will not be paid by Barney's insurance contract, and why.

11.4   While attending classes at her college, Lisa parks her Corvette on the street and locks it. When she returns, it is gone. She reports its loss to her insurer and notifies the police immediately. Because she must commute to school and to work, she rents a car for $180 per week, or $28 per day for any part of a week. Twenty-three days after her car disappeared, it is recovered. It has been driven over 12,000 miles, its right rear fender has been destroyed in an accident, and the interior has been vandalized. The low estimate for repair of the exterior and interior damage is $23,000. The actual cash value of her car is $16,000. Lisa has a PAP with other than collision coverage and a $200 deductible. Explain her coverage to her, noting what she can expect to recover from her insurer, and why.

NOTES

1. *The I.I.I. Fact Book 2002.*
2. See Jeffrey O'Connell, "No-Fault Auto Insurance: Back by Popular (Market) Demand," *San Diego Law Review* 26 (1989). Most studies regarding these aspects of fault-based laws are now old. Emphasis has turned recently to premium levels, as discussed.
3. *The I.I.I. Fact Book 2002,* p. 47.
4. *The I.I.I. Fact Book 2002,* p. 45.
5. *The I.I.I. Fact Book 2002,* pp. 100 and 101.

CHAPTER 12

Business Insurance

In the preceding four chapters, you read about property and liability exposures generally, and how families insure home and auto exposures specifically. Now, we will delve briefly into business insurance. Commercial insurance is a topic for an extensive separate course, but its importance has been reflected to a great extent throughout the previous chapters. Employers who take unnecessary risks or do not practice prudent risk management may not only cause job losses, they also may cause the loss of pensions and important benefits such as health insurance (discussed in later chapters).

As members of the work force, we drive our employers' cars and spend many of our waking hours operating machines and computers on business premises. There are risks involved in these activities that require insurance coverage. A case in point is the damage caused by mold in many commercial buildings and schools, as well as in homes, as noted in prior chapters. Mold can cause headaches, discomfort, and more serious problems. Employer's property coverage was of great help in remedying the problem. However, as a result of the many claims, insurers have excluded mold coverage or provide very low limits. This and more pertinent issues in commercial coverages will be discussed in this chapter. Some highlights of the commercial policies, provided in Appendices C and D, will also be briefly discussed to provide you with a glimpse into the complexities of commercial coverages. The main new endorsements for mold, e-commerce, and terrorism are also included in appendices in the back of the text. Issues such as directors and officers coverage complexities in the year 2002 due to the fraudulent behavior of executives in many large corporations such as Enron and WorldCom will be discussed in this chapter's "Important Issues," and the dispute over the limits of coverage of the World Trade Center will be the topic of the "Ethical Dilemma." The interested student is invited to study the policies in the appendices in depth and explore the risk and insurance news media for current commercial coverages issues. Also, Case 3 at the back of the textbook relates to commercial coverages embedded in integrated risk programs. The programs described in the case use similar commercial packaged policies that are described in this chapter, which covers the following:

1. Connection
2. Commercial package policy
3. Commercial property coverages
4. Other property coverages
5. Commercial general liability policy
6. Commercial umbrella liability policy
7. Other property coverages
8. Other liability risks

CONNECTION

At this point in our study, we are drilling further down into specific, more complex coverages of the commercial world. Many coverages are customized to the need of the business, but many more use the policies designed by the Insurance Service Office (ISO), which have been approved in most states. We have moved from the narrow realm of personal line coverages, but the basic premises are still the same. The business risks as shown in our puzzle figure do not clearly differentiate between commercial risk and personal hazards. The perils of fire and windstorm do not separate personal homes from commercial buildings. Our business may be sued for mistakes we make as employees since the business is a separate legal entity. We cannot separate between the commercial world and our personal world when it comes to completing our risk management puzzle to ensure holistic coverage.

Figure 12.1 shows how the picture of our risk puzzles connect to the commercial coverages available as a package by ISO. We use the Common Policy Declarations Page, which illustrates the mechanism of this packaged policy. This program permits businesses to select among a variety of insurance options, like a cafeteria where we can choose the items we want and reject those we do not need. The program is considered a "package" because it combines both property and liability options in the same policy, as well as additional coverages as listed in the Common Policy Declarations Page in Figure 12.1. Further, within each of the property and liability coverages are various options available to tailor protection to the particular needs of the insured, as you will see in this chapter.

As stated in prior chapters, hard market conditions have predominated in the early 2000s as shown in Table 12.1. In 2001, the combined ratio (the loss ratio = losses divided by premiums plus the expense ratio = expenses divided by premiums) for the various commercial property/casualty lines covered a wide range: 114.5 for commercial automobile, 132 for the commercial package, 135.5 for general and product liability, and 143 for medical malpractice. These levels of losses were the impetus behind new coverage exclusions (see Table 12.1). Among the changes (mentioned in prior chapters) are the terrorism and mold endorsements, as well as the e-commerce endorsement discussed in

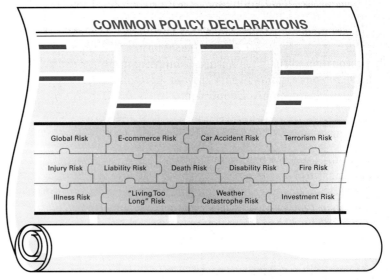

FIGURE 12.1

Connecting the Risks and Insurance Coverage Available in the Commercial Policy Package

(Continued)

FIGURE 12.1 Connecting the Risks and Insurance Coverage Available in the Commercial Policy Package (Continued)

COMPANY NAME AREA	PRODUCER NAME AREA

NAMED INSURED: _____

MAILING ADDRESS: _____

POLICY PERIOD: FROM _____ TO _____ AT 12:01 A.M. STANDARD
TIME AT YOUR MAILING ADDRESS SHOWN ABOVE: _____

BUSINESS DESCRIPTION	

IN RETURN FOR THE PAYMENT OF THE PREMIUM, AND SUBJECT TO ALL THE TERMS OF
THIS POLICY, WE AGREE WITH YOU TO PROVIDE THE INSURANCE AS STATED IN THIS

THIS POLICY CONSISTS OF THE FOLLOWING COVERAGE PARTS FOR WHICH A PREMIUM IS INDICATED. THIS PREMIUM MAY BE SUBJECT TO ADJUSTMENT.

	PREMIUM
BOILER AND MACHINERY COVERAGE PART	$
CAPITAL ASSETS PROGRAM (OUTPUT POLICY) COVERAGE PART	$
COMMERCIAL AUTOMOBILE COVERAGE PART	$
COMMERCIAL GENERAL LIABILITY COVERAGE PART	$
COMMERCIAL INLAND MARINE COVERAGE PART	$
COMMERCIAL PROPERTY COVERAGE PART	$
CRIME AND FIDELITY COVERAGE PART	$
EMPLOYMENT-RELATED PRACTICES LIABILITY COVERAGE PART	$
FARM COVERAGE PART	$
LIQUOR LIABILITY COVERAGE PART	$
POLLUTION LIABILITY COVERAGE PART	$
PROFESSIONAL LIABILITY COVERAGE PART	$
	$
TOTAL:	$

Premium shown is payable: $ at inception. $

FORMS APPLICABLE TO ALL COVERAGE PARTS (SHOW NUMBERS):
_____
_____
_____
_____
_____

Countersigned: _____   By: _____
             (Date)   (Authorized Representative)

NOTE OFFICERS' FACSIMILE SIGNATURES MAY BE INSERTED HERE, ON THE POLICY COVER OR ELSEWHERE AT THE COMPANY'S OPTION.

Source: ISO Common Policy Declaration from ILDS 00 07 02. Reprinted with permission. All ISO samples in this text are shown with special licensing agreement for this text.

Chapter 8. In the process of understanding the complete risk management steps needed, the pieces of the puzzle are beginning to fit together for the property/casualty lines. Case 3 for larger businesses at the back of the textbook is designed to bring the concepts together for complete commercial coverage. This chapter and the next for workers' compensation will complete the holistic risk management picture for the property/casualty lines of business.

TABLE 12.1
Estimated Combined
Ratios by Product
Line for the
Property/Casualty
Industry

Line of Business	A.M. Best Combined Ratio Estimates		
	2001	2002	Breakeven
Homeowners	126.0	117.5	103
Personal Auto	107.0	106.3	105
Fire and Allied Lines	130.5	105.0	102
Commercial Package	132.0	116.5	107
Commercial Auto	114.5	110.0	107
General and Product Liability	135.5	117.0	113
Workers' Comp	129.0	107.8	112
Medical Malpractice	143.0	122.0	115
Inland Marine	102.5	95.0	107
All Lines Other	109.5	95.0	106
Total All Lines	117.0	107.5	107

* NPW = Net Premium Written

Source: A.M. Best Review/Preview. Used with permission.

COMMERCIAL PACKAGE POLICY

The commercial package policy (CPP) program was begun by the Insurance Services Office (ISO) in 1986. Every policy includes three standard elements: the cover page, common policy conditions, and common declarations (shown in Figure 12.1, as of July 2002). It is important to elaborate on the discussion of the declaration page since it provides a visual aid of the various coverages that can be selected by a business in this package, depending on the needs. Some businesses may not need specific parts of the package, but all the elements are listed for the choice of the potential insured. More specifically, the package may include the following commercial coverage parts: boiler and machinery, capital assets program, commercial automobile, commercial general liability, commercial inland marine, commercial property, crime and fidelity, employment-related practices liability, farm liability, liquor liability, pollution liability, and professional liability. Some of these coverages were discussed in prior chapters. The rest of the coverages will be described here.

Most commercial organizations have similar property exposures. These exposures, along with business income exposures, can be insured through the commercial property policy form of the CPP. A sample of the 2002 ISO CPP policy is included in Appendix C. The liability module of the CPP is the **commercial general liability (CGL) policy.** It replaced the liability coverage previously available through the comprehensive general liability policy. In 1986, the CGL was made part of the new modular approach introduced by ISO in the form of the CPP.

COMMERCIAL PROPERTY COVERAGES

The commercial property policy form of the CPP begins with property declarations and conditions. These provisions identify the covered location, property values (and limits), premiums, deductibles, and other specific aspects of the coverage. These pages make the insurance unique for a given policyholder by identifying that policyholder's specific exposures. The information in the declarations must be accurate for the desired protection to exist.

The remainder of the commercial property coverage consists of:

■ the building and personal property coverage form (BPP)

The remainder of the commercial property coverage consists of:

- the building and personal property coverage form (BPP)
- one of three causes of loss forms for the BPP
- business income coverage form (BIC)
- endorsements—Appendices C-1 and C-2

Direct Property Coverage: The Building and Personal Property (BPP) Form

The BPP provides coverage for direct physical loss to buildings and/or contents as described in the policy. Separate sections with distinct limits of insurance are available for both buildings and contents to account for differing needs of insureds. Some insureds will be tenants, who do not need building coverage. Others will be landlords, who have limited or no need for contents coverage. Many insureds, of course, will need both in varying degrees. Thus, relating to our example of the September 11 loss case of the Worlding department store in the introduction of this book, we recall that the coverage was only for the stock, but not for the building since the store rented the four-story space.

Covered Property

What constitutes a "building" and "business personal property" may appear obvious. The insurer, however, must be very precise in defining its intent because, as you know, insurance is a contract of adhesion. Ambiguities, therefore, are generally construed in favor of the insured. Table 12.2 lists the items defined as "buildings." Table 12.3 lists those items defined as "business personal property."

TABLE 12.2 Building as Defined in ISO Building and Personal Coverage Form, 2002	a. Building, meaning the building or structure described in the Declarations, including: 1. Completed additions; 2. Fixtures, including outdoor fixtures; 3. Permanently installed Machinery and Equipment; 4. Personal property, including fire extinguishing equipment; Outdoor furniture; Floor coverings; and Appliances used for refrigerating, ventilating, cooking, dishwashing or laundering; 5. If not covered by other insurance: additions under construction, alterations and repairs to the building or structure; Materials, equipment, supplies and temporary structures, on or within 100 feet of the described premises, used for making additions, alterations or repairs to the building or structure.
TABLE 12.3 Business Personal Property as Defined in ISO Building and Personal Coverage Form, 2002	b. Your Business Personal Property located in or on the building described in the Declarations or in the open (or in a vehicle) within 100 feet of the described premises: 1. Furniture and fixtures; 2. Machinery and equipment; 3. "Stock"; 4. All other personal property owned by you and used in your business; 5. Labor, materials or services furnished or arranged by you on personal property of others; 6. Your use interest as tenant in improvements and betterments. 7. Leased personal property for which you have a contractual responsibility to insure, unless otherwise provided for under Personal Property of Others. c. Personal Property of Others that is: In your care, custody or control; and located in or on the building described in the Declarations or in the open (or in a vehicle) within 100 feet of the described premises.

In addition to limiting coverage by defining building and business personal property, the BPP lists specific property that is excluded from protection. These items are listed in Table 12.4. Reasons for exclusions in insurance were discussed earlier. Note in Table 12.4 and in the corresponding section in the policy the exclusion of "Electronic data, except as provided under additional coverages." In part f (4) of Additional Coverages, discussed below and in Table 12.5, the electronic data that is covered is limited to a loss of up to

TABLE 12.4

Listed Property Not Covered as Defined in ISO Building and Personal Coverage Form, 2002

2. Property Not Covered

a. Accounts, bills, currency, food stamps or other evidences of debt, money, notes or securities. Lottery tickets held for sale are not securities;

b. Animals;

c. Automobiles held for sale;

d. Bridges, roadways, walks, patios or other paved surfaces;

e. Contraband, or property in the course of illegal transportation or trade;

f. The cost of excavations, grading, backfilling or filling;

g. Foundations of buildings, structures, machinery or boilers if their foundations are below;

h. Land (including land on which the property is located), water, growing crops or lawns;

i. Personal property while airborne or waterborne;

j. Bulkheads, pilings, piers, wharves or docks;

k. Property that is covered under another coverage form;

l. Retaining walls that are not part of a building;

m. Underground pipes, flues or drains;

n. Electronic data, except as provided under Additional Coverages;

o. The cost to replace or restore the information on valuable papers and records, including those which exist as electronic data;

p. Vehicles or self-propelled machines;

q. The following property while outside of buildings:

1. Grain, hay, straw or other crops;

2. Fences, radio or television antennas

TABLE 12.5

Additional Coverage and Coverage Extension as Defined in ISO Building and Personal Coverage Form, 2002

Additional Coverages

a. Debris Removal

b. Preservation of Property

c. Fire Department Service Charge

d. Pollutant Clean Up and Removal

e. Increased Cost of Construction

f. Electronic Data—up to $2,500

Coverage Extensions

a. Newly Acquired or Constructed Property

b. Personal Effects and Property of Others

c. Valuable Papers and Records (Other than Electronic Data)

d. Property Off-Premises

e. Outdoor Property

f. Non-owned Detached Trailers

$2,500 sustained in one year. The low limit on electronic equipment and data losses have propelled many businesses to buy the e-commerce endorsement shown in Appendix C-1 and discussed in Chapter 8. This exclusion is not always noticed by businesses. To assure adequate coverage, insurers began to offer education programs to risk managers about their cyber-risk exposures.[1]

Additional Coverages and Coverage Extensions

In addition to paying for repair or replacement of the listed property when caused by a covered peril, the BPP pays for other related costs. The BPP also extends coverage under specified conditions. These coverage additions and extensions are listed in Table 12.5.

The value of these additional and extended coverages can be significant. **Debris removal,** for example, is a cost that is often overlooked by insureds, but can involve thousands of dollars. Recent tornadoes in the Midwestern United States caused heavy property damage; yet for many insureds, the most significant costs involved removal of tree limbs and other debris.

An interesting additional coverage is **pollutant cleanup and removal.** This provision specifies the conditions under which and the extent to which protection for clean-up costs are paid by the insurer. Because of large potential liabilities, coverage is narrowly defined to those situations caused by a covered loss, and only for losses at the described premises. The amount of available protection is also limited.

The extended coverages primarily offer protection on properties not included in the definition of covered buildings and personal property. The intent is to provide specific and limited insurance for these properties, which is why they are separated from the general provision. Newly acquired property and property of others, for instance, involve exposures distinct from the general exposures, requiring special attention in the coverage extensions. Some of the coverage extensions offer protection against loss caused by a short list of causes to property otherwise excluded. Outdoor equipment is an example.

Valuation

As has been discussed in prior chapters, property insurance payments may be made on either a replacement cost new (RCN) basis or an actual cash value (ACV) basis. If the insured chooses actual cash value, then the **provision 7 valuation** of **section E, loss conditions** applies. Note that the valuation provision involves a number of parts.[2] Parts (b) through (f) explain the insurer's intent for valuation in situations on RCN when ACV may be difficult to measure or inappropriate. Part (b), for instance, permits payment at RCN for relatively small losses, those valued at $2,500 or less.

If the insured chooses **replacement cost new,** this optional coverage must be designated in the declarations. Further, the insured ought to recognize the need for higher limits than if ACV is used. Typically, the insurer does not charge a higher rate for RCN coverage; however, more coverage is needed, which translates into a higher premium. For RCN to be paid, the insured must actually repair or replace the covered property. Otherwise, the insurer will pay on an ACV basis.

Limits of Insurance

As just discussed, we need to be cautious when selecting an amount of insurance that will cover our potential losses. The insurer will not pay more than the limit of insurance, except for the coverage extensions and coverage additions (fire department charges, pollution cleanup, and electronic data). In addition to concern over having a sufficient amount of insurance to cover the value of any loss, some insureds will need to worry about violation of the **coinsurance provision,** which is found under section F, **additional conditions** on page 11 of the BPP. The policy provides examples of coinsurance. An example of underinsurance in the policy is as follows:

Example No. 1 (Underinsurance):

When:		
	The value of the property is	$250,000
	The Coinsurance percentage for it is	80%
	The Limit of Insurance for it is	$100,000
	The Deductible is	$250
	The amount of loss is	$40,000

Step (1): $250,000 x 80% = $200,000 (the minimum amount of insurance to meet your Coinsurance requirements)

Step (2): $100,000 ÷ $200,000 = .50

Step (3): $40,000 × .50 = $20,000

Step (4): $20,000 − $250 = $19,750

We (the insurer) will pay no more than $19,750. The remaining $20,250 is not covered.

Reading of the policy will show that the BPP continues to include a coinsurance provision as a major condition of coverage. Most insureds, however, choose to override the coinsurance clause with an **agreed value option,** found in section G, **optional coverages.** The agreed value option requires the policyholder to buy insurance equal to 100 percent of the value of the property, as determined at the start of the policy. If the insured does so, then the coinsurance provision does not apply and all losses are paid in full, up to the limit of insurance. The wording of the policy is as follows:

1. Agreed Value
   a. The Additional Condition, Coinsurance, does not apply to Covered Property to which this Optional Coverage applies. We will pay no more for loss of or damage to that property than the proportion that the Limit of Insurance under this Coverage Part for the property bears to the Agreed Value shown for it in the Declarations.

The agreed value option, however, does not assure that the policyholder will have sufficient limits of insurance to cover a total loss, especially in times of high inflation. To ward off unwanted retention of loss values above the limit of insurance, the insured can purchase the **inflation guard option** found in section G, optional coverages. The inflation guard provides for automatic periodic increases in limits, with the intent of keeping pace with inflation. The amount of the annual increase is shown on a percentage basis in the declarations.

Causes of Loss

We have just described the major elements of the BPP form. A full understanding of the coverage requires a thorough reading and consideration of the impact of each provision. As for which perils are covered, the property section of the CPP offers three options: the **basic causes of loss** form; the **broad causes of loss** form; and the **special causes of loss** form.

Causes of Loss—Basic Form

The basic causes of loss form is a named-perils option that covers eleven named perils, listed in Table 12.6. Some perils are defined and others are not. When no definition exists, the common use of the term, supplemented by court opinions, will provide its meaning.

Fire, for example, is not defined, because it has a generally accepted legal meaning. Insurance policies cover only certain fires. While excessive heat may be sufficient for the fire protection to apply, oxidation that results in a flame or glow is typically required. Further, the flame must be "hostile," not within some intended container. For instance, if I throw something into a fireplace, intentionally or not, that fire is not hostile, and the loss likely is not covered.

A review of the policy and Chapter 10, where many of these same perils were discussed as they apply to homeowners coverage, may clarify which loss situations are payable on the basic causes of loss form. Review of the exclusions is just as important.

Exclusions found in the basic causes of loss form can be categorized as follows:

- Ordinance of law
- Earth movement
- Governmental action
- Nuclear hazards
- Power failure
- War and military action (note the terrorism exclusion endorsement form in Appendix C-2)
- Water damage
- "Fungus," wet rot, dry rot and bacteria
- "Other," involving primarily steam, electrical, and mechanical breakdown

Most of these exclusions involve events with catastrophic potential.

Causes of Loss—Broad Form

The broad causes of loss form is also a named-perils coverage. It differs from the basic form in adding some perils, as listed in Table 12. 6. Geography may dictate to some extent preference for the broad form, because of its ice and snow coverage. Further, note that the water damage peril is for the "sudden and accidental leakage of water or steam that results from the breaking or cracking of part of an appliance or system containing water or steam

TABLE 12.6	Basic Form	Broad Form
Causes of Loss Forms, ISO Commercial Property Policy, 2002	• fire • lightning • explosion • windstorm or hail • smoke • aircraft or vehicles • riot or civil commotion • vandalism • sinkhole collapse • volcanic action	Basic form perils, plus: • weight of snow, ice, or sleet • water damage • falling objects • breakage of glass

(not a sprinkler system)." It does not cover floods or other similar types of catastrophic water damage.

In addition to adding these perils, the broad form includes a provision to cover "collapse" caused by the named perils or by hidden decay; hidden insect or vermin damage; weight of people or personal property; weight of rain that collects on a roof; or use of defective materials in construction, remodeling, or renovation. While this "collapse" additional coverage does not increase the amount of coverage available (as the other additional coverages do), it does expand the list of covered-loss situations.

The "mold" exclusion was discussed in prior chapters. The exact wording of the exclusion from ISO Causes of Loss—Broad Form is as follows:

> h. "Fungus", Wet Rot, Dry Rot And Bacteria
>
> Presence, growth, proliferation, spread or any activity of "fungus", wet or dry rot or bacteria.
>
> But if "fungus", wet or dry rot or bacteria results in a Covered Cause of Loss, we will pay for the loss or damage caused by that Covered Cause of Loss.
>
> This exclusion does not apply:
> 1. When "fungus", wet or dry rot or bacteria results from fire or lightning; or
> 2. To the extent that coverage is provided in the Additional Coverage—Limited Coverage For "Fungus", Wet Rot, Dry Rot And Bacteria with respect to loss or damage by a cause of loss other than fire or lightning.

The Additional Coverage in the policy permits a coverage limit for mold for only up to $15,000 as noted in Section D: Additional Coverage—Limited Coverage For "Fungus", Wet Rot, Dry Rot And Bacteria.

> The coverage described under D.2. of this Limited Coverage is limited to $15,000. Regardless of the number of claims, this limit is the most we will pay for the total of all loss or damage arising out of all occurrences of Covered Causes of Loss (other than fire or lightning) and Flood which take place in a 12-month period (starting with the beginning of the present annual policy period). With respect to a particular occurrence of loss which results in "fungus", wet or dry rot or bacteria, we will not pay more than a total of $15,000 even if the "fungus", wet or dry rot or bacteria continues to be present or active, or recurs, in a later policy period.

Business income coverage will be discussed in the next section. For now, it is important to note that under the mold exclusion and extension of coverage, business interruption income is provided for only thirty days. The days do not need to be consecutive (see Part D, 6, a and b).

After September 11, as noted earlier, the insurance industry was able to obtain the approval from many states to exclude terrorism. The Exclusion of Terrorism (With Limited Exception) and Exclusion of War and Military Action ISO 2002 form is in Appendix C-2. The exclusion defines terrorism and provides for a limit of up to $25 million in property coverage. More specifically, the Endorsement states (in Part B):

> In determining whether the $25,000,000 threshold is exceeded, we will include all insured damage sustained by property of all persons and entities affected by the terrorism and business interruption losses sustained by owners or occupants of the damaged property.... Multiple incidents of terrorism which occur within a 72-hour period and appear to be carried out in concert or to have related purpose or common leadership will be deemed to be one incident.

Ethical Dilemma

Liability Limits: One Event or Two?

Did the September 11 terrorist attacks on the World Trade Center constitute one loss or two? The answer to this question could be worth $3.5 billion, but the resolution is far from simple. The controversy surrounding this issue illustrates the ambiguities inherent in some business insurance contracts.

When the two hijacked airplanes struck the World Trade Center towers on the morning of September 11, 2001, the insurance and reinsurance contracts for the property were still under binder agreements. Thus, the wording of the binder agreements has become the central issue of this case. Real estate executive Larry A. Silverstein's company had only recently acquired a ninety-nine-year lease on the World Trade Center and had not yet finalized insurance coverage, which provided up to $3.5 billion in property and liability damage per occurrence. With policies of such size, which have large reinsurance requirements, it is not uncommon for the final policies to not be in place when the insured begins operations.

The United Kingdom-based reinsurer Swiss Re had agreed to underwrite 22 percent of coverage on the property once the loss exceeded $10 million, translating into $3.5 billion per occurrence in this case. After the attacks, Swiss Re argued that its preliminary agreement with the lessee defined occurrence as "all losses or damages that are attributable directly or indirectly to one cause or one series of similar causes" and that "all such losses will be added together and the total amount of such losses will be treated as one occurrence irrespective of the period of time or area over which such losses occur." Silverstein, however, argued that each of the airplane crashes was a separate occurrence and his company was due $7 billion for the two attacks.

A court ruling involving three of the primary insurers of the WTC property supports Swiss Re's position. In September 2002, U.S. District Court Judge John S. Martin Jr., in Manhattan, found in favor of Hartford Fire Insurance Co., Royal Indemnity Co., and The St. Paul Fire and Marine Insurance Co., who together were responsible for approximately $112 million of the losses. The insurers argued that in issuing coverage binders to the WTC leaseholders just before the September 11 terrorist attack, they had agreed to be bound by the so-called WilProp form, a proprietary policy form provided by the Willis Group of New York Inc., the insurance brokers for Silverstein Properties. The judge agreed with the insurers that the WilProp form unambiguously defined "occurrence" as a single occurrence, rejecting Silverstein's contention that the binders were only "binding preliminary commitments," and thus subject to further negotiations.

Silverstein Properties is expected to appeal. If this ruling is not overturned, however, Swiss Re can probably expect a similar outcome when its own case comes to trial, since the reinsurance was also covered by the WilProp form, defining the WTC collapse as one event.

This case illustrates the difficulties that can arise in insurance contracts. Liability contracts, especially those negotiated between insureds and insurers, are considered the most complex and most prone to disputes, but even standard contracts can contain clauses that are open to interpretation, leaving the courts to make the final decision.

Questions for Discussion

1. If the insurance contract on the WTC were not negotiated, it would have been considered a contract of adhesion. Under those circumstances, do you think the federal judge would have ruled in favor of the insurer?

2. Do you agree with the judge's ruling in this complex case? What is the justification for the ruling against the leaseholder in this case? Do you think this ruling is ethical in light of the massive loss?

3. In ethical terms, who should really suffer the burden of the attack on America on September 11? Should it be any private citizen or the private insurance industry?

Sources: E.E. Mazier, "Swiss Re Presses 'One Attack' Theory," *National Underwriter,* Property & Casualty/Risk & Benefits Management Edition, 29 October 2001; E.E. Mazier, "Experts View Swiss Re WTC Lawsuit as Unprecedented Legal Quagmire," *National Underwriter* Online News Service, 31 October 2001; Mark E. Ruquet, "Insurers to Lose WTC Case: Agent Univ.," *National Underwriter* Online News Service, 22 July 200; E.E. Mazier, "Judges Sends WTC Claim to Jury Trial," *National Underwriter,* Property & Casualty/Risk & Benefits Management Edition, 10 June 2002; E.E. Mazier, "Judge Rules WTC Terror is One Event," *National Underwriter* Online News Service, 25 September 2002; E.E. Mazier, "Swiss Re Silverstein WTC Case in Shambles," *National Underwriter* Online News Service, 27 September 2002.

The wording leaves no ambiguities. If such wording were in the policy used for the World Trade Center, there would not have been a dispute between its leaseholder and Swiss Re, as described in "Ethical Dilemma: Liability Limits—One Event or Two?" in this chapter. The terrorism endorsement further states that "if terrorism results in fire, we will pay for the loss or damage caused by that fire. However, this exception for fire applies only to direct loss or damage by fire to Covered Property. Therefore, for example, the exception does not apply to insurance "provided under Business Income and/or Extra Expense coverage forms…."

Note, that the two exclusions described here are for cause of loss exclusions, while the exclusion for electronic data noted above is to the actual property.

Causes of Loss—Special Form

The special form causes of loss is an "open perils" or "all risk" coverage form. That is, instead of listing those perils that are covered, the special form provides protection for all causes of loss not specifically excluded. In this form, then, the exclusions define the coverage. Remember that all those exclusions listed for the basic form, except for the "other" category and some aspects of the water damage exclusion, apply to the special form.

Most of the additional exclusions found in the special form relate either to catastrophic potentials or to nonfortuitous events. Among the catastrophe exclusions are boiler or machinery explosions. Nonfortuitous exclusions relate to such things as wear and tear, smoke from agricultural smudging, and damage to a building interior caused by weather conditions, unless the building exterior is damaged first.

Some experts believe that the greatest benefit of the special form over the broad form is coverage against theft. You may recall that theft is not a listed peril in the broad (nor in the basic) form. Coverage of theft from any cause, however, is too costly for most policyholders. The special form, therefore, includes some limitations on this protection. For instance, employee dishonesty and loss of property that appears to have been stolen but for which there is no physical evidence of theft ("mysterious disappearance") are not covered. In addition, certain types of property such as patterns, dyes, furs, jewelry, and tickets are covered against theft only up to specified amounts. The special form also provides coverage for property in transit.

Consequential Property Coverage: Business Income Coverage (BIC)

As noted in prior chapters, in addition to the cost of repairing and/or replacing damaged or lost property, a business is likely to experience some negative consequences of being unable to use the damaged or lost property. Those negative consequences typically involve reduced revenues (sales) or increased expenses, both of which reduce net income (profit). The commercial property policy provides coverage for net income losses through the **business income coverage** (BIC) form. The BIC protects against both business interruption and **extra expense** losses.

Business Interruption

When operations shut down (are interrupted) because of loss to physical property, a business likely loses income. The BIC covers:

1. Business Income

   Business Income means the:

   a. Net Income (Net Profit or Loss before income taxes) that would have been earned or incurred; and

   b. Continuing normal operating expenses incurred, including payroll.

Normal operating expenses are those costs associated with the activity of the business, not the materials that may be consumed by the business. Included among operating expenses are payroll, heat and lighting, advertising, and interest expenses.

The intent of the BIC is to maintain the insured's same financial position with or without a loss. Payment, therefore, does not cover all lost revenues, because those revenues generally cover expenses, some of which will not continue. Yet because some expenses continue, coverage of net income alone is insufficient. An example of a BIC loss is given in "Business Income Coverage (BIC) Hypothetical Loss".

It is important to note the wording in the 2002 policy. The coverage applies only to business interruption for damages to the property in the declaration. More specifically, the policy states:

> We will pay for the actual loss of Business Income you sustain due to the necessary "suspension" of your "operations" during the "period of restoration". The "suspension" must be caused by direct physical loss of or damage to property at premises which are described in the Declarations and for which a Business Income Limit of Insurance is shown in the Declaration.

Under this policy, businesses that sustained losses because of the economic backlash and fear after September 11, 2001 would not be covered for their loss of income. For discussion of this issue review please review "Important Issues: Business Interruption Without Direct Physical Loss" in Chapter 8.

As noted above while discussing the BPP policy, this part of the Commercial package also limits coverage for interruption to computer operations as follows under Section 4.

> Additional Limitation—Interruption Of Computer Operations
>
> a. Coverage for Business Income does not apply when a "suspension" of "operations" is caused by destruction or corruption of electronic data, or any loss or damage to electronic data, except as provided under the Additional Coverage—Interruption Of Computer Operations.
>
> b. Coverage for Extra Expense does not apply when action is taken to avoid or minimize a "suspension" of "operations" caused by destruction or corruption of electronic data, or any loss or damage to electronic data, except as provided under the Additional Coverage—Interruption Of Computer Operations.
>
> c. Electronic data means information, facts or computer programs stored as or on, created or used on, or transmitted to or from computer software (including systems and applications software), on hard or floppy disks, CD-ROMs, tapes, drives, cells, data processing devices or any other repositories of computer software which are used with electronically controlled equipment. The term computer programs, referred to in the foregoing description of electronic data, means a set of related electronic instructions which direct the operations and functions of a computer or device connected to it, which enable the computer or device to receive, process, store, retrieve or send data.

In Additional Coverage, the amount available for interruption of computer operation is $2,500. No wonder many businesses today purchase the e-commerce endorsement, such as the ISO 2002 endorsement in Appendix C-1, or buy the new policies from the companies described in Chapters 8 and 9.

Extra Expense

In addition to losing sales, a business may need to incur various expenses following property damage in order to minimize further loss of sales. These extra expenses are also covered by the BIC. A bank, for example, could not simply shut down operations if a fire destroyed its building, because the bank's customers rely on having ready access to financial services. As a result, the bank is likely to set up operations at a temporary location (thus reducing the extent of lost revenues) while the damaged property is being repaired. The rent at the temporary location plus any increase in other expenses would be considered covered extra expenses.

Causes of Loss

The same three perils options available for the BPP are also available for the BIC. Because the BIC requires that the covered income loss result from direct physical loss or damage to property described in the declarations, most insureds choose the same causes of loss form for both the BPP and the BIC.

An example of business interruption was provided in the introduction. The example was applicable to September 11 attacks. Now, we show a more detailed example of a hypothetical loss that occurred during the Chicago flood in 1992.

Business Income Coverage (BIC) Hypothetical Loss

In the spring of 1992, Chicago experienced an unusual "flood," apparently caused by damage to an underground tunnel system. Many firms were required to shut down offices in the damaged area. Among them were large accounting organizations, just two weeks before the tax deadline of April 15. Thus, the losses were magnified by the fact that the flood occurred during the tax season. Assume the following hypothetical conditions for one of those firms.

Pre-Loss Financial Information

Average monthly revenues	$500,000
Average April revenues (stated in 1992 dollars)	700,000
Average monthly payroll	300,000
Average April payroll	550,000
Monthly heat, electricity, water	25,000
Monthly rent for leased office	45,000
Monthly interest expense	10,000
Monthly marketing expense	15,000
Monthly other expenses	$10,000
Net Income in April	$45,000

Post-Loss Financial Information for April 1992

Revenues	$600,000
Payroll	540,000
Utilities	30,000
Rent on downtown space	0
Rent for temporary space	50,000
Interest expense	10,000
Marketing expense	22,000
Other expenses	$20,000
Net Loss	($72,000)

This firm experienced both a reduction in revenue and an increase in expenses. The resulting profit (net income) loss is the covered loss in the BIC.

For this example, the loss equals $117,000, the sum of the income not received ($45,000) that would have been expected without a loss, plus the actual lost income ($72,000) incurred. Such a substantial loss for a two-week period is not unusual.

Coinsurance

The coinsurance provision of the BIC is one of the more confusing parts of any insurance policy. Its purpose is the same as that discussed earlier, which is to maintain equity in pricing. Its application is also similar. The difficulty comes in defining the underlying value of the full exposure, which is needed to apply any coinsurance provision. Following is an underinsurance example from a BIC policy. More examples are provided in the policy sample.

Example No. 1 (Underinsurance):

When: The Net Income and operating expenses for the 12 months following the inception, or last previous anniversary date, of this policy at the described premises would have been $400,000

The Coinsurance percentage is   50%

The Limit of Insurance is $150,000

The amount of loss is $80,000

Step 1: $400,000 × 50% = $200,000 (the minimum amount of insurance to meet your Coinsurance requirements)

Step 2: $150,000 ÷ $200,000 = .75

Step 3: $80,000 × .75 = $60,000

We (the insurer) will pay no more than $60,000. The remaining $20,000 is not covered.

Remember that a BIC loss equals net income plus continuing operating expenses. Coinsurance, however, applies to net income plus all operating expenses, a larger value. The amount of insurance required to meet the coinsurance provision is some percentage of this value, with the percentage determined by what the insured expects to be the maximum period of interruption. If a maximum interruption of six months is expected, for example, the proper coinsurance percentage is 50 percent (6/12). If it is nine months, a coinsurance percentage of 75 percent (9/12) is appropriate.

Because of the complexity of the coinsurance provision, however, many insureds choose an agreed value option. This option works under the same principles as those discussed with regard to the BPP. Using the example illustrated in "Business Income Coverage (BIC) Hypothetical Loss," we can demonstrate the application of the coinsurance provision. Coinsurance requirements apply to net income plus operating expenses ($95,000 plus $405,000 per month on average, or $6,000,000 for the year). If a 50 percent coinsurance provision is used because the expected maximum period of interruption is six months, then the amount of insurance required is $3,000,000 (.50 × $6,000,000). If the April example is representative (which is really not the case with a tax accounting office), a six-month interruption would result in a much lower loss.

Other Options

The BIC includes a number of options designed to modify coverage for the insured's specific needs. Three options that affect the coinsurance provision are the **monthly limit of**

indemnity; maximum period of indemnity; and **payroll endorsements.** For better clarity, the student is invited to read the policy in addition to reading the following explanations.

The monthly limit of indemnity negates the coinsurance provision. Instead, a total limit is listed, as is the percentage of that limit available each month. The policy uses the example of a $120,000 limit and 1/4 monthly amount. For this example, only $30,000 (1/4 × 120,000) is available each month. An organization with stable earnings and expectations of a short period of restoration would likely find this option of interest.

The maximum period of indemnity option also negates the coinsurance provision of the BIC. Instead of limiting the amount payable per month, however, this option limits the duration of coverage to 120 days (or until the limit is reached, whichever comes first). Both the maximum period of indemnity and monthly limit of indemnity address the fact that the standard policy cannot be used with a coinsurance provision of less than 50 percent (6 months).

Instead of negating the coinsurance provision, as do the two options just discussed, the payroll endorsements allow the insured to deduct some or all of its payroll from the value of operating expenses before calculating the coinsurance requirement. Doing so will allow the insured to purchase less insurance (and pay lower premiums, usually) and still meet the coinsurance provision. It also excludes payroll from covered expenses, however, so the insured must feel confident that payroll would not be maintained during a shutdown. A common payroll endorsement includes ninety days of payroll expense in the coinsurance calculation (and BIC coverage), assuming that a short shutdown might allow the insured to continue to pay employees. For a longer shutdown, termination of employment might be more cost effective.

OTHER PROPERTY COVERAGES

The commercial package policy is designed to accommodate separate and sometimes special property needs of insureds as shown in Figure 12.1.

Commercial Crime and Fidelity Coverage

The program includes enhancements that protect businesses and government entities against:

- Employee theft
- Burglary
- Other workplace crimes

Historically, crime losses have been insured separately from other property losses. Perhaps the separation has been intended to standardize the risk; exposure to crime loss may involve quite different loss control needs and frequency and severity estimates, from exposure to fire, weather damage, or other BPP type losses. Furthermore, within the crime coverage, employee dishonesty has typically been insured separately from other property crimes, likely also in an effort to recognize variations in risk and loss control needs between the two. Furthermore, employee dishonesty protection began as a bond (called a **fidelity bond**), which was a guarantee provided to employers by each employee promising loyalty and faithfulness, and stipulating a mechanism for financial recovery should the promise be broken. As a result, bonding companies developed to protect against employee crimes, while insurers expanded their coverage separately to protect against other property-related crimes.

Today, ISO has a **Crime and Fidelity insurance** program.[3] The ISO enhancements include coverage for losses caused by employee theft of:

- Money
- Securities
- Other property of the insured
- Clients' property on the clients' premises

Also available is coverage for additional perils, including:

- Forgery or alteration of negotiable instruments
- Loss through transferring money and securities by fraudulent telephone or fax instructions
- Extortion threats targeting the insured's property

Inland Marine

You may recall that the BPP covers personal property while it is located at the described premises. Many businesses, however, move property from one location to another or have specialized personal property that requires insurance coverage not intended by the BPP. These needs are often met by **inland marine** (IM) insurance. Despite its name, inland marine insurance covers non-water forms of transportation such as rails and trucking.

Inland marine insurance is an outgrowth of **ocean marine insurance,** which is coverage for property while being transported by water (including coverage for the vessels doing the transporting). IM tends to be broad coverage, often on an open-perils basis, and generally for replacement cost. Exclusions tend to involve nonfortuitous events, such as wear and tear and intentionally caused loss. The protection IM provides is for inland transportation and specialized equipment.

Boiler and Machinery Coverage

When a boiler or similar piece of machinery explodes, the cost tends to be enormous. Typically, the entire building is destroyed, as are surrounding properties. Anyone in or near the building may be killed or badly injured. Furthermore, the overwhelming majority of such explosions can be prevented through periodic inspection and excellent maintenance. As a result, a boiler inspection industry developed, and ultimately became an inspection and insurance industry.

Boiler and machinery (B&M) coverage protects against loss that results from property damage to the insured's own property and to nonowned property (bodily injury liability coverage can be added by endorsement) caused by explosions or other sudden breakdowns of boilers and machinery. The bulk of the premium, however, goes toward costs of inspection and loss control. Any business that uses a boiler or similar type of machinery needs to consider purchase of this coverage, because the potential loss is large while the probability of loss is low if proper care is maintained.

Capital Assets Program

The Insurance Services Office introduced "the ISO **Capital Assets Program**—a manufacturer's output type policy—that enables insurers to provide large and medium commercial accounts superior coverage and pricing flexibility for buildings and business personal property."[4]

The program provides businesses coverage on a blanket, replacement-cost basis without a coinsurance provision. The program also provides options to value property at actual cash value, agreed value, or, for buildings, functional replacement cost. Under the program, "business income and extra expense coverages are written into the form and can be activated by entries on the policy declaration page."

Business Owners Policy

In 1976, the ISO developed its first **business owners policy** (BOP), which was designed for small businesses in the office, mercantile, and processing categories and for apartment houses and condominium associations. The intent was to provide a comprehensive policy that would omit the need for small businesses to make numerous decisions, while also incorporating coverage on exposures often overlooked. The original BOP was one policy covering both property and liability exposures. The current program incorporates the BOP into the commercial package policy through separate property and liability policies designed for small businesses. When these coverages are combined, they provide protection nearly identical to the old BOP policy.

The property portion of the business owners program covers both direct and consequential losses, combining the types of coverage found in the BPP and BIC. An inflation guard is standard, as is a **seasonal fluctuation** for personal property. The inflation guard increases the building's coverage limit by some stated percentage automatically each year. The seasonal fluctuation permits recovery of lost personal property up to 125 percent of the declared limit, as long as the average value of the personal property over the prior twelve months is not greater than the limit. For organizations with fluctuating stock values, this provision is helpful. Coverage is on a replacement cost new basis without a coinsurance provision.

The policy also provides business income loss for one year of interruption without a stated dollar limit or coinsurance requirement. Many small businesses are prone to ignore this exposure, which is why the coverage is included automatically.

Coverage can be purchased either on a named-perils basis or open risk. The named-perils form covers the causes of loss listed in Table 12.6, which are the same perils available in other coverage forms. One additional peril, "transportation," is also covered in the BOP. The transportation peril affords some inland marine protection.

The newest "business owners program" was released by ISO in June 2002.[5] The BOP 2002 expanded some risk categories eligible for coverage with a new section, "Commercial Lines Manual." The new BOP includes "computer coverage, business income from dependent properties coverage, and fire extinguisher system recharge expense." There are some new optional endorsements, such as "coverage for food contamination, water backup and sump overflow, functional building and personal property valuation, liquor liability, employee benefits liability, and several coverage and exclusion options for pollution liability." The BOP also has terrorism endorsements as described for the CPP above and for the CGL below.[6]

COMMERCIAL GENERAL LIABILITY POLICY

As discussed in Chapter 9, businesses have a wide variety of liability exposures. Many of these are insurable through the CGL.

CGL Policy Format

The format of the CGL is very similar to that of the BPP and BIC. The CGL contract includes:

- CGL declaration form
- CGL coverage form
- Any appropriate endorsements, such as the mold exclusion endorsement in Appendix D

The CGL itself is comprised of five sections:

1. Coverages
2. Who is an insured
3. Limits of insurance
4. CGL conditions
5. Definitions

Coverage is available either on an **occurrence** or on a claims-made basis. Claims-made basis is a policy that limits the period in which the claims for injuries need to be made. Under such a program, claims for injuries that occurred 30 years ago cannot be covered. The claim needs to be filed (made) during the coverage period for injuries that occur during the same period or designated retroactive time. This limitation is the result of insurers having to pay for asbestos injuries that occurred years before knowledge of the exposure outcome was discovered. Insurers that provided coverage for those injuries 30 years ago were required to pay regardless of when the claims were made. Claims for past unforeseen injuries were not included in the loss development (discussed in Chapter 4) and caused major unexpected losses to the insurance industry. If the claims-made option is chosen, a sixth section is incorporated into the policy, the extended reporting periods provision.

Coverages

The CGL provides three coverages:

- Bodily injury and property damage liability
- Personal and advertising injury liability
- Medical payments

Each coverage involves its own insuring agreement and set of exclusions. Each also provides a distinct limit of insurance, although an aggregate limit may apply to the sum of all costs under each coverage for the policy period. Other aggregates also apply, as discussed in the policy limits section below.

Coverage A—Bodily Injury and Property Damage Liability

The CGL provides open-perils coverage for the insured's liabilities due to "bodily injury" or "property damage" experienced by others. The bodily injury or property damage must arise out of an "occurrence," which is "an accident, including continuous or repeated exposure to substantially the same general harmful conditions." If the policy is a **claims-made** policy, the event must take place after a designated **retroactive date,** and a claim for damages must be made during the policy period. Under the claims-made policy, an insured's liability is covered (assuming no other applicable exclusions) if the event causing liability occurs after some specified retroactive date and the claim for payment by the plaintiff is made within the policy period. This differs from an **occurrence policy,** which covers liability for events that take place within the policy period, regardless of when the plaintiff makes a claim. The claims-made policy may lessen the insurer's uncertainty about likely future payments, because the time lag between premium payments and loss payments generally is smaller with claims-made than with occurrence.

If the claims-made policy is purchased, a retroactive date must be defined. In addition, an **extended reporting period** must be included for the policy to be legal. The extended reporting period applies if a claims-made policy is cancelled. It provides coverage for claims brought after the policy period has expired for events that occurred between the retroactive date and the end of the policy period. An example is shown in Table 12.7. The standard extended reporting form is very limited, and so insureds may purchase additional extensions.

The claims-made policy was introduced (first in medical malpractice insurance, later in other policies) in response to increased uncertainty about future liabilities. As explained above, an occurrence policy could be sold today, and liability associated with it determined thirty or more years later. With changing legal and social norms, the inability of insurers to feel confident with their estimates of ultimate liabilities (for pricing purposes) led them to develop the claims-made coverage.

Bodily injury (BI) is defined as bodily injury, sickness, or disease sustained by a person, including death resulting from any of these at any time. **Property damage** (PD) is defined as (a) physical injury to tangible property, including all resulting loss of use of that property; or (b) loss of use of tangible property that is not physically injured.

In addition to covering an insured's liability due to bodily injury or property damage, the insurer promises to defend against suits claiming such injuries. The **cost of defense** is provided in addition to the limits of insurance available for payment of settlements or judgments, as is payment of interest that accrues after entry of the judgment against the insured. The insurer, however, has the general right to settle any suit as it deems appropriate. Further, the insurer's obligation to defend against liability ends when it has paid out its limits for any of the coverages in settlements or judgments.

So far, this coverage sounds extremely broad, and it is. A long list of exclusions, however, defines the coverage more specifically. Table 12.8 provides the list of exclusions.

We can discuss the exclusions as they relate to the four general reasons for exclusions, as presented earlier. Several relate to situations that may be nonfortuitous. Exclusion (a), which denies coverage for intentionally caused harm, clearly limits nonfortuitous events. Exclusion (b), an exclusion of contractually assumed liability, also could be considered a nonfortuitous event because the insured chose to enter into the relevant contract. Pollution liability (exclusion f), likewise, may arise from activities that were known to be dangerous. Damage to the insured's own products or work (exclusions k and l) indicates that the insurer is not willing to provide a product warranty to cover the insured's poor workmanship, a controllable situation.

TABLE 12.7
Claims-Made Coverage Example

Assume a policy purchased on January 1, 1990, that provides $1,000,000 per occurrence of claims-made coverage with a retroactive date of January 1, 1988, and a one-year policy period. Further assume that the policy was canceled on December 31, 1990, and that the insured purchased a one-year extended reporting period.

The following losses occur:

Amount	Date of Injury	Date of Claim	Insurer responsibility
$100,000	3/15/88	3/15/89	—0[1]
100,000	3/15/88	3/15/90	100,000[2]
100,000	3/15/90	3/15/91	100,000[3]
100,000	3/15/90	3/15/92	—0[4]
100,000	3/15/91	3/15/91	—0[5]

[1] The claim precedes the coverage period. No coverage exists under this policy.
[2] The event follows the retroactive date and the claim is brought during the policy period.
[3] The event follows the retroactive date and the claim is brought in the extended reporting period.
[4] The claim follows the end of the reporting period (assuming our date of claim is date of notice to the insurer). No coverage exists under this policy.
[5] Even though the claim is brought within the extended reporting period, the event occurs

A number of exclusions are intended to standardize the risk and/or limit duplicate coverage when other coverage does or should exist. Liquor liability (exclusion c), for instance, is not standard across insureds. Entities with a liquor exposure must purchase separate coverage to protect against it. Likewise, we know that workers' compensation and employers' liability (exclusions d and e) all are covered by specialized contracts. Separate policies also exist for autos, aircraft, watercraft, and mobile equipment (exclusions g and h), because these "risks" will not be standard for organizations with similar general liability exposures.

The category of property owned by or in the care, custody, and control of the insured is also excluded (exclusion m). These are exposures best handled in a property insurance policy, in part because the insured cannot be liable to itself for damage, and in part because the damage should be covered whether or not caused by the insured's carelessness.

Some exclusions apply because of the catastrophic potential of certain situations. In addition to the possible nonfortuity of pollution losses, the potential damages are catastrophic. Cost estimates to clean hazardous waste sites in the U.S. run into the hundreds of billions of dollars as discussed in Chapter 9. Similarly, war-related injuries (exclusion i) are likely to affect thousands, possibly hundreds of thousands of people simultaneously.

After September 11, as noted earlier, many states approved various ISO terrorism endorsements which also excluded terrorism liability coverage from the commercial general liability policies.[7] The NAIC Bulletin[8] to all insurers writing CGL policies after September 11 noted that for policies providing liability insurance coverage the following limitations apply:

- Exclusion for acts of terrorism only apply if the acts of terrorism result in industry-wide insured losses
- Fifty or more persons sustain death or serious physical injury. For purposes of this provision serious physical injury means:
  - Physical injury that involves a substantial risk of death;
  - Protracted and obvious physical disfigurement; or
  - Protracted loss of or impairment of the function of a bodily member or organ.

TABLE 12.8

Exclusions to Coverage A—Bodily Injury and Property Damage Liability in the CGL ISO Policy , 2001

a. Expected or Intended Injury—"bodily injury" or "property damage" expected or intended from the standpoint of the insured.
b. Contractual Liability
c. Liquor Liability
d. Workers' Compensation and Similar Laws
e. Employer's Liability
f. Pollution
g. Aircraft, Auto or Watercraft
h. Mobile Equipment
i. War
j. Damage to Property you own, rent, or occupy, including any costs or expenses incurred by you, Premises you sell, give away or abandon, Property loaned to you; Personal property in the care, custody or control of the insured;
k. Damage to Your Product
l. Damage to Your Work
m. Damage to Impaired Property or Property Not Physically Injured
n. Recall of Products, Work or Impaired Property
o. Personal and Advertising Injury

- Exclusions for acts of terrorism are not subject to limitations above if:
  - The act involves the use, release or escape of nuclear materials, or that directly or indirectly results in nuclear reaction or radiation or radioactive contamination;
  - The act is carried out by means of the dispersal or application of pathogenic or poisonous biological or chemical materials; or
  - Pathogenic or poisonous biological or chemical materials are released, and it appears that one purpose of the terrorism was to release such materials.

The Bulletin also provided the following definition of terrorism.

Terrorism means activities against persons, organizations or property of any nature:

1. That involve the following or preparation for the following:
   a. Use or threat of force or violence; or
   b. Commission or threat of a dangerous act; or
   c. Commission or threat of an act that interferes with or disrupts an electronic, communication, information, or mechanical system; and

2. When one or both of the following applies:
   a. The effect is to intimidate or coerce a government or the civilian population or any segment thereof, or to disrupt any segment of the economy; or
   b. It appears that the intent is to intimidate or coerce a government, or to further political, ideological, religious, social or economic objectives or to express (or to express opposition to) a philosophy or ideology.

The terrorism exclusion, its implications, and the debate about governmental terrorism reinsurance pool were discussed in prior chapters and in more detail in the Ethical Dilemma discussion of Chapter 2.

The war risk as well as today's terrorism risk practically defines catastrophe, because it affects so many people from a single situation, not too unlike a product recall (exclusion n). Most manufacturers produce tens of thousands of products in each batch. If a recall is necessary, the whole batch generally is affected. This situation also has some element of nonfortuity, in that the insured has some control over deciding upon a recall, although limited separate coverage is available for this exposure. A memorable example occurred when Johnson & Johnson recalled all of its Tylenol products following the lethal tampering of several boxes. Even though Johnson & Johnson undertook the recall to prevent future injury (and possible liability), its insurer denied coverage for the recall costs. Insureds can buy an endorsement for product recall.

Another new exclusion is the "Fungi and Bacteria Exclusion," shown in Appendix D in the back of the text. As noted for the property coverage, the CGL also has a new mold exclusion that applies to bodily injury and property damage only. The endorsement states that payment for liability is excluded for

a. "Bodily injury" or "property damage" which would not have occurred, in whole or in part, but for the actual, alleged or threatened inhalation of, ingestion of, contact with, exposure to, existence of, or presence of, any "fungi" or bacteria on or within a building or structure, including its contents, regardless of whether any other cause, event, material or product contributed concurrently or in any sequence to such injury or damage.

b. Any loss, cost or expenses arising out of the abating, testing for, monitoring, cleaning up, removing, containing, treating, detoxifying, neutralizing, remediating or disposing of, or in any way responding to, or assessing the effects of, "fungi" or bacteria, by any insured or by any other person or entity.

Coverage B—Personal and Advertising Injury Liability

Coverage A provides protection against physical injury or damage due to the insured's activities. Despite the many exclusions, it provides broad coverage for premises, products, completed work, and other liabilities. It does not, however, provide protection against the liabilities arising out of nonphysical injuries. Coverage B does provide that protection. The policy states:

> We will pay those sums that the insured becomes legally obligated to pay as damages because of "personal and advertising injury" to which this insurance applies. We will have the right and duty to defend the insured against any "suit" seeking those damages. However, we will have no duty to defend the insured against any "suit" seeking damages for "personal and advertising injury" to which this insurance does not apply. We may, at our discretion, investigate any offense and settle any claim or "suit" that may result.

The exclusions for Coverage B, Personal and Advertising Injury Liability, are listed in Table 12.9.

The exclusions eliminate intentional acts (non-accidental acts), acts that occurred before the coverage began, criminal acts, and contractual liability. False statements and failure to conform to statements and infringements of copyrights and trademarks are also excluded. As in other coverages, electronic chat rooms and Internet businesses are excluded, as was noted in Chapter 9. In this context, insureds in the Internet and media businesses are completely excluded from coverage B under the 2001 CGL policy. The particular exclusion of unauthorized use of other's name and product was also noted in Chapter 9. Since pollution and pollution related risks are considered catastrophic, they are excluded as well.

TABLE 12.9 Exclusions to Coverage B—Personal and Advertising Injury Liability in the CGL ISO Policy, 2001	a. Knowing Violation of Rights of Another b. Material Published with Knowledge of Falsity c. Material Published Prior to Policy Period d. Criminal Acts e. Contractual Liability f. Breach of Contract g. Quality or Performance of Goods — Failure to Conform to Statements h. Wrong Description of Prices i. Infringement of Copyright, Patent, Trademark, or Trade Secret j. Insureds in Media and Internet-Type Businesses k. Electronic Chatrooms or Bulletin Boards l. Unauthorized Use of Another's Name or Product m. Pollution n. Pollution-Related

Coverage C—Medical Payments

We have discussed medical payments coverage in both the homeowners and auto policy. The CGL medical payments coverage is similar to what is found in the homeowners policy. It provides payment for first aid, necessary medical and dental treatment, ambulance, hospital, professional nursing, and funeral services to persons other than the "insured." The intent is to pay these amounts to people injured on the insured's premises or due to the insured's operations, regardless of fault. That is, medical payments coverage is not a liability protection.

The medical payments coverage is not intended to provide health insurance to the insured nor to any employees of the insured (or anyone eligible for workers' compensation). Nor will it duplicate coverage provided in other sections of the CGL or fill in where coverage A excludes protection. War is also excluded. A list of exclusions to coverage C is provided in Table 12.10.

Supplementary Payments

Supplementary payments are for bodily injury, property damage, and personal injury coverages. The insurer pays for the claim or suit, the cost for bonds up to $250, all expenses for investigation it conducts, and "all reasonable expenses incurred by the insured." As long as the list of conditions detailed in the policy are met (see Appendix D), the insurer pays all attorneys' fees it incurs in the defense of the insured. The obligation to defend and to pay for attorneys' fees and necessary litigation expenses as supplementary payments ends when the insurer has reached the applicable limit of insurance in the payment of judgments or settlements.

Who Is an Insured?

Section II of the 2001 CGL is very specific and detailed in defining whose liability is covered. The following are insureds:

- An individual
- A partnership or joint venture
- A limited liability company
- An organization other than a partnership, joint venture or limited liability company
- A trust

The "volunteer workers" of the business are also insured. However, none of the employees or volunteer workers are insureds for bodily injury or personal and advertising injury to the insured or property damage to property that is owned or occupied by the insured. More detail can be gleaned in the policy in Appendix D in the back of the textbook.

TABLE 12.10 Exclusions to Coverage C—Medical Payment in the CGL ISO Policy, 2001	a. Any Insured b. Hired Person c. Injury on Normally Occupied Premises d. Workers Compensation and Similar Laws e. Athletics Activities f. Products-Completed Operations Hazard g. Coverage A Exclusions h. War

Limits of Insurance

The limits of insurance, as you know by now, define the maximum responsibility of the insurer under specified situations. A portion of the declaration for CGL is shown in Figure 12.2

The policy clarifies the limits of insurance shown in the declarations and the applicable rules. The general aggregate limit is the most that the insurer pays for the sum of:

- Medical expenses under Coverage C, plus
- Damages under Coverage A, except damages because of "bodily injury" or "property damage" included in the "products-completed operations hazard," plus
- Damages under Coverage B

The limits are paid regardless of the number of insureds, claims made, or suits brought, or persons or organizations making claims or bringing suits. The limits apply separately to each consecutive annual period.

CGL Conditions

Like all other policies, the CGL includes an extensive conditions section, primarily outlining the duties of the insured and insurer. Subrogation, other insurance, proper action in the event of loss, and similar provisions are spelled out in the conditions section.

Definitions

Words used in insurance policies might not have the same interpretation as when used in other documents or conversations. To specify its intent, insurers define significant terms (remember that insurance is a contract of adhesion, so ambiguities are read in the manner most favorable to the insured). Some defined terms in the CGL have already been discussed, including "bodily injury," "property damage," **"personal injury," "advertising injury,"** and "occurrence." In total, twenty two terms are defined in the CGL. Like the rest of the policy, a full interpretation of coverage requires reading and analyzing these definitions. The problems that arise out of interpretation of the CGL policy wording is discussed in the "Ethical Dilemma: Liability Limits—One Event or Two?" in this chapter.

COMMERCIAL UMBRELLA LIABILITY POLICY

Today, $1,000,000 of liability coverage, the standard limit for a CGL, is insufficient for many businesses. Furthermore, liabilities other than those covered by the CGL may be of

FIGURE 12.2

Section of the ISO CGL Declaration Page

LIMITS OF INSURANCE		
EACH OCCURRENCE LIMIT	$ _____	
DAMAGE TO PREMISES RENTED TO YOU LIMIT	$ _____	Any one premises
MEDICAL EXPENSE LIMIT	$ _____	Any one person
PERSONAL ADVERTISING INJURY LIMIT	$ _____	Any one person or organization
GENERAL AGGREGATE LIMIT	$ _____	
PRODUCTS/COMPLETED OPERATIONS AGGREGATE LIMIT	$ _____	

significant importance to a business. To obtain additional amounts and a broader scope of coverage, a business can purchase a commercial **umbrella liability policy.**

The umbrella liability policy provides excess coverage over underlying insurance. Except for excluded risks, it also provides excess over a specified amount, such as $25,000, for which there is no underlying coverage. Typically, you are required to have specified amounts of underlying coverage, such as the CGL with a $1,000,000 limit and automobile insurance with the same limit. When a loss occurs, the basic contracts pay within their limits and then the umbrella policy pays until its limits are exhausted. If there is no underlying coverage for a loss covered by the umbrella, you pay the first $25,000 (or whatever is the specified retention) and the umbrella insurer pays the excess.

The umbrella policy covers bodily injury, property damage, personal injury, and advertising injury liability, similar to what is provided in the CGL. Medical expense coverage is not included. The limits of coverage, however, are intended to be quite high, and the exclusions are not as extensive as those found in the CGL. Most businesses find umbrella liability coverage an essential part of their risk management operations.

It is important to note that ISO designed a separate terrorism exclusion endorsement for the umbrella policy in "Commercial Liability Umbrella Endorsement."

OTHER LIABILITY RISKS

What about the business liability exposures not covered by the CGL? Space limitations prohibit discussing all of them, but several merit some attention: automobile, professional liability, and workers' compensation. Workers' compensation is discussed in Chapter 13.

Automobile Liability

If the business is a proprietorship and the only vehicles used are private passenger automobiles, the personal auto policy or a similar policy is available to cover the automobile exposure. If the business is a partnership or corporation or uses other types of vehicles, other forms of automobile insurance must be purchased if the exposure is to be insured. The coverages are similar to the automobile insurance discussed in Chapter 11.

Professional Liability

The nature and significance of the professional liability risk were discussed in Chapter 9. Most professionals insure this exposure separately with **malpractice insurance, errors and omissions insurance,** or **directors and officers insurance (D&O).** These liability coverages were discussed in Chapter 9. You are urged to review the current conditions of the D&O coverage featured in the "Important Issues: Directors and Officers Coverage in the Limelight" in this chapter.

Employment Practices Liability

The ISO's **Employment-Related Practices Liability Program,** which is available to all ISO-participating insurance companies, was filed with state insurance regulators for approval effective April 1, 1998.[9] It was the newest line introduced in more than 20 years. Because of an increase in the number of lawsuits filed for sexual harassment and many more employment-related liability suits, the coverage became imperative to most businesses. The ISO is considered a base line program. "The policy covers insureds' lia-

IMPORTANT ISSUES

Directors and Officers Coverage in the Limelight

William Webster had enjoyed a long and distinguished career in public service, most notably as the only person ever to head both the FBI (under President Carter) and the CIA (under President Reagan). The onetime U.S. District Court judge retired from public office in 1991, at age sixty-seven, and devoted his time to practicing law in Washington, D.C., and sitting on the boards of several large corporations. One of them was U.S. Technologies, which develops and supports emerging Internet companies. But in July 2002, Webster was told the company could no longer provide adequate liability insurance to its directors and officers. He resigned.

All publicly traded companies must have a board of directors, a group of people elected by the stockholders to govern the company. Generally the board is charged with selecting and supervising the executive officers, setting overall corporate policy, and overseeing the preparation of financial statements. This role leaves directors vulnerable to lawsuits from shareholders, creditors, customers, or employees on such charges as abuse of authority, libel or slander, and—the biggest concern these days—financial mismanagement. Board members at many corporations became concerned about their personal liability and started taking a closer look at the insurance, known as "directors and officers coverage" or simply "D&O," that is supposed to protect them.

Not surprisingly, the corporate scandals of 2001 and 2002 had driven up the cost of D&O insurance. Following WorldCom's June 2002 announcement that it had "inappropriately classified" nearly $4 billion in expenses, D&O insurers pulled back from covering not just WorldCom but also its banks, its suppliers, and its business customers. Another reason for the shrinking D&O insurance pool was the late-'90s trend toward astronomical settlements in class-action securities lawsuits. By 2002, "high-risk" companies—in the aircraft, financial, health care, technology, and telecommunications industries—were paying triple what they used to for D&O, if they could find coverage at all.

Directors and officers were made even more vulnerable with the passage of the Sarbanes-Oxley Act in July 2002. With this key piece of legislation, Congress hoped to restore the public's confidence in U.S. financial markets by holding chief executives, directors, and outside auditors more responsible—even criminally liable—for the accuracy of financial reports. Sarbanes-Oxley was passed just one month after Enron's outside auditor, the accounting firm Arthur Andersen, was convicted on obstruction of justice charges for its role in the financial fraud. Thus the star of the act was its provision for a corporate-accounting oversight board to "audit the auditors"—to set and enforce standards for financial reporting, and to scrutinize accounting firms to make sure they are in compliance.

As the October deadline neared for appointing a board chairman, William Webster seemed the perfect choice. It was under Webster's directorship that the FBI had exposed the massive U.S. savings and loan scandal of the early 1980s, so he had experience with large-scale financial law enforcement. Webster's integrity was unimpeachable, and he was widely admired by both Democrats and Republicans. But just days after Webster's appointment, questions began to surface about his tenure at U.S. Technologies. The company had not fared well; it was all but bankrupt, and its chief executive officer was being sued by investors who claimed they had been defrauded of millions of dollars. The company's auditors, BDO Seidman, charged that Webster had made "false and misleading statements" about how much he knew about the company's financial problems.

Webster denied any wrongdoing, and to date he is not the target of any government investigation. But, as he said in his resignation letter, "I now believe my continued presence on the Board will only generate more distractions which will not be helpful to the important mission of the Board." Some see a double irony: that the chairman of the board established to stamp out corporate fraud should be accused of corporate fraud, and that the reason he resigned from U.S. Technologies was that it lacked liability insurance to cover such a situation as this.

Explore the Internet

If you'd like, you can read all sixty-six pages of the Sarbanes-Oxley Act at www.loc.gov/law/guide/pl107204.pdf. The American Institute of Certified Public Accountants offers a manageable ten-page
(Continued)

IMPORTANT ISSUES (CONTINUED)

summary at www.aicpa.org/info/sarbanes_oxley_summary.htm, and a look at how the act will affect the accounting/auditing profession at www.aicpa.org/info/Sarbanes-Oxley2002.asp. For the latest SEC implementations of Sarbanes-Oxley, see www.sec.gov /news/press.shtml.

Sources: Roberto Ceniceros, "WorldCom Adds to D&O Ills," *Business Insurance*, 8 July 2002; Rodd Zolkos and Mark A. Hofmann, "Crises Spur Push for Reform," *Business Insurance*, 15 July 2002; Richard B. Schmitt, Michael Schroeder, and Shailagh Murray, "Corporate-Oversight Bill Passes, Smoothing Way for New Lawsuits," *The Wall Street Journal*, 26 July 2002; Stephen LaBaton, "S.E.C. Orders Investigation into Webster Appointment," *New York Times*, 31 October 2002; Carrie Coolidge, "D&O Insurance Gets Closer Scrutiny," *Forbes*, 22 November 2002.

bility for claims arising out of an injury to an employee because of an employment-related offense, as well as providing legal defense for the insured. Injury may result from discrimination that results in refusal to hire; failure to promote; termination; demotion; discipline or defamation. Injury also can include coercion of an employee to perform an unlawful act; work-related sexual harassment; or verbal, physical, mental or emotional abuse."

The ISO program excludes:

- Criminal, fraudulent or malicious acts;
- Violations of the accommodations requirement of the Americans with Disabilities Act;
- Liability of the perpetrator of sexual harassment; and
- Injury arising out of strikes and lock-outs, employment termination from specified business decisions and retaliatory actions taken against "whistle blowers."

The program makes available a number of optional coverages including:

- Extending the claims-reporting period to three years;
- Extending coverage beyond managers and supervisors to all of a firm's employees;
- Insuring organizations that are newly formed or acquired by the insured during the policy period for 90 days;
- Insuring persons or organizations with financial control over the insured or the insured's employment-related practices.

KEY TERMS

commercial general liability policy	business income coverage	claims-made policy
debris removal	extra expense	retroactive date
pollutant cleanup and removal	monthly limit of indemnity	extended reporting period
provision 7 valuation	maximum period of indemnity	bodily injury
section E, loss conditions	payroll endorsements	property damage
replacement cost new	fidelity bond	cost of defense
coinsurance provision	crime and fidelity insurance	personal injury
additional conditions	ocean marine insurance	advertising injury
agreed value option	inland marine	umbrella liability policy
optional coverages	boiler and machinery	malpractice insurance
inflation guard option	capital asset program	errors and omission insurance
basic causes of loss	business owners policy	directors and officers insurance
broad causes of loss	seasonal fluctuation	employment related practices policy
special causes of loss	occurrence policy	

DISCUSSION QUESTIONS

1. What types of property are covered in the BPP? What are some examples of excluded property, and why are they excluded?
2. How can an insured get around the coinsurance provision in the BPP? Why might an insured prefer to do this?
3. What are the primary differences among the three causes of loss forms available in the commercial property policy? Why not always choose the special form?
4. What kinds of losses are covered in the BIC? Provide examples.
5. How does the insured choose a limit of insurance for the BIC?
6. When would the monthly limit of indemnity, maximum period of indemnity, or payroll endorsement be appropriate?
7. What is a fidelity bond?
8. What is inland marine insurance?
9. What are the advantages of using a business owners policy?
10. Provide an example of expenses that would be covered under each of the three CGL coverages.
11. Compare occurrence and claims-made policies.
12. What responsibility does a CGL insurer have with regard to litigation expenses for a lawsuit that, if successfully pursued by the plaintiff, would result in payment of damages under the terms of the policy?
13. Provide a detailed rationale for excluding pollution, auto accidents, and liquor liability in the CGL.
14. How does "personal injury" differ from "bodily injury?"
15. Who needs an umbrella liability policy? Why?
16. How does malpractice differ from errors and omissions?
17. Compare the endorsements included in Appendices C-1, C-2, and D. What is the specific intention of each endorsement? How does each contribute to complete the holistic risk management program of a business?
18. How much will be paid to a business that suffered a large mold loss under the current ISO commercial coverage program? Explain your answer.

EXERCISES

12.1 Assume that the Seinfeld Shoe Station owns the $1 million building in which it operates, maintains inventory and other business properties in the building worth $700,000, and often has possession of people's properties up to a value of $50,000 while they are being repaired. For each of the following losses, what if anything will Seinfeld's BPP insurer pay? Limits are $1 million on coverage A and $800,000 on coverage B. The broad causes-of-loss form is used and there was no e-commerce endorsement. Explain your answers.
   a. Wind damage rips off tiles from the roof, costing $20,000 to replace. The actual cash value is $17,000.
   b. An angry arsonist starts a fire. The building requires repairs of $15,000, $17,000 of inventory is destroyed, and $2,000 of other people's property is burned.
   c. A water pipe bursts, destroying $22,000 of inventory and requiring $10,000 to repair the pipe.

    d.   The computer system crashed for three days.

12.2 Seinfeld also bought a BIC with a limit of $250,000 and a 50 percent coinsurance clause. No other endorsements are used. A limited income statement for last year is shown below.

Revenues		$2,000,000
Cost of Goods Sold	800,000	
Utilities	200,000	
Payroll	400,000	
Other Expenses	300,000	$1,700,000
Profit		$300,000

    a.   How much in expenses does Seinfeld expect to be noncontinuing in the event of a shutdown? Explain.

    b.   What is the longest shutdown period Seinfeld would expect following a loss?

    c.   If a three-month closing occurred following the roof collapsing due to the weight of snow, what do you think would be the loss? Explain.

12.3 Hurricane Iniki in 1992 caused extensive damage to one of the Hawaiian Islands. A significant loss in tourist activity resulted. Assume the Koehn Hotel experienced $500,000 in damage to its property. Furthermore, assume Koehn typically brought in $100,000 of revenue per month, on which it incurred $80,000 of fixed and variable expenses. For two months following Iniki, the Koehn Hotel was shut down, but still incurred expenses of $50,000. The hotel further spent $15,000 more than usual on advertising before reopening. Based on this information, what would be the insurable consequential losses of the Koehn Hotel from Hurricane Iniki? What could be done to reduce those losses?

12.4 Assume the Koehn Kitchen Corporation, a manufacturer of kitchen gadgets, experiences the following losses:

    a.   A consumer chops off his finger while using Koehn's Cutlery Gizmo. The consumer sues Koehn for medical expenses, lost income, pain and suffering, and punitive damages.

    b.   An employee of Koehn is injured while delivering goods to a wholesaler. The employee sues for medical expenses and punitive damages.

    c.   Koehn uses toxic substances in its manufacturing process. Neighbors of its plant bring suit against Koehn, claiming that a higher rate of stillbirths is occurring in the area because of Koehn's use of toxics. (Consider the variation that an explosion emitted toxics, rather than normal operations).

    d.   Koehn's Mighty Mate Slicing Machine must be recalled because of a product defect. The recall causes massive losses.

    Based on information in this chapter, which parts of any of these losses are covered by Koehn's CGL? Explain your answer.

12.5 Assume that the Baker-Leetch Pet Store has a CGL with a $1,000,000 aggregate limit. The policy commences July 1, 2001, and ends June 30, 2002.

    a.   If claims-made, the retroactive date is July 1, 2000, and a one-year extended reporting period applies. Under both occurrence and claims-made scenarios, would the following losses be covered? The pet shop sold a diseased gerbil in August 2000. The gerbil ultimately infected the owner's twenty cats and dogs (kept for breeding purposes), who all died. The owner filed a lawsuit against Baker-Leetch in September 2001. What if the lawsuit were filed in September 2002? September 2003?

b. The pet shop provided dog training in July 2001 and guaranteed the results of the training. In December 2001, one of the trained dogs attacked a mail carrier, causing severe injuries. The mail carrier immediately sued Baker-Leetch.

c. The pet store sold an inoculated rare and expensive cat in October 2001. The cat contracted a disease in October 2002 that would not have occurred if the animal truly had been properly inoculated. The owners sued in December 2002.

12.6 The Goldman Cat House is a pet store catering to the needs of felines. The store is a sole proprietorship, taking in revenues of approximately $1,700,000 annually. Products available include kittens, cat food, cat toys, cages, collars, cat litter and litter boxes, and manuals on cat care. One manual was written by the store owner, who also makes up his own concoction for cat litter. All other goods are purchased from national wholesalers. Two part-time and two full-time employees work for Goldman. Sometimes the employees deliver goods to Goldman customers.

a. Identify some of Goldman Cat House's liability exposures.

b. Would Goldman be best advised to purchase an occurrence-based or claims-made liability policy?

c. What liability loss control techniques would you recommend for Goldman?

NOTES

1. "Hartford Offers Free Cyber-Risk Course," *National Underwriter* Online News Service, 21 August 2002. "The Hartford Financial Services Group announced it will offer a free online course to insurance agents to help them identify and protect their clients from cyber risks."
2. A detailed description of this part of the policy is beyond the scope of this text. Interested students are invited to study the policy in the appendix.
3. ISO press release at: www.iso.com/products/2200/prod2241.html.
4. ISO press release at: www.iso.com/press_releases/2002/01_22_02.html, January 22, 2002.
5. "New ISO Offering For Smaller Businesses," *National Underwriter* Online News Service, 3 June 2002. The press release by ISO "ISO's NEW BUSINESSOWNERS PROGRAM SIMPLIFIES RATING AND EXPANDS COVERAGE ELIGIBILITY—ISO IntegRater™ and AscendantOne™ Updated for the New BOP" is available at: www.iso.com/press_releases/2002/06_03_02.html.
6. Businessowners Endorsement: Bp 05 11 01 02 (N/A To Standard Fire Policy States); Businessowners Endorsement: Bp 05 12 02 (Applies In Standard Fire Policy States); Businessowners Endorsement: Bp 05 13 01 02.
7. Commercial General Liability Endorsement: Cg 21 69 0102; Commercial General Liability Endorsement: Cg 31 42 01 02; Commercial General Liability Endorsement: Cg 31 43 01 02.
8. National Association of Insurance Commissioners, www.naic.org.
9. ISO press release as of August 19, 1997 at: www.iso.com/press_releases/1997/08_19_97.html.

CHAPTER 13

Workers' and Unemployment Compensation

Workers' compensation is a state mandated coverage that is exclusively related to the workplace. Unemployment compensation is also a mandated program required of employers. Both are considered social insurance programs, as is Social Security. Social Security is featured in Chapter 15 as a foundation program for employee benefits (covered in Chapters 16 through 18). Social insurance programs are required coverages as a matter of law. The programs are based only on the connection to the labor force, and not on need. Both workers' compensation and unemployment compensation are part of the risk management of businesses in the United States. The use of workers' compensation as part of an integrated risk program is featured in Case 3 at the back of the text as well as in Chapter 3.

Remember from the Introduction to this text that workers' compensation was one of the coverages that helped the families who lost their breadwinners in the attacks of September 11. New York City and the state of New York suffered their largest-ever loss of human lives. Since most of the occurrences were while the employees were at work, those injured received medical care, rehabilitation, and disability income under the New York workers' compensation system, and families of the deceased received survivors' benefits. The huge payouts raised the question of what would happen to workers' compensation rates. The National Council on Compensation Insurance (NCCI) predicted a grim outlook.[1] 2001 was one of the worst years in the market's history, with the largest human catastrophe ever, with approximately 3,000 people dead at the World Trade Center and thousands more injured. There were nearly 6,000 workers' compensation claims from employees at the WTC, estimated to cost $1.3 billion.[2] The good news in this grim picture was the fact that frequency of income claims declined by 4 percent in 2001, but medical severity of claims increased by 11 percent.

New York is known to be a generous state for workers' compensation. It was estimated that the surviving relatives of those killed in the disaster would receive $500,000 per claim.[3] The system in New York, as noted in the Introduction, provides $10,000 for funeral expenses, and a surviving spouse and each surviving child is entitled to $400 a week. The spouse is eligible to receive the benefit for the rest of her/his life unless remarrying. In this case, the benefits stop after two years. The children receive the benefits until age 21. Under certain circumstances, such as being a student or disabled, the benefits are extended. The September 11 losses were so massive that a second such attack could wipe out the workers' compensation fund.[4] Regardless of these factors, the average workers' compensation rate will probably not rise, but insurers are allowed to build in new "catastrophe loads" into their loss development (see Chapter 4) for their rates proposals to regulators and for reserves.[5]

Workers' compensation is considered a social insurance program. Another social insurance program is the unemployment compensation offered in all the states. This chapter includes a brief explanation of this program as well. To better understand how workers' compensation and unemployment compensation work, this chapter includes the following:

1. Connection to the holistic risk management puzzle
2. Workers' compensation laws and benefits
3. Workers' compensation insurance
4. Self-insurance of workers' compensation costs
5. State funds and second-injury funds.
6. Workers' compensation issues
7. Unemployment compensation

CONNECTION

At this point in our study we look at the coverage employers provide for you and your family in case you are hurt on the job (workers' compensation) or lose your job involuntarily (unemployment compensation). As noted above, these coverages are mandatory in most states. Workers' compensation is not mandatory in New Jersey and Texas (though most employers in these states provide it anyway). In later chapters you will see the employer-provided group life, health, disability, and pensions as part of non-cash compensation programs. These coverages complete important parts of your holistic risk management. You know that, at least for work-related injury, you have protection and if you are laid off, limited unemployment compensation is available to you for six months. These coverages are paid completely by the employer; the rates for workers' compensation are based on your occupational classification.

In some cases the employer does not purchase workers' compensation coverage from a private insurer, but buys it from a state's monopolistic fund or self-insures the coverage. For unemployment compensation, the coverage is (in most cases) provided by the states.[6] Regardless of the method of obtaining the coverage, you are assured by statutes to receive the benefits.

As with the coverages discussed in Chapters 10–12, external market conditions are a very important indication of the cost of coverage to your employer. As shown in Table 5.2, the combined ratio for workers' compensation in 2001 was extremely high, at 129. When rates increase dramatically, many employers will opt to self-insure and use a third-party administrator (TPA) to manage the claims. The example of NEXCOM in Chapter 3 is of an employer who self-insures and also administers the claims on its own. In workers' compensation, loss control and safety engineering are important parts of the risk management process. One of the causes of loss is ergonomics, particularly as related to computers. See "Ethical Dilemma: Should Ergonomic Standards Be Mandatory?" for a discussion. You would like to minimize your injury at work, and your employer is obligated under federal and state laws to secure a safe workplace for you.

Thus, in your pursuit for a holistic risk management, workers' compensation coverage is an important piece of the puzzle that completes your risk mitigation. The coverages you receive are only for work-related injuries. What happens if you are injured away from work? This will be discussed in later chapters. One trend is **integrated benefits,** in which the employer integrates the disability and medical coverages of workers' compensation with voluntary health and disability insurance. Integrated benefits are part of the effort to provide **24-hour coverage** regardless if an injury occurred at work or outside of work. Currently, non-work-related injuries are covered for medical procedures by the employer-provided health insurance and for loss of income by group disability insurance. Integrating the benefits is assumed to prevent "double dipping" (receiving benefits under workers' compensation and also under health insurance or disability insurance) and to assure security of coverage regardless of being at work or not. (See "Important Issues: Integrated Benefits—The 24-Hour Coverage Concept" in this chapter.) Health and disability coverages are provided voluntarily by your employer and it is your responsibility to seek individual coverages when the pieces that are offered are insufficient to complete your holistic risk management. Figure 13.1 shows how your holistic risk pieces relate to the risk management parts available under workers' compensation and unemployment compensation.

WORKERS' COMPENSATION LAWS AND BENEFITS

Each state, and certain other jurisdictions such as the District of Columbia and other U.S. territories, has a workers' compensation system to enforce a series of state laws designed to pay workers for their work-related injuries and illnesses.

FIGURE 13.1 Connection Between Risks and Workers' Compensation and Unemployment Compensation

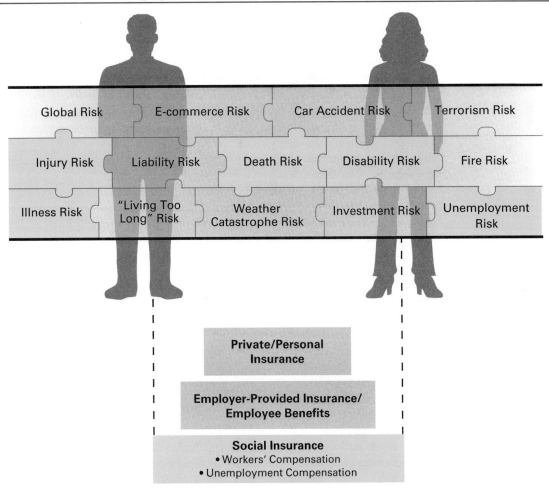

History and Purpose

In the nineteenth century, before implementation of workers' compensation laws in the United States, employees were seldom paid for work-related injuries. A major barrier to payment was that a worker had to prove an injury was the fault of his or her employer in order to recover damages. The typical employee was reluctant to sue his or her employer out of fear of losing the job. For the same reason, fellow workers typically refused to testify on behalf of an injured colleague about the circumstances surrounding an accident. If the injured employee could not prove fault, the employer had no responsibility. The injured employee's ability to recover damages was hindered further by the fact that even a negligent employer could use three **common law defenses**: the fellow-servant rule, the doctrine of assumption of risk, and the doctrine of contributory negligence.

Under the **fellow-servant rule,** an employee who was injured as a result of the conduct of a fellow worker could not recover damages from the employer. The **assumption of risk doctrine** provided that an employee who knew, or should have known, of unsafe conditions of employment assumed the risk by remaining on the job. Further, it was argued that the employee's compensation recognized the risk of the job. Therefore, he or she could not recover damages from the employer when injured because of such conditions. If an employee was injured through negligence of the employer but was partly at fault, the employee was guilty of **contributory negligence.** Any contributory negligence, regardless of how slight, relieved the employer of responsibility for the injury.

These defenses made recovery of damages by injured employees virtually impossible, placing the cost of work-related injuries on the employee. As a result, during the latter part of the nineteenth century, various **employer liability laws** were adopted to modify existing laws and improve the legal position of injured workers. The system of negligence liability was retained, however, and injured employees still had to prove that their employer was at fault to recover damages.

Even with modifications, the negligence system proved costly to administer and inefficient in protecting employees from the financial burdens of workplace injuries.[7] The need for more extensive reform was recognized, with many European countries instituting social insurance programs during the latter half of the 1800s. Beginning with Wisconsin in 1911,[8] U.S. jurisdictions developed the concept of workers' compensation that compensated workers without the requirement that employers' negligence must be proved (that is, with strict employer liability). Costs were borne directly by employers (generally in the form of workers' compensation insurance premiums) and indirectly by employees who accepted lower wages in exchange for benefits. To the extent, if any, that total labor costs were increased, consumers (who benefit from industrialization) shared in the burden of industrial accidents through higher prices for goods and services. Employees demanded higher total compensation (wages plus benefits) to engage in high-risk occupations, resulting in incentives for employers to adopt safety programs. By 1948, each jurisdiction had similar laws.

In compromising between the interests of employees and employers, the originators of workers' compensation systems limited the benefits available to employees to some amount less than the full loss. They also made those benefits the sole recourse of the employee against the employer for work-related injuries. This give-and-take of rights and duties between employers and employees is termed a **quid pro quo,** literally meaning "this for that." The intent was for the give-and-take to have an equal value, on the average. You will see in our discussion of current workers' compensation issues that some doubt exists as to whether or not equity has been maintained. An exception to the sole recourse concept exists in some states for the few employees who elect, prior to injury, not to be covered by workers' compensation. Such employees, upon injury, can sue their employer; however, the employer in these instances retains the three defenses described earlier.

Integrated Benefits—The 24-Hour Coverage Concept

Are your wrists painful? Or numb? (If you think about it long enough, you'll convince yourself they're one or the other.) Perhaps you have a repetitive stress injury or carpal tunnel syndrome. Maybe it's now painful enough that you need to take a few days off. But wait—you use a computer at work, so this could be a work-related injury. Better go talk to the risk manager about filing a workers' compensation claim. But wait—you spend hours at home every night playing computer games. If this is an off-hours injury, you should call your HMO for an appointment with your primary care physician, so you can arrange for short-term disability. But wait—when your boss is not looking, you surf the Internet at work. How do you decide what to do?

If you worked for Steelcase Inc., an office-furniture manufacturer based in Grand Rapids, Michigan, your wrists might still hurt but you would not have to worry about whom to call. Steelcase used to handle its medical benefits like most companies do: The risk management department handled workers' compensation, the human resources department handled health insurance, short-term disability, and long-term disability, and four separate insurers provided the separate coverages. Several events caused top management to rethink this disintegrated strategy: rising

medical costs, a slowdown in the economy that forced a look at cost-savings measures, and the results of a survey showing that employees simply did not understand their benefits. "The employees hammered us in terms of not understanding who to call or what they get," Steelcase manager Libby Child told *Employee Benefit News* in June 2001.

In 1997, Steelcase became one of the first U.S. companies to implement an integrated benefits program. It combined long- and short-term disability, workers' compensation, medical case management, and Family and Medical Leave Act administration, and outsourced the recordkeeping duties. Now a disabled employee—whether the injury is work-related or not—can make one phone call and talk to a representative who collects information, files any necessary claims, and assigns the worker to a medical case manager. The case manager ensures that the employee is receiving proper medical treatment and appropriate benefits, and helps him or her return to work as soon as possible.

The integrated plan has been a hit with employees, who like the one-call system, and with managers, because lost-time days decreased by a third after the program was implemented. Steelcase's financial executives are happy, too: The combined cost of short-term

(Continued)

In addition to every state and territory having a workers' compensation law, there are federal laws applicable to longshore workers and harbor workers, to non-government workers in the District of Columbia, and to civilian employees of the federal government. Workers' compensation laws differ from jurisdiction to jurisdiction, but they all have the purpose of assuring that injured workers and their dependents will receive benefits without question of fault.

Coverage

Coverage under workers' compensation is either inclusive or exclusive. Further, it is compulsory or elective, depending upon state law. A major feature is that only injuries and illnesses that "arise out of and in the course of employment" are covered.

Inclusive or Exclusive

Inclusive laws list all the employments that are covered; **exclusive laws** cover all employments except those that are excluded. Typically, domestic service and casual labor (for some small jobs) are excluded. Agricultural workers are excluded in nineteen jurisdictions, whereas their coverage is compulsory in twenty-seven jurisdictions and entirely voluntary in four jurisdictions. Some states limit coverage to occupations classified as hazardous. The disability, long-term disability, and workers' compensation dropped 13 percent in the program's first three years.

With Steelcase and other pioneers proving the success of integrated benefits, it is a wonder that all companies have not jumped on the bandwagon. Many are, but there are still some obstacles to overcome:

- The shift from paper recordkeeping to computer databases raises concerns over privacy.

- Risk managers and human resources personnel may have "turf wars" over the combination of their duties.

- To fully integrate, and to be able to generate meaningful data, all computer systems must be compatible and their operators trained; however, human resource departments and the treasurer (where risk management resides) may not have the same systems.

- Workers' compensation is provided by property/casualty insurers while health and disability are provided by life/health insurers, so integration may be complicated.

- Regulations vary widely for workers' compensation and employee benefits.

In the past few years, many companies large and small have taken the leap toward integrating benefits. Recent converts include Pacific Bell, San Bernardino County in California, Pitney Bowes, and even an insurance company, Nationwide. For any business that wants to reduce sick time off and disability benefits—which cost the average company 14.3 percent of payroll—the question of integrating benefits is not "whether" but "when."

Explore the Internet

San Francisco-based Integrated Benefits Institute (IBI) is a national non-profit research and education organization focusing on the issues surrounding health, productivity and the bottom line. Learn more about integrated benefits and read case studies at www.ibiweb.org.

Sources: Annmarie Geddes Lipold, "Benefit Integration Boosts Productivity and Profits," Workforce.com, www.workforce.com/section/02/feature/23/36/89/; Karen Lee, "Pioneers Return Data on Integrated Benefits," *Employee Benefit News,* June 2001; Lee Ann Gjertsen, "Brokers Positive on Integrated Benefits," *National Underwriter,* Property & Casualty/Risk & Benefits Management Edition, 7 July 1997; Leo D. Tinkham Jr., "Making the Case for Integrated Disability Management," *National Underwriter,* Life & Health/Financial Services Edition, 13 May 2002, Myers, Phyllis S. and Etti G. Baranoff, "Workers' Compensation: On the Cutting Edge," Academy of Insurance Education, Washington D.C., Instructional video with supplemental study guide. (Video produced by the Center for Video Education, 1997.)

laws of thirty-nine states apply to all employers in the employments covered; others apply only to employers with more than a specified number of employees. Any employer can comply voluntarily.

Compulsory or Elective

In all but two states, the laws regarding workers' compensation are compulsory. In these two states (New Jersey and Texas) with **elective laws,** either the employer or the employee can elect not to be covered under the law. An employer who opts out loses the common law defenses discussed earlier. If the employer does not opt out but an employee does, the employer retains those defenses as far as that employee is concerned. If both opt out, the employer loses the defenses. It is unusual for employees to opt out, since those who do must prove negligence in order to collect and must overcome the employer's defenses.

An employer who does not opt out must pay benefits to injured employees in accordance with the requirements of the law, but that is the employer's sole responsibility. Thus, an employee who is covered by the law cannot sue his or her employer for damages. The law is the employee's **sole remedy,** also called "exclusive remedy." (In fact, workers' compensation is losing its status as the employee's sole remedy against the employer. Later in this chapter, we will discuss some of the current methods used by employees to negate the exclusive remedy rule.) By coming under the law, the employer avoids the cost of litigation and the risk of having to pay a large judgment in the event an injured employee's suit for damages is successful.

In Texas, 65 percent of employers opted to stay in the system despite the fact that workers' compensation is not mandatory.[9] It is likely that as insurance rates rise, more companies will opt to stay out of the system. Virtually all employers that opt out reduce their likelihood of being sued by providing an alternative employee benefit plan which includes medical and disability income benefits as well as accidental death and dismemberment benefits for work-related injuries and illnesses.[10] In addition, the employer purchases employers' liability insurance to cover the possibility of being sued by injured employees who are not satisfied with the alternative benefits.

Proponents of an opt-out provision argue that competition from alternative coverage provides market discipline to lower workers' compensation insurance prices. Furthermore, greater exposure to common law liability suits may encourage workplace safety. Opponents see several drawbacks of opt-out provisions:

- Some employers may fail to provide medical benefits or provide only modest ones, resulting in cost shifting to other segments of society.

- The right of the employee to sue may be illusory because some employers may have few assets and no liability insurance.

- Employees may be reluctant to sue the employer, especially when the opportunity to return to work exists or if family members may be affected.

- Safety incentives may not be enhanced for employers with few assets at risk.[11]

Covered Injuries

In order to limit benefits to situations in which a definite relationship exists between an employee's work and the injury, most laws provide coverage only for injuries "arising out of and in the course of employment." This phrase describes two limitations. First, the injury must **arise out of employment,** meaning that the job environment was the cause. For example, the family of someone who has a relatively non-stressful job but dies of cardiac arrest at work would have trouble proving the work connection, and therefore would not be eligible for workers' compensation benefits. A police officer or firefighter, on the other hand, who suffers a heart attack (even while not on duty) is presumed in many states to have suffered from work-related stress.

The second limitation on coverage is that the injury must occur **while in the course of employment.** That is, the loss-causing event must take place while the employee is on the job. An employee injured while engaged in horseplay, therefore, might not be eligible for workers' compensation because the injury did not occur while the employee was "in the course of employment." Likewise, coverage does not apply while traveling the normal commute between home and work. Along these same lines of reasoning, certain injuries generally are explicitly excluded, such as those caused by willful misconduct or deliberate failure to follow safety rules, those resulting from intoxication, and those that are self-inflicted.

Subject to these limitations, all work-related injuries are covered, even if due to employee negligence. In addition, every state provides benefits for **occupational disease,** which is defined in terms such as "an injury arising out of employment and due to causes and conditions characteristic of, and peculiar to, the particular trade, occupation, process or employment, and excluding all ordinary diseases to which the general public is exposed."[12] Some states list particular diseases covered, whereas others simply follow general guidelines.

Benefits

Workers' compensation laws provide for four types of benefits: medical, income replacement, survivors', and rehabilitation.

Medical

All laws provide unlimited **medical care benefits** for accidental injuries. Many cases do not involve large expenses, but it is not unusual for medical bills to run into many thousands of dollars. Medical expenses resulting from occupational illnesses may be covered in full for a specified period of time and then terminated. Unlike non-occupational health insurance, workers' compensation does not impose deductibles and coinsurance to create incentives for individuals to control their demand for medical services.

When you study about health care in Chapters 17 and 19, you will become very familiar with managed care. To save on the escalating costs of medical care in workers' compensation, the medical coverage also uses managed care. Briefly, managed care limits the choice of doctors. The doctors' decisions are reviewed by the insurer, and many procedures require pre-approval. Doctors who take care of injured employees under workers' compensation coverage are asked to try to get the employees back to work as soon as possible. Florida has been drafting a new law making managed-care programs optional for the employer. In Texas, a new law instructs providers of care under the workers' compensation program to keep a "return to work" mind set and limit the time out of work. The return-to-work objective is to ensure employees' presence at work under any capacity, thus incurring less workers' compensation losses. The industry is attempting to monitor itself for managing the care in a more cost-saving manner.[13] One area that causes major increase in workers' compensation rate is the cost of drugs.[14] The anti-inflammatory drugs Vioxx and Celebrex are among the most used drugs and are extremely expensive. Table 13.1 shows the costs of medical claims under workers' compensation from 1991 to 2001. As you can see, severity of claims (losses per claim) has increased every year since 1994.

Income Replacement

All workers' compensation laws provide an injured employee with a weekly income while disabled as the result of a covered injury or disease. Income replacement benefits are commonly referred to by industry personnel as indemnity benefits. The amount and duration of **indemnity payments** depend upon the following factors:

- Whether the disability is total or partial, and temporary or permanent
- Employee's compensation
- Each state's maximum duration of benefits
- Waiting period
- Cost-of-living adjustments

Degree and Length of Disability   **Total disability** refers to the condition of an employee who misses work because he or she is unable to perform any of the important duties of the occupation. **Partial disability,** on the other hand, means the employee can perform some, but not all, of the duties of his or her occupation. In either case, disability may be permanent or temporary. **Permanent total disability** means the person is not expected to be able to work again. **Temporary total disability** means the employee is expected to be able to return to work at some future time.[15]

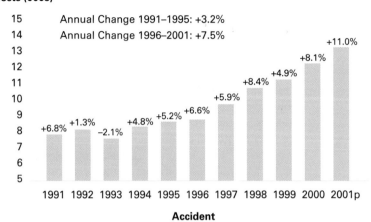

TABLE 13.1

Workers' Compensation Medical Claims Severity

p: Preliminary

Based on data through 12/31/2001, developed to ultimate

Based on the states where NCCI provides ratemaking services

Excludes the effects of deductible policies

Source: © 2002 National Council on Compensation Insurance, Inc. All rights reserved. Reprinted with permission.

Partial disability may be either temporary or permanent. **Temporary partial** payments are most likely to be made following a period of temporary total disability. A person who can perform some but not all work duties qualifies for temporary partial benefits. Such benefits are based on the difference between wages earned before and after an injury. They account for a minor portion of total claim payments.

Most laws specify that the loss of certain body parts constitutes **permanent partial disability.** These cases are called **scheduled injuries.** Benefits expressed in terms of number of weeks of total disability payments are usually provided in such cases. For example, the loss of an arm might entitle the injured worker to two hundred weeks of total disability benefits; the loss of a finger might entitle him or her to thirty-five weeks of benefits. No actual loss of time from work or income is required, under the assumption that loss of a body part causes a loss of future income.

Table 13.2 shows the number of claims for the fifteen largest classes of occupation. As you can see, the frequency of lost-time-only claims has declined, which is the good news in the workers' compensation field. The largest drop is in the convalescent/nursing home claims. The least decline is in the drivers/chauffeurs and college professional classifications.

Amount of Benefit Weekly benefits for death, disability, and, often, disfigurement are primarily based on the employee's **average weekly wage** (average earned income per week during some specified period prior to disability) multiplied by a **replacement ratio,** expressed as a percentage of the average weekly wage. Jurisdictions also set **minimum** and **maximum weekly benefits.**

The replacement percentage for disability benefits ranges from sixty in one jurisdiction to seventy in two others, but in most jurisdictions it is 66 ⅔. The percentage reflects the intent to replace income after taxes and other work-related expenses, since workers' compensation benefits are not subject to income taxation. The amount in New York City

CHAPTER 13 WORKERS' AND UNEMPLOYMENT COMPENSATION **309**

| TABLE 13.2 | | Lost Time Claims by Occupation | | | | |

Countrywide		Latest		Four Years		
Class*	Payroll ($M)	Lost-Time Only Claims	Frequency	Lost-Time Only Claims	Frequency	Frequency Change
Clerical	$ 397,020	29,358	0.07	32,267	0.10	−26%
Salesperson—outside	95,602	11,051	0.12	11,662	0.14	−19%
College Professional	54,507	7,298	0.13	7,636	0.16	−16%
Retail Store	25,884	15,786	0.61	19,257	0.89	−31%
Hospital Professional	18,904	7,180	0.38	9,960	0.51	−25%
Auto Service/Repair	12,884	12,118	0.94	14,206	1.24	−24%
Store—Meat/Grocery	10,086	11,714	1.16	14,542	1.64	−29%
Drivers/Chauffeurs	9,581	13,813	1.44	15,016	1.72	−16%
Electrical Wiring	9,164	9,110	0.99	8,584	1.28	−22%
Convalescent/Nursing Home	8,929	14,190	1.59	17,610	2.47	−36%
Machine Shop	8,212	9,291	1.13	9,904	1.47	−23%
Plumbing	7,768	8,726	1.12	9,190	1.43	−22%
Store—Wholesale	7,716	11,642	1.51	12,163	2.01	−25%
Hotel	6,827	8,471	1.24	10,975	1.79	−31%
Trucking	11,310	25,559	2.26	5,875	2.85	−21%
Total	684,393	195,307	0.29	198,847	0.35	−19%
All Class Total	1,209,061	633,342	0.52	750,801	0.72	−27%

*Based on a recent study

Note: Frequency = Lost-Time Claims/Payroll; prior payroll adjusted for inflation

Source: © 2002 National Council on Compensation Insurance, Inc. All rights reserved. Reprinted with permission.

after September 11 was $400 per week, as noted above. The amount provided in Texas has increased from $428 in 1991 to $536 in 2002.[16]

Twenty jurisdictions lower their permanent partial maximum payment per week below their maximum for total disability. For these jurisdictions, the average permanent partial maximum is 60.7 percent of their total disability maximum. With respect to death benefits, thirty-one jurisdictions use 66⅔ percentage in determining survivor benefits for a spouse only; five of these use a higher percentage for a spouse plus children. The range of survivor benefits for a spouse plus children ranges from 60 percent in Idaho to 75 percent in Texas. Examples of Texas benefits calculations are demonstrated in hypothetical incomes in Tables 13.3A–D. As shown, in Texas, temporary income benefits equal 70 percent of the difference between a worker's average weekly wage and the weekly wage after the injury. If a worker's average weekly wage was $400, and an injury caused the worker to lose all of his or her income, temporary income benefits would be $280 a week.

The next example is demonstrated in Table 13.3B for supplemental income when the injured Texas employee

- has an impairment rating of 15 percent or more; and
- has not returned to work because of the impairment, or has returned to work but is earning less than 80 percent of the average weekly wage because of the impairment;
- did not take a lump sum payment of impairment income benefits; and

TABLE 13.3

Hypothetical Examples of Texas Workers' Compensaton Income Calculations

13-3A Calculation of Temporary Income Benefits

Average weekly wage	$ 400
Less wage after injury	0
Equals	$ 400
Temporary income benefit (70 percent of the equal amount)	$ 280

13-3B Calculation of Supplemental Income Benefits

Average weekly wage	$ 400
80 percent of weekly wage	$ 320
Less the current wage	0
Equals	$ 320
Supplemental benefit (80 percent of the equal amount)	$ 256

13-3C Calculation of Lifetime Income Benefits for Disability with a Loss of Limb

Average weekly wage	$ 400
Lifetime income benefit (75 percent of weekly wage)	$ 300

13-3D Calculation of Death Benefits

Average weekly wage	$ 400
Death benefit (75 percent of weekly wage)	$ 300

Source: Texas Workers Compensation Commission, www.twcc.state.tx.us

■ has tried to find a job that matches his or her ability to work.[17]

As you can see, if the employee is not earning at least 80 percent of the prior-to-injury income, the employee is eligible to receive 80 percent of the 80 percent ($.80 \times .80 = .64$) of the prior weekly wage as supplemental income ($.64 \times \$400 = \$256$)

In Texas, an injured worker may get lifetime income benefits if the worker has an injury or illness that results in the loss of the hands, feet, or eyesight, or if the worker meets the conditions of the Texas Workers' Compensation Act. Table 13.3C provides an example of benefits for lifetime in such a case.

Duration of Benefits   In thirty-nine jurisdictions, no limit is put on the duration of temporary total disability. Nine jurisdictions, however, allow benefits for less than 500 weeks; two specify a 500-week maximum. The limits are seldom reached in practice because the typical injured worker's condition reaches "maximum medical improvement" that terminates temporary total benefits earlier. Maximum medical improvement is reached when additional medical treatment is not expected to result in improvement of the person's condition.

In forty-three jurisdictions, permanent total benefits are paid for the duration of disability/lifetime. These jurisdictions generally do not impose a maximum dollar limit on the aggregate amount that can be paid.

Waiting Periods   Every jurisdiction has a **waiting period** before indemnity payments (but not medical benefits) for temporary disability to begin; the range is from three to seven days. The waiting period feature has the advantages of giving a financial incentive to work, reducing administrative costs, and reducing the cost of benefits. If disability continues for a specified period (typically, two to four weeks), benefits are retroactive to the date disability began. Moral hazard is created among employees who reach maximum medical improvement just before the time of the retroactive trigger. Some employees will malinger long enough to waive the waiting period. Hawaii does not allow retroactive benefits.

Cost-of-Living Adjustment   Fifteen jurisdictions have an automatic cost-of-living adjustment (COLA) for weekly benefits. In some cases, the COLA takes effect only after disability has continued for one or two years. Because benefit rates are usually set by law, those rates in jurisdictions that lack automatic increases for permanent benefits become out-of-date rapidly during periods of inflation.

Survivor Benefits   In the event of a work-related death, all jurisdictions provide **survivor income benefits** for the surviving spouse and dependent children, as well as a burial allowance. The survivor income benefit for a spouse plus children is typically (in thirty jurisdictions) 66⅔ percent of the worker's average weekly wage. Several jurisdictions provide additional income for one child only. Table 13.3D provides an example of the death benefits in Texas. Burial benefits pay up to $2,500 of the worker's funeral expenses. Burial benefits are paid to the person who paid the worker's funeral expenses. The death benefits in New York were discussed earlier. In the example case for Texas, the replacement of lost income is 75 percent, as shown in Table 13.3D

Rehabilitation   Most people who are disabled by injury or disease make a complete recovery with ordinary medical care and return to work able to resume their former duties. Many workers, however, suffer disability of such a nature that something more than income payments and ordinary medical services is required to restore them, to the greatest extent possible, to their former economic and social situation. **Rehabilitation** is the process of accomplishing this objective.

Rehabilitation involves the following:

- Physical-medical attention in an effort to restore workers as nearly as possible to their state of health prior to the injury
- Vocational training to enable them to perform a new occupational function
- Psychological aid to help them adjust to their new situation and be able to perform a useful function for society

About one-fourth of the workers' compensation laws place this responsibility on the employer (or the insurer, if applicable). Most of the laws require special maintenance benefits to encourage disabled workers to cooperate in a rehabilitation program. Nearly all states reduce or stop income payments entirely to workers who refuse to participate.

HOW BENEFITS ARE PROVIDED

Workers' compensation laws hold the employer responsible for providing benefits to injured employees. Employees do not contribute directly to this cost. In most states, employers may insure with a private insurance company or qualify as self-insurers. In some states, state funds act as insurers. Following is a discussion of coverage through insurance programs and through the residual markets (part of insurance programs for difficult-to-insure employers), self-insurance, and state funds.

Workers' Compensation Insurance

Employers' risks can be transferred to an insurer by purchasing a workers' compensation and employers' liability policy.

Coverage

The workers' compensation and employers' liability policy has three parts. Under part I, Workers' Compensation, the insurer agrees to pay promptly when due all compensation and other benefits required of the insured by the workers' compensation law.

The policy defines "workers' compensation law" as the law of any state designated in the declarations, and specifically includes any occupational disease law of that state. The workers' compensation portion of the policy is directly for the benefit of employees covered by the law. The insurer assumes the obligations of the insured (that is, the employer) under the law and is bound by the terms of the law as well as the actions of the workers' compensation commission or other governmental body having jurisdiction. Any changes in the workers' compensation law are automatically covered by the policy.

Four limitations, or "exclusions," apply to part 1. These limitations include any payments in excess of the benefits regularly required by workers' compensation statutes due to (1) serious and willful misconduct by the insured; (2) the knowing employment of a person in violation of the law; (3) failure to comply with health or safety laws or regulations; or (4) the discharge, coercion, or other discrimination against employees in violation of the workers' compensation law. In addition, the policy refers only to state laws and that of the District of Columbia; thus, coverage under any of the federal programs requires special provisions.

Part 2, **Employers' Liability,** protects against potential liabilities not within the scope of the workers' compensation law, yet arising out of employee injuries. The insurer agrees to pay damages for which the employer becomes legally obligated because of

> bodily injury by accident or disease, including death at any time resulting there from ... by any employee of the insured arising out of and in the course of his employment by the insured either in operations in a state designated in ... the declarations or in operations necessary or incidental thereto.

Examples of liabilities covered under part 2 are those to employees excluded from the law, such as domestic and farm laborers. Part 2 might also be applicable if the injury is not considered work-related, even if it occurs on-the-job.

Part 3 of the workers' compensation policy provides **Other States Insurance.** Previously, this protection was available by endorsement. Part 1 applies only if the state imposing responsibility is listed in the declarations. An employee injured while working out of state may be covered by that state's compensation law. To account for this potential gap, part 3 allows the insured to list states (perhaps all) where the employees may have potential exposure. Coverage is extended to these named locales.

Cost

Based on Payroll   The premium for workers' compensation insurance typically is based on the payroll paid by the employer. A charge is made for each $100 of payroll for each classification of employee. This rate varies with the degree of hazard of the occupation.[18] Large employers can elect to have **experience rating,** which takes a company's prior losses into account in determining its current rates.

Factors Affecting Rate   The rate for workers' compensation insurance is influenced not only by the degree of hazard of the occupational classification but also by the nature of the law and its administration and, of course, by prior losses such as the catastrophic events of September 11. If the benefits of the law are high, rates will tend to be high. If they are low, rates will tend to be low. Moreover, given any law, no matter its benefits level, its administration will affect premium rates. If those who administer the law are conservative in their evaluation of borderline cases, premium rates will be lower than in instances where administrators are less circumspect in parceling out employers' and insurers' money. Most laws provide that either the claimant or the insurer may appeal a decision of the administrative board in court on questions of law, but if both the board and the courts are inclined toward generosity, the effect is to increase workers' compensation costs.

Workers' compensation may be a significant expense for the employer. Given any particular law and its administration, costs for the firm are influenced by the frequency and severity of injuries suffered by workers covered. The more injuries there are, the more workers will be receiving benefits. The more severe such injuries, the longer such benefits must be paid. It is not unusual to find firms in hazardous industries having workers' compensation costs running from 10 to 30 percent of payroll. This can be a significant component of labor costs. Moreover, there are many other non-wage costs for employers, such as Social Security, unemployment compensation taxes, and voluntary employee benefits (group life and health insurance or group pensions).

Whatever their size, however, these costs are only part of the total cost of occupational injury and disease. The premium paid is the firm's direct cost, but indirect costs of industrial accidents, such as lost time, spoiled materials, and impairment of worker morale, can be just as significant. These costs can be reduced by loss prevention and reduction, and by self-insuring the risk.

Loss Prevention and Reduction

Most industrial accidents are caused by a combination of physical hazard and faulty behavior. Once an accident begins to occur, the ultimate severity is largely a matter of chance. Total loss costs are a function of accident frequency and severity. Frequency is a better indicator of safety performance than severity, because chance plays a greater part in determining the seriousness of an injury than it does in determining frequency.

Accident Prevention   The first consideration is to reduce frequency by preventing accidents. Safety must be part of your thinking, along with planning and supervising. Any safety program should be designed to do two things: (1) reduce hazards to a minimum and (2) develop safe behavior in every employee. A safety engineer from your workers' compensation insurer (or a consultant if you are self-insured) can give you expert advice and help with your program. He or she can identify hazards so they can be corrected. This involves plant inspection, job safety analysis, and accident investigation.

The safety engineer can inspect your plant to observe housekeeping, machinery guarding, maintenance, and safety equipment. He or she can help you organize and implement a safety training program to develop employee awareness and safe practices. He or she can analyze job safety to determine safe work methods, and can set job standards that promote safety. Your insurer will provide you with accident report forms and instructions on accident investigation. This is essential because every accident demonstrates a hazardous condition or an unsafe practice, or both. The causes of accidents must be known if you are going to prevent them. Inspections, job safety analysis, and accident investigations that lead consistently to corrective action are the foundations of accident prevention. "Ethical Dilemma: Should Ergonomic Standards Be Mandatory?" in this chapter discusses the issues of job safety in the area of posture and position in the workplace.

Loss Reduction   Accident frequency cannot be reduced to zero because not all losses can be prevented. After an employee has suffered an injury, however, action may reduce the loss. First, if you provide immediate medical attention, you may save a life. Moreover, recovery will be expedited. This is why many large plants have their own medical staff. It is also why you should provide first-aid instruction for your employees. Second, you or your insurer should manage the care of the injured worker, including referrals to low-cost, high-quality medical providers. Third, arrange for an injured worker to take advantage of rehabilitation. Rehabilitation is not always successful but experience has shown that remarkable progress is possible, especially if it is started soon enough after an injury. The effort is worthwhile from both the economic and humanitarian points of view. All of society benefits.

Ethical Dilemma

Should Ergonomic Standards Be Mandatory?

In the waning days of the Clinton administration, the Occupational Safety and Health Administration (OSHA) issued sweeping new guidelines for *ergonomics* in the workplace. Ergonomics refers to the design and arrangement of workplace equipment in order to maximize worker safety, health, comfort, and efficiency. The new standards, which applied to all industries and nearly all types of businesses, both large and small, placed the ergonomic burden on employers (and, through them, on the states' workers' compensation insurance industry, which would be responsible for implementing the new rules). Every company was required to set up a program to manage ergonomics, including worker training, analysis and elimination of risk factors, and identification of musculoskeletal disorder (MSD) injuries. Of most concern to the insurance industry was a provision that mandated a set level of compensation for MSD injuries. By requiring compensation for ergonomic injuries to be between 90 and 100 percent of a worker's salary, OSHA was infringing upon state workers' compensation systems, which, on average, awarded injured workers only 67 percent of their salaries up to a certain maximum.

Controversial from the start, the ergonomic standards were overturned by Congress in April 2001 just after George W. Bush took office. Working with the insurance industry, OSHA has since launched a voluntary program to reduce ergonomic injuries. While some of the details are still vague, the new guidelines include more cooperation with business, including technical support, and an education campaign. However, not everyone is pleased with the new voluntary standards, with labor advocates rejecting them as not providing enough protection for workers.

In the spring of 2002 a new bill (S. 2184) was introduced in the Senate that would require a new ergonomics rule to be written within two years. With the introduction of this new legislation, the controversy came to life again, with business and insurance groups opposing any "one size fits all" regulation. Referred to the Senate Committee on Health, Education, Labor, and Pensions in June 2002, no further action has been taken as of the writing of this text.

Today, if you visit OSHA's website, osha.gov/ergonomics/ergotools.html, you can view the educational component of the voluntary program for yourself. Along with description of potential hazards and solutions, the site contains pictures (some animated) of both the incorrect and correct ways to undertake various work activities, including delivering beverages, handling luggage, processing poultry, and working at a computer workstation.

Questions for Discussion

1. Can too much workplace regulation put employees out of work? In the face of hard-to-meet standards, might some employers decide not to stay in business, or to move their businesses to a country without such strict rules?

2. Is it ethically correct to require the same workplace standards from small start-up companies and large, well-established ones?

3. Should the states be the only entities allowed to set workers' compensation rules? Why not the federal government?

4. Do voluntary programs work, or do they allow businesses to get away with ignoring workers' injuries?

Sources: Steven Brostoff, "Senate Sidesteps Ergonomics Mandate," *National Underwriter,* Property & Casualty/Risk & Benefits Management Edition, 29 July 2002; Bruce C. Wood, "Federal Regs Threaten State WC System," *National Underwriter,* Property & Casualty/Risk & Benefits Management Edition, 19 August 2002; Mark A. Hofmann, "Senate Committee Approves Ergo Rule Bill," *Business Insurance,* 19 June 2002; Steven Brostoff, "Ergonomic Rule Bill Moves," *National Underwriter* Online News Service, 19 June 2002; Steven Brostoff, "Insurance Groups Support Ergo Plan," *National Underwriter,* Online News Service, 27 August 2002; Arlene Ryndak and Julie L. Gackenbach, "Congress Should Not Tie OSHA's Hands on Ergonomic Regulations," *National Underwriter,* Property & Casualty/Risk & Benefits Management Edition, 20 May 2002; "Risk Managers, Insurers Get a Break on Ergonomics," *National Underwriter,* Property & Casualty/Risk & Benefits Management Edition, 22 April 2002; Steven Brostoff, "New Ergonomics Bill Draws Insurer Ire," *National Underwriter,* Property & Casualty/Risk & Benefits Management Edition, 29 April 2002; Caroline McDonald, "Insurers: New OSHA Ergo Plan Okay," *National Underwriter* Online News Service, 5 April 2002.

Residual Market

Various **residual market** mechanisms, such as assigned risk pools and reinsurance facilities, allow employers that are considered uninsurable access to workers' compensation insurance. Usually employers with large losses depicted by high experience rating are considered high risk. These employers encounter difficulty in finding workers' compensation coverage. The way to obtain coverage is through the residual or **involuntary market** (a market where insurers are required to provide coverage on an involuntary basis). Insurers are required to participate, and insureds are assigned to an insurer in various ways. Even though rates for this residual market segment are substantially higher than those for the regular market, the approximately 25 percent of total workers' compensation premiums in this market produces large losses that must be absorbed solely by private insurers.

As reported in the NCCI "State of the Line" report, Table 13.4 provides the workers' compensation residual market premiums from 1985 to 2001; Table 13.5 provides the residual market combined ratio for the same period.

Eighteen jurisdictions have **state operated workers' compensation funds.** In six of these, the state fund is exclusive; that is, employers are not permitted to buy compensation insurance from a private insurance company but must insure with the state fund or self-insure.[19] Where the state fund is competitive (that is, optional), employers may choose to self-insure or to insure through either the state fund or a private insurer.

Employer's Risk

Industrial accidents create two possible losses for employers. First, employers are responsible to employees covered by the workers' compensation law for the benefits required by law. Second, they may become liable for injuries to employees not covered by the law.[20] The risks associated with these exposures cannot be avoided without suspending operations—hardly a practical alternative.

TABLE 13.4	Residual Market Premiums as of December 31, 2001

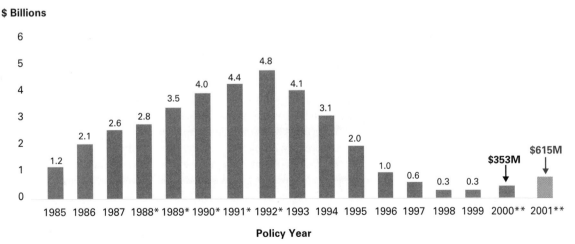

* Excludes Maine Residual Market Pool

** Projected to ultimate

Source: © 2002 National Council on Compensation Insurance, Inc. All rights reserved. Reprinted with permission.

| TABLE 13.5 | Residual Market Combined Ratio as of September 30, 2001 |

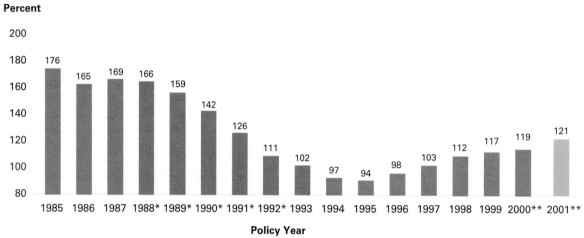

* Excludes Maine Residual Market Pool

** Projected to ultimate

Source: © 2002 National Council on Compensation Insurance, Inc. All rights reserved. Reprinted with permission.

Where permitted, self-insurance of this exposure is common. Self-insurance is desirable in part because of the predictability afforded by legislated benefits. In addition, employers can buy coverage (called excess loss insurance) for very large losses similar to the commercial umbrella liability policy discussed in Chapter 12.

Self-Insurance

Most state workers' compensation laws permit an employer to retain the workers' compensation risk if it can be proved that the employer is financially able to pay claims. Some states permit the risk to be retained only by employers who furnish a bond guaranteeing payment of benefits.

The major question for the self-insurance of the workers' compensation risk is whether the firm has a large enough number of exposure units (employees) so that its losses are reasonably stable and can be predicted with some accuracy. Clearly, an employer with ten employees cannot make an accurate prediction of workers' compensation benefit costs for next year. Such costs may be zero one year and several thousand dollars another year. On the other hand, as the number of the firm's employees increases, workers' compensation losses become more stable and predictable. Just how stable losses must be in order for self-insurance to be feasible depends upon the employer's ability and willingness to pay for losses that exceed expectations. The employer's ability to pay for loss is a second important factor considered by regulators in determining whether or not to permit self-insurance. Captives are also used by many employers for this coverage. Of course, all types of self-insurance require the use of stop loss coverage through reinsurance. The reinsurance is best for use with captives as explained in Chapter 5.

Insurance or Self-Insurance?

Is your firm large enough to self-insure and, if so, can you save money by doing so? Unless you have at least several hundred employees and your workers' compensation losses have a low correlation with other types of retained exposures, self-insurance is not feasible. The low correlation implies diversification of the retained risk exposures. Unless self-insurance will save money, it is not worthwhile. Most employers who decide to self-insure use third-party administrators to administer the claims or contract with an insurer to provide administrative services only.

What are the possible sources for saving money? Ask yourself the following questions about your present arrangement:

- Does your insurer pay benefits too liberally?
- Does it bear the risk of excessive losses?
- Does it bear the risk of employers' liability?
- Does it administer the program?
- How large is the premium tax paid by the insurer?
- How large is the insurer's profit on your business?
- What is your share of losses in the assigned risk plan?
- Can the third-party administrator be a good buffer in disputes with angry employees?

As a self-insured firm, you will still provide the benefits specified by the workers' compensation law(s) in the state(s) where you operate. Therefore, self-insuring reduces benefits only if you or your outside self-insurance administrator will settle claims more efficiently than your insurer.

Unless your firm is very large you probably would decide to buy stop-loss insurance for excessive losses, and you would buy insurance for your employer's liability (part B of a workers' compensation insurance policy). Would you administer the self-insured program? Yes, unless you hire an outside administrator. In either event, your administrative expenses might be similar to those of your insurer. As a self-insurer, you would save the typical premium tax of between 2 and 3 percent that your insurer is required to pay to the state(s) where you do business. Profits are difficult to calculate because the insurer's investment income must be factored in along with premiums, benefit payments, expenses, and your own opportunity cost of funds. While the workers' compensation line of business produces losses in some years and profits in others, over a period of several years you would expect the insurer to make a profit on your business. You could retain this profit by self-insuring.

Firms that do not qualify for insurance based on normal underwriting guidelines and premiums can buy insurance through an assigned risk plan, that is, the residual market. Because of inadequate rates and other problems, large operating losses are often realized in the residual market. These losses become an additional cost to be borne by insurers and passed on to insureds in the form of higher premiums. Assigned risk pool losses are allocated to insurers on the basis of their share of the voluntary (non-assigned risk) market by state and year. These losses can be 15 to 30 percent or more of premiums for employers insured in the voluntary market. This "burden" can be avoided by self-insuring. Many firms have self-insured for this reason, resulting in a smaller base over which to spread the residual market burden.

If your firm is large enough to self-insure, your workers' compensation premium is experience rated. What you pay this year is influenced by your loss experience during the past three years. The extent to which your rate goes up or down to reflect bad or good experience depends upon the credibility assigned by the insurer. This statistical credibility is primarily determined by the size of your firm. The larger your firm, the more your experience influences the rate you pay during succeeding years.

If you want this year's experience to influence what you pay this year, you can insure on a **retrospective plan.** It involves payment of a premium between a minimum and a maximum, depending on your loss experience. Regardless of how favorable your experience is, you must pay at least the minimum premium. On the other hand, regardless of how bad your experience is, you pay no more than the maximum. Between the minimum and the maximum, your actual cost for the year depends on your experience that year.

Several plans with various minimum and maximum premium stipulations are available. If you are conservative with respect to risk, you will prefer a low minimum and a low maximum, but that is the most expensive. Low minimum and high maximum is cheaper, but this puts most of the burden of your experience on you. If you have an effective loss prevention and reduction program, you may choose the high maximum and save money on your workers' compensation insurance.

In choosing between insurance and self-insurance, you should consider the experience rating plans provided by insurers, as well as the advantages and disadvantages of self-insurance. The process of making this comparison will, undoubtedly, be worthwhile.

State Funds

A third method of assuring benefit payments to injured workers is the state fund. State funds are similar to private insurers except that they are operated by an agency of the state government, and most are concerned only with benefit payments under the workers' compensation law and do not assume the employers' liability risk. This usually must be insured privately. The employer pays a premium (or tax) to the state fund and the fund, in turn, provides the benefits to which injured employees are entitled. Some state funds decrease rates for certain employers or classes of employers if their experience warrants it.

Cost comparisons between commercial insurers and state funds are difficult because the state fund may be subsidized. Moreover, in some states, the fund may exist primarily to provide insurance to employers in high-risk industries—for example, coal mining—that are not acceptable to commercial insurers. In any case, employers who have access to a state fund should consider it part of the market and compare its rates with those of private insurers.

SECOND-INJURY FUNDS

Nature and Purpose

If two employees with the same income each lost one eye in an industrial accident, the cost in workers' compensation benefits for each would be equal. If one of these employees had previously lost an eye, however, the cost of benefits for him or her would be much greater than for the other worker (probably more than double the cost). Obviously, the loss of both eyes is a much greater handicap than the loss of one. To encourage employment in these situations, **second-injury funds** are part of most workers' compensation laws. When a subsequent injury occurs, the employee is compensated for the disability resulting from the combined injuries. The insurer (or employer) who pays the benefit is then reimbursed by the second-injury fund for the amount by which the combined disability benefits exceed the benefit that would have been paid only for the last injury.

Financing

Second-injury funds are financed in a variety of ways. Some receive appropriations from the state. Others receive money from a charge made against an employer or an insurer when a worker who has been killed on the job does not leave any dependents. Some states finance the fund by annual assessments on insurers and self-insurers. These assessments can be burdensome.

WORKERS' COMPENSATION ISSUES

In "Critical Issues Facing Workers Compensation," a report by NCCI,[21] the critical issues as of 2002 were

- Cost drivers and reform
- Decreasing capacity
- Reserve deficiency
- Privacy
- Erosion of exclusive remedy and scope of coverage
- Mental health claims
- Black lung
- The Americans with Disabilities Act (ADA)
- Ergonomics

As noted earlier, medical inflation in addition to increased benefits through reforms in the states and attorney fees have cost the system a substantial amount of extra expenses and cause escalation in the combined ratio for the workers' compensation line.

All medical care costs have, for decades, grown much faster than the overall Consumer Price Index. Workers' compensation medical care costs are of special concern. The high reimbursement rate (100 percent of allowable charges) by workers' compensation relative to lower rates (generally 80 to 90 percent) in non-occupational medical plans creates a preference for workers' compensation among employees and medical care providers who influence some decisions about whether or not a claim is deemed work-related. The managed care option mentioned above is used, but, since medical inflation is so high, the system cannot resolve the issue on its own.

Attorney involvement varies substantially among the states. It is encouraged by factors such as:

- The complexity of the law
- Weak early communication to injured workers
- Advertisements by attorneys
- Failure to begin claim payments soon after the start of disability
- Employee distrust of some employers and insurers
- Employee concern that some employers will not rehire injured workers
- The subjective nature of benefit determination (for example, encouraging both parties to produce conflicting medical evidence concerning the degree of impairment)

The solution may be a system that settles claims equitably and efficiently through promoting agreement and timely return to work. The Wisconsin system may be the best example of this type of system, characterized by prompt delivery of benefits, low transaction costs, and clear communication between employers and employees.

The workers' compensation combined ratio per calendar year since 1990 is shown in Table 13.6. It is clear that the growth from 2000 to 2001 is due to the September 11 catastrophe.

As noted in Chapter 5, the property/casualty industry as a whole has suffered from decreased capacity. The reasons are poor underwriting results, as described, but also poor

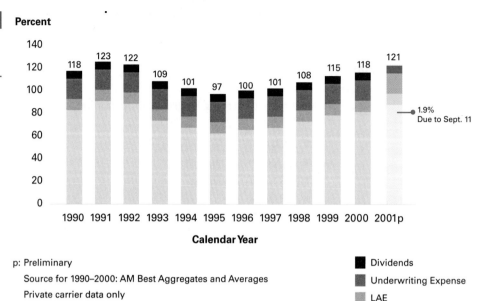

TABLE 13.6

Workers' Compensation Combined Ratios

p: Preliminary

    Source for 1990–2000: AM Best Aggregates and Averages

    Private carrier data only

Source: © 2002 National Council on Compensation Insurance, Inc. All rights reserved. Reprinted with permission.

As noted in Chapter 5, the property/casualty industry as a whole has suffered from decreased capacity. The reasons are poor underwriting results, as described, but also poor investment income results. The bearish stock market has, no doubt, affected insurers as well. Workers' compensation reserve deficiencies climbed to $21 billion in 2001 from a low of $.5 billion in 1994. The poor investment results are shown in Table 13.7.

The next issue, privacy, has been discussed in prior chapters. This is an issue engulfing the whole industry and is relevant to the workers' compensation line because of the

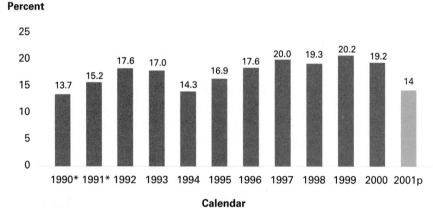

TABLE 13.7

Workers' Compensation Ratios of Investment Gain and Other Income to Premium

p: Preliminary

    Investment gain includes investment income and realized capital gains

* Adjusted to include realized capital gains to be consistent with 1992 and after

    Private carrier data only

Source: © 2002 National Council on Compensation Insurance, Inc. All rights reserved. Reprinted with permission.

medical and health components of this coverage. How to protect the individuals' health information from being identified and transmitted is the industry concern.

Employers, of course, benefit from having their liabilities limited to what is stipulated in workers' compensation laws. When the benefits received by workers are a close approximation of what would be received under common law, employees receive a clear advantage as well from the law. Today, however, there is a perception that workers' compensation provides inadequate compensation for many injuries. With high awards for punitive and general damages (neither available in workers' compensation) in tort claims, workers often perceive the exclusivity of compensation laws as inequitable.

As a result, workers attempt to circumvent the exclusivity rule. One method is to claim the employer acts in a **dual capacity,** permitting the employee an action against the employer in the second relationship as well as a workers' compensation claim. For example, an employee injured while using a product manufactured by another division of the company might seek a products liability claim against the employer. Dual capacity has received limited acceptance. Think about an employee of Firestone tires using the employer's commercial auto with Firestone tires to make deliveries. If the tire exploded, the employee has a workers' compensation claim as well as a case against the manufacturer of the tire—his own employer.

A second means of circumventing the exclusivity of workers' compensation is to claim that the employer intentionally caused the injury. Frequently, this claim is made with respect to exposure to toxic substances. Employees claim that employers knew of the danger, but encouraged employees to work in the hazardous environment anyway. This argument, too, has received limited acceptance, yet litigation of these cases is costly. Further, their mere existence likely indicates at least a perception of faults in the workers' compensation system.

A third circumvention of the exclusivity of workers' compensation is the third-party over action. It begins with an employee's claim against a third party (not the employer). For example, the employee may sue a machine manufacturer for products liability if the employee is injured while using the manufacturer's machine. In turn, the third party (the manufacturer in our example) brings an action against the employer for contribution or indemnification. The action against the employer might be based on the theory that the employer contributed to the loss by failing to supervise its employees properly. The end result is an erosion of the **exclusive remedy rule**—as if the employee had sued the employer directly.

Another current issue in workers' compensation is the broadening of the scope of covered claims. The original intent of workers' compensation laws was to cover only work-related physical injuries. Later, coverage was extended to occupational illnesses that often are not clearly work-related. Claims for stress and cases involving mental health claims, especially after September 11, are on the increase. Black lung disease from mold is another explosive issue, as discussed in prior chapters.

The Supreme Court in 2002 clarified that only the inability to perform daily living activities is a disability under the Americans with Disabilities Act (ADA) and not the inability to perform a job. The ADA forbids employers with more than fifteen employees from discriminating against disabled persons in employment. Disabled persons are those with physical or mental impairments limiting major life activities such as walking, seeing, or hearing. The ADA requires that employee benefits, as a privilege of employment, be provided in a nondiscriminatory manner as well. Employees with disabilities must be given equal access to medical expense insurance coverage and disability coverage. If the medical plan does not cover certain treatment needed by persons with disabilities, such as vision care, the employer does not have to add vision care treatment. However, if vision care is provided by the plan, then vision care must also be offered to employees with disabilities. In addition, specific disabilities, such as vision impairment, or disability in general cannot be excluded from coverage.

The other issue regarding repetitive activities that cause stress and carpal tunnel syndrome was still under consideration at the time of writing this text, as noted in the Ethical Dilemma box of this chapter.

UNEMPLOYMENT COMPENSATION

While workers' compensation is quasi-social private insurance of significant concern to its many stakeholders, unemployment compensation is a purely social insurance program. Because of the high risk associated with projecting future rates of unemployment and associated claims, private insurers are not willing to provide this type of insurance. **Unemployment compensation** programs pay weekly cash benefits to workers who are involuntarily unemployed. The following sections cover state laws, coverage, how benefits are financed, and administration of unemployment compensation.

State Laws

State unemployment compensation programs were established as a result of federal legislation. However, each state creates, finances, and administers its own law. Like workers' compensation, the law transfers to the employer at least part of the financial element of a risk faced by the employee. Unlike most workers' compensation programs, however, the firm's risk manager has no choice with regard to how the risk is handled. Neither private insurance nor self-insurance is permitted. Management can, however, reduce the cost by stabilizing the firm's employment and preventing payment of unjustified benefits.

Employers Subject to Tax

The federal tax applies to firms that have one or more employees in each of twenty weeks during a calendar year, or firms that pay $1,500 or more in wages during any calendar quarter. As of January 1987, coverage was extended to agricultural employers that have ten or more employees in each of twenty weeks during the year or that pay $20,000 or more in wages during any calendar quarter. New provisions to include domestic and municipal employees, as well as employees of nonprofit organizations, have also been added.

Coverage

The federal law established minimum standards for coverage and benefits. Unless a state law meets the standards, no tax offset is permitted. Every state meets the standards, and in many cases they are exceeded. Today, all states cover state and local government employees, several cover farm workers, and a few cover domestic workers. About 97 percent of the civilian labor force is covered. In some cases, the unemployment compensation is self-insured in a pool, as is the case with the unemployment compensation of employees of many Texas school districts that opted to use the pool administered by the Texas Association of School Boards.[22]

Unemployment compensation is designed to relieve workers in certain industries and occupations of part of the economic burden of temporary unemployment. Three aspects of benefit payments are important: (1) amount and duration, (2) qualifications for benefits, and (3) disqualifications.

Amount and Duration

The amount of the weekly benefit payment a worker may receive while unemployed varies according to the **benefit formula** in the law of each state. Usually the amount is about one-half of the worker's full-time weekly pay within specified limits. The maximum is low and is easily accessible on the Web site of your state unemployment compensation agency (usually a division of the employment commission). Some states provide an additional allowance for certain dependents of the unemployed worker. With the passage of the 1986 Tax Reform Act, all unemployment benefits became fully taxable to the recipient for federal income tax purposes.

Most state laws have a waiting period—typically one week—between the time an unemployed worker files a claim for benefits and the time benefit payments begin. This is designed to place the burden of short-term temporary unemployment on the worker as well as to decrease the cost of the plan, thereby making possible greater coverage of more significant unemployment losses.

In most states, the maximum number of weeks benefits can be paid is twenty-six. A federal–state program of extended benefits may continue payments for another thirteen weeks during periods of high unemployment, such as occurred in the early 1990s. In an "economic emergency," federal funding may continue payments for another twenty-six weeks.

Qualifications for Benefits

In order to qualify for benefits, unemployed workers must fulfill certain conditions. They must first be involuntarily unemployed. Once they are involuntarily unemployed, they are required to register for work at a public employment office and file a claim for benefits. They must have been employed in a job covered by the state unemployment compensation law.[23] They must have earned a specified amount of pay or worked for a specified length of time, or both. They must be able to work (this is important in order to differentiate unemployment benefit from disability benefits), be available for work, and be willing to take a suitable job if it is offered to them. In most states, an unemployed worker who is sick and, therefore, unable to work is not entitled to unemployment compensation benefits. Some states permit payments to disabled workers under a separate disability program.[24]

Disqualifications

Unemployed workers may be disqualified from benefits even if they meet the qualifications described above. As noted above, most state laws disqualify those who quit voluntarily without good cause or who were discharged for just cause. Those who refuse to apply for or accept suitable work, or are unemployed because of a work stoppage caused by a labor dispute may be disqualified. Other causes for disqualification are receiving pay from a former employer, receiving workers' compensation benefits, receiving Social Security benefits, or being deemed an independent contractor and, therefore, not an employee.

The effect of disqualification varies from state to state. In some cases, it means that the unemployed worker receives no benefits until he or she has again qualified by being employed for a specified length of time in covered work. In other cases, disqualification results in an increase in the waiting period. Some state laws not only increase the waiting period but also decrease the benefits.

How Benefits Are Financed

Noncontributory

Most unemployment compensation insurance is *noncontributory*: employers pay all the cost in most states.[25] The **Federal Unemployment Tax Act** places a tax on employers at the rate of 6.2 percent of workers' pay in covered jobs, excluding anything over $7,000 paid to a worker in a year. Up to 5.4 percent can be offset by employers who pay a state tax or have been excused through experience rating. So, in effect, the federal tax may be only (6.2 – 5.4 =) 1.2 percent. Revenue from this tax is deposited in the Federal Unemployment Trust Fund and credited to the state for the payment of benefits under its plan. Each state has its own trust fund. The remaining part of the federal tax goes into general federal revenues. Congress appropriates money for grants to the states for their administration of the program. If appropriations for this purpose are less than the federal share of the payroll tax, the remainder of such revenue is put into a reserve fund for aid to the states in payment of benefits when state reserves are low.

Experience Rating

All states have experience rating; that is, they reduce the contribution of employers whose workers have little unemployment. The theory of this rating system is that it encourages employers to reduce unemployment and stabilize employment to the extent that they can. One other effect, however, is to make employers interested in disqualifying workers who apply for benefits, because it is benefits paid out of their account that reflect their experience under the plan.[26] This has led to considerable discussion of disqualification standards and administration and to many hearings and disputes.

Administration

The federal portion of the unemployment compensation insurance program is administered by the Employment and Training Administration in the Department of Labor. Every state has its own employment security agency: some are independent; others are in the State Department of Labor or some other state agency. Typically, the agency is also responsible for the administration of state employment search offices. There are more than 2,500 such offices in the United States where claims for benefits may be filed. Claimants apply for benefits and register for employment at the same time. The function of the office is to find employment for claimants or provide benefits.

KEY TERMS

workers' compensation	exclusive laws	permanent total disability
integrated benefits	elective laws	temporary total disability
24-hour coverage	sole remedy	temporary partial
common law defenses	arise out of employment	permanent partial
fellow-servant rule	while in the course of	disability
assumption of risk	employment	scheduled injuries
doctrine	occupational disease	average weekly wage
contributory negligence	medical care benefits	replacement ratio
employer liability laws	indemnity benefits	minimum weekly benefits
quid pro quo	total disability	maximum weekly benefits
inclusive laws	partial disability	waiting period

survivor income benefits
rehabilitation
employers' liability
other states insurance
experience rating
residual market

involuntary market
state operated workers'
  compensation funds
retrospective plan
second-injury funds
dual capacity

exclusive remedy rule
unemployment
  compensation
benefit formula
Federal Unemployment
  Tax Act

DISCUSSION QUESTIONS

1. A worker is entitled to workers' compensation benefits when disability "arises out of and in the course of employment." A pregnant employee applies for medical and income benefits, alleging that her condition arose out of and in the course of the company's annual Christmas party. Is she entitled to benefits? Why, or why not?

2. Is the rationale for workers' compensation laws the same as that for no-fault auto insurance plans?

3. What are the arguments for and against allowing employers to opt out of the workers' compensation systems in Texas and New Jersey?

4. Given the rapid increases in workers' compensation costs, would you argue that other states should return to offering an opt-out provision? (Note: In the early days of workers' compensation laws in the United States, opt-out provisions were common because of concern about whether making workers' compensation mandatory was constitutional—now, a non-issue.)

5. The frequency of workers' compensation claims due to stress has increased. How can the law provide for legitimate stress claims while reducing illegitimate ones?

6. Ann and Dick both have excellent jobs in Boston. She is transferred to Los Angeles. Dick quits his job so he can go with her. Should he receive unemployment compensation benefits? Why, or why not?

7. Do unemployment compensation benefits help stabilize our economy? Please explain.

8. Do you think experience rating of unemployment compensation contributions helps stabilize employment? Why, or why not?

EXERCISES

13.1 The Baylor Crane Construction Co. is a Virginia-based builder with 1,750 full-time and 300 part-time employees. The company provides all the social insurance benefits required by law and most other employee benefits plans. Last year, Baylor suffered high severity of losses when the top five floors of a high rise collapsed in Virginia Beach during strong winds. Three workers sustained severe injuries and Johnny Kendel, the 64-year old supervisor, was killed. All of the injured workers are back at work except for Tom Leroy, who is still on disability; his prognosis is not good.

   a. Compare the benefits provided by workers' compensation and unemployment compensation.

   b. Compare the method of financing of workers' compensation and unemployment compensation.

   c. Describe the benefits of each of the injured and killed employees.

13.2 As risk manager for Titanic Corp., you want to embark on a stringent work safety program that would cost the business at least $500,000 per year for the next three years, and $300,000 per year thereafter. Workers' compensation losses average about $600,000 per year, and you estimate that you can reduce them by one-third. Your plan is opposed by the financial vice president as a "bleeding heart" program that is not even close to being cost efficient.

    a. In light of your knowledge of workers' compensation costs, employers' liability exposures, and trends in court decisions, what arguments can you make in favor of the safety program?

    b. Give some examples of activities you might include in this safety program.

13.3 Jeanne quits her job because her boss continually makes advances to her. She applies for unemployment compensation benefits while she looks for another job, but her former employer challenges her benefits on the grounds that her unemployment was voluntary because she quit her job with his firm.

    a. What do you think her chances of collecting benefits are?

    b. Do you think she should be able to collect?

    c. Could an employer make a workplace so hostile as to force resignations in order to escape unemployment compensation costs?

13.4 Franco Chen, a production foreman for Acme Machine Company, was discussing an unusual situation with Bill Johnson, a line supervisor. "Bill, I've got a bit of a problem. That new applicant for the number 7 drill press job seems to be just the person we need. He has the skill and experience to handle the job. The fact that he has sight in only one eye doesn't affect his ability to perform adequately. Yet I am worried about two things. First, he said he lost his sight in the bad eye because of a steel shaving from a drill press ten years ago. That bothers me about this job, and a possible reoccurrence. Second, I know that management would be upset if he lost his only good eye, because he would be totally blind and the workers' compensation settlement would be much higher for him than for a less experienced worker with two good eyes. It's a hard decision for me to make." Bill replied, "I don't know much about the technical aspects of that problem, but I think I would hire the experienced fellow. In fact, the Americans with Disabilities Act requires that we not discriminate against him."

    a. What obligation (if any) does the company have toward the new worker, if he is hired, to make his workplace "extra" safe?

    b. How much added workers' compensation risk will the company be assuming by hiring the one-eyed worker rather than a worker with normal vision?

NOTES

1. Daniel Hays, "WC Loss Picture 'Grim,' Says NCCI," *National Underwriter* Online News, 9 May 2002.
2. Chapin Clark, "Critical Issues Facing Workers' Compensation," in *Issues Report 2002* (Boca Raton, Fla.: National Council on Compensation Insurance, 2002). Chapin Clark is president and CEO of NCCI Holdings, Inc., www.NCCI.com.
3. Dennis Kelly, "The Cost of Terror: Workers' Comp Costs Could Reach $6 Billion," *Best's Review,* October 2001.
4. Daniel Hays, "Second Terrorism Hit Could 'Ruin' WC," *National Underwriter,* Property & Casualty/Risk & Benefits Management Edition, 20 May 2002.
5. Meg Fletcher, "Average N.Y. Comp Rates Static Despite New Cat Factor," *Business Insurance,* 12 July 2002. As you know, rates are regulated for workers' compensation and the method of calculating the rates is tightly regulated as well.
6. Exceptions are taxing governmental entities that may be allowed to self-insure unemployment compensation such as the school districts in Texas. They have a pool administered by the Texas Association of School Boards.

7. A counterargument is postulated in "Challenges to Workers' Compensation: A Historical Analysis," by Edward D. and Monroe Berkowitz, in *Workers' Compensation Adequacy, Equity & Efficiency,* eds. John D. Worral and David Appel (Ithaca, N.Y.: ILR Press, 1985). The authors contend that workers were becoming successful in suing employers. Thus, workers' compensation developed as an aid to employers in limiting their responsibilities to employees.

8. For a detailed history of workers' compensation laws see the *Encyclopedia of Economic and Business History:* http://eh.net/encyclopedia/fishback.workers.compensation.php//eh.net/encyclopedia/fishback.workers.compensation.php

9. Daniel Hays, "Despite Option, More Texas Firms Offer Comp," *National Underwriter* Online News Service, 1 February 2002. The results were obtained through a survey of 2,808 employers between August and October 2001, following the passage of a measure that outlawed the use of pre injury liability waivers by employees.

10. Employee benefits are discussed in Chapters 16–18. Alternative coverage never exactly duplicates a state's workers' compensation benefits.

11. Various concepts and statistics in this chapter are based on research described in S. Travis Pritchett, Scott E. Harrington, Helen I. Doerpinghaus, and Greg Niehaus, *An Economic Analysis of Workers' Compensation in South Carolina* (Columbia, S.C.: Division of Research, College of Business Administration, University of South Carolina, 1994).

12. J.D. Long and D.W. Gregg, eds., *Property and Liability Insurance Handbook* (Homewood, Ill.: Richard D. Irwin, Inc., 1965), p. 521. At times we shorten our description of covered perils to "injuries" rather than "injuries and illnesses" because state laws often define occupational illnesses to be injuries.

13. Peter Rousmaniere and Dale Chadwick, "Managing Workers' Comp: The workers' compensation managed-care industry is doing a better job of monitoring itself, but it needs to figure out what to do with the information," *Best's Review,* November 2001.

14. Daniel Hays, "Insurer: Costly Drugs Jack Comp Cost," *National Underwriter* Online News Service, 17 April 2002.

15. The amount of weekly income benefits is the same for both permanent and temporary total disability.

16. Each state workers' compensation commission has a Web site that shows its benefit amounts.

17. Eligibility to receive supplemental income benefits ends 401 weeks from the date of injury. If the worker has an occupational illness, eligibility ends 401 weeks from the date the worker first became eligible to receive income benefits.

18. Rates are made for each state and depend upon the experience under the law in that state. Thus, the rate for the same occupational classification may differ from state to state.

19. Three of the six permit self-insurance. Exclusive funds are called monopolistic state funds.

20. For example, many workers' compensation laws exclude workers hired for temporary jobs, known as casual workers. Injured employees who are classified as casual workers are not entitled to benefits under the law but may recover damages from the employer if they can prove that their injuries were caused by the employer's negligence. The employer's liability risk with regard to excluded employees is the same as it would be if there were no workers' compensation law.

21. Chapin Clark, CEO of NCCI Holdings, Inc., in *Workers' Compensation Issues Report,* 2002. www.ncci.com.

22. This is first-hand information by the author, who was employed by the Texas Association of School Boards in 1994–95.

23. An unemployed federal civilian or ex-serviceperson may be entitled to benefits under the conditions of a state law for determining benefit eligibility. The amount he or she may receive will be the same as if federal pay had been covered under the state law. Costs of the benefits are paid by the federal government.

24. Several states have compulsory temporary disability insurance laws to provide income (and, in one state, medical) benefits for disabled workers who are not receiving unemployment benefits. Some of these plans pay partial benefits to workers receiving workers' compensation benefits. Others exclude these workers.

25. Employees contribute in Alabama, Alaska, and New Jersey.

26. This does not necessarily mean that employers try to cheat employees out of benefits. There are many borderline cases in which there is room for argument about whether or not the unemployed worker is really *involuntarily* unemployed. Experience rating emphasizes the fact that employers pay the cost of benefits and motivates them to be interested in disqualifications. As in other human relations situations, one can find examples of bad behavior by both employers and employees.

PART V

LIFE, HEALTH, AND RETIREMENT RISKS

CHAPTER 14

Life Insurance

Up to this point we concentrated on the property/casualty coverages. With this chapter we begin our expedition into the life and health industry and products, along with the explanation of Social Security in Chapter 15 as the social insurance foundation for life and health insurance and retirement programs. The life/health industry is a separate industry altogether. As you saw in Chapter 4, reserve and pricing are based on mortality tables for life insurance and annuities, while we use morbidity tables and loss data for calculating health and disability rates. This part of the text also delves into retirement programs and contains, in addition to life insurance products and Social Security, coverage of employee benefits programs in Chapters 16, 17, and 18 and individual coverages and need analysis in Chapter 19. In this chapter we will learn about the myriad of life insurance products available—term life, whole life, universal life, variable life, and universal variable life products. The way these products fit into the risk management portfolio of the Smith family is featured in Case 1 at the end of the text. How to determine the amount of life insurance needed for another family is discussed in detail in Chapter 19. This chapter concentrates on the life products themselves.

Life insurance can be thought of as a contract providing a hedge against an untimely death. When purchasing life insurance, the policyowner buys a contract for the future delivery of dollars. This also provides liquidity. The death, whenever it occurs, will create final expenses, such as funeral costs and debt payment, and estate taxes if the estate is large enough, that must be paid immediately. Most people, no matter how wealthy, will not have this much cash on hand. Life insurance provides the necessary liquidity because its payment is triggered by death. Smart decisions about life insurance require understanding both the nature of life insurance and the different types available. In this chapter we cover the most widely used products.

This chapter covers:

1. Connection
2. How life insurance works
3. The life insurance market
4. Term Insurance
5. Universal life
6. Variable life
7. Variable universal life
8. Current assumption whole life
9. Taxation
10. Policy provisions for whole life and universal life policies
11. Riders
12. Adjusting life insurance for inflation

CONNECTION

For our holistic risk management we need to look at all sources of coverages available. Understanding each coverage will complete our ability to manage our risk. In this chapter we delve into the various types of life insurance coverages that are available in the market. Some focus on covering the risk of mortality alone, while others offer also a savings element along with covering the risk of dying. This means that at any point in time, there is a cash value to the policy. This savings element is critical to the choices we make among such policies as whole life, universal life, or universal variable life policies. Our savings with insurance companies, via life products or annuities, makes this industry one of the largest financial intermediaries globally. As explained in Chapter 4, the investment part of the operation of an insurer is as important as the underwriting part.

In this chapter, the drilling down into the life policies is just a piece of the products puzzle that helps us complete the bigger picture of our risks. All of the steps of the three-step stool in Figure 14.1 include some elements of death benefits coverages. In this chapter we delve into the top step for individual life coverages. Figure 14.1 provides us with the connection of the life policies of this chapter into the holistic risk picture.

HOW LIFE INSURANCE WORKS

Life insurance, like other forms of insurance, is based on three concepts: pooling many exposures into a group, accumulating a fund by contributions (premiums) from the members of the group, and paying from this fund for the losses of those who die each year. That is, life insurance involves the group sharing of individual losses. To set premium rates, the insurer must be able to calculate the probability of death at various ages among its insureds, based on pooling. The simplest illustration of pooling is one-year term life insurance. If an insurer promises to pay $100,000 at the death of each insured who dies during the year, it must collect enough money to pay the claims. If past experience indicates that 0.1 percent of a group of young people will die during the year, one death may be expected for every 1,000 persons in the group. If a group of 300,000 is insured, 300 claims (300,000 × .001) are expected. Because each contract is for $100,000, the total expected amount of death claims is $30 million (300 claims × $100,000). To collect enough premiums to cover mortality costs (the cost of claims), the insurer must collect $100 per policyowner ($30 million in claims ÷ 300,000 policyowners).

Other Premium Elements

In addition to covering mortality costs, a life insurance premium must reflect several adjustments. First, the premium is reduced to recognize that the insurer expects to earn investment income on premiums paid in advance. In this manner, most of an insurer's investment income benefits consumers. Second, the premium is increased to cover the insurer's marketing and administrative expenses. Taxes levied on the insurer also must be recovered. In calculating premiums, an actuary usually increases the premium to cover the insurer's risk and expected profits. Risk charges cover any deviations above the predicted level of losses and expenses. The major **premium elements** for term life insurance and the actual prediction of deaths and the estimation of other premium elements are complicated actuarial processes, as discussed in Chapter 4.

FIGURE 14.1   Connection between Risks and Life Insurance Policies

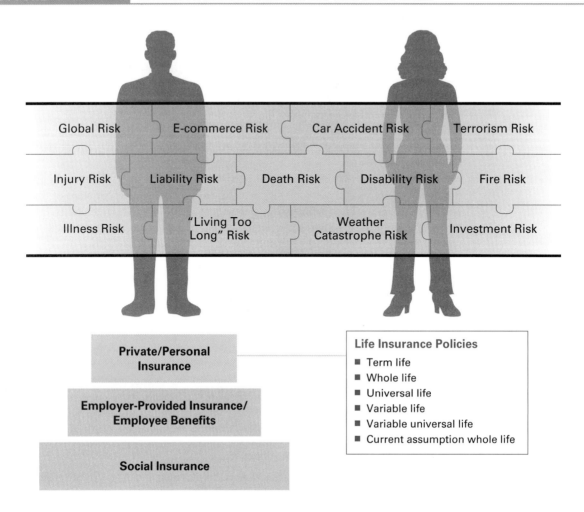

The mortality curve (Figure 4.2) discussed in Chapter 4 also shows why life insurance for a term of one year costs relatively little for young people. The probability that a death benefit payment will be made during that year is very low. The mortality curve also indicates why the cost of **yearly renewable term** life insurance, purchased on a year-by-year basis, becomes prohibitive for most people's budgets beyond the middle years. The theory of insurance is that the losses of the few can be paid for by relatively small contributions from the many. If, however, a large percentage of those in the group suffer losses (say, because all members of the group are old), the burden on one's budget becomes too great, substantial adverse selection is experienced, and the insurance mechanism fails.

Level-Premium Plan

The mortality curve shows that yearly renewable term life insurance, where premiums increase each year as mortality increases, becomes prohibitively expensive at advanced ages. For example, the mortality table shows a mortality rate of .06419 for a male age 75. Thus, just the mortality element of the annual premium for a $100,000 yearly renewable term life insurance policy would be $6,419 (.06419 × 100,000). At age 90, ignoring other premium elements and adverse selection, the mortality cost would be $22,177 (.22177 × 100,000). This high cost, from a budget perspective, coupled with adverse selection, can leave the insurer with a group of insureds whose mortality is even higher than would be anticipated in the absence of adverse selection. Healthy people tend to drop the insurance, while unhealthy people try to pay premiums because they think their beneficiaries may soon have a claim. This behavior is built into renewal rates on term insurance, resulting in renewal rates that rise substantially above rates for new term insurance for healthy people of the same age. A system of spreading the cost for life insurance protection, over a long period or for the entire life span, without a rise in premiums, is essential for most individuals. This is the function of level-premium life insurance.

A **level premium** remains constant throughout the premium-paying period, instead of rising from year to year. Mathematically, the level premium is the amount of the constant *periodic payment* over a specified period (ending before the specified date in the event of death), equivalent to a hypothetical *single premium* that could be paid at the beginning of the contract, discounting for interest and mortality. The hypothetical single premium at the beginning can be thought of as similar to a mortgage that is paid for by periodic level premiums.

As Figure 14.2 shows, the level premium for an **ordinary (whole) life** policy (which provides lifetime protection, issued at age 25 in the illustration) is greater during the early years than premiums for a yearly renewable term policy for the same period. The excess (see the shaded area between age 25 and a little before age 50 in Figure 14.2) and its investment earnings are available to help pay claims as they occur. It is this accumulation of funds, combined with a decreasing amount of true insurance protection (which is the net amount at risk to the insurance mechanism), that makes possible a premium that remains level even though the probability of death rises as the insured grows older. In later years, the true cost of insurance protection (the probability of death at a particular age times the decreased amount of protection) is paid for by the level premium plus a portion of the investment earnings produced by the policy's cash value. In summary, the level premium is higher than necessary to pay claims and other expenses during the early years of the contract, but less than the cost of protection equal to the total death benefit during the later years. The concept of a level premium is basic to an understanding of financing death benefits at advanced ages.

The accumulation of funds is a mathematical side effect of leveling the premium to accommodate consumers' budgets. Beginning in the 1950s, however, insurers began to refer to the accumulated funds as *cash value* that could meet various savings needs. Today, the payment of premiums greater than the amount required to pay for a yearly renewable term policy often is motivated, at least in the minds of consumers, by the objective of creating savings or investment funds.

Effects of the Level-Premium Plan

From an economic standpoint, the level-premium plan does two things. First, the insurer offers an installment payment plan with equal payments over time. Second, the level-premium policies are made up of two elements: protection and investment.[1]

As discussed, although the periodic premium payments exceed death benefits and other expenses for an insured group during the early years of the policy, they fall short during later years (see Figure 14.2). The insurer accumulates a **reserve** to offset this deficiency. The insurer's reserve is similar in amount, but not identical, to the sum of cash values for the insured group. The reserve is a liability on the insurer's balance sheet, representing the insurer's obligation and reflecting the extent to which future premiums and the insurer's assumed investment income will not be sufficient to cover the present value of future claims on a policy. At any point, the present value of the reserve fund, future investment

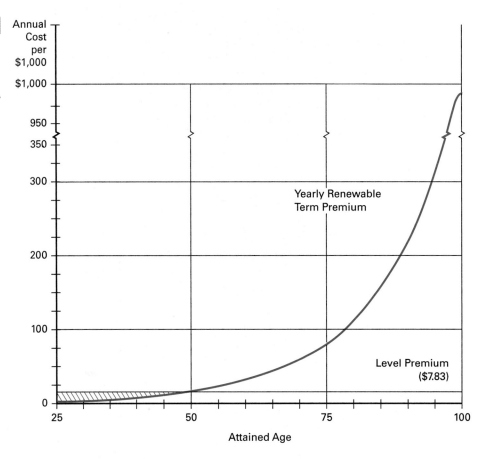

Premiums that exceed the cost of yearly renewable term life insurance.
Based on nonsmoker rates for a $50,000 policy with a selected company.

earnings, and future premiums are sufficient to pay the present value of all future death claims for a group of insureds. When an insured dies, the insurer is obligated to pay the beneficiary the face amount (death benefit) of the policy. Part of this payment is an amount equal to the reserve.

The difference between the reserve at any point in time and the face amount of the policy is known as the **net amount at risk** for the insurer, and the **protection element** for the insured. As Figure 14.2 illustrates, this element declines each year because the reserve (investment or **cash value**) increases. The protection/net-amount-at-risk element is analogous to decreasing term insurance. All level premium life policies have a combination of cash value and protection.

The amount at risk for the insurer (that is, the protection element) decreases as the cash value element increases with age; thus, less true insurance (protection) is purchased each year. This decreasing amount of insurance is one of the reasons why the annual cost of pure insurance (that is, the protection element) to the insurer is less than the sum of the level premium plus investment earnings, even at advanced ages when mortality rates significantly exceed the premium per $1,000 of death benefit. Over time, the growing amount of investment earnings (due to increasing cash value) more than offsets the inadequacy of the level premium. The periodic addition of part of these investment earnings to cash value explains why the cash value in the policy continues to grow throughout the life of the contract (see Figure 14.3).

From an insurer's perspective, the reserve is a liability that will have to be paid when the insured either dies or surrenders the policy. The separation of a whole life policy into protection and investment elements is an economic or personal finance concept, rather than an actuarial one. Actuaries deal with large groups of insureds rather than individual policies and look at an individual policy as an indivisible contract.

The cash value is classified as an asset on the policyholder's personal balance sheet, because it is the policyowner's money. There are three ways to realize the cash value:

1. Surrender (discontinue) the policy and receive the cash value as a refund
2. Take a loan from for an amount not to exceed the cash value
3. Leave the cash value in the contract and eventually let it mature as part of the death claim

THE LIFE INSURANCE MARKET AND PRODUCTS

The life insurance industry is one of the largest industries in the world. In 2000, there was $16 trillion of life insurance coverage in force in the United States.[2] Life insurance net premiums (after reinsurance) for individual policies were $102 billion and for group life (discussed in Chapter 16) were $26 billion for 2000.[3]

Between 1990 and 2000, purchases of variable life insurance grew from $5.9 billion to $20.6 billion, universal life decreased from $261.4 billion to $146.3 billion, and variable universal life increased dramatically from $27.9 billion to $336.6 billion.[4] Detailed explanation of each of the products follows. See Table 14.2 for a side-by-side comparison. The focus here is only to provide a description of the life insurance marketplace in the early 2000s.

The tremendous growth in variable life products is the result of the bull stock market during the mid to late 1990s. This dramatic increase turned its trend into a major decrease in the sales of these products when the stock market turned bearish. Changes in new sales of individual life insurance are shown in Table 14.1.

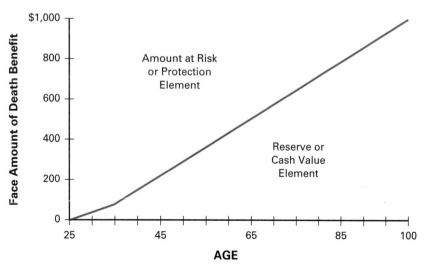

FIGURE 14.3

Proportion of Protection and Cash Value in Ordinary Life Contract (Issued to a Male Age 25)

This table show the cash value (investment) figures for a selected ordinary life policy. The insurer's reserve would be slightly higher than the cash value in the early contract years.

TABLE 14.1		Annualized Premiums	Face Amount	Number of Policies
Increase (Decrease) in Individual Life Insurance Sales, 2000–2001	Universal Life	18.0%	10.0%	7.0%
	Variable Life	(33.0%)	(31.0%)	(34.0%)
	Variable Universal Life	(10.0%)	(16.0%)	(18.0%)
	Term Life	(9.0%)	(8.0%)	(9.0%)
	Whole Life	5.0%	7.0%	2.0%
	Average	(3.0%)	(7.0%)	(5.0%)

Source: Linda Koco, "UL Sales Soared, VL Plunged Last Year," *National Underwriter* Life and Health/Financial Services Edition, 4 March 2002.

TERM INSURANCE

Term life insurance provides protection for a specified period, called the policy's term (or duration). When a company issues a one-year term life policy, it promises to pay the face amount of the policy in the event of death during that year.

TABLE 14.2 — Characteristics of Major Types of Life Insurance Policies

	Distinguishing Feature	Premiums	Cash Value	Death Benefit
Term life	Provides protection for a specific period (term)	Fixed, but increase at each renewal	None, thus no provision for loans or withdrawals	Pays face amount of policy if death occurs within term
Whole life (see policy in Appendix E)	Lifetime protection: As long as premiums are paid, policy stays in force	Fixed	Guaranteed	Pays face amount if policy is in force when death occurs
Universal life (see policy in Appendix F)	Guaranteed minimum interest rate on the investments accumulated in the accounts. Interest rates are based on bonds only—not stocks—and can be higher than the minimum guaranteed	Flexible, set by policyholder; used to pay mortality rate and expenses, then remainder is invested	Depends on the account value minus surrender charges (see policy for the complex calculations)	Option A: Maintains level death benefit Option B: Face amount increases as accumulated cash value grows (see Figure 14.6)
Variable life	The "mutual fund" policy, intended to keep death benefits apace with inflation; technically, a security as well as insurance	Fixed	Not guaranteed; depends on investment performance of stocks	Minimum face amount that can be greater as cash value changes (see Figure 14.7)
Variable universal life	Combines the premium and death benefit flexibility of a universal life policy with the investment choices in stocks of variable life	Flexible, as in universal life	Not guaranteed; depends on investment performance of stocks	Same options as universal life

Duration

The length of term policies varies; common terms are one-, five-, ten-, fifteen-, and twenty-year. Term policies are often not renewable beyond age 65 or 70 because of adverse selection that increases with age. Yet increasingly, yearly renewable term policies are renewable to age 95 or 100, although it would be unusual for a policy to stay in effect at advanced ages because of the amount of premium. Yearly renewable term policies are subject to high **lapse rates** (that is, failure to be renewed) and low profitability for the insurer.

Short-term life policies involve no investment element. Long-term contracts (for example, term to age 65) when accompanied by a level premium can accumulate a small cash value element in the early years, but this is depleted during the latter part of the term because then the cost of mortality exceeds the sum of the level premium and the investment earnings. Two options are typically available with term insurance sold directly to individuals: renewability and convertibility.

Renewability

If the policyholder wishes to continue the protection for more than one term, the insurer will require a new application and new evidence of insurability. The risk of being turned down may be handled by purchasing renewable term insurance. The **renewability option** gives the right to renew the policy for a specified number of additional periods of protection, at a predetermined schedule of premium rates, without new evidence of insurability. Renewability protects insurability for the period specified. After that period has elapsed, the insured must again submit a new application and prove insurability.

Each time the policy is renewed, the premium increases because of the insured's increasing age. Because the least healthy tend to renew and the most healthy tend to discontinue, the renewable feature increases the cost of protection. The renewable feature, however, is valuable in term life insurance.

Convertibility

A term policy with a **convertibility option** provides the right to convert the term policy to a whole life or another type of insurance, before a specified time, without proving insurability. If, for example, at age 28 you buy a term policy renewable to age 65 and convertible for twenty years, you may renew each year for several years and then, perhaps at age 36, decide you prefer cash-value life insurance. Your motivation may be that the premium, though higher than that of the term policy at the age of conversion, will remain the same year after year; the policy can be kept in force indefinitely; or you may want to include cash values among your investments. If you become uninsurable or insurable only at higher-than-standard (called substandard) rates, you will find the convertibility feature very valuable.

Most conversions are made at **attained age** premium rates. That is, the premium for the new policy is based on the age at the time of the conversion. The insured or policyowner pays the same rate as anyone else who could qualify for standard rates based on good health and other insurability factors. The option results in no questions about your insurability.

Death Benefit Pattern

The death benefit in a term policy either remains level, decreases, or increases over time. Each pattern of protection fits specific needs. For example, a decreasing term policy may be used as collateral for a loan on which the principal is being reduced by periodic payments.

An increasing amount of protection helps maintain purchasing power during inflation. The increasing benefit is likely to be sold as a rider to a level benefit policy.

Mortgage protection insurance is decreasing term insurance; with each mortgage payment, the face value of the insurance decreases to correspond to the amount of the loan that is outstanding. Otherwise, mortgage protection is like other decreasing term policies.[5] **Credit life** insurance is similar to mortgage protection. Its death benefit changes, up or down, as the balance changes on an installment loan or other type of consumer loan.

Premium Patterns

An insurer's rates for nonsmokers may be 40 percent or so lower than those for smokers. Rates for women are less than for men, as discussed in "Ethical Dilemma: Should Life Rates Be Based on Gender?" of this chapter. The yearly renewable term contract usually has a table of premiums that increase each year as the insured ages and as time elapses since insurability was established.

Reentry term allows the insured to re-demonstrate insurability periodically, perhaps every five years, and qualify for a new (lower) select category of rates that are not initially loaded for adverse selection. If the insured cannot qualify for the new rates, usually because of worsening health, he/she can either pay the higher rates of the initial premium table ("ultimate rates") or drop the policy and try to find better rates with another insurer.

Summary: Features of Term Life

In summary, in term life we see the following features (also see Table 14.2):

- Death benefits: Level or decreasing
- Cash value: None
- Premiums: Increase at each renewal
- Policy loans: Not allowed
- Partial withdrawals: Not allowed
- Surrender charges: None

WHOLE LIFE INSURANCE

Whole life insurance, as its name suggests, provides for payment of the face value upon death regardless of when the death may occur. As long as the premiums are paid, the policy stays in force. Thus, whole life insurance is referred to as "permanent insurance." This ability to maintain the policy throughout one's life, instead of for a specific term, is the key characteristic of whole life insurance.

There are three traditional types of whole life insurance: (1) ordinary or straight life, (2) limited-payment life, and (3) single-premium life. The difference between them is in the arrangements for premium payment. (See Appendix E for a sample straight whole life policy.)

Straight Life

The premiums for a **straight life** policy are paid in equal periodic amounts over the life of the insured. The rate is based on the assumption that the insured will live to an advanced age (such as age 90 or 100). In effect, the insured is buying the policy on an installment basis and the installments are spread over the balance of the lifetime, as explained earlier in our discussion of the level-premium concept. This provides the lowest possible level outlay for permanent protection.

Ethical Dilemma

Should Life Rates Be Based on Gender?

As a group, young male drivers cause more automobile insurance losses than young female drivers. A few states, however, no longer allow automobile insurers to charge different rates for males and females. Similarly, over a decade ago, the Supreme Court ruled that employers using annuities to fund retirement benefits could no longer collect higher contributions from women, who were expected to live longer than men, in order to make equal annuity payments during retirement. Employers continuing to pay retirement benefits through annuities were forced by the Supreme Court to use unisex tables. That is, the mortality rates of men and women were pooled to produce an average life expectancy greater than that for men alone and less than that for women alone. Retirement benefits went up for the women and down for the men involved.

Should life insurance rates be made gender neutral as well? The quotes displayed here were requested from Insweb (www.insweb.com), an online insurance quotes and distribution company, in December 2002. They show that the premiums for a ten-year term life insurance policy of $200,000 for a 25-year old male of perfect health and family history, weight appropriate to height, and no tobacco use, are higher than those for a female with the same attributes. For example, the rate is $9.80 per month for a male as opposed to $8.67 for a female as shown in the table of quotes below.

When we compare a particular man to a particular woman of the same age and seemingly the same state of insurability (health, lifestyle, occupation, financial condition, and so forth), the man may outlive the woman, but, as you know, insurers pool cohorts of insureds rather than the individual. Insurers observe difference in average experience for large groups of males and females to justify different life rates based on gender, arguing that doing so creates actuarial equity. That is, premiums should differ because expected outcomes (death benefits multiplied by probabilities) are different for groups of males and females.

In the past two decades, the gender mortality gap has begun to close. While female longevity has risen, male life spans have increased at a faster rate, due in part to medical advances in treating conditions like heart disease, which traditionally kills more men than women. Many insurers, however, still base their insurance rates on actuarial data from the 1970s. Because of AIDS and the uncertainties that accompanied it, insurers were reluctant to use data from the 1980s. Only recently have companies begun to incorporate data from the early 1990s. Yet even with a smaller gap between men's and women's longevity, insurance rates for women are still lower than for equally aged and healthy men.

Questions for Discussion

1. Is it ethical for life insurers to charge different rates for men and women? If it is not legal to charge different rates based on race, why should gender be different?

2. Does this practice represent unreasonable discrimination (sometimes called "social inequity") against males based on a factor over which they have no control?

3. Given the possibility that the gap between male and female mortality may close during the next few decades, is it really fair to charge different rates to men and women for a policy that runs twenty, thirty, or more years?

Sources: Ron Panko, "Closing the Gender Gap," *Best's Review,* August 2000; Insweb, www.insweb.com.

Monthly premium for a 10-year level term Life Insurance policy*

Male Coverage	25	35	45	Female Coverage	25	35	45
$ 100,000	$ 7.06	$7.09	$11.29	$ 100,000	$ 6.46	$6.56	$ 8.67
200,000	9.80	9.80	16.64	200,000	8.67	8.75	13.09
300,000	10.70	11.22	21.63	300,000	10.12	10.15	16.75
400,000	12.96	13.66	26.61	400,000	12.07	12.07	20.91
500,000	14.17	14.58	30.26	500,000	12.08	12.08	24.65

* Quotes based on a composite of participating carriers, which have at least an A–rating by S&P. Your premium may differ due to your health, smoking, or other activities. Rates subject to underwriting and state availability. InsWeb is a service offered by InsWeb Insurance Services, Inc., a licensed agency in most states (CA #0C24350)

As shown in Figure 14.3, the level-premium policy consists of a protection element and a cash value element. The cash value builds over time, and, eventually, when the insured is 90 or 100, the cash value will equal the face value of the policy. If the insured is still alive at this advanced age, the insurer will pay the death benefit as if death occurred. By this time, no real insurance element exists. The options available with regard to this value are discussed later in this chapter. A basic straight life policy typically has a face amount (death benefit) that remains level over the lifetime. The pattern can change, however, by using dividends to buy additional amounts of insurance or by purchasing a cost of living adjustment rider. In 2000, 3.7 million traditional whole life policies were sold. This figure represents more than half of the individual permanent insurance sold.

Limited-Payment Life

Like straight life, **limited-payment life** offers lifetime protection but limits premium payments to a specified period of years or to a specified age. After premiums have been paid during the specified period, the policy remains in force for the balance of life without further premium payment. The policy is "paid up." A 20-pay life policy becomes paid up after premiums have been paid for 20 years, a life-paid-up-at-65 becomes paid up at age 65, and so on (see Figure 14.4). The shorter premium payment period appeals to some buyers. For example, a life-paid-up-at-65 policy ends premiums around the time many people expect to begin living on retirement pay. If the insured dies before the end of the premium-paying period, premium payments stop and the face amount is paid. These policies are mainly sold as business insurance where there is a need to fully pay for a policy by a certain date, such as the time an employee will retire.

Single-Premium Life

Whole life insurance may be bought for a **single premium**—the ultimate in limited payment. Mathematically, the single premium is the present value of future benefits, with discounts both for investment earnings and mortality. Cash and loan values are high compared with policies bought on the installment plan (see Figure 14.4). Single-premium life insurance is bought almost exclusively for its investment features; protection is viewed as a secondary benefit of the transaction.

Investment Aspects

The typical buyer of life insurance, however, does not expect to pay income taxes on proceeds from his or her policy. Instead, the expectation is for the policy to mature eventually as a death claim. At that point, all proceeds (protection plus cash value) of life insurance death claims are exempt from income taxes under Section 101(a)(1). In practice, most policies terminate by being lapsed or surrendered prior to death as needs for life insurance change.

Life insurers offer participation in portfolios of moderate-yield investments (such as high-grade industrial bonds, mortgages, real estate, and common stock) in which cash values are invested, with potentially no income tax on the realized investment returns. Part of each premium, for all types of cash-value life insurance, is used to make payments on the protection element of the contract, but the protection element also has an expected return. This return is equal to the probability of death multiplied by the amount of protection. Thus, the need to pay for protection in order to gain access to the cash value element of a single-premium or other investment-oriented plan should not be viewed as a consumer disadvantage if there is a need for additional life insurance protection. The participation (dividend) feature of a policy has a major effect on its cost and worth.

FIGURE 14.4

Protection and Cash
Value Elements for
Single Premium and
Installment Forms of
Cash Value Life
Insurance

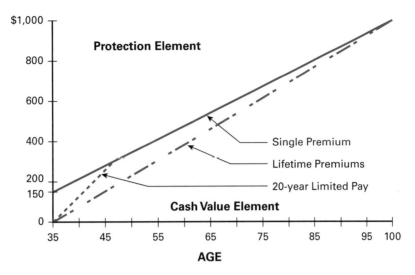

Note: Hypothetical values not drawn to scale.

Participation Feature

Mutual life insurers have always sold their term and cash-value life products on a participation basis. Stock life companies have also made limited use of participating policies.
Participating contracts pay **dividends** for the purpose of refunding higher-than-necessary
premiums and sharing company profits with policyowners. Thus, as investment returns
escalate above previous expectations, or as mortality rates decline, the policyowners share
in the success of the insurer.

Dividends allow the sharing of current profits from investments, mortality assumptions, expense estimates, and lapse experience with the policyholder. Investment returns
usually have more influence on the size of dividends than do the other factors. The fact
that insurer investment portfolios tend to have many medium- and long-term bonds and
mortgages that do not turn over quickly creates a substantial lag, however, between the
insurer's realization of higher yields on new investments and the effect of those higher
yields on average **portfolio returns** that affect dividends.

Participating whole life insurance continues to be a major product line for mutual
insurers. Sales illustrations are used by agents in presenting the product to the consumer.
For products with the participation feature, dividends projected for long periods into the
future are a significant part of the sales illustration. Generally, the illustrations are based
on the current experience of the insurer with respect to its investment returns, mortality
experience, expenses, and lapse rates.

Summary: Features of Whole Life

In summary, in whole life we see the following features (also see Table 14.2):

- Death benefits: Fixed level
- Cash value: Guaranteed amounts
- Premiums: Fixed level
- Policy loans: Allowed
- Partial withdrawals: Not allowed
- Surrender charges: None

UNIVERSAL LIFE INSURANCE

Universal life insurance contracts were introduced to the market in 1979 to bolster the profits of stock insurance companies. Universal policies were advertised as offering competitive investment features and the flexibility to meet changing consumer needs. When expense charges (such as mortality rates) are set at reasonable levels, the investment part of the universal life contract can be competitive on an after-tax basis with money market mutual funds, certificates of deposit, and other short-term instruments offered by investment companies, banks, and other financial institutions. Most insurers invest funds from their universal life contracts primarily in short-term investments so they can have the liquidity to meet policyholder demands for cash values. Some other insurers use investment portfolios that are competitive with medium- and long-term investment returns.

A key feature of the product is its flexibility. The policyowner can:

- Change the amount of premium periodically
- Discontinue premiums and resume them at a later date without lapsing the policy
- Change the amount of death protection (subject to restrictions)

Universal life was introduced during a period of historically high, double-digit interest rates. Sales illustrations often projected high investment returns for many years into the future, resulting in illustrated cash values that surpassed those of traditional cash value policies. Traditional policy illustrations projected dividends and cash values using average investment returns for a portfolio of securities and mortgages purchased during periods of low, medium, and high interest rates. Consumers were attracted to the high new money rates of the early 1980s, which resulted in universal life growing to a sizable market with $146.3 billion of face amount in 2000. The share of the market declined when interest rates declined and increased as the stock market became bearish.

Separation of Elements

Traditional cash-value life insurance products do not clearly show the separate effect of their mortality, investment, and expense components. The distinguishing characteristic of universal life contracts is a clear separation of these three elements. This is called **unbundling.** The separation is reported at least annually, by a **disclosure statement.** The disclosure statement shows:

- The gross rate of investment return credited to the account[6]
- The charge for death protection
- Expense charges
- The resulting changes in accumulation value and in cash value

This **transparency** permits seeing how the policy operates internally, after the fact.

The insurer maintains separate accounting for each policyowner. The account has three income items:

- New premiums paid
- Guaranteed interest credited
- Excess interest credited

The cash outflow items, from a consumer perspective, consist of:

- A mortality charge for death protection
- Administrative and marketing expenses
- Withdrawals or loans

The difference between income and outflow becomes a new contribution to (or deduction from) the **accumulation value** account. Visualize this as the level of liquid in an open container where the three income items flow in at the top and the outflow items are extracted through a spigot at the bottom. Accounting usually occurs on a monthly basis, followed by annual disclosure of the monthly cash flows. The steps in the periodic **flow of funds** for a universal life policy are shown in Figure 14.5. The first premium is at least a minimum amount specified by the insurer; subsequent premiums are flexible in amount, even zero if the cash value is large enough to cover the current cost of death protection and any applicable expense charges.

Administrative and marketing expense charges are subtracted each period. Some policies do not make explicit deductions. Instead, they recover their expenses by lowering investment credits or increasing mortality charges (limited by guaranteed maximums). Another periodic deduction is for mortality. The policyowner decides whether withdrawals (that is, partial surrenders of cash values) or policy loans are made. They cannot exceed the current cash value. If the entire cash value is withdrawn, the contract terminates. Withdrawals and loans reduce the death benefit as well as the cash value.

After deductions at the beginning of each accounting period for expenses, mortality, and withdrawals, the accumulation value is increased periodically by the percentage that reflects the insurer's current investment experience (subject to a guaranteed minimum rate) for the portfolio underlying universal life policies.

The difference between the accumulation value and what can be withdrawn in cash (the cash value) at any point in time is determined by surrender expenses. "Surrender expenses" and other terms will become clearer as aspects of universal life are discussed in more detail in the next few pages.

FIGURE 14.5

Flow of Funds for Universal Life

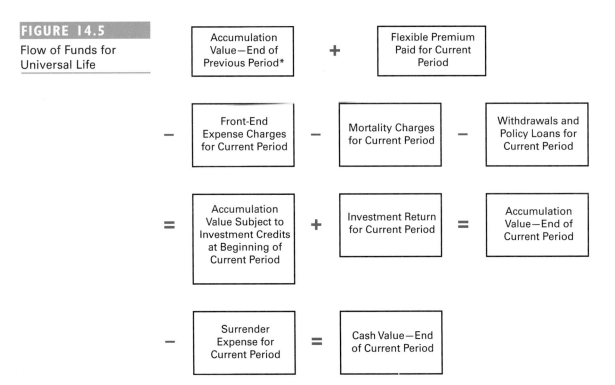

* This accumulation value is zero for a new policy.

Death Benefit Options

Figure 14.6 shows two **death benefit options** that are typically available. Type A keeps a level death benefit by making dollar-for-dollar changes in the amount of protection as the investment (cash value account) increases or decreases. This option is expected to produce a pattern of cash values and protection like that of a traditional, ordinary life contract. When a traditional, straight life contract is issued, the policy stipulates exactly what the

FIGURE 14.6

Two Universal Death
Benefit Options

Type A—Level Death Benefit

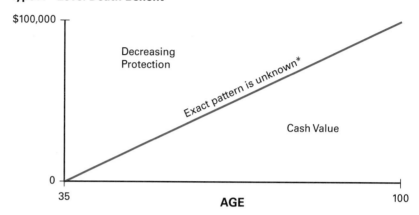

Type B—Increasing Death Benefit

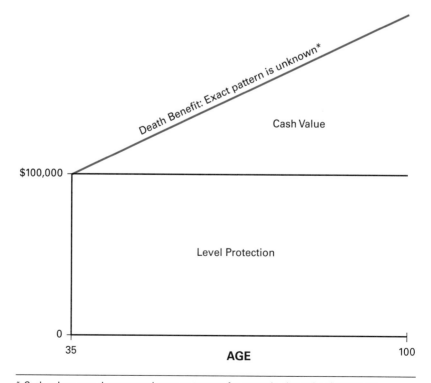

* Cash values may decrease and even go to zero, for example, due to low investment
returns or inadequate premium payments.

pattern of cash values will be and guarantees them. In universal life contracts, there are illustrations of cash values for thirty years or so, assuming:

- A specified level of premium payments
- A guaranteed minimum investment return
- Guaranteed maximum mortality rates

Another column of the illustration will show values based on current investment and mortality experience. Company illustration practices also usually provide a column of accumulation and cash values based on an intermediate investment return (that is, a return between the guaranteed and current rates).

The type B option is intended to produce an increasing death benefit. The exact amount of increase will depend on future non-guaranteed changes in cash value, as described in the discussion of type A policies. The type B alternative is analogous to buying a yearly, renewable level term insurance contract and creating a separate investment account.

With either type the policyowner may use the contract's flexibility to change the amount of protection as the needs for insurance change. Like traditional life insurance contracts, additional amounts of protection require evidence of insurability, including good health, to protect the insurer against adverse selection. Decreases in protection are made without evidence of insurability. The insurer simply acknowledges the request for a different death benefit by sending notification of the change. The contract will specify a minimum amount of protection to comply with federal tax guidelines. These guidelines must be met to shelter the contract's investment earnings (commonly called inside interest build-up) from income taxes.

Cost of living adjustment (COLA) riders and options to purchase additional insurance are available from most insurers, as you will see at end of this chapter. **COLA riders** increase the death benefit annually, consistent with the previous year's increase in the Consumer Price Index. Thus, if inflation is 3 percent, a $100,000 type A policy reflects a $103,000 death benefit in the second year. Of course, future mortality charges will reflect the higher amount at risk to the insurer, resulting in higher costs of death protection and lower cash values, unless premiums or investment returns increase concomitantly. Options to purchase additional insurance give the contractual right to purchase stipulated amounts of insurance at specified future ages (generally limited to age 40) and events (for example, the birth of a child) without evidence of insurability.

Premium Payments

Most universal policies require a minimum premium in the first policy year. In subsequent years, the amount paid is the policyowner's decision, subject to minimums and maximums set by insurers and influenced by IRS rules.

Mortality Charges

Almost all universal life insurance policies specify that mortality charges be levied monthly. The charge for a particular month is determined by multiplying the **current mortality rate** by the current amount of protection (net amount at risk to the insurer). The current mortality charge can be any amount determined periodically by the insurer as long as the charge does not exceed the guaranteed **maximum mortality rate** specified in the contract. Maximum mortality rates typically are those in the conservative 1980 CSO Mortality Table. Updated mortality tables are expected to be adopted in 2004, as discussed in this chapter's "Important Issues: New Mortality Tables."

The current practice among most insurers is to set current mortality rates below the specified maximums. Mortality charges vary widely among insurers and may change after a policy is issued. Consumers should not, however, choose an insurer solely by a low mortality charge. Expense charges and investment returns also factor into any determination of a policy's price. It is also unwise to choose a policy solely on the basis of low expenses or high advertised gross investment returns.

Expense Charges

Insurers levy expense charges to help cover their costs of marketing and administering the policies. The charges can be grouped into **front-end expenses** and **surrender expenses** (back-end expenses). Front-end expenses are applied at the beginning of each month or year. They consist of some combination of: (1) a percentage of new premiums paid (for

---

IMPORTANT ISSUES

New Mortality Tables

As of January 1, 2004, in life insurance terms, you may be able to think of yourself as three years younger. According to newly revised mortality tables, American adults can expect to live, on average, two to four years longer than their parents. The new tables, dated 2001 but scheduled to be adopted by the states beginning in 2004, are updates of the 1980 Commissioners Standard Ordinary Mortality Tables, which life insurers consult for underwriting and setting premiums. They were prepared by the Society of Actuaries and the American Academy of Actuaries at the request of the National Association of Insurance Commissioners (NAIC).

Age is a very important factor when life insurers assess the classification of an insurance applicant. Others include gender, tobacco use, and health. Like the 1980 tables, the 2001 tables are categorized by gender, and show that women as a group live several years longer than men do. (See "Ethical Dilemma: Should Life Rates Be Based on Gender?") Sub-tables separate tobacco users from nonusers, and reflect the decrease in male smokers since 1980 but a slight increase in female smokers. Mortality rates for female smokers in their fifties and sixties are now higher than they were in 1980. Women in that group can expect to pay higher life insurance premiums when the new tables are adopted.

Changes in aggregate health status are difficult to determine (and the tables do not even try), but it is generally accepted that any improvements are offset by more and better medical testing. That is, if more seventy-year-olds are diagnosed with prostate cancer in 2002 than there were in 1982, it is possible the cancer rate has increased—but also true that the detection

test is more widely given these days, and that men in 1982 were more likely to die of other causes before even reaching that age. One factor that has clearly worsened since 1980—in fact, it has more than doubled—is the nation's rate of obesity. Since overweight people are very likely to develop health problems as they grow older, most life insurers will charge higher premiums or even decline to cover people who weigh 30 percent or more above their ideal (see "Ethical Dilemma: Obesity and Insurance—Should Size Matter? in Chapter 9).

Other factors contributing to America's overall life expectancy have clearly progressed in the last twenty years: medical breakthroughs, including antibiotics and vaccines; public health and environmental efforts; and increased standards of living such as better housing and safer foods. Thanks to developments like these and more, the general mortality rate in the United States has improved about 1 percent per year since early last century. If this trend holds, in 2020 you can take another three years off your age.

Explore the Internet

How much longer do you have to live? Check out the Annuity 2000 Mortality Table at Insure.com, www.insure.com/life/annuity2000-2.html.

Sources: Dr. Rick Rogers, "Will Mortality Improvements Continue?" *National Underwriter,* Life & Health/Financial Services Edition, 26 August 2002; American Academy of Actuaries, "June 2002 CSO Task Force Report," www.actuary.org/life/cso_0702.htm; National Association of Insurance Commissioners, "Recognition of the 2001 CSO Mortality Table for Use in Determining Minimum Reserve Liabilities and Nonforfeiture Benefits Model Regulation," www.naic.org/1papers/models/htms/cso-summary.htm.

example, 5 percent, with 2 percent covering premium taxes paid by the insurer to the state), (2) a small flat dollar amount per month or year (for example, $1.50 per month), and (3) a larger flat dollar amount in the first policy year (for example, $50). Universal life policies began with high front-end expenses, but the trend has been toward much lower or no front-end expenses due to competition among companies. Those that levy front-end expenses tend to use only a percentage of premium load in both first and renewal policy years. Policies with large front-end loads seldom levy surrender expenses.

As most early issuers of universal policies lowered their front-end charges, they added surrender charges. Whereas front-end expenses reduce values for all insureds, surrender expenses transfer their negative impact to policyowners who terminate their policies. Surrender charges help the insurer recover its heavy front-end underwriting expenses and sales commissions. Questions exist about whether or not they create equity between short-term and persisting policyholders. A few insurers issue universal policies with neither front-end nor surrender charges. These insurers, of course, still incur operating expenses. Some lower operating expenses by distributing their products directly to consumers or through financial planners who charge separate fees to clients. These "no-load" products still incur marketing expenses for the insurers that must promote (advertise) their products through direct mail, television, and other channels. They plan to recover expenses and make a profit by margins on actual mortality charges (current charges greater than company death claim experience) and margins on investment returns (crediting current interest rates below what the company is earning on its investment portfolio). Thus, even "no-load" contracts have hidden expense loads. Expense charges of all types, like current mortality rates, vary widely among insurers. Advertised investment returns are likely to vary in a narrower range.

Investment Returns

Insurers reserve the right to change the current rate of return periodically. Some guarantee a new rate for a year; others only commit to the new rate for a month or a quarter.

The **indexed investment strategy** used by some insurers ties the rate of return on cash values to a published index, such as rates on 90-day U.S. Treasury bills or Moody's Bond Index, rather than leaving it to the insurer's discretion and its actual investment portfolio returns. This approach also provides a guarantee between 4 and 5 percent.

Some insurers use a **new money rate** for universal contracts. As explained earlier, this approach credits the account with the return an insurer earns on its latest new investments. The practice dictates investment of universal life funds in assets with relatively short maturities in order to match assets with liabilities. When short-term rates are relatively high, such as in the early 1980s, the new money approach produces attractive returns. When short-term returns drop, as they did after the mid-1980s, the approach is not attractive, as noted earlier.

Summary: Features of Universal Life

In summary, in universal life we see the following features (also see Table 14.2):

- Death benefits: Level or increasing
- Cash value: Guaranteed minimum cash value plus additional interest when rates are higher than guaranteed
- Premiums: Flexible
- Policy loans: Yes, but the interest credited to the account is reduced
- Partial withdrawals: Allowed
- Surrender charges: Yes

VARIABLE LIFE INSURANCE

To overcome policyholder fears that inflation will erode life insurance values, **variable life** provides the opportunity to invest funds in the stock market.

The theory of variable life insurance (and variable annuities) is that the prices of the stock and other equities purchased by the insurer for this product will provide insureds with access to any investment vehicle available in the marketplace and not be limited to fixed-income products. Investments supporting variable life insurance are held in one or more account(s) separate from the general accounts of the insurer. This distinguishes them from investments underlying other life and health insurance contracts.

Each variable life consumer has a choice of investing in a combination of between five and twenty different separate accounts with varying investment objectives and strategies. For example, you might add more short-term stability by placing part of your money in a short-term bond fund, while maintaining a significant equity element in one or more common stock funds. Each separate account makes investments in publicly traded securities that have readily determinable market values. Market values are needed to determine the current values of cash/accumulation values and death benefits. Cash values will vary daily, and death benefits will vary daily, monthly, or annually.

Variable life transfers all investment risks to the policyowner. Unlike universal life, for example, which guarantees the fixed-dollar value of your accumulation fund and a minimum return, variable insurance products make no guarantee of either principal or returns. All the investment risk (upside or downside) is yours. Cash values (but not death benefits) can go to zero as a result of adverse investment experience.

How It Works

The *Model Variable Life Insurance Regulation,* produced by the National Association of Insurance Commissioners, sets guidelines that help establish the form of the product. Certain basic characteristics can be identified.

Variable life is, in essence, a whole life product that provides variable amounts of benefit for the entire life. It requires a level premium; therefore, the out-of-pocket contributions will not change with changes in the cost of living. This limits the extent to which death benefits can increase over time, since no new amounts of insurance can be financed by defining the premium in constant dollars. All increases in death benefits must come from favorable investment performance.

Contracts specify a minimum death benefit, called the face amount. In one design, this minimum stays level during the life of the contract. Another design uses increasing term insurance to provide automatic increases of 3 percent per year for fourteen years, at which point the minimum face amount becomes level at 150 percent of its original face value. Assuming continuation of premium payments, the face amount can never go below the guaranteed minimum.

Each separate account is, in essence, a different mutual fund. For example, one contract offers five investment accounts: (1) guaranteed interest, (2) money market, (3) a balance of bonds and stocks, (4) conservative common stock, and (5) aggressive common stock. The policyowner could allocate all net premiums (new premiums minus expense and mortality charges) to one account or divide them among any two or more accounts. Currently, approximately 75 percent of separate account assets are in common stocks. Some policies limit the number of changes among the available accounts. For example, some contracts set a limit of four changes per year. Administrative charges may accompany switches among accounts, especially when one exceeds the limit. Since the changes are made inside a life insurance product where investment gains are not subject to income taxes (unless the contract is surrendered), gains at the time of transfer among accounts are not taxable.

It is assumed that investments in the underlying separate accounts will earn a modest compound return, such as 4 percent. This **assumed rate of return** is generally a rate necessary to maintain the level of cash values found in a traditional fixed-dollar straight life contract. Then, if actual investment returns exceed the assumed rate, (1) cash values increase more than assumed, and (2) these increases are used partly to purchase additional death benefits.

The additional death benefits are usually in the form of term insurance. The amount of term insurance can change (upward or downward) daily, monthly, or yearly, depending on the provisions of the contract. The total death benefit, at a point in time, becomes the amount of traditional straight life insurance that would be supported by a reserve equal to the policy's current cash value.

If separate account values fall below the assumed rate, (1) the cash value falls, and (2) one-year term elements of death protection are automatically surrendered. The net result is a new death benefit that corresponds to the amount of straight life that could be supported by the new cash value, subject to the minimum death benefit. These variable aspects are what give the contract its name. The nature of variable life insurance, with one-year term additions, is depicted in Figure 14.7.

Policy loans and contract surrenders can be handled by transferring funds out of the separate account. Loans are typically limited to 90 percent of the cash value at the time of the latest loan. Surrenders equal to the entire cash value minus any applicable surrender charge.

Some variable contracts are issued on a participating basis. Since investment experience is reflected directly in cash values, dividends reflect only unanticipated experience with respect to mortality and operating expenses.

Variable life insurance is technically a security as well as insurance. Therefore, it is regulated by the Securities and Exchange Commission (SEC)—which enforces the Investment Company Act of 1940, the Securities Act of 1933, and the Securities Exchange Act of 1934—as well as by state insurance departments. The SEC requires that an applicant be given a **prospectus** before being asked to sign an application for variable life. The prospectus explains the risks and usually illustrates how the death benefit and cash values would perform if future investment experience results in returns of 0, 4, 6, 8, 10, and 12 percent. Returns also can be illustrated based on historical experience of the Standard and Poor's 500 Stock Price Index. Because the product is a security, it can be sold only by agents who register with and pass an investments examination given by the National Association of Security Dealers.

A mid-range assumption (for example, 4 percent) produces a contract that performs exactly like traditional straight life insurance. The zero percent return would produce the minimum face amount; the cash value would be below normal for a period and go to zero at an advanced age. Because cash values cannot be negative, the policy would continue from the time the cash values reach zero until the death without cash values. At death, the minimum face amount would be paid. The 8 and 12 percent returns would produce cash values that grow much faster than those normal for an ordinary life policy; the total death benefit would continue to grow above the minimum face amount. These illustrations all assume continuous payment of the fixed annual premium.

Summary: Features of Variable Life

The cash value in a variable life policy fluctuates with the market value of one or more separate accounts. Death benefits, subject to a minimum face amount, vary up or down as the cash value changes. Success in achieving the objective of maintaining a death benefit that

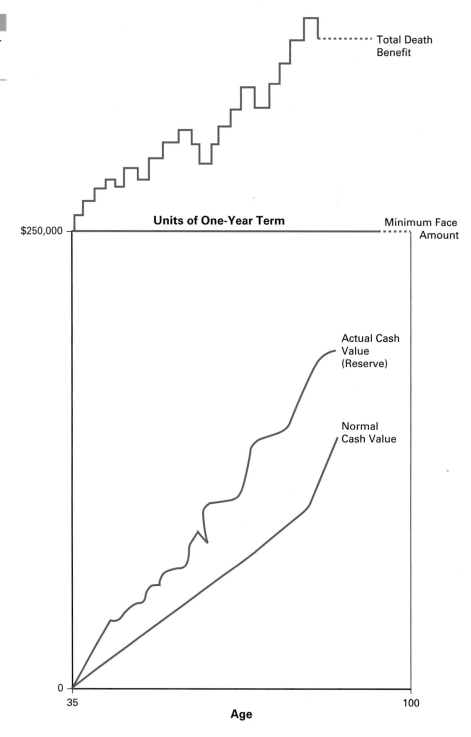

FIGURE 14.7

Hypothetical Values for
a Variable Life
Insurance Contract

Note: The relationship depicted between the Actual Cash Value and the Total Death Benefit is approximate. It has not been drawn precisely to scale.

keeps pace with inflation depends on the validity of the theory that certain investments are good inflation hedges.

All investment risks are borne by the policyowner, rather than by the insurer. The issuer of a variable life policy assumes only mortality and expense risks. Variable life is decreasing in popularity, probably because its fixed premium at a guaranteed level is higher initially than premiums on competing products. As you saw in Table 14.1, with the decline in the stock market, sales of variable life products are declining dramatically.

In summary, in variable life we see the following features (also see Table 14.2):

- Death benefits: Guaranteed minimum plus increases from investments
- Cash value: Minimum not guaranteed; depends on investment performance
- Premiums: Fixed level
- Policy loans: Yes
- Partial withdrawals: Not allowed
- Surrender charges: Yes

VARIABLE UNIVERSAL LIFE INSURANCE

In 1985, **variable universal life** was marketed for the first time. It combines the premium and death benefit flexibility of a universal policy design with the investment choices of variable life. This policy is also called flexible premium variable life insurance. Some insurers allow all premiums to vary after the first year of the contract. Others specify minimum premiums that would, if paid, continue death protection at least through age 65. Premiums can exceed these minimums. Single-premium policies are also available.

Like the universal life policyowner, the variable universal life policyowner decides periodically whether to decrease death protection (subject to the contract's minimum face amount) or increase death benefits (subject to evidence of insurability). One design specifies a fixed face amount, like universal life's type A design (see Figure 14.6), and allows investment experience to affect only cash values. Another design, like variable life, allows the total amount of protection to increase when cash values exceed their normal level for a straight life contract.

As with variable life, the assets backing variable universal policies are invested in separate accounts. The choices are like those for variable life policies, and the policyowner continues to assume all investment risks. The flow of funds due to expenses, mortality charges, and policy loans for both variable and variable universal work like those in universal policies. The outlook for the sale of variable universal policies is bright because the contract combines:

- The premium flexibility of universal life
- The death benefit flexibility of universal life
- Greater investment flexibility than universal life.
- The disclosure of universal and variable life
- The ability to withdraw cash values as policy loans without any tax penalties. (This is an advantage in comparison to annuities, rather than to other types of life insurance.)

Separate accounts are not general assets of an insurer. Therefore, they are protected in the event of the insurer's insolvency. The major drawback of variable universal life, as with variable life, is the transfer of all investment risk to the policyowner.

Summary: Features of Variable Universal Life

In summary, in variable universal life we see the following features:

- Death benefits: Guaranteed minimum plus increases from investments
- Cash value: Minimum not guaranteed; depends on investment performance
- Premiums: Flexible
- Policy loans: Allowed
- Partial withdrawals: Allowed
- Surrender charges: Yes

CURRENT ASSUMPTION WHOLE LIFE INSURANCE

In most respects, **current assumption whole life** policies work like universal life. The major difference is that, similar to traditional whole life contracts, the premiums are fixed. These policies do not have the flexible premium arrangements characteristic of universal life. Some current assumption designs emphasize low premiums (for example, $6 per year per $1,000 at age 25) and expect the premiums, with periodic adjustments, to be paid over the entire lifetime. Low-premium policies emphasize protection and appeal primarily to families or businesses with modest incomes. Medium- and high-premium alternatives for the same initial face amount might have premiums of $10 and $15 respectively. They emphasize cash values in the protection/investment mix and reduce the chances of the insurer having to request higher premiums to avoid the contract lapsing in later years.

After a current assumption contract is issued, the outlook for prospective (future) mortality and expenses can result in periodic increases or decreases in premiums. Some insurers adjust premiums annually; others make changes at three- or five-year intervals.

The higher-premium versions of current assumption policies usually include a contract provision allowing the policyowner to stop premium payments and essentially have a non-guaranteed, paid-up contract for the initial face amount. This **vanishing premiums provision** is triggered when the cash-value account has a balance equal to a net single premium for this amount of death benefit at the attained age. The net single premium is determined with current (at the time of vanish) investment and mortality assumptions. If future experience with the insurer's investments and mortality turns out to be less favorable, the single premium may prove to be insufficient. The policyowner could either resume premium payments or let the policy lapse. Thus, the policyowner retains some financial risk even for higher-premium current assumption policies where premiums have vanished. See the discussion of vanishing premiums in Chapter 6.

As is characteristic of universal life policies, minimum guaranteed interest rates are typically 4.0, 4.5, or 5.0 percent. Current assumption whole life is technically a non-participating policy, as is most universal life. Yet, like universal life, it shares the insurer's investment and mortality expectations with the insured (through excess interest credits). It is sometimes referred to as **interest-sensitive whole life** because of its participatory investment feature. The accumulation value and cash value are determined in the same manner as was described earlier for universal life policies.

The death benefit is usually a fixed, level amount, analogous to a type A universal life contract. Some insurers, however, offer an alternative death benefit equal to the original stated face amount plus the accumulation fund balance, analogous to a type B universal life design.

An annual disclosure statement shows the current investment credit, mortality charge, any applicable expenses, and surrender charges. Although the premium is not flexible, the current assumption product provides far more flexibility and transparency for consumers than is available in traditional whole life policies.

Summary: Features of Current Assumption Life

In summary, in current assumption life we see the following features:

- Death benefits: Fixed
- Cash value: Guaranteed minimum plus excess interest (like universal life)
- Premiums: Vary according to experience, but no higher than a set maximum
- Policy loans: Yes
- Partial withdrawals: Allowed
- Surrender charges: Yes

TAXATION

In the United States, we typically pay individual life insurance premiums out of funds on which we previously had paid income taxes. That is, premiums are paid from after-tax income. Therefore, there are no income taxes on the death benefits proceeds.

In general, when premiums are paid from after-tax income, death benefits are not part of the beneficiary's or anyone else's gross income.[7] Therefore, whether the death is soon or long after purchasing a $100,000 life insurance policy on life, the named beneficiary, irrespective of relationship, would not incur any federal income taxes on the proceeds, including gains within the cash value portion of the policy. Nontaxable proceeds also include non-basic benefits such as term riders, accidental death benefits, and paid-up additions. There are some exclusions, but a discussion of those is beyond the scope of this text. Some life insurance policies include dividends, and these policyholder dividends are excluded from federal income taxation. The federal government reasons that dividends constitute the return of an original overcharge of premiums. The premiums were paid with after-tax dollars, so any portion of those premiums, returned as a dividend, must have already been taxed as well. More will be said about dividends later in this chapter.

Except for single-premium life insurance, the purchase of most life insurance is motivated primarily by a need for death protection. The availability of private life insurance reduces pressures on government to provide welfare to families that experience premature deaths of wage earners. Furthermore, life insurance is owned by a broad cross section of U.S. society. This, along with effective lobbying by life insurers, may help explain the tax treatment of life insurance.

MAJOR POLICY PROVISIONS

The major policy provisions are listed in Table 14.3 for the sample whole life policy in Appendix E and in Table 14.4 for the sample universal life policy in Appendix F. Most of the explanations of the provisions relate to these sample policies, but also apply to other whole life and universal life policies of other insurers. For more comprehensive comparisons of each of the provisions you are invited to study the policies themselves.

TABLE 14.3	These provisions apply to most types of life insurance policies. The highlighted provision is the only one unique to whole life.
Main Policy Provisions in the Whole Life Policy in Appendix E	

Policy identification	Payment of benefits provisions
Schedule of benefits	Premium provisions
Schedule of premiums	Dividend provisions
Schedule of insurance and values	Guaranteed value provisions
Definitions	Policy loan provisions
Ownership provisions	General provisions

Both sample policies begin with a cover page (similar to any policy's declarations page) indicating the amounts of coverage and premiums. Since universal life has flexible premiums, the page also includes the monthly deduction statement. The second page in both policies relate to guarantees. While in the whole life policy the guaranteed cash value is shown along with other options (discussed later), the universal life provides a schedule of surrender charges and the maximum monthly cost of insurance rates as explained in the universal life section above.

The next section defines the terms in both of the sample policies. The definitions are preceded by an explanation of ownership.

Policy Ownership

The whole and universal life policies have similar ownership sections. **Ownership** refers to rights. The owner of a life insurance policy has rights, such as the right to assign the policy to someone else, to designate the beneficiary, to make a policy loan, or to surrender the policy for its cash value. When filling out the initial policy application, the policyowner designates whether the rights should stay with the insured or be assigned to another person, such as a spouse, or perhaps to a trust. The **ownership provision,** sometimes simply labeled "rights," shows this designation.

Death Benefits and Death Benefits Options Provisions

This section is unique to universal life policy, as would be expected from the lengthy explanation above regarding the two options of death benefits. On page 6 of Appendix F, you can see the wording of these options, the amounts of coverage, and changes to the amounts.

The **changes in basic amount provision** specifies the conditions under which a policyowner can change the total face amount of the policy. Any requested decreases take place on a monthly anniversary date and reduce the most recent additions to coverage (if any)

TABLE 14.4	These provisions apply to most types of life insurance policies. Those unique to universal life are highlighted.
Main Policy Provisions of the Universal Life Policy in Appendix F	

Policy identification	Ownership provisions
Schedule of benefits	**Death benefit and death benefit options provisions**
Schedule of premiums	
Monthly deductions	Payment of benefits provisions
Schedule of surrender charges	Premium provisions
Cost of insurance rates and monthly charges	Guaranteed value provisions
Definitions	Policy loan provisions
	General provisions

before affecting the initial face amount. Requests for increases in coverage must be made on a supplemental application and are subject to evidence of insurability.

Payment of Benefits Provisions

This section applies to both the sample whole life and the sample universal life policies and to other policies in general. The purpose of the **payment of benefits provision** is to enable the owner of the policy to designate to whom the proceeds shall be paid when the insured dies. If no beneficiary is named, the proceeds will go to the owner's estate. A **revocable beneficiary** can be changed at will by the policyowner. Most people prefer the revocable provision. **Irrevocable beneficiary** designations, on the other hand, can be changed only with the consent of the beneficiary. For example, a divorced spouse, as part of a property settlement, may be given an irrevocable interest in life insurance on his or her former spouse. The former spouse, as the insured and policyowner, would be required to continue premium payments but could not make a policy loan or other changes that would diminish the rights of the irrevocable beneficiary.

A beneficiary must survive the insured in order to be entitled to the proceeds of the policy. It is customary, therefore, to name one or more beneficiaries who are entitled to the proceeds in the event that the primary (first-named) beneficiary does not survive the insured. These are known as secondary or tertiary **contingent beneficiaries.** Such beneficiaries are named and listed in the order of their priority.

If the insured and the primary beneficiary die in the same accident and no evidence shows who died first, there is a question as to whether the proceeds shall be paid to the estate of the primary beneficiary or to a contingent beneficiary. In states where the Uniform Simultaneous Death Act has been enacted, the proceeds are distributed as if the insured had survived the beneficiary. Where this act is not in effect, the courts have usually reached the same conclusion. If no contingent beneficiary has been named, the proceeds go to the estate of the policyowner, thus subjecting them to estate taxes (discussed in Chapter 19), probate costs, and the claims of creditors. Probate costs are levied by the court that certifies that an estate has been settled properly. Probate costs (but not estate taxes) are avoided when benefits go to a named beneficiary.

A similar problem arises when the primary beneficiary survives the insured by only a short period. In such a case, the proceeds may be depleted by taxes and costs associated with the beneficiary's estate settlement or because an annuity-type settlement option had been selected. This problem can be solved by adding a **common disaster provision** (or survivorship clause), which provides that the beneficiary must survive the insured by a specified period of time (for example, seven to thirty days) or must be alive at the time of payment to be entitled to the proceeds. If neither of these conditions is fulfilled, the proceeds go to a contingent beneficiary or to the estate of the policyowner if a contingent beneficiary has not been named.

policyowners should designate the beneficiary clearly. No questions should exist about the identity of the beneficiary at the time of the insured's death. In designating children as beneficiaries, one must keep in mind that a minor is not competent to receive payment. In the event of the death of the insured prior to the maturity of a beneficiary child, a guardian may have to be appointed to receive the proceeds on behalf of the child. As a general rule, policyowners should avoid naming minors as beneficiaries. Where the objective is a substantial estate to benefit a child or children, the preferable approach would be to name a trust as beneficiary. The child or children (the ones already born and those to be born or join the family unit after a divorce and remarriage) could be the beneficiary(ies) of the trust.

Payment Methods

Life insurance is designed to create a sum of money that can be used when the insured dies or the owner surrenders a cash-value policy. In the early days of life insurance, the only form in which the death proceeds or cash value of a policy were paid was in a lump sum. Because a lump-sum payment is not desirable in all circumstances, several additional **settlement options** (also called payment plans) have been developed and are now included in most policies. The owner may select an option in advance or leave the choice to the beneficiary. The owner may also change the option from time to time if the beneficiary designation is revocable. The payment plans have the following methods for death proceeds (for detailed explanation see pages 6 and 7 of the sample whole life policy in Appendix E and pages 7 and 8 in the sample universal life policy in Appendix F):

- Interest method—The beneficiary leaves the proceeds with the insurer and collects only the interest
- Fixed years method—even distribution of the proceeds over a certain number of years
- Life income method—even distribution of the proceeds over the life of the beneficiary
- Fixed amount method—even distribution of the proceeds until depleted
- Joint life income method—even distribution of the proceeds over the life of the beneficiary with continued distribution to his/her beneficiary at the same or reduced level
- One-sum method—a lump-sum distribution
- Other method as agreed upon

Premium Provisions

This section also applies to both the whole and the universal life policies. Premiums are payable on the due date on a monthly, quarterly, semiannual, or annual basis. The first premium must be paid in advance while the insured is in good health and otherwise insurable. Subsequent premiums are due in advance of the period to which they apply. Insurance companies send a notice to the policyowner indicating when the premium is due. The time horizon over which premiums are payable depends on the type of policy (for example, through age 99 for a straight life policy), and will be stated on the cover page. Note in the sample universal life policy that the premium limitations section allows the insurer to refund any overpayment of premiums. As you know, such possibility may occur because of the flexible premium allowed for universal life policies.

Grace Period

The law requires that the contract contain a provision entitling the policyowner to a **grace period** within which payment of a past-due premium (excluding the first premium) must be accepted by the insurer. The grace period is thirty-one days in the whole life sample in Appendix E. Although the premium is past due during this period, the policy remains in force. If the insured dies during the grace period, the face amount of the policy minus the amount of the premium past due will be paid to the beneficiary. If the premium is not paid during the grace period of a traditional policy, a nonforfeiture option (to be discussed later) becomes effective. The purpose of the grace period is to prevent unintentional lapses. If it were not for this provision, an insured whose premium was paid one day late would have to prove his or her insurability in order to have the policy reinstated.

In variable, universal, and other flexible-premium policies, the grace period is usually sixty days, as seen in the universal life policy in Appendix F. This has meaning only when the cash value is not large enough to cover expense and mortality deductions for the next period. Most insurers notify the policyowner of such a situation. The cash surrender value in the first few policy years may be zero due to surrender charges. In that event, most universal and variable policies also contain a grace period exception clause. This clause states that during a specified period of time (generally the first few policy years, even if the policy has a negative surrender value), as long as at least the stated minimum premium has been paid during the grace period, the policy will continue in force.

Nonpayment of Premium, Accumulation to Avoid Lapse, and Automatic Premium Loans

The nonpayment of premium, accumulation to avoid lapse, and automatic premium loans sections apply only to whole life policies, as should be clear from the nature of inflexible premiums. Regarding **automatic premium loans,** if the owner selects this option, at the end of the grace period, loans are taken automatically from the cash value to pay the premiums. The owner is charged interest and can cancel this provision at any time.

Reinstatement

This section applies to both sample policies. If the grace period has expired with a premium still due, the policy is considered to have lapsed. An owner who wants to reinstate the policy, rather than apply for new insurance, must follow certain requirements. The **reinstatement provision** provides that unless the policy has been surrendered for cash, it may be reinstated at any time within five (in some cases, three, ten, or more) years after premium payments were stopped. Payment of all overdue premiums on the policy and other indebtedness to the insurer, plus interest on these items, is required along with payment of the current premium. Usually, the insured must provide satisfactory evidence of current insurability. This provision is shown on page 8 of the sample whole life policy in Appendix E, and page 9 of the universal life sample in Appendix F.

Evidence of insurability may be as strict in the case of reinstatement as it is for obtaining new life insurance. The insurer may be interested in health, occupation, hobbies, and any other factors that may affect the probability of early death. For recently lapsed policies, most insurers require only a personal health statement from the insured. Universal and variable policies typically provide reinstatement without requiring payment of back premiums as noted in Appendix F. In this event, the cash value of the reinstated policy equals the amount provided by the premium paid, after deductions for the cost of insurance protection and expenses.

Premium Adjustment When the Insured Dies

In whole life policies only, after the death of the insured the insurers refund any premium paid but unearned. For example, if an annual premium was paid on January 1 and the insured died on September 30, 25 percent (reflecting the remaining three months of the year) of the premium would be refunded. Most insurers explain their practice in a contract **premium refund provision.**

Dividend Options

Participating policies of mutual insurers, such as State Farm, share in the profits the insurer earns because of lower-than-anticipated expenses, lower-than-expected mortality, and greater-than-expected investment earnings. The amounts returned to policyowners are called dividends. Dividends also involve the return of any premium overpayment. Dividends are payable annually on the policy anniversary. They are not guaranteed, but are a highly significant element in many policies.

When purchasing a participating life insurance policy, the policyowner can choose how the dividend money should be spent, from one or more of the following **dividend options** (see page 9 in Appendix E):

- Applied toward the next premium
- Used to buy paid-up additional insurance
- Left with the insurer to accumulate interest
- Paid to the policyholder

The majority of companies offer these four options. The selection of the appropriate dividend option is an important decision.

Guaranteed Values Provisions

This section illustrates the major differences between the whole life and universal life policies. A whole life policy guarantees that a policyholder who decides to cancel the policy can either take cash for the surrender (cash) value or continue the policy in force as extended term insurance and paid-up insurance. These provisions are also called **nonforfeiture options** in other policies. The sample whole life policy lists these amounts in the Schedule of Insurance and Values on page 4 of Appendix E.

As pointed out earlier, the cash value life plan results in the accumulation of a savings (or cash value element, from the insured's perspective) that usually increases as each year passes. If the contract is terminated, the policyholder can receive the cash value or the policy can be converted to **extended term insurance** or **paid up insurance.** Under the extended term insurance option, the death benefit continues at its previous level for as long as the cash value supports this amount of term insurance (like a single premium life). Under the paid-up insurance option, it is as if there is a new policy with a lower lifetime death benefit than the old one did. The death benefits are paid up completely without expiration date. Both extended term and paid-up options are nonforfeiture options.

With universal, current assumption, and variable universal life policies, the policyowner may discontinue premium payments at any time without lapsing the policy, as long as the surrender value is sufficient to cover the next deduction for cost of insurance and expenses. In the universal life policy there is a description of the account value at the end of the first month. It is 95 percent of the initial premium less the monthly deduction. Thereafter, there are adjustments that take the interest rate into account. The following sections are covered in the sample universal life in Appendix F:

- Account value
- Monthly deduction
- Cost of insurance
- Monthly cost of insurance rates (maximum rates are shown on page 4)
- Interest (guaranteed at 4 percent in the sample policy)
- Cash surrender value
- Withdrawals
- Surrender charges
- Basis of computation, which includes the table of surrender charges

Policy Loan Provisions

Policy loan provisions apply to both the whole life and the universal life policies. The owner can borrow an amount up to the cash value from the insurer at a rate of interest specified in the policy, and up to the account value in universal life. In the sample universal life policy in Appendix F, the interest rate is set at 8 percent. In the whole life policy, the majority of insurers use a fixed rate of interest or a variable rate as indicated in the sample whole life policy in Appendix E, page 11.

General Provisions

Both the whole life and the universal life sample policies conclude with general provisions sections that include the following:

- The contract
- Annual report (universal life only)
- Projection of benefits and values (universal life only)
- Annual dividend (universal life only)
- Dividend options (universal life only as part of this section; see dividends for whole life above as a separate section)
- Assignment
- Error in age or sex
- Incontestability
- Limited death benefits (suicide clause)

The Contract

The written policy and the attached application constitute the entire agreement between the insurer and the policyowner. Because of this contract provision, agents cannot, orally or in writing, change or waive any terms of the contract. Statements in the application are considered representations, rather than warranties. This means that only those material statements that would have caused the insurer to make a different decision about issuance of the policy, its terms, or premiums will be considered valid grounds to void the contract.

Annual Report and Projection of Benefits and Values

As would be expected from the discussion above, the changes in the universal life values require reporting to the policyowner on a regular basis. These provisions state the obligation of the insurer to provide such annual reports. The projection of death benefits is not automatic. The policyowner can request it and may be charged $25 as shown in the sample policy in Appendix F, page 12.

Assignment

As mentioned, the owner of a life insurance policy can transfer part or all of the rights to someone else. The **assignment provision** provides, however, that the company will not be bound by any assignment until it has received notice, that any indebtedness to the company shall have priority over any assignment, and that the company is not responsible for the validity of any assignment. This provision helps the company avoid litigation about who is entitled to policy benefits, and it protects the insurer from paying twice. As you can see in the sample policies in Appendices E and F, the "assignment may limit the interest of the beneficiary."

Errors in Age and Sex

Age and sex have a direct bearing on the cost of life insurance. They are, therefore, material facts. Thus, the **misstatement of age or sex** would ordinarily provide grounds, within the contestable period, for rescinding the contract. Most state laws, however, require that all policies include a provision that if age or sex has been misstated, the amount of the insurance will be adjusted to that which the premium paid would have covered correctly.

Incontestability

A typical **incontestable provision** makes a contract incontestable after it has been in force for two years during the lifetime of the insured. If the insured dies before the end of the two years, the policy is contestable on the basis of material misrepresentations, concealment, and fraud in the application. If the insured survives beyond the contestable period, the policy cannot be contested even for fraud. An exception is fraud of a gross nature, such as letting someone else take the medical exam. While the incontestable clause may force the insurer to do considerably more investigating (part of the underwriting process) before contracts are issued than would otherwise be the case, and perhaps does result in some claims being paid that should not be, it is important to the honest policyowner who wants to be confident that his or her insurance proceeds will be paid upon death.

Limited Death Benefits (Suicide Clause)

In both sample policies, the insured is not to be paid death benefits in case of suicide within two years. (In some policies, the duration is only one year.) This is sometimes called the **suicide clause.** As you can see in the sample universal life policy in Appendix F, page 13, when coverage is increased, the additional insurance is subject to a new suicide exclusion period. If the company wishes to deny a claim on the grounds that death was caused by suicide during the period of exclusion, it must prove conclusively that the death was suicide.

LIFE INSURANCE RIDERS

Through the use of **riders,** life insurance policies may be modified to provide special benefits. Under specified circumstances, these riders may waive premiums if the policyholder becomes disabled, provide disability income, provide accidental death benefits, guarantee issuance of additional life insurance, and pay accelerated death benefits (before death).

Waiver of Premium

The **waiver of premium rider** is offered by all life insurance companies and is included in about half of the policies sold. Some companies automatically provide it without charging an explicit amount of additional premium. The rider provides that premiums due after commencement of the insured's total disability shall be waived for a period of time. A waiting period of six months must be satisfied first. In flexible premium contracts such as universal and variable universal life, the waiver of premium provision specifies that the target premium to keep the policy in force will be credited to the insured's account during disability.[8] If a premium was paid after disability began and before the expiration of a waiting period, the premium is refunded. When disability begins before a certain age, usually age 60, premiums are waived as long as the insured remains totally disabled.

Definition of Disability

To qualify for disability benefits, the disability must be total and permanent, and must occur prior to a specified age. Disability may be caused by either accidental injury or sickness; no distinction is made. Typically, for the first two years of benefit payments, the insured is considered totally disabled whenever, because of injury or disease, he or she is unable to perform the duties of the regular occupation. Beyond two years, benefits usually continue only if the insured is unable to perform the duties of any occupation for which he or she qualified by reason of education, training, and experience. A minority of insurers uses this more restrictive definition from the beginning of the waiver period. Most insurers and courts interpret the definition liberally. Most riders define blindness or loss of both hands, both feet, or one hand and one foot as presumptive total disability. Typically, disability longer than six months is considered to be permanent. Circumstances may later contradict this assumption, as proof (generally in the form of a physician's statement) of continued disability is usually required once a year up to age 65.

Disability Income

The **disability income rider** provides a typical income benefit of $10 per month per $1,000 of initial face amount of life insurance for as long as total disability continues and after the first six months of such disability, provided it commences before age 55 or 60. Disability payments are usually made for the balance of the insured's life as long as total disability continues. Under some contracts, payments stop at age 65 and the policy matures as an **endowment,** but this is less favorable than continuation of income benefits.

The definitions of disability for these riders are like those for waiver of premium provisions. Most disability income insurance is now sold either through a group plan (for an example, see Chapter 16 and Case 2) or as separate individual policies. Most life insurers do not offer this rider.

Accidental Death Benefit

The **accidental death benefit rider** is sometimes called **double indemnity.** It usually provides that double the face amount of the policy will be paid if the insured's death is caused by accident, and, sometimes, triple the face amount if death occurs while the insured is riding as a paying passenger in a public conveyance.[9] Figure 14.8 illustrates the accidental death benefit rider.

A typical definition of accidental death is, "Death resulting from bodily injury independently and exclusively of all other causes and within ninety days after such injury." Certain causes of death are typically excluded: suicide, violations of the law, gas or poison, war, and certain aviation activities other than as a passenger on a scheduled airline. This rider is usually in effect to the insured's age 70.

Guaranteed Insurability Option

Many insurers will add a **guaranteed insurability option** (GIO) to policies for an additional premium. This gives the policyowner the right to buy additional amounts of insurance, usually at three-year intervals up to a specified age, without new proof of insurability.

FIGURE 14.8

Accidental Death
Benefits Rider

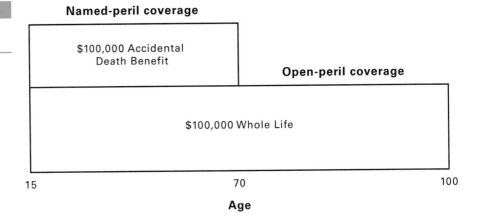

The usual age of the last option is 40; a small number of insurers allow it up to age 65. The amount of each additional purchase is usually equal to or less than the face amount of the original policy. If a $50,000 straight or interest-sensitive life policy with the GIO rider is purchased at age 21, the policyowner can buy an additional $50,000 every three years thereafter to age 40, whether or not the insured is still insurable. By age 40, the total death benefit would equal $350,000. The new insurance is issued at standard rates on the basis of the insured's attained age when the option is exercised. The GIO rider ensures one's insurability. It becomes valuable if the insured becomes uninsurable or develops a condition that would prevent the purchase of new life insurance at standard rates.

Accelerated Death Benefits

Some medical conditions regularly result in high medical expenses for the insured and his or her family or other caregivers. The need for funds may significantly exceed benefits provided by medical and disability insurance because of deductibles, coinsurance, caps on benefits, and exclusions, and (perhaps primarily) because of having purchased inadequate coverage. **Accelerated death benefits** are triggered by either the occurrence of a catastrophic (dread) illness or the diagnosis of a terminal illness, resulting in payment of a portion of a life insurance policy's face amount prior to death.

The accelerated benefits are also called **living benefits,** or **terminal illness rider.** Usually, the terminally ill insured can receive up to 50 percent of the death benefits to improve life quality before death. Often, the coverage is provided without an additional premium. The benefit can usually be claimed when two doctors agree that the insured has six months or less to live. When the insured desires greater amounts, he or she may use a **viatical settlement** company to transfer the ownership of the policy to a third party in return for a higher percentage of the death benefits, perhaps 80 percent. A more detailed discussion of viaticals is provided in Chapter 16 and in that chapter's "Ethical Dilemma: Do Viatical Settlements Have a Place in Today's Market?"

Catastrophic Illness Coverage

When a **catastrophic illness rider** is added to a life insurance policy (usually requiring an additional premium), a portion (usually 25 to 50 percent) of the face amount is payable upon diagnosis of specified illnesses. The named illnesses differ among insurers, but typically include organ transplantation.

As benefits are paid out under either a catastrophic or terminal illness rider, the face amount of the basic policy is reduced an equal amount and an interest charge applies in some policies. Cash values are reduced either in proportion to the death benefit reduction or on a dollar-for-dollar basis.

ADJUSTING LIFE INSURANCE FOR INFLATION

Participating policies, current assumption whole life policies, and universal life policies recognize inflation in a limited manner. Participating contracts can respond to inflation through dividends. Dividends can be used each year to purchase additional amounts of paid-up life insurance, but these small amounts of additional protection seldom keep pace with inflation.

Interest-sensitive contracts partly recognize inflation by crediting investment earnings directly to cash values. We say "partly recognize" because cash values in these policies are primarily invested in short-term debt instruments like government securities and in short-term corporate bonds, and the interest rates for these have an expected inflation component at the time they are issued. The expected inflation component is there because, in addition to a basic return on the money being loaned and an increase to reflect financial risks of failure, investors in debt instruments require an incremental return to cover their projections of future inflation rates. Thus, contracts with direct crediting of insurer investment returns to cash values give some recognition to inflation. The recognition is weak, however, for two reasons. First, the protection element of these contracts does not respond quickly, or at all for type A contracts, to inflation.[10] The protection element is expressed in fixed dollars and, as a storehouse of value and purchasing power, the dollar certainly is not ideal. Second, in a portfolio of primarily debt instruments, all except newly purchased parts reflect inflation expectations formed in the past. These expectations can grossly underestimate current and future rates of inflation.

Buy More Life Insurance

As long as you are insurable, you can buy more life insurance as your needs increase. What if you become uninsurable? You can protect yourself against that possibility by buying a policy with a guaranteed insurability option; however, this has drawbacks. First, the option is limited to a specified age, such as 40, and you may need more insurance after that age. Second, you must buy the same kind of insurance as the policy you have. Third, the premium will be higher due to your age.

Buy a Cost-of-Living Rider or Policy

Another alternative is the **inflation rider** or **cost-of-living rider,** which automatically increases the amount of insurance as the Consumer Price Index rises. It provides term insurance as an addition to the face amount of your permanent or term policy up to a point such as age 55. If, for example, you have a $100,000 whole life policy and the CPI goes up 5 percent this year, $5,000 of one-year term insurance is automatically written for next year at the premium rate for your age. You are billed for it along with the premium notice for your basic policy. Since your premium increases with each increase in coverage, you may conclude that you bear the risk of keeping your coverage up with inflation. Keep in mind that no evidence of insurability is required. You do not have to accept (and pay for) the additional insurance if you don't want it. If you refuse to exercise the option, however, it is no longer available. In other words, you can't say, "I'm short of funds this year,

TABLE 14.5 Inflation Rider Option (at 5 Percent Annual Inflation)	**Year**	**Consumer Price Index**	**Basic Insurance Amount**	**Option Amount**	**Total Death Benefit**

Year	Consumer Price Index	Basic Insurance Amount	Option Amount	Total Death Benefit
1995	1.00000	$100,000		$100,000
1996	1.05000	100,000	$5,000	105,000
1997	1.10250	100,000	10,250	110,250
1998	1.15763	100,000	15,763	115,763
1995	1.21551	100,000	21,551	121,551
1996	1.27628	100,000	27,628	127,628
1997	1.34010	100,000	34,010	134,010
1998	1.40710	100,000	40,710	140,710
1999	1.47746	100,000	47,746	147,746
2000	1.55133	100,000	55,133	155,133
2001	1.62889	100,000	62,889	162,889
2002	1.71034	100,000	71,034	171,034
2003	1.79586	100,000	79,586	179,586
2004	1.88565	100,000	88,565	188,565
2005	1.97993	100,000	97,993	197,993
2006	2.07893	100,000	107,893	207,893
2007	2.18287	100,000	118,287	218,287
2008	2.29202	100,000	129,202	229,202
2009	2.40662	100,000	140,662	240,662
2010	2.52659	100,000	152,659	252,659
2011	2.65330	100,000	165,330	265,330

but I will exercise the option next year." Table 14.5 illustrates how the inflation rider option would affect your total amount of insurance if you had bought a $100,000 whole life policy in 1995 and the inflation rate was 5 percent every year.

Buy a Variable or Variable Universal Life Policy

The face amount of variable life and variable universal life (except for the level face amount type) policies fluctuates with the performance of one or more separate accounts. You have the option of directing most of your premiums into common stock accounts where long-run returns are expected to offset CPI increases.

If you buy a variable life policy, you assume the risk that the equity markets may be going down at the same time that the CPI is going up. Should you buy a variable life policy? The answer depends on you. How much investment risk are you willing to take in coping with inflation?

KEY TERMS

premium elements	term life	whole life
yearly renewable term	lapse rates	straight life
level premium	renewability option	limited-payment life
ordinary (whole) life	convertibility option	single premium
reserve	attained age	dividends
net amount at risk	mortgage protection	portfolio returns
protection element	credit life	universal life
cash value	reentry term	unbundling

disclosure statement
transparency
accumulation value
flow of funds
death benefit options
COLA riders
current mortality rate
maximum mortality rate
front-end expenses
surrender expenses
indexed investment
 strategy
new money rate
variable life
assumed rate of return
prospectus
variable universal life
current assumption whole
 life
vanishing premiums
 provision

interest-sensitive whole life
ownership
ownership provision
changes in basic amount
 provision
payment of benefits
 provision
revocable beneficiary
irrevocable beneficiary
contingent beneficiaries
common disaster provision
settlement options
grace period
automatic premium loan
reinstatement provision
premium refund provision
dividend options
nonforfeiture options
extended term insurance
paid-up insurance
policy loan provision

assignment provision
misstatement of age or sex
incontestable provision
suicide clause
riders
waiver of premium rider
disability income rider
endowments
accidental death benefit
 rider (double indemnity)
guaranteed insurability
 option
accelerated death benefits
living benefits
terminal illness
viatical settlement
catastrophic illness rider
inflation rider (cost of
 living rider)

DISCUSSION QUESTIONS

1. Would you expect one-year term insurance that is renewable and convertible to require a higher premium than one-year term insurance without these features? Explain.

2. Explain why an investment (cash value) segment becomes a part of a level-premium life insurance contract.

3. In what way is the reentry feature of term insurance desirable to policyholders? Is it a valuable policy feature after you become unhealthy?

4. How may the participating whole life policy share higher-than-expected investment earnings?

5. Explain the nature of the reserve an insurer accumulates in connection with its level-premium life insurance policies.

6. Compare term life to universal life and to variable life insurance in terms of (a) death benefits, (b) cash value, (c) premium, and (d) policy loans. Refer to the sample policies in Appendices E and F.

7. What elements of a universal life contract are separated or unbundled relative to their treatment in a traditional life insurance policy? How does a "disclosure statement" help implement the separation and create transparency?

8. Explain the two death benefit options that are available to you when you purchase a universal life or current assumption policy.

9. When the dollar value of your home increases because of inflation, the insurer normally automatically increases the amount of insurance on your dwelling and its contents. Why does your life insurer require evidence of insurability before allowing you to increase the face value of your universal life insurance policy? (Assume no cost of living rider or guaranteed insurability rider.) How do you explain this difference between insuring homes and human lives?

10. What is the major difference between a current assumption life policy and a universal life policy? Why might a life insurer prefer issuing current assumption policies?

11. What is the objective of variable life insurance? Can this objective be achieved through a variable universal life policy with a level face amount (i.e., one like a type A universal life contract)?

12. Who bears the investment risk in variable life and universal variable life policies? How does this differ from investment risks borne by the buyer of a universal life policy?

13. The premium on Bill Brown's traditional whole life policy was due September 1. On September 15, he mailed a check to the insurance company. On September 26, he died. When the insurance company presented the check to the bank for collection, it was returned because there were insufficient funds in Bill's account. Does the company have to pay the claim presented by Bill's beneficiary? Why, or why not? What provisions might result in payment?

14. Clancy knew he could not meet the physical requirements for insurability, so he had his twin brother, Clarence, take the physical examination in his place. A policy was issued, and three years later, Clancy died. The insurance company claims manager learned that Clancy's twin took the examination in his place and refused to pay the claim. Clancy's beneficiary sued the company for the proceeds, claiming that the two-year contestable period had expired. Did the company have to pay? Why, or why not?

15. If you don't need life insurance now but realize you may need it sometime in the future, would you be interested in buying a guaranteed insurability option, if it were available, without buying a policy now? Why, or why not?

16. What desirable features characterize the policy loan provision of a cash-value life insurance policy relative, for example, to borrowing money from a bank? How do policy loans affect death benefits?

17. Explain how universal life policies transfer mortality risk (subject to a limit) to you. Does the provision that creates this risk have an "up side" that may allow you to participate in your insurer's good fortunes?

18. Describe the nature of what is purchased by the dividend on a life insurance policy when it is used to buy "paid-up additions."

EXERCISES

14.1 George and Mary Keys are very excited over the news that they are to be parents. Since their graduation from college three years ago, they have purchased a new house and a new car. They owe $130,000 on the house and $8,000 on the car. Their only life insurance consists of $75,000 of term coverage on George and $50,000 on Mary. This coverage is provided by their employers as an employee benefit. Their personal balance sheet shows a net worth (assets minus liabilities) of $80,000. George is rapidly moving up within his company as special projects engineer. His current annual salary is $60,000. In anticipation of the new arrival, George is considering the purchase of additional life insurance. He feels that he needs at least $500,000 in coverage, but his budget for life insurance is somewhat limited. The couple has decided that Mary will stay at home with the new baby and put her career on hold for ten years or so while this baby and perhaps a later sibling or two are young.

    a. As George's agent, advise him as to the type(s) of life insurance that seem(s) most appropriate for his situation.

    b. George indicates to you that his financial situation will change in five years when he receives a one-time payment of approximately $100,000 from his uncle's estate. In what way would this affect the type of life insurance you recommend to George?

14.2 Your wealthy Aunt Mabel, age 64, recently talked to you, her life insurance agent, regarding her desire to see that her great-niece has the funds to attend college. Aunt Mabel is in very good health and expects to live for many years to come. She does not know if she should put aside money in certificates of deposit at the bank, buy more insurance on herself, or choose some other plan of action. She simply knows that her great-niece will need at least $80,000 to pay for her college education in ten years. What type of investment and/or insurance program would you recommend for her? Why?

14.3 Phil Pratt has decided that the lowest-premium form of life insurance is definitely the best buy. Consequently, he has purchased a $250,000 yearly renewable term life insurance policy as his only life insurance.

Explain why you agree or disagree with Phil's philosophy.

a. Will his decision have any possible adverse effects in later years?

b. Are there any realistic alternatives available to him without making premiums too high at a young age?

14.4 Betty Bick, age 40, is considering the purchase of a limited-payment participating life insurance policy which would be paid up at age 60. She plans to work until then and does not wish to pay any premiums after she retires, but she definitely wants whole life insurance protection. Betty earns $45,000 per year as a branch manager for a commercial bank. As a single mother she has been unable to accumulate much wealth. At this time, Betty has dependent children ages 10 and 14.

a. Explain to her any alternatives that would meet the criteria she has established.

b. Why do you think her choice is a good (or bad) one? What additional information would you like to have before feeling confident about your answer?

14.5 Lane Golden has just purchased a universal life insurance policy from Midwest Great Life. Initially, Lane pays a first-month premium of $100. Her policy has (1) a front-end load of $2.00 per month, (2) a surrender charge equal to 100 percent of the minimum first-year premiums of $1,200 ($100 per month), decreasing 20 percent of the original surrender charge per year until it disappears after five years, (3) a current monthly mortality rate of $0.15 per $1,000 of protection (amount at risk), and (4) a current monthly investment return of 0.667 percent. Her policy is a type B one, with a level $100,000 protection element.

a. Construct a flow of funds statement, like the one in Figure 14.6, for the first month of Lane's policy.

b. Explain why her accumulation value and cash value will be equal if she continues her policy for more than five years.

14.6 The following insureds have accidental death benefit riders on their life insurance policies. Discuss why you think this rider will or will not pay the beneficiary in each of the following situations.

a. The insured dies from a fall through a dormitory window on the tenth floor. The door to his room is locked from the inside, and the window has no ledge. There is no suicide note. He had not appeared despondent.

b. The insured dies in a high-speed single-car automobile accident, on a clear day and with no apparent mechanical malfunction in the vehicle. He had been very depressed about his job and had undergone therapy with a counselor, during which he had discussed suicide; however, there is no note.

c. The insured contracts pneumonia after she is hospitalized due to injuries received from a fall from a ladder while rescuing a cat from a tree. She has a history of pneumonia and other serious respiratory problems. She dies of pneumonia thirty days after the fall.

NOTES

1. Some insurers use one provision to correct misstatements of age or sex to cover the possible misstatement of either.
2. *Life Insurance Fact Book,* American Council of Life Insurers, 2002, p. 3.
3. *Life Insurance Fact Book,* American Council of Life Insurers, 2002, p. 54
4. *Life Insurance Fact Book,* American Council of Life Insurers, 2002, p. 100.
5. Before buying a mortgage protection policy, consider the pros and cons of paying off your mortgage at the time of death. Will your spouse's income be sufficient to meet the mortgage payments? Is the interest rate likely to be attractive in the future? Will the after-tax interest rate be less than the rate of growth in the value of the house, resulting in favorable leverage?
6. The advertised rate of return credited to the account is likely to be higher than the true rate of return being earned on the cash value element of the contract. This issue was discussed at length in Chapter 7 regarding vanishing premiums and market conduct.
7. Tax law changes in 1988 made single-premium surrenders and policy loans undesirable because any gain over net premiums becomes taxable immediately. Furthermore, gains are subject to an additional 10 percent tax penalty if the policyowner is less than age 59½. Thus, the tendency of single-premium buyers is to let the policy mature as a death claim. At that time there are no adverse income tax effects.
8. An alternative to the waiver of premium rider for flexible premium contracts waives only the amount required to cover mortality cost and expense deductions.
9. Policies with flexible face amounts usually issue the accidental death rider for a fixed amount equal to the basic policy's initial face amount.
10. Small recognition in total death benefits exists in type B universal policies because any increases in cash values as a result of higher interest rates are added to a level amount of protection. Dividends may be used to buy additional amounts of insurance, but the relationship to inflation is weak.

CHAPTER 15

Social Security

The mandatory coverage for life cycle events risk is Social Security. As noted in Chapter 13, **Social Security** is a major social insurance program that was created in 1935 as an outcome of the depression era. Originally, this program was a compulsory pension plan known as Old Age Insurance, or OAI. Later, survivors' benefits were added and the program became known as Old Age and Survivors' Insurance, or OASI. When disability benefits were added, it became OASDI, and, with the addition of hospital and medical benefits, it became the **OASDHI** program. Social Security is not need-based and is dependent upon a person's employment history. Its objective is to provide a "floor of protection" or a "reasonable level of living." Figure 15.1 illustrates the idea of a "floor of protection." Social Security is the foundation upon which retirement, survivors', and disability benefits should be designed. In addition, the program is the foundation of health benefits for the retired population under Medicare Parts A and B. This chapter is positioned here in the text to emphasize the importance of Social Security as a foundation to employer-provided benefits, such as group life, disability, and health insurance and retirement programs.

Most U.S. workers—full-time, part-time, self-employed, and temporary employees—are part of the Social Security program. Every employer and employee is required to contribute in the form of payroll taxes. Social Security provides income in the event of retirement, disability, or death. It also provides medical expense benefits for disabled or retired persons and their specified dependents.[1] As of December 2001, 39 million people were receiving Old Age and Survivors' Insurance (OASI, retirement) benefits, 6.9 million were receiving disability benefits, and about 40 million were covered under Medicare. In 2001, non-interest income to the Social Security Trust Fund exceeded disbursements by $90 billion; income exceeded disbursements from the Medicare Hospital Insurance Trust Fund by $17 billion.[2]

This chapter includes the following discussion points:

1. Connection
2. Definition of Social Security
3. Coverage and eligibility requirements
4. Types and amounts of benefits
5. Financing of benefits
6. Medicare
7. Issues
8. Global trends

FIGURE 15.1   Connection between Risks and Social Security Benefits

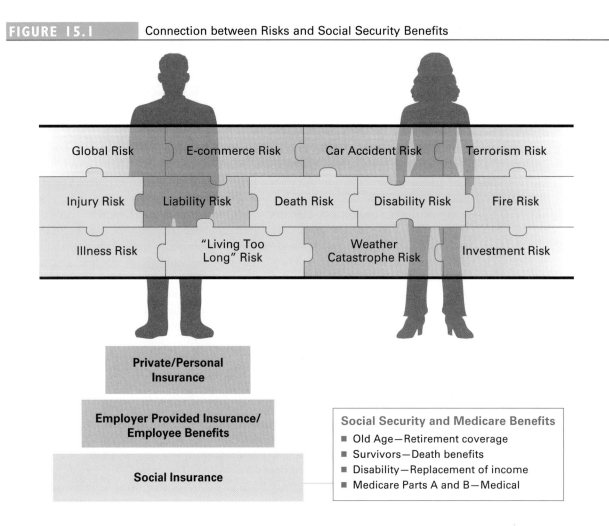

CONNECTION

At this point in our study, we get into the foundation of coverages for many of the life cycle, injury, and illness risks. While in Chapter 14 we talked about life insurance policies provided through individual purchases, now we are moving into a basic mandatory package of coverages that is tied to belonging to the workforce in the United States. Social Security's mandatory coverages are the first step in building the pyramid of coverages to assure our complete holistic risk management process. In Figure 15.1, using the familiar stepstool, you can see that Social Security is the basic foundation of coverages for life cycle risks, depicted in our holistic risk picture.

As before, for our holistic risk management we need to look at all sources of coverages available. Understanding each component of the coverages from the various sources is critical to completing the picture and ensuring we have adequately managed all our risks. Social insurance programs (including workers' compensation and unemployment compensation discussed in Chapter 13) play an important role in financial planning and should be considered when assessing the risk of economic loss due to premature death, disability, or retirement. The amount each individual must save for such situations is effectively reduced by the expected benefits from social insurance programs. The Social Security Administration sends an annual statement to all workers that includes earning history and projected future benefits. Table 15.1A provides a rough estimate of retirement benefits for various income levels and Table 15.1B provides the estimated average income by beneficiary category.

DEFINITION OF SOCIAL SECURITY

There are many governmental programs designed to provide economic security for individuals and families. Both public assistance (also referred to as welfare programs) and **social insurance** programs are organized and undertaken by the government and have the broad social purpose of reducing want and destitution. However, social insurance is different from public assistance: Social insurance is an insurance program that is compulsory for nearly all Americans; eligibility criteria and benefits are specified by law; and financing is wholly or partially covered by the employer. Unlike public assistance, employers and employees pay into the social insurance system to earn their rights to benefits. Some examples of social insurance programs include workers' compensation and unemployment compensation, which were covered in Chapter 13, and Social Security.

Welfare benefits are financed through general revenues that come from both federal and state funds. Benefits received from welfare are not based on contributions made by or on behalf of the recipients. Medicaid is an example of welfare benefit solely based on need. While public assistance programs have a role in providing economic security, they are not insurance programs. The insurance principles of assessing and pooling risk do not apply to welfare programs.

The types of benefits available from Social Security are apparent from the acronym OASDHI: old age (or retirement), survivors', disability, and health (or Medicare) benefits, which include hospital insurance and supplemental medical insurance. The program can be separated into two broad parts. The first part is the old-age, survivors', and disability insurance program known as Social Security. The second part of the program is Medicare.

We will begin the discussion about Social Security and Medicare with a description of each social program, its benefits, and its eligibility requirements. Following the general discussion is an explanation of how the programs are financed. We will introduce the two programs separately because there are many differences between Social Security and Medicare. We begin with the eligibility requirements and then discuss the benefits available to eligible employees.

COVERAGE AND ELIGIBILITY REQUIREMENTS

Today, nearly all employees in private industry, most self-employed persons, and members of the armed forces are covered by Social Security. Coverage is compulsory for more than

TABLE 15.1A Monthly Benefits for Various Levels of Earnings	Worker with steady earnings since age 22 and retirement at age 65			
	Low Retirement Benefits	Average Retirement Benefits	High Retirement Benefits	Maximum Retirement Benefits
2000	$598	$ 987	$1,279	$1,433
2001	636	1,051	1,364	1,467
2002	682	1,126	1,467	1,660
2003	701	1,158	1,513	1,741

Source: Social Security Administration, www.ssa.gov.

TABLE 15.1B		Before 1.4% COLA	After 1.4% COLA
Estimated Average Monthly Social Security Benefits Payable in January 2003	All Retired Workers	$ 882	$ 895
	Aged Couple, Both Receiving Benefits	$1,463	$1,483
	Widowed Mother and Two Children	$1,812	$1,838
	Aged Widow(er) Alone	$ 850	$ 862
	Disabled Worker, Spouse and One or More Children	$1,376	$1,395
	All Disabled Workers	$ 822	$ 833

Source: Social Security Administration, www.ssa.gov.

90 percent of all workers in the United States, meaning that Social Security taxes must be paid on their wages. The major exceptions are railroad workers, who are covered by the Railroad Retirement Act, and federal government employees who, before 1984, were covered by other programs. Prior to 1984, state and local government bodies could elect not to cover certain employees under Social Security. With few exceptions, this option is no longer allowed. Municipal governments that elected out prior to 1984 do have the option to voluntarily join the Social Security program. Ministers are covered automatically unless they request a waiver on religious grounds. Members of religious sects whose beliefs prohibit acceptance of benefits are exempt.

Eligibility

In order to be eligible to receive benefits, a worker must achieve insured status. There are three levels of insured status: fully insured, currently insured, or disability insured. If the worker is **fully insured,** most types of Social Security benefits are payable. If the worker does not have enough work tenure to be fully insured, he or she may be **currently insured,** which still allows eligibility for some survivor benefits.

A person must be in the workforce for a minimum number of quarters during which his or her earnings meet minimum criteria. The required earnings per quarter in 2002 is a minimum of $870, and in 2003 that amount increases to $890. The amount is adjusted every year. An employee can earn a maximum of four credits per year, even if he or she did not work the full four quarters, as long as he or she made enough even in one month (4 × $870). A beneficiary is fully insured once forty credits of coverage are earned, or when the retiree has a minimum of six credits of coverage and, if greater, at least as many quarters of coverage as there are years elapsing after 1950 (or after age 21, if later). For example, a person age 25 who has six credits of coverage is fully insured, whereas a person age 40 needs nineteen credits to be fully insured. Currently insured status is achieved if the beneficiary has at least six credits in the thirteen-quarter period ending with the quarter of death. **Disability insured** status is gained by having twenty credits in the ten years before disability begins. Less rigorous disability requirements apply to a beneficiary who is under age 31 or blind.

TYPES OF BENEFITS

As noted, Social Security pays four types of benefits: old age (or retirement), survivors', disability, and Medicare. Following is a more detailed description of each of these benefits.

<table>
<tr><td>**TABLE 15.2**
Who Gets Monthly Benefits if a Fully Insured Worker Retires?</td><td>

- Retired worker who is at least 62 years old
- Spouse of retired worker who either (1) has a child under age 16 or a disabled child in his or her care or (2) is at least 62 years old; applies also to divorced spouse if the marriage lasted at least 10 years
- Dependent child of retired worker, either under age 18, under 19 if a full-time student, or disabled before age 22

</td></tr>
</table>

Retirement (Old Age) Benefits

A fully insured worker is eligible to receive benefits, including retirement income benefits. A spouse or divorced spouse of a retired worker is entitled to a monthly benefit if he or she is (1) at least age 62 or (2) caring for at least one child of the retired worker (under age 16, or disabled if disability began before age 22). A dependent child, grandchild, or great-grandchild of a retired worker who is (1) under age 18, (2) a full-time student between 18 and 19, or (3) disabled, if disability began before age 22, is also entitled to a benefit. Table 15.2 summarizes these benefits.

Normal retirement age ranges from 65 (for people born before 1938) to 67 (for those born in or after 1960). A fully insured worker can elect to receive full **retirement benefits** at the normal retirement age, or reduced benefits as early as age 62. A schedule of the new retirement ages is shown in Table 15.3.

Early Retirement

Early retirement benefits are permanently reduced in amount, since the expected benefit pay-out period is longer than it would have been starting from normal retirement age. In the case of **early retirement,** a benefit is reduced 5/9 of one percent for each month before the normal retirement age. The earliest a person can retire is age 62. Beyond 36 months, the benefit is reduced 5/12 of one percent per month.

For example, assume the normal retirement age is exactly age 67 and a person decides to retire at exactly age 62. There are a total of 60 months of reduction to the worker's expected benefit. The reduction for the first 36 months is 5/9 of one percent times 36, or 20 percent. The reduction for the remaining 24 months is 5/12 of one percent times 24, or 10 percent. Thus, in this example, the total benefit reduction is 30 percent.

	Year of Birth	Normal Retirement Age
TABLE 15.3 Schedule of Normal Social Security Retirement Ages	1937 or before	65
	1938	65 and 2 months
	1939	65 and 4 months
	1940	65 and 6 months
	1941	65 and 8 months
	1942	65 and 10 months
	1943–54	66
	1955	66 and 2 months
	1956	66 and 4 months
	1957	66 and 6 months
	1958	66 and 8 months
	1959	66 and 10 months
	1960 and later	67

Note: Persons born on January 1 of any year should refer to the credit percentage for the previous year.
Source: Social Security Administration, www.ssa.gov/OACT/ProgData/nra.html.

Late Retirement

Likewise, postponing retirement past the normal retirement age, **late retirement,** results in a permanently increased benefit amount to compensate for the shortened length of the pay-out period and to encourage older workers to continue working full-time. No delayed retirement credit is granted for retiring past age 69.

Survivors' Benefits

Survivors' benefits protect the surviving dependents of a fully or currently insured deceased worker. The surviving spouse is entitled to monthly income payments if caring for a child who is under age 16 or a child who is disabled by a disability that began before age 22. A child of a fully or currently insured deceased worker is entitled to benefits if he or she (1) is under age 18, is disabled by a disability that began before age 22, or is age 18 or 19 and a full-time student attending an elementary or secondary school, (2) was dependent on the deceased worker, and (3) is not married. Table 15.4 summarizes who gets monthly benefits if a fully insured or currently insured worker dies.

A widow or widower of a fully insured deceased worker is qualified for benefits at age 50 if disabled, and otherwise at age 60. A divorced spouse also qualifies, subject to having been married to the worker for at least ten years and not being remarried. A parent of a fully insured deceased worker is entitled to benefits if he or she (1) is at least age 62, (2) was receiving at least half of his or her support from the child, (3) has not remarried since the child's death, and (4) is not entitled to a retirement or disability benefit equal to or larger than this survivors' benefit.

In addition to these monthly benefits, a small lump-sum death benefit of $255 is paid upon the death of a worker who is fully or currently insured. It is paid to the spouse living with the worker at the time of death, or a spouse otherwise entitled, or children entitled as described above. In the absence of a spouse or children, the death benefit is not paid. It is the only benefit that has not increased since the Social Security legislation was passed in 1935.

Disability Benefits

A fully insured worker who has a medically determinable physical or mental condition that prevents any substantial gainful work is entitled to monthly **disability benefits** after a waiting period of five full months if he or she is under age 65 and has been disabled for twelve months, is expected to be disabled for at least twelve months, or has a disability that is expected to result in death. The definition of disability for a widow or widower of a deceased worker is even more restrictive. A spouse or child of a disabled worker is entitled to a monthly benefit upon meeting the same qualifications as those previously listed in connection with retirement benefits. Table 15.5 shows who gets monthly benefits if a fully insured worker is disabled. Note that to receive benefits the worker must be fully insured, meet the disability insured status, and meet the definition of disability, which is the inability to do work and not expected to survive more than 12 months.

TABLE 15.4 Who Gets Monthly Benefits if a Fully Insured Worker Dies?	■ Dependent child of deceased worker ■ Aged widow(er) who is at least 60 years old ■ Young widow(er) caring for a dependent child under age 16 or a disabled child ■ Disabled widow(er) who is disabled and 50 years or older (converted to aged widow(er) upon attainment of age 65) ■ Parent who was a dependent of the deceased worker and is at least 62 years old

TABLE 15.5

Who Gets Monthly Benefits if a Fully Insured Worker is Disabled?

- Disabled worker who had been working recently in covered employment prior to disability
- Spouse of disabled worker who either (1) has a child under age 16 or a disabled child in his or her care, or (2) is at least 62 years old; applies also to divorced spouse if the marriage lasted at least 10 years
- Dependent child of disabled worker

More specifically, a non-blind person earning more than $800 in 2003 is considered to be engaging in *substantial gainful activities* and is not eligible for Social Security benefits. The amount of earnings allowable if the person is blind is $1,330 in 2003. These amounts are indexed annually with increases in the national wage index.[3] It is extremely difficult to qualify to receive Social Security disability benefits.

Disability benefits may be stopped if the disabled worker refuses to participate in rehabilitation. They may be reduced if disability benefits are received from workers' compensation or under a federal, state, or local law. At the end of 2001, about 817,000 persons were receiving monthly benefits from the OASI Trust Fund due to disability or the disability of children under the custodial care of the beneficiary. Benefits paid from this trust fund to the beneficiaries totaled $5.5 billion in 2001.[4]

AMOUNT OF BENEFITS

Primary Insurance Amount

The **primary insurance amount** (PIA) is the basic unit used to determine the amount of monthly benefits. PIA is computed from a person's **average indexed monthly earnings** (AIME). In the calculation of the AIME, earnings for prior years, up to the maximum Social Security wage base (see Tables 15.6 and 15.11 for the wage base), are adjusted to what they would have been if wage levels in earlier years had been the same as they are now. This is the indexed amount.

We compute the AIME by first finding the sum of the highest 35 years of indexed earnings and the corresponding average monthly amounts of such earnings. We get the average indexed monthly amount by dividing the sum of the 35 highest amounts by the number of months in 35 years. The result is the AIME.

Consequently, there is no easy way to make an estimate of one's PIA. It is not as simple as finding average wages and consulting a table. The Social Security Administration has computerized wage histories for all workers, and the PIA calculation is made by the computer when an application for benefits is processed. The Social Security Administration furnishes annually the calculation of each insured's PIA. If a person has not received the statement, the Social Security Administration will furnish a record of the historical Social Security earnings and PIA upon request.[5] The Social Security Administration Web site also has an online calculator.

After the AIME is determined, an individual's PIA in 2003 would be determined by the formula in Table 15.7. The formula shows that benefit levels, expressed as **replacement ratios,** are weighted in favor of lower-income workers. Here a replacement ratio is defined as the Social Security benefit divided by the AIME.

The three AIME ranges represented in the formula are known as **bend points.** The bend points represent the dollar amount at which the PIA formula changes. The bend points increase as average wages in the economy increase. This is seen in Figure 15.2. The bend points in 2003 are $606 and $3,653, as can be seen from Table 15.7. These bend

TABLE 15.6	Year	Indexing Factor	Earnings (High)	Indexed Earnings (High)	Maximum (Wage Base)
Indexed Earnings for a Hypothetical Worker Age 62 in 2002	1962	7.49285	$ 4,800	$35,966	$35,966
	1963	7.31350	4,800	35,105	35,105
	1964	7.02635	4,800	33,726	33,726
	1965	6.90207	4,800	33,130	33,130
	1966	6.51123	6,600	42,974	42,974
	1967	6.16768	6,600	40,707	40,707
	1968	5.77103	7,800	45,014	45,014
	1969	5.45574	7,800	42,555	42,555
	1970	5.19780	7,800	40,543	40,543
	1971	4.94912	7,800	38,603	38,603
	1972	4.50739	9,000	40,567	40,567
	1973	4.24197	10,800	45,813	45,813
	1974	4.00396	12,849	51,448	52,852
	1975	3.72554	13,809	51,448	52,530
	1976	3.48506	14,762	51,448	53,321
	1977	3.28800	15,647	51,448	54,252
	1978	3.04611	16,890	51,448	53,916
	1979	2.80107	18,367	51,448	64,145
	1980	2.56962	20,022	51,448	66,553
	1981	2.33461	22,037	51,448	69,338
	1982	2.21279	23,250	51,448	71,694
	1983	2.11000	24,383	51,448	75,327
	1984	1.99285	25,816	51,448	75,330
	1985	1.91142	26,916	51,448	75,692
	1986	1.85632	27,715	51,448	77,965
	1987	1.74503	29,482	51,448	76,432
	1988	1.66312	30,934	51,448	74,840
	1989	1.59978	32,159	51,448	76,789
	1990	1.52914	33,645	51,448	78,445
	1991	1.47421	34,899	51,448	78,723
	1992	1.40197	36,697	51,448	77,809
	1993	1.39002	37,012	51,448	80,065
	1994	1.35369	38,006	51,448	82,033
	1995	1.30152	39,529	51,448	79,653
	1996	1.24083	41,462	51,448	77,800
	1997	1.17242	43,882	51,448	76,676
	1998	1.11411	46,178	51,448	76,205
	1999	1.05530	48,752	51,448	76,615
	2000	1.00000	51,448	51,448	76,200
	2001	1.00000	53,889	53,889	80,400
	Highest-35 total		507,125	1,741,149	2,309,776
	AIME		1,207	4,145	5,499

Source: Social Security Administration.

TABLE 15.7	■ 90 percent of the first $606 of his/her average indexed monthly earnings, plus
PIA Formula for Individual, 2003	■ 32 percent of his/her average indexed monthly earnings over $606 and through $3,653, plus
	■ 15 percent of his/her average indexed monthly earnings over $3,653.

Source: Social Security Administration, Formulas for the Primary Insurance Amount for 2003, www.ssa.gov/OACT/COLA/BenForm.html.

FIGURE 15.2	
Graph of PIA Formula Showing Bend Points	

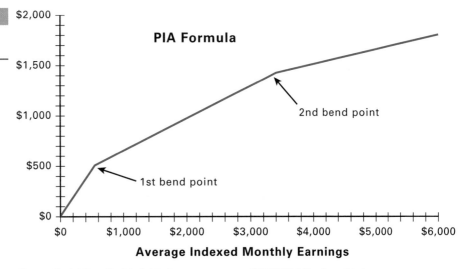

Source: Social Security Administration, www.ssa.gov/OACT/COLA/BenForm.html.

points apply to workers who become eligible for benefits in 2003. A table of bend points for past years is available at www.ssa.gov.

Other Factors Affecting Benefit Amounts

As described above, the AIME determines the PIA of a retired or disabled worker; the benefit levels for other beneficiaries are a percentage of the PIA. If an individual qualifies as both a worker and as the spouse of a worker, the beneficiary will receive whichever PIA is greater, but not both. Other factors also may affect the benefit amount.

The maximum family benefit is the maximum monthly amount that can be paid on a worker's earnings record. The formula for the maximum family benefit, shown in Table 15.8, is based on the worker's primary insurance amount (PIA). The maximum PIA for the family is computed based on the bend points shown in Table 15.8. When the family reaches its maximum family benefit, the worker's benefit is not reduced but the benefits of the survivors or dependents are reduced proportionately. There is also a minimum PIA for very-low-wage workers who have been covered by Social Security for at least ten years. This attempts to address the broad social purpose of Social Security: reducing want and destitution by providing an adequate income to insured workers.[6]

TABLE 15.8
The PIA Formula for Maximum Family Benefit, 2003

- 150 percent of the first $774 of the worker's PIA, plus
- 272 percent of the worker's PIA over $774 through $1,118, plus
- 134 percent of the worker's PIA over $1,118 through $1,458, plus
- 175 percent of the worker's PIA over $1,458.

Cost of Living Adjustment (COLA)

Benefit amounts are also affected by automatic cost-of-living adjustments linked to increases in the Consumer Price Index. In addition, workers receiving Social Security disability income may have Social Security benefits reduced to offset other disability benefits received from governmental programs, such as workers' compensation, to reduce the moral hazard of malingering.

Legislation enacted in 1973 provides for **automatic cost-of-living adjustments,** or **COLAs.** The theory is to prevent inflation from eroding the value of Social Security and Supplemental Security Income (SSI) benefits. The COLA for 2002 is 1.4 percent for both Social Security benefits and SSI payments, as you can see in Table 15.9.

Many people retire before or after the normal retirement age, which affects the PIA for those individuals. The COLA is always computed based on the PIA, so for an individual retiring early, the final benefit amount is reduced from what the PIA formula shows. For an individual retiring past the normal retirement age, the final benefit amount is higher than the PIA formula reveals.

The Earnings Test

The retirement benefit may be reduced for a retiree who is younger than normal retirement age and whose annual earned income exceeds the retirement earnings exempt amount. This provision is called the **earnings test.** Its purpose is to limit monthly cash benefits for retirees who have earned income and to reduce the cost of the Social Security program. As Table 15.10 shows, a beneficiary attaining the normal retirement age after 2002 is exempt from reduction of social security benefits regardless of amount of earned income. The earning test applies only to early retirement.

TABLE 15.9
Automatic Cost-of-Living Adjustments

Year	COLA	Year	COLA	Year	COLA
1975	8.0%	1985	3.1%	1995	2.6%
1976	6.4%	1986	1.3%	1996	2.9%
1977	5.9%	1987	4.2%	1997	2.1%
1978	6.5%	1988	4.0%	1998	1.3%
1979	9.9%	1989	4.7%	1999	2.5%
1980	14.3%	1990	5.4%	2000	3.5%
1981	11.2%	1991	3.7%	2001	2.6%
1982	7.4%	1992	3.0%	2002	1.4%
1983	3.5%	1993	2.6%		
1984	3.5%	1994	2.8%		

Source: Social Security Administration: Automatic Cost of Living Adjustment, www.ssa.gov/OACT/COLA/colasummary.html.

	Year	Lower amount*	Higher amount†
TABLE 15.10 Annual Retirement Earnings Test Exempt Amounts for Persons under the Normal Retirement Age	2000	$10,080	$17,000
	2001	10,680	25,000
	2002	11,280	30,000
	2003	11,520	30,720

*Applies in years before the year of attaining the NRA.
†Applies in the year of attaining the NRA, for months prior to such attainment.

In 2003, a beneficiary under the normal retirement age would lose $1 of benefits for every $2 earned above $11,520. The beneficiary would also lose $1 for every $3 above the higher exempt amount, $30,720.

FINANCING OF BENEFITS

Taxation

Social Security benefits are financed through payroll taxes paid by employers and employees and by a special tax on earnings paid by the self-employed. The tax rate for employers and employees is 6.2 percent for OASDI up to a certain amount of earnings called the **wage base level,** as shown in Table 15.11, and 1.45 percent for HI (Medicare Part A) on all earnings. Self-employed workers pay both employer and employee shares. The tax rates scheduled under current law are shown in Table 15.12. Those who elect Medicare Part B coverage pay monthly premiums via deductions from their Social Security benefits checks.

TABLE 15.11 OASDI Annual Wage Base for Tax Purposes

Year	Amount	Year	Amount	Year	Amount
1937-50	$3,000	1981	$29,700	1996	$62,700
1951-54	3,600	1982	32,400	1997	65,400
1955-58	4,200	1983	35,700	1998	68,400
1959-65	4,800	1984	37,800	1999	72,600
1966-67	6,600	1985	39,600	2000	76,200
1968-71	7,800	1986	42,000	2001	80,400
1972	9,000	1987	43,800	2002	84,900
1973	10,800	1988	45,000	2003	87,000
1974	13,200	1989	48,000		
1975	14,100	1990	51,300		
1976	15,300	1991	53,400		
1977	16,500	1992	55,500		
1978	17,700	1993	57,600		
1979	22,900	1994	60,600		
1980	25,900	1995	61,200		

Source: Social Security Administration

TABLE 15.12 Tax Rates Paid on Wages and Earnings since 1990

	OASI	DI	OASDI	Medicare A
Tax rate for employees and employers, each (percent)*	5.30	0.90	6.20	1.45
Tax rate for self-employed persons (percent)*	10.60	1.80	12.40	2.90

*Up to wage base level for OASDI; unlimited earnings for Medicare A.

Social Security taxes, sometimes called FICA taxes (after the Federal Insurance Contributions Act of 1939), are automatically withheld on wages up to a set amount, adjusted annually for inflation. Any wages earned over this wage base are not taxed for Social Security, though Medicare Part A taxes will still be deducted.

The tax rates are intended to remain constant (the last hike was in 1990), but the taxable wage base is adjusted annually to reflect increases in average wages. As you can see in Table 15.11, the 2003 annual wage base is $87,000, meaning that employers, employees, and the self-employed paid OASDI taxes on individual wages up to $87,000. If wages increase 5 percent the following year, the tax rates would remain the same but the taxable wage base would increase by 5 percent, thus increasing total Social Security tax revenue (all else being equal). Wages beyond the threshold are not subject to the OASDI tax, but they are subject to the Medicare Part A tax.

Social Security benefits are subject to income taxes. More specifically, taxes are payable on 50 percent of the Social Security benefit by single persons whose taxable incomes (including 50 percent of Social Security benefits and any interest on tax-exempt bonds) are between $25,000 and $34,000 (between $32,000 and $44,000 for married couples filing joint returns). If income exceeds $34,000 for single persons (or $44,000 for married couples filing jointly), up to 85 percent of the Social Security benefit received at retirement as income is taxable.

Trust Funds

The funds collected from payroll taxes are allocated among three trust funds. One trust fund is for retirement and survivors' benefits, the second is for disability insurance, and the third is for hospital insurance, or Medicare Part A. Medicare Part B, supplementary medical benefits, is financed by monthly premiums from persons enrolled in the program, along with amounts appropriated from the general revenue of the federal government. These funds are deposited in a fourth trust fund, the supplementary medical insurance trust fund.

The Social Security system is primarily a pay-as-you-go system. For the most part, current tax revenues are used to pay the current benefits of Social Security recipients. This is quite different from financing with traditional, private insurance, where funds are set aside in advance to accumulate over time and benefits are paid to those who contributed to the fund.

Income to the trust funds consists of:

- Employment taxes paid by employees, their employers, and self-employed persons
- Income from the taxation of benefits
- Interest on investments made by the program
- Other income such as donations and Treasury reimbursements

Over 98 percent of expenditures from the combined OASI and DI trust funds in 2001 went to pay retirement, survivor and disability benefits totaling $431.9 billion.[7] In 2001, 86 percent of total income ($516.4 billion) to the trust funds consisted of taxes paid by employees, employers, and the self-employed on earnings covered by the Social Security program.[8]

In 2001, revenue from the taxing of benefits represented two percent of total income, or $12.7 billion.[9] All revenue from the added tax (from 50 percent to 85 percent of income) is directed into Medicare's Hospital Insurance Trust Fund.

MEDICARE

Medicare Part A: Hospital Benefits

Anyone who is eligible for Social Security or railroad retirement benefits at age 65 is also eligible for **Medicare Part A—hospital insurance benefits.** No premium is required, because workers have already paid Medicare A taxes. A worker does not have to retire to be covered for hospital benefits; however, Medicare is the secondary payer for persons who continue to work between ages 65 and 69 and have medical coverage through their employers. Individuals age 65 and over who are not eligible for Social Security or railroad retirement benefits may enroll in Medicare Part A by paying premiums. The Medicare Part A plan provides the following hospital-related benefits:

- Inpatient hospital services
- Post-hospital home health services
- Hospice care

For Medicare Part A, the deductible paid by the beneficiary will be $840 in 2003, up 3.5 percent from 2002's $812 deductible.

Medicare Part B: Medical Benefits

Anyone eligible for Part A, the basic hospital benefits plan, and anyone age 65 or over is eligible for **Medicare Part B—medical benefits.** Those receiving Social Security or railroad retirement benefits are enrolled automatically unless they elect not to be covered. The monthly premium paid by beneficiaries enrolled in Medicare Part B, which covers physician services, outpatient hospital services, certain home health services, durable medical equipment, and other items, is $58.70 in 2003, an increase of 8.7 percent over the $54.00 premium for 2002.[10] People who turn down coverage at age 65 and enroll later pay a higher premium.[11] The benefits provided under Medicare Part B are listed in Table 15.13.

Charges that are not covered include routine physical examinations; routine care of the eyes, ears, and feet; prescription drugs; most immunizations; and cosmetic surgery.

TABLE 15.13 Medical Expenses Covered by Medicare Part B	

- Doctor's services, including house calls, office visits, and services in the hospital and other institutions
- Hospital diagnostic studies and other services on an outpatient basis
- Services and supplies to outpatients
- Outpatient physical therapy and speech pathology furnished by specified agencies
- Dentists' bills for bone surgery
- Outpatient psychiatric treatment
- Home health services, up to 100 visits per year
- Diagnostic tests
- Radiation therapy
- Surgical dressings and similar items
- Ambulance service under certain circumstances
- Dialysis services and supplies
- Outpatient rehabilitation services
- Non–self-administered drugs

Doctors must bill Medicare directly, rather than having patients file Medicare claims. Some physicians and surgeons accept as full payment the amount that Medicare considers reasonable, but others charge patients an additional fee. However, doctors are limited in the additional amount they may charge patients.

ADMINISTRATION

The Social Security program is administered by the Social Security Administration, an agency of the United States Department of Health and Human Services. Local service is provided by offices located in the principal cities and towns of the fifty states and Puerto Rico. Applications for Social Security numbers and the various benefits as well as the enrollment for the medical insurance plan are processed by the district office.

Disability determination—the decision as to whether or not an applicant for disability benefits is disabled as defined in the law—is made by a state agency (usually the vocational rehabilitation agency) under agreements between the state and the secretary of the Department of Health and Human Services. Qualification for hospital and medical benefits is determined by the district office, but claims for such benefits are processed through private insurer intermediaries under contract with the Social Security Administration.

The first decision concerning a person's qualification for benefits under the various parts of the program is made at the local level. Simple, effective procedures exist for appeal by any applicant for whom the decision is unsatisfactory. There is no charge for such appeals, and the agency strives to provide courteous assistance to the claimant.

SOCIAL SECURITY ISSUES

During the 2000 presidential election campaign, Social Security financing was the most heated issue in the election, with the debate focusing on privatization and moving away from the **pay-as-you-go system.** Pay-as-you-go means that the current workers finance the benefits of the current recipients. When the stock market was booming and everyone believed they could do better by investing their own funds, the idea of moving away from the current system became very appealing. Today (in late 2002) the tune is different after the large decline in the stock market.

Another major issue that is debated is the cost of drugs for Medicare recipients since Medicare does not pay for self-administered drugs.[12] Some Medicare recipients end up paying more for drugs than for food, and it has reached a crisis level as the general cost of medical care has increased, as discussed in Chapter 17's "Ethical Dilemma: What is the Tradeoff between Health Care Cost and Benefits?" Also, another crisis in Medicare is the departure of many providers from the plan because of low reimbursement levels.

Social Security and Medicare were originally designed to operate with advance funding, but it has for many years operated on an unfunded, pay-as-you-go basis. As a result, this generation of workers is paying for the benefits of current beneficiaries. Social Security taxes have increased much faster than the general level of prices and even faster than the cost of health care during the past two decades.

As described in the "Ethical Dilemma: Does Privatization Provide a More Equitable Solution?" and depicted in Figure 15.3, the number of retired workers has increased faster than the number of those working. In 1945, there were forty-two workers per retiree. Currently, this has decreased to approximately three workers per retiree and is expected to decline to two by the year 2020. The Social Security funding burden is being borne by a shrinking sector of society as birth rates have declined and longevity has

Ethical Dilemma

Does Privatization Provide a More Equitable Solution?

> The threat to the stability of Social Security has been apparent for decades. For years, political leaders have agreed that something must be done....We can postpone action no longer. Social Security is a challenge now; if we fail to act, it will become a crisis. We must save Social Security and we now have the opportunity to do so.

With these words, on May 2, 2001, President George W. Bush established the Presidential Commission to Strengthen Social Security.

The crisis President Bush was referring to is the declining numbers of new workers paying into the Social Security system. Fewer births and longer life expectancies are both to blame. In 1940, when the first benefits were paid, there were more than forty workers paying in for each retiree receiving benefits. In 1960, there were five workers for each retiree. Today there are 3.4 workers paying in for each beneficiary. With the baby boom generation set to retire over the next few decades, that number is expected to fall even further. The Presidential Commission's report estimates that the ratio will be 2.2:1 in 2025 and just 2:1 by 2050.

These demographic changes mean that the burden of paying for Social Security will fall ever more heavily on the younger generation of workers. When polled, 41 percent of young people (ages eighteen to thirty-four) said that they do not expect to receive Social Security benefits at today's level when they retire, while 31 percent expected to receive no benefits at all.

Certainly current benefit levels cannot be maintained without raising Social Security withholding taxes. But is it fair to tax younger workers more heavily to pay for their parents' retirement? Will there even be any money left for their own? One solution that has been proposed is individual investment accounts that would allow individuals to invest a percentage of their social security savings themselves. Proponents of privatization argue that it would allow greater returns than the traditional Social Security system.

In the heady days of soaring stock prices and budget surpluses, just before President Bush created the commission, privatization was a popular solution. Workers, it was argued, could invest their Social Security funds in the stock market and see great returns. Low-wage workers would become shareholders in the U.S. economy and be able to accumulate wealth. Money would flow into the economy.

With the stock market slump that began in mid 2000, the wind has been taken out of privatization's sail. But even when the plan was first proposed, it faced opposition on a number of grounds. The pay-as-you-go system is a guaranteed benefit. With many retirees depending on Social Security as their main source of income, this guarantee is crucial. Yet what happens if an individual invested unwisely? Proponents of a private system argue that an education campaign along with requirements for diversification and safeguards against high-risk investments should prevent such losses.

Another argument against privatization is the distortion it could cause in the stock market. With a large number of funds flowing into mutual funds from Social Security investors, prices might be driven up artificially. "Government Approved" mutual funds would receive a huge windfall in fees.

Interestingly, most young people, who politicians have argued would benefit the most from privatization, do not support changing the Social Security system but would rather see the existing system strengthened. A majority polled say that "making sure that people receive a decent, guaranteed monthly retirement benefit" is a higher priority than "making sure that people receive a better rate of return."

Questions for Discussion

1. Who should be responsible for the welfare of the retired population? The current workers? Or the savings of the retirees?

2. Is it appropriate for the government to mandate forced savings in private accounts in lieu of the pay-as-you-go Social Security system? In effect, wouldn't this action change the nature of the requirements from tax to private saving?

3. If part of the individual accounts would be administered by the government, is it ethical for the government to essentially become a major shareholder in private companies?

Sources: Key findings from Hart Research Poll, 24 July 1998; "Young Americans and Social Security: A public opinion study conducted for the 2030 Center by Peter D. Hart, Research Associates," July 1999 (www.2030.org/pdf/report1.pdf); Strengthening Social Security and Creating Personal Wealth for All Americans, the Final Report of the President's Commission to Strengthen Social Security, Released December 21, 2001. This document includes all appendices and Estimates of Financial Effects for Three Models Developed by the President's Commission to Strengthen Social Security, prepared by the Office of the Chief Actuary, Social Security Administration; May 2, 2001: Remarks By The President In Social Security Announcement; www.socialsecurity.org/ [CATO Institute]; Gary Burtless, "Social Security Privatization and Financial Market Risk," Center on Social and Economic Dynamics, Working Paper No. 10, February 2000.

FIGURE 15.3
Number of Workers per
OASDI Beneficiary

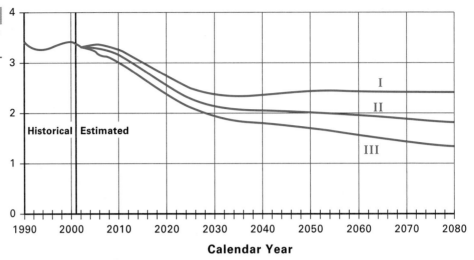

Source: OASDI Trustees Report, www.ssa.gov/OACT/COLA/CBB.html.

increased. This trend will continue as the "baby boomers" move out of the work force and into retirement. Retired workers are concerned about the certainty of their benefits and future required tax rates. The current generation of taxpayers has serious doubts about the ability of the Social Security system to deliver benefits at current inflation-adjusted levels.

Such doubts are understandable, considering recent problems of the OASI program, which is by far the largest part of the system. Each year the trustees of the Social Security and Medicare trust funds report on the funds' status and their projected condition over the

FIGURE 15.4
Long-Range OASI and
DI Annual Income
Rates and Cost Rates
(As a Percentage of
Taxable Payroll)

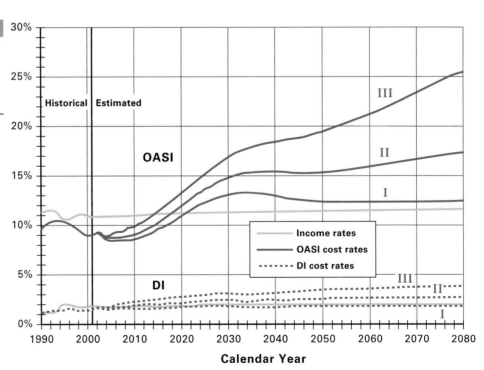

Source: 2002 OASDI Trustees Report, www.ssa.gov/OACT/TR/TR02/IV_LRest.html#219007.

IMPORTANT ISSUES

The Future of Social Security

A quick glance at Figure 15.4: Long-Range OASI and DI Annual Income Rates and Cost Rates reveals one important fact: The costs of Social Security are rising faster than its income. But this figure also shows much more—some things you already know from your reading in this chapter, some new information, and some assumptions about the future of Social Security. It is worth spending a little extra time on a second look.

Figure 15.4 comes from the 2002 OASDI Trustees Report on the current and projected financial condition of the Social Security program. (The six trustees of the board are the Secretary of the Treasury, the Secretary of Labor, the Secretary of Health and Human Services, the Commissioner of Social Security, and two members appointed by the president.) The program, as is explained in Chapter 15, is financed through two separate trust funds: The Old-Age and Survivors Insurance (OASI) Trust Fund pays monthly benefits to retired workers and their families and to survivors of deceased workers; the Disability Insurance (DI) Trust Fund pays monthly benefits to disabled workers and their families. For 2001, the funds paid out total benefits of $432 billion and received an income of $602 billion from payroll taxes. At the end of 2001, the funds held $1.2 trillion in special issue U.S. Treasury securities. In 2010 the baby-boom generation will begin retiring, which will both decrease income (they'll no longer pay into the system) and increase costs (but they will take plenty out).

To project future effects on the bottom line, the trustees review available evidence and gather expert opinion about all the factors that affect income and expenditures: demographic (birth rate, mortality, immigration), economic (unemployment rates, inflation), and program-specific (retirement patterns, disability incidence). The trustees make both short-range (ten year) and long-range (seventy-five year) predictions; for the long-range predictions, they propose three sets of assumptions, marked on Figure 15.4 as I, II, and III. Alternative II is the trustees' best guess; the optimistic Alternative I assumes rapid economic growth and low inflation; the pessimistic Alternative III assumes slow economic growth and high inflation. But as Figure 15.4 shows, even the optimistic projection postpones the inevitable for just five years, showing OASI losses beginning in the year 2020 as opposed to the pessimistic view's 2015. Using the mid-range

Alternative II assumptions, annual costs will exceed tax income starting in 2017.

These scenarios assume that the trust funds' income will remain constant in terms of percentage of taxable income. That is, as taxable payroll increases—whether by new jobs or higher wages—the dollar amounts contributed to the funds will increase, but the percentage is assumed to stay the same. The 2001 tax rate, employers and employees combined, is 10.6 percent for OASI and 1.8 percent for DI (the income lines in Figure 15.4 are a bit higher because they include income from interest and from taxes on benefits).

Traditional solutions to the looming Social Security budget crisis have focused on increasing these taxes and cutting benefits. By some calculations, raising payroll taxes an additional 2.5 percentage points would eliminate the projected shortfall, but many feel that would disproportionately burden younger workers (and be political suicide for any representative who voted for it). Another option, also politically suicidal, is means testing—reducing or eliminating benefits to retirees above a certain income level.

President Bush and many members of Congress believe the answer is privatization (discussed in the Ethical Dilemma of this chapter)—allowing workers to invest some or all of their own (private) Social Security funds in the stock market, which historically yields greater returns over long investment periods than Treasury securities do. After Chile's successful move to privatization in 1981, almost every South American country has followed suit, with positive results. Countries from Singapore to Hungary have also converted successfully. But there are many arguments on both sides, and it remains to be seen what, if anything, will save the Social Security system.

Exploring the Internet

The Board of Trustees of the Social Security Trust Funds reports each year on the current and projected financial condition of the Social Security program. Find current and past reports at www.ssa.gov/OACT/TR/. A summary of the latest report is available at www.ssa.gov/OACT/TRSUM/trsummary.html.

Sources: Merrill Matthews Jr., "A 12-Step Plan for Social Security Reform," National Center for Policy Analysis, 4 June 1998, www.ncpa.org/ba/ba267.html; The 2002 OASDI Trustees Report, www.ssa.gov/OACT/TR/TR02/index.html.

next 75 years. The 2002 Annual Reports show that both Social Security and Medicare need serious reform.[13] In 2001, both programs faced a long-term financing gap. Closing the gap between monies going into the Social Security and Medicare funds and monies coming out of the funds will be a challenge. It will force the government to come up with innovative solutions to fixing the long-term deficits.

As Figure 15.4 shows, the OASI and DI trust funds are expected to be adequately financed for only the next ten years (depending on the actuarial assumptions).[14] An explanation of the figure with outlook to the future is discussed in "Important Issues: The Future of Social Security."

Whether the objective of the Social Security program should be to provide a "floor of protection" or a "reasonable level of living" remains debatable. Reform, however, will require agreement by politicians and the public on not only what benefits citizens are entitled to, but what benefits taxpayers are willing to fund.

GLOBAL TRENDS IN SOCIAL SECURITY SYSTEMS

In many countries, financing the government social security system has become increasingly difficult. There are several reasons for this. Benefit levels have increased in many nations through the political process to the point where the tax rates necessary to support benefits are at an all-time high. For example, free or very-low-cost medical care may be available to everyone; disability benefits may require little proof of inability to work, and generous disability payments may result in the moral hazard of malingering. Demographic trends in other industrialized nations mirror those in the United States: The population is aging, so fewer workers finance the pay-as-you-go system for retirees; the declining birthrate suggests that this trend is unlikely to be reversed. In addition, other governments also face the problem of growing budget deficits. Governments in some developing countries may be perceived as unable to administer the social security system fairly and efficiently.

Experts anticipate a shift from public sector social insurance plans to private sector plans, especially for retirement benefits. Private sector organizations, particularly insurance companies, have successfully managed retirement savings and income for decades and are in a position to improve management and funding practices. Several countries have already begun to privatize the social security system, namely, Chile, Peru, Mexico, Italy, and Japan. In Chile (beginning in 1981) and Peru (in 1993), for example, workers are required to contribute to their own retirement fund, and contributions are invested by a private pension fund manager selected by the worker. In both these countries, the pre-funded privatized system appears to be working well. Some countries also are moving toward privatized medical care systems.

The trend toward privatization is worldwide, including both industrialized and developing countries. The potential for market expansion for insurers and other financial institutions is tremendous.

KEY TERMS

Social Security	late retirement	automatic cost-of-living
OASDHI	survivors' benefits	adjustments (COLAs)
social insurance	disability benefits	earnings test
fully insured	primary insurance amount	wage base level
currently insured	(PIA)	Medicare Part A—hospital
disability insured	average indexed monthly	insurance benefits
normal retirement age	earnings (AIME)	Medicare Part B—medical
retirement benefits	replacement ratio	benefits
early retirement	bend points	pay as you go system

DISCUSSION QUESTIONS

1. How does a worker become fully insured under Social Security? What benefits are fully insured workers entitled to?

2. What is the difference between Medicare Part A and Medicare Part B? Does a retiree need both?

3. Why is it important to index earnings in calculating AIME? What does the PIA represent?

4. How does the earnings test affect Social Security benefits?

5. Social Security benefits are financed largely through payroll taxes. Up to the maximum earnings base, the more you earn, the more tax you pay. Income benefits, however, favor lower-income workers. You may earn twice as much as I do and pay twice as much tax, but you will not receive twice as much income benefit. Do you think this is fair? If not, should it be changed? How?

6. Do you think Social Security coverage should be voluntary? Why, or why not?

7. From time to time, you may hear that Social Security is in financial trouble and that you may not receive the benefits you expect. Do you think this is true? If it is true, what should be done about it?

8. Would you favor privatization of the Social Security retirement program, as other countries have done? Please explain.

EXERCISES

15.1 C.J. Abbott worked hard all his life and built up a successful business. His daily routine involves helping with management decisions in the business, even though the majority of it is now owned and managed by his sons. He continues to draw a salary from the company sufficient to cover his expenses each month. C.J. is fully insured under Social Security and applied for benefits at age 62. However, he does not presently receive, nor has he ever received, Social Security benefits. He celebrated his 64th birthday last May.

 a. Why doesn't C.J. receive any Social Security benefits? Does this tell you anything about how much he is earning at the business?

 b. Why do you think C.J. continues to work?

 c. Will C.J.'s benefits be increased any for his work beyond age 65? (Assume he starts drawing benefits at age 70.)

 d. What is the logic behind the provision in the Social Security law that leads to a fully insured individual like C.J. not receiving Social Security retirement benefits after age 65?

15.2 Your father-in-law was employed by a state agency for forty years before his retirement last year. He was not covered by Social Security on his state job. During the last five years of his career with the state government, however, you employed him on a part-time basis to do some surveying work on a housing development for which you had an engineering contract. You withheld Social Security tax from his wages and turned his share plus yours as his employer over to the government.

When he retired, he applied for Social Security retirement benefits. Several months later, he was notified that he was not entitled to benefits because the work he did for you was "in the family," and not bona fide employment. The implication in the notice he received was that the job you gave him was designed to qualify him for Social Security benefits rather than to provide him with "real" employment.

    a.   What should your father-in-law do?

    b.   How can you help him?

15.3 Medicare costs have turned out to be much greater than expected when the program was first enacted. The number of people eligible for Medicare and the benefit amounts have increased through the years. For example, Medicare covers not only medical expenses for eligible retirees, but also kidney dialysis and kidney transplants for persons of all ages.

    a.   Why does Medicare have deductibles, coinsurance, and limitations on benefits that create gaps in coverage for insureds?

    b.   Considering the fact that many older people worry about what is not covered by Medicare, do you think the gaps should be eliminated?

    c.   Should Medicare be expanded to cover everyone for a broad array of medical services without regard to age or work history? Do you favor expanding Medicare into a national health insurance plan?

15.4 The Baylor Crane Construction Co. is a Virginia-based builder with 1,750 full time and 300 part time employees. The company provides all the social insurance programs required by law and most standard employee benefits plans. Last year Baylor Crane suffered a high severity of losses when the top five floors of a high rise collapsed in Virginia Beach during strong winds. Luckily, most workers escaped injuries, except six workers who stayed to secure the building. Three of them sustained severe injuries and Johnny Kendle, the 64-year-old supervisor, was killed. The injured workers are back at work except for Tom Leroy, who is still on disability. His prognosis is not good.

    a.   What social insurance programs are provided by the company?

    b.   Compare the benefits provided by each of the social programs.

15.5 Dan Wolf, Duncan Smith, and Jim Lavell are employees of the Happy Wood Company. Fifteen months ago Dan Wolf was injured when a log fell on him and hurt his back. He has not been able to work since. Duncan, who had 15 years of service with the company, was killed in that accident. He left a wife and five children. About a month later, Jim injured his back at home and he, too, has been unable to work since the accident. Respond to the following questions:

    a.   Based on the benefits of the social insurance programs you described above, compare the type of benefits Dan, Duncan, and Jim (or their families) are receiving.

    b.   What are the eligibility conditions to receiving these benefits?

NOTES

1.   All statistics in this chapter are from the Social Security Administration (www.ssa.gov) and the Department of Health and Human Service's Medicare site (www.medicare.gov).

2.   Social Security and Medicare Board of Trustees, "Status of the Social Security and Medicare Programs: A Summary of the 2002 Annual Social Security and Medicare Trust Fund Reports." This summary was released on March 29, 2002, and analyzes data relating to the Social Security and Medicare Trust Funds through December 2001. www.ssa.gov/OACT/TRSUM/trsummary.html.

3.   Social Security Administration: Substantial Gainful Activity Amounts for 2002, www.ssa.gov/OACT/COLA/SGA.html.

4.   Social Security Administration: 2002 OASDI Trustees Report, Section VI(F): Analysis of Benefit Disbursements From the OASI Trust Fund With Respect to Disabled Beneficiaries, www.ssa.gov/OACT/TR/TR02/VI_OASIforDI.html#94768.

5.   https://s00dace.ssa.gov/pro/batch-pebes/bp-7004home.shtml.

6. To be eligible for "special minimum" benefits, a worker must earn at least a certain portion (25 percent in years 1990 and before, and 15 percent in years following 1990) of the "old law" contribution and benefit base. In 2002, the "old law" contribution and benefit base is $63,000.

7. Except where noted, all figures for the OASDI trust fund financing are from the 2002 OASDI Trustees Report, section IIB: Trust Fund and Financial Operations in 2001, www.ssa.gov/OACT/TR/TR02/II_cyoper.html#87137.

8. 2002 OASDI Trustees Report, section IIIA: Operations of the Combined OASI and DI Trust Funds, Calendar year 2001, www.ssa.gov/OACT/TR/TR02/III_fyoper.html#84778.

9. See note 15.

10. Press Release: Friday, Oct. 18, 2002, HHS ANNOUNCES MEDICARE PREMIUM AND DEDUCTIBLE RATES FOR 2003 at: www.hhs.gov/news/press/2002pres/20021018.html

11. U.S. Department of Health and Human Services: "What is Medicare?" www.medicare.gov/Basics/WhatIs.asp.

12. Jerry Geisel, "Medicare drug benefit seen as unlikely this year," *Business Insurance,* 8 July 2002.

13. Social Security and Medicare Board of Trustees' Summary of the 2002 Annual Reports on the status of the Social Security and Medicare Programs. The goal of the public trustees is to approach the current state of Social Security and Medicare in a nonpartisan way. They aim to ensure the integrity of the reports, both in methods of preparation and in the credibility of the information they contain. Realizing that numerous assumptions must be made to predict the future condition of the funds, the trustees prepare these reports because they believe the reports paint the most reliable picture available today. This summary is available online at www.ssa.gov/OACT/TRSUM/trsummary.html.

14. 2002 OASDI Trustees Report, Section II: Overview, www.ssa.gov/OACT/TR/TR02/II_highlights.html#76460.

15. 2002 OASDI Trustees Report, section IIIA: Operations of the Combined OASI and DI Trust Funds, Calendar year 2001. http://www.ssa.gov/OACT/TR/TR02/III_fyoper.html#84778.

CHAPTER 16

Employee Benefits: Fundamentals, Life, and Disability Risks

The mandatory benefits that employees obtain through the workplace—workers' compensation, unemployment compensation, and Social Security—were discussed in earlier chapters. With this chapter we move into the voluntary benefits area of group insurance coverages offered by employers. We begin with an overall explanation of the **employee benefits** field and group insurance in this chapter. Our next step is to delve into the specific group benefits provided by employers through insurance or self-insurance. In addition to being regulated by the states as insurance products, employee benefits are also regulated by the federal government (under The Employee Retirement Income Security Act of 1974), especially when the employer self-insures and is not subject to state insurance regulation. Because there are many tax incentives available to employers that provide employee benefits, there are many nondiscrimination laws and specific limitations on the tax advantages. Employee benefits are regulated by the Department of Labor and the Internal Revenue Service.

To ensure your clear understanding of the main features of employee benefits, this chapter will include a general discussion of group insurance. The second part of the chapter will include a discussion of group life, group disability, and cafeteria plans. Some federal laws affecting employee benefits, such as the Americans with Disabilities Act, the Age Discrimination in Employment Act, and the Pregnancy Discrimination Act, are also covered. Chapter 17 will delve into the most expensive noncash benefit, the health care coverage. All types of managed care plans will be discussed along with the newest program of defined contribution health care plans. Relating to health insurance are long-term care and dental care, also discussed in Chapter 17. Two important federal laws, the Health Insurance Portability and Accountability Act of 1996 and the Consolidated Omnibus Budget Reconciliation Act of 1986, commonly known as COBRA, will also be explained in Chapter 17. Chapter 18 is devoted to employer-provided qualified pension plans under The Employee Retirement Income Security Act of 1974 (ERISA) and subsequent reforms such as the Tax Reform Act of 1986 and the most recent Economic Growth Tax Reform and Reconciliation Act of 2001 (EGTRRA). Chapter 18 also describes deferred compensation plans such as 403(b), 457, IRA, and Roth IRA. We will focus on qualified retirement plans, in which the employer contributes on the employee's behalf and receives tax benefits while the employee is not taxed until retirement.

The field of employee benefits is a topic of more than one full course. Therefore, your study in this and the following two chapters, along with the employee benefits case number 2 at the end of the text is just a short introduction to the field. This chapter covers the following:

1. Connection
2. Overview of employee benefits
3. Employer's objectives
4. Nature of group insurance
5. Federal laws regarding employee benefits
6. Group life insurance plans
7. Group disability insurance plans
8. Cafeteria plans and flexible spending accounts
9. Multinational employee benefit plans

CONNECTION

At this point in our study we are ready to discuss what the employer is doing for us in the overall process of our holistic risk management. Employers became involved in securing benefits for their employees during the industrial era when employees left the security of their homes and families and moved to the cities. The employer became the caretaker for health needs, burial, disability, and retirement. As the years passed, the government began giving employers tax incentives to continue to provide the "fringe" benefits. Today, these benefits are called noncash compensation and are very significant in the completeness of our risk management puzzle.

As noted in our complete risk management puzzle of Figure 16.1, we need to have coverage for the risks of health, premature death, disability, and living too long. These benefits and more are provided by most employers to their full-time employees. These coverages are the second stage in our stepstool. As you saw in the cases described in the introduction to this text of the hypothetical families affected by the attacks of September 11, the benefits offered by employers are critical in the build-up of our coverages. As you will see in the next section of this chapter, there is no individual underwriting when we are covered in the group contract of our employer. As such, for some employees with medical problems, the group life, disability, and health coverages are irreplaceable.

In our drill down into the specific pieces of the puzzle, we will learn again in this chapter that each risk is covered separately and that coverages from many sources protect each risk. It is up to us to pull together these separate pieces to provide a complete risk management portfolio. Whether the employer pays all, or requires us to participate in the cost of the coverages, the offers are important to consider and will not allow us a complete understanding of the holistic risk management process without these pieces. Better yet, some of the benefits provide wonderful tax breaks that should be well recognized.

OVERVIEW OF EMPLOYEE BENEFITS

Noncash compensation, or employee benefits, today is a large portion of the employer's cost of employment. The Employee Benefit Research Institute (EBRI), an important research organization in the area of employee benefits, reported that in 2000, employers spent $5.7 trillion in total compensation, out of which $874.4 billion was in the form of benefits (excluding paid leave and supplemental pay such as bonuses).[1] The complete picture of employee benefits cost per hour worked and as a percent of compensation is provided in Table 16.1 As you can see in this table, benefits make up a significant amount of the pay from employers with 27.2 percent of the total pay. The largest shares of the benefits go towards legally required benefits (social insurance), paid leave, and health insurance.

FIGURE 16.1   Connection between Risks and Employee Benefits: Group Life and Group Disability

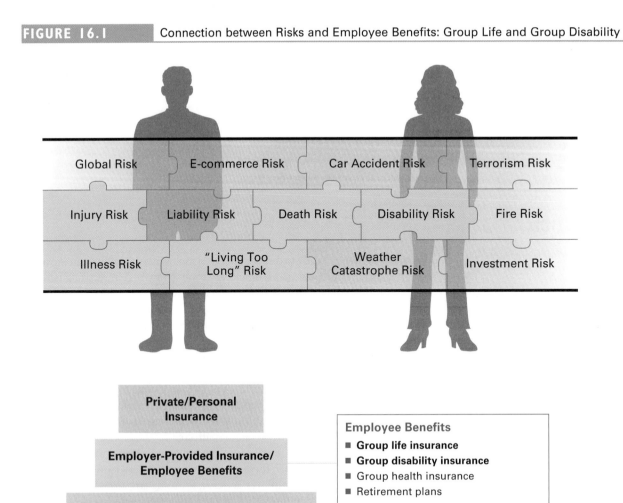

As noted above, employee benefits have tax incentives. Some benefits such as health-care, educational assistance, legal assistance, childcare, discounts, parking, cafeteria facility, and meals are deductible to the employer and completely tax exempt to the employees. Retirement benefits, both the contributions and earnings on the contributions, are tax deductible to the employer and tax deferred to the employees until their retirement. Some of the benefits paid by employees themselves are tax deferred, such as investment in 401(k) plans (discussed in Chapter 18). Other benefits are partially tax exempt, such as group life. The employee is not required to pay taxes on the cost of life insurance up to coverage in the amount of $50,000 in death benefits. For larger death benefits, the employer's contributed premiums (based on IRS Table 1) are counted as taxable income to the employee. This will be discussed later in this chapter.

When we do not pay taxes, the government is forgoing income. Each year, the White House Office of Management and Budget calculates the amounts forgone by the tax benefits. EBRI reports that the total amount for 2001 was $240.8 billion; for 2007, it is projected to be $360.95 billion.[2]

With the tax incentives comes a very stringent set of rules for nondiscrimination to ensure that employers provide the benefits to all employees, not only to executives and top

TABLE 16.1

Compensation Costs, Private Industry, Employer Costs per Hour Worked for Employee Compensation, Selected Years 1987–2002

Compensation Components	1987	1999	2001	2002
		Costs per hour worked		
Total Compensation	$13.42	$19.00	$20.81	$21.71
Wages and salaries	9.83	13.87	15.18	15.80
Total benefits	3.60	5.13	5.63	5.90
Paid leave	0.93	1.20	1.37	1.44
Vacation pay	a	0.59	0.68	0.72
Holiday pay	a	0.41	0.47	0.49
Sick leave	a	0.14	0.17	0.17
Other	a	0.05	0.06	0.06
Supplemental pay	0.32	0.55	0.61	0.62
Premium pay	a	0.23	0.24	0.24
Nonproduction bonus	a	0.05	0.05	0.06
Shift pay	a	0.28	0.32	0.32
Insurance	0.72	1.13	1.28	1.40
Life	a	0.04	0.05	0.04
Health	a	1.03	1.16	1.29
Short-term disability[b]	a	0.04	0.04	0.04
Long-term disability	a	0.02	0.03	0.03
Retirement and savings	0.48	0.57	0.62	0.63
Defined benefit plans	a	0.25	0.21	0.23
Defined contribution plans	a	0.32	0.40	0.40
Legally required[c]	1.13	1.65	1.73	1.80
Social Security	a	1.16	1.26	1.32
OASDI[d]	a	0.93	1.02	1.06
Medicare	a	0.23	0.25	0.26
Federal unemployment	a	0.03	0.03	0.03
State unemployment	a	0.10	0.09	0.10
Workers' compensation	a	0.36	0.33	0.35
Other benefits	0.02	0.03	0.02	0.03
		Percentage of total compensation		
Total compensation	100.0%	100.0%	100.0%	100.0%
Wages and salaries	73.2	73.0	72.9	72.8
Total benefits	26.8	27.0	27.1	27.2
Paid leave	6.9	6.3	6.6	6.6
Vacation pay	a	3.1	3.3	3.3
Holiday pay	a	2.2	2.3	2.3
Sick leave	a	0.7	0.8	0.8
Other	a	0.3	0.3	0.3
Supplemental pay	2.4	2.9	2.9	2.9
Premium pay	a	1.2	1.2	1.1
Nonproduction bonus	a	0.3	0.2	0.3
Shift pay	a	1.5	1.5	1.5
Insurance	5.4	5.9	6.2	6.4
Life	a	0.2	0.2	0.2
Health	a	5.4	5.6	5.9
Short-term disability[b]	a	0.2	0.2	0.2
Long-term disability	a	0.1	0.1	0.1
Retirement and savings	3.6	3.0	3.0	2.9
Defined benefit plans	a	1.3	1.0	1.1
Defined contribution plans	a	1.7	1.9	1.8
Legally required[c]	8.4	8.7	8.3	8.3
Social Security	a	6.1	6.1	6.1
OASDI[d]	a	4.9	4.9	4.9
Medicare	a	1.2	1.2	1.2
Federal unemployment	a	0.2	0.1	0.1
State unemployment	a	0.5	0.4	0.5
Workers' compensation	a	1.9	1.6	1.6
Other benefits[e]	0.1	0.2	0.1	0.1

This table is as of July 2002 and was provided by EBRI by special request. *Source:* U.S. Department of Labor, Bureau of Labor Statistics, Employer Costs for Employee Compensation, 1986-1999 and Employer Costs for Employee Compensation, March 2001 and March 2002 (Washington, DC: U.S. Government Printing Office, 2001 and 2002). www.bls.gov/ncs/ect/.

[a]Data not available. [b]Short-term disability (previously, sickness and accident insurance) includes all insured, self-insured, and state mandated plans that provide benefits for each disability, including unfunded plans. [c]Includes railroad retirement and supplemental retirement, railroad unemployment, and other legally required benefits in addition to those benefits shown. [d]Old-Age, Survivors, and Disability Insurance. [e]Includes severance pay and supplemental unemployment benefits. [f]Costs per hour is $0.01 or less.

management. The most stringent rules are per the Employee Retirement Income Security Act,[3] which will be explored briefly in Chapter 18 in the discussion of pensions. Keep in mind that employee benefits are a balance of tax incentives as long as employers do not break **nondiscrimination rules** and act in good faith for the protection of the employees in their **fiduciary** capacity. The efforts to protect employees in cases of bankruptcies are featured in "Important Issues: Fast Action on Bankruptcy from the PWBA."

EMPLOYER OBJECTIVES

The first step in managing an effective employee benefit program, as with the other aspects of risk management discussed in Chapter 3, is setting objectives. Objectives take into account both (1) the economic security needs of employees and (2) the financial constraints of the employer. Without objectives, a plan is likely to develop incrementally into a haphazard program. An employer who does not have an on-staff specialist in this field would be wise to engage an employee benefits consulting firm.

Employers can use several methods to set objectives for benefit plans. They may investigate what other organizations in the region or within the industry are doing, and then design a competitive package of their own to recruit and retain qualified employees. Benefits may be designed to compete with plans offered for unionized workers. Employers may survey employees to find out what benefits are most desired and then design the benefits package with employees' responses in mind.

Employer objectives are developed by answering questions such as the following:

- Who is eligible for each type of benefit?
- Should seniority, position, salary, and other characteristics influence the amount of each employee's benefit? Care with nondiscrimination rules is very important in this area.
- How might a specific benefit affect employee turnover, absenteeism, and morale?
- How should benefits be funded? Should the employer buy insurance or self-insure?
- Should the benefits program be designed to adjust to differing needs among employees?
- How do laws and regulations influence benefit plan design?
- To what extent should tax preferences affect plan design?

In answering questions like these, management must keep in mind the effect of its benefits decisions on the organization's prime need to operate at an efficient level of total expenditure with a competitive product price. Efficiency requires management of total labor costs, wages plus benefits. Thus, if benefits are made more generous, this can have a dampening effect on wages, all else being equal. Financial constraints are a major factor in benefit plan design.

NATURE OF GROUP INSURANCE

Individuals receive economic security from individually purchased insurance and from group insurance. Both types of coverage may provide protection against economic loss caused by death, disability, or sickness. To the covered person, the differences between the two types of coverage (shown in Table 16.2) may not be noticeable.

IMPORTANT ISSUES

Fast Action on Bankruptcy from the PWBA

A division of the U.S. Department of Labor, the Pension and Welfare Benefits Administration (PWBA), educates and assists the nation's 200 million participants and beneficiaries in pension, health, and other employee benefit plans and the more than 3 million sponsors of those plans. In carrying out its responsibility to protect participants' and beneficiaries' benefits, PWBA has targeted populations of plan participants who are potentially exposed to the greatest risk of loss. One such group of individuals is participants and beneficiaries of plans whose sponsor has filed for bankruptcy.

In bankruptcy situations, it is common to find employers holding assets that belong to or are owed to plans, occasionally intermingling those assets with the employers' own assets. Because of the tight time frames and the intricacies of the bankruptcy laws, plan assets and employee benefits could be lost because of the plan fiduciaries' failure to identify plan contributions that have not been paid to the plan's trust.

The new REACT (Rapid ERISA Action Team) initiative allows PWBA to respond quickly to protect the rights and benefits of plan participants when the plan sponsor faces severe financial hardship or bankruptcy and the assets of the employee benefit plan are in jeopardy. Under REACT, when a company has declared bankruptcy PWBA will take immediate action to ascertain whether there are plan contributions that have not been paid to the plans' trust, to advise all affected plans of the bankruptcy filing, and to provide assistance in filing proofs of claim to protect the plans, the participants, and the beneficiaries.

PWBA also attempts to identify the assets of the responsible fiduciaries and evaluate whether a lawsuit should be filed against those fiduciaries to ensure that the plans are made whole and the benefits secured.

An example that best illustrates the types of assistance the Rapid ERISA Action Team will deliver occurred in Chicago when a bank foreclosed on the line of credit of a struggling manufacturer. In order to meet its debt obligations, the employer used employee pension plan contributions. PWBA promptly intervened and nearly $75,000 in delinquent employee contributions were restored to the 401(k) plan.

Exploring the Internet

For more on pension plans and ERISA, see www.dol.gov/pwba/faqs/faq_consumer_pension.html. The home page of the PWBA, www.dol.gov/pwba/, has links to information on health care fraud, retirement savings, COBRA, HIPAA, and similar topics.

Portions reprinted from "Rapid ERISA Action Team for Bankruptcy," U.S. Department of Labor, Pension and Welfare Benefits Administration, www.dol.gov/pwba/newsroom/fs0102.html.

Administration

The administration of group insurance differs from individual insurance in that the contract is made with the employer rather than with each individual. The employer receives a **master contract** that describes all the terms and conditions of the group policy. The employer, in turn, provides each insured employee with a **certificate of insurance** as evidence of participation. **Participants** in the benefit plan may include employees, their dependents (including a spouse and children under a specified age, such as 21, when enrolled in school), retirees, and their dependents. Participants receive a booklet describing the plan, distributed by the employer at the time the plan goes into effect or when eligibility begins, whichever is later.

Administration of group insurance also differs from individual insurance in that the employer may be responsible for the record keeping ordinarily done by the insurer, especially if the group is large. Administration is simplified by the employer paying periodic premiums directly to the insurer. If employees are required to contribute toward the premium, the employer is responsible for collection or payroll deduction of employee contributions, as well as for payment to the insurer of the total group premium amount.

Many large employer plans are **self-insured,** and employers, rather than insurers, pay claims and bear the risk that actual claims will exceed expected claims. Some employers

TABLE 16.2	Comparison of Group Insurance and Individual Insurance	
	Individual Insurance Contract	**Group Insurance Contract**
Administration/Contract	Issued to the person insured	Master contract issued to employer or a trust; each employee is issued a certificate of insurance (not a contract)
Underwriting	Evidence of insurability	Characteristic of the group to minimize adverse selection and administrative costs
Eligibility	At inception of contract	Related to employment periods
Experience Rating/Pricing	Experience of the insurance company	Experience of the large group

with self-insured plans also administer the benefits themselves. However, insurers and **third-party administrators (TPAs)** administer many (even large) self-funded plans under an **administrative services only (ASO)** contract. The employer transfers record keeping and claim payment functions to the insurer or TPA, paying about 5 to 10 percent of the normal premium for administrative services.

In addition, the employer may purchase **stop loss insurance** from the same or another insurer through the TPA for protection against unexpectedly high claims. Stop loss coverage is a form of reinsurance or excess insurance for self-insured plans. The two basic forms of coverage are **specific stop loss,** in which a limit is set per claim, and **aggregate stop loss,** in which a limit is set for the total claims in a year. The insurer reimburses the employer for claim amounts above the limit, also called the "attachment point." Purchase of an ASO contract and stop loss insurance gives the employer the potential cash flow and expense advantage of self-funding, while reducing the employer's administrative burden and potential for catastrophic risk.

Underwriting

Individually purchased life and health insurance involve individual underwriting. The purchaser files an application and, in some cases, takes a medical examination. On the basis of this and other information, the underwriter decides whether or not to issue insurance, and on what terms. The merits of each application are decided individually. **Group underwriting** does not involve an application to the insurer by each participant, or a medical examination (except in some very small employer groups). The group as a whole is being underwritten. The employer makes one application for the entire group, and, instead of selecting individual insureds, the insurer makes an underwriting decision based on group characteristics.

Characteristics of the Group as Key Underwriting Determinants

Reason for the Group's Existence   It is imperative that the group was not created for insurance purposes. Insurance should be incidental to the group's formation. Under state laws, the following are eligible groups for group insurance:

- Individual employer groups
- Negotiated trusteeships
- Trade associations
- Labor union groups

■   Multiple-employer trusts (METs) or multiple employer welfare arrangements

Some, mostly smaller, employers may have trouble finding an insurance carrier willing to service their group if one or more individuals are in ill health. Many of these firms, however, have access to group insurance by participating in a multiple employer trust (MET). The MET makes available to small employers, often in the same industry group and with as few as one or two employees each, benefits similar to those available to large groups. METs often are organized for a trade association, union, or other sponsoring organization by an insurer or third-party administrator. When small employers come together through an MET to purchase insurance, they have access to group underwriting treatment, products, and services similar to those available to large employers.[4]

Financial Stability of the Employer   Insurers prefer to work with firms that will exist during the year and be able to pay the premium. Since the cash flow is moving very fast in group insurance such as health insurance, financial stability is critical to underwriters accepting the business. This requirement is really fundamental to all types of underwriting, not only group underwriting.

Prior Experience of the Plan   This factor is important not only in accepting a group for coverage, but also in pricing the group plan. Insurers look at past losses—the frequency, severity, and length of illnesses or disabilities—when deciding whether to accept a business and then how to price it. Pricing factors will be discussed later in this section.

Size of the Group   As you recall from the first two chapters of this text, the law of large numbers is very important to the functioning of insurance. Therefore, large groups can be rated on their own experience while small groups have to be rated based on the insurer's experience with groups of similar type and size.

Source and Method of Premium Payment   Insurance laws may require that a minimum percentage of the group be enrolled in the benefit plan to ensure that there are enough healthy employees and dependents to help offset the high claims that can be expected from unhealthy employees or dependents. Every group, insured or self-insured, can anticipate enrollment by the unhealthy. The likelihood of achieving minimum participation (meaning at least 75 percent) is increased by **employer sharing of costs.** Most states and insurers require that noncontributory plans, in which employees do not pay for the cost of their coverage, enroll 100 percent of employees. In contributory plans, where employees pay all or part of the premium amount, 75 percent of employees must participate. This helps protect the plan from adverse selection.

Stability of the Group   To avoid the problems associated with high employee turnover, employers use waiting periods or probationary periods before insurance coverage begins. There are some advantages to turnover, however; for one, the age composition does not get older when more new employees join the plan.

Persistency of the Group   Group business is costly for the insurer in the first year. An employer that changes carriers every year will be an undesirable client. Insurers look for more permanent relationship with the employers.

Method of Determining Benefits   To avoid adverse selection, employers are required under nondiscrimination laws to offer the same benefits package to all employees. In reality, many groups provide **flexible benefit programs,** which allow employee input into the amount of each benefit, and **supplemental plans,** which allow employees to purchase additional amounts of a specific benefit on a fully contributory basis. These options undoubtedly invite adverse selection, which is reflected in higher rates for flexible and supplemental benefits. However, given the diversity in needs among single, married, divorced, younger, older, male, and female employees in the typical group, the advantages of giving employees a voice in benefit decisions may well outweigh the cost of some adverse selection. Flexible benefit programs, also known as cafeteria plans, are discussed later in this chapter.

Supplemental plans allow employees to choose additional group insurance coverage paid for entirely by themselves. For example, supplemental life coverage can allow an employee to increase the face amount of group life insurance coverage, and supplemental group disability coverage can allow for a cost-of-living benefit increase for periods of long-term disability. In recent years, the use of supplemental plans has grown, largely due to the flexibility they provide to employees at little or no cost to employers other than facilitating the payroll deductions.

The potential for adverse selection may be greater with supplemental benefits than with nonsupplemental benefits. Since employees pay the premium for supplemental coverage, it is likely that those who anticipate to need the benefit are more willing to participate. Despite this, supplemental plans are popular because they allow employees to tailor benefits to meet their individual needs through a convenient payroll deduction plan.

Provisions for Determining Eligibility   Generally, employees are first eligible for benefits either immediately upon hiring or following a three- to six-month **probationary period.** Following hiring or the probationary period (whichever the employer requires), the employee's **eligibility period** usually extends for thirty-one days, during which employees may sign up for group insurance coverage. This period is called **open enrollment.** In order for coverage to become effective, most group plans require that the employee be **actively at work** on the day that coverage would normally become effective. Being at work provides some evidence of good health and helps reduce adverse selection.

Enrollment after the eligibility period usually means that the employee will have to provide evidence of insurability. The employee may have to complete a questionnaire or have a medical examination to show that he or she is in good health. This provision helps reduce adverse selection. Most employers allow only full-time employees to participate in the benefit plan. (The definition of full-time differs from employer to employer; the minimum may be as low as 20 hours per week, but it is more often 32 to 35 hours.) To lower adverse selection, part-time employees are not included, as some part-time employees join the work force only for the benefits. Some employers provide minimal benefits for part-time employees, such as burial cost only instead of full death benefits.

Administrative Aspects   The most important part of this requirement is to what extent the employer plans to help in the enrollment and claims process.

The last few factors in underwriting are self-explanatory. They are (1) the age and gender composition of the group, (2) the industry represented by the group, and (3) the geographical location of the group.

Pricing

Some employers pay the entire cost of the group insurance premium. These are **noncontributory plans.** In **contributory plans,** employees pay part of the cost. Frequently, group life and disability insurance plans are noncontributory, but require the employees to contribute if other family members are covered. Health insurance, because of rising premiums as described in the "Ethical Dilemma: What Is the Tradeoff Between Health Care Cost and Benefits?" of Chapter 17, is more and more likely to be contributory. The employer makes the premium payment to the insurer; contributory amounts, if any, are deducted from the employee's paycheck.

Group insurance is usually less expensive than individual insurance for several reasons: (1) with group coverage, the insurer deals with one insured instead of many, streamlining marketing costs; (2) the employer takes care of much of the administrative detail; (3) commission scales on group business are lower than they are on individual policies; (4) medical examinations are not needed, because the employees are at least healthy enough to work; (5) the employer collects the premiums and pays the insurer in one lump sum, which is more efficient for the insurer; and (6) the employer often does some monitoring to eliminate false or unnecessary claims for health care benefits. In addition, group insurance theory maintains that the replacement by younger employees of employees who retire or quit keeps average mortality and morbidity rates from rising to prohibitive levels. That is, a flow of persons through the group tends to keep average costs down. This is often true when the number of employees in a group is growing, but is less true for an organization that is downsizing.

Group life and health insurance rates are usually quoted by insurers as one monthly rate (for example, $0.15 per $1,000 of coverage in the case of life insurance) for all employees. This rate is based on a weighted average, taking into account the age, sex, and accompanying mortality and morbidity rates for each employee in the group. Since mortality and morbidity rates increase with age, life insurance rates are quoted in age brackets. Someone in the 31–35 age bracket will pay slightly more than someone in the 26–30 bracket. Thus groups with a higher proportion of older people will have relatively higher premiums.

Most small organizations, for example, those with fewer than fifty employees, have their entire premium based on pooled claims experience for similar-sized firms. However, larger employers are likely to have **experience-rated premiums,** in which the group's own claims experience affects the cost of coverage as described in Chapter 13 for workers' compensation. Experience rating allows employer groups to benefit directly from their own good claims experience, and provides a direct economic incentive for risk managers to control claims.

With experience rating, the weight or credibility given to a group's own experience increases with the number of participants. The experience of smaller groups (for example, those with fewer than 500 or 1,000 employees) is not considered sufficiently statistically credible or reliable to determine premiums completely. Insurers, therefore, use a weighted average of the group's loss experience and the pooled experience for groups of similar size and characteristics in developing the claims charge. For example, the group's actual loss experience may be weighted at 70 percent of the claims charge and the pooled experience for groups of similar attributes may carry a weight of 30 percent. If the group had a loss experience of $80,000 and the pool experience was $100,000, then the claims charge for the experience-rated premium would be $86,000 per year. A larger group would have more statistically reliable experience and might receive an 80 percent weighting for its own experience and a 20 percent weighting for the pooled experience, resulting in a claims charge of $84,000. Thus, the larger the group, the more credit the group receives for its own claims experience. The experience-rated claims charge makes up the bulk of the total premium due, but the final experience-rated premium also includes administrative charges and fees.

Premiums for larger organizations, however, may reflect only the group's own loss experience. With prospective experience rating, the group's claims experience for the previous few years, plus an inflation factor, partly or completely determines the premium for the current year. A retrospective experience rating plan uses loss experience to determine whether premium refunds (or dividends) should be paid at the end of each policy year.

Group insurance premiums paid by the employer are a deductible business expense and are not taxable income to employees except for amounts of term life insurance in excess of $50,000 per person and all group property–liability insurance. Employee premium contributions are not tax deductible, except if allowed to be used in a cafeteria program under a **premium conversion plan** or **flexible spending account (FSA)** discussed later in this chapter. The other tax-sheltered accounts available under health reimbursement arrangement (HRA) or medical savings account (MSA) plans are discussed in Chapter 17. Proceeds paid from group life insurance at death are not taxable income to the beneficiary, as noted in Chapter 14, but are included in the estate of the insured, if he or she is the owner, for federal estate tax purposes.

Group disability insurance premiums paid by the employer are also a deductible business expense for the employer, and do not result in an immediate tax liability for the employee. If an employee receives disability benefits, the portion paid for by the employer is taxable to the employee. For example, if the employer pays one-third of the premium amount for disability coverage, and if the employee becomes disabled and receives benefits, one-third of the benefits are taxable income to the employee. Benefits attributable to coverage paid for by the employee with after-tax dollars are not taxable. Thus, in this example, two-thirds of the disability benefit amount would not be taxable income. Explaining taxation of disability income to employees can be a challenge to the benefits manager. However, many employers are successful in conveying the importance of after tax premium payment to the level of benefits that may result in case of disability. The tax savings on the premiums are very small relative to the tax savings on the disability benefits.

FEDERAL REGULATION: COMPLIANCE WITH NONDISCRIMINATION LAWS

As noted above, administration and design of group employee benefit plans have been affected by federal regulation through ERISA, EGTRRA, 2001 (discussed in Chapter 18), the Age Discrimination in Employment Act, the Civil Rights Act (which includes pregnancy nondiscrimination), and the Americans with Disabilities Act. The Social Security Act was discussed in Chapter 15; the Health Maintenance Organization Act is discussed in Chapter 17 with medical care delivery systems. Federal legislation is concerned with nondiscrimination in coverage and benefit amounts for plan participants.

Age Discrimination in Employment Act

The **Age Discrimination in Employment Act (ADEA)** was first passed in 1967 and is known primarily for eliminating mandatory retirement on the basis of age. That is, employees cannot be forced to retire at any age, with the exception of some executives who may be subject to compulsory retirement. Employee benefits are also affected by the ADEA, since the law was amended to require that benefits must be continued for older workers. Most benefits can be reduced to the point where the cost of providing benefits for older workers is no greater than for younger workers except health care benefits. The Act makes this an option; employers are not required to reduce benefits for older workers. Employers choosing to reduce some benefits for older workers generally do not reduce benefits except for workers over age 65, even though reductions prior to age 65 may be legally allowed based on cost.

The employer may reduce benefits on a benefit-by-benefit basis based on the cost of coverage, or may reduce them across the board based on the overall cost of the package. For example, with the benefit-by-benefit approach, the amount of life insurance in force might be reduced at older ages to compensate for the extra cost of term coverage at advanced ages. Alternatively, several different benefits for an older worker might be reduced to make the total cost of the older worker's package commensurate with the cost of younger workers' packages.

Life and disability insurance may be reduced for older workers. Acceptable amounts of life insurance reductions are specified by law. For example, employees age 65 to 69 may be eligible for life insurance benefit amounts equal to 65 percent of the amounts available to eligible employees under age 65; employees age 70 to 74 may receive only 45 percent. Disability benefits provided through sick leave plans may not be reduced on the basis of age. Reductions in benefit amounts for short-term disability insured plans are allowed, but are relatively uncommon in actual practice. Long-term disability benefits may be reduced for older workers through two methods. Benefit amounts may be reduced and duration remain the same, or benefit duration may be curtailed and amounts remain the same. This is justified on the basis of cost, since the probability of disability and the average length of disability increase at older ages.

Medical benefits may not be reduced for older employees. Employers must offer older workers private group medical benefits that are equal to those offered to younger participants, even if active workers over age 65 are eligible for Medicare. Medicare is the secondary payer for active employees over age 65, covering only those expenses not covered by the primary payer, the employee's group medical insurance.

The Civil Rights Act

Traditionally, employee benefit plans have not been required to provide benefits for pregnancy and other related conditions. Including disability and medical benefits for pregnancy can significantly increase costs. However, in 1978 the **Civil Rights Act** was amended to require employers to provide the same benefits for pregnancy and related medical conditions as are provided for other medical conditions. If an employer provides sick leave, disability, or medical insurance, then the employer must provide these benefits in the event of employee pregnancy. Spouses of employees must also be treated equally with respect to pregnancy-related conditions. This federal regulation applies only to plans with more than fifteen employees, but some states impose similar requirements on smaller employers.

Americans with Disabilities Act

As described in Chapter 13, the 1990 **Americans with Disabilities Act (ADA)** forbids employers with more than fifteen employees from discriminating against disabled persons in employment. Disabled persons are those with physical or mental impairments limiting major life activities such as walking, seeing, or hearing. The ADA has important implications for employee benefits. The ADA is not supposed to disturb the current regulatory system or alter industry practices such as underwriting. Therefore, under ADA, disabled employees must have equal access to the same health benefits as other employees with the same allowances for coverage limitations. The guidelines allow blanket pre-existing conditions, but not "disability-based" provisions. For example, if the medical plan does not cover vision care, the employer does not have to offer vision care treatment to disabled employees. However, if vision care is provided by the plan, then vision care must also be offered to employees with disabilities. Recent Supreme Court cases clarified the intent of the ADA. Most important is the clarification that the ADA is concerned with a person's ability to perform regular daily living activities and not his or her ability to perform a specific job.

Family Medical Leave Act

Under the **Family Medical Leave Act** (FMLA) of 1993, an employer with fifty or more employees must grant an eligible employee (one who has been employed by the employer for at least twelve months) up to a total of twelve work-weeks of unpaid leave during any twelve-month period for one or more of the following reasons:

- For the birth and care of the employee's newborn child
- For placement with the employee of a child for adoption or foster care
- To care for an immediate family member (spouse, child, or parent) with a serious health condition
- To take medical leave when the employee is unable to work because of a serious health condition

This law may sometimes create conflicting interpretations, especially in relationship to workers' compensation and disability leaves. Employee benefits administrators are advised to track the leave taken by employees under different programs and ensure compliance with the law.[5] Compliance issues require clarifications; a recent Supreme Court decision clarified that only material denial of the FMLA statute should trigger penalties.[6]

GROUP LIFE INSURANCE

Group life insurance is the oldest of the employer-sponsored group insurance benefits, dating from 1912. The most common type of group life insurance offered by employers is yearly renewable term coverage. It is the least expensive form of protection the employer can provide for employees during their working years. Due to a shorter average life expectancy, older employees and males have relatively higher premium rates. The premium for the entire group is the sum of the appropriate age- or sex-based premium for each member of the group. Obviously, a particular employee's premium will increase yearly with age. However, if younger employees continue to be hired, the lower premium for new hires can offset increases due to aging employees hired some years earlier. Also, if young employees replace older ones, premiums will tend to stabilize or decrease. This flow of covered lives helps maintain a fairly stable average total premium for the employer group.

Benefits

Most group term life insurance provides death benefit amounts equal to the employee's annual salary, one and a half times the salary, or twice the salary. Some provide three or four times the salary, but some states and many insurers set limits on maximum benefits. Some provide a flat amount, such as $10,000 or $50,000. Other employers base the amount on the position of the employee, but they have to be careful to adhere to the nondiscrimination laws. An amount equal to some multiplier of the salary is most common and reduces the possibilities of discrimination. Insurers' underwriting limitations are usually related to the total volume of insurance on the group.

Additional amounts of term life insurance may be available on a supplemental basis. Employers sponsor the supplemental plan, and employees usually pay the entire premium through payroll deduction. This allows employees to increase life insurance based on their individual needs. Supplemental coverages are usually subject to insurability evidence to avoid adverse selection. Accidental death and dismemberment insurance is also part of added benefits. This coverage provides an additional principal sum paid for accidental death. The death must occur within ninety days of the accident. The coverage also comes in multipliers of salary. The dismemberment part of the coverage is for loss of limb or eyesight. Dependent life insurance is available for low amounts for burial and funeral expenses. Benefits are small for children and spouses. Most employers also add waiver of premiums so that in the event the employee becomes disabled, premiums are waived. Added benefits are also called voluntary coverage, since the employee always pays for the coverage.

Beneficiary designation is determined by the insured persons; in some states, the employer may not be the beneficiary. The beneficiary can choose from the settlement options detailed in Chapter 14. Any mistake in age made by the employer is corrected by premium adjustment, unlike individual coverage, which adjusts the death benefit. There is a grace period of thirty days for the premiums.

Life insurance policies have changed to meet the changing needs of policyholders. Many life insurance policies today allow benefits to be paid early in the event that the insured has a terminal illness or catastrophic medical expenses, as noted in Chapter 14. The insured must provide evidence that life expectancy is less than six months or one year, or proof of catastrophic illness such as cancer or liver failure. The insured can then receive living benefits or accelerated death benefits rather than the traditional death benefit. Living benefits are limited in amount, typically from 25 to 50 percent of the face amount of the life insurance policy. The balance of the benefit (minus insurer expenses) is paid to beneficiaries after the death of the insured. Generally, adding the living benefits rider does not increase total group costs, and employers and employees will not pay more for the option.

Since living benefits may not provide enough funds to the terminally ill person, some may prefer to sell their policy to a **viatical settlement** company, which gives more funds up front, up to 80 percent of the face amount. Viatical settlements used to be very controversial, as you can read in the "Ethical Dilemma: Do Viatical Settlements Have a Place in Today's Market?" of this chapter.

Many group plans terminate an employee's group life insurance benefit when he or she retires. Those that allow employees to maintain coverage after retirement usually reduce substantially the amount of insurance available. If an employee is insurable at retirement, additional life insurance may be purchased on an individual basis. Alternatively, the employee can use the **conversion privilege** in most group plans (regardless of the reason that employment terminates) to buy an equal or lower amount of permanent life insurance with level premiums based on the employee's attained age. Conversion takes place without demonstrating evidence of insurability. Because mortality rates increase rapidly after middle age, the costs of conversion are high as well.

Taxation of the group life is subject to IRS section 79, which states that the employer's premium contribution of up to $50,000 of death coverage is not considered income to the employee for income tax purposes. For any premiums for an amount of death benefits greater than $50,000, the employee has to pay taxes on the premiums as an income for income tax purposes. The premiums for the income calculations are based on the Uniform Premium Table I (revised in 1999 for lower rates) shown in Table 16.3.

Ethical Dilemma

Do Viatical Settlements Have a Place in Today's Market?

Viatical settlements involve the sale of an existing life insurance policy by a terminally ill person to a third party. Viaticals saw their heyday during the late 1980s as AIDS patients, with little time left, sought funds to live out their final days or months with dignity. Numerous companies were formed in which individuals invested in the life insurance policies of AIDS patients, essentially betting on the short life expectancy of the policyholder. The investor would give the insured about 80 percent of the death benefits, expecting to generate a large return in less than a year when the insured passed away and the proceeds would be collected by the investor/beneficiary.

With the advent of protease inhibitors in the mid-1990s, the life expectancy of people with AIDS increased dramatically. AIDS viaticals no longer looked like such a good investment. But the industry has not disappeared. Today, companies selling viaticals seek out individuals with other terminal illnesses, such as cancer or ALS (Lou Gehrig's disease). They also market very similar products, called life settlements, to the elderly with short life expectancy.

Viatical settlements are possible because ownership of life insurance may be transferred at its owners' discretion. Viatical settlement firms typically buy insurance policies worth $10,000 and more from individuals with one to four years left to live. Both individual and employer-provided life insurance (group life) policies can be sold. Once sold, the new owner pays the premiums. The former owner uses the settlement money for anything from health expenses to taking that last dream vacation.

The option to receive a portion of the life proceeds before death is not new. The accelerated benefit option in life policies allows terminally ill policyholders access to the death benefits of their policies before they die. In such a case, a percentage of the face value (usually 50 percent or less) is paid in a lump sum to the policyholder. The rest of the insurance is paid to the beneficiary at the time of death. The low amount available under the accelerated benefit option is the impetus to the development of the viatical settlement companies. With transfer of ownership, the insured can get much more than 50 percent of the policy amount.

While viatical and life settlements can provide greatly needed funds to terminally ill individuals, they are not without pitfalls. They pay less than the face value of the policy. Life settlements usually provide higher amounts than the "cash value" of a policy, but still less than the face value of the policy. Settlement money may be subject to taxation, while life insurance benefits are not. Because beneficiaries may contest the sale of life insurance, which will reduce their inheritance, their advance approval is required. Seniors whose beneficiaries have died, however, often have no reason to continue paying premiums and may let their policies lapse anyway. In this case, selling their policy may provide them with funds they would otherwise never see.

Concerned that insureds may be taken advantage of, insurance regulators are busy establishing regulations over the viatical and life settlement industry. The National Association of Insurance Commissioners (NAIC) has developed model viatical settlement regulation for states to adopt.

Questions for Discussion

1. Is it ethical to profit from someone else's misfortune by buying their life insurance at a discount?

2. Are viaticals a good idea for the policyholder? What are their advantages and disadvantages?

3. Do you think there is a need for viatical or life settlements when accelerated benefits are available?

Sources: Ron Panko, "Is There Still Room for Viaticals?" *Best's Review,* April 2002; Lynn Asinof, "Is Selling Your Life Insurance Good Policy in the Long Term?" *The Wall Street Journal,* 15 May 2002; Karen Stevenson Brown, "Life Insurance Accelerated Benefits," www.elderweb.com/, National Association of Insurance Commissioners, www.naic.org; Life Partners Inc., www.lifepartnersinc.com/Viaticals.htm.

Group universal life insurance is available from many employers. This insurance is usually offered as a supplement to a separate program of group term benefits. Universal life premiums are paid by employees and are administered through payroll deduction. A substantial amount of coverage (for example, twice the annual salary up to a maximum of $100,000 in face amount) is available without evidence of insurability. Low administrative expenses and low agents' commissions usually result in reasonably priced insurance. Group universal life insurance plans have become increasingly popular with both employers and employees. Employers are able to sponsor a life insurance plan that covers workers during their active years and into retirement, at little or no cost to the employer.

Age	Cost per Month per $1,000 Coverage
24 and under	$ .05
25–29	.06
30–34	.08
35–39	.09
40–44	.10
45–49	.15
50–54	.23
55–59	.43
60–64	.66
65–69	1.27
70 and over	2.06

TABLE 16.3
Uniform Premium
IRS Table I

For example, the employer's expense may be limited to the costs of providing explanatory material to new employees, making payroll deductions of premiums, and sending a monthly check for total premiums to the insurer. Group universal life insurance is also popular with employees, largely because of the flexibility of the product.

GROUP DISABILITY INSURANCE

Group disability income coverage provides economic security for employees who are unable to work due to illness or injury. The coverage is to replace lost income. Disability income coverage is important, since employee disability can mean not only lost or reduced income but also added medical and rehabilitation expenses. An extended disability may result in greater economic hardship for the family than does the premature death of the employee. Employers, however, are less likely to provide group disability insurance than group life or medical expense insurance.

Disability income may be provided on a short- or long-term basis. The flow of a seamless coverage of group disability income without gaps is shown in Table 16.4. It used to be that employers would offer only sick leave and long-term disability, leaving employees without coverage for a period of time. Consultants and employee benefits specialists urge employers to close the gap and provide seamless coverage as noted in Table 16.4.

Group Short-Term Disability Plans

The first step in short-term disability coverage is sick leave plans (also called **salary continuation plans).** With sick leave plans, employees accumulate leave, typically at a rate of one day per month of work up to a maximum of twenty-six weeks. In the event of illness or disability, the employee uses sick leave and receives 100 percent income replacement beginning on the first day of illness or disability. Today, many employers do not offer sick leave separately from vacation. The combined time off is called **paid time off (PTO).** Under PTO there is less incentive to abuse sick leave and more reward to employees who never use sick leave. PTO consolidates sick leave, personal leave, and vacation leave into a total number of personal days off each year.

Short-term disability income replacement through insured plans generally includes all full-time employees after meeting some probationary period, such as three months. Unlike sick leave, these plans do not pay benefits until after an **elimination period,** typically from one to seven days of absence from work due to disability. The employee may be required periodically to provide medical evidence of continuing disability. These plans pay

TABLE 16.4		Seamless Coverage of Group Disability Insurance	
Coverage	Salary Continuation/ Sick Leave	Short-Term Disability (STD)	Long-Term Disability (LTD)
Length of coverage	7 or more days paid time off	From 7 days up to 3, 6, 12 months or 2 years (flexibility)	From expiration of STD to age 65 or to lifetime
Replacement of income	100% of pay	May be as high as 100% of pay, but 65–75% is more common (up to a maximum)	Usually 60%–70% of pay coordinated with Social Security and workers' compensation (up to a maximum)
Definition of disability	Inability to do your own job	Inability to do your own job or a job for which you are qualified by education and training; nonoccupational	Inability to do a job for which you are qualified by education and training, or inability to work at all; occupational and nonoccupational

for the duration stipulated in the employer's policy, usually ranging from three months to two years (although the majority pay for one year at most). Group short-term disability insurance plans do not provide full income replacement, but pay 65 to 75 percent of salary. This provision reduces moral hazard and encourages employees to return to work.

The **definition of disability** determines when the employee is eligible for benefits. Short-term disability insurance policies generally define disability as the inability of the employee to perform any and every duty of the job. This liberal definition allows disabled workers to qualify for benefits relatively easily when compared with the definition of disability used by most group long-term disability insurance policies. Some STD policies require a more stringent definition of disability, especially those that provide coverage for a year or more. Under this definition, the employee will receive benefits only if unable to perform a job for which he or she is qualified by education and training. Generally, group short-term disability policies pay only for nonoccupational disability, and workers' compensation benefits cover employees for short-term occupational income loss.

Group Long-Term Disability Plans

The eligibility criteria for group **long-term disability insurance** are often different from those for short-term insured plans. Unlike short-term insured plans, which generally cover all full-time workers, long-term disability plans usually cover mostly salaried workers after they meet a probationary period lasting from three months to one year. Long-term disability plans also have an elimination period prior to payment of benefits, ranging from three to six months. The elimination period is often equivalent to the benefit period for the short-term disability plan. If the elimination period is longer than the period covered by short-term income replacement, the employee may have a gap in coverage.

The definition of disability used for long-term plans is generally more restrictive than for short-term plans. Most contracts pay only if the employee is unable to engage in the material duties of the job. Under this definition the employee will receive benefits only if he or she cannot perform a job for which he or she is qualified by education, experience, and training. For example, a surgeon who can no longer perform surgery because of a hand injury may be able to manage the surgery room. This employee will not be eligible for LTD.

Some group STD and LTD policies use a dual definition of disability. For example, benefits are payable while the own-occupation definition applies for a relatively short period of time, for example, two or three years. After that, long-term benefits are paid only if the employee is unable to engage in any reasonable occupation for which he or she is or can become qualified. Use of both definitions provides economic security to the employee and an economic incentive to find reasonable, gainful employment.

The benefit period for LTD policies can vary greatly. Employees may be covered only for five or ten years, or they may be covered until retirement age or for life. Typically, group LTD plans pay no more than 60 to 70 percent of salary to disabled employees. In addition, a maximum dollar benefit amount may apply. Group disability benefits are usually coordinated with other disability income from Social Security or workers' compensation to ensure that the overall benefits are still below the level earned prior to disability. Employees may be able to obtain additional nongroup disability insurance in the individual market to increase their total amount of protection, although seldom to the level of full income replacement. This ensures that the disabled person has an economic incentive to return to work.

Most group LTD contracts include a rehabilitation provision. This allows insureds to return to work on a trial basis for one or two years while partial long-term disability benefits continue. If disabled employees are unable to perform in the new job, long-term disability benefits are fully restored. By providing this safety net, insurers encourage disabled workers to attempt to return to work through rehabilitative employment. Insurers may also assist with training and rehabilitation costs, since these can be far less than continuing benefit payments for those who do not return to work.

LTD benefit amounts may also be affected by supplemental benefits made available to employees through payroll deduction. Cost-of-living adjustments can be added to prevent the erosion of purchasing power of the disability income benefit. Survivors' benefits can protect employee dependents after the death of the disabled employee.

Group LTD contracts contain several important exclusions. Benefits are not paid unless the employee is under a physician's care. Benefits are not paid for self-inflicted injuries, and **preexisting condition clauses** may restrict coverage. Generally, benefits are not paid if the employee is gainfully employed elsewhere.

In the past, long-term disability claims experience (both frequency and duration) for hourly workers has been especially unfavorable (relative to salaried employees). This may be because hourly workers are more likely to be in jobs that are monotonous and produce lower satisfaction, factors which do not help keep employees at work or encourage them to return quickly. Disability claim frequency among hourly workers has risen especially during periods of economic recession, when job security is threatened. Hourly employees may choose to make a disability claim rather than to be laid off with temporary and minimal unemployment benefits. Because of unfavorable claims experience, employers and insurers are reluctant to provide hourly workers with long-term disability insurance.

For salaried workers, too, there has been a shift in long-term disability claims experience in the last few years. The frequency and duration of claims by salaried employees and highly paid professionals, particularly physicians, have increased significantly. The rise in claims among physicians may be due in part to an increasingly litigious environment for practicing medicine and to health care financing reform initiatives that threaten the traditional practice of medicine, factors that can negatively affect physician job satisfaction. Among non-medical professionals, the increased incidence may be due to a more stressful business environment characterized by firm downsizing, especially among mid- and upper-management employees. Employers and insurers are paying attention to the increased incidence of claims among salaried employees, and in some cases are limiting the amount of benefits payable for long-term disability to reduce any potential moral hazard problems.

Whether group disability benefits are taxable income to the employee depends on who pays the premiums. If the employer pays the premium, the employee will be taxed on the benefits. If the employee pays with after-tax income, the employee will not have to pay taxes on the benefits. Thus many employers advise their employees to pay for this coverage themselves with after-tax income through payroll deduction.

Traditionally, disability insurance has never been easy to sell. However, the need for such a product is always clearer during hard times. It is known that financial planners look at the lack of disability coverage as a gap in the complete coverage for a person. A downturn in the economy is helpful in pushing the sales of disability income policies.[7]

THE FLEXIBILITY ISSUE

Employers have been interested in flexible benefit plans since the early 1970s. These plans give the employee choices among an array of benefits or cash and benefits. Few flexible plans were adopted until tax issues were clarified in 1984. At that time, it became clear that employees could choose between taxable cash income and nontaxable benefits without adversely affecting the favorable tax status of a benefit plan. However, since then the rules regarding **cafeteria plans** and flexible spending accounts have continued to change, resulting in some employer hesitancy to adopt these plans. Despite the uncertain legislative environment, flexible plans became very popular in the mid-1980s, particularly among large employers. Employers are attracted to flexible benefit plans because, relative to traditional designs, they:

- Increase employee awareness of the cost and value of benefit plans
- Meet diverse employee economic security needs
- Help control total employer costs for the benefit plan
- Improve employee morale and job satisfaction

How flexible benefit plans accomplish these goals will become clear through discussion of cafeteria plans and flexible spending accounts.

Cafeteria Plans

Flexible benefit plans frequently are called **cafeteria plans** because they allow selection of the types and amounts of desired benefits. A cafeteria plan usually involves five elements: flexible benefit credits, minimum levels of certain benefits, optional benefits, cash credits, and tax deferral.

In a cafeteria plan, the employer generally allows each employee to spend a specified number of flexible credits, usually expressed in dollar amounts. The number of credits assigned each year may vary with employee salary, length of service, and age. Some employers allow the employee to spend the flexible credits on a combination of benefits and cash, whereas others require that all credits be applied to benefits. The cash element is necessary to be considered a cafeteria plan for tax purposes.

Cafeteria plans are under Section 125 of the Internal Revenue Code. Under the plan, all participants may choose between two or more benefits consisting of qualified benefits and cash. Qualified benefits in a cafeteria plan are any welfare benefits excluded from taxation under the Internal Revenue Code. Long-term care is not included, while a 401(k) plan is included.

Benefit election must be made prior to the beginning of the plan year and cannot be changed during the plan year unless allowed by the plan and for changes in the following:

1. Legal marital status
2. Number of dependents

3. Employment status
4. Work schedule
5. Dependent status under a health plan for unmarried dependents
6. Residence or worksite of the employee, spouse, or dependent

The employer may restrict employee benefit choice to some degree, since the employer has a vested interest in making sure that some minimal level of economic security is provided to employees. For example, the organization might be embarrassed if the employee did not elect health coverage and was subsequently unable to pay a large hospital bill. Most flexible benefit plans specify a minimum level of certain benefits judged to be essential. For example, a core of medical, death, and disability benefits may be specified for all employees. The employee can elect out of a core benefit by supplying written evidence that similar benefits are available from another source, such as the spouse's employer or the military retirement system.

Each benefit will have a per unit price. For example, group term life insurance, above a core level equal to one year's pay, may be available in units of $10,000 up to a maximum of five times the employee's annual pay. The price of a unit may vary with the employee's age and sex. Evidence of insurability may be required at some level, such as three times annual pay. If the employee chooses additional units of an optional benefit, the employee spends credits equal to the price of each selected unit. After the credits are exhausted, the employee may be allowed to select additional benefits on a payroll deduction basis. Through the selection process, employees become aware of the cost and value of their benefits.

Cafeteria plans also help control employer benefit costs. Employers set a dollar amount on benefit expenditures per employee, and employees choose within that framework. This maximizes employee appreciation, since employees choose what they want, and minimizes employer cost, since employers do not have to increase coverage for all employees in order to satisfy the needs of certain workers.

Cafeteria plans have been especially effective in controlling group medical expense insurance costs. Employees often are offered several alternative medical plans, including an HMO and a PPO, plans designed to control costs (discussed in Chapter 17). In addition, employees may be charged lower prices for traditional plans with more cost containment features. For example, a comprehensive medical insurance plan may have an option with a $100 deductible, 90 percent coinsurance, a $1,000 out-of-pocket or stop loss provision, and a $1 million maximum benefit. A lower-priced comprehensive plan may offer the same maximum benefit with a $2,000 deductible, 80 percent coinsurance, and a $4,000 stop loss provision. The employee uses fewer benefit credits to get the lower option plan, and the cost sharing requirements likely reduce claim costs, too. Likewise, long-term disability insurance choices will attach lower prices per $100 of monthly benefit with an option that insures 50 percent of income rather than 60 or 70 percent. Here again, lower prices attract employees to options with more cost sharing, and the cost sharing helps contain claims.

Cafeteria plans are well suited to meet the needs of a demographically diverse work force. The number of women, single heads of households, and dual career couples in the work force has increased dramatically in the past decade, and benefit needs vary across employees more than ever before. A single employee with no dependents may prefer fewer benefits and more cash income. Someone covered by medical benefits through a spouse's employer may prefer to use benefit dollars on more generous disability coverage. An older worker may prefer more generous medical benefits and fewer life insurance benefits, once the children are grown. Clearly, economic security needs vary, and job satisfaction and morale may improve by giving employees some voice in how benefits, a significant percentage of total compensation, are spent.

However, both higher administrative costs and adverse selection discourage employers from implementing cafeteria plans. Record keeping increases significantly when benefit packages vary for each employee. Computers help, but do not eliminate the administrative cost factor. Communication with employees is both more important and more complicated, since employees are selecting their own benefits and all choices must be thoroughly explained. Employers are careful to explain but not to advise about benefit choices, because then the employer would be liable for any adverse effect of benefit selection on the employee.

Cafeteria plans may have some adverse selection effects, since an employee selects benefits that he or she is more likely to need. Those with eye problems, for example, are more likely to choose vision care benefits, while other employees may skip vision care and select dental care to cover orthodontia. The result is higher claims per employee selecting each benefit. Adverse selection can be reduced by plan design and pricing. The employer may require, for example, that those selecting vision care must also choose dental care, thus bringing more healthy people into both plans. Pricing helps by setting each benefit's unit price high enough to cover the true average claim cost per employee or dependent, while trying to avoid excessive pricing that would discourage the enrollment of healthy employees.

Flexible Spending Accounts

Flexible spending accounts (FSAs) allow employees to pay for specified benefits (which are defined by law) with before-tax dollars. In the absence of a flexible spending account, the employee would have purchased the same services with after-tax dollars. An FSA can either add flexibility to a cafeteria plan or can accompany traditional benefit plans with little other employee choice. The employer may fund the FSA exclusively, the employee may fund the account through a salary reduction agreement, or both may contribute to the FSA.

The employee decides at the beginning of each year how much to personally contribute to the FSA, and then signs a salary reduction agreement for this amount. The legal document establishing the employer's program of flexible spending accounts will specify how funds can be spent, subject to the constraints of Section 125 in the Internal Revenue Code. For example, the simplest kind of FSA is funded solely by an employee salary reduction agreement and covers only employee contributions to a group medical insurance plan. The salary reduction agreement transforms the employee contribution from after-tax dollars to before-tax dollars, often a significant savings. A more comprehensive FSA, for example, may allow the employee to cover medical premium contributions, uninsured medical expenses, child care, and legal expenses. Dependent care is a nice addition in the FSA. The catch with an FSA plan is that the employee forfeits to the employer any balance in the account at year's end. This results in flexible spending accounts primarily being used to prefund highly predictable expenses on a before-tax basis.

Employees also pay their portion of the health premium in a premium conversion plan, which allows the funds to be collected on a pre-tax basis. These are usually the premiums for dependents.

MULTINATIONAL EMPLOYEE BENEFIT PLANS

Multinational corporations manage the human resource risk across national boundaries. The most common concern of multinational employers is the benefit needs of **expatriates,**

U.S. citizens working outside the United States. However, the employer is also concerned with managing benefits for employees who are not U.S. citizens, but who are working in the United States. In addition, benefits must be considered for employees who are not U.S. citizens and who work outside the United States.

The corporation designs multinational benefit policy to achieve several objectives. First, the plans need to be sufficient to attract, retain, and reward workers in locations around the world where a corporate presence is required. The plan needs to be fair for all employees, within the corporation itself, within the industry, and within the country where employees are located. In addition, the multinational benefit policy needs to facilitate the transfer of workers across national boundaries whenever necessary, with a minimum of overall transaction costs.

Typically, the multinational employer tries to protect the expatriate from losing benefits when the employee transfers outside the United States. A premium may be paid at the time of the move to compensate the employee for international relocation. The corporation often provides the expatriate with the same life, long-term disability, medical, and pension benefits as those provided to their U.S. employees. However, in some cases the employee may receive medical care or short-term disability benefits like those of the host country. When employers provide benefits in several international locations, they may use an **international benefit network** to cover employees across countries under one master insurance contract. This can simplify international benefit administration. The employer also must take into consideration the social insurance systems of the host country, and coordinate coverage as necessary with the employee's home country's system.

Cultural and regulatory factors differ among countries and affect benefit design, financing, and communication. This makes international employee benefits management a dynamic and challenging field. With the continued globalization of business in the new millennium, career opportunities in international benefits management are likely to grow.

KEY TERMS

employee benefits
nondiscrimination rules
fiduciary
master contract
certificate of insurance
participants
self-insured
third-party administrator (TPA)
administrative services only (ASO)
stop loss insurance
specific stop loss
aggregate stop loss
group underwriting
multiple employer trust (MET)
employer sharing of costs
flexible benefit programs

supplemental plans
probationary period
eligibility period
open enrollment
actively at work
noncontributory plans
contributory plans
experience-rated premiums
premium conversion plan
flexible spending account (FSA)
Age Discrimination in Employment Act (ADEA)
Civil Rights Act
Americans with Disabilities Act (ADA)
Family Medical Leave Act (FMLA)
viatical settlement

conversion privilege
group universal life insurance
salary continuation plan
paid time off (PTO)
short-term disability income
elimination period
definition of disability
long-term disability insurance
preexisting condition clauses
cafeteria plans
expatriates
international benefit network

DISCUSSION QUESTIONS

1. What methods do employers use to set objectives for a benefits plan?

2. What is the difference between the "probationary period" and the "eligibility period" in group insurance? What is an "elimination period" in group disability insurance?

3. How do employers protect themselves from the risk of catastrophic financial loss when they self-insure a benefits program?

4. What factors do underwriters consider when accepting an employer group plan? What are the factors for pricing a group plan?

5. Describe three group insurance underwriting requirements that reduce the potential for adverse selection.

6. Why do most group disability insurance plans limit income replacement to no more than 70 percent of salary, even if employees are willing to pay more to get 100 percent coverage? Does this seem fair to you? Why, or why not?

7. Cafeteria plans have become increasingly popular. What factors contributed to the increased use of these plans?

8. How might a flexible benefit plan achieve desirable goals for your employer as well as for you?

9. Why might the benefits manager of a multinational corporation use an international benefits network?

10. Recall the discussion of integrated benefits in Chapter 13. How do you think a good integrated benefits program would be coordinated with workers' compensation, FLMA, ADA, and group disability benefits? See "Important Issues: Integrated Benefits—The 24-Hour Coverage Concept" in Chapter 13.

EXERCISES

16.1 The Midland Construction Co. is a Virginia-based builder with 750 full-time employees and 300 part-time employees. The company provides all the social insurance programs required by law and most other employee benefits plans. Last year Midland Construction Co. suffered high severity of losses when the cranes on the Kerville high rise in Washington D.C. collapsed. Six workers sustained severe injuries and Johnny Kyle, the 64-year old supervisor, was killed. Five of the injured workers are back at work except for Tom Lovelace who is still on disability and his future prognosis is not good.

The CEO of the Midland Construction Co. decided to reevaluate the group life and disability programs offered to the employees. He hired the EB Solution group to help redesign the programs. As a member of the consulting group, provide the Midland Construction Company with the following proposals:

a. Two alternative proposals for the group term life insurance. Include in this proposal all important elements such as the definition of the benefit, amounts of coverage, eligibility, basic and supplemental benefits, all added coverages, costs, who pays for the coverage, and tax implications.

b. One proposal for group short-term and long-term disability. Include details about the definition of the benefits, definition of disability, amounts and duration of each coverage, waiting periods, eligibility, cost and tax implications, the employer or employees' contributions, integration and all possible additions to the basic coverage.

c.   Under your proposals, what benefits would have been available to the injured employees or their families?

16.2 John and Dan are full-time employees (for the past three years) of a local pizza parlor. During a fire in the kitchen, John was killed and Dan was severely disabled. Both John and Dan were married, and John also had a two-year-old daughter. Their employer provided group life and group disability insurance in addition to all the required social insurance. Based on the proposals you created in Exercise 16.1, what benefits are available to Dan and to John's family?

16.3 Rosa Sanchez, single and 25, received two job offers after college graduation. Both were with organizations that she respected, and the nature of the work at each place sounded very interesting to her. One job was with a larger, well-established firm and offered $22,000 per year in salary plus noncontributory benefits worth $7,000 per year. The other job was with a small business and offered a salary of $30,000 per year without employer voluntary benefits (the employer is required to pay for social insurance programs). Rosa's mother suggested that she make the choice between the two jobs based on which offered better total compensation.

a.   What factors should Rosa consider in determining the better package? Which package do you think maximizes her total compensation?

b.   Which employer is economically better off (all else being equal), the one offering salary plus benefits or the one offering salary only? Explain your answer.

16.4 Henry Zantow, the comptroller for Kado Industries, was discussing the supposed advantages of a true cafeteria plan versus a "traditional" plan with Lloyd Olsen. Lloyd agreed with Henry that a cafeteria plan certainly seemed the better of the two plans. Both Henry and Lloyd looked at each other and in the same breath said, "I wonder why anyone would choose a traditional plan?"

a.   What is your answer to this question?

b.   If the corporation decides to use a cafeteria plan, why might it want a minimum level of core benefits?

16.5 Jan Czyrmer, the employee benefits manager at Ludlow Enterprises, wants to restructure the leave policy for the company. He is concerned that employees abuse sick leave policy, taking sick leave time for personal reasons not related to illness. He wants to abolish particular types of leave (such as sick leave, vacation leave, personal leave) and give employees a certain number of general leave days per year to use as they choose.

a.   What advantages might Jan cite to convince upper management that consolidating leave may be helpful for Ludlow Enterprises?

b.   If upper management rejects Jan's idea of a major restructuring of leave, what can he do to prevent abuse of current sick leave policy? Are there steps that can be taken to reduce moral hazard within the traditional leave system?

16.6 Yolanda Freeman is evaluating whether federal nondiscrimination laws have helped or hurt employees.

a.   Which federal laws particularly affect employee benefits? Which workers are particularly affected by each law?

b.   Who pays the cost of requiring that benefits be paid on a nondiscriminatory basis? Do additional benefit costs have any effect on employee wage levels?

      c.   If federal laws did not require coverage for certain employees and their dependents, who would pay for benefits for these individuals? Do you think that social welfare is maximized by mandating coverage for certain workers and their dependents through these nondiscrimination laws?

NOTES

1. Employee Benefit Research Institute, "Employer Spending on Benefits 2000," *Facts from EBRI,* April 2002. www.ebri.org. More information can also be found in the U.S. Chamber of Commerce Survey at Uschamber.com at: www.uschamber.org/Research+and+Statistics/Publications/Employee+Benefits+Study.htm

2. See note 1 above.

3. For detailed explanation see the U.S. Department of Labor, Department Of Pension and Welfare Benefits Administration at: www.dol.gov/pwba.

4. See footnote 3

5. Rebecca Auerbach, "Your Message To Employers: Manage FLMA With Other Benefit Programs," *National Underwriter,* Life & Health/Financial Services Edition, 22 April 2002.

6. This case, *Ragsdale v. Wolverine World Wide,* No. 00-6029 (U.S. March 19, 2002), hinged on to what extent employers are obligated to inform employees of their rights when they begin a leave of absence. Wolverine had given Tracy Ragsdale time off for cancer treatment, but when she was unable to return to work after 30 weeks, Wolverine ended her employment. Ragsdale filed suit, citing a FMLA regulation that a leave of absence counts against the employee's FMLA allowance only if the employer specifically designated it as FMLA leave. She claimed she was still entitled to her 12 weeks of FMLA leave. The Court disagreed, and declared that regulation invalid. One of the Court's reasonings was that Ragsdale had not been harmed—she would not have been better off if Wolverine had designated her original leave as FMLA. See Steven Brostoff, "U.S. High Court Ruling Helps RMs," *National Underwriter* Online News Service, 20 March 2002.

7. Jeff Sadler, "Down Economy Can Push DI Sales Up," *National Underwriter,* Life & Health/Financial Services Edition, 25 February 2002.

CHAPTER 17

Employee Benefits: Medical Care

The costs of health care and health insurance have been of major social concern in the United States in the last two decades. The year 2003 is projected to be the fifth straight year of double-digit increases in group health care cost, with a report of an average increase of 14.7 percent in 2002 translating to an average cost per employee of $5,646.[1] The 1980s were a decade of double-digit rate increases in health insurance, which was the impetus for the birth of managed care plans such as preferred provider organizations (PPOs) and for the boom in health maintenance organizations (HMOs). The new idea of the new millennium is the **defined contribution health plan,** also called **consumer-driven health coverage** and health reimbursement accounts, under which the consumer negotiates prices with healthcare providers. The idea received a recent boost from the Internal Revenue Service, as you will see later in this chapter. The issues of high cost and the impact on benefits are discussed in more details in "Ethical Dilemma: What is the Tradeoff Between Health Care Cost and Benefits?" later in this chapter.

Most nongovernmental health insurance is provided through employer groups. Health insurance is a substantial percentage of the employer's total benefits expenditures. As shown in Table 16.1 in Chapter 16, out of the $5.90 spent for each employee's benefits per hour on average, $1.29 goes toward health insurance ($0.11 is spent on life and disability insurances, and $0.63 for retirement programs; the rest is for social insurance and time off). Health insurance is a substantial expense for employers and a major concern of society. Just think about your own situation. Do you have health insurance coverage? If you responded positively, you probably feel very comfortable. If you do not have coverage, you probably are making a note to yourself to go check how you can get the coverage and be able to afford the cost. In this chapter, you will learn about health insurance from the point of view of a risk manager or an employee benefits specialist. You will gain an understanding of the choices an employee has to make when given the option to select among various health plans such as PPOs or HMOs. A practical application is provided in both Cases 1 and 2 at the back of the text. Thus, this chapter covers:

1. Connection
2. Group health coverage, including indemnity health plans and managed care plans
3. Federal laws, including COBRA and HIPAA
4. Group dental
5. Group long-term care
6. Other health plans: medical savings accounts and health care reimbursement arrangements.
7. Medical insurance policy provisions
8. Medical care systems worldwide

CONNECTION

Among the risks shown in the holistic risk puzzle, the risk of illness or injury is the leading personal risk. The desire to mitigate this risk—a cause of major expense—is why many employees would not take a job without health insurance as part of the compensation package. In the big picture of risk management in our lives, taking care of health insurance is ranked rather high. If you have surveyed your friends or classmates, you have probably learned that the few who do not have health insurance coverage are not comfortable about it. They are likely aware that a serious accident or severe illness could cause them deep financial trouble.

Like the air we breathe, we believe that we are entitled to the best health care possible to save our lives and keep us well. While in the old days, the town's doctor visited the patient's home to provide help and accepted any payment, today's medical care is an impersonal business wherein doctors and emergency rooms require patients to show proof of capacity to pay. Health care coverage is rather expensive and deserves a careful consideration in completing our holistic risk management. In Figure 17.1, the connection among the health risk and the possible coverage available from the employer is depicted. It is important to note that if health care coverage is not available from an employer, it is the responsibility of the individual to obtain individual coverage, as discussed in Chapter 19. Group health is covered in detail in Case 2 of employer-provided benefits and in Case 1 of the risk management portfolio of the Smith family.

It is no wonder that health care issues have been high on the agendas of Congress and state governments, notably the Patients' Bill of Rights, the costs of prescription drugs for the elderly, and the 39 million Americans who are currently uninsured. On the "good news" side are two important federal laws that will be discussed later in this chapter: COBRA, the Consolidated Omnibus Budget Reconciliation Act of 1986, which provides for continuing health care coverage when an employee leaves a job or a breadwinner dies; and HIPAA, the Health Insurance Portability and Accountability Act of 1996, which enforces coverage for pre-existing conditions when a person changes jobs. The student can see the enormous importance of this coverage in the holistic picture of risk management.

GROUP HEALTH INSURANCE: AN OVERVIEW

Today, health insurance is very different from what it was two or three decades ago. Most of us do not pay providers of health care directly and fill out an insurance form for reimbursement. And most of us do not have complete freedom in choosing our physicians, but must select from a list of "in-network providers." The days of seeing any doctor and being reimbursed for any procedure the doctor ordered are long gone. We live in the era of mostly receiving health care under managed care: controlled access to doctors, procedures, and medicines. While limited access is the disadvantage of the managed care systems, there are many advantages. The most important is cost containment through efficiency. Another advantage is that most patients no longer have to deal with paperwork. Insureds simply make a co-payment to the healthcare provider, and the remaining reimbursements are done behind the scenes. Additional advantages are preventive care and higher standards for quality care.

But the costs are no longer controlled, because the underlying issues that created medical cost inflations never disappeared. The underlying main factors are medical technology development, medical malpractice lawsuits, drug and medication development, and the fact that a

FIGURE 17.1   Connection between Risks and Group Health Insurance

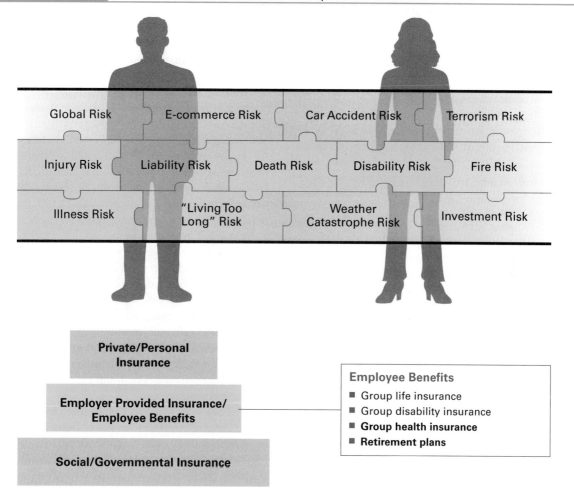

third party pays for the cost of obtaining medical services. These underlying cost factors did not disappear. Under managed care, while people transitioned from the open choice of indemnity plans into the more controlled managed care plans such as PPOs, point of service plans (POS), and the various types of HMOs, medical technology improvements, new medications, aging of the population, and medical malpractice continued in full swing. The cost-control factors of managed care that eased medical cost inflation during the transition period no longer stop the medical cost inflation. Once most of the U.S. population enrolled in managed care plans, the cost saving factors no longer surpassed medical cost inflation factors. The situation in the health market is discussed in "Ethical Dilemma: What is the Tradeoff Between Health Care Cost and Benefits?" in this chapter.

It appears that the old managed care ideas no longer work and new ideas are emerging. While the old systems are considered "defined benefit" health programs, because the benefits are defined and are provided under the plans, the new ideas call for "defined contribution health plans" in which the consumer/employee receives a certain amount of money from the employer and then selects the desired healthcare components. Rather than employers negotiating with insurers or managed care organizations for the group health plans, consumers are encouraged to negotiate directly with providers.

What Is the Tradeoff between Health Care Cost and Benefits?

Health care coverage costs are growing at a faster pace than almost any other segment of the economy. 2003 is expected to be the fifth straight year in which group health insurance costs go up by double digits. One of the nation's largest benefits purchasing groups, the California Public Employee Retirement Systems, expects its PPO rates to rise 20 percent while its HMO plans will increase by 26 percent. Many other employers are seeing similar increases. To balance their books, employers will have to either pass these additional costs along to employees or find ways to cut benefits.

HMOs were once seen as the saviors of the health insurance system. Offering lower costs, they often attracted younger, healthy workers. But now, as their costs are rising as well, even HMOs no longer look like good deals and many of the benefits they once offered are also being cut as well. For many older individuals, or those with greater health needs, HMOs do not provide the level of care and flexibility they desire. The PPOs they prefer, however, are becoming more and more expensive. And even with PPOs, benefits such as low co-pays for drugs, are now being reduced.

At the same time, doctors are also feeling the pinch. Pressured by insurance companies to cut costs, they are forced to see more patients in less time, which can lead to medical mistakes. Increasingly, insurance companies are also questioning expensive tests and medical procedures and refusing to pay doctors the full amount submitted. Soaring medical malpractice costs are causing some doctors to leave the profession.

And those individuals who have insurance, primarily through their employers, are the lucky ones. Some 38 million Americans have no insurance at all. Those who earn too much to qualify for Medicaid, but not enough to purchase private health insurance often find themselves paying huge out-of-pocket bills. Often, uninsured patients neglect treatment until their condition becomes an emergency. When they cannot pay, hospitals and doctors pick up the cost, and make up for it by raising prices elsewhere, contributing to escalating health care costs.

Is rationing health care the answer? Canada and many European countries have adopted systems of universal coverage, but such coverage comes with a price. Benefits, while universal, are often lower. It is often difficult to see

specialists, especially about non-emergency conditions. Long waits are the norm. A Universal Health Care system proposed during the first Clinton Administration never got off the ground.

Legislation aimed at giving patients a greater voice in determining what procedures health insurers will cover came close to passing in 2002 before it was derailed. Conditions under which patients could sue HMOs and how much the damage amount could be differed under the House and Senate versions of the Patients' Bill of Rights. The Senate bill favored patients' rights and the House bill favored the rights of the insurers. Both bills would have allowed for greater access to specialists and require payment of emergency room services.

Even if it is eventually passed, however, a Patients' Bill of Rights is not likely to solve the problem of escalating costs. It could even contribute to them. With patients demanding the best care, is there even a solution?

Some employers are looking to cut costs through disease management programs. With the majority of costs resulting from chronic conditions, such as asthma, diabetes, heart disease, and arthritis, human resource executives believe that they can reduce costs by developing better ways to manage the health care of employees with such conditions.

For healthier workers, a new option for cutting costs is the defined-contribution plan. These plans provide employees with a health-reimbursement account funded by the employer to pay for all their routine health care expenses. Using these funds, employees can see any doctor they wish. Once the money runs out, however, they must pay for their own health care until the cost reaches a certain level. Then catastrophic coverage kicks in. A recent IRS ruling that allows employees to roll over any unused cash in the account at the end of the year into the next year tax-free has increased the appeal of such plans to employees. A number of federal agencies have recently added these plans to the options their employees can select.

Questions for Discussion

1. Who should be responsible for individuals' health care coverage? The employer? The individual? The government?

2. How would it be possible to solve the health care crisis under the current health care system in the

(Continued)

Ethical Dilemma (Continued)

United States? Should it be socialized as in many European countries and Canada?

3. Would passage of a patients' bill of rights solve the cost crisis? Reduce the number of uninsured?

Sources: Lucette Lagnado, "Uninsured and Ill, a Woman Is Forced to Ration Her Care," *The Wall Street Journal,* 12 November 2002; Allison Bell, "Group Health Rates Still Rocketing," *National Underwriter,* Life & Health/Financial Services Edition, 19 August 2002; Lori Chordas, "Multiple-Choice Question: Disease management, cost shifting and prescription-drug initiatives are some of the strategies insurers are using to stabilize health-care expenses," *Best's Review,* August 2002; Barbara Martinez, "Insurer Software Shaves Bills, Leaves Doctors Feeling Frayed," *The Wall Street Journal,* 31 July 2002; Frances X. Clines, "Insurance-Squeezed Doctors Folding Tents in West Virginia," *New York Times,* 13 June 2002; "Survey: HMO Rate Increases Are Highest in 11 Years" *Best Wire,* 2 July 2002; "Dueling Legislation on Patients' Rights in the House and Senate," *The Washington Post,* 5 August 2001; Mark Hofmann, "Senators, White House Deadlock on Patient Rights," *Business Insurance,* 2 August 2002.

Table 17.1 describes the health care plans prevalent in the marketplace today. Note, however, that the various health plans are not as distinct from one another as they appear in the table. Since these plans were introduced, changes in health care regulations coupled with new laws concerned with patients' rights have eliminated some of the differences among the plans, and they now overlap greatly. (It is no longer true, for example, that HMOs are necessarily cheaper than PPOs.) Figure 17.2 provides the five more striking illustrations of the health plans on a continuum of choice and cost. There are other health care plans, such as **Exclusive Physician Organizations (EPO)** where doctors have created their own networks in response to the competitive environment.[2] The physicians organize their own healthcare networks in response to hospital chains, medical centers, and insurance companies acquiring group practices. These networks do not provide access to out-of-network providers.

The student who is new to this topic might best comprehend the changes of the past three decades by first understanding the HMOs and the indemnity plans of the late 1970s and early 1980s. In those days, these two types of plans were truly far apart. Patients had unlimited provider choice in the indemnity plans and the least choice in the HMOs. The HMOs supplied a person's medical needs for about $5 a visit. The subscriber to the staff model HMO would visit a clinic-like facility and see a doctor who was paid a salary. Well baby, eye, and dental care were included. A new baby would cost a family very little. On the other side of the spectrum, the subscribers of the indemnity plans could see any provider, pay for the services, and later apply for reimbursement. The premiums for HMOs were substantially lower than those for the indemnity plan. In most cases, the employer paid the full premium for HMO and would ask the employee to supplement the higher cost of the indemnity plan.

FIGURE 17.2 Continuum of Health Plans

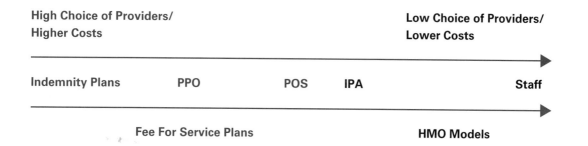

TABLE 17.1		Spectrum of Health Plans			
	Indemnity	Indemnity w/Network	PPO	POS	HMO‡
Choice level	Highest				Lowest
Cost Level	Highest				Lowest
Access to providers	Access to any provider—no restriction	Access to any provider in a large network; out-of-networks with penalties	Access to any provider in a large network; out-of-networks with penalties	Same as PPO but required to see primary care physician (PCP) first; referral from PCP to see a specialist. (PPO + PCP)	Staff model: Facility only; Other models: In networks only with PCP as a gatekeeper
Methods of reimbursing the providers	Fee-for-service: Patient pays total fee directly to the doctor for service rendered	Fee-for-service: subject to usual, customary, and reasonable (UCR) limits	Discounted fee-for-service (FFS)	PCPs by capitation; specialists by discounted FFS	Staff model: salaries Other models: capitations Individual Practice Association: capitation for PCP, discounted FFS for specialists
What is required of the patient?	Patient files claim forms; insurer reimburses co-insurance after the deductible	Same as indemnity, but reimbursement is only for UCR	Co-pays* in networks; out of networks are similar to indemnity with penalties	Same as PPO	Co-pay only; traditionally, no out-of-networks reimbursement
The benefits – levels of preventive care†	Comprehensive medical package with minimal preventive care	Comprehensive medical package with minimal preventive care	Same as indemnity, with increased preventive care and well baby care	Same as PPO	Same as PPO with most preventive care, well-baby, physical exams, immunizations, extended dental, vision, & prescription plans†
Prevalence	Lowest	Low	High	High	High

*   Co-pays can run from $10 for PCP to $30 for specialists. Each plan is negotiated, so co-pays may differ.
†   All plans are required to provide preventive care such as mammography screenings and Pap tests.
‡   The distinction among the managed care plans—PPO, POS and HMO—has become more fuzzy in recent years as HMOs are required to provide emergency out of network benefits and more choice. HMOs have begun unbundling the preventive care services and charge additional premiums for more benefits such as vision and dental care.
Note: not all types of plans are included. Exclusive Physician Organization (EPO) is another plan that does not permit access to "out of network" providers.

Of these two extremes, who would select the HMO and who would select the indemnity plan? You answered correctly if you said that young and healthy employees most likely selected the HMOs. It turned out that there was adverse selection against the indemnity plans, which saw the more mature and less healthy employees. The manager of the indemnity plans began looking at the other extreme of the continuum for help in reducing costs. This is how managed care in traditional indemnity plans began. First, there were indemnity plans with large networks limiting access to providers and reimbursing only for **"usual, customary, and reasonable"** (UCR) costs for that area based on studies of the appropriate cost for each medical procedure. But this was only the first step.

The low co-pay that HMOs asked were very desirable. The newly formed Preferred Provider Organizations (PPOs) adopted the co-pay method and used managed-care organizations to negotiate with doctors and all providers for large discounts, with some more than 50 percent of the usual, customary and reasonable. The next step was to bring the gatekeeper, the primary care physician, which the HMOs used in most of their models (discussed later in this chapter), into the structure of the PPO. So when a gatekeeper is introduced, the new plan is called a **Point of Service** (POS) plan. They are the PPO plus a gatekeeper or the IPA HMO model as discussed later in the chapter.

The HMOs also evolved. The model of one facility with doctors on staff (the staff model) expanded to a few types of modes: (1) the group model, (2) the network model of doctors, and (3) the individual practice association (IPA) of many doctors in one practice. The doctors in an IPA could see HMO and non-HMO patients. In many cases the POS and IPA are very similar from the point of view of the patients, except that when the POS is based on a preferred provider organization rather than an HMO, there is more access to out-of-network providers (but with penalties). These days many IPAs may allow some out-of-network access as well, especially in cases of emergencies. In both the PPO and IPA-based networks with a gatekeeper (POS), the provider specialists receive discounted fee for service while the gatekeepers (primary care physicians) receive **capitation** (a set amount paid to each provider based on the number of subscribers in the plan). These are the areas where the distinctions among the plans become fuzzy. HMOs were forced to give more choice and services. Their subscribers, originally young, healthy employees, had become aging baby boomers who needed more quality care. The House and Senate have each passed a version of the Patients' Bill of Rights regarding managed care plans (see "Ethical Dilemma: What is the Tradeoff between Health Care Cost and Benefits?"). Many states have passed bills requiring HMOs to loosen many of their restrictions. With all these changes came a price. HMOs became more expensive; with the best practices widely emulated, the offerings of all plans converged. The pendulum of choice versus cost has probably landed at this point somewhere in the middle of the continuum shown in Figure 17.2. For learning purposes, this chapter will regard HMOs as the plans with minimal access to out-of-networks providers. A comparison of the actual benefits under the various plans is available in the employee benefits portfolio Case 2 at the back of the text.

We will now give more detailed descriptions of the plans featured in Table 17.1 and Figure 17.2. Following these descriptions, additional plans such as group dental and long-term-care plans will be discussed. The chapter will conclude with health-related laws affecting group medical insurance (some are also featured in "Important Issues: Recent Laws Affecting Health Care."

INDEMNITY HEALTH PLANS: THE TRADITIONAL FEE-FOR-SERVICE PLANS

The traditional method for providing group medical expense benefits has been by paying **health care providers** a fee for services rendered. Health care providers include health professionals, such as physicians and surgeons, as well as health facilities, such as hospitals and outpatient surgery centers. Medical expense benefits may be provided on an indemnity, service, or valued basis.

Indemnity benefits apply the principle of indemnity by providing payment for loss. The insured (the covered employee or dependent) would receive, for example, the actual costs incurred up to but not exceeding $300 per day for up to ninety days while confined in a hospital. Other dollar limits would be placed on benefits for other types of charges, such as those for ancillary charges (such as x-ray, laboratory, and drugs) made by the hospital.

There are five major classifications of traditional fee-for-service medical expense insurance: (1) hospital expense, (2) surgical expense, (3) medical expense, (4) major medical, and (5) comprehensive medical insurance. The first three types are called "basic" coverage and provide a limited set of services or reimburse a limited dollar amount. As the names suggest, major medical and comprehensive medical insurance provide coverage for large losses.

Basic Health Care Benefits

Basic health care benefits cover hospital, surgical, and medical expenses. These coverages are limited in terms of the types of services (or expenditure reimbursements) they provide, as well as the dollar limits of protection. As Figure 17.3 shows, basic medical coverage generally provides first-dollar coverage instead of protection against large losses.

The **basic hospital policy** covers room and board (for a specified number of days) and hospital ancillary charges, such as those for x-ray imaging and laboratory tests. The basic hospital policy primarily provides benefits during a hospital confinement. In addition, it covers outpatient surgery and limited emergency care in case of an accident. Many policies have a small deductible. Ancillary charges may be covered on a schedule basis, or more commonly on a blanket basis for all x-rays, laboratory work, and other ancillary charges, with a maximum limit such as $5,000 for all such charges. Maternity coverage is included in group medical expense insurance policies, since the Civil Rights Act forbids employer-sponsored health insurance plans from treating pregnancy differently from any other medical condition.

The **basic surgical policy** usually pays providers according to a schedule of procedures, regardless of whether the surgery is performed in a hospital or elsewhere. The policy lists the maximum benefit for each type of operation. A second approach sometimes used by insurers is to pay benefits up to the UCR surgical charges in the geographical region where the operation is performed. UCR charges are defined as those below the ninetieth percentile of charges by all surgeons in a geographical region for the same procedure.

A **basic medical expense policy** covers all or part of doctors' fees for hospital, office, or home visits due to nonsurgical care. Often a plan provides benefits only when the insured is confined to a hospital. Most policies have an overall limit of a daily rate multiplied by the number of days in the hospital. Common exclusions are routine examinations, eye examinations, x-rays, and prescription drugs.

Basic health care coverage has been criticized for encouraging treatment in the hospital, the most expensive site for medical care delivery. For example, both the basic hospital and medical policies cover services primarily delivered on an inpatient basis. Newer basic

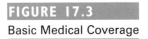

FIGURE 17.3

Basic Medical Coverage

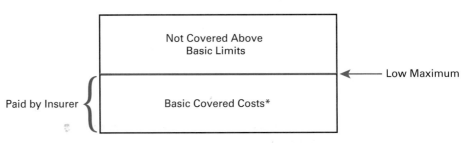

*Basic coverage excludes some expenses, and some policies have a small deductible.

policies provide better coverage for outpatient services. For example, some provide x-ray and laboratory benefits on an outpatient basis (up to a small maximum benefit) and cover the cost of preadmission tests, done on an outpatient basis prior to hospital admission.

Major Medical and Comprehensive Insurance

The hospital, surgical, and medical expense insurance policies previously discussed are basic contracts in the sense that they provide for many of the medical expenses on a somewhat selective basis and with rather low limits. They are weak in the breadth of their coverage, as well as their maximum benefit limits. Two health insurance plans have been developed to correct for these weaknesses: major medical insurance and comprehensive medical insurance.

Major Medical Insurance

Major medical insurance covers the expense of almost all medical services prescribed by a doctor. It provides coverage for virtually all charges for hospitals, doctors, medicines, blood, wheelchairs, and other medically necessary items. Major medical policies have four fundamental features: high maximum limits (such as $1 million) or no limits, a large deductible, coverage of a broad range of different medical services, and coinsurance provisions.

Maximum limits apply to the total amount the insurer will pay over the insured's lifetime. It may apply to each injury or illness separately, but typically applies to all injuries and illnesses irrespective of whether they are related.

Internal policy limits often apply to specified services. Hospital room and board charges are usually limited to the hospital's most prevalent semi-private rate. All charges are subject to a usual and customary test.

As Figure 17.4 shows, the deductible in policies is large, ranging from $300 to $2,000. The purpose of the deductible is to eliminate small claims and restrict benefits to the more financially burdensome expenses, thus making possible high limits and broad coverage at a reasonable premium rate. A new deductible must be satisfied each **benefit period.** In group insurance, the benefit period is usually a calendar year. The deductible applies to each individual; however, many policies require only that two or three family members meet the deductible each year. This reduces the possibility of deductibles causing financial hardship when several family members have serious illnesses or injuries during the same year.

The **coinsurance provision** gives the percentage of expenses the insurer will pay in excess of the deductible. It may vary from 70 to 90 percent; 80 percent is common. The

FIGURE 17.4

Major Medical
Insurance

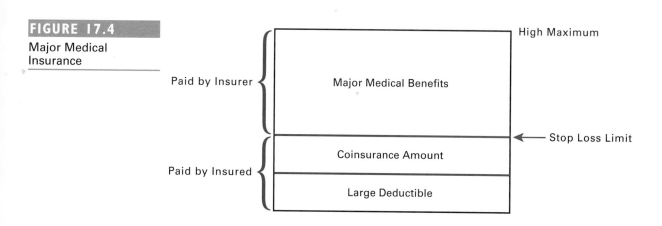

insured bears the remainder of the burden up to a **stop loss limit,** for example, $3,000, after which 100 percent of covered charges are reimbursed. Some group contracts include the deductible in the stop loss limit and others do not (Figure 17.4 shows the deductible included in the stop loss limit).

Deductibles and coinsurance requirements are **cost sharing** provisions that increase the personal cost to the insured of using medical services. When insureds pay part of the cost, they tend to use fewer unnecessary or discretionary medical services. That is, deductibles and coinsurance provisions reduce moral hazard and help keep group insurance premiums affordable. The stop loss limit protects the insured from excessive cost sharing, which could be financially devastating.

Comprehensive Medical Insurance

With major medical policies, the insurer pays most of the cost for medical services. However, major medical policy cost sharing still may be sizeable, putting a heavy financial burden on the insured. **Comprehensive medical insurance** deals with this problem by providing smaller deductibles, typically $100 to $300 per individual per calendar year (see Figure 17.4). Comprehensive medical insurance is designed as a stand-alone policy that provides broad coverage for a range of inpatient and outpatient services. Except for the smaller deductible, the provisions of a comprehensive plan are usually the same as those in a major medical plan. The comprehensive policy is sold mainly on a group basis.

Coordination of Benefits

Many employees and their dependents are eligible for group medical expense coverage under more than one plan. For example, a husband and wife may each be eligible on their own employer's plan as well as their spouse's. Children may be eligible under both the father's and the mother's plan. Workers with more than one permanent part-time job may be eligible for coverage with more than one employer. Coordination is needed to prevent duplicate payment of medical expenses when employees or their dependents are covered under more than one group policy.

The **coordination of benefits provision** establishes a system of primary and secondary insurers. The primary insurer pays the normal benefit amount, as if no other insurance were in force. Then the secondary insurer pays the balance of the covered health care expenses. The total payments by the primary and secondary insurers are limited to 100 percent of the covered charges for the applicable policies. Estimates are that coordination of benefits reduces the total cost of health insurance by over 10 percent by reducing duplicate payment.

An employee's group plan is always considered primary for expenses incurred by the employee. For example, a husband's primary coverage is with his employer, a wife's with her employer, and each has secondary coverage through the spouse's plan. When a child is insured under both parents' plans, the policy of the parent whose birthday falls first in the year is the primary policy. However, in the case of separation or divorce, the primary coverage for the child is through the custodial parent. Secondary coverage is through stepparents, and coverage through the non-custodial parent pays last. In some cases, these rules may not establish a priority of payment, and then the policy in effect for the longest period of time is primary. Any group plan that does not include a coordination of benefits provision is considered the primary insurer by all insurers that have such provisions. This encourages almost universal use of the coordination of benefits provision.

Allowing insureds to be covered under more than one policy means that these insureds may not have to pay deductible or coinsurance requirements. However, group policies sometimes stipulate that the secondary payer cannot reimburse the deductible amounts required by the primary policy. This is designed to preserve the effect of the cost-sharing requirement, namely, to control the use of unnecessary or excess services by the insured and to reduce moral hazard.

Following is an example of a dependent insured who has double coverage. Sharon and John Shank are both covered by indemnity health plans under their respective employers. They also cover their three children. Sharon is born on October 1, 1970 and John on November 30, 1968. On January 3, 2003 their son, Josh, was hurt in a soccer tournament and had to have surgery on his ankle. The cost of the procedure was $5,000. John's plan provides for a $250 deductible and 90 percent coinsurance, while Sharon's plan has $400 deductible with 80 percent coinsurance. Since Sharon's birthday is earlier in the year, her insurer is the primary carrier. The reimbursement under her carrier is ($5,000 – $ 400) × 0.80 = $3,680. The **out-of-pocket** cost would be $1,320. But, since the family is covered by both parents' health plans, the amount will be covered in full under the plan of John's employer. John's employer, as a secondary payer, does not impose the deductibles and coinsurance. The student is invited to calculate what the payment of John's insurer would be if he had an earlier birthday during the year. Note, that if Sharon's health plan were self-insured, her plan would not be the primary regardless of her birthday.

COST CONTAINMENT INITIATIVES FOR TRADITIONAL FEE-FOR-SERVICE POLICIES

As noted above, escalating medical costs propelled high-cost plans to look for effective methods to control costs. These **cost containment techniques** can be categorized as follows:

1. Plan design techniques
2. Administration and funding techniques
3. Utilization review

Plan Design Techniques

Plan design techniques relate to deductibles, coinsurance, limits on coverage, and exclusions such as experimental procedures or purely cosmetic surgeries. Most of the plans charge extra for coverage of routine eye examinations, eyeglasses, hearing examinations, and most dental expenses.

Administrative and Funding Techniques

When employers decide to self-insure their employees' group coverage, insurers continue to have an administrative role. The insurers enroll the employees, pay claims, and reinsure catastrophic claims. Through self-insurance, employers may be able to avoid state premium taxes (usually 1 or 2 percent of premiums) levied on insurance, eliminate most of the insurers' potential profits, and, in some cases, earn higher investment returns on reserves for health claims than those normally earned by group insurers. In addition, self-insured plans do not have to comply with state laws mandating coverage of medical care benefits (for example, alcoholism and infertility benefits). A small percentage of employers administer their plans themselves, eliminating any insurer involvement. The overall effect of these changes on the cost of health care can be characterized as significant in absolute dollar savings, yet minor as a percentage of total costs.

Utilization Review

Efforts to control costs include utilization review techniques developed by insurers and employers to reduce the use of the most costly forms of health care—hospitalization and surgery. Some of these techniques are listed in Table 17.2. Most group plans use some or all of these methods to control costs. The first ten are discussed briefly in this section, and the others are described later in more detail.

Insurers will pay full coverage when the insured seeks a **second surgical opinion** before undergoing elective or non-emergency surgery, and a lower percentage or no coverage if the insured proceeds with surgery after only one opinion. Second surgical opinions do not require that two surgeons agree that surgery needs to be done before the insurer will pay for the procedure. A second surgical opinion provision only requires that the insured get a second opinion to increase the information available before making a decision about whether to have the surgery.

Insurers encourage patients to use **ambulatory surgical centers** or have outpatient surgery at the hospital or surgeon's office rather than a hospital stay. The reimbursement rates also encourage **preadmission testing,** where patients have diagnostic tests done on an outpatient basis prior to surgery to reduce the total time spent in the hospital.

Most group fee-for-service plans require **preadmission certification** for hospitalization for any non-emergency condition. The insured or the physician of the insured contacts the plan administrator for approval for hospital admission for a specified number of days. The administrative review is usually made by a nurse or other health professional. The recommendations are based on practice patterns of physicians in the region, and an appeals process is available for patients with conditions that require admissions and lengths of stay outside of the norm.

Extended care facilities or nursing facilities, **hospice care** for the dying, or **home health care** following hospital discharge may be recommended to reduce the length of hospitalization. Extended care facilities provide basic medical care needed during some recoveries, rather than the intensive and more expensive medical service of a hospital. With hospice care, volunteers and family members help to care for a dying person in the hospital, at home, or in a dedicated hospice facility. Home health care is an organized system of care at home that substitutes for a hospital admission or allows early discharge from the hospital. The insurer covers the cost of physicians' visits, nurses' visits, respiratory therapy, prescription drugs, physical and speech therapy, home health aids, and other essentials.

TABLE 17.2
Health Care Cost Containment Methods

- Second surgical opinions
- Ambulatory surgical centers
- Preadmission testing
- Preadmission certification
- Extended care facilities
- Hospice care
- Home health care
- Utilization review organizations
- Statistical analysis of claims
- Prospective payment
- Business coalitions
- Wellness programs
- Health maintenance organizations
- Preferred provider organizations
- Managed care plans

Cancer, diabetes, fractures, AIDS, heart ailments, and many other illnesses can be treated as effectively and less expensively with home health, hospice, and extended care.

Employers or their insurers often contract for reviews by an outside **utilization review organization,** sometimes called a professional review organization (PRO). Utilization review organizations, run by physicians, surgeons, and nurses, offer peer judgments on whether a hospital admission is necessary, whether the length of the hospital stay is appropriate for the medical condition, and whether the quality of care is commensurate with the patient's needs. When problems are identified, the utilization review organization may contact the hospital administrator, the chief of the medical staff, or the personal physician. When treatment deviates substantially from the norm, the physician may be asked to discuss the case before a peer review panel. The medical insurance policy may refuse to pay for care considered unnecessary by the reviewing organization.

Utilization review organizations, third-party administrators, and many large employers collect and analyze data on health care claims. This **statistical analysis of claims** has the purpose of identifying any over utilization or excessive charges by providers of medical care. These studies usually establish standard costs for a variety of **diagnostic related groups (DRGs).** Each DRG is a medical or surgical condition that recognizes age, sex, and other determinants of treatment costs. By looking at each provider's charges on a DRG basis, the analyses can identify high- and low-cost providers.

Another cost containment technique using DRGs is **prospective payment.** In 1983, the federal government adopted the practice of paying a flat fee for each Medicare patient based on the patient's DRG. Prospective payment provided an economic incentive to providers, specifically hospitals, to minimize length of stay and other cost parameters. Use of prospective payment proved effective, and other insurers and employers now use similar methods. But the down side is that the level of reimbursement is too low and many providers do not accept Medicare patients. Assignment of incorrect or multiple DRGs to obtain higher fees can be problematic, and monitoring is necessary to keep costs as low as possible.

Another cost containment initiative by employers has been to sponsor **wellness programs** designed to promote healthy lifestyles and reduce the incidence and severity of employee medical expenses. The programs vary greatly in scope. Some are limited to educational sessions on good health habits and screening for high blood pressure, cholesterol, diabetes, cancer symptoms, and other treatable conditions. More extensive programs provide physical fitness gymnasiums for aerobic exercise such as biking, running, and walking. Counseling is available, usually on a confidential basis, as an aid in the management of stress, nutrition, alcoholism, or smoking.

MANAGED CARE PLANS

The central concept in the area of health care cost containment is **managed care.** As the concept of managed care has grown in the last fifteen to twenty years, several characteristics are common across health care plans. Managed care plans control access to providers in various ways. Managed care fee-for-service plans control access to procedures through provisions such as preadmission certification; PPOs control access by providing insureds with economic incentives to choose efficient providers; and HMOs control access by covering services only from HMO providers. Managed care plans typically engage in utilization review, monitoring service usage and costs on a case-by-case basis. In addition, managed care plans usually give economic incentives to stay in networks by charging penalties when nonpreferred providers are seen.

Preferred Provider Organizations

Preferred provider organizations (PPOs) were first formed in the 1980s as another approach to containing costs in group health insurance programs. PPOs are groups of hospitals, physicians, and other health care providers that contract with insurers, third-party administrators, or directly with employers to provide medical care to members of the contracting group(s) at discounted prices. They provide a mechanism for organizing, marketing, and managing fee-for-service medical care.

Unlike most HMOs, PPOs give employees and their dependents a broad choice of providers. The insured can go to any provider on an extensive list, known as the in-networks list, supplied by the employer or insurer. The insured can also go to a provider not on the list, known as going out of network. If the insured goes to a preferred provider, most PPOs waive most or all of the coinsurance, which is a percent of the fee paid to the doctor by the insurer. PPOs always charge a co-pay that can range from $10 to $30 or more depending on the specialty or the contract the employer negotiated with the insurance company. Providers such as doctors and hospitals are in abundant supply in most urban areas. Most operate on a fee-for-service basis and are concerned about competition from HMOs. In order to maintain their market share of patients, providers are willing to cooperate with PPOs. The income they give up in price discounts, they expect to gain through an increase of patients. Employers and insurers like PPOs because they are not expensive to organize and they direct employees to low-cost providers. The primary incentive for employees to use preferred providers is being able to avoid deductibles and coinsurance provisions and only having to make co-payments.

Cost effectiveness would not be achieved, even with discounts, if providers got insureds to accept more service(s) than necessary for the proper treatment of injury or illness. Therefore, many PPOs monitor their use of services.

Health Maintenance Organizations

Health maintenance organizations (HMOs) have been around for over sixty years. In the 1970s, they gained national attention for their potential to reduce health care costs.

History of HMOs

The HMO concept is generally traced back to the Ross-Loos group, which was a temporary medical unit that provided medical services to Los Angeles construction workers building an aqueduct in a California desert in 1933. Henry J. Kaiser offered the same service to construction workers for the Grand Coulee Dam in Washington state. During World War II, what is now called the Kaiser Permanente plan was used for employees in Kaiser shipyards.[3] The major turning point in popularity for HMOs occurred with the passage of the Health Maintenance Organization Act of 1973.

This act required an employer to subscribe exclusively to an HMO or to make this form of health care available as one of the options to the employees, provided an HMO that qualified under the act was located nearby and requested consideration. By the time this requirement was retired, employers were in the habit of offering HMOs to their employees. Sponsors of HMOs include insurance companies, government units, Blue Cross Blue Shield, hospitals, medical schools, consumer groups, unions, and other organizations.

Nature of HMOs

As noted above and featured in Table 17.1, HMOs provide a comprehensive range of medical services, including physicians, surgeons, hospitals, and other providers, emphasizing preventive care. The HMO either employs providers directly or sets up contracts with outside providers to care for subscribers. Thus, the HMO both finances care (like an insurer) and provides care (unlike an insurer).

The scope of HMO coverage is broader than that of most fee-for-service plans. For example, HMOs cover routine checkups even when the employee is not ill. Co-payments apply only to minor cost items, such as physician office visits and prescription drugs (for example, a $10 co-payment may be required for each of these services). The employee has lower cost sharing requirements than with traditional fee-for-service plans.

Two basic types of HMOs are available. Some of the oldest and largest plans are the not-for-profit **group practice association** and the staff model. In this arrangement, HMO physicians and other providers work for salaries or capitation. In **individual practice associations** (IPAs), which can be either for-profit or not-for-profit organizations, contractual arrangements are made with physicians and other providers in a community who practice out of their own offices and treat both HMO and non-HMO members. A physician selected as an HMO member's primary physician is often paid a fixed fee per HMO member, known as capitation fee.[4] When physicians are paid by salary or per patient, the primary physician acts as a gatekeeper between the patient, specialists, hospitals, and other providers. The group association, the staff model, and the individual practice association all pay for and refer subscribers to specialists when they consider this necessary. However, if the HMO subscriber sees a specialist without a referral from the HMO, the subscriber is responsible for paying the specialist for the full cost of care. HMOs either own their own hospitals or contract with outside hospitals to serve subscribers.

Cost-Saving Motivation

Because the HMO providers receive an essentially fixed annual income and has promised to provide all the care the subscriber needs (with a few exclusions), they are financially at risk. If the HMO providers overtreat subscribers, they will lose money. Consequently, no economic incentive exists to have subscribers return for unnecessary visits, to enter the hospital if treatment can be done in an ambulatory setting, or to undergo surgery that is unlikely to improve quality of life. This is the key aspect of an HMO that is supposed to increase efficiency relative to traditional fee-for-service plans.

A major criticism of HMOs is the limited choice of providers for subscribers. The number of physicians, hospitals, and other providers in the HMO may be quite small with group, staff, and individual practice models. Some individual practice plans overcome the criticism by enrolling almost every physician and hospital in a geographic region, and then paying providers on a fee-for-service basis. Paying on a fee-for-service basis, however, may destroy the main mechanism that helps HMOs control costs. Another concern expressed by critics is that HMOs do not have proper incentives to provide high-quality care. A disadvantage for many of the baby boomers is the inability to seek the best health care possible. As noted in the connection section, health care is a social commodity. Every person believes he/she deserve the best health care. Thus, if M.D. Anderson were the best place to receive cancer treatment, everyone would want to go to Houston for such treatment. Under HMOs, there would not be any reimbursement for this selection. Under a PPO or POS plan, the insured may use the out-of-network option and pay more, but at least receive some reimbursement. However, a recent national survey of 1,000 insureds under age 65 revealed that customer dissatisfaction with HMOs is lessening.[5] The explanation may be the narrowing gap in services and access to out-of network providers that has resulted from an increased concern for patient rights, such as the 2002 Supreme Court decision that allows the states to challenge HMOs' treatment decisions.[6] Many states have subsequently created independent boards to review coverage decisions.[7]

CONTINUATION PROVISIONS

Continuity: COBRA

The Consolidated Omnibus Budget Reconciliation Act of 1986, known as **COBRA,** directs that employers of more than twenty employees who maintain a group medical plan must allow certain minimum **continuation provisions.** COBRA's continuation provisions require that former employees, their spouses, divorced spouses, and dependent children be allowed to continue coverage at the individual's own expense upon the occurrence of a qualifying event (one that otherwise would have resulted in the loss of medical insurance). The qualifying events are listed in Table 17.3. Most terminations of employment, except for gross misconduct, activate a thirty-one-day right to convert the health insurance that the employee or dependent had before the qualifying event (vision and dental benefits need not be offered). The employer can charge for the cost of conversion coverage, but the charge cannot exceed 102 percent of the cost of coverage for employees, generally (including the portion the employer paid). Some events require coverage continuation for eighteen months, and others require thirty-six months of coverage.

The employee has a valuable right with COBRA, because continuation of insurance is provided without evidence of insurability. In addition, the group rate may be lower than individual rates in the marketplace. However, COBRA subjects employers to adverse selection costs and administrative costs beyond the additional 2 percent of premium collected. Many terminated healthy employees and dependents will immediately have access to satisfactory insurance with another employer, but many unhealthy employees may not. This is because of the preexisting condition clauses that many group insurance plans have (though this is less of a concern since the passage of HIPAA, as you will see below). After September 11, Congress worked on creating subsidies for the payment of COBRA premiums to laid-off employees. This law is part of the 2002 trade legislation. As of 2003, the new law provides subsidies of 65 percent of the premiums to people who lose their jobs because of foreign competition.[8]

TABLE 17.3

COBRA Qualifying Events for Continuation of Health Insurance

1. Voluntary (and in some cases involuntary) termination of employee's employment.
2. Employee death.
3. Reduction of hours worked resulting in coverage termination.
4. Divorce or legal separation from an employee.
5. Entitlement by an employee for Medicare.
6. Dependent child ceases to meet dependent child definition.
7. Employer filing for Chapter 11 bankruptcy.

Note: For each event, it is assumed that the person was covered for group medical benefits immediately prior to the qualifying event.
Source: COBRA

Retiree Eligibility for Group Medical Benefits

As discussed in Chapter 16, most active, permanent, full-time employees are eligible for group coverage. Employers that offer group medical insurance are required to offer it to active workers over age 65, under the Age Discrimination in Employment Act (ADEA) discussed in chapter 16. For these employees, Medicare becomes a secondary payer. Some employers choose to offer continuation of group medical benefits to employees who have retired. This coverage is like Medigap insurance (discussed in Chapter 19), where Medicare is the primary payer and the group plan is secondary. Typically, the retiree plan is less generous than the plan for active workers, since it is designed to simply "fill the gaps" left by Medicare.

Historically, employers have paid medical premiums or benefits for retirees out of current revenues, recognizing the expense in the period that it was paid out. However, in 1993 the Financial Accounting Standards Board (FASB 106) began phasing in a requirement that employers recognize the present value of future retiree medical expense benefits on the balance sheet during the employees' active working years rather than the old pay-as-you-go system. The negative effect of these new rules on corporate earnings has been significant. Consequently, most employers have been cutting back on health benefits promised to retirees, and only about a third of the companies that had retiree health care in 1990 have them in 2002.

Portability: HIPAA

Title I of the Health Insurance Portability and Accountability Act of 1996, or **HIPAA,** protects employees who change jobs from having to start a new waiting period before a preexisting condition is covered. For example, before HIPAA, a person with diabetes might not want to change jobs, even for a much better position, since it would mean going for a time without coverage for daily insulin shots and possible complications of the illness. Many employees were trapped in such situations before HIPAA. After the enactment of HIPAA, a person with diabetes could change jobs, and health insurance providers, without fear of losing coverage on that specific condition.

HIPAA provides protection for both group and individual health insurance. In essence, it provides **portability** of coverage.[9] That means that when an employee leaves one job and starts a new job, the coverage of health insurance under the new employer's program cannot exclude benefits for pre-existing condition, as long as the break in health coverage is no longer than sixty-three days. Portability does not mean carrying the actual coverage of the old employer to the new employment, but rather carrying forward the qualification for pre-existing conditions. For example, Joe was employed with company A for ten years and had health coverage under that employer. He accepted a job offer from company B. One month before changing his job he broke his leg in a skiing accident. Under HIPAA, the new employer cannot limit coverage for the injured leg. If Joe needs surgery on this leg in three months, the health coverage under employer B will pay for the surgery. Before HIPAA, Joe would have had to stay covered under his old employer, paying the full amount himself through COBRA, until the pre-existing condition period of the new employer was met. That could have been six months, a year, or even longer.

Under HIPAA, an employer can impose only up to twelve months pre-existing conditions exclusions for regular enrollment and up to eighteen months for late enrollment. During an exclusion period, the health plan has to pay for all other conditions except the pre-existing condition. Prior group health coverage applies to these limits. Thus, if an employee's only previous group health coverage was for six months with Company A, the pre-existing conditions exclusion from new employer B would last for just six additional months rather than the full twelve. Under HIPAA, a pre-existing condition is defined as a condition for which the employee received any treatment within the six-month period before enrolling with the new employer.

The details of HIPAA are complex, but the gist is that an employee without a break in health coverage will never have to meet a pre-existing condition period more than once in a lifetime, if at all. When an employee leaves a job, the employer is required to provide a certificate of health coverage. This certificate is then taken to the next employer to ensure that no pre-existing conditions are imposed on the employee. Employers who neglect to give the certificate are subject to penalties of $100 per day. More on HIPAA and other recent health care-related laws is included in the "Important Issues: Recent Laws Affecting Health Care" of this chapter.

GROUP DENTAL INSURANCE

Most medical insurance policies do not cover dental expenses. **Dental insurance policies,** available in both the individual and group market, typically pay for normal diagnostic, preventive, restorative, and orthodontic services, as well as services required because of accidents. Diagnostic and preventive services include checkups and x-rays. Restorative services include procedures such as fillings, crowns, and bridges, and orthodontia includes braces and realignment of teeth.

Group dental insurance is available from insurance companies under fee-for-service plans, from dental service plans, from Blue Cross and Blue Shield and from managed care dental plans such as dental HMOs, dental PPOs, and dental POS plans. The rules under these plans are similar to that of medical expense plans. Most of the dental plans cover all types of treatment with a schedule of maximum benefits for each procedure, such as no more than $2,000 for orthodontic treatment. Benefits are subject to coinsurance and deductibles, and the limitation may be for a calendar maximum ($500 to $2,000) or a lifetime maximum ($1,000 to $5,000), or both. Teeth cleaning may be paid for once every six months. COBRA rules apply to dental plans. An example of a dental plan is available in the employee benefits case in the back of the text.

GROUP LONG-TERM CARE

A significant risk that individuals face later in life is the risk of insufficient resources to pay for nursing home services. This risk applies also to a need for nursing home or skilled nursing facilities in case of an injury that requires lengthy recovery time for any age group, not only the elderly. Generally, wealthy individuals are able to pay these expenses from their private income or savings. Those with few resources may qualify for Medicaid and public assistance. Long-term care services can be very expensive. According to the U.S. General Accounting Office, the national average cost for nursing home care is $55,000 and more in some areas. Nursing home costs are likely to increase dramatically over the next thirty years and are estimated to reach $190,000 annually.[10] Some people mistakenly think that long-term nursing care is covered by Medicare; as you learned in Chapter 15, Medicare covers only a limited number of days of skilled nursing care after a period of hospitalization. Group long-term care insurance is being offered by an increasing number of employers, but it is still only a small part of the long-term care insurance market. HIPAA gave tax incentives to employers offering group LTC.

IMPORTANT ISSUES

Recent Laws Affecting Health Care

The Health Insurance Portability and Accountability Act (HIPAA)

The Health Insurance Portability and Accountability Act (HIPAA) provides rights and protections for participants and beneficiaries in group health plans. HIPAA was signed into law on August 21, 1996, and became effective for all plans and issuers beginning June 1, 1997. The act protects workers and their families by:

- Limiting exclusions for preexisting medical conditions
- Providing credit against exclusion periods for prior health coverage and a process for showing periods of prior coverage to a new group health plan or health insurance issuer
- Providing new rights that allow individuals to enroll for health coverage when they lose other health coverage, get married, or add a new dependent
- Prohibiting discrimination in enrollment and in premiums charged to employees and their dependents based on health status-related factors
- Guaranteeing availability of health insurance coverage for small employers and renewability of health insurance coverage for both small and large employers

Newborns' and Mothers' Health Protection Act

The Newborns' and Mothers' Health Protection Act of 1996 requires plans that offer maternity coverage to pay for at least a 48-hour hospital stay following childbirth (96-hour stay in the case of a cesarean section). It was signed into law on September 26, 1996, and became effective for group health plans for plan years beginning on or after January 1, 1998.

All group health plans that provide maternity or newborn infant coverage must include a statement in their summary plan description advising individuals of the Newborns' Act requirements: A mother may not be encouraged to accept less than the minimum protections available to her under the Newborns' Act, and an attending provider may not be induced to discharge a mother or newborn earlier than 48 or 96 hours after delivery.

Women's Health and Cancer Rights Act

The Women's Health and Cancer Rights Act (WHCRA) contains protections for patients who elect breast reconstruction in connection with a mastectomy. It was signed into law on October 21, 1998, and became effective immediately. WHCRA requires that any plan offering mastectomy coverage must also include coverage for:

- Reconstruction of the breast on which the mastectomy was performed
- Surgery and reconstruction of the other breast to produce a symmetrical appearance
- Prostheses and physical complications at all stages of mastectomy, including lymphedemas

Under WHCRA, mastectomy benefits may be subject to annual deductibles and coinsurance consistent with those established for other benefits under the plan or coverage. Group health plans covered by the law must notify individuals of the coverage required by WHCRA upon enrollment, and annually thereafter.

Mental Health Parity Act

The Mental Health Parity Act (MHPA), signed into law on September 26, 1996, requires that annual or lifetime dollar limits on mental health benefits be no lower than any such dollar limits for medical and surgical benefits offered by a group health plan or health insurance issuer offering coverage in connection with a group health plan. The law does not apply to benefits for substance abuse or chemical dependency.

Exploring the Internet

More information on each of these important health care laws can be found in the booklet "Questions and Answers: Recent Changes in Health Care Law" (www.dol.gov/pwba/pubs/hippa.pdf) published by the Pension and Welfare Benefits Administration of the U.S. Department of Labor. See the Publications and Reports page at www.dol.gov/pwba/publications/main.html for a complete list of the PWBA's reports.

Adapted from publications of the U.S. Department of Labor, Pension and Welfare Benefits Administration, www.dol.gov/pwba/publications/main.html.

Group long-term care insurance (LTC) covers the costs of the following levels of care:

- Skilled nursing care
- Intermediate care
- Custodial care help needed to handle personal needs
- Home health care
- Adult day care

Generally, benefits are expressed as a maximum daily benefit, such as $50 or $100 per day, with an overall policy limit, such as five years of benefits or a $100,000 lifetime maximum. Waiting or elimination periods are not uncommon; for example, a policy may not pay the first ninety days of nursing home expenses.

Eligibility for benefits usually is based on the inability to perform a certain number of **activities of daily living** (ADL) such as getting out of bed, dressing, eating, and being able to use the bathroom. Some LTC policies recognize cognitive impairment. Most cover skilled nursing care, which requires medical professionals to treat the patient on a twenty-four-hour basis under the direction of a physician. Patients typically need this type of attention for a relatively short period of time, immediately after hospitalization or following an acute illness. However, some individuals may require skilled nursing care for longer periods. Skilled nursing care is the most expensive kind of long-term care. Intermediate nursing care is for those not requiring around-the-clock assistance by medical professionals. This type of care typically extends for longer periods than skilled nursing care does.

Custodial care provides individuals with assistance in activities of daily living, such as bathing, dressing, and eating. Medical staff are not required. Although it is the least intensive kind of care, custodial care is often needed for the longest period of time and thus can be the most costly care overall. Coverage of custodial care varies across policies. Some contracts cover custodial care only if a doctor states that it is medically necessary. Others cover only if the insured is unable to perform a certain number of activities of daily living.

Group LTC insurance typically covers skilled, intermediate, and/or custodial nursing care in a nursing home facility. Some group policies also cover **home health care,** in which all or a portion of these services are provided in the insured's own home. Coverage of home health care is becoming increasingly common, since insureds generally prefer to be at home and total costs may be lower than if care is provided in a medical facility.

If an employer offers group LTC, eligibility may be restricted to active employees and their spouses, though sometimes retired employees up to age 80 are included. In most cases, employers do not pay for or contribute to this benefit, and the premiums paid by the employee cannot be included in a cafeteria plan or flexible spending account (explained in Chapter 16). Thus, the premiums cannot be paid with before-tax income. But HIPAA provides some tax relief if the group plan meets stringent qualification of the benefits. If the employer pays the premium, the amount is not taxable to the employees, as the premiums for health insurance are not included in taxable income. Under the act, the benefits are tax-free, as are the benefits of health insurance, as long as the benefit payment per day does not exceed a certain amount. At the time of enactment of HIPAA, the amount per day was limited to $190. The qualification requirements are that the group LTC policies cover only what is considered LTC service; benefits are paid to chronically ill people who cannot perform two out of five or six daily living activities; and the services of an LTC facility is required because of substantial cognitive impairment. These factors make the group LTC policies that qualify for the tax break very stringent and undesirable. These factors may be the main reason for the slow growth of group LTC market. Individual LTC policies are not so limiting in the definition of the qualified recipient of the benefits.

OTHER HEALTH PLANS

Medical Savings Accounts (MSAs)

Another way in which employers may provide for coverage of employee medical expenses is through use of individual employee **medical savings accounts,** also called MSAs. MSAs are similar to individual retirement accounts (IRAs) in that deposits are made to an account for the employee, who uses the fund to cover medical expenses (rather than retirement expenses). MSAs provide an economic incentive to employees to be cost conscious and use only necessary care, since employees retain the balance of their own accounts.

A catastrophic medical expense insurance policy (a high-deductible policy) is usually purchased in conjunction with an MSA. For example, the catastrophic policy may have a deductible of $3,000, so that all medical expenses less than $3,000 are paid from the MSA, but in the event of medical costs exceeding $3,000, the catastrophic policy offers full protection. A catastrophic policy is less expensive than traditional policies or HMOs and PPOs. When insurers do not have to deal with many small claims, the administrative cost of health claims is reduced dramatically. The premium saved by purchasing only catastrophic coverage can be used to fund the MSA.

Employer and employee contributions to the MSA are limited in amount. The enactment of HIPAA made MSA contributions tax-exempt, as demonstrated in Table 17.4. These plans are available to the self-employed and to workers in businesses with fifty or fewer employees. Under an approved MSA plan, individuals or employers (but not both) can make deposits into the MSA plan's savings account after obtaining a high-deductible insurance policy. The annual insurance deductible ranges from $1,650 to $2,500 for individuals, of which no more than 65 percent can be deposited into an MSA. The range is $3,300 to $4,950 for families, of which no more than 75 percent can be deposited in an MSA. (These figures are as of 2002; the amounts increase each year.) The MSA accounts are to be used only for medical expenses; unused amounts are carried over from year to year. Before age 65, no money can be withdrawn without penalty of 15 percent.

Health Care Reimbursement Arrangements

The move to consumer-driven health care plans described in "Ethical Dilemma: What is the Tradeoff Between Health Care Cost and Benefits?" received a boost in the summer of 2002. The IRS gave the green light to employers that prefer to sponsor "catastrophic plans"—defined-contribution health programs accompanied by high-deductible indemnity insurance, similar to MSAs. The employers are required to contribute to the employees' **personal care accounts,** also called **health care reimbursement arrangements** (HRAs). The employees use the accounts to pay their medical expenses or COBRA premium, and they have their choice of health care providers. Under the IRS ruling, accounts funded completely by the employer are not taxable to the employees and can be carried over from year to year like the MSA accounts. The IRS ruling is considered an important step towards creating the innovative ideas of defined contribution health plans.[11] These plans are considered consumer-driven plans that combine a high deductible (at least $1,000 and often $2,000 or more) with an employee reimbursement account. It gives more freedom of choice of providers and, as noted, are funded by the employer.

TABLE 17.4 Medical Savings Accounts	**HIPAA 1996**	The Health Insurance Portability and Accountability Act of 1996 includes provisions that allow self-employed individuals to pay for their health care with tax-exempt funds.
	Annual carryover	The medical savings accounts, or MSAs, can be carried over year to year and accumulate interest tax-deferred. MSA deposits remain tax-exempt as long as they are used to cover qualified medical expenses.
	Pre-tax dollars	Under the law, the accounts must be paired with a qualifying high-deductible health policy. That means users will pay their first few thousand dollars of covered health expenses from pretax dollars (the money in the savings accounts), cover the next several hundred from their own pockets, and receive reimbursement for covered expenses exceeding a high deductible.
	Maximum deposits	Individuals are permitted to deposit up to 65% of that deductible in a savings account (families would be allowed 75% of the deductible), and deduct that sum from their taxable income for the year. In other words, if a family bought an MSA-qualified policy with a $4,000 deductible, they could deposit up to $3,000 in their MSA. For a family in the 27% tax bracket, the tax savings would be $810 a year.
	Example	1. John Bright, a computer software consultant, buys a health insurance policy with a $4,650 deductible for his family. 2. Over the course of the year, the family deposits $3,488 (75% of deductible) in the bank for an MSA. 3. Total medical expenses for the year are $1,000. The Bright family withdraws $1,000 from the MSA to pay medical bills. 4. On the Bright family's federal tax form, the $3,488 contributed to the MSA is listed as a tax deduction. 5. There is $2,488 left in the MSA at year-end. It can be used to pay future medical bills. An additional $3,488 can be contributed each successive year. Interest on the account is tax-deferred. MSA money can be withdrawn at any time to pay medical bills and is tax-free. Using the funds for any other purpose prior to age 65 makes them subject to regular income tax plus a 15% penalty.

Adapted from HealthcareShopper.com, www.healthcareshopper.com/msa.htm.

MEDICAL CARE SYSTEMS WORLDWIDE

The level of health care services within a country varies with the level of economic development. Countries that are more developed or industrialized have modern health services available to most of the population, whereas in poorer countries, health care systems are very limited. Among the countries with more extensive health care systems, financing methods vary greatly. Some nations have a public, nationalized health service, some have social insurance programs, and some finance health services through private, voluntary insurance plans.

With a purely public, nationalized health service model, the state owns and operates the health care system. Hospitals are owned by the state and doctors are employees of the state. The state provides universal coverage (or care to everyone), funded through general tax revenues. The system in the United Kingdom most closely follows this model.

The social insurance model integrates the public and private sectors to finance health care. Employers and employees pay a payroll tax to private insurers, who in turn contract with physician groups to provide care. Hospitals may be publicly or privately owned. Those people not covered by employment (such as the unemployed or elderly) are insured by the state. Germany uses a social insurance program to provide most health care services.

The private, voluntary system does not require employers, employees, or individuals to participate in a health insurance plan. Typically, larger employers provide health insurance for employees. Individuals not covered at work may buy health insurance themselves. A portion of the population, however, may be uninsured, which limits their access to medical services. Insurers, physicians, and hospitals operate in the private sector to provide services. The United States is the principal example of a private, voluntary system.

Most countries finance health care primarily through one of these systems. However, most countries also have sub-systems in place. For example, in the United Kingdom, the national health service covers everyone, but about 10 percent of the population also has private, supplemental health insurance. Private policies cover services that may not be readily accessible otherwise. Likewise, the social insurance system is often supplemented by private insurance that covers deductibles or coinsurance costs. Canada, Germany, and France have social insurance systems augmented by voluntary, private insurance. In the United States, although private insurance predominates, more than 40 percent of medical care is provided by governmental programs (for example, for the poor and elderly). Combination systems allow adjustment of a country's health care system to provide service for those not well served by the predominant system.

Although there are many different approaches to health care financing, the objectives across systems are similar: to provide high-quality care to many people at an affordable price. Achieving these objectives is of great concern, not only in the United States, but worldwide. As we learn more about other health care systems, we have an excellent opportunity to consider the effects of different systems on the availability, quality, and price of health care.

KEY TERMS

defined contribution health plan
consumer driven health coverage
Exclusive Physician Organization (EPO)
usual, customary, and reasonable (UCR)
Point of Service (POS)
capitation
health care providers
indemnity benefits
basic health care benefits
basic hospital policy
basic surgical policy
basic medical expense policy
major medical insurance
maximum limits
internal policy limits
benefit period
coinsurance provision

stop loss limit
cost sharing
comprehensive medical insurance
coordination of benefits provision
cost containment techniques
second surgical opinion
ambulatory surgical center
preadmission testing
preadmission certification
extended care facilities
hospice care
home health care
utilization review organization
statistical analysis of claims
diagnostic related group (DRG)
prospective payment
wellness programs
managed care

preferred provider organization (PPO)
health maintenance organization (HMO)
group practice associations
individual practice associations (IPA)
COBRA
continuation provisions
HIPPAA
portability
dental insurance policy
group long-term care insurance (LTC)
activities of daily living (ADL)
home health care
medical savings account (MSA)
personal care account
healthcare reimbursement arrangement (HRA)

DISCUSSION QUESTIONS

1. What is the purpose of including deductible and coinsurance provisions in group medical insurance policies?

2. Explain how second surgical opinion provisions work to control health care costs.

3. What services are provided by a home health service? How do home health services reduce overall health care expenses?

4. How do PPOs differ from group practice HMOs? Is there much difference between a PPO and an individual practice HMO that pays its providers on a fee-for-service basis?

5. How does a PPO differ from a POS?

6. What characteristics should be contained in a managed care plan?

7. What are the advantages and disadvantages of managed care plans?

8. The intent behind passage of COBRA was to reduce the number of uninsured persons. How does COBRA work to achieve this objective?

9. Now that we have HIPAA, do we need COBRA? Use an example.

10. Describe medical saving accounts.

11. Describe group long-term care.

12. Describe group dental coverage.

EXERCISES

17.1 The Meridian Advertising Agency has 1,340 employees in six states. The main office is in Richmond, Virginia. Fifty percent of the employees are women in their childbearing years. Most employees are in good health. The major medical losses last year incurred from Jack Denton's heart surgery, fifteen baby deliveries, and four cases of cancer treatment. Jack Denton is the creative director of the agency.

Meridian is using EB-Consulting to assist in choosing health care and dental coverages. Currently the agency fully insures five options of health plans as follows (use some of the information from the Employee Benefits Case in the back of the text):

- A staff model HMO available only in Richmond (premium per employee, $145 per month)
- An IPA HMO available in many but not all locations ($155 per month)
- A POS available in all locations ($160 per month)
- A PPO available in all locations ($175 per month)
- An indemnity plan available in all locations ($190 per month)

The Meridian Agency pays $145 of each monthly premium.

a. Compare the current health care programs that are used by the Meridian Agency in terms of:

- Benefits provided under each plan
- Possible out-of-pocket expenses for the employees and their families for illnesses and injuries
- Choice of providers
- The ways providers are being reimbursed

b. Jack Denton (the employee with the heart surgery) has two children. He lives twenty miles west of Richmond in a rural community of 100 people and farms his land on the weekends. His wife is expecting another baby in four months.

Before his surgery, Jack and his wife evaluated the plans and selected the one that best fit their needs.

- Which health plan do you think they selected? Explain.
- Do you think now, after his surgery, Jack is still happy with this choice? Explain.

c. The Meridian Agency has employed Dan Smith for the last ten years. Three months ago Dan had a foot injury for which he is still being treated. He accepted a job offer from a Washington, D.C., advertising agency. Before Dan leaves, Meridian's human resources department invites him for an exit interview. If you were Meridian's employee benefits specialist, what would you tell Dan about his rights? Explain to Dan about COBRA and HIPAA.

d. Meridian is considering adding a dental plan.

- What type of dental plan you think EB-Consulting would suggest?
- Why are dental insurance plans more likely than medical expense plans to include benefits for routine examinations and preventive medicine?

e. EB-Consulting is trying to convince the Meridian Agency to add long-term care insurance to their employee benefits package. Explain long-term care coverage.

17.2 Anna Claire's Costumes, Inc., has experienced medical benefit cost increases of 16 and 19 percent over the last two years. The benefits manager believes that high hospitalization rates and unnecessarily long hospital stays may explain this. The company wants to control costs by reducing hospitalization costs.

a. What cost control methods could be implemented to achieve this objective?

b. Would employees still have adequate protection with these new techniques in place?

c. How do employees gain in the long run if the company contains medical benefit costs?

17.3 Marguerite Thomas, a Canadian, and Margaret Phythian, a Minnesotan, each tried to convince the other that the health care system in her country was superior. In Canada, Marguerite enjoys nationalized health care, where everyone is covered. She does not worry that she may need care she can't afford. She is willing to pay the taxes necessary to support the system. She doesn't mind waiting several weeks to get certain elective procedures done because she knows that everyone is getting the care they need and she is willing to wait her turn. Margaret, however, likes the high-quality, high-tech care available to her in the Twin Cities through her employer-provided HMO. She gets high quality care and never needs to wait for treatment. She also likes the lower tax rate she pays, partly because the U.S. government isn't funding a nationalized health system.

a. If Marguerite and Margaret were unemployed or had low income, which system might they prefer? Would this change if they were in high income tax brackets? Please explain.

b. Which system would you prefer? What trade-offs are you willing to make to have this type of health care system?

NOTES

1.   Jerry Geisel, "Health plan costs up 14.7% in 2002: Mercer," *Business Insurance*, 9 December 2002.

2.   Managed Care Information Center at: www.themcic.com/company/press/press01.htm.

3. Today, Kaiser Permanente is one of the largest HMOs in the United States, with operations scattered across the country.

4. An example of calculation of capitation provided by the American Society of Dermatology is featured in "DEVELOP A REALISTIC CAPITATION RATE" at the Society's web site: www.asd.org/realrate.html.

5. "HMOs Tightening Consumer Satisfaction Gap: Survey," NU Online News Service, July 15, 11:20 a.m., 2002.

6. Sarah Lueck, Robert S. Greenberger, and Rhonda L. Rundle, "Supreme Court Rules Against HMOs On Paying for Rejected Treatments," *Wall Street Journal,* 21 June 2002.

7. Steven Brostoff, "High Court Upholds States' HMO Rules," *National Underwriter* Online News Service, 20 June 2002.

8. Jerry Geisel, "COBRA Subsidy Could Increase Beneficiaries: Survey," *Business Insurance,* 30 August 2002.

9. Health Care Financing Administration, www.hcfa.gov.

10. From TIAA-CREF Web Center "How Much Does Long-Term Care Cost, and Who Pays for It?" at: www.tiaa-cref.org/ltc/ltcosts.html.

11. "Hewitt Praises New IRS Health Account Rules," *National Underwriter* Online News Service, 2 July 2002. The IRS has posted more information about the HRA guidelines on the Internet at www.ustreas .gov/press/releases/po3204.htm.

CHAPTER 18

Employee Benefits: Retirement Plans

As noted earlier in this text, individuals rely on several sources for income during retirement: Social Security, employer-sponsored retirement plans, and individual savings (depicted in our familiar three-stepped stool). In Chapter 15, we discussed how Social Security, a public retirement program, provides a foundation of economic security for retired workers and their families. Social Security provides only a basic floor of income; it was never intended to be the sole source of retirement income.

Employees may receive additional retirement income from employer-sponsored retirement plans. As you saw in Table 16.1 of Chapter 16 (which described the fundamentals of employee benefits), the employer's share of the cost for pensions in 2002 was estimated at 2.9 percent of total cash and non-cash compensation. Clearly, private retirement benefits are an important component of employee compensation. In this chapter we discuss the objectives of group retirement plans, how plans are structured, and current issues important to employers and employees.

The chapter presents:

- Connection
- The nature of qualified pension plans
- Types of qualified plans
- Other qualified defined contribution plans
- Other qualified plans
- Pension plan funding techniques
- Nonqualified, tax-favored retirement plans

CONNECTION

In our search to complete the risk management puzzle of Figure 18.1, we now add an important layer that is represented by the second step of the three-stepped stool: employer-sponsored pension plans. The pension plans provided by the employer (in the second step of the three-stepped stool) can be either **defined benefit** or **defined contribution.** Defined benefit pension plans assure employees of a certain amount at retirement, leaving all risk to the employer who has to meet the specified commitment. Defined contribution, on the other hand, is a promise only to contribute an amount to the employee's separate, or individual, account. The employee has the investment risk and no assurances of the level of retirement amount. Defined benefit plans are insured by the **Pension Benefit Guaranty Corporation (PBGC),** a federal agency that ensures the benefits up to a limit in case the pension plan cannot meet its obligations. The maximum amount of benefits guaranteed under the PBGC for 2003 is $3,664.77 per month, up from $3,579 in 2002.[1] The employee never contributes to this plan. The prevalence of this plan is on the decline. It accounted for 1.4 percent of all compensation in 1997 and declined to 1.1 percent in 2002, as you saw in Table 16.1. Another trend that became prevalent and has received Congressional attention is the move from the traditional defined benefit plans to cash balance plans. These plans are defined benefit plans, though they are in a way a hybrid between defined benefit and defined contribution plans. More on cash balance plans, and all other plans, will be explained in this chapter and in "Ethical Dilemma: Cash Balance Conversions—Who Gets Hurt?" In December 2002, the Treasury Department and Internal Revenue Service proposed rules that regard the method of crediting each employee with the same percentage of salary under the cash balance plans as non-discriminatory under the federal age discrimination law explained in Chapter 16.[2]

The most common plans are the defined contribution pension plans. As noted above, under this type of plan, the employer provides us with the money and we invest the funds. If we do well with our investments, we may be able to enjoy a prosperous retirement. Under defined contribution plans, in most cases we have some choices for investments.

FIGURE 18.1 Connection between Risks and Employee Benefits: Retirement Plans

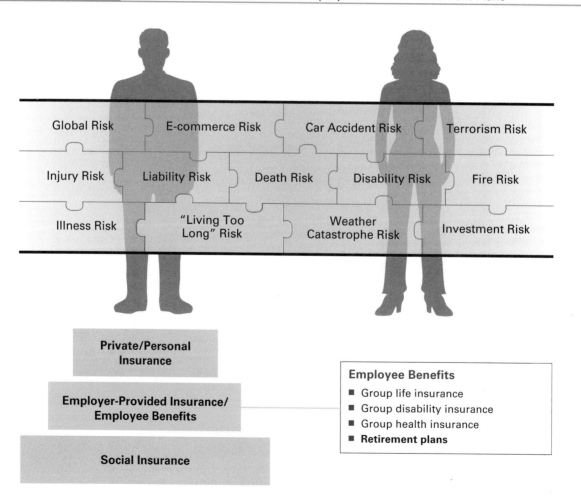

Plans such as money purchase, profit sharing, and target plans are funded by employers. In another type of defined contribution plan, we contribute towards our retirement by forgoing our income or deferring it on a pre-tax basis such as into 401(k), 403(b) or 457 plans. These plans are sponsored by employers and the employer may match some portion of our contribution in some of these deferred compensation plans. Since it is our own savings, we can say that it belongs in the third step of Figure 18.1. However, since it is done through the employer, it is also part of the second step. The pension plans discussed in this chapter are featured in Figure 18.2.

As you can see, we need to know what we are doing when we invest our defined-contribution retirement funds. During the stock market boom of the late 1990s, many small investors put most of their retirement funds in stocks. As of summer 2002, the stock market saw some of the worst declines in its history. Among the reasons for the decline were the downturn in the economy, September 11, and investors' loss of trust in the integrity of the accounting numbers of many corporations. The fraudulent behavior of executives in companies such as Enron, WorldCom, and others led investors to consider their funds not just lost but stolen.[3] On July 29, 2002, President George W. Bush signed a bill for corporate governance or corporate responsibility to re-build the trust in corporate America and punish fraudulent executives.[4] "The legislation, among other things, will bring the accounting industry under federal supervision and stiffen penalties for corporate executives who misrepresent company finances."[5] Congress has also been working on legislation to safeguard employee 401(k)s in an effort to prevent future disasters like the one suffered

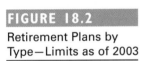

FIGURE 18.2

Retirement Plans by Type—Limits as of 2003

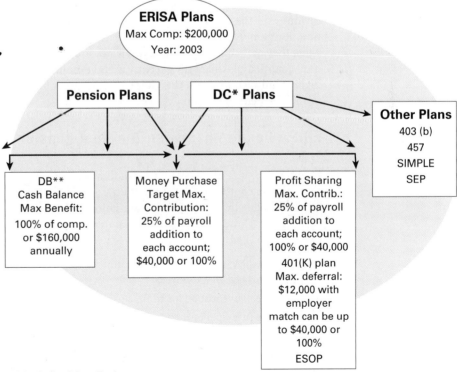

*   DC = Defined Contribution

** DB = Defined Benefits

Source: Adapted from Etti G. Baranoff, "Teaching Pensions Through Case Study: How to Evaluate the Differences Among Qualified Retirement Plans for a Small Medical Office," working paper.

by Enron employees, who were not allowed (under the blackout period) to diversify their 401(k) investments and lost the funds when Enron declared bankruptcy.[6] The reform objective is to give more oversight and safety measures to defined contribution plans, as these plans do not enjoy the oversight and protection of the PGBC.

In this chapter, our drill-down into the specific pieces of the puzzle brings us into areas of many challenges. But we do need to complete the holistic risk management process we have started. This chapter delivers only a brief insight into the very broad and challenging area of pensions. Pensions are also featured as part of Case 2 at the back of the textbook.

THE NATURE OF QUALIFIED PENSION PLANS

A retirement plan may be qualified or nonqualified. The distinction is important to both employer and employee, because qualification produces a plan with a favorable tax status. In a **qualified plan,** employer contributions to an employee's pension during the employee's working years are deductible as a business expense but are not taxable income to the employee until they are received as benefits. Moreover, investment earnings on funds held by the trustee for the plan are not subject to income taxes as they are earned.

Most nonqualified plans do not allow employer funding contributions to be deducted as a business expense unless they are classified as compensation to the employee, in which case they become taxable income for the employee. Investment earnings on these nonqualified accumulated pension funds are also subject to taxation. Retirement benefits from a nonqualified plan are a deductible business expense when they are paid to the employee, if not previously classified as compensation. Most non-qualified plans are for executives and designed to benefit only a small number of highly paid executives. In this chapter we discuss non-qualified plans briefly at the end of the chapter.

ERISA Requirements for Qualified Pension Plans

In order to be qualified, a plan must fulfill various requirements. These requirements prevent those in control of the organization from using the plan primarily for their own benefit. The following requirements are enforced by the United States Internal Revenue Service, the United States Department of Labor, and the Pension Benefit Guaranty Corporation (PBGC).

- The plan must be legally binding, in writing, and must be communicated clearly to all employees.
- The plan must be for the exclusive benefit of the employees or their beneficiaries.
- The principal or income of the pension plan cannot be diverted to any other purpose, unless the assets exceed those required to cover accrued pension benefits.
- The plan must benefit a broad class of employees and not discriminate in favor of highly compensated employees.
- The plan must be designed to be permanent and have continuing contributions.

IMPORTANT ISSUES

Warning Signs that Pension Contributions Are Being Misused

Increasingly, employees are asked to make voluntary or mandatory contributions to pension and other benefit plans. This is particularly true for 401(k) savings plans. These plans allow you to deduct from your paycheck a portion of pretax income every year, invest it, and pay no taxes on those contributions until the money is withdrawn at retirement.

An anti-fraud campaign by the Department of Labor uncovered a small fraction of employers who abused employee contributions by either using the money for corporate purposes or holding on to the money too long. Here are ten warning signs that your pension contributions are being misused.

- Your 401(k) or individual account statement is consistently late or comes at irregular intervals.
- Your account balance does not appear to be accurate.
- Your employer failed to transmit your contribution to the plan on a timely basis.
- You notice a significant drop in account balance that cannot be explained by normal market ups and downs.
- Your 401(k) or individual account statement does not reflect a contribution from your paycheck.
- Investments listed on your statement are not what you authorized.
- Former employees are having trouble getting their benefits paid on time or in the correct amounts.
- You notice unusual transactions, such as a loan to the employer, a corporate officer, or one of the plan trustees.
- Investment managers or consultants change frequently and without explanation.
- Your employer has recently experienced severe financial difficulty.

If you think the plan trustees or others responsible for investing your pension money have been violating the rules, you should call or write the nearest field office of the U.S. Department of Labor's Pension and Welfare Benefits Administration (PWBA). The Labor Department has authority to investigate complaints of fund mismanagement. If an investigation reveals wrongdoing, the department can take action to correct the violation, including asking a court to compel plan trustees and others to put money back in the plan. Courts can also impose penalties of up to 20 percent of the recovered amount and bar individuals from serving as trustees and plan money managers.

If you suspect that individuals providing services to the plans have gotten loans or otherwise taken advantage of their relationship to the plan, the Employee Plans Division of the Internal Revenue Service may want to take a closer look. The Internal Revenue Service is authorized to impose tax penalties on people involved in unlawful "party in interest" transactions.

Cases of embezzlement or stealing of pension money, kickbacks, or extortion should be referred to the Federal Bureau of Investigation or the Labor Department field office in your area. If illegal activities are found, the case can be referred to the U.S. Department of Justice for prosecution. Criminal penalties can include fines and prison sentences, or both.

Federal pension law makes it unlawful for employers to fire or otherwise retaliate against employees who provide the government with information about their pension funds' investment practices.

Explore the Internet

For more information on managing your pension, including explanations of the rules that pension managers must follow, see "Protect Your Pension," a handbook from the U.S. Department of Labor, at www.dol.gov/pwba/pubs/protect/guidetoc.htm. For updates on bills debated in Congress, such as Senate Bill S.1971, ensuring that pension assets are adequately diversified and employees have access to change their investments, see http://thomas.loc.gov.

Sources: Portions reprinted from "10 Warning Signs," U.S. Department of Labor, Pension and Welfare Benefits Administration, www.dol.gov/pwba/publications/10warningsigns.html, and from "Protect Your Pension," a handbook from the U.S. Department of Labor, at www.dol.gov/pwba/pubs/protect/guidetoc.htm.

- The plan must comply with the Employee Retirement Income Security Act and subsequent federal laws.

The Employee Retirement Income Security Act of 1974 (**ERISA**) and subsequent amendments and laws—in particular, the Tax Reform Act of 1986 (TRA86)—are federal laws that regulate the design, funding, and communication aspects of private, qualified retirement plans. The most recent amendment is the Economic Growth and Tax Relief Reconciliation Act of 2001 (EGTRRA 2001). In practice, the term ERISA is used to refer to the 1974 act and all subsequent amendments and related laws. The purpose of ERISA is two-fold: to protect the benefits of plan participants and to prevent discrimination in favor of highly compensated employees (that is, those who control the organization).[7]

Within the guidelines and standards established by ERISA and subsequent federal laws, the employer must make some choices regarding the design of a qualified retirement plan. The main items covered by ERISA and subsequent laws and amendments, particularly the Tax Reform Act of 1986 (TRA86), are:

- Employee rights
- Reporting and disclosure rules
- Participation coverage
- Vesting
- Funding
- Fiduciary responsibilities
- Amounts contributed or withdrawn
- Nondiscrimination
- Tax penalties

ERISA provides significant protection to plan participants. As time elapsed and the nature of the work force changed from stable and permanent positions to mobile and transient positions, it appeared that ERISA failed to address portability issues when employees change jobs. ERISA and subsequent laws are also considered to have administrative difficulties and to be a burden on employers. While the percentage of working population covered is still unchanged since 1974, the number of defined benefit plans has dropped below 70,000 from a high of 175,000 plans in 1983 and more employees are covered under defined contribution plans. ERISA has a safety valve for defined benefit plans with the insurance provided by the PBGC. Plans such as 401(k) do not have such safety valve. For example, Enron's fiasco with its employees' 401(k) funds occurred because the company imposed a "blackout" period during which they were not allowed to change their investments.[8] This brought the question of whether ERISA rules are adequate for defined contribution plans. As noted earlier, at the time of writing of this text, Congress has been looking into safeguard measures in this area.[9] Information on how to protect your pensions is available from the Department of Labor and is featured in "Important Issues: Warning Signs that Pension Contributions are Being Misused."

In 2001, EGTRRA addressed some of ERISA's shortfalls. The new law offers employers sponsoring plans more flexibility in plan funding and incentives by allowing greater tax deductions. The changes are expected to result in a 4 percent revenue loss to the Department of the Treasury. The major benefits of EGTRRA are the increases in retirement savings limits and mandates of faster participant vesting in employers' matching contributions to 401(k) plans. Also important are the increases in portability, increase in flexibility in plan funding and design, and administrative simplification. It is estimated that the adoption of EGTRRA provisions by employers and worker utilization will result in contributions increasing in range from $2.07 to $4.62 billion in 2002 to $4.55 to $11.37 billion in 2006. There is, however, a ten-year sunset provision that may reverse the changes to the original level at the time of enactment of the law, unless Congress passes additional laws.[10]

Eligibility and Coverage Requirements

A pension plan must establish **eligibility criteria** for determining who is covered. Most plans exclude certain classes of employees. For example, part-time or seasonal employees may not be covered. Separate plans may be set up for those paid on an hourly basis. Excluding certain classes of employees is allowed, provided the plan does not discriminate in favor of highly compensated employees, meets minimum eligibility requirements, and passes the tests noted below.

Under ERISA, the minimum eligibility requirements are the attainment of age 21 and one year of service. A year of service is defined as working at least 1,000 hours within a calendar year.[11] This is partly to reduce costs of enrolling employees who leave employment shortly after being hired, and partly because most younger employees attach a low value to benefits they will receive many years in the future. The Age Discrimination in Employment Act eliminates all maximum age limits for eligibility. Even when an employee is hired at an advanced age, such as 71, the employee must be eligible for the pension plan within the first year of service if the plan is offered to other, younger hires in the same job.

In addition to eligibility rules, ERISA has **coverage requirements,** designed to improve participation by non-highly compensated employees. All employees of businesses with related ownership (called a **controlled group**) are treated for coverage requirements as if they were employees of one plan.

Retirement Age Limits

In order to reasonably estimate the cost of some retirement plans, mainly defined benefit plans, it is necessary to establish a retirement age for plan participants. For other types of plans, mainly defined contribution plans, setting a retirement age clarifies the age at which no additional employer contributions will be made to the employee's plan. The **normal retirement age** is the age at which full retirement benefits become available to retirees. Most private retirement plans specify age 65 as the normal retirement age.

Early retirement may be allowed, but that option must be specified in the pension plan description. Usually, early retirement permanently reduces the benefit amount. For example, an early retirement provision may allow the participant to retire as early as age 55 if he or she also has at least thirty years of service with the employer. The pension benefit amount, however, would be reduced to take into account the shorter time available for fund accumulation and the likely longer period that benefits will be paid out.

Early-retirement plans used to be very appealing both to longtimers and to employers who saw replenishment of the work force. In 2001, companies such as Procter & Gamble, Tribune Co., and Lucent Technologies used early retirement as an alternative to layoffs. Since the decline of old-fashioned defined-benefit pensions, employees have less incentive to take early retirement. With defined contribution plans, employees continue to receive the employer's contribution or defer their compensation in a 401(k) plan as long as they work. The benefits are not frozen at a certain point as in the traditional defined benefit plans. At the time of writing of this text, it appears that fewer and fewer people can think about early retirement when they have defined contribution plans that were invested in the stock market. The bear stock market is a major contributor to the situation.[12]

Mandatory retirement is considered age discrimination, except for executives in high policy-making positions. Thus, a plan must allow for late retirement. Deferral of retirement beyond the normal retirement age does not interfere with the accumulation of benefits. That is, working beyond normal retirement age may produce a pension benefit greater than would have been received at normal retirement age. However, a plan can set some limits on total benefits (for example, $50,000 per year) or on total years of plan participation (for example, 35 years). These limits help control employer costs.

Vesting Provisions

A pension plan may be contributory or noncontributory. A **contributory plan** requires the employee to pay all or part of the pension fund contribution. A noncontributory plan is funded only by employer contributions; that is, the employee does not contribute at all to the plan. ERISA requires that if an employee contributes to a pension plan, the employee must be able to recover all these contributions, with or without interest, if she or he leaves the firm.

Employer contributions may be recovered by an employee leaving the organization if the employee is vested. **Vesting,** or the employee's right to benefits for which the *employer* has made contributions, depends on the plan provisions. The TRA86 amendment to the original ERISA vesting schedule and EGTRRA 2001 established minimum standards to assure full vesting within a reasonable period of time. The employer usually chooses one of the two minimum vesting schedules as follows:

- Cliff vesting: Full vesting of employer contributions after five years. In top-heavy plans and the employer-matching portion of 401(k) plans, full vesting after three years.
- Graded vesting: 20 percent vesting of employer contributions after three years, 40 percent after four years, 60 percent after five years, 80 percent after six years and 100 percent after seven years. In top-heavy plans and employer-matching portion of 401(k) plans, graded vesting begins after two years and 100 percent at the sixth year.

Top-heavy plans are those in which the owners or highest-paid employees hold over 60 percent of the value of the pension plan. Key employees under EGTRRA 2001 are those who earn $130,000 or more annually in 2003.

Some plans provide a cash settlement at termination of employment. This distribution is taxable income in the year it is made, unless the employee moves the funds directly into a rollover individual retirement account (IRA). Employees not rolling the funds over must pay penalties in addition to income taxes in the year pension funds are received unless they are 59½ years old.

Nondiscrimination Tests

The employer's plan must meet one of the coverage requirements as follows:

- Percentage ratio test: The percentage of covered non-highly compensated employees must be at least 70 percent of highly compensated employees who are covered under the pension plan. For example if only 90 percent of the highly compensated employees are in the pension plan, only 63 percent (70 percent times 90 percent) of non-highly compensated employees must be included.
- Average benefit test: The average benefit (expressed as a percentage of pay) for non-highly compensated employees must be at least 70 percent of the average benefit for the highly compensated group.

In 2003, highly compensated employees are those earning $90,000 or more annually. Although the objective of coverage rules is to improve participation by non-highly compensated employees, the expense and administrative burden of compliance discourages small employers from having a qualified retirement plan.

Distributions

Distributions are benefits paid out to participants or their beneficiaries, usually at retirement. Tax penalties are imposed on plan participants who receive distributions (except for disability benefits) prior to age 59½. However, the law requires that benefits begin by age 70½, whether retirement occurs or not. Depending on the provisions of the particular plan, distributions may be made (1) as a lump sum, (2) as one of several life annuity options (as explained in the settlement options in Chapter 14), or (3) over the participant's life expectancy. At age 70½, the distribution requirements under ERISA direct the retiree to collect a minimum amount each year based on longevity tables.[13] Because of recent census data, Congress directed changes in the required minimum distribution calculations under EGTRRA 2001.[14]

The longest time period over which benefits may extend is the participant's life expectancy. ERISA requires that pension plan design make spousal benefits available. Once the participant becomes vested, the spouse automatically is eligible for a qualified **pre-retirement survivor annuity.** This provision gives lifetime benefits to the spouse if the participant dies before the earliest retirement age allowed by the plan. Once the participant reaches the earliest retirement age allowed by the plan, the spouse becomes eligible for benefits under a **joint and survivor annuity** option. This qualifies the spouse for a lifetime benefit in the event of the participant's death. In most cases, the spouse receives 50 percent of the annuity. Upon the employee's retirement, the spouse remains eligible for this benefit. These benefits may be waived only if the spouse signs a notarized waiver.

Loans

Employees who need to use their account balances are advised to take a loan rather than terminate their employment and receive distribution. The distribution results not only in tax liability but also in a 10 percent penalty if the employee is under 59½ years old. The loan provisions require that an employee can take only up to 50 percent of the vested account balance for not more than $50,000. A loan of $10,000 may be made even if it is greater than 50 percent of the vested account. The number of loans are not limited as long as the total amount is within the required limits. Some employers do not provide loan provisions in their retirement plan.

TYPES OF QUALIFIED PLANS

As noted above and shown in Figure 18.2, employers choose a pension plan from two types, defined benefit or defined contribution. Both are qualified plans that provide tax-favored arrangements for retirement savings.

Figure 18.2 displays the different qualified retirement plans. Defined benefit (DB) and defined contribution (DC) pension plans are shown in the first two left-hand squares. The defined contribution profit sharing (PS) plan is shown in the third left-hand rectangle. The left-most square represents the highest level of financial commitment by an employer; the "Profit Sharing" rectangle represents the least commitment. The profit sharing plan is funded at the discretion of the employer during periods of profits, whereas pension plans require annual minimum funding. This is why the employer is giving greater commitment to pension plans—contributions are required even in "bad" years. Among the pension plans, the traditional defined benefit plan represents the highest level of employer's commitment. It is a promise that the employee will receive a certain amount of income replacement at retirement. The benefits are defined by mathematical formula as will be shown later. Actuaries calculate the amount of annual contribution necessary to fund the retirement promise given by the employer. The PBGC provides insurance to guarantee these benefits (up to the maximum shown above) at a cost to the employer of $19 per employee per year. Since the traditional defined benefit pension plan is the plan with the greatest commitment, usually a high level of contribution is allowed for older employees. The allowed benefit at retirement in 2003, shown in Figure 18.2, is up to $160,000 or 100 percent of compensation for retirement at age 65 (up from $140,000 in 2001). Since the maximum allowed compensation level for pensions in 2003 is $200,000 (up from $170,000 in 2001), a maximum income at retirement of $160,000 would represent an 80 percent replacement of income. The amounts are shown in Figure 18.2.

Another defined benefit plan is the **cash balance plan.** As discussed above, it is a hybrid of the traditional defined benefit plan and defined contribution plans. In a cash balance plan the employer commits to contribute a certain percentage of compensation each year and guarantees a rate of return. Under this arrangement, employees are able to calculate the exact lump sum that will be available to them at retirement since the employer guarantees both contributions and earnings. This plan favors younger employees and is currently the topic of major debate and Congressional deliberation since many large corporations such as IBM converted their traditional defined benefits plans to cash balance, grandfathering the older employees' benefits under the plan.[15] See "Ethical Dilemma: Cash Balance Conversions—Who Gets Hurt?" in this chapter.

A cash balance plan is considered a hybrid plan because the contributions are guaranteed. The benefits are not explicitly defined, but are the outcome of the length of time the employee is in the pension plan. Since both the contributions and rate of returns are guaranteed, the amount available at retirement is therefore also guaranteed. It is an insured plan under the PBGC and all funds are kept in one large account administered by the employer. The employees have only hypothetical accounts that are made of the contributions and the guaranteed returns. As noted above, it is a defined benefit plan that looks like a defined contribution plan.

The simplest of the defined contribution pension plans is the money purchase pension plan. Under this plan, the employer guarantees only the annual contribution, but not any returns. As opposed to a defined benefit plan, where the employer keeps all the monies in one account, the defined contribution plan has separate accounts under the control of the employees. The investment vehicles in these accounts are limited to those selected by the employer who contracts with various financial institutions to administer the investments. If employees are successful in their investment strategy, their retirement benefits will be larger. The employees are not assured an amount at retirement and they have the investment risk, not the employer. Since the employer is at less of an investment risk here and its commitment is lower, the tax benefit is not as great (especially for older employees). The maximum annual allowed contribution per employee is the lesser of $40,000 or 100 percent of the employee's compensation in 2003 (up from $35,000 or 25 percent in 2001). The limits were increased pursuant to the Economic Growth and Tax Relief and Reconciliation Act of 2001 (EGTRRA) and was not changed in 2003. An employee who is receiving the maximum contribution of $40,000 and is earning the maximum allowed compensation of $200,000, will receive a contribution of 20 percent of income per year.

Another defined contribution plan is the target pension plan, which favors older employees. This is another hybrid plan, but this is actually a defined contribution plan (subject to the $40,000 and 100 percent limitation) that looks like a traditional defined benefits plan in its first year only. Details about this plan are beyond the scope of this text.

For employers seeking the least amount of commitment, profit sharing plans are the solution. These are defined contribution plans that are not pension plans. There is no minimum funding requirements each year. As of 2003, the maximum allowed tax

Ethical Dilemma

Cash Balance Conversions—Who Gets Hurt?

Over the past decade and a half, a number of employers have switched their traditional defined benefit pension plans to cash balance plans. By 2000, at least 20 percent of the *Fortune* 500 had shifted to cash balance plans. Employers like cash balance plans because they are less expensive than traditional plans. This is, in part, because they do not require the high administrative cost and large contributions for employees who are near retirement. Also, cash balance benefit plans may pay out less, because they base their benefits on an employee's career earnings while defined benefit plans are based on the final years of salary, when earnings usually peak.

In November 2002, Delta Airlines joined the cash balance trend, citing the soaring costs of its underfunded traditional pension plan as the reason. The airline expects to save $500 million over the next five years through the conversion of the plans of 60,000 non-pilot employees from defined benefits to cash balance.

Like Delta, many companies have implemented cash balance plans by "converting" their old defined benefit plans. In doing so, they determine an employee's accrued benefit under the old plan and use it to set an opening balance for a cash balance account. While the opening account of a cash balance account can end up less than the actual present value of the benefits an employee has already accrued (called "wear away"), cash balance plans have the advantage of portability. While the traditional defined benefits plan is not portable, in that an employee who leaves a job may need to leave the accrued and vested benefits with the employer until retirement, cash balance plans are considered very portable. The plan is similar to defined contribution plans in that the employee knows at any moment what is the value of his or her hypothetical account that is built up as an accumulation of employer's contributions and guaranteed rate of return. For this reason, cash balance plans are advertised as advantageous for today's mobile work force. Also, cash balance plans are considered best for younger workers since these employees have many years to accumulate their hypothetical account balances.

However, these conversions have not been free of major controversies. Older employees, who do not have a long enough time to accumulate the account balance, in most cases are granted continuation under the old plan, under a grandfather clause. Mid-career employees in their forties have most to risk, because it is uncertain whether the new cash balance plans can actually catch up to the old promise of defined benefits at age sixty-five. "Plan critics have repeatedly charged that pay credits discriminate against older employees because the credits they receive

would purchase a smaller annuity at normal retirement age than would those received by younger employees. Numerous lawsuits alleging discrimination have been filed against employers offering the plans." Regardless of these allegations, the IRS and the Department of the Treasury published proposed rules in December 2002 that consider the equal contributions in the cash balance plans not discriminatory under the federal age discrimination act.

IBM's conversion in 1999 provides a notorious example of the pitfalls of conversion for mid-career employees. When IBM announced the conversion, it was inundated with hundreds of thousand of e-mails complaining about the change, resulting in the company's repeated tweaking of its plan. Still, many employees are not satisfied when they compare the new plan with the defined benefit plan they might otherwise have received. (See examples of comparisons at www.cashpensions.com/samples.html.)

To soften the effects of cash balance conversion, many companies offer transitional benefits to older employers. Some companies allow their workers to choose between the traditional plan and the cash balance plan. Others offer stock options or increased contributions to employee 401(k) plans to offset the reduction to pension benefits.

Questions for Discussion

1. Who actually is the beneficiary of the conversions? The employer? All employees? Or only some? Is it ethical to change promises to employees?

2. Are conversion to cash balance plans a reflection of the lowering of the non-cash compensation (pension offering) of employers in the last two decades? Or are they just a smart move to accommodate the mobile work force? Is it ethical to make non-cash compensation reduction without agreement with employees?

3. As many employers try to get away from the traditional defined benefits plans that are similar to the current Social Security system, can this be a signal to privatizing Social Security? Would it be ethical to make changes that may not be clear to employees (see Chapter 15)?

Sources: Jerry Geisel, "Delta's New Pension Plan to Generate Big Savings," *Business Insurance*, 25 November 2002; Jonathan Barry Forman, "Legal Issues in Cash Balance Pension Plan Conversions," *Benefits Quarterly*, 1 January 2001; Lawrence J. Sher, "Survey of Cash Balance Conversions," *Benefits Quarterly*, 1 January 2001; Robert L. Clark, John J. Haley, and Sylvester J. Schieber, "Adopting Hybrid Pension Plans: Financial and Communication Issues," *Benefits Quarterly*, 1 January 2001; "IBM Employee and Investor Issues Summary Highlights," www.ibmemployee.com/Highlights001007.htm; "Cash Balance Plans Questions & Answers," U.S. Department of Labor, www.dol.gov/pwba/pubs/cashbq&a.htm, Jerry Geisel, "Proposed rules clarify cash balance plan status," *Business Insurance*, 10 December, 2002.

deductible contribution by employer per year is 25 percent of payroll. This is also a major change in effect after the enactment of EGTRRA 2001. The level used to be only 15 percent of payroll with limits of annual addition to each account of $35,000 or 25 percent in 2001. The additions to each account are up to the lesser of $40,000 or 100 percent of compensation. Since the maximum compensation allowed for computation of pensions is $200,000 for 2003, in effect the maximum contribution cannot exceed 20 percent of compensation. The 401(k) is part of the tax code for a profit sharing plan, but it is not designed as an employer contribution. Rather, it is a pre-tax deferred compensation contribution by the employee with possible matching by an employer. Maximum allowed employee contribution as of 2003 is $12,000 if the employer meets the discrimination testing or falls under certain safe harbor provisions. EGTRRA 2001 increased the permitted deferred compensation under 401(k) plans gradually up to $15,000 (in 2006) from the level of $10,500 in 2001 (see Tables 18.6 and 18.7). The Act also has catch-up provisions. The explanation of the 401(k) plan includes an example of the Average Deferral Percentage (ADP) discrimination test used for 401(k) plans. When an employer adds matching or profit sharing, or any other defined contribution plans, the amount of annual additions to the individual accounts cannot exceed the lesser of $40,000 or 100 percent of compensation including the 401(k) deferral. The combination of 401(k) and any other profit-sharing contributions cannot exceed 25 percent of payroll. Employee stock ownership plan (ESOP) is another type of profit sharing plan. ESOP is covered only briefly in this text. This chapter also provides a brief description of other qualified plans such as 403(b), 457, SIMPLE, SEP (included in the most right square in Figure 18.2), traditional IRA and Roth IRA. EGTRRA made major changes to these plans as well as to the plans discussed so far. Traditional IRA and Roth IRA are not sponsored by the employer, but require employee compensation through employment.

Defined Benefit Plans

A defined benefit plan has the distinguishing characteristic of clearly defining, by its benefit formula, the amount of benefit that will be available at retirement. That is, the benefit amount is specified in the written plan document, although the amount that must be contributed to fund the plan is not specified.

Traditional Defined Benefit Plan

In a defined benefit plan, any of several benefit formulas may be used:

- A flat dollar amount
- A flat percentage of pay
- A flat amount unit benefit
- A percentage unit benefit

Each type has advantages and disadvantages, and the employer selects the formula that best meets both the needs of employees for economic security and the budget constraints of the employer.

The defined benefit formula may specify a flat dollar amount, such as $500 per month. It may provide a formula by which the amount can be calculated, yielding a flat percentage of current annual salary (or the average salary of the past five or so years). For example, a plan may specify that each employee with at least twenty years of participation in the plan receives 50 percent of his or her average annual earnings during the three consecutive years of employment with the highest earnings. A flat amount unit benefit formula assigns a flat amount (for example, $25) with each unit of service, usually with each year. Thus, an employee with thirty units of service at retirement would receive a benefit equal to thirty times the unit amount.

The most popular defined benefit formula is the percentage unit benefit plan. It recognizes both the employee's years of service and level of compensation. See Table 18.1 for an example. Tables 18.1 through 18.5 feature different qualified retirement plans for the Slone-Jones Dental Office. The dental office is used to demonstrate how each plan would work for the same mix of employees.

When the compensation base is described as compensation for a recent number of years (for example, the last three or highest consecutive five years), the formula is referred to as a **final average formula.** Relative to a **career average formula,** which bases benefits on average compensation for all years of service in the plan, a final average plan tends to keep the initial retirement benefit in line with inflation.

Two types of service are involved in the benefit formula: past service and future service. Past service refers to service prior to the installation of the plan. Future service refers to service subsequent to the installation of the plan. If credit is given for past service, the plan starts with an initial past service liability at the date of installation. To reduce the size of this liability, the percentage of credit for past service may be less than that for future service, or a limit may be put on the number of years of past service credit. Initial past service liability may be a serious financial problem for the employer starting or installing a pension plan. Past service liability (**supplemental liability**) can be amortized over a certain number of years, not to exceed thirty years for a single employer.

Cash Balance Plan

The cash balance plan does not provide an amount of benefit that will be available for the employee at retirement. Instead, the cash balance plan sets up a hypothetical individual account for each employee, and credits each participant annually with a plan contribution (usually a percentage of compensation). The employer also guarantees a minimum interest credit on the account balance. For example, an employer might contribute 10 percent of an employee's salary to the employee's plan each year, and guarantee a minimum rate of return of 4 percent on the fund, as shown in Table 18.2. If investment returns turn out to be higher than 4 percent, the employer may credit the employee account with the higher rate. The amount available to the employee at retirement varies, based on wage rates and investment rates of return. Although the cash balance plan is technically a defined benefit plan, it has many of the same characteristics as defined contribution plans. These characteristics

TABLE 18.1   The Slone-Jones Dental Office: Standard Defined Benefit Pension Plan (Service Unit Formula, 2003)

Employees	(1) Current Age	(2) Current Salary	(3) Allowable Compensation	(4) Years of Service	(5) Years of Service to Age 65	(6) Maximum Allowed Benefit	(7) Expected Benefit at Age 65 2%×(3)×(5)
Dr. Slone	55	$240,000	$200,000	20	30	$160,000	$120,000
Diane	45	55,000	55,000	10	30	55,000	33,000
Jack	25	30,000	30,000	5	45	30,000	27,000

Source: Adapted from Etti G. Baranoff, "Teaching Pensions Through Case Study: How to Evaluate the Differences Among Qualified Retirement Plans for a Small Medical Office," working paper.

TABLE 18.2   The Slone-Jones Dental Office: Standard Cash Balance Plan (2003)

Employees	(1) Current Age	(2) Current Salary	(3) Allowed Compensation	(4) Maximum Benefit	(5) Contribution Year (10%)	(6) Years to Retirement	Future Value of $1 Annuity at 4%	Lump Sum at Age 65 (7)×(5)
Dr. Slone	55	$240,000	$200,000	$160,000	$20,000	10	12.006	$240,122
Diane	45	55,000	55,000	55,000	5,500	20	29.778	163,779
Jack	25	30,000	30,000	30,000	3,000	40	95.024	285,077

Source: Adapted from Etti G. Baranoff, "Teaching Pensions Through Case Study: How to Evaluate the Differences Among Qualified Retirement Plans for a Small Medical Office," working paper.

include "hypothetical" individual employee accounts, a fixed employer contribution rate, and an indeterminate final benefit amount, since employee compensation changes over time and interest rates may turn out to be well above the minimum guaranteed rate.

Features of Defined Benefit Plans

All defined benefit plans may provide for adjustments to account for inflation during the retirement years. A plan that includes a **cost-of-living adjustment (COLA)** clause has the ideal design feature. Benefits increase automatically with changes in a cost-of-living or wage index.

Many plans integrate the retirement benefit with Social Security benefits. An **integrated plan** coordinates Social Security benefits (or contributions) with the private plan's benefit (or contribution) formula. Integration reduces private retirement benefits based on the amount received through Social Security, thus reducing the cost to employers of the private plan. Or, on the other hand, integration allows employees with higher income to receive greater benefits or contributions depending on the formula. The scope of this text is too limited to explore the exact mechanism of integrated plans. There are two kinds of plans. The offset method reduces the private plan benefit by a set fraction. This approach is applicable only to defined benefit plans. The second method is the integration-level method. Here, a threshold of compensation, such as the wage base level shown in Chapter 15, is specified, and the rate of benefits or contributions provided below this compensation threshold is lower than the rate for compensation above the threshold. The integration-level method may be used for defined benefit or defined contribution pension plans.

As noted above, defined benefits up to specified levels (for 2003 it is $3,664.77 per month, up from $3,579 in 2002[16]) are guaranteed by the PBGC , a federal insurance program somewhat like the Federal Deposit Insurance Corporation (FDIC) for commercial bank accounts, and like the Guarantee Funds for Insurance. All defined benefit plans contribute an annual fee (or premium) per pension plan participant to finance benefits for members of insolvent terminated plans. The premium amount takes into account, to a degree, the financial soundness of the particular plan, measured by the plan's unfunded vested benefit. Thus, plans with a greater unfunded vested benefit pay a greater PBGC premium (up to a maximum amount), providing an incentive to employers to adequately fund their pension plans. Despite this incentive, there is national concern about the number of seriously underfunded pension plans insured by the PBGC. If these plans were unable to pay promised retirement benefits, the PBGC would be liable, and PBGC funds may be insufficient to cover the claims. Taxpayers could end up bailing out the PBGC. Careful monitoring of PBGC fund adequacy continues, and funding rules may be tightened to keep the PBGC financially sound.

Defined Benefit Cost Factors

Annual pension contributions and plan liabilities for a defined benefit plan must be estimated by an actuary. (Actuaries with pension specialties are called enrolled actuaries.) The defined amount of benefits becomes the employer's obligation, and contributions must equal whatever amount is necessary to fund the obligation. The estimate of cost depends on factors such as salary levels; normal retirement age; current employee ages; and assumptions about mortality, turnover, investment earnings, administrative expenses, and salary adjustment factors (for inflation and productivity). These factors determine estimates of how many employees will receive retirement benefits, how much they will receive, when benefits will begin, and how long benefits will be paid.

Normal costs reflect the annual amount needed to fund the pension benefit during the employee's working years. **Supplemental costs** are the amounts necessary to amortize any past service liability, explained above, over a period that may vary from ten to thirty years. Total cost for a year is the sum of normal and supplemental costs. Under some methods of calculation, normal and supplemental costs are estimated as one item. Costs may be estimated for each employee and then summed to yield total cost, or a calculation may be made for all participants on an aggregate basis.

Defined benefit plan administration is expensive compared with defined contribution plans, because of actuarial expense and complicated ERISA regulations. This explains in part why about 75 percent of the plans established since the passage of ERISA have been defined contribution plans.

Qualified Defined Contribution Plans

A defined contribution plan is a qualified pension plan in which the contribution amount is defined but the benefit amount available at retirement varies. This is in direct contrast to a defined benefit plan, in which the benefit is defined and the contribution amount varies. As with the defined benefit plan, when the defined contribution plan is initially designed, the employer makes decisions about eligibility, retirement age, integration, vesting schedules, and funding methods.

The most common type of defined contribution plan is the **money purchase plan.** This plan establishes an annual rate of employer contribution, usually expressed as a percentage of current compensation; for example, a plan may specify that the employer will contribute 10 percent of an employee's salary, as shown in the example in Table 18.3. Separate accounts are maintained to track the current balance attributable to each employee, but contributions may be commingled for investment purposes.

The benefit available at retirement varies with the contribution amount, the length of covered service, investment earnings, and retirement age, as you can see in Column 9 of Table 18.3. Some plans allow employees to direct the investment of their own pension funds, offering several investment options. Generally, retirement age has no effect on a distribution received as a lump sum, fixed amount, or fixed period annuity. Retirement age affects the amount of income received only under a life annuity option.

From the perspective of an employer or employee concerned with the adequacy of retirement income, the contributions that typically have the longest time to accumulate with compound investment returns are the smaller ones. They are smaller because the compensation base (to which the contribution percentage is applied) is lowest in an employee's younger years. This is perhaps the major disadvantage of defined contribution plans. It is also difficult to project the amount of retirement benefit until retirement is near, which complicates planning. In addition, the speculative risk of investment performance (positive or negative returns) is borne directly by employees.

From an employer's perspective, however, such plans have the distinct advantage of a reasonably predictable level of pension cost, because they are expressed as a percentage of current payroll. Since the employer promises only to specify a rate of contribution and prudently manage the plan, actuarial estimates of annual contributions and liabilities are unnecessary. The employer also does not contribute to the Pension Benefit Guaranty Corporation, which applies only to defined benefit plans. Most new plans today are defined contribution plans, not surprising given their simplicity, lower administrative cost, and limited employer liability for funding.

OTHER QUALIFIED DEFINED CONTRIBUTION PLANS

Employers may offer a variety of defined contribution plans other than money purchase plans to assist employees in saving for retirement. These may be the only retirement plans offered by the organization, or they may be offered in addition to a defined benefit plan or a defined contribution money purchase plan, as you can see in the Employee Benefits Case 2 at the back of the textbook. One such defined contribution plan is the **target plan,** which is an age-weighted pension plan. Under this plan, each employee is targeted to receive the same formula of benefit at retirement (age 65), but the benefits are not guaranteed. Since older employees have less time to accumulate the funds to retirement, they receive a larger contribution as a percent of compensation than the younger employees do. The target plan is a hybrid of defined benefits and defined contribution plans, but it is a defined contribution pension plan with the same limits and requirements as defined contribution plans. The limit of contribution in 2003 is 100 percent of compensation up to $40,000 per employee per year.

Profit-Sharing Plans

All profit-sharing plans are defined contribution plans. They are considered incentive plans rather than pension plans, because they do not have annual funding requirements. Profit-sharing plans provide economic incentives for employees, since firm profits are distributed directly to employees. In a **deferred profit-sharing plan,** a firm puts part of its profits in trust for the benefit of employees. Typically, the share of profit allocated is related to salary; that is, the share each year is the percentage determined by the employee's salary

| TABLE 18.3 | The Slone-Jones Dental Office: Standard Money Purchase Plan (2003) |

Employees	(1) Current Age	(2) Current Salary	(3) Allowable Compensation	(4) Service	(5) Maximum Contribution Allowed	(6) Contribution 10.00% (3)×0.10	(7) Years to Retirement	(8) Future value of $1 Annuity at 10%	(9) Lump Sum at Retirement (6)×(8)
Dr. Slone	55	$240,000	$200,000	10	$40,000	$20,000	10	15.937	$318,748
Diane	45	55,000	55,000	20	40,000	5,500	20	57.274	315,012
Jack	25	30,000	30,000	40	30,000	3,000	40	442.580	1.327.778

Source: Adapted from Etti G. Baranoff, "Teaching Pensions Through Case Study: How to Evaluate the Differences Among Qualified Retirement Plans for a Small Medical Office," *Benefits Quarterly* (forthcoming, 3rd quarter, 2003).

divided by total salaries for all participants in the plan. Per EGTRRA 2001, the maximum amount of contribution is 25 percent of the total payroll of all employees.

Table 18.4, featuring again the Slone-Jones Dental Office, shows an allocation of profit sharing should the employer decide to contribute $30,000 to the profit sharing plan. The allocation is based on the percentage of each employee's pay from total payroll allowed (see Column (4) in Table 18.4). The maximum profits to be shared in 2003 cannot be greater than an allocation of $40,000 for top employees. If the maximum compensation allowed is $200,000 and the maximum contribution $40,000, in essence the contribution to the account of an employee making $200,000 or more would not be more than 20 percent.

401(k) Plans

Another qualified defined contribution plan is the **401(k) plan,** which allows employees to defer compensation for retirement before taxes. See an example of deferral in Table 18.5. As you see, contributions to a 401(k) plan are limited per the description in Figure 18.2 and Tables 18.6 and 18.7. The total contribution amount to a 401(k) plan, by both employee and employer, cannot exceed $40,000 or 100 percent of the employee's income. In 2003, the deferral by the employee cannot exceed $12,000, unless over age 50.

To receive the tax credits for 401(k), employers have to pass the Average Deferral Test (ADP test), unless they either (1) match 100 percent of the employee contribution up to 3 percent of compensation and 50 percent of the employee contribution between 3 percent and 5 percent of compensation, or (2) make a nonelective (nonmatching) contribution for all eligible non-highly compensated employees equal to at least 3 percent of compensation. These employer's contributions are considered a safe harbor. The Average Deferral Percentage Test (ADP test) is shown in Table 18.5 for a hypothetical elective deferral of the employees of the Slone-Jones Dental Office.

As you can see, there are two parts to the ADP test as follows:

- Average the deferral percentages of the non-highly compensated employees. Multiply this figure by 1.25. Is the result greater than the average for the highly compensated employees? If yes, the employer passed the test. If no, proceed to the next test.

- Take the average of the deferral percentages of non-highly compensated employees. Double this percentage, or add two percentage points, whichever is less. Is the result greater than the average for the highly compensated employees?

TABLE 18.4 The Slone-Jones Dental Office: Standard Profit-Sharing Plan (2003)	Employees	(1) Current Age	(2) Salary	(3) Maximum Allowed Comp.	(4) % of Pay from Total Adj. Payroll (3)/285.000	(5) Allocation of $30,000 profits (4)×30,000
	Dr. Slone	55	$240,000	$200,000	70.18%	$21,053
	Diane	45	55,000	55,000	19.30	5,789
	Jack	25	30,000	30,000	10.53	3,158
	Total			$285,000	100.00%	$30,000

Source: Adapted from Etti G. Baranoff, "Teaching Pensions Through Case Study: How to Evaluate the Differences Among Qualified Retirement Plans for a Small Medical Office," *Benefits Quarterly* (forthcoming, 3rd quarter, 2003).

TABLE 18.5	Employees	(1) Current Age	(2) Salary	(3) Allowable Compensation	(4) Voluntary 401(k) Contribution	(5) Contribution % of Compensation (4)/(3)
The Slone-Jones Dental Office: ADP Testing for 401(k) Plan (2003)	Dr. Slone	55	$240,000	$200,000	$11,000	5.50%
	Diane	45	55,000	55,000	3,000	5.45
	Jack	25	30,000	30,000	1,200	4.00

ADP Test 1: Average Jack's and Diane's contributions [(5.45% + 4.00%)/2] = 4.73%; multiply 4.73% × 1.25 = 5.91%. This figure is greater than Dr. Slone's contribution. **Passed.**

ADP Test 2: 4.73% × 2 = 9.45%. 4.73% + 2 = 6.73%. The lesser of these is greater than Dr. Slone's contribution. **Passed.**

Source: Adapted from Etti G. Baranoff, "Teaching Pensions Through Case Study: How to Evaluate the Differences Among Qualified Retirement Plans for a Small Medical Office," *Benefits Quarterly* (forthcoming, 3rd quarter, 2003).

If the answer is no, the employer did not pass the ADP test and the highly compensated employees have to pay taxes on the amounts they cannot defer. Most employers give incentive to employees to voluntarily defer greater amounts.

As noted, strict requirements are put on withdrawals, such as only allowing them for hardships (that is, heavy and immediate financial needs), disability, death, retirement, termination of employment, or reaching age 59½. As in all other qualified retirement plans, a 10 percent penalty tax applies to withdrawals before age 59½. The penalty undoubtedly discourages contributions from employees who want easier access to their savings. Most employees would rather take loans.

Employee Stock Ownership Plans

An **employee stock ownership plan (ESOP)** is a special form of profit sharing plan. The unique feature of an ESOP is that all investments are in the employer's common stock. Proponents of ESOPs claim that this ownership participation increases employee morale and productivity. Critics regard it as tie-in of human and economic capital in a single firm, which may lead to complete losses when the firm is in trouble. An illustration of the hardship that can occur when employees invest in their company is the Enron case noted earlier.

An ESOP represents the ultimate in investment concentration, since all contributions are invested in one security. This is distinctly different from the investment diversification found in the typical pension or profit-sharing plan. To alleviate the ESOP investment risk for older employees, employers are required to allow at least three diversified investment portfolios for persons over age 55 who also have at least ten years of participation in the plan. Each diversified portfolio would contain several issues of non-employer securities, such as common stocks or bonds. One option might even be a very low-risk investment, such as bank certificates of deposit. This allows use of an incentive-type qualified retirement plan without unnecessarily jeopardizing the retiree's benefit.

Other Qualified Plans: 403(b) and 457 Plans

Tax-deferred programs for employees include individual retirement accounts (IRAs); employer-sponsored Internal Revenue Code (IRC) Section 401(k) savings/profit sharing plans, discussed above; IRC Section 403(b) tax-sheltered annuity (TSA) plans for employees of educational and certain other tax-exempt organizations; and IRC Section 457 plans for state and local government employees. The TSA is a retirement plan of tax-exempt organizations and educational organizations of state or local governments. Employees of tax-exempt groups, such as hospitals or public schools, can elect to defer a portion of their salaries for retirement in what are called **403(b) plans.** They are similar to 401(k) plans. Section **457 plans,** offered to employees of state and local governments and nonprofit, noneducational institutions, were created in 1978. They are similar to 401(k) and 403(b) plans in that the money in the plan must be held separately from employer assets, in a trust, custodial account, or annuity contract. The 457 plan may be offered in conjunction with another defined-contribution plan such as a 401(k) or 403(b), or a defined-benefit pension plan. EGTRRA 2001 changed the 457's unique features and made it more comparable to the 401(k) and 403(b). Employees of governmental educational institutions can defer compensation in both 403(b) and 457 plans up to the maximum of each. Tables 18.6 and 18.7 show the new maximums for the plans under EGTRRA 2001.

Self-employed workers can make tax-deferred contributions through a Keogh plan or a simplified employee plan (SEP). Small employers also can establish a SEP or a savings incentive match plan for employees of small employers (SIMPLE).

Keogh Plans

Keogh plans (also known as HR-10 plans) are for people who earn self-employment income. Contributions can be made based on either full- or part-time employment. Even if the employee is a retirement plan participant with an organization that has one or more qualified defined benefit or defined contribution plans, the employee can establish a Keogh plan based on self-employment earned income. For example, the employee may work full-time for wages or salary but part-time as a consultant or accountant in the evenings and on weekends. Saving part of net income from self-employment is what Keogh is all about. Proprietors, partners, and employees can be covered in the same plan. The Keogh plan may be designed as either a regular defined benefit or money purchase plans, with the same contribution limits.

	Taxable Year Beginning in	Salary Reduction Limit
TABLE 18.6 Limits for 401(k), 403(b), and 457 Plans under EGTRRA 2001	2002	$ 11,000
	2003	12,000
	2004	13,000
	2005	14,000
	2006	15,000
	After 2006	$15,000, indexed for cost of living increases in $500 increments

	Taxable Year Beginning in	50-or-over Additional Deferral Permitted
TABLE 18.7 Additional Limits for Employees over 50 Years Old for 401(k), 403(b), and 457 Plans under EGTRRA 2001	2002	$ 1,000
	2003	2,000
	2004	3,000
	2005	4,000
	2006	5,000
	After 2006	$5,000, indexed for cost of living increases in $500 increments

Simplified Employee Pension Plans

A **simplified employee pension (SEP)** is similar to an employer-sponsored individual retirement account (IRA). With a SEP, the employer makes a deductible contribution to the IRA, but the contribution limit is much higher than the annual deduction limit of the typical IRA (explained in the next section). The SEP contribution is limited to the lesser of $40,000 or 25 percent of the employee's compensation. Coverage requirements ensure that a broad cross-section of employees is included in the SEP. Employers are not locked into an annual contribution amount, but when contributions are made, they must be allocated in a way that does not discriminate in favor of highly compensated employees. The main advantage of the SEP is low administrative cost.

SEPs allow an employer to establish and make contributions to IRAs.[17] The two critical differences between SEP-IRAs and other IRAs are that SEP contributions are generally made by employers, not employees, and that the limits of SEP are substantially larger.

SIMPLE Plans

SIMPLE (Savings Incentive Match Plan for Employees of Small Employers) plans are for employers with 100 employees or less.[18] This plan was authorized by the Small Business Job Protection Act of 1996. Small businesses comprise over 38 percent of the nation's private workforce. The maximum contributions under EGTRRA 2001 are shown in Tables 18.8 and 18.9. Under the new limits, eligible employees can contribute up to $8,000 in 2003 through convenient payroll deductions. Employers offer matching contributions equal to employee contributions (up to 3 percent of employee wages) or fixed contributions equal to 2 percent of employee wages. This plan, like SEP, eliminates many of the administrative costs associated with larger retirement plans. The employees who can participate are those who earned $5,000 or more during the preceding calendar year. This plan cannot be established with other qualified plans. As in all other defined contributions plans, the employee may make the initial choice of financial institution to receive contributions.

Individual Retirement Accounts (Traditional IRA and Roth IRA)

When discussing other retirement plans, we include **traditional IRA** and **Roth IRA** despite the fact that these programs are not provided by the employer. But they do require some level of income for participation. An employee cannot make contributions to an IRA account without some level of compensation. An employee is not part of an employer's program can defer compensation by establishing an individual retirement account (IRA) or Roth IRA. This is also the vehicle for rolling over employers' sponsored retirement accounts in order to avoid penalties and tax issues. An employee who participates in the employer's retirement plans but earns a low income can open an IRA or a Roth IRA. A traditional IRA allows the employee to defer taxes on the contributions and the earning on the contributions until the accounts are withdrawn. A Roth IRA is funded with after-tax dollars, but the earnings on the account are never taxed, even after the employee retires and begins drawing from the account. The Roth IRA is considered a wonderful program from taxation planning point of view, especially during low earning years when tax rate is very low. The maximum allowed contributions to traditional IRA and Roth IRA are featured in Tables 18.10 and 18.11.

Who is eligible to make tax-deferred IRA contributions? An employee who does not participate in an employer-sponsored retirement plan in a particular year can make contributions up to the amount shown in Tables 18.10 and 18.11 (or 100 percent of the employee's earned income if making less than shown in Tables 18.10 and 18.11). If the employee participates in an employer-sponsored retirement plan (that is, an employer makes contributions or provides credits on the employee's behalf), the maximum amount of tax-deferred IRA contribution depends on income earned from work, but not from investments, Social Security, and other nonemployment sources. The maximum contributions are for the following income level:

- Single people earning less than $25,000 and married couples filing a joint income tax return with less than $40,000 are eligible not to pay current income taxes on IRA contributions up.

TABLE 18.8 SIMPLE Plan Limits under EGTRRA 2001	Taxable Year Beginning in	SIMPLE Salary Reduction Limit
	2002	$ 7,000
	2003	8,000
	2004	9,000
	2005	10,000
	After 2005	$10,000, indexed for cost of living increases in $500 increments

TABLE 18.9 SIMPLE Plan Limits for Employees over 50 Years Old under EGTRRA 2001	Taxable Year Beginning in	50-or-over Additional Deferral Permitted (SIMPLE)
	2002	$ 500
	2003	1,000
	2004	1,500
	2005	2,000
	2006	2,500
	After 2006	$2,500, indexed for cost of living increases in $500 increments[8]

TABLE 18.10 Traditional IRA and Roth IRA Limits per EGTRRA 2001	Taxable Year Beginning in	Deductible Amount
	2001	$2,000
	2002 through 2004	3,000
	2005 through 2007	4,000
	2008 and thereafter	5,000

TABLE 18.11 IRA and Roth IRA Limits for Age 50 and Older per EGTRRA 2001	Year	Deductible Amount
	2001	$2,000
	2002 through 2004	3,500
	2005	4,500
	2006 and 2007	5,000
	2008 and thereafter	$6,000 adjusted for COLA

- Single people earning more than $35,000 and married couples earning in excess of $50,000 have zero tax-deferred contribution limits.

For earnings between $25,000 and $35,000, there is an adjustment to the level of maximum tax deferral allowed. For example, a single employee earning $30,000 was eligible to contribute $1,500 on a pre-tax basis in 2002, calculated as follows:

Tax-deferred (for 2002)
$$[(\$30,000 - \$25,000) \div 10,000] \times \$3,000 = \$1,500$$

The advantage of making tax-deferred contributions to any of the several tax-deferred, "qualified" programs is the deferral of income taxes until the employee withdraws the funds from the annuity (or other tax-deferred plan such as a mutual fund). Ideally, withdrawal takes place in retirement, many years in the future. If the employee had not made the qualified contributions, a significant portion would have gone to government treasuries in the years they were earned. When contributions are made to qualified plans, the money that would otherwise have gone to pay income taxes earns investment returns, along with the remainder of the employee's contributions.

Further, a 10 percent federal penalty tax applies to premature withdrawals (those made prior to age 59½). The penalty does not apply to:

- Withdrawals due to death
- Withdrawals due to disability
- Payments taken in essentially equal installments over the employee's life expectancy (or the joint life expectancy of the employee and the employee's spouse)
- Withdrawals allocable to contributions made before August 14, 1982
- Withdrawals from a structured settlement contract

The Roth IRA is a program for retirement without tax implication upon distribution, but the contributions are made with after-tax income.[19] The Roth IRA was born on January 1, 1998, as a result of the Taxpayer Relief Act of 1997.[20] It provides no tax deduction for contributions, which is not a great incentive to save, but instead provides a benefit that is not available for any other form of retirement savings. If certain earning requirements are met, all earnings are tax free when withdrawn. Other benefits included under the Roth IRA are avoiding the early distribution penalty on certain withdrawals and avoiding the need to take minimum distributions after age 70½. Roth IRA is not a pre-tax-contribution type of retirement savings account. But it is the only plan that allows earnings to accumulate without tax implication ever. A regular IRA provides a pre-tax saving, but the earnings are taxed when they are withdrawn.

Eligibility for Roth IRA is available even if the employee participates in a retirement plan maintained by the employer. The contribution limits are shown in Tables 18.10 and 18.11. There are earning requirements: (1) For the maximum contribution, the income limits are $95,000 for single individuals and $150,000 for married individuals filing joint returns. (2) The amount that can be contributed is reduced gradually and then completely eliminated when adjusted gross income exceeds $110,000 (single) or $160,000 (married filing jointly).

A regular IRA can be converted to a Roth IRA if (a) the modified adjusted gross income is $100,000 or less, and (b) the employee is single or files jointly with a spouse. Taxes will have to be paid in the year of the conversion.

Since the brief description here is just an introductory level, for more details you are advised to consult the many sources for each pension plan on the Internet and in many books written on the topic.

PENSION PLAN FUNDING TECHNIQUES

ERISA requires advance funding of qualified pension plans. An advance funded plan accumulates funds during the period in which employees are actively working for the organization. Pension expense is charged against earned income while pension obligations are accumulating, instead of being deferred until employees have retired. Pension plans are funded either through noninsured trust plans or insured plans.

Noninsured Trust Plans

With a **noninsured trust plan,** the employer creates a trust to accumulate funds and disburse benefits. The trustee may be an individual, a bank, a trust company, an insurer, or some combination of co-trustees. The duties of the trustee are to invest the funds contributed by the employer to the trust (and by the employees, if contributory), accumulate the earnings, and pay benefits to eligible employees. The trustee makes no guarantee with regard to earnings or investments.

Under a defined benefit trust plan, a consulting actuary is employed to estimate the sums that should be put into the trust. The employer is in effect a self-insurer. The consulting actuary does not guarantee that the estimates will be accurate. There is also no guarantee as to the expense of operating the plan. Thus, the employer that chooses a noninsured trust to fund a defined benefit plan should be large enough and financially strong enough to absorb differences between actual experience and past estimates of mortality, investment returns, and other cost factors.

Insured Plans

Several insurer options are available for funding pension plans. These are group deferred annuity contracts, group deposit administration contracts, immediate participation guarantee contract, separate accounts, and guaranteed investment contracts.

Group Deferred Annuity Contracts

The **group deferred annuity** is a contract between insurer and employer to provide for the purchase of specified amounts of deferred annuity for employees each year. For example, an annuity that would pay retirees $50 per month beginning at age 65 might be purchased by the employer from the insurer each year for each employee. The employer receives a master deferred annuity contract, and certificates of participation are given to individuals covered by the plan. Group plans usually require some minimum number of participants, to lower administrative expenses per employee.

Under this plan, all actuarial work is done by the insurer, which also provides administrative and investment services. Neither the employees nor the employer are subject to risk of investment return fluctuations. The only risk is the possible failure of the insurers. The employer's sole responsibility is to report essential information to the insurer and pay the premiums.

Group Deposit Administration Contracts

The **deposit administration** arrangement requires the employer to make regular payments to the insurance company on behalf of employees, and these contributions accumulate at interest. An actuary estimates the amount of annual employer deposits necessary to accumulate sufficient funds to purchase annuities when employees retire. The insurer guarantees the principal of funds deposited, as well as a specified minimum rate of interest. However, the insurer has no direct responsibility to employees until they retire, at which time an annuity is purchased for them. Before retirement, the employee's position is similar to that under an uninsured trust plan. After retirement, the employee's position is the same as with a group deferred annuity contract.

Immediate Participation Guarantee Contracts

The **immediate participation guarantee contract (IPG)** plan is a form of deposit administration; the employer makes regular deposits to a fund managed by the insurance company. The insurer receives deposits and makes investments. An IPG may be structured like a trust plan in that the insurer makes no guarantee concerning the safety of investments or their rate of return. However, some IPGs may guarantee the fund principal and a minimum rate of return.

The IPG is distinctive from other deposit administration contracts and attractive to employers, in that it gives employers more flexibility after an employee retires. The employer has the option to pay retirement benefits directly from the IPG fund, rather than locking into an annuity purchased from the insurer. This gives the employer control over the funds longer. The employer can also purchase an annuity for the retired employee.

Separate Accounts

Separate account plans are another modification of deposit administration contracts and are designed to give the insurer greater investment flexibility. The contributions are not commingled with the insurer's other assets, and therefore are not subject to the same investment limitations. At least part of the employer's contributions are placed in separate accounts for investment in common stocks. Other separate accounts pool money for investment in bonds, mortgages, real estate, and other assets. Usually the funds of many employers are pooled for investment purposes, although a large firm may arrange for a special, separate account exclusively for its own funds. Separate accounts may be used to fund either fixed-dollar or variable annuity benefits.

Guaranteed Investment Contracts

Guaranteed investment contracts (GICs) are arrangements used by insurers to guarantee competitive rates of return on large, lump-sum transfers (usually $100,000 or more) of pension funds, usually from another type of funding instrument. For example, an employer may terminate a trust plan and transfer all the funds in the trust to an insurer who promises to pay an investment return of 7 percent for each of the next ten years. At the end of the specified period, the GIC arrangement ends and the fund balance is paid to the original investor, who may decide to reinvest in another GIC.

NONQUALIFIED, TAX-FAVORED RETIREMENT PLANS

In addition to the qualified pension and profit-sharing plans previously discussed, other tax-favored retirement income plans are available. While these other plans technically are not qualified, they allow employers to deduct contributions, accumulations to the fund accrue tax-free, and employees are taxed on employer contributions and investment accumulations only when benefits are received. These plans are usually considered part of executive compensation, which is beyond the scope of this text.

KEY TERMS

defined benefit
defined contribution
Pension Benefit Guaranty
  Corporation (PBGC)
qualified plan
ERISA
eligibility criteria
coverage requirements
controlled group
normal retirement age
contributory plan
vesting
top-heavy plan
pre-retirement survivor
  annuity
joint and survivor annuity

cash balance plan
final average formula
career average formula
supplemental liability
cost-of-living adjustment
  (COLA)
integrated plan
normal costs
supplemental costs
money purchase plan
target plan
deferred profit-sharing
  plan
401(k) plan
employee stock ownership
  plan (ESOP)

403(b) plan
457 plan
Keogh plan
simplified employee pen-
  sion (SEP)
SIMPLE plan
traditional IRA
Roth IRA
noninsured trust plan
group deferred annuity
deposit administration
immediate participation
  guarantee contract (IPG)
separate account plans
guaranteed investment
  contracts (GIC)

DISCUSSION QUESTIONS

1. There has been a proposal that all private pension plans be required to provide full vesting at the end of one year of participation. If you were the owner of a firm employing fifty people and had a qualified pension plan, how would you react to this proposal? Please explain.

2. List ERISA requirements for qualified pension plans.

3. What is the PBGC? Why is it an important agency?

4. As an employee with a defined benefit pension plan, which would you prefer: a flat amount benefit formula that specifies $1,000 per month, or a percentage unit benefit formula that says your benefit will be 1.5 percent per year times your average annual salary for your highest three consecutive years of employment? Please explain.

5. As an employer, would you prefer a defined contribution pension plan or a defined benefit plan? Please explain.

6. Which is preferable from an employee's point of view: a defined contribution or a defined benefit pension plan? Please explain.

7. As an employee, would you prefer a deferred or an immediate (cash at the end of the year) profit-sharing plan? If your income doubled, would your choice change? Please explain.

8. Some employers have deferred profit-sharing plans instead of defined benefit or defined contribution money purchase plans. Why?

9. As an employee benefits manager, you must recommend to the firm's CEO a defined contribution plan to add to the existing defined benefit retirement plan. First describe a hypothetical firm, giving firm size, profitability, and stability of the work force. Then explain your choice of a deferred profit-sharing plan, a 401(k), a money purchase plan, or some combination of these.

10. Cash balance plans have become increasingly popular in recent years. Why do employers like cash balance plans relative to other types of defined benefit plans?

11. Explain the difference between a group deferred annuity contract and a deposit administration contract. Which offers more protection to employers against the risk of inadequate funding of a promised defined benefit?

12. Prepare a matrix comparing 401(k) with 403(b), 457, SEP, and SIMPLE.

13. Compare the traditional IRA with the Roth IRA.

EXERCISES

18.1 The law firm of Dewey, Cheetham & Howe has five employees. Following is information regarding these employees:

Employees	Age	Salary	Position
Dewey	57	$240,000	partner
Cheetham	34	$180,000	partner
Howe	58	$110,000	partner
Perez	38	$60,000	associate
McCall	27	$40,000	paralegal

The partners talked to Rollings Benefits Consultants about the best-qualified pension plan for the firm in light of their major success in and anticipated growth in profits in the coming years. Rollings Benefits created a presentation of a possible plan that showed the maximum possible contributions for the highly paid employees (the partners).

Please answer the following question:

a. Under this proposal, what qualified plan do you think Rollings consultants suggested to Dewey, Cheetham & Howe? The objective is to give highly paid employees the highest possible contributions. Explain the proposal.

18.2 The law firm of Tayka, Mooney & Ruhn has the following five employees. Following is information regarding these employees:

Employees	Age	Salary	Position
Tayka	37	$210,000	partner
Mooney	34	$160,000	partner
Ruhn	28	$110,000	partner
Davies	38	$60,000	Associate
Edmundsen	27	$40,000	paralegal

a. Rollings consultants explain to the owners of Tayka, Mooney & Ruhn the problems that may occur with 401(k) plans. They show an example of how the company can fail the ADP test and how highly paid employees would not be able to take all the deductions they want. Pretend you are the Rollings consultant: Show such an example and give the firm some methods to overcome this problem. Use the table above to calculate an example, and explain your answer.

b. If the company decides to start a profit sharing plan with $35,000 the first year, how much will be allocated to each employee?

18.3 Jackson Appliances has twelve employees. The owner, Zena Jackson, is considering some system to reward them for their loyalty and to provide some funds to help them with their living expenses after they retire. Explain why a SEP might be a good choice for the company and explain how it works. Are there other alternatives Zena should consider?

18.4   Henry Wooster meets with the employee benefits manager to discuss enrolling in the company's 401(k) plan. He finds that if he enrolls, he must choose the amount of salary to defer and also direct his fund investment. Having no college education and no business experience, Henry lacks confidence about making these decisions.

    a.   Should Henry enroll in the 401(k)? Do the advantages outweigh the difficulties he may have in managing the plan?

    b.   What would you recommend that Henry do to educate himself about fund management? How can the benefits manager help?

    c.   Is it appropriate for the employer to establish a plan that requires employees to take this much responsibility for retirement planning? Please explain.

NOTES

1. See the PBGC News at www.pbgc.gov.
2. Jerry Geisel, "Proposed rules clarify cash balance plan status," *Business Insurance,* 10 December, 2002.
3. Kara Scannell, "Public Pensions Come Up Short as Stocks' Swoon Drains Funds," *The Wall Street Journal* 16 August 2002.
4. Elisabeth Bumiller, "Bush Signs Bill Aimed at Fraud in Corporations," *The New York Times,* 30 July 2002.
5. Greg Hitt, "Bush Signs Sweeping Legislation Aimed at Curbing Business Fraud," *Wall Street Journal,* 21 July 2002.
6. Jerry Geisel, "Senate Finance Committee passes 401(k) safeguards," *Business Insurance,* 11 July 2002.
7. ERISA defines highly compensated and non-highly compensated employees based on factors such as employee salary, ownership share of the firm, and whether the employee is an officer in the organization.
8. Enron matched employees' salary deferrals only in company stocks and barred participants from selling shares until age 50. In addition, as the value of Enron shares was plummeting last year, Enron imposed a blackout period while it was changing plan administrators, leaving the employees powerless to make any changes.
9. The following information is provided from http://thomas.loc.gov/cgi-bin/bdquery/z?d107:SN01971 :@@@L&summ2=m& for Senate Bill S.1971: Sponsor: Sen. Grassley, Charles E. (introduced 2/27/2002). Latest Major Action: 8/2/2002 Senate preparation for floor. Status: Placed on Senate Legislative Calendar under General Orders. Calendar No. 552. Title: A bill to amend the Internal Revenue Code of 1986 and the Employee Retirement Income Security Act of 1974 to protect the retirement security of American workers by ensuring that pension assets are adequately diversified and by providing workers with adequate access to, and information about, their pension plans, and for other purposes.
10. The overview provided is based on many sources, among them Vineeta Anand, "Lawyer Steven J. Sacher Says that for the Most Part ERISA Has Performed 'Smashingly Well,'" *Pensions & Investments,* 6 September 1999, p19; Barry B. Burr, "Reviewing Options: Enron Fallout Sparks Much Soul-Searching; Experts Debate Need for Change Following Huge Losses in 401(k)," *Pensions & Investments,* 4 February 2002, v30 p1; William G. Gale et. al, "ERISA after 25 Years: A Framework for Evaluating Pension Reform," *Benefits Quarterly,* 1 October 1998; Lynn Miller, "The Ongoing Growth of Defined Contribution and Individual Account Plans: Issues and Implications," *EBRI Issue Brief* No. 243, March 2002; Martha Priddy Patterson, "A New Millennium for Retirement Plans: The 2001 Tax Act and Employer Flexibility," *Benefits Quarterly,* 1 January 2002.
11. The service requirement may be extended to two years in the small minority of plans that have immediate vesting. Vesting is defined later in the chapter.
12. Carlos Tejada, "Early-Retirement Plans Become Thing of the Past," *Wall Street Journal,* 31 July 2002.
13. April K. Caudill, "More Clarity and Simplicity in New Required Minimum Distribution Rules," *National Underwriter,* Life & Health/Financial Services Edition, 13 May 2002.
14. The regulations state that the new method can be used to calculate substantially equal periodic payments under Section 72(t)—distributions of retirement funds after age 70½.

15. For more information, see coverage of this topic in the following sample of articles: "Sun Moves to Cash Balance Pensions," *Employee Benefit Plan Review* 45(9): 50-51, March 1991; Arleen Jacobius, "Motorola Workers Embrace New Hybrid Pension Plan," *Business Insurance* 34(45): 36-37, November 2000; Karl Frieden, "The Cash Balance Pension Plan: Wave of the Future or Shooting Star?" CFO: *The Magazine for Chief Financial Officers* 3(9): 53-54, September 1987; Avra Wing, "Employers Wary of Cash Balance Pensions," *Business Insurance* 20(39): 15-20, 29 September 1986; Arleen Jacobius, "60% of Workers at Motorola Inc. Embrace Firm's New PEP Plan," *Pensions & Investment Age* 28(19): 3, 58, 18 September 2000; Jerry Geisel, "Survey Aims to Find Facts about Cash Balance Plans," *Business Insurance* 34(21): 10-12, 22 May 2000; "American Benefits Council President Discusses Cash Balance Plans, Pension Reform," *Employee Benefit Plan Review* 55(4): 11-13, October 2000; Donna Ritter Mark, "Planning to Implement a Cash Balance Pension Plan? Examine the Issues First," *Compensation & Benefits Review* 32(5): 15-16, September/October 2000; Vineeta Anand, "Young and Old Hurt in Switch to Cash Balance," *Pensions & Investment Age* 28(20): 1, 77, October 2000; Vineeta Anand, "Employees Win Another One in Cash Balance Court Cases," Pensions & Investment Age 28(19): 2, 59, 18 September 2000; Regina Shanney-Saborsky, "The Cash Balance Controversy: Navigating the Issues," *Journal of Financial Planning* 13(9): 44–48, September 2000.

16. See footnote 1.

17. Department of Labor www.dol.gov/pwba/pubs/seps97.htm.

18. Department of Labor, www.dol.gov/pwba/pubs/simple.htm.

19. www.rothira-advisor.com/taxfreegrowth.htm.

20. www.fairmark.com/rothira/roth101.htm.

CHAPTER 19

Annuities, Individual Health Products, and Need Analysis

Individual contracts are an important source of insurance for unemployed people, those without employer-sponsored benefits, or those employed but with inadequate employee benefits. Some of the policy characteristics of individual contracts are similar to those of group contracts; however, there are differences. In this chapter we explore the individual contract and also investigate various health policies, such as individual dental and cancer policies, long-term care insurance, and Medigap insurance. Supplementing Chapter 18 on pensions is the discussion of annuities discussed in this chapter.

In general, risk management on a personal or commercial basis requires needs analysis as was indicated in Chapter 3. In this chapter, as the concluding chapter of this textbook and a starting point for the four cases featured immediately after this chapter, we provide a need analysis for life insurance for the hypothetical Dowd family. This need analysis is followed by the complete portfolio of risk management of the Smith family in Case 1. Each coverage requires some level of need analysis and a careful consideration of the appropriate amounts. Over-insurance is too costly and inappropriate, as is featured in the "Ethical Dilemma: When Is Coverage Really Needed?" of this chapter. This chapter also briefly explores the need to protect the estate of the insured. Further study of estate planning and applicable tax issues is a topic for an advanced course in life insurance.

This chapter is structured as follows:

1. Connection
2. Annuities
3. Individual medical expense insurance
4. Individual dental insurance
5. Cancer or dread disease policies
6. Individual disability income insurance
7. Individual long-term care insurance
8. Medicare supplement
9. How much life insurance to buy?
10. Estate planning in relation to life insurance

CONNECTION

Finally, we come full circle into individual risk management. The emphasis is on the individual—the third step in the three-step stool. This is the time to plan for holistic risk management using individual contracts such as individual health, dental, cancer, disability, Medicare supplement (Medigap), long-term care (LTC) products and annuities, as well as hybrid products such as LTC-annuities or life-acceleration LTC. Individual life policies were discussed in Chapter 14. Thus, this chapter covers individual products in the area of life and health insurance that were not discussed thus far. Once the understanding of the life-cycle products are clarified to some extent, a need analysis is important. Deciding how much insurance to buy is featured in the last part of this chapter, and is explored further in Case 1 of the Smith family. Case 1 is designed to provide a complete risk management portfolio of the life/health and property/casualty products necessary for the family. The case is a cumulative portfolio of the pieces of puzzle discussed throughout this textbook. Case 2 focuses on the group products and pensions from the employer's point of view, while Cases 3 and 4 are designed for commercial business and are in the more advanced risk management area.

In Chapter 18, we discussed retirement plans provided by employers and those we can fund on our own such as traditional IRA and Roth IRA accounts. Retirement benefits from Social Security were discussed in Chapter 15. In this chapter we add annuity products to our tool kit for retirement. These products were created by the insurance industry in response to the need to mitigate the risk of "living too long." The products are investment instruments with mortality elements. They are designed to compete in the investments marketplace with mutual funds and any types of investments.

With the added individual products discussed in this chapter, we provide the final step in the three-step stool shown in Figure 19.1 and complete our study of holistic risk management. Individual arrangements for health, dental, disability, life, and pensions are necessary when all other programs represented in the bottom two steps do not complete the risk management program of a family.

ANNUITIES

Chapter 18's discussion of employer-provided pensions and IRAs emphasized the importance of selecting the right investment vehicle for the individual. Annuities, which offer features not available in any other investment product, are provided by insurance companies to help individuals accumulate funds for retirement. During preretirement years, annuities are primarily investment vehicles. During retirement years, the product provides a periodic payment that continues throughout a fixed period and/or for the duration of a life or lives. Although annuities are frequently used to save for retirement, their unique function is the scientific (actuarially computed) liquidation of a principal sum, usually during retirement years. During this period, they protect against the risk of outliving the financial resources invested earlier in the annuity. If the duration depends upon the expected length of a life or lives, the contract is known as a **life annuity.**

Parties to an Annuity

The person or entity that purchases an annuity is the **owner.** The person on whose life expectancy payments are based is known as the **annuitant.** For annuities sold directly to individuals, the owner and annuitant are usually the same person. The **beneficiary** is the person or entity who receives any death benefits due at the death of the annuitant.

FIGURE 19.1 Connection between Risks and Individual Annuities and Life/Health Insurance Products

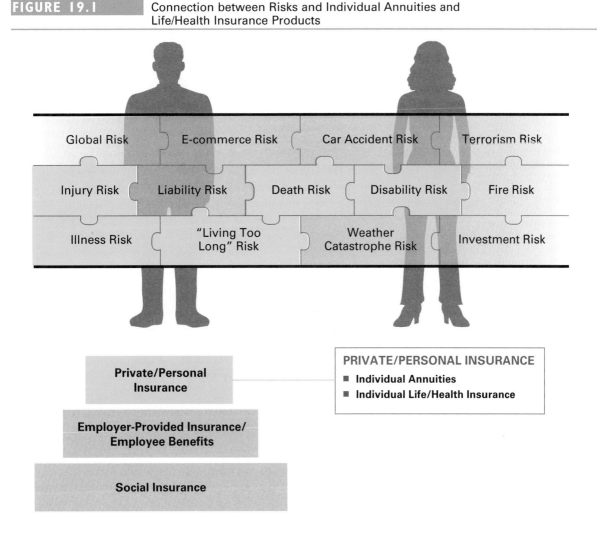

Mechanics of Annuities

Accumulation versus Liquidation

The time during which premiums are being paid and benefits (distribution) have not begun is called the **accumulation period.** The value of the contract during this period consists of premiums plus investment earnings minus expenses and is called the **accumulation value.** The time during which the accumulation value and future investment returns are being liquidated by benefit payments is called the **liquidation period.**

Premium Payments

Annuities may be bought either on the **installment plan** or with a **single premium.** Most people use the installment plan. Usually, the owner chooses a flexible plan where premiums may vary in amount and frequency. In the event the annuitant dies before benefit payments begin, deferred annuities sold to individuals promise to return the accumulation value at the time of death.

Deferred annuity on the installment plan is a savings program during the accumulation period. There is no protection (insurance) element involved—not any more than would be the case of monthly deposits in savings account at the bank. The insurance or mortality element is only part of the distribution over the life of the annuitant. The payments are promised to last for the life of the annuitant even in cases of living longer than the life expectancy.

Commencement of Benefits

Annuities may be classified as either immediate or deferred, reflecting when benefit payments begin. An **immediate annuity** begins payments at the next payment interval (for example, month, quarter, or year) after purchase. They require a single premium. **Deferred annuities** begin payments sometime in the future as elected by the owner, such as at age 65. Deferred annuities may be funded by a single premium, equal installments, or, more commonly, by flexible premiums.

Level of Benefits

During the accumulation period and the liquidation period, the annuity is classified as either a **fixed dollar annuity** or a **variable annuity.** Fixed dollar annuities earn investment returns at rates guaranteed by the insurer, subject to periodic changes in the guaranteed rate for the next period. A set amount of benefit per dollar of accumulation (varying also by life expectancy when benefits begin) is paid during the liquidation period. Variable annuity returns vary with the investment performance of special investment accounts. The amount of benefit payment may vary from month to month or at another interval.

Settlement Options

Generally, an annuity owner does not set a precise retirement income goal in advance. The retirement benefit is whatever amount has accumulated by retirement time. Further, the amount accumulated is a function of the amount of contributions, their timing, and the rates of investment return credited to the account over time. This concept is illustrated in Figure 19.2. If the annuitant dies before beginning the annuity payments, the accumulation value is returned to the beneficiary. When the annuitant lives until the liquidation period and selects an income option based on the life expectancy of the annuitant alone, it is considered a **single life annuity.**

The originally specified retirement date can be changed after the annuity is purchased. Upon retirement, there are several options for settlement, similar to the ones shown in Chapter 14 for life insurance proceeds:

- Lump sum cash payment
- Fixed period payment
- Fixed amount payment
- Life annuity
- Refund annuity
- Temporary life annuity
- Period certain life annuity
- Joint life annuity
- Joint and survivor annuity

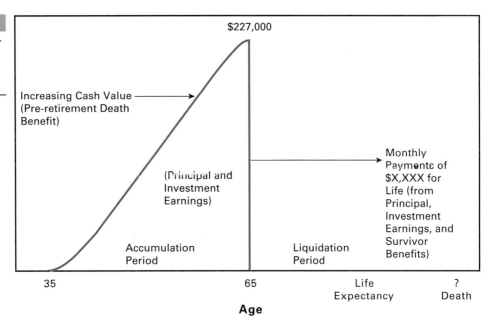

FIGURE 19.2

Hypothetical Values for the Flexible Premium, Deferred Annuity Concept

$227,000

Increasing Cash Value (Pre-retirement Death Benefit)

(Principal and Investment Earnings)

Accumulation Period

Liquidation Period

Monthly Payments of $X,XXX for Life (from Principal, Investment Earnings, and Survivor Benefits)

35   65   Life Expectancy   ?   Death

Age

The typical options include taking cash in a lump sum equal to the accumulation value of the contract. A **fixed period annuity** makes payments for a specified period, such as twenty years, and then ceases. A **fixed amount annuity** pays benefits of a set amount per period until the accumulation value at the time benefits begin plus investment earning during the liquidation period are exhausted. The amount paid under these three options is not influenced by anyone's life expectancy.

As with whole life or universal life policies, there are mortality factors and investment return factors that are guaranteed. The mortality guarantee is in case a person lives longer than expected. Unlike a regular savings account where the recipient of the money gets only the total amount in the account, in annuities the payments are promised for the duration of the annuitant's life. The insurance company is taking the risk of paying more to someone who lives longer than expected according to mortality tables. This is the mortality guarantee.

An annuity in which benefit payments are guaranteed for life, but cease and the premium considered fully earned upon the death of the annuitant, is known as a **life annuity.** In this case, no beneficiary will receive any more payments even if the annuitant dies very early. While this annuity pays the maximum periodic benefit per dollar accumulated at the time benefits begin (or per immediate single premium), far more common is the selection of a payment option that provides continuation of payments to beneficiaries for a certain amount of time such as ten or twenty years following the death of the annuitant. Most people do not like the idea that they might die shortly after beginning to receive benefit payments from an annuity in which they have made a large investment. Insurers have, therefore, made available refund annuities, period-certain life annuities, and annuities like joint and survivor that reflect the life expectancies of more than one person.

A **temporary life annuity** is a combination of a fixed period annuity and a life annuity. Payments stop at the end of a specified period or at the death of the annuitant, whichever comes first. A **period-certain option** guarantees a minimum number of annuity payments whether the annuitant lives or dies. Thus, a person can purchase a life annuity with five years certain, ten years certain, or some other period certain. If the annuitant dies before the end of the specified period, payments continue to a beneficiary for at least the period specified. A cash payment may be available to the beneficiary equal to the present value of the remaining payments. If the annuitant lives through the period certain, payments continue until death.

A **refund annuity** guarantees that the annuitant and/or beneficiary will receive, during the liquidation period, minimum payments equal to the single premium in an immediate annuity or the accumulation value in a deferred annuity. For example, assume an accumulation value of $250,000 at the time of annuitization and that the annuitant receives $100,000 before death. The beneficiary would receive a lump sum payment of $150,000. The annuitant is also promised lifetime benefits. Consequently, benefits can far exceed the accumulation value of $250,000 at the time of annuitization, plus future investment earnings on this amount. The annuitant pays for the refund feature by taking a reduced amount of periodic benefit compared to what he or she would receive for a life annuity. He or she would also pay for any other options to guarantee certain payments to beneficiaries are paid with reduced amount of periodic payments.

With a **joint annuity,** two people are named and payments stop when the first joint annuitant dies. In contrast to the joint annuity, a **joint-and-survivor annuity** continues payments as long as at least one annuitant is alive. You may recall from Chapter 18 that the joint-and-survivor annuity is the mode required in pensions unless the spouse relinquishes this benefit. In annuities sold by insurers, husbands and wives are the typical users of the joint-and-survivor option. They can decide at the time of annuitization whether payments should continue at the same amount after one spouse dies, or if the amount should be reduced (perhaps to half or two-thirds of the original amount). Some annuitants want the full refund guaranteed by the refund option, while others are satisfied with a period certain guaranteed. Others select a joint or joint-and-survivor option because of concern for another person, possibly over their lifetime. The effect of such guarantees is to reduce the monthly installments that can be purchased with any given sum of money. The option selected depends upon one's situation and viewpoint.

Types of Contracts

Annuities commonly used to help fund retirement include:

- Flexible premium annuity
- Single premium deferred annuity
- Single premium immediate annuity

All are available with fixed-dollar guarantees, as a variable or as index annuities.

The **flexible premium deferred annuity** allows you to change the amount of contributions, stop contributions, and resume them at will. For example, you may use a payroll deduction plan in which you authorize your employer to transfer $100 per pay period to the insurer. For a period of time you may want to discontinue these contributions and later resume them at $200 per pay period. Without payroll deductions you might prefer to submit premiums on a monthly, quarterly, annual, or some other basis. Earlier in the chapter, we referred to this as the installment plan.

For fixed dollar annuities, the insurer guarantees a minimum rate of interest. Initially, a current rate of return will be promised on funds in your account for a certain time (for example, two years) during the accumulation period. As returns vary over time on your insurer's investments that support fixed dollar annuities, the guarantee for future periods is likely to change. The degree of change may, in part, reflect the need for your insurer to remain competitive with annuity returns offered by other insurers, bank certificates of deposit, and other competing investment vehicles. Often, two or more interest guarantees are made by the insurer. One set of guarantees applies to funds contributed to the account in past periods. The other rate applies to funds contributed during a future period.

The **single premium deferred annuity** differs from a flexible premium deferred annuity primarily in the manner of premium payments. As the name implies, only one premium is paid. The motivation for purchase usually is driven more by the tax deferral of interest on earnings than by the promise of lifetime income during retirement. Another difference between the single premium deferred annuity and its flexible premium cousin is the longer period to which the current rate of interest is guaranteed

Many insurers have either a low or no sales load, which is basically a surrender charge (a percentage attached to withdrawals) that applies during the first five or more years. For example, 7 percent of the amount withdrawn can be retained by the insurer if the contract is surrendered for its cash value in the first year. The penalty decreases 1 percent per year, disappearing at the end of the seventh year. The surrender charge has two purposes. First, it discourages withdrawals. Second, it allows the insurer to recover some of its costs if the contract is terminated early.

The agent or broker may receive a normal level of sales commission on no-load and low-load annuities, but the commission is not deducted directly from the contributions. Annual expense charges levied on all assets are usually around 2 percent. Part of this charge is used to pay marketing expenses.

The **single premium immediate annuity** is best understood by emphasizing the word "immediate." Benefit payments to the annuitant begin on the next payment date following the premium payment, usually a large sum. The primary purchase motive would typically be interest in lifetime income. A primary source of funds for these annuities is lump sum distributions from corporate retirement plans (Chapter 18). Other sources of funds include various forms of personal investment and life insurance death benefits.

Another use of annuities arises out of legal liability judgments. Liability insurers are increasingly interested in making periodic payments to the plaintiff, to lower the total cost of the liability. A **structured settlement annuity** is a special type of single premium immediate annuity that achieves the goal. Issued by a life insurer, its terms are negotiated by the plaintiff, the defendant, their attorneys, and a structured settlement specialist. The market for structured settlement annuities is highly competitive. Consequently, the successful insurer in this market is likely to have a high rating for financial soundness, a competitive assumed rate of investment return, and a mortality assumption that reflects the plaintiff's life expectancy.

Variable Annuities

Variable annuities are more complicated than fixed-dollar annuities and are similar in concept to variable life insurance, discussed in Chapter 14. They are available as single premium annuity or immediate or deferred annuities.

In the variable annuity, two types of units are employed: accumulation units and annuity units. Some accounts invest primarily in variable-dollar assets such as common stocks and real estate. Investments are made in accounts that are kept separate from the insurers' general funds. These are called **separate accounts** in the insurer's annual statement. The value of each unit varies with the current market value of the underlying investments in the portfolio.

As premiums are paid, the account is credited with a number of **accumulation units,** the number to be determined by (1) the amount of premium and (2) the current market value of an accumulation unit. For example, if the monthly premium after expenses is $50 and the current value of a unit is $10, the account is credited with five units. If the current value of a unit has changed to $9.52, the account is credited with 5.25 units. The surrender value, or maximum withdrawal, at a specific point in the accumulation period is

$$\text{(Total number of units} \times \text{Current market value per unit)}$$
$$- \text{Surrender charge, if any} = \text{Surrender value}$$

This same calculation determines the death benefit received by the beneficiary in case of the annuitant's death during the accumulation period.

During the liquidation or distribution period, **annuity units** are exchanged for accumulation units. The determinants of the dollar income are (1) the current market value of each unit, (2) an assumed investment return, such as 4 percent, and (3) the number of units considering the age, gender, and settlement option of the annuitant. Since women's mortality is longer, gender is important in determining the periodic amount paid. Women of the same age as men will receive less periodic payment for equal accumulated account. If the investments perform better than the assumed return, the income will be greater. Many variable annuities offer a choice of investment mediums. The choices are similar to those for a family of mutual funds. In fact, some variable annuities are funded by a family of mutual funds rather than by separate accounts maintained by the insurer. For example, your variable annuity might offer the following separate accounts:

- Money market
- Long-term commercial bond fund
- High-grade common stocks
- Balanced fund with bonds and stocks
- Growth stocks

The funds can be divided among two or more accounts in a manner that reflects your personal risk propensity.

Index Annuities

Equity indexed annuities are annuities with returns linked to the S&P 500 with guarantees of investment or to some fixed interest rate indices. Some index annuities have several "buckets" of investments mixes, including one that has a fixed interest rate. The appeal of these annuities is the opportunity to earn more returns, but still have the minimum guarantees. Some agents sell these products instead of fixed annuities, not in lieu of variable annuities. Since the year 2002 saw growth in these products, it appears that more insurers are interested in creating such structures to compete in the marketplace.[1]

TAXATION OF ANNUITIES

The first major tax question is: Can individuals deduct annuity contributions (premiums) from adjusted gross income each year? Generally, premiums are not deductible. The exception is when annuities are invested in any of the pension plans described in Chapter 18.

When an annuity is purchased separately from any pension plan by individuals, the premiums paid are from after-tax income. With these annuities, during the accumulation period, no income taxes are due on the returns unless the annuitant is making withdrawals or surrenders. When the annuity is distributed to the annuitant, only the earnings (not the premiums) are subject to income tax. When annuities are used as investment instruments in pensions or in IRA accounts, they are considered tax-deferred annuities. The premiums are paid with before-tax income. Distributions from tax-deferred annuities are subject to income taxation on the whole account. All payments from a tax-deferred annuity are subject to ordinary income taxes during the liquidation period.

For annuities that are bought with after-tax money by individuals, ordinary income taxes are paid on the return of (previously untaxed) investment earnings. The amount of each payment returned during the distribution of the annuity represents previously taxed contributions. These are not taxed again. Each payment is, therefore, divided between taxable and nontaxable amounts at the beginning of the payout period by calculating an **exclusion ratio.** The ratio is then multiplied by each periodic payment to determine the amount of each annuity payment that is excluded from gross income. The exclusion ratio is

$$\frac{\text{Investment in Contract}}{\text{Expected Return}}$$

INDIVIDUAL HEALTH INSURANCE CONTRACTS

The individual health insurance products mirror closely the group market products. Since most of these policies are very close to the structure of the group health, we provide here examples of individual health policies available to 22-year-old male and female college students in Richmond, Virginia. Figure 19.3 shows the plans offered by some insurers using the Internet site of e-health insurance, retrieved in September 2002 from eHealthInsurance.com.

As you can see, the lowest price is for a catastrophic plan with $5,000 deductible with co-insurance of 20 percent. The price of the coverage increases as the deductible decreases. A more detailed example of one of the plans is provided for Trigon Blue Cross/Blue Shield for the same 22-year-old individual in Figure 19.4. Figure 19.5 features a Trigon policy for a female student age 22. A comparison between the two plans can be very educational, especially since the man's policy is a PPO type, while the woman's policy is a comprehensive major medical. Both of them receive a list of physicians to choose from. Both have deductibles; hers is higher and she has no limit to the annual out-of-pocket expense. Her co-insurance is mostly 0 percent and there is no distinction between in and out of networks. The student is invited to make a thorough comparison of the plans. It will be important to compare the policies based on the benefit package, cost sharing, such as co-pays, coinsurance, and deductibles, and factors such as gender.

The most noticeable difference between the individual plan and the group plan featured in Case 2 at the back of the text regards the maternity benefits. They are available as a rider, or optional coverage, in the individual policy, but cannot be optional in group insurance because of the Civil Rights Act described in Chapter 17. The act requires employers to treat pregnancies as any other illnesses.

FIGURE 19.3   Individual Health Insurance Options for a Full-Time Male Student, Age 22, Richmond, Virginia, September, 2002

Company	Monthly Premium	Plan Type	Deductible	Coinsurance	Copay
Golden Rule Basic Plan I	$27.03	PPO	$5,000	20%	N/A
Golden Rule Basic Plan II	$31.12	PPO	$2,500	20%	N/A
UNICARE Saver 2000	$33.00	PPO	$2,000	30%	$30
TRIGON Individual Basic KeyCare	$56.00	PPO	$ 750	20%	N/A

Source: eHealthInsurance.com® (a registered trademark of eHealthInsurance Services, Inc.).

FIGURE 19.4	Individual Health Insurance from TRIGON BC/BS for a Full-Time Male Student, Age 22, Richmond, Virginia, September, 2002

Plan Summary

Company	TRIGON
Plan Name	Individual Basic KeyCare
Estimated Monthly Premium	$56.00
Plan Type	PPO
Office Visit	In Network: You pay 20% coinsurance per office visit
	Out of Network: You pay 30% coinsurance.
Deductible	$750 Single/ $1,500 Family (Aggregate)
Coinsurance	In Network: You pay 20% coinsurance after deductible unless otherwise stated
	Out of Network: 30% coinsurance after deductible unless otherwise stated.
Out-of-Pocket Limit	In Network: 2,000 Single, $4,000 Family (Aggregate)
	Out of Network: $4,000 Single, $8,000 Family (Aggregate)
Lifetime Maximum	$2 million regardless of providers or facilities.
Exclusions and limitations	Exclusions and Limitations—more details are available in a separate Internet page.
Online Physician Directory	Physician's Directory

Outpatient Benefits

Prescription Drugs	Prescription card: you pay the greater of a $10 copayment or 40% coinsurance; $5,000 annual maximum. You receive maximum benefits when you choose generic drugs, when available. $200 separate deductible.
Emergency Room	You pay 20% coinsurance in or out of network.
Periodic Health Exam	In Network: 2 office visits per year. You pay 20% coinsurance for covered screenings and up to $150 per calendar year for immunizations, labs, and x-rays
	Out of Network: You pay 30% coinsurance.
Periodic OB-GYN Exam	See benefits for Periodic Health Exam
Lab/X-Ray	In Network: You pay 20% coinsurance
	Out of Network: You pay 30% coinsurance.
Outpatient Surgery	In Network: You pay 20% coinsurance
	Out of Network: You pay 30% coinsurance.
Maternity – Prenatal/Postnatal	Rider Available
Well Baby Care	You pay 0% coinsurance in or out of network. No deductible.
Physical Therapy	In Network: You pay 20% coinsurance for outpatient physical/occupational therapy up to $2,000 per calendar year
	Out of Network: You pay 30% coinsurance.
Skilled Nursing	In Network: You pay 20% coinsurance up to 100 days per calendar year
	Out of Network: You pay 30% coinsurance.
Home Health Care	In Network: You pay 20% coinsurance up to 90 visits per calendar year
	Out of Network: You pay 30% coinsurance.
Mental Health Office Visits	In Network: You pay 20% coinsurance for first 5 visits, and 50% coinsurance amount for visits 6–20
	Out of Network: You pay 30% coinsurance for first 5 visits and 50% coinsurance amount for visits 6–20.

Inpatient Benefits

Hospitalization	In Network: You pay 20% coinsurance
	Out of Network: You pay 30% coinsurance.
Maternity	Rider available
Mental Health	In Network: You pay 20% coinsurance up to a 25 day maximum per calendar year
	Out of Network: You pay 30% coinsurance.
Chemical Dependency	See benefits for Mental Health

Additional Benefits

Optional Benefits (Dental, Maternity, Life Insurance, etc.)	Optional Benefit Quotes

Source: eHealthInsurance.com® (a registered trademark of eHealthInsurance Services, Inc.).

FIGURE 19.5   Comprehensive Major Medical Insurance Plan from TRIGON for a Full-Time Female Student, Age 22, Richmond, Virginia, September, 2002

Plan Summary

Company	TRIGON
Plan Name	Individual Basic BlueCare
Estimated Monthly Premium	$70.00
Plan Type	Comprehensive Major Medical
Office Visit	You pay 0% coinsurance.
Deductible	$1,500 Single/ $3,000 Family (Aggregate)
Coinsurance	You pay 0% coinsurance after deductible unless otherwise stated.
Out-of-Pocket Limit	None
Lifetime Maximum	$2 million regardless of providers or facilities.
Exclusions and limitations	Exclusions and Limitations (separate details)
Online Physician Directory	Physician's Directory

Outpatient Benefits

Prescription Drugs	Prescription card: you pay the greater of a $10 copayment or 40% coinsurance; $5,000 annual maximum. You receive maximum benefits when you choose generic drugs, when available. $200 separate deductible.
Emergency Room	You pay 0% coinsurance.
Periodic Health Exam	2 office visits per year. You pay 0%* coinsurance for covered screenings and up to $150 per calendar year for immunizations, labs, and x-rays.
Periodic OB-GYN Exam	See benefits for Periodic Health Exam
Lab/X-Ray	You pay 0% coinsurance.
Outpatient Surgery	You pay 0% coinsurance.
Maternity - Prenatal/Postnatal	Rider Available
Well Baby Care	You pay 0% coinsurance. No deductible.
Physical Therapy	You pay 20% coinsurance for outpatient physical/occupational therapy up to $2,000 per calendar year.
Skilled Nursing	You pay 20% coinsurance up to 100 days per calendar year.
Home Health Care	You pay 20% coinsurance up to 90 visits per calendar year.
Mental Health Office Visits	You pay 20% coinsurance for first 5 visits, and 50% coinsurance amount for visits 6–20.

Inpatient Benefits

Hospitalization	You pay 0% coinsurance
Maternity	Rider Available
Mental Health	You pay 0% coinsurance up to a 25 day maximum per calendar year
Chemical Dependency	See benefits for Mental Health

Additional Benefits

Optional Benefits (Dental, Maternity, Life Insurance, etc.)	Optional Benefit Quotes

Source: eHealthInsurance.com® (a registered trademark of eHealthInsurance Services, Inc.).

CANCER AND CRITICAL ILLNESS POLICIES

Some health policies reimburse only for specific illnesses (such as cancer), pay only a per diem amount for medical expenses, or are otherwise very limited in coverage. The consumer needs to read individual policies carefully. These policies are not for reimbursement of medical services.

"Critical illness insurance is one of those product areas that is almost guaranteed to spark a spirited debate when insurance folks get together and talk about sales," said *National*

Underwriter reporter Linda Koco in "Critical Illness Insurance: Real Or Gimmick?"[2] "Some producers call it a brand-new kind of policy—the fourth leg of the living benefits stool (life, health, and disability insurance being the other three). But others aren't so kind. They sniff at it and walk away baffled about why it's even here. Some dismiss it outright, as a gimmick or some sort of warmed-over cancer insurance." A cancer or critical illness policy is designed to pay for the extra expenses incurred during the period of medical treatment. It does not pay the doctors or any of the medical bills that are paid by health insurance. It is not a disability income policy for lost time at work, or accelerated benefits available in a life insurance policy. It is to cover the travel expenses associated with the illness such as parents staying at a hotel next to the hospital of the child if the hospital is in a different city. It will also pay for adaptive equipment expenses such as reconfiguration of a bathroom. One of the attributes that make this coverage interesting to buyers is the critical illness policy's lump sum payment upon diagnosis of a dread or critical illness. Insureds believe that the coverage helps them cope with the health crisis and recovery.[3] But, like all coverages, a detailed need analysis should accompany the decision to buy such coverage.

Critical illness policies were introduced in the United States in the mid-1990s. Numerous insurance companies offer the product. One that you may be familiar with is AFLAC. The duck quacking in the commercials of AFLAC for supplemental expense or cancer policies is a household feature. (According to an AFLAC spokesperson, the duck was selected to represent the companies because the quacking sounds like AFLAC.) The products are vastly different across the states because of varying regulation, but typically, the policy pays a lump sum when the insured is diagnosed with a qualified illness. Individual contracts usually require insurability evidence. There are several important questions that should be asked when evaluating a critical illness policy, including how many illnesses it covers and whether the definitions of illness are precise.

The American Cancer Society regards these policies as supplementing medical coverage. The co-insurance and deductibles of a major medical policy are a major source of financial burden to families inflicted with a critical illness. As the example of the medical coverage in Figure 19.5 shows, a major medical policy has no limits on out-of-pocket expenses. Such a policy may cause substantial hardship to a family.[4] The supplemental expense policies are available to ease this hardship. They are not to replace the health insurance, but only to help with catastrophic out-of-pocket costs. The policy also provides an initial sum of money to help cope with a critical illness. The student is advised to not use such a policy in lieu of health insurance since a critical illness policy does not provide medical insurance and the debate about the real need for such policies has never subsided.

DENTAL INSURANCE

Most individual medical insurance policies do not cover dental expenses. Dental plans are offered on an individual basis as separate policies, though they can be offered as an option attached to the health insurance too. Figures 19.6 and 19.7 show the dental plans offered to our 22-year-old female student residing in Richmond, close to school. A sample of a few plans (out of many) that are available to the student are shown in Figure 19.6. Details of a PPO dental plan is shown in Figure 19.7. In many ways, there is no difference between the individual dental plan featured here and the group dental plan featured in Case 2 at the back of the text.

Dental insurance policies encourage better dental health by not applying a deductible or coinsurance to charges for checkups and cleaning. By having first-dollar coverage, insureds are more likely to seek routine diagnostic care, which enables early detection of problems and may reduce total expenditures. Dental policies not only cover routine care

FIGURE 19.6 Dental Plans for a Full-Time Female Student, Age 22, Richmond, Virginia, September 2002

Company and Plan	Premium Per month	Type	Annual Max	Deductible	Co-insurance
Security Life Insurance Company of America Security Life Plan	$23.01	PPO	$750 per person	$50 yearly	30%–80%
Security Life Insurance Company of America Security Life Plan III	$28.65	PPO	$1,000 per person	$50 yearly	0%–50%
Security Life Insurance Company of America Security Life Plan IV	$30.20	Indemnity	$750 per person	$50 yearly	10%–50%
Monumental Life Insurance Company Multiflex Dental $1,000 Benefit	$37.61	Indemnity	$1,000 per person	$50–$75 yearly	0%–50%
Monumental Life Insurance Company Multiflex Dental $2,000 Benefit	$42.51	Indemnity	$2,000 per person	$50–$75 yearly	0%–50%

Source: eHealthInsurance.com® (a registered trademark of eHealthInsurance Services, Inc.).

but also protect insureds against more expensive procedures such as restorative services. For restorative and orthodontic services, insureds usually pay a deductible or coinsurance amount. A fee schedule limits the amount paid per procedure, so the insured may also pay out-of-pocket for the cost of services above the scheduled amount. Policy maximums are specified on an annual and lifetime basis, such as $2,000 per year and $50,000 during a lifetime.

Many dentists consult with the insured in advance of the procedure to determine what will be paid by insurance. The dentist lists what needs to be done and then the dentist or the insured checks with the insurer to determine coverage. Most policies exclude coverage for purely cosmetic purposes, losses caused by war, and occupational injuries or sickness.

INDIVIDUAL DISABILITY INCOME INSURANCE CONTRACTS

Disability income insurance replaces lost income when the insured is unable to work. Income replacement is especially critical with disability because the individual faces not only the risk of reduced earnings but also the risk of additional expenses resulting from medical or therapeutic services. In Chapter 15 we discussed the Social Security disability program, which covers most employees in the United States. However, qualifying under the Social Security definition for disability is difficult. Workers' compensation is another source of disability insurance, but only for disability arising from employment-related injury or illness (see Chapter 13). Some employers provide private group disability insurance, as discussed in Chapter 17, but this employee benefit is much less commonly offered than life, medical, and retirement benefits. If it is offered, it may not be sufficient to replace lost income. Individuals may want to purchase disability coverage on their own, in case they are not eligible for Social Security, workers' compensation, or private employer-sponsored plans, or simply because they want additional protection. Again, it is important to have a need analysis done to determine whether a layer of individual coverage is necessary over the employer-provided disability and Social Security.

FIGURE 19.7	PPO Dental Plan from Security Life Insurance Company of America for a Full-Time Female Student, Age 22, Richmond, Virginia, September, 2002

Plan Elements	Benefits
Estimated Monthly Cost	$23.01
Plan Type	PPO
Annual Maximum	$750
Deductible	$50
Exclusions and Limitations	See Exclusions and Limitations in a separate Internet site
Office Visit	70% deductible waived in Network. Benefit increases to 80% 2nd year, 90% 3rd year
Teeth Cleaning	70% deductible waived in Network. Benefit increases to 80% 2nd year, 90% 3rd year
Topical Fluoride	Benefit limited to family members 16 years of age and younger. 70% deductible waived in Network. Benefit increases to 80% 2nd year, 90% 3rd year
Sealants	Not covered
Restorative Dentistry/Fillings	6 month waiting period applies 40% 1st year Benefit increases to 50% 2nd year, 60% 3rd year and beyond
Extractions	6 month waiting period applies 40% 1st year Benefit increases to 50% 2nd year, 60% 3rd year and beyond
Oral Surgery	6 month waiting period applies 40% 1st year Benefit increases to 50% 2nd year, 60% 3rd year and beyond
X-Rays	6 month waiting period applies 40% 1st year Benefit increases to 50% 2nd year, 60% 3rd year and beyond
Crown	6 month waiting period applies 20% 1st year Benefit increases to 35% 2nd year, 50% 3rd year
Bridges	6 month waiting period applies 20% 1st year Benefit increases to 35% 2nd year, 50% 3rd year
Dentures	6 month waiting period applies 20% 1st year Benefit increases to 35% 2nd year, 50% 3rd year
Root Canals	6 month waiting period applies 20% 1st year Benefit increases to 35% 2nd year, 50% 3rd year
Periodontics	6 month waiting period applies 20% 1st year Benefit increases to 35% 2nd year, 50% 3rd year
Endodontics	6 month waiting period applies 20% 1st year Benefit increases to 35% 2nd year, 50% 3rd year

Source: eHealthInsurance.com® (a registered trademark of eHealthInsurance Services, Inc.).

Definition and Cause of Disability

Definitions of disability vary more among individual policies than among group policies. **Total disability** may be defined as the complete inability to perform "any and every duty" of the individual's own job. Alternatively, it may be defined as the inability to engage in any "reasonable and gainful occupation" for which the individual is (or could become) qualified by education, training, or experience. Some policies combine these two definitions, with the more liberal (from the insured's point of view) "own occupation" definition satisfying the requirement for total disability during an initial short-term period (for example, two years), and the more stringent definition being used thereafter. **Partial disability** is even more difficult to define than total disability. It is usually measured in terms of the inability to perform some of the important duties of the job. Some policies pay partial disability only if partial disability follows total disability or only if a loss of income results.

Some contracts provide income benefits for disability caused by accident only, others for both accident and sickness. It is necessary to distinguish between losses caused by accident and those caused by sickness, because the benefits can differ. Some policies provide that income losses resulting from injuries due to accident must start within ninety days after the injury. Losses resulting from injuries that begin after the ninety-day period are deemed to have resulted from sickness. Moreover, a loss is not considered caused by accident unless it results "directly and independently of all other causes." This provision is designed to eliminate from the definition of accidental bodily injury income losses actually caused by illness. For example, a person who suffers a heart attack and is injured when falling to the ground would not qualify for accident benefits but would qualify for sickness benefits.

The debate about the definition of disability is an old one. Figure 19.8 provides a list of definitions of disability. It is not always clear which definition best serves the individual policyholder. In reality, it is desirable to have a true needs assessment of the individual in this market.

Benefits

As with group insurance, both short-term disability and long-term disability policies are available for individuals. **Short-term disability policies (STD)** are those with benefits payable up to two years. Short-term plans may restrict benefits to periods as short as thirteen or twenty-six weeks. Individual STD plans may limit benefit duration to six months for the same cause of disability, sometimes requiring the insured to return to work for up to ninety days before establishing a new maximum benefit period for disability from the same cause.

FIGURE 19.8   Definitions of Disability

Own Occ: Means insureds can return to work in another occupation, with no offsets on the disability benefit, if they are unable to perform their own occupation.

Any Occ: Means insureds can return to work in any occupation for which they are qualified (based on education level and prior work experience).

Gainful Occ: Means insureds can return to work in any occupation where they can earn 50% to 60% of their former income (based on education level and prior work experience).

Loss of Earnings: Means insureds qualify for one of the above definitions if their earnings are diminished.

Loss of Time or Duties: Means insureds qualify for one of the above definitions if the amount of time they can spend at the job is reduced or if the number of duties they perform are reduced.

Flexible: Refers to newer approach that allows insureds to flex coverage between a range of definitions contained in the policy as their needs change. For instance, the more affordable any occ or gainful occ options may appeal to younger clients, but own occ (working or not) may be needed when skills are more specialized.

Source: James Foley, "Look Beyond The Definition Of Disability," *National Underwriter* Life & Health/Financial Services Edition, 29 July 2002.

Long-term disability policies (LTD) are those that pay benefits for longer periods, such as five years, ten years, until a set retirement age, or for life. Long-term disability policies often assume that the insured will become eligible for retirement benefits from Social Security or private retirement plans at age 65. To coordinate benefits, the disability policy defines the maximum duration as age 65. LTD benefits for any shorter period would expose the insured to a potentially devastating income loss, since neither disability nor retirement income would be provided for this period.

Long-term benefits do not cost proportionately more than short-term coverage. From the consumer's point of view, the longer term policy is a better buy. It protects against an unbearable risk: the long-term loss of income. This is a good example of the "large loss principle," where insurance purchase should be governed by the potential severity of loss, rather than the frequency of loss. The large loss principle should govern disability income insurance purchases even though most disabilities are of relatively short duration.

Policies pay benefits after an elimination or waiting period. The **elimination period,** like a deductible in medical insurance, reduces moral hazard. For STD policies the elimination period typically extends from a few days to two weeks; for LTD policies the period extends from one month to one year. Here, as in group coverage, the insured may be covered during the LTD waiting period by benefits from the STD policy or a salary continuation plan (such as sick leave).

Individual contracts generally state the amount of the benefit in terms of dollars per week or month, unlike group policies that state benefits as a percentage of the insured's basic earnings. In either case, the insurer is wary of having the benefit equal to anything approaching full earnings. Typically, the amount is limited to about two-thirds of earned income because benefits under individual disability policies are typically not taxable. The benefits are not taxable because the premiums are paid from after tax income. The purpose of this limitation is to reduce moral hazard by providing an economic incentive for employees to return to work.

Benefits may differ for disabilities resulting from accident rather than sickness. Benefits for sickness are not as generous as those for accidents. For example, a policy may provide benefit payments for five years if disability is caused by accident, but only two years if caused by sickness. Some long-term policies pay to age 65 for sickness, but for life when the cause of disability is accidental. Benefits for partial disability, which are more likely to be provided by individual contracts rather than group contracts, often are only for disability caused by accident. Some policies pay no benefits if the sickness or accident is work-connected and the employee receives workers' compensation benefits. Such policies are called non-occupational. Others supplement workers' compensation benefits up to the point at which the insured gets the same payment for occupational and non-occupational disabilities. Some individual policies specify a maximum combined benefit for Social Security and the private policy. The insured can purchase a plan with a **social insurance substitute,** which replaces Social Security benefits if the individual does not qualify under their strict definition of disability.

Often, individual policies are not coordinated with other disability income benefits. The relatively few individual policies that coordinate disability benefits use the **average earnings provision.** This provision addresses the problem of over insurance, which may occur when a person has more than one policy. (In group insurance, coordination of benefits provisions address the problem of over-insurance.) For example, a person whose salary is $2,000 per month may have two disability income policies, each of which provides $1,200 per month income benefits. In the event of total disability, assuming no coordination provision, the insured loses $2,000 per month in salary and receives $2,400 in benefits. This reduces the incentive to return to work and may lead to benefit payment for a longer time than anticipated when the premium rate was established.

The average earnings clause provides for a reduction in benefit payments if the total amount of income payments under all insurance policies covering the loss exceeds earnings at the time disability commences, or exceeds the average earnings for two years preceding disability, whichever is greater. The amount of the reduction is the proportion by which all benefits would have to be reduced in order to prevent total benefits from exceeding average earned income. In the preceding illustration, for example, total insurance exceeded income by one-fifth, in which case the benefits of each policy containing an average earnings clause would be reduced so that disability benefits do not exceed pre-disability earnings. A reduction of the payment provided by each policy from $1,200 to $1,000 per month eliminates the excess.

The insured may have policies in place that do not have an average earnings clause, and could receive benefits in excess of pre-disability earnings. This provides an income advantage during a period of disability. As noted above, a further advantage to the insured is the absence of federal income taxes on disability benefits from individual policies (as well as employee-paid group policies). In addition, the disabled insured has few, if any, work expenses, such as clothing and transportation costs. Insurance underwriters recognize these advantages, as well as the potential for moral hazard, and may be unwilling to issue a large policy when benefits are otherwise available.

In 2002, the individual disability market in the United States included eighteen carriers. In 2001, there was a modest revenue growth and an 11 percent increase in sales.[5]

LONG-TERM CARE INSURANCE

We discussed group **long-term care (LTC) insurance** in Chapter 17. This is one coverage that is more prevalent in the individual market since more older people are interested in such coverage than younger working individuals. As noted in Chapter 17, the inability to perform the regular daily living activities are never covered by health insurance or Medicare. The gap in coverage is closed by the development of LTC policies.

The American Association of Retired Persons (AARP) helps to promote long-term care and provides information regarding the coverage on its Web site. The Web site notes, "Typically, policies reimburse the insured for long-term care expenses up to a fixed amount, such as $100 per day for nursing home care and $50 per day for home care. To receive benefits, however, the insured must meet the policy's disability [long-term care] criteria. For example, some policies require the individual to be severely cognitively impaired or to need help in performing two 'activities of daily living' (such as bathing and dressing). Other policies will pay benefits based on the loosely defined term "medical necessity."[6]

Long-term care insurance began as a basic form of nursing care insurance in the 1960s, and expanded into custodial and home care in the 1980s. During the 1990s the product began developing into today's LTC insurance. The current policies expanded the coverage and differentiated themselves.[7] Today's LTC policies include favorable changes such as:

- Adding assisted living facility (ALF) coverage to policies that had nursing home and home care coverage
- Broadening the definitions of activities of daily living to include stand-by assistance

- Expanding bed reservation coverage to include reasons beyond hospitalization
- Lowering existing premiums
- Removing restrictions such as three-day prior hospitalization as well as inorganic mental and nervous exclusions
- Upgrading to add home care coverage and assisted living facility coverage[8]

Many of these changes have pricing consequences.

The cost of individual long-term care insurance is based on cohorts of individuals. The factors for the costs are duration of benefits, the length of waiting periods, and the types of triggers of benefits. Compared with group long-term care, the definition of the triggers is not as stringent in individual LTC policies. Many policies provide for inflation protection. Cost factors vary by age, as would be expected.

The passage of HIPAA, discussed in Chapter 17, also affected individual long-term care policies. Only the more stringent, federally qualified long-term care policies meet the favorable tax treatment of health policies. Those who use these policies can deduct the premiums up to a maximum (provided the taxpayer itemizes deductions and has medical costs in excess of 7.5 percent of "adjusted gross income").

LTC Annuities

In the world of insurance, change and new products are the constant state of the world. There is a new interest in **LTC-annuity** products.[9] The product is similar to life insurance with an LTC rider. This rider covers the costs of nursing home stays, home health care treatment, and other LTC services typically covered by stand-alone LTC policies.[10] The tax implications of the portion of the premiums attributed to LTC are not yet determined. The LTC risk and "living too long" risk are inversely related since those needing LTC are expected to have a shorter life span. This provides the insurer a type of hedge.

LTC Acceleration Life Rider

Like living benefits, accelerated LTC benefits fit well with life insurance. LTC benefits are provided to the needy insureds while still living, like living benefits. Traditional life insurance policies are considered best suited for LTC riders because of the guarantees.

Insurers such as National Life and Interstate entered this market with various universal and variable life insurance products. The development activity is more pronounced in the variable universal life. These integrated VUL/LTC products pose many challenges since LTC requires more guarantees than those provided by universal variable life products. To overcome some of the challenges, the LTC benefits are designed as a percentage of the death benefit or other specified amount.[11] Some products provide a minimum death benefit guarantee, and the LTC monthly maximum benefit reflects the death benefit guarantee.

MEDICARE SUPPLEMENTARY INSURANCE

Medicare health insurance is provided through the Social Security system for covered persons over age 65, as well as those under 65 with kidney disease and those eligible to receive Social Security disability. Medicare, however, does not completely cover the cost of all medical services needed by elderly people. Figure 19.9 lists top reasons to buy Medicare supplement.

Private individual health contracts, known as **Medigap insurance,** supplement the coverage provided by Medicare. Various Medigap policies are available, representing a

FIGURE 19.9   Top Eight Reasons to Buy Medigap Insurance

1. Without Medigap coverage, if you spend one night in the hospital, it will likely cost you $812 (the Medicare hospital deductible).
2. If you are sick or hospitalized while traveling abroad, you will need to pay 100% of all costs because Medicare does not have foreign emergency medical coverage.
3. If you develop a chronic illness, you can easily spend 10% or more of your annual income on prescription drugs because Medicare has no prescription drug benefit.
4. Medicare does not cover many medical services, like routine check-ups, cholesterol screenings, hearing tests, eye exams, and at-home recovery.
5. Even for the services that Medicare covers, you may have to pay up to 15% of the bill because doctors and hospitals can charge more than what Medicare finds is "reasonable."
6. If you don't buy Medigap coverage within 6 months of enrolling in Medicare Part B, you may be declined and you may be charged significantly higher premiums due to pre-existing conditions that you have or may develop.
7. As long as you keep paying your Medigap premiums, the insurance company must renew your policy, regardless of your health.
8. All Medigap policies come with a 30-day "free look"—if, within 30 days of purchasing a Medigap policy, you decide you don't want it, you can get a full refund.

Source: eHealthInsurance.com® (a registered trademark of eHealthInsurance Services, Inc.).

range of benefits and premiums. In the past, the wide variety of products, as well as unethical sales practices by agents, made it difficult for consumers to understand policy provisions or compare contracts. Lengthy preexisting condition requirements limited the protection offered by many policies. Many people purchased duplicate coverage, not realizing that the additional policies provided no extra protection. Many of the policies were not good buys, returning less than 60 cents in benefits for each dollar of premium. See "Ethical Dilemma: When Is Coverage Really Needed?" in this chapter for tips on how to avoid Medicare Supplements scams.

In 1990, legislation required standardization of Medigap policies to make it easier for consumers to understand and compare various policy provisions. Ten standardized policies (developed by the National Association of Insurance Commissioners) are now approved for sale in the individual Medigap market. Preexisting condition clauses cannot exceed six months. In addition, loss ratios, the ratio of benefits paid to premiums received, are required to be at least 60 percent. Legislation outlawed the sale of duplicate policies, and agents can be fined for deceptive sales practices.

The ten standard Medigap plans range from Plan A to Plan J. Plan A, the least expensive contract, is the basic policy and covers a core of benefits. Benefits increase as one moves toward Plan J, which provides the most coverage and has the highest premium. Comparing the ten standardized policies on the basis of benefits and price is straightforward, and the insured can simply decide what to purchase based on need for coverage and willingness or ability to pay. However, not all insurers selling Medigap coverage sell all of the plans.

Like long-term care insurance, Medigap insurance can provide an important element of economic security for elderly people. Given the current funding shortfalls of Medicare and the national concern with the federal budget deficit (discussed in Chapter 15), additional public funding of medical care for the elderly is unlikely. Thus, the importance of Medigap insurance is not likely to diminish anytime soon.

Every state provides Medicare supplements booklets to educate the public. The booklets provide rate comparisons and details about the difference among the various policies. Many can be found online at your state's department of insurance.[12]

Ethical Dilemma

When Is Coverage Really Needed?

How much insurance is adequate? How much is too much? Agents prefer to sell you more and may try to take advantage of vulnerable older people in order to collect more commission. But most agents truly try to do a thorough need analysis for every coverage. To help consumers learn more about how to identify potential scams, every state insurance regulatory body has created educational booklets for most coverages from homeowners, automobile, health, and life insurance. One area that is receiving more attention is the educational tips for the elderly population regarding Medicare supplement and long-term care coverages. Most business journals and many Web sites provide good insurance advice.

The following is one example of a "guidance" article from MSN Money/CNBC.

How to Avoid Medicare Scams: Five Tips

When health-maintenance organizations "dump" Medicare patients, worried seniors can become easy targets for unscrupulous agents, officials say. This was especially apparent in December 2000, when 115 health insurance companies stopped offering Medicare HMO coverage, leaving more than 930,000 elderly and disabled Americans looking for new health plans.

Many of those who lose their HMO coverage wind up enrolling in a traditional Medicare fee-for-service program. Because there are large gaps in traditional Medicare program coverage, seniors often buy Medigap policies from private insurers to obtain additional benefits, such as prescription-drug coverage. Some insurance agents see this as an opportunity to use high-pressure sales tactics to convince unsuspecting seniors to buy Medigap policies they don't need, or buy before they need them. Agents benefit by receiving commissions, and insurers receive more premiums.

Shady agents use misleading advertisements or target seniors who attend seminars seeking information about new coverage options, says Joe Baker, executive vice president of the Medicare Rights Center, a not-for-profit organization that helps older adults and disabled people find affordable health coverage.

"If they go to a marketing seminar run by a private company, they have to understand what those seminars are all about," Baker cautions. "And they're about selling products."

How to Avoid Being Snookered

If you are losing your Medicare HMO coverage, don't panic, says Baker. And certainly, he warns, don't be pressured into buying a Medigap policy too soon; you'll only pay for coverage you don't need yet, and you'll lose some important protections if you drop your HMO coverage prematurely.

Those protections include the right to buy a specified Medigap plan without coverage exclusions or higher premiums based on your health or claims experience, and in some cases the right to buy any Medigap plan of your choice. For more information about your rights, visit the government's question-and-answer page on Medicare HMO withdrawals. Medicare's Web site offers further information, as well as information on government-sponsored seminars in your area.

Protect yourself by taking a few basic precautions.

- Know who is running a seminar about Medicare. If it's a private company, remember that its ultimate goal, Baker says, is to sell its products to you.
- If someone tells you to sign a policy before you leave the seminar, refuse. Instead, offer to take the material home, where you'll be able to read it carefully.

Shop around. Although Medigap plans are standard in most states, premiums can vary widely.

- If in doubt, call Medicare officials at (800) MEDICARE for advice or help.
- Report suspicious agents to your state insurance department.

Questions for Discussion

1. While it is not considered criminal activity to sell more than one policy of the same type, would it be considered unethical in all situations?

2. As you learned in this text, complete risk management includes a composition of many insurance policies to assure holistic coverage. When would you know if an additional policy is too much?

Source: MSN Money / CNBC, "The Basics: How to Avoid Medicare Scams: 5 Tips," http://moneycentral.msn.com/articles/insure/health/5907.asp

HOW MUCH LIFE INSURANCE TO BUY?

In this section, the income continuation needs for a single-parent family, the Dowds, will be evaluated to see how much life insurance is necessary. The risk management component of the financial planning process will be used to look at the family's present resources, income needs, and insurance needs in the event of the wage earner's death. Coverages for property and casualty, health, disability, and retirement are covered in Case 1 at the back of this text. Also, the rights of individuals called to military duty and their families regarding health and pension coverages are discussed in "Important Issues: Individual Coverage Rights When Called to Military Duty" of this chapter.

Data Collection

The Dowd family has three members:

- Sharon, age 35
- Liz, age 6
- Bob, age 4

Liz and Bob see a pediatrician at least once a year. Sharon had a routine check-up about six months ago. All three are apparently healthy.

Financial Situation

Sharon is a branch bank manager whose gross yearly income is $50,000. Her former husband lives in another state and does not pay alimony or contribute to child support.

A balance sheet and cash flow statement are important in evaluating Sharon's current ability to meet her needs and in establishing post-loss objectives. Sharon has constructed Tables 19.1 and 19.2. On the balance sheet, you may wonder why the value of furniture and other personal property is only $10,000. The sums listed are liquidation values; these items probably have a replacement value between $30,000 and $40,000. But our concern, in the event of Sharon's death, is how much the items would sell for if they had to be liquidated to meet family income needs. Unlike houses and automobiles, limited demand exists for used furniture and clothing.

The family has four types of basic resources in addition to the assets shown in Table 19.1. These resources are provided by:

- Social Security
- Sharon's employer
- Individual insurance
- Personal savings and investments

Based on Sharon's earnings history, we estimate that the following Social Security benefits would be available to her and/or the children in the event of her death. Survivor benefits are expected (based on the current Social Security law) to keep pace with inflation.

- Sharon's death: $255 burial allowance plus $600 per month survivor benefits to each child until each is age 18 (or age 19 if still a full-time high school student)

IMPORTANT ISSUES

Individual Coverage Rights When Called to Military Duty

As a result of the September 11 attacks, many veterans, National Guard members, and reservists have been activated for military service. The Department of Labor's Veterans Employment and Training Service (VETS) explains the benefits-related rights and responsibilities of those called to active duty and their civilian employers.

My family had health coverage through my employer when I was called for active duty in the military. What are my rights to health coverage now?

If you are on active duty for more than thirty days, you and your dependents should be covered by military health care. In addition, two laws protect your right to continue health coverage under an employment-based group health plan. The Consolidated Omnibus Budget Reconciliation Act (COBRA) provides health coverage continuation rights to employees and their families after an event such as reduction in employment hours. The Uniformed Services Employment and Reemployment Rights Act of 1994 (USERRA) is intended to minimize the disadvantages that occur when a person needs to be absent from civilian employment to serve in the uniformed services. Both COBRA and USERRA generally allow individuals called for active duty to continue coverage for themselves and their dependents under an employment-based group health plan for up to eighteen months. The Health Insurance Portability and Accountability Act (HIPAA) may give you and your family the right to enroll in other group health plan coverage if it is available to you (for example, if your spouse's employer sponsors a group health plan).

My family and I had health coverage under my employer's group health plan before I was called on active duty. We let this coverage lapse while I was away and took military health coverage. When I return to my employer from active duty, what are our rights to health coverage under my old plan?

Under USERRA, you and your family should be able to reenter your employer's health plan. In addition, your plan generally cannot impose a waiting period or other exclusion period if health coverage would have been provided were it not for military service.

While I am on active duty, is my employer required to continue making employer contributions to my 401(k) plan?

USERRA requires that returning service members who meet the law's eligibility criteria must be treated as if they had been continuously employed for pension purposes, regardless of the type of pension plan the employer has adopted. This applies to vesting (determining when the employee qualifies for a pension) and also to benefit computation (determining the amount of the employee's monthly pension payment).

Under the Soldiers' and Sailors' Civil Relief Act, creditors are required to drop interest charges down to 6 percent on debt owed by those called to active duty. Does this apply to a loan from my pension plan?

Yes. Under the Soldiers' and Sailors' Civil Relief Act (SSCRA), creditors, including a pension plan, are required to drop interest rates down to no more than 6 percent on debt owed by those entering military service for the period of such military service. Further, under the Employee Retirement Income Security Act (ERISA), the loan will not fail to be a qualified loan under ERISA solely because the interest rate is capped by SSCRA.

Exploring the Internet

For more information on USERRA, visit the USERRA Employee/Employer Advisor at www.dol.gov /elaws/aud_veteran.asp. The VETS Web site, www.dol .gov/vets/, has links to resources and services to help returning servicemen and women maximize their employment opportunities and protect their employment rights.

Sources: Adapted from "Reservists Being Called to Active Duty," U.S. Department of Labor, Pension and Welfare Benefits Administration, www.dol.gov /pwba/faqs/faq_911_2.html.

TABLE 19.1		
Sharon Dowd's Balance Sheet (End of Year Market Value)		

Assets

Checking account	$	500
Certificates of deposit		3,000
Life insurance cash values		4,500
401(k) retirement plan (vested value)		15,000
Automobile		10,000
House		85,000
Furniture and other personal property		10,000
Total		$ 128,000

Liabilities

Credit card balances	$	1,000
Other household account balances		500
Automobile loan balance		8,000
Life insurance loan against cash values		4,000
Home mortgage balance		75,000
Total		$ 88,500
Net Worth		$ 39,500

TABLE 19.2		
Sharon Dowd's Annual Cash Flow Statement		

Income

Sharon's salary	$	50,000
Investment income		*
Total cash flow		$ 50,000

Taxes

Social Security	$	3,825
Federal income		4,300
State income		1,700
Total SS and income taxes		$ 9,825
Disposable personal income		$ 40,175

Expenses

State sales taxes	$	1,300
Personal property taxes (home and auto)		1,175
401(k) retirement savings contribution		2,000
Dependent medical & dental insurance		1,500
House payments, including homeowner's insurance		8,900
Utilities		2,700
Food		3,200
Automobile payments and expenses		3,600
Child care		4,500
Clothes		1,800
Miscellaneous expenses		9,000
Total		$ 39,675
Savings	$	500

*Investment earnings of approximately $1,500 are being reinvested in the certificates of deposit and 401(k) plan.

Sharon's employee benefit plan at the bank provides her and the children with the benefits outlined in Table 19.3.

Individual Coverage

Sharon has a $15,000 whole life policy that her parents purchased when she was young and turned over to Sharon when she finished college. Sharon recently borrowed most of the policy's $4,500 cash value to help make the down payment on the family home. She purchased credit life insurance to cover the balance of her automobile loan. She has not purchased life or disability insurance associated with her home mortgage.

Personal Savings and Investments

At the present time, Sharon's personal savings and investments are small, consisting of $3,000 in certificates of deposit at her bank and a $15,000 vested value in her 401(k) plan.

TABLE 19.3
Sharon Dowd's Employee Benefits

Group Life Insurance

—Term insurance equal to two times annual salary for active employees.
—$5,000 term insurance for retirees.

Short-Term Disability

—Paid sick leave equal to income for ninety days.

Long-Term Disability

—Long-term disability (LTD) income to age 70 equal to two-thirds of annual salary in last year of employment, minus total Social Security and employer-provided pension benefits; 90-day waiting period; no adjustment for inflation.

Group Comprehensive Preferred Provider Medical Care

—$200 annual deductible per family member.
—90 percent coinsurance for preferred providers; 75 percent coinsurance for non-network providers.
—$1 million aggregate lifetime limit.
—Stop-loss provision after $1,000 out-of-pocket coinsurance expenses per person per year.
—Benefits terminate upon job termination or retirement.

Dental Coverage

—$50 per person annual deductible; no deductible on preventive care.
—80 percent coinsurance.
—$1,000 per person per year limit.
—$1,000 per person lifetime limit on orthodontic work.
—$50,000 aggregate family lifetime limit on other care.
—Benefits terminate upon job termination or retirement.

401(k) Plan

—Employer matches 50 percent of employee contributions up to a maximum employee contribution of 6 percent of basic pay, subject to the annual maximum limit on 401(k) contributions.

Defined-Benefit Pension Plan

—Pension at age 65 equal to 40 percent of average final three years salary, minus half of primary Social Security retirement benefit, with no provision for benefits to increase after retirement. Early retirement is allowed between ages 60 and 65, subject to a reduction in benefits. Reductions equal 4 percent for each year the retiree is below age 65.

Her yearly savings of $500 are 1 percent of her gross income. In addition, she is contributing 4 percent of gross income to her 401(k) plan and her employer matches 50 percent of this amount. If these savings rates can be continued over time and earn reasonable returns, her total savings and investments will grow quickly.

Objectives

In Case of Death

In the event of her premature death, Sharon would like her children to live with her sister, Kay, and Kay's husband, Robert, who have expressed willingness to assume these responsibilities. Sharon has not, however, formally created a legal document expressing this wish. Kay and Robert have three small children of their own, and Sharon would not want her children to be a financial burden to them. Taking care of her children's nonfinancial needs is all that Sharon expects from Kay and Robert.

Sharon's values influence her objectives. Her parents paid almost all her expenses, including upkeep of a car, while she earned a bachelor's degree. Sharon recognizes that her children are currently benefiting from her well-above-average income. When they reach college, she wants them to concentrate on their studies and enjoy extracurricular activities without having to work during the academic year. They would be expected to work during the summers to earn part of their spending money for school. Sharon decides that, if she dies prematurely, she wants to provide $12,000 per year before taxes for each child through age 17 when they will graduate from high school, both having been born in August. During their four years of college, Sharon wants $18,000 per year available for each child. She realizes that inflation can devastate a given level of income in only a few years. Thus, she wants her expressed objectives to be fulfilled in real (uninflated) dollars. We will present a simple planning solution to this problem.

Alternative Solutions/Exposure Evaluation

The next step in the financial planning process requires determining:

- The amount of money required to meet Sharon's objectives
- Any gaps that exist between what is desired and Sharon's current financial resources
- Alternatives available to fill the gaps

Money Required for Death

Determination of the amount of money required to meet Sharon's objectives for her children in the event of her premature death is complicated by the following:

- We do not know when Sharon will die.
- The family's income needs extend into the future possibly eighteen years (assuming Sharon dies now and income is provided until her younger child is age 22).
- Social Security will make its payments monthly over fourteen of the eighteen years.
- Sharon's two life insurance policies (and any new policies) would, most likely, make lump-sum payments at the time of her death, although her objective calls for the provision of support over many years.

- Lump sums may be liquidated over the period of income need, but we need to be sure the money does not run out before the period ends.
- The effects of inflation must be recognized.

Life Insurance Planning and Need Analysis

With some simplifying assumptions, these problems can be solved by a technique that we will call **life insurance planning.** The technique is static in the sense that it considers only the worst possible scenario: Sharon dies this year. Also, the technique does not recognize various changes (for example, remarriage and a third child) that could occur at some point during the planning period.

Figure 19.10 reflects the assumption that Sharon dies today by showing Liz's and Bob's current ages at the left, on the horizontal axis. The figure continues until Sharon's objectives are met when Bob is assumed to complete college at age 22.

The vertical axis of Figure 19.10 shows Sharon's real income objective of $12,000 per year per child prior to age 18. Sharon plans for much of this money to be spent by her sister and brother-in-law for her children's food, utilities, transportation, childcare, school expenses, and other basic needs. She does not plan for her children to have excessive amounts of spending money. During college, each child has $18,000 per year, which will provide financial access to modestly priced private colleges and out-of-state universities. The maximum annual need of $36,000 per year, depicted in Figure 19.10, occurs during the last two

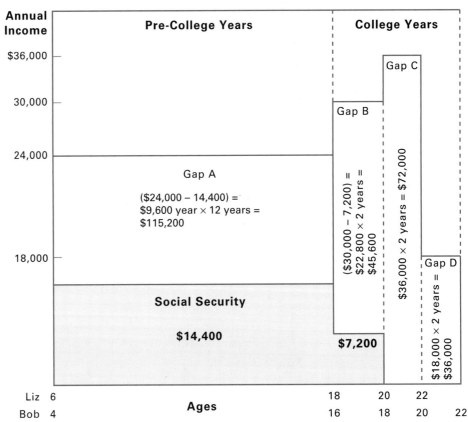

FIGURE 19.10

Family Income Objectives if Sharon Dies—Hypothetical Date (Social Security amounts are not actual)

Both the required amounts of income and Social Security benefits are shown in real (uninflated) dollars.

years of Liz's planned college period, when it is assumed that Bob also will have begun college. Social Security benefits begin at $14,400 and remain at this level (in real terms) until Liz's benefit terminates at age 18. Bob's benefit of $7,200 continues until he is 18.

Looking at the differences (gaps) between Sharon's objectives and the income expected from Social Security (see gaps A through D in Figure 19.10), we see an increase in the size of the gaps as Social Security payments decline and then stop as Bob's college years begin. The simplest way to summarize the amount of the gaps is to add the following:

($24,000 – 14,400) × (12 years) =	$115,200
($30,000 – 7,200) × (2 years) =	45,600
($36,000) × (2 years) =	72,000
($18,000) × (2 years) =	36,000
Total =	$268,800

This period while children remain dependent is called the **family dependency period.** A subsequent period during which support might be provided to a spouse is not depicted since Sharon is not married. Such a period may be called a **spousal dependency period.**

What are the problems with saying $268,800 is needed to fulfill Sharon's objectives, assuming she dies now? Reviewing our list of seven complications, we can recognize two major problems. First, inflation is likely to increase her nominal (inflated dollar) needs. Current Social Security legislation provides for annual benefit increases to reflect the lesser of inflation or wage increases over time. Thus, we can assume that real-dollar Social Security benefits will increase approximately at the rate of inflation. Our concern becomes the effect of inflation on the gap between total income needs and Social Security. In the first year, we know this gap is $9,600. If there is 4 percent inflation, the gap in nominal dollars would be $13,664 by the beginning of the tenth year and $64,834 by the beginning of the sixteenth year, the second year when both Liz and Bob are expected to be in college. Our $268,800 total understates the nominal dollar need substantially.

Second, we have ignored the opportunity to invest the lump-sum insurance benefits (existing and yet-to-be-purchased) and net worth. With such an opportunity, investment earnings would provide part of the future cash flow needs. Unlike the possibility of inflation, the failure to recognize this time value of money overstates the size of the gaps.

Sharon may use the $268,800 figure depicted in Figure 19.10 if she is willing to assume that the net return on investments will be just sufficient to cover the rate of expected inflation. This is not an unrealistic assumption for the conservative investor who would make "low-to-medium risk/low-to-medium expected return" investments. Relatively conservative investments may be suitable where the purpose is safety of principal in the interest of supporting two children, following the death of their sole financial support (other than Social Security). The static life insurance planning technique produces approximate, rather than exact, estimates of death needs.

At this point, we have only estimated Sharon's gross death needs for the family dependency period.

Total Needs

Total death needs for most situations can be grouped into four categories:

- Final expenses
- Family dependency period
- Spousal dependency period
- Special needs

We have looked only at the family dependency period. To complete Sharon's financial planning for death, assume that her **final expenses** consist of funeral costs of $4,500, $1,500 to pay her current bills, and $3,000 for an executor to settle her estate. Nothing is required to fund a spousal dependency period in Sharon's case. The **special needs** category could include college expenses that we have placed in the family dependency period, care of a dependent parent, or other expenses that do not fit neatly in the other three categories.

Sharon's total needs above Social Security are

Final expenses	$ 9,000
Family dependency period	268,800
Total needs	$277,800

Net Needs

Life insurance is a substitute for other assets that for one reason or another, at the current time, have not been accumulated. Thus, the need for new life insurance as a result of the life insurance planning process consists of:

Net Needs = Gross Death Needs − Resources

Consideration of Existing Resources

Are Sharon's current net worth and life insurance adequate to meet her objectives if she dies now? From the balance sheet provided earlier, we know that she has a net worth of $39,500.[13] This is a liquidation value that is net of sales commissions, depreciation, and other value-reducing factors. Her current life insurance consists of a $100,000 term policy through her employer and a $15,000 individual policy. The proceeds from the individual policy will be $11,000 after the insurer deducts the $4,000 loan. Her automobile loan will be paid by credit life insurance. We show this loan repayment below as a life insurance resource. Sharon's net needs after recognizing existing resources are:

Total needs		$277,800
Resources (minus):		
Net worth	$ 39,500	
Group life insurance	100,000	
Individual life insurance	11,000	
Credit life insurance	8,000	158,500
Net needs		$119,300

Solutions

Sharon could resolve this $119,300 shortage in one of three ways. First, she could reevaluate her objectives, decide to lower the amount of financial support for Liz and Bob, and calculate a lower total. Second, she could decide to tighten her budget and increase her savings/investment program. Third, she could buy an additional life insurance policy in the amount of, let's say, $125,000. Life insurance premiums would vary upward from approximately $175 for next year for an annual renewable term policy to higher amounts for other types of insurance. Buying additional life insurance is probably Sharon's best option. Savings as an alternative to life insurance is not a good solution because she could die before contributing much to her savings program. Nevertheless, she should continue to save.

Other Life Insurance Planning Issues

Sharon's situation certainly does not cover all planning possibilities. For example, a person with a disabled child might want to extend the family dependency period far beyond age 22. Another person might want to contribute to a spouse's support for the remainder of his or her life. In this case, a good option is using the life insurance planning technique to quantify the need up to an advanced age, such as 65, and getting price quotations on a life annuity for the remainder of the person's lifetime.

ESTATE PLANNING

Estate planning is the process of arranging for the conservation and transfer of property—the estate—to heirs upon death. The basic tools are wills, trusts, life insurance, and gifts. When the estate holder dies, the estate is settled in accordance with the provisions of a will or, if there is no will, in accordance with the state's "laws of descent and distribution." The settlement process, called **probate,** is carried out by an **executor** or **administrator** under the supervision of a probate court judge.[14] The executor is named in the will, but when there is no will or the person named as executor cannot serve, the court appoints an administrator to assist with probate. The functions of an executor or administrator are to assemble the assets, pay all the debts and taxes, and make proper distribution of the remaining property. The executor or administrator may hire an attorney to do the paperwork, provide guidance on complicated matters, obtain court approval of potentially questionable actions, and prepare final reports to the probate court and the United States Internal Revenue Service.

Objectives

The estate planning process holds several objectives:

- Conserve property values between the time of death and transfer to heirs.
- Transfer property to certain persons or entities in accordance with wishes.
- Assure that heirs who are dependents receive the advice and help.
- Accomplish the transfer with minimum administration and legal fees.
- Keep taxes at a minimum, consistent with the achievement of other objectives.

Wills

The major reason to have a will is to assure that the estate will be distributed in accordance with the deceased's wishes. A valid will must usually be in writing, signed by the **testator** (the person for whom the will is written) while mentally competent, and signed by two or more witnesses. Requirements vary by state, resulting in the need to revise the will when moving from one state to another. Someone who dies without a will is said to have died **intestate.** In such a case, the estate is distributed in accordance with the laws of the state in which the deceased was a resident. If the deceased was married with two or more children, many states would provide that one-third of the estate go to the spouse and two-thirds be distributed to the children. If the deceased was married with no children, one half might go to the spouse and the remainder to the parents and siblings. The state's division, in the condition of intestacy, might be quite different from the deceased's wishes. Further, dying intestate might reduce marital deduction and thereby increase estate taxes.

A frequently overlooked complication to dying intestate involves minor beneficiaries. It may be difficult for the surviving spouse to manage property inherited by minor children. Unless he or she is the **guardian** of the child's estate, which does not occur automatically, a sale of such property may be impossible.

Trusts

Suppose you were given $100,000 and asked to invest it and give the income to the giver's daughter. As holder of the property, you are the **trustee.** A trustee is obligated to administer the trust in accordance with the terms of the trust agreement. Often, the **trust agreement** (that is, the legal document) gives the trustee discretionary power to use both income and principal solely for the needs of the trust beneficiary or beneficiaries. The person giving the property is called the **grantor, donor, trustor, settlor,** or **creator** of the trust. The daughter, as recipient of the income earned under your management, is the **beneficiary.** The property (money) is the corpus of the trust. The arrangement between the trustor and trustee is known as a **trust.**

Testamentary Trust

The most widely used trusts are **testamentary trusts.** They are part of a will and become effective after the death of the testator. For example, a testamentary trust can be created in a will to handle the problem previously mentioned in connection with minor beneficiaries. People who want to leave property to their children but want their spouse to manage it can create a testamentary trust and designate the spouse as trustee, or the spouse and a bank as co-trustees. The trustee or co-trustees would have whatever authority the creator granted in the provisions of the trust.

In the Dowd family case, Sharon should consider creating a testamentary trust with her children as beneficiaries. A big decision for Sharon would be who to name as trustee. Logical options include: her sister Kay and brother-in-law Robert as co-trustees, Kay alone, Robert alone, Kay and/or Robert and a bank or trust company as co-trustees, and a bank as the sole trustee. If a bank is named, it appoints a bank employee, usually with the title of "trust officer," to see that the wishes of the trust creator are carried out. Sharon obviously thinks Kay and Robert have good judgment or she would not have appointed them guardians of her children. If one or both are named trustees without the involvement of a bank, they must be capable of prudent investment decisions with respect to large sums of money. They may or may not have this financial knowledge. Banks or trust companies are often made trustee or co-trustee because of their expertise in the management of the trust. When the major trust asset is life insurance proceeds (as in the Dowd case), the trust is called an insurance trust. The trust would be named as beneficiary of any policy proceeds that the grantor wants as part of the trust.

Living Trust

A **living trust** is a legal document that holds title or ownership to real property and assets. The creator of the trust transfers ownership of assets to the trust, but is still in full control of all assets or property in the trust. Like a will, a trust contains instructions for disposition of the creator's estate after death. However, a trust does not go through probate, which reduces administrative and legal costs.

Another advantage of a living trust is that trust income and assets are just as readily available after the creator's death as they were before. In contrast, income and assets of an estate may be temporarily unavailable while the probate process grinds along at what may be a snail's pace. If a spouse has to ask the court to approve a partial distribution or special living allowance during probate in order to have money to live on, that request adds to legal costs and, sometimes, causes further delay in settling the estate.

Life Insurance

Upon a person's death, taxes, administrative costs, mortgages, and all bills must be paid before the remainder of the estate is transferred to heirs. If estate assets have to be sold to meet these obligations, the amount available for the heirs is reduced. Furthermore, it may be difficult to sell certain assets for their true worth, especially if business assets or real estate are involved. Additional life insurance (above that needed to continue income) can be purchased to pay these obligations and protect the estate.

When the estate is large enough to be subject to estate taxes (more than $1 million in 2003, increasing half a million each year to $3.5 million by 2009 with sunset provisions after ten years as explained in Chapter 18 pursuant to EGTRRA, 2001), the proceeds of life insurance policies on the policyowner's life will be included in the estate for tax purposes, regardless of how the beneficiary is named, as long as the insured is also the owner of the policies when he or she died. When taxes are a factor, it is advisable to consider having the policies owned by an irrevocable living trust or another person. Thus, in considering the ways to handle life insurance, the needs the policies are designed to meet are critical to the coverage and contractual design. At a minimum, it is important that the executor has sufficient liquidity to pay debts, taxes, and other administrative costs without selling assets at prices that may be depreciated during the relatively short period available for estate settlement.

In calculating federal estate taxes, the deceased is given an unlimited marital deduction. This means that any amount passing to a spouse escapes taxation. This may, however, simply defer the tax problem until the death of the spouse (assuming he or she has not remarried and has not consumed or given away assets). A couple may want to avoid the liquidation of a family business, real estate, or other illiquid assets on short notice by having life insurance provide the necessary estate settlement costs. Since insurance proceeds to cover estate taxes are needed only at the death of the second of the two spouses, the preferred policy may be **second-to-die life insurance,** which pays the death benefits only after the death of the second spouse. When the first spouse dies there is no payment.[15]

KEY TERMS

life annuity	single premium	life annuity
owner	immediate annuity	temporary life annuity
annuitant	deferred annuity	period-certain option
beneficiary	fixed dollar annuity	refund annuity
accumulation period	variable annuity	joint annuity
accumulation value	single life annuity	joint-and-survivor annuity
liquidation period	fixed period annuity	flexible premium deferred
installment plan	fixed amount annuity	annuity

single premium deferred annuity	long-term disability (LTD) policies	probate
single premium immediate annuity	elimination period	executor/administrator
structured settlement annuity	social insurance substitute	testator
	average earnings provision	intestate
separate accounts	long-term care (LTC) insurance	guardian
accumulation units	LTC-annuity	trustee
annuity units	Medigap insurance	trust agreement
exclusion ratio	life insurance planning	grantor/donor/trustor/ settlor/creator
disability income insurance	family dependency period	beneficiary
total disability	spousal dependency period	trust
partial disability	final expenses	testamentary trust
short-term disability (STD) policies	special needs	living trust
	estate planning	second-to-die life insurance

DISCUSSION QUESTIONS

1. Why do you suppose the flexible premium annuity is the most popular form of deferred annuity?

2. Who assumes the investment risk in variable annuities? Does the same party assume mortality and operating expense risk?

3. What is the primary way in which a single premium deferred annuity differs from a flexible premium deferred annuity? How might the typical motivations for purchase differ for investors in these two types of annuities?

4. Compare variable annuities with index annuities.

5. How do individual and group medical insurance policies differ regarding maternity benefits?

6. Compare the benefits of the 22-year-old female student to that of the 22-year-old male student featured in Figures 19.4 and 19.5. Which policy would you choose?

7. What types of services are covered by dental insurance contracts? Why are individuals given first-dollar coverage for some services but not for others? Evaluate the dental policy featured in Figure 19.7. Would you buy it?

8. Would someone with Social Security, workers' compensation, and an employer-provided group disability plan have any reason to purchase disability insurance in the individual market? Please explain.

9. What is meant by the statement: "The benefits of a disability income policy are no better than the definition of disability"?

10. Describe the nature of cancer or critical illness insurance policies.

11. What are individual long-term care policies? Why are they needed?

12. What is LTC-annuity?

13. If custodial care is the least expensive type of service covered by long-term care insurance, is it important to make sure your contract covers this type of care?

14. What are Medicare Supplement (Medigap) policies? Why are they needed?

15. Describe how family cash flow is changed by the death or total, permanent disability of a major income producer. Why is an investment program not a workable solution to these potential cash flow problems?

16. Explain how life insurance, Social Security survivor benefits, and family net worth are complements and substitutes for each other.

17. With respect to life insurance planning, discuss several factors that complicate the determination of the amount of life insurance needed by a family.

18. Why is it important for most adults to have a will? What does it mean to die intestate? Can this influence the size of one's marital deduction in the calculation of federal estate taxes?

19. Distinguish between living and testamentary trusts.

20. What role can life insurance play in estate planning for wealthy people?

EXERCISES

19.1 Mrs. Abigail Dozier, age 66, is asking your advice about how to use a lump-sum distribution of $500,000 she expects in three months from her employer's money purchase retirement plan. She is single, has no close relatives, lives in a rented condominium, and has nonretirement certificates of deposit valued at $75,000. She wants to leave, at her death, the balance of her nonretirement fund assets to Bard College, her alma mater. She hopes the balance will be substantially more than the current $75,000 value. In addition to Social Security benefits, her lifestyle, including travel and treatment of a chronic (non-life-threatening) health problem, will require liquidation of approximately 90 percent of the $500,000 lump-sum distribution over her twenty-year life expectancy.

   a. What financial instrument is designed to keep Mrs. Dozier (and others) from being without income because of having lived beyond the time a principal sum is liquidated by periodic withdrawals that include principal?

   b. Help Mrs. Dozier decide between fixed dollar and variable annuities, or a combination of the two.

19.2 Diana Antonopolos, your friend from high school, is trying to determine the best health insurance policy to buy. She has offers for a cancer policy with a low premium, a major medical policy with a higher premium, and a PPO policy with a premium that falls midway between the other two. All policies are noncancelable until age 65.

   a. Discuss the major features that will affect Diana's decision. Explain what you would look for, and why.

   b. If you were to buy only one policy and had a limited—but adequate—budget, which product would you choose?

19.3 Talitha Byrd has a long-term disability income insurance contract and is disabled. After the sixty-day waiting period, she begins receiving the $1,200 per month in benefits. Although this is less than her pre-disability income of $2,000 per month, she is able to get along quite nicely. Even though she is not eligible for Social Security disability benefits, after two years the insurer tells her that it is stopping payment under the contract.

   a. Why might the insurer stop payment after two years?

   b. What might Talitha do to receive payments again?

   c. How could she have prevented this problem when she was selecting a disability income policy?

19.4 Darnell Walker's mother is surprised when he tells her she may want to look into buying an individual long-term care contract. She is 71 years old and already has Medicare coverage.

    a.   Does Medicare pay for long-term care?

    b.   What types of services should she make sure are covered by the policy? What policy provisions may be important for her?

    c.   Darnell is 50 years old. The long-term care premium at his age is low. Do you think he should buy it now while it is inexpensive?

19.5 Bill Masters, age 55, has accumulated a sizable estate. Included are a $250,000 home, with only $20,000 in unpaid mortgage balance; his personally owned business, which has assets of $4 million and liabilities of $2.5 million; a common stock portfolio with a market value of $1.5 million; and $250,000 of personally owned life insurance. He has a wife, Jane, age 53, and three children, all of whom are married college graduates.

    a.   Why should Bill plan his estate?

    b.   Is there any reason to consider additional life insurance in this plan?

NOTES

1. Linda Koco, "1st Half Index Annuity Sales Hit New Record of Nearly $5 Billion" *National Underwriter*, Life & Health/Financial Services Edition, 16 September 2002.
2. Linda Koco, "Critical Illness Insurance: Real or Gimmick?" *National Underwriter* Life & Health/Financial Services Edition, 1 January 2002.
3. Patrick D. Lusk, "Critical Illness Insurance Ideal for Worksite," *National Underwriter* Life & Health/Financial Services Edition, 31 August 1998.
4. IEEE Financial Advantage Program, Insurance Articles of Interest at: www.ieeeinsurance.com/articles/artlcei.asp.
5. Allison Bell, "Individual Disability Sales Were Up 11% Last Year" *National Underwriter*, Life & Health/Financial Services Edition, 24 June 2002.
6. AARP, http://research.aarp.org/health/fs7r99_long_term.html.
7. Cheryl McNamara and Mary Madigan, "Insuring an Independent Lifestyle," *Best's Review*, 1 April 2002.
8. Claude Thau, "Surveying Industry Practices On Changes To In-Force LTCI Policies," *National Underwriter* Life & Health/Financial Services Edition, 29 March 2002.
9. Craig R. Springfield and Chelsea K. Bachrach, "LTC-Annuities: Two Birds, One Stone," *National Underwriter* Life & Health/Financial Services Edition, 2 September 2002.
10. Cary Lakenbach, "Traditional Life: A Chassis For LTC Riders," *National Underwriter* Life & Health/Financial Services Edition, 13 September 1999.
11. Cary Lakenbach, "Integrated VL/LTCs Pose Some Challenges," *National Underwriter* Life & Health/Financial Services Edition, 21 February 2000.
12. For examples, see the Texas Department of Insurance's Web site at www.tdi.state.tx.us/index.html; the North Dakota Department of Insurance's Web site at www.state.nd.us/ndins//consinfo/medicare.html; or the Nebraska Department of Insurance's Web site at www.state.ne.us/home/NDOI/nica/medsup/med-supin.htm. Details are also provided at the AARP's site at www.aarp.org/hcchoices/medicare/supplement/home.html.
13. It is feasible that all furniture, jewelry, and so on would be liquidated. In a two-parent family, the surviving spouse might want to retain the house and all furnishings.
14. In some states the person who settles the estate is called the "personal representative," irrespective of whether there is a will.
15. The use of a buy-sell agreement, often funded by life insurance, to avoid liquidation of a small business is not discussed in this text. For those interested, please refer to higher level estate-planning resources.

The Smith Family's Insurance Portfolio

PREFACE

The purpose of this project is to build a portfolio of risk management and insurance coverages for a hypothetical family. This report is typical of those produced by students as a group project in the author's risk and insurance classes. The students present sections of the coverages throughout the semester and the complete project at the end of the semester as part of their final grade. The students "live" the project during the semester and provide creativity, along with hands-on knowledge and information, about the best risk management for their "created" families. Many groups develop special relationships with helpful agents who volunteer to speak to the class. The help agents provide can be immeasurable to the students.

This report, as all the others produced by the students, considers property, auto, disability, life, health, and long-term-care insurance, as well as retirement planning. The group project presented here does not involve the agent-customer relationship. Many other reports do include the relationship as a reason to buy from a specific company.

INTRODUCTION

We[1] examined different types of insurance and selected the best coverage for our hypothetical family—the Smith family. Several insurance quotes were found through the Internet and others were from the benefits package offered by Virginia Power. We also talked to some agents.

FAMILY DESCRIPTION

John is a thirty-five-year-old nuclear engineer who has been working for Virginia Power since 1990. His wife, Karen, is a thirty-year-old homemaker. They have been married for five years. John and Karen have a nine-month-old infant named Tristian. John and Karen are in good health. They are looking forward to having another child, but Karen is likely to have a high risk pregnancy. This must be taken into consideration when selecting health insurance coverage for this family. Their annual net income is $72,000 (John's salary of $100,000, less taxes and other deductions). They have two cars. John drives a 1996 Toyota Corolla and Karen drives a 1997 Toyota Camry. They need good insurance coverage since John is the only one who is working. All of the insurance providers examined have an "A" or better rating from AM Best and Standard and Poor (S&P) ratings.

INSURANCE COVERAGE

Homeowners Insurance

John and Karen purchased a two-story single-family home for $150,000 in 1996. The house is located on 7313 Pineleaf Drive in Richmond, Virginia. The total footage is 2,014 sq. ft. There is a two-car attached garage. John and Karen decided not to renew their homeowner's insurance with AllState Insurance because of the high premium and unacceptable customer service they received in the past. John did research on the Internet and found quotes from different companies. He was asked to give detailed information on the house. The house is located within 1,000 feet of a fire hydrant and is four blocks from a fire station. John promised to install a security system to prevent theft. Karen wanted extra protection on her precious jewelry worth $10,000, Ming china worth $5,000, and antique paintings valued at $7,000. They needed to have scheduled personal property endorsements. Over the last five years, John and Karen's house has appreciated by $10,000. They wanted to insure the home to 100% of its estimated replacement cost, which is $160,000, rather than 80%. In case of a total loss, the insurer will replace the home exactly as it was before the loss took place, even if the replacement exceeds the amount of insurance stated in the policy. Table C1.1 summarizes the coverage offered by three insurance companies.

The Smith family decided to choose the insurance coverage provided by Travelers' Insurance Company because of its good rating and low premium, and a water-back coverage. Under this HO 3 (special form), dwelling and other structures are covered against risk of direct loss to property. All losses are covered except certain losses that are specifically excluded.

Auto Insurance

John drives a 1996 Toyota Corolla, which he purchased new for $18,109. He has had one accident in the past four years in which he was hit by another driver. This estimated driving mileage within a year is 10,000 miles. He drives 190 miles weekly to work. His car is not used for business purposes. Karen bought a new Toyota Camry in 1997 for $20,109. She has never had an accident. Her estimated mileage within a year is 7,500 miles and her weekly driving is 100 miles.

The Smiths used the Internet and found several quotes from various insurance companies that fit their needs. Table C1.2 summarizes the results of their research. Their premiums are not the preferred rate.

The Smith family decided to choose the insurance coverage provided by Harford Insurance Company. Harford has an A+ rating, the coverage is more comprehensive and the premium is significantly lower than the other two companies.

Loss Scenario #1

John has had this auto insurance for almost six months. On the way to a business meeting one day, he is hit by an uninsured motorist. John's car is badly damaged and he is rushed to the emergency room. Luckily, John has only minor cuts and bruises. John reports this accident to the police and notifies his insurer. The insurance company inspects and appraises the wrecked car. The Smiths' uninsured motorist's coverage covers John's medical expenses (under bodily injury) and property damages caused by the accident. Harford Insurance considers John's car a total loss and pays him $14,000 (fair market value less the deductible).

Long-Term Disability

The Smith family decided to purchase long-term disability (LTD) insurance for John because he is the only breadwinner in the family. In the event of an accident that would disable John and leave him unable to work, the family would need adequate coverage of all their expenses. The LTD benefit provided by John's employer, Virginia Power, would pay 50% of John's salary, up to $2,000 per month, in case of his total disability; however, the family would like to have more coverage.

TransAmerica, an insurance broker that prepares coverage for Erie and Prudential Life, prepared two plans for the Smiths as shown in Table C1.3. Both plans provided benefits to age sixty-five with a ninety-day waiting period. Both plans offer the same level of optional benefits, including residual disability and an inflation rider.

The Smith family chose additional disability coverage provided by Erie because of the lower premium, lower residual disability cost, and lower inflation rider cost.

TABLE C1.1   Homeowners Insurance Plan Options (Year = 2000)

	Geico	Travelers	Nationwide
Coverage A: Dwelling Replacement	$ 160,000.00	$ 160,000.00	$ 160,000.00
Coverage B: Other Structures	16,000.00	16,000.00	16,000.00
Coverage C: Personal Property	112,000.00	112,000.00	112,000.00
Coverage D: Loss of Use	48,000.00	48,000.00	48,000.00
Coverage E: Personal Liability	300,000.00	300,000.00	300,000.00
Coverage F: Guest Medical	2,000.00	2,000.00	2,000.00
Deductible	500.00	250.00	500.00
Endorsements for Collectibles and Inflation Guard	Yes	Yes	Yes
Annual Premium	568.00	512.00	560.00
S&P Rating	AAA	AA	AA-

TABLE C1.2	Auto Insurance Plan Options (Year = 2000)		
Companies	**Harford**	**Integon Indemnity**	**Dairyland**
A.M. Best Rating	A+	A+	AA+
Liability	100000/300000/100000	100000/300000/100000	100000/300000/100000
Medical Payments	$5000	$5000	$5000
Uninsured/Underinsured Motorist	100000/300000/100000	100000/300000/100000	100000/300000/100000
Collision	$250 Deductible	$250 Deductible	$250 Deductible
Other than Collision	$500 Deductible	$500 Deductible	$500 Deductible
Monthly Premium	$160	$210	$295

Life Insurance

The Smith family realized they needed to invest in additional term life insurance for John (they were not ready to invest in permanent level life insurance) since his employer provided only group term life coverage in the amount of one time his salary, $100,000. They did not need to worry about life insurance for Karen since her parents bought a 10-year level term coverage in the amount of $250,000 on Karen's life when Tristian was born. They told Karen that an untimely death would mean an economic loss to the family, as John would likely have to hire help for housekeeping and childcare.

As noted earlier, John is thirty-five years old and in very good health. He enjoys working out at the gym after work at least three times a week and has never been a smoker. John's family history shows no serious health problems, and most relatives have lived well into their seventies.

In order to decide how much life insurance is needed for John, he and Karen worked on a need analysis with some friends who are familiar with financial planning. They came to the conclusion that he will need to purchase $300,000 of additional coverage. A breakdown of why they believe they need this amount of coverage can be seen in Table C1.4.

TABLE C1.3	Long-Term Disability Plan Options (Year = 2000)	
	Erie	**Prudential**
Benefit Period	To age 65	To age 65
Waiting Period	90 Days	90 Days
Monthly Benefit	$2,917.00	$3,700
Base Annual Premium	$1,003.49	$1,262.10
Total Annual Premium	$1,414.88	$1,783.92
Optional Benefits		
Residual Disability	$183.25	$232.43
Inflation Rider	$228.14	$289.38

Virginia Power offers additional life insurance that their employees can purchase through North American Life. The Smiths wanted to compare prices of additional coverage, so they looked on the Web. They found Western-Southern Life and John Hancock plans to fit their budget and their needs. The three plans are compared in Table C1.5.

The Smith family decided to go with Western-Southern Life because of its higher rating, low premiums, and guaranteed initial rate for twenty years. John

TABLE C1.4	Need Analysis for Life Insurance	
Cash needs		
Funeral expenses	$12,000	
Probating will and attorney fees	3,000	
Income needs		
To get Karen and Tristian on their feet	192,000	($4,000 monthly for four years*)
Special needs		
Balance on mortgage and Karen's car loan	120,000	
College fund for Tristian	50,000	
Emergency fund	75,000	
Total family needs		**$452,000**
Current financial assets		
Savings balance	$20,000	
401(k) current balance	32,000	
Group term insurance	100,000	
Total current financial assets		**$152,000**
Additional coverage needed		**$300,000**

* They assume that Karen will adjust their standard of living to her own income after four years.

TABLE C1.5	Life Insurance Plan Options (Year = 2000)		
	North American (VA Power)	**Western-Southern Life**	**John Hancock**
Amount	$300,000	$300,000	$300,000
Term Period	20 years	20 years	20 years
Initial Monthly Premium	$21.00	$19.95	$18.50
Initial Rate Guarantee	5 years	20 years	20 years
S&P Rating	AA	AAA	AA+

will have to prove his insurability when he purchases the coverage (unlike the group life coverage provided by the employer). This is not a big issue to John as he is in excellent health.

Health Insurance

Virginia Power offers its employees two PPO (preferred provider organization) options and one HMO (health maintenance organization) option. The Smith family decided to choose one of the PPO plans as opposed to an HMO plan because Karen and John are planning to have another child and, considering her high-risk status, prefer to have more choices and an out-of-network option

if necessary. They also like the dental coverage that is included in Medical Plan 1 (shown in Table C1.6).

A PPO is a network of health care providers who have agreed to accept a lower fee for their services. A PPO plan gives the flexibility to select a network provider without having to select a primary care physician to coordinate care, or to go out-of-network with higher cost. All of Virginia Power's benefit coverages are provided by Trigon Blue Cross Blue Shield Company of Virginia with an A.M. Best rating of A++. Employees of Virginia Power and their family members are covered on the date of employment. In-network participants must receive preventative care benefits from PPO providers. Participants who live outside the network's

TABLE C1.6	Health Insurance Plan Options	
Feature	**Medical Plan 1**	**Medical Plan 2**
	In-Network/Out-of Network	**In-Network/Out-of Network**
Annual Deductible	$572	$1,146
Monthly Premiums (employee's portion for the whole family)	$91.41	$41.13
Out-of-Pocket Maximum	$2,288/4,004	$4,584/8,022
Lifetime Maximum Benefits	Unlimited	$1,000,000
Participant Coinsurance	20%/40%	20%/40%
Preventative Care	100% after $10 co-pay for generalist; $20 co-pay for Specialist	
Prescription Drugs		
Deductible	None	None
Participant Coinsurance	20%	20%
Out-of-Pocket Maximum	$700	$700
Out-Patient Mental Health	After deductible, next 20% of $500 of expenses, then 50% of the balance for the remainder of the plan year; no out-of-pocket maximum	
In-Patient Mental Health	Up to 30 days per person per year; 60 days maximum per person per lifetime for substance abuse	
Chiropractic	Maximum benefits $500 per person per year	
Dental	Up to 2 cleanings per year; 50% co-insurance on all procedures with $200 deductible; maximum annual benefits, $4,500	None

geographic area may receive these services from PPO and non-PPO providers. Table C1.6 compares the benefits and cost of the two PPO options.

The Smith family chose Medical Plan 1 because of the lower deductible and lower out-of-pocket maximum, the unlimited lifetime maximum benefit, and the dental coverage.

Health premiums are paid on a pre-tax basis into a Premium Conversion Plan. Even though the employer offers a Flexible Spending Account, the Smiths decided not to use it since they do not have day care needs for Tristian and they are usually in very good health.

Loss Example #2

While vacationing with his family in Orlando, Florida, John keeps up his routine jogs. On the third day of the vacation John suffers chest pains while running and collapses. John is rushed by ambulance to a nearby hospital where he is diagnosed with a bronchial infection. X-rays and lab work total $300. The family pays 20 percent of the bill since they had met their deductible for the year. Their total out-of-pocket expenses for the visit are $60. Though disappointed that he can't jog for a week or two, John is thankful that, even out of state, he is able to have expert medical care and return to his family to enjoy the remainder of his vacation.

Long-Term Care

John and Karen are very young, so they do not perceive the need for investing in long-term care. Virginia Power doesn't offer this plan. However, John has heard rumors that long-term care might be offered next year. If Virginia Power offers long-term care next year, John will consider participating in it.

Retirement

The Smiths decided to invest in the 401(k) plan offered by Virginia Power. Virginia Power will match contributions 50 percent. John chose to invest $240 monthly; added to Virginia Power's 50 percent match of $120, the monthly total is $360. The contributions are invested in two mutual funds, one is a growth fund and the other a conservative fund. John's 401(k) current balance is $32,000 and he hopes he will be able to invest it smartly. When he is fifty-nine and a half he can begin withdrawing his retirement benefits if he wishes without the 10 percent penalty.

ANNUAL BUDGET AND NET ASSETS

Tables C1.7 and C1.8 depict the Smith family's finances. Figure C1.1 shows the costs of insurance premiums in reference to the Smiths' income.

CONCLUSION

With the help from all group members, the Smith family is able to choose the best coverage they can get from various insurance plans. Their homeowners insurance is provided by Travelers Insurance Company; their auto is covered by Harford Insurance Company. They bought additional life insurance from Western–Southern Life

TABLE C1.7	Smith Family Income Statement	
Monthly salary after taxes		$6,000
Mortgage and car payment	$1,900	
Utilities	350	
Homeowners insurance	42.67	
Car insurance	160	
Life insurance	19.95	
Health insurance	91.41*	
401(k) plan	240	
Disability insurance	117.91	
Baby needs	300	
Groceries	500	
College fund	100	
Entertainment	400	
Other expenses	200	
Possible expenses	800	
Potential savings	778.07	
Total		$6,000

* Health premiums are paid on a pre-tax basis into a Premium Conversion plan

TABLE C1.8	Smith Family Net Worth
Assets	
Savings	$ 20,000
401(k) current balance	32,000
House	160,000
Collectibles	22,000
Total assets	**234,000**
Liability	
Mortgage and car loans payable	120,000
Net assets	**114,000**

FIGURE C1.1 Insurance Premium Allocator

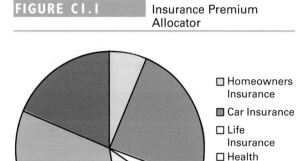

- □ Homeowners Insurance
- ◼ Car Insurance
- □ Life Insurance
- □ Health Insurance
- ◻ 401(K)
- ◼ Disability Insurance

Company and additional long-term disability from Erie. Virginia Power provides good health care coverage, term life insurance, a 401(k) retirement plan, and long-term disability. The Smith family chose insurance plans that best fit their needs.

NOTES

1. This project was prepared by Kristy L. Blankenship, Crystal Jones, Jason C. Lemley, and Fei W. Turner, students in the author's Fall 2000 class in risk and insurance. Many other groups also prepared excellent projects, which are available upon request from the author.

CASE **2**

Galaxy Max Employee Benefits

PREFACE

As it was in Case 1, this case is a group project that is part of employee benefits classes taught by the author of this textbook. The case presented here is a typical project that lives with the students throughout the semester. The students present portions of the case as the material is covered in class. In most cases, the whole employee benefits portfolio of the hypothetical company created by the students is presented at the conclusion of the semester as part of the final grade.[1] Following is the employee benefits portfolio of a compilation of the ten groups of the Fall 2002 class (and some of the Fall 2000),[2] in the words of the students.[3]

WELCOME, GALAXY MAX EMPLOYEES

The Board of Directors and the corporate executives of Galaxy Max, Inc., have developed a comprehensive benefits package to meet the needs of our employees and their families. This handbook includes a brief overview of the organization and its structure and a detailed description of benefits related to group life and disability insurance, health care, dental and vision coverage, flexible spending account, and retirement benefits. The information provided will enable you to understand your benefits. General information may be secured from the Company's Web site, www.galaxymax.com. Additional questions may be addressed to the Human Resources Department, 7500 Galaxy Max Road, Richmond, VA 23228; telephone (800) 674-2900; e-mail hrgalaxymax@vcu.edu. Suggestions are always welcome as we continue to improve services.

DESCRIPTION OF THE COMPANY

Background and Current Information

- Galaxy Max, Inc., is a multimillion-dollar business equipment retail chain established in 1985 to service the needs of companies and consumers.
- The company specializes in direct sales and e-commerce of office equipment, business accessories, and computer hardware and software and provides technical support for all facets of the industry involved in maintaining the business environment. The company plans to expand its service capabilities throughout the global marketplace.
- The corporation is headquartered in the city of Richmond and has one retail outlet and two regional stores in northern Virginia and the Tidewater area. (See Figure C2.1.)

Employee Description

Galaxy Max employs 758 staff members: 338 full-time salaried and 420 hourly employees. Our rapid growth in size and value allows us to provide a substantial benefit package to full-time employees.

Employee Benefits

Galaxy Max has developed a competitive and comprehensive benefits package for our employees because we value their service to the organization and want to maintain a healthy, motivated, and high-quality staff. Our commitment to employees is to support their personal needs and financial goals and to reward dedicated individuals. The benefits package is shown in Table C2.1.

Mission Statement

Galaxy Max is committed to providing superior customer satisfaction in administering sales and service to consumers while maintaining competitive prices, quality products, and active growth within the international business community. We strive for technological advancement, excellence in the delivery of services, and promoting partnerships.

PART I: GROUP INSURANCE BENEFITS

Life Insurance

Galaxy Max provides you with basic life insurance at one times your annual base pay (1 × annual salary), at

FIGURE C2.1 Organizational Structure

no cost to you. Benefits are rounded to the next higher $1,000. The minimum benefit is $5,000. You may purchase supplemental coverage. The maximum benefit is five times your current annual base pay or $1,000,000, whichever is less. Table C2.2 outlines the main features of the company's life insurance plan. The cost of supplemental life insurance coverage is shown in Table C2.3.

Beneficiary

The employee names the beneficiary. It cannot be the employer.

Termination

Coverage shall terminate automatically when any of the following conditions exist:

- The employee terminates employment.
- The employee ceases to be eligible.
- The policyholder terminates the master contract.
- The insurer terminates the master contract.
- Contributions have not been made.

Important Features of Your Life Insurance Plans

- Waiver of the payment of your premium if you become disabled
- The right to convert to an individual policy if you terminate your employment
- Accelerated benefits if you become terminally ill

TABLE C2.1 Galaxy Max Benefits Package

Benefits	Full-Time Salaried Employees (32 or more hours per week)	Hourly and Part-Time Employees
Group term life insurance	Yes	No
Short- and long-term disability	Yes	No
Health	Yes	Optional
Dental	Yes	Optional
Flexible spending account	Yes	Yes
Defined benefit plan	Yes	Defined benefit plan available for those working more than 1,000 hours per year
Profit sharing plan	Yes	Profit sharing plan available for those working more than 1,000 hours per year
401(k) plan with matching	Yes	401(k) plan with matching available for those working more than 1,000 hours per year

TABLE C2.2	Group Term Life Insurance: Major Plan Provisions
Benefits	Basic life insurance is equal to one times your annual base pay—employer pays
	Additional coverage up to five times your annual base pay as supplemental coverage—you pay (see costs in Table C2.3)
	Added coverage for dependents—you pay (see costs in Table C2.3)
	Accidental Death and Dismemberment (AD&D)—employer pays
	Waiver of premium in case of disability (life coverage continues without charge)—part of the basic coverage
	Convertibility (in case of termination of the term life, you can convert the policy to whole life policy without evidence of insurability)—part of basic coverage
	Accelerated benefits (living benefits)—in case of becoming terminally ill, you can collect up to 50 percent of the policy benefits while still living—part of basic coverage
Eligibility	Regular, full-time employees (working 32 per week or more) who are active at work
Enrollment	Coverage is automatic
When coverage begins	30 days after employment date
Cost	The Company pays the full cost of basic life insurance; you pay for any additional coverage (supplements of 2, 3, 4, or 5 times annual salary, and for dependent coverage)
Evidence of Insurability	For basic coverage paid by the employer, no evidence of insurability is required
	For supplemental amounts greater than $150,000, evidence of insurability is required
Provider, A.M. Best Rating	Minnesota Life (Minnesota, U.S.A), A++ Rating
Taxes	Premiums on coverage greater than $50,000 are taxable income to you (based on IRS Table PS-58)
	Death benefits paid to the beneficiary are not taxed

Accelerated Benefits If a covered employee is diagnosed with a qualifying condition, the employee may request that an accelerated benefit be paid immediately. The amount payable is 50 percent to a maximum benefit of $50,000. Qualifying conditions include:

- The diagnosis of a terminal illness that is expected to result in death within six to twelve months
- The occurrence of a specified catastrophic illness, such as AIDS, a stroke, or Alzheimer's disease

Dependent Life Insurance

Life insurance on a spouse can be purchased by full-time employees in increments of $5,000 up to $25,000. Life insurance on children can be purchased in the amount of $5,000 per child.

Accidental Death & Dismemberment

Benefits under the Accidental Death and Dismemberment (AD&D) plan are in addition to any benefits payable under the life insurance plan. AD&D benefits are payable in the event of an accident resulting in:

- Your death
- Loss of one or more of your body parts (such as hand or foot)
- Loss of sight in one or both eyes

Table C2.4 outlines the main features of the company's AD&D plan. If you survive an accident, but sustain certain injuries, AD&D benefits would be payable as shown in Table C2.5.

Life insurance will not pay out if you survive an accident; it pays only in the event of your death.

Losses not covered under AD&D include:

- Bodily or mental infirmity
- Disease or bacterial infection, unless resulting directly from the injury or any resulting surgery
- Medical or surgical treatment, unless resulting directly from the injury or any resulting surgery
- Suicide or attempted suicide while sane or insane
- Intentionally self-inflicted injury
- War or any act of war, whether declared or undeclared

TABLE C2.3		Costs for Supplemental Life and Dependent Life			

Supplemental Term   **Dependent: Rates for Spouse**

Age	Cost per month per $1,000 of coverage	Age	Cost per month per $1,000 of coverage	Amount	Cost
29 & under	$0.06	50–54	$0.42	$5,000	$0.58
30–34	$0.07	55–59	$0.69	$10,000	$1.15
35–39	$0.09	60–64	$1.10	$15,000	$1.73
40–44	$0.15	65–69	$2.00	$20,000	$2.31
45–49	$0.25	70 & over	$3.60	$25,000	$2.88

TABLE C2.4	AD&D Plan Provisions

Benefit	In case of accidental death, the basic and supplemental amounts are doubled (in case of a loss, see Table C2.5)
Eligibility	Regular, full-time employees (working 32 hours per week or more) who are active at work
Enrollment	Coverage is automatic
When coverage begins	30 days after employment date
Cost	The company pays the full cost of basic AD&D insurance; you pay for any additional coverage (supplements of 2, 3, 4, or 5 times annual salary)
Evidence of Insurability	Same as for regular group term life
Provider, A.M. Best Rating	Minnesota Life, A++ Rating

TABLE C2.5	AD&D Loss Provisions

If you have this loss	You will receive this percentage of your AD&D coverage
Loss of hand	50%
Loss of foot	50%
Loss of eye	50%
Multiple loss	100%

- 1 times pay ($45,000) from Minnesota Life for basic life
- 1 times pay ($45,000) from Minnesota Life for AD&D
- 1 times pay ($45,000) for his supplemental life
- 1 times pay ($45,000) for his supplemental AD&D

Total received is $180,000.

Provider

Life insurance is provided by Minnesota Life Insurance Company, which is rated A++ by A.M. Best.

Life Insurance Loss/Benefit Examples

Life Insurance Example 1   A forty-year-old employee making an annual base salary of $45,000 dies in an automobile accident. He had chosen to purchase supplemental insurance for both life (one times salary) and AD&D (one times salary). Beneficiary will receive:

Life Insurance Example 2   A life insurance claim was filed by Mary Jones after the death of her husband, Robert, in June 2002. He died after a short battle with cancer. He was a full-time employee of Galaxy Max for five years and his current salary was $55,000 annually. He has life insurance in the amount of three times his salary: $55,000 × 3 = $165,000. Therefore his benefit is $165,000, payable to his beneficiary, his spouse, Mary Jones. Mrs. Jones filed the claim within two weeks of Mr. Jones's death. Mrs. Jones had to present a copy of his death certificate and fill out the required forms. She was informed that she would receive her benefit within sixty days from the date of the claim.

Mrs. Jones has chosen to receive the life insurance benefit in a lump sum payment. She received this payment fifty-eight days from the date of the claim.

Internal Revenue Service Code Section 101 provides that the death benefits are not counted toward taxable income.

Sick Leave, Short-Term Disability, and Long-Term Disability

Table C2.6 provides a summary of all disability plans provided by Galaxy Max.

Sick Leave

Benefits The employee will receive regular pay for time missed due to illness or injury (non-occupational), up to seven days per calendar year.

Cost of Sick Time Galaxy Max pays for sick leave from its operating budget.

Short-Term Disability

Definition of Disability "Disability" is the total and continuous inability of the employee to perform each and every duty of his or her regular occupation.

Benefits Short-term disability (STD) benefits are 80 percent of salary up to $5,000 per month after a seven-day waiting period. The maximum length of the benefit is six months. There is no integration of benefits under short-term disability.

Premium Galaxy Max self-insures and deducts such as a normal business expense.

Exclusions An employee cannot collect STD benefits under the following conditions:

- For any period during which the employee is not under the care of a physician
- For any disability caused by an intentionally self-inflicted injury
- If the employee is engaged in any other occupation for remuneration
- If the disability was incurred during war, whether declared or undeclared
- If the disability was incurred while participating in an assault or felony
- If the disability is mental disease, alcoholism, or drug addiction

Termination Disabled employees will not be considered terminated and, when able to return to work, will not have to satisfy any waiting period for coverage.

TABLE C2.6	Sick Leave, Group Short-Term Disability, and Group Long-Term Disability Major Plan Provisions
Benefits	Sick leave—7 days, 100% of pay
	STD (7 days to 6 months)—80% of pay up to $5,000 benefit per month
	LTD (6 months to age 65)—60% of pay up to $6,000 benefit per month coordinated with workers' compensation and Social Security
Eligibility	Regular, full-time employees (working 32 hours per week or more) who are actively at work
Enrollment	Coverage is automatic
When coverage begins	30 days after employment date
Cost	The company pays the full cost of STD; employee pays for LTD through payroll reduction
Definition of disability	Sick leave and STD—unable to do your own job due to non-occupational injury or illness
	LTD—from 6 months to 2 years, unable to do any job relating to your training and education; after two years, unable to do any job
Evidence of Insurability	Required if joining after open enrollment
Provider, A.M. Best Rating	Sick leave and STD—Self-insured
	LTD—Aetna (rated "A" for excellent by A.M. Best)
Taxes	Employees do not pay taxes on the cost of STD, but in case of receiving benefits, taxes will be paid on the benefits
	For LTD, employee pays the premium from income after taxes, and benefits in case of disability are not taxable

Long-Term Disability

Definition of Disability   Long-term disability (LTD) is defined as the total and continuous inability of the employee to engage in any and every gainful occupation for which he or she is qualified or shall reasonably become qualified by reason of training, education, or experience for the first two years. After two years, it is the inability to engage in any gainful employment.

Benefits

- LTD benefit amount is 60 percent of your basic monthly earnings, to a maximum monthly benefit of $6,000.
- Monthly LTD benefit will be reduced by amounts received from other benefit programs such as Social Security, workers' compensation, and any other coinciding retirement plan. However, your monthly benefit can never be less than 10 percent of the gross benefit or $100, whichever is greater.

"Basic monthly earnings" means your monthly salary in effect just prior to the date disability begins. It includes earnings received from commissions and incentive bonuses, but not overtime pay or other extra compensation. Commissions and incentive bonuses will be averaged for the thirty-six month period of employment just prior to the date disability begins.

Cost of Coverage   The employee will pay the full cost through payroll deduction. The human resources representative will advise of the contribution amount that is based on a rate per $1,000 of your annual base pay. The cost of coverage is determined by the insurance company, Aetna (rated "A" for excellent by A.M. Best). Galaxy Max will notify you in advance in the event of a rate change.

LTD Exclusions   An employee cannot collect LTD benefits under the following conditions:

- Any disability caused intentionally
- Any period not under the care of a physician
- Active participation in a riot
- War, declared or undeclared, or any act of war

Taxation   Since the employee pays the entire premium from income after taxes, benefits are not taxable to the employee.

Rehabilitation   A disabled employee may enter a trial work period of up to two years in rehabilitative employment. During this time, benefits will be reduced by 50 percent. If the trial is unsuccessful, original long-term benefits will resume without penalty.

Termination   Disabled employees will not be considered terminated and, if able to return to work, will not have to satisfy any waiting period for coverage. Long-term disability coverage cannot be converted at end of employment.

Health Insurance Coverage

Galaxy Max offers two plans for health insurance, an HMO and PPO. The broad benefits are described in Table C2.7. The medical plans pay the cost of necessary and reasonable medical expenses for non-work related illness or injury and are completely optional.

Insurers

Galaxy Max has chosen Healthkeepers Inc. for HMO coverage. Healthkeepers' most recent A.M. Best rating is 'A' (excellent). Cigna Healthcare of Virginia Inc. is Galaxy Max's PPO provider, and has also earned A.M. Best's rating of 'A.'

Benefits

The benefits under each plan are explained in Table C2.8.

Financing

Galaxy Max will pay a generous part of the health care premiums. Table C2.9 lists employee obligations.

Coverage Area

The PPO is comprised of specific in-network offices. Consult your benefits liaison for a complete list of providers in your area. All employees residing in Virginia are considered in-area. HMO offices are also shown in the booklet of providers.

TABLE C2.7	Health Plan Provisions
Benefits	You have a choice between an HMO and a PPO plan.
Eligibility	Regular, full-time salaried and part-time employees scheduled to work at least 32 hours per week and their eligible dependents: spouse; unmarried dependent child under 19, or 25 in school full-time; disabled dependent child; eligible child with qualified medical child support order
Enrollment	You may enroll when eligible. You may elect to enroll eligible dependents for extra charges provided they meet the qualifications of a "dependent." Annual open enrollment period is October 1–November 1 every year. Changes effective January 1 the following year.
Waiting Period	30 days
Coverage Categories	Employee only Employee and child(ren) Employee and spouse Employee and family
Cost	You and Galaxy Max share the cost of coverage (see Table C2.9)
What Is Covered	Medically necessary services and supplies Inpatient and outpatient hospital care Doctors' care and treatment Home or office visits Prescription drugs Inpatient and outpatient mental health care Routine physical exams and preventative care (in network only)

Exclusions

The following items, among others, are not covered in any of the plans. If you have any questions regarding the coverage of a treatment or service you must contact the appropriate provider.

- Treatment that is not medically necessary in accordance with the designated insurers
- Experimental drugs or investigative procedures

Termination of Coverage

Coverage is terminated at the following times (unless COBRA is selected):

- The date on which employment terminates
- The date in which the employee becomes ineligible
- The end of the last period for which the employee has made any required contributions

Dependent coverage is terminated in the following cases (unless COBRA is selected):

- The date on which the dependent ceases to meet the definition of a dependent

- The date on which the dependent receives the maximum benefit of major medical coverage

Conversion

The employee may convert to individual health coverage within thirty-one days of losing eligibility. Galaxy Max complies with all local, state, and federal legislation with regard to group health plans as described in the following:

COBRA The Consolidated Omnibus Budget Reconciliation Act (COBRA) extends coverage for eighteen to thirty-six months following a qualifying event[4] that causes the employee to lose eligibility. The employer does not have to pay the premium, and the premium may be increased to a maximum of 102 percent of the group rate. The employee may elect COBRA within sixty days of the qualifying event. As noted above, the thirty-one day period of conversion may be applied after COBRA coverage.

HIPAA The Health Insurance Portability and Accountability Act (HIPAA) forbids insurers from imposing "preexisting conditions" exclusions when an

TABLE C2.8	HMO and PPO Plan Benefits

	HMO	PPO in Network	PPO out of Network
Annual Deductible			
	None	None	$300/individual, $600/family
Outpatient Care			
	Copay per visit ($)	Coinsurance (%) or copay ($) per visit	Coinsurance (%) per visit
Primary care physician	$10	$15*	30%
Diagnostic labs/x-rays	Fully covered	10%	30%
Preventive care	$10	$15†	30%
Well-baby care	$10; no age limit	$15 plus 10% of screening and diagnostic tests; through child's seventh birthday‡	30%
Maternity care for all routine pre- and postnatal care of mother rendered by ob/gyn	Routine care fully covered; $10 for diagnostic testing	$15 for initial visit if doctor submits one bill after delivery	30%
Mammogram screenings	$20	20%	30%
Ob/gyn visit (includes pelvic exam, breast exam, and pap smear	$10	$15	30%
Specialist office visit	$20 with PCP referral	$15	30%
Emergency services	$50 (waived if admitted)	$50 plus 20%; $15 for doctor's services	30%
Annual vision exams	$10	no	
Outpatient surgery	$75	$50 plus 20%; $15 for doctor's services	30%
Outpatient nonsurgical services	$20	$50 plus 20%; $15 for doctor's services	30%
Mental health & substance abuse	$20	26 visits per calendar year: $15 for visits 1–13; 50% for visits 14–26	30%
Home health care	Fully covered	Fully covered	30%
Outpatient physical, speech, and occupational therapy	$20 (90 days maximum)	Limits per calendar year: physical, $2,000; speech, $750; occupational, $2,000	30%
Inpatient Care (Preauthorization Required)			
	Copay per visit ($)	Coinsurance (%) or copay ($) per visit	Coinsurance (%) per visit
Hospital care for illness, injury, or maternity in a semi-private room	$250 per admission	$250 plus 10% per admission	30%
In-hospital physician's services	Fully covered	10%	30%
Inpatient mental health and substance abuse	$250 per admission	$250 plus 10% per admission	30%
Skilled nursing facility care	Fully covered (limited to 100 days per illness or condition)	20% (limited to 100 days per illness or condition)	30%

TABLE C2.8 CONTINUED	HMO and PPO Plan Benefits		
Durable medical equipment and supplies	Fully covered up to $1,000 per calendar year	10%; limited to $5,000 per calendar year	30%
Hospice services	Fully covered for patients diagnosed with a terminal illness with a life expectancy of 6 months or less	Fully covered for patients diagnosed with a terminal illness with a life expectancy of 6 months or less	30%
Annual Out-of-Pocket Expense Limit Through Deductibles, Coinsurances, and Copayments for Covered Services			
Individual	$1,000	$2,000	$4,000
Family	$2,000	$4,000	$8,000
Lifetime Maximum			
	$500,000	$750,000	$750,000

* Primary care physician or specialist visit.

† Coverage includes annual check-ups, annual gynecological exam and pap smear, prostate specific antigen (PSA) test and prostate exams for men age 40 and over, one baseline mammogram for women ages 35–39, annual mammogram for women age 40 and over, and annual colorectal cancer screening; up to $200 per calendar year for family members age seven and older for all other routine immunizations, labs, and x-rays done in connection with annual check-ups whether received in-network or out-of-network.

‡ No coinsurance for immunizations.

TABLE C2.9	Employee Premiums	
Plan	HMO	PPO
Bi-weekly premium per insured	$35.67	$51.09
Each additional dependent	$12.00	$18.00

eligible individual transfers from one plan to another. After you have been covered in a health plan for twelve months, "preexisting conditions" exclusions are no longer in effect. Prior coverage would not qualify if there is a break of health insurance for more than sixty-three days.

Group Dental

Group dental provides coverage for any dental work you may incur. Like group medical, group dental has many variations, and coverage can be obtained from two different providers. However, there are some clear differences between the two plans. For example, group dental plans are more likely to provide benefits on a

fee-for-service basis but provide the benefits with a managed care approach.

Eligibility

Full-time (thirty-two hours or more per week) and salaried employees are eligible to enroll for group dental coverage. You may enroll your spouse and child(ren) for an additional premium.

Waiting Period

Same as for health plans.

Plan Highlights

Table C2.10 summarizes the key features of the dental plan, including benefits, types of service, and cost information.

Conversion

Dental coverage cannot be converted to an individual policy if employment terminates. You, your spouse, or your dependent children may elect to continue coverage under the company's dental plan as provided by

TABLE C2.10	Major Dental Plan Provisions

Annual Deductible	$30 per person with $90 family maximum
Cost	You and the company share the cost
Plan Maximums	$1,000 per person per year $1,000 lifetime under 19 for orthodontics

Coverage	Examples of Items Covered	Plan Pays Up to
Preventive	Non-orthodontics x-rays, oral exams, and cleaning of teeth	100% of reasonable and customary fees (R&C) for cleanings, X-rays, exams, fluoride treatments
Restorative	Fillings, extractions	80% R&C fillings, extractions
Prosthodontics	Replacement of natural teeth with bridgework or dentures	50% R&C for bridgework
Orthodontics	Straightening of teeth	50% of R&C for orthodontic services with braces

COBRA if the original coverage ends because of one of the following life events:

- Termination of employment by employee
- Retirement
- Disability
- Death
- Reduction in hours

Provider

Galaxy Max has chosen Cigna Corp. for dental coverage because the company has a strong presence in the insurance business and has been one of the leaders in coverage.

Flexible Spending Account

To accommodate the needs of our diverse work force, Galaxy Max has created a Flexible Spending Account (FSA) plan to help employees to meet expenses that are not covered under any benefit plan. Money deposited in these accounts is not taxed when it goes into the accounts or when it is paid back to you. Employees can use these pre-tax dollars to pay for miscellaneous items such as eyeglasses or unreimbursed medical/dental expenses. This plan also allows employees to pay for dependent care expenses with pretax dollars. Any amount not spent at the end of the plan year is lost to the employee. The rule: Use it or lose it. See Table C2.11 for details.

In addition, a premium conversion plan is offered to employees for premium payments for health insurance on a pre-tax basis.

PART II: PENSION PLAN

Galaxy Max offers a defined-benefit pension plan to its eligible employees. The pension plan is designed to provide you or your beneficiary with monthly benefit payments at retirement. The pension plan is funded entirely by the company; employees do not contribute. In addition, Galaxy Max offers a 401(k) plan and a profit sharing plan.

Defined Benefit Plan

A defined benefit plan clearly defines the amount of benefit available at retirement. Table C2.12 summarizes the major pension program provisions.

Payments

Your pension benefit is paid to you in monthly installments at the end of the month. Your benefits will be

TABLE C2.11	Summary of FSA: Major Plan Provisions
Eligibility	Regular, full-time salaried employees and part-time employees
When Coverage Begins	Employment date; or each January, following annual open enrollment; or date of life event
When Coverage Ends	Employment termination or your pay ceases for any reason (death, retired, or disabled)
	You or your survivors may continue to submit claims expenses incurred prior to the date you left the payroll
Contributions	Your selected contributions will be deducted from each pay before federal income tax and, in most cases, state income tax and Social Security tax are withheld
	Minimum annual contribution: Health Care and/or Dependent Day Care: $120
	Maximum annual contribution: Health Care and/or Dependent Day Care:$5,000
Accounts	Health care accounts for tax-deductible health care expenses
	Dependent day care accounts for work-related dependent day care expenses
	Maximum of $2,500 if married and filing separate returns
Reimbursement	Eligible claims paid monthly
	Minimum claim of $10/month
	Claims must be received by administrator by April 1 for prior year's expenses
	Unclaimed account balances must be forfeited

TABLE C2.12	Defined Benefit Plan
Benefit formula	(1.3% of your final average salary up to the Social Security–covered Compensation Level) + (1.8% of your final average salary in excess of the Social Security–covered compensation level, if any) × (years of creditable service). See example in Table C2.13.
Eligibility	Full or part-time employees who are scheduled to work or who actually work at least 1,000 hours in a twelve-month period are eligible.
	Participation begins on your date of hire or your twenty-first birthday, whichever is later.
Normal Retirement	You may retire and receive normal retirement benefits the first day of the month on or after your sixty-fifth birthday.
Early Retirement	You may retire and receive an early retirement benefit on or before you reach age sixty-five.
	You are eligible for early retirement on the first day of the month on or after your fifty-fifth birthday with three years of vesting service.
Insured	Plan is insured by the Pension Benefit Guaranty Corporation.
Vesting	You become fully vested when you complete three years of vesting service (including vesting service with an acquired company) or reach age sixty-five.
	Vesting credit begins when you are eligible for the pension program.

paid as a lump-sum payment if the present value of your pension is $5,000 or less. The normal form of benefit paid by the retirement plan is based on your marital status. Unless you elect a different option, you will receive your benefit in one of the following forms, which are actuarially equivalent:

- If you are single, you will receive a single life pension.
- If you are married, you will receive a 50 percent survivorship pension with your spouse as the beneficiary. If you are married and would like to receive your benefit in another form, you will need to provide your spouse's written and notarized consent.

The survivorship option pays you for as long as you live. When you die, benefits continue to be paid to your designated beneficiary, assuming your beneficiary survives you. Written spousal consent is required before you can designate a beneficiary other than your spouse. Benefits are reduced for the survivorship option since payments will be made over two lives rather than one. Payments depend on your age and your beneficiary's age when you begin receiving payments. If you choose the survivorship option and your beneficiary dies before you, your payment will be increased to the amount that you would have received under the single life option. Additionally, you may choose the amount (50 percent, 75 percent, or 100 percent) your surviving beneficiary will receive after you die.

Formula and Calculations

The traditional formula used in calculating your retirement benefit is based on your final average salary, your creditable service, and the Social Security–covered compensation level based on your age. Your retirement pension benefit may not be more than 100 percent of your final average salary, or $160,000 in 2002. These formula components are outlined below. See Table C2.13 for an example of how the formula works.

Final Average Salary Your final average salary is your highest average annual compensation during any consecutive sixty-month period. It includes base pay, commission payments, bonuses, and overtime.

Creditable Service Your service with Galaxy Max, including approved leaves of absence up to six months, certain periods of military and public service, and periods in which you are totally disabled (as defined in the LTD Plan), is considered your creditable service. Service for part-time work is reduced to the equivalent portion of the year worked.

Social Security Compensation Level The average of the Social Security wage bases (maximum amount on which you pay Social Security taxes) for the thirty-five years before the date of your retirement is the Social Security compensation level that is used to calculate your benefits. These amounts change each year according to the Covered Compensation Table provided by the Social Security Administration.

Vesting

We at Galaxy Max chose to use a cliff vesting option. You become 100 percent vested after three years of creditable service. Our plan provides you with a cash settlement option if your employment at Galaxy Max is terminated. The cash settlement option is effective on your termination date. This distribution is considered taxable income in the year the distribution is made. The only exception to this rule is if you choose to roll this payment into an IRA.

Loans

Loans are not available under the retirement plan

Distributions

As a valued employee of Galaxy Max, you or your beneficiaries may choose, in addition to those described in the "Payments" section earlier, the option of guaranteed payment. You may choose to have your pension payments guaranteed for a certain period of time after retirement. The payment options include either five or ten years for a single life pension or five years for a survivorship pension benefit. This is usually used for single employees.

So...When Can I Retire and Receive Benefits?

Depending on your age and length of service, you may choose normal retirement or early retirement.

Normal retirement is when you retire at or after age sixty-five. If you choose this option, you will receive normal retirement pension benefits.

Early retirement is the first of any month on or after you reach age fifty-five after completing three years of vesting service. Benefits for early retirement are less than normal retirement benefits because the plan

TABLE C2.13   Example of Defined Benefit Formula

Suppose Joe, a sales representative for Galaxy Max, was born in 1942 and retired after thirty years of service to Galaxy Max with a final average salary of $40,000. At the time of Joe's retirement, the Social Security–covered compensation level is $37,212. To calculate Joe's benefit:

1. Multiply Joe's final average salary, up to Social Security–covered compensation level, by the benefit percentage — $37,212 × 1.3% = $484
2. Multiply Joe's final average salary in excess of Social Security–covered compensation level by the excess benefit percentage — ($40,000 − $37,212) × 1.8% = $50
3. Add amounts calculated — $448 + $50 = $534
4. Multiply by years of service to calculate Joe's annual retirement benefit — $534 × 30 = $16,018

Thus, Joe's annual pension is $16,018.

adjusts the payment amount to allow the benefits to be paid over a longer period of time.

Early Retirement

You become eligible for early retirement benefits when you reach age fifty-five with three years of vested service. You can retire on the first day of any month on or after your fifty-fifth birthday. If you retire before you reach age sixty-five, the date you retire will be known as your early retirement date.

The amount of your normal retirement benefit is available to you, without reduction, if you retire early—on or after your sixtieth birthday. If you retire on or after your fifty-fifth birthday and before your sixtieth birthday, your pension benefit will be reduced as explained in Table C2.14.

The benefit in Galaxy Max's defined plan is protected by the Pension Benefit Guaranty Corporation (PBGC). The cost of $19 per year per employee is paid by Galaxy Max.

401(k) Plan

Galaxy Max offers you a Section 401(k) plan, hereinafter the Galaxy Max 401(k) Plan, as a supplement to the retirement plan. You have the opportunity to put aside salary dollars on a pre-tax basis, and Galaxy Max makes employer-matching contributions to help build retirement savings more quickly. You can choose your own level of deferral, if any. The plan also offers you several investment options with varying portfolios to allow your savings to grow over time. Taxes are deferred on employer matching contributions, your pre-tax deferral, and investment returns until you withdraw the funds from your account.

Eligibility

All full-time and part-time employees are eligible. You become eligible for the Galaxy Max 401(k) Plan after completing one year of continuous service and must complete at least 1,000 hours of service during the year. Your enrollment commences on the first day of the month following the completion of that first year of service.

Maximum Contributions

For employees under the age of fifty, the 2002 contribution limit is $11,000. If you are fifty years old or older, these limits are $12,000 in 2002 and $14,000 in 2003.

Employer Matching

During each of your first five years of service, Galaxy Max will match 80 percent ($0.80 for every $1.00) that you contribute to the plan, up to 6 percent of your salary. After five years of service, our matching increases to 100 percent ($1.00 for every $1.00) that you contribute to the plan, up to 6 percent of your salary.

Vesting

Vesting is your right to the money in your 401(k) account. You are always 100 percent vested in the value

---

TABLE C2.14 Early retirement reduction in Defined Benefit Plan

If you retire between the ages of fifty-eight and sixty, your pension benefit will be reduced by 0.25% for each month that remains until your sixtieth birthday. For example, if you retire on your fifty-eighth birthday, your pension will be reduced by 6 percent (24 months × 0.25% per month). If you retire between the ages of fifty-five and fifty-eight, your pension will be reduced by that 6 percent plus an additional 0.50% percent for each month that remains until your fifty-eighth birthday. For example, if you retire on your fifty-sixth birthday, your benefit will be reduced by 18 percent [6% + (24 months × 0.50% per month)]. This table shows the percentage your benefit would be reduced if you retired on your birthday.

Retirement Age	Benefit Reduction
60 or older	None
59	3%
58	6%
57	12%
56	18%
55	24%

of your own contributions and the earnings on your investments. You are vested on Galaxy Max's matching contributions at the rate of 20 percent for each year of service, and thus fully vested after five years. For example, if you left Galaxy Max three full years after joining the 401(k) plan, you would have the right to all your investments and their earnings and to 60 percent of the matching funds plus their earnings.

Withdrawals

In-service withdrawals for certain hardships are permitted under the Galaxy Max 401(k) Plan, as long as two conditions are met:

1. The withdrawal must be necessary and follow severe financial hardships. Examples include the following:
   a. Purchasing your primary residence
   b. Preventing foreclosure or eviction from your primary residence
   c. Paying for major uninsured medical expenses for you or your eligible dependents
   d. Paying tuition, room and board, and related education expenses for the next twelve months for you or your eligible dependent to attend college.
2. The funds are not reasonably available from any other resources. The requirements are met if the following circumstances exist:
   a. The distribution does not exceed the amount of the severe financial hardship.
   b. The employee has obtained all other forms of distributions other than hardship distributions.

Contributions will be suspended twelve months after the distribution and the maximum contribution in the next year will be reduced by the amount contributed in the prior year.

Loans

The minimum loan amount is $1,000. The maximum loan amount is the lesser of $50,000 or 50 percent of your vested balance. The following two types of loans are available under the plan.

General Purpose   You can take between six and sixty months to repay a general purpose loan.

Primary Residence   You can take between sixty-one and 180 months to repay this loan. Eligible residences include house, condominium, co-op, mobile home, new home construction, or land for new construction or mobile home.

Investment and Investment Risk

You bear the risk of investments in your Galaxy Max 401(k) Savings Account. However, you can choose from several investment funds through the SunTrust Classic Funds Family, commonly referred to as the STI Classic Funds. These funds were rated one of the top ten mutual fund families in the nation for 2001. This will enable you to select your own desired level of risk.

Investment funds range from a fixed income fund with very low risk and corresponding low return potential to higher risk equity funds with higher return potential. The funds that you may choose from are as listed:

- Galaxy Max Stock Fund
- STI Classic Small Cap Growth Stock Fund
- STI Classic Mid-Cap Equity Fund
- STI Classic Appreciation Fund
- SunTrust 500 Index Fund
- STI Classic Growth & Income Fund
- STI Classic Value Income Stock Fund
- STI Classic Investment Grade Bond Fund
- STI Classic Short-Term Bond Fund
- STI Classic Prime Quality Money Market Fund

Termination

You will be terminated from the Galaxy Max 401(k) Plan if you cease to be employed by Galaxy Max.

Profit Sharing Plan

Over the past five years, Galaxy Max has been financially successful because of the dedication and talent of our valued employees. We started the profit sharing program to give you the opportunity to share in the success of our wonderful company. The primary purpose of this plan is to help you build retirement income. Along with the Galaxy Max 401(k) Plan and the defined benefit plan, the profit sharing plan can provide you with the foundation for a financially secure retirement.

A profit sharing plan is a qualified, defined contribution plan that features a flexible contribution by us. When you become eligible to participate, Galaxy Max will set up an individual account in your name. In other words, you do not need to enroll in the plan. Participation in the plan is automatic and you are not required or permitted to contribute personal funds into the plan.

Eligibility

The eligibility requirements for the Galaxy Max Profit Sharing Plan are the same as the Galaxy Max 401(k) Plan. Please refer to that section.

Contributions

Each year, Galaxy Max will contribute a portion of its pre-tax income for profit sharing purposes. The contribution is made after the end of each fiscal year. The amount allocated to your account is based on a formula that includes your compensation during the fiscal year. This contribution is made at the discretion of Galaxy Max and cannot be guaranteed every year.

Profit Sharing Formula

Here is how the allocation formula works. Once you become a participant, we evaluate your eligible compensation (base pay, commissions, and bonuses) and the eligible compensation of all Galaxy Max employees. Your portion of the amount of profits we contribute is the proportion of your eligible compensation to that of all employees. For example, suppose Galaxy Max will contribute $200,000 to the profit sharing plan, your eligible compensation is $35,000, and the eligible compensation of all employees is $950,000. Your share would be $35,000/$950,000, or 3.68 percent, of $200,000. Therefore, the allocation to your account would be $7,368.42. Remember, these numbers are just used to create a simple example. The total contribution from Galaxy Max and eligible compensation from all employees is much larger.

Investing Your Profit Sharing Account

The plan's trustee, SunTrust Bank (located in Atlanta, Georgia), will invest contributions to your account. At the end of each fiscal year, investment earnings are allocated to your profit sharing Account. Since the value of your investments will fluctuate, you will assume the investment risk. Therefore, your account balance will increase or decrease in value from year to year.

Profit Sharing Account Balance

Once all accounts have been reconciled for the fiscal year, you will receive an annual statement of your account. It will include your beginning balance, allocation of investment income, contributions, and ending balance. These statements are typically distributed to you four to five months after the fiscal year end.

Vesting

Vesting means earning ownership rights to the value of your individual account. You begin earning ownership rights to your account once you complete three continuous years of service. After your third full year you are 20 percent vested, and you earn another 20 percent each year. Once you complete seven years of service you are fully vested. If your employment ends because you become permanently disabled, die, or leave Galaxy Max after age sixty-five with at least five years of service, you will be entitled to receive the full value of your account, regardless of your vesting.

Loans

You may borrow from your profit sharing account under the same provisions that apply to 401(k) loans. Please refer to that section for details.

Distributions

You can receive the vested portion of your account after you leave Galaxy Max, retire, or become permanently and totally disabled. Your designated beneficiary will receive your vested account balance if you die before receiving your benefit.

If your vested account balance is $6,000 or less, you or your beneficiary will receive the payment in a single lump sum. If your account balance is more than $6,000, you or your beneficiary can take a single lump sum, receive annual installments for up to five years, or delay receiving distributions until a later time. Generally, you can roll over the vested portion of your account balance into another qualified retirement account or individual retirement account (IRA) so that you can defer paying federal income taxes.

Termination from Plan

You will be terminated from the plan if you cease to be employed by Galaxy Max.

Limitations on Contributions

For all three plans, certain legal limits are placed on contributions to your account. The combined contributions to your retirement plans cannot exceed $40,000 or 100 percent of your compensation, whichever is lower. This limit applies to both your and Galaxy Max's contributions to your 401(k), profit sharing, and defined benefit plans, unless the defined benefit plan requires (under the minimum required annual contribution) a greater annual contribution. Thus, in summary, all qualified retirement plans combined cannot exceed the $40,000 or 100 percent of compensation annual limit, unless more contribution is necessary to meet the minimum requirements under the defined benefit plans.

CONCLUSION

The management of Galaxy Max hopes that the benefits we offer are clear to you. Our studies indicate that our benefit package far exceeds the norms of our industry. We are very interested in your well being, and this motivated us to exceed our peer group's offerings. Should you have questions, please contact the Human Resources Department, 7500 Galaxy Max Road, Richmond, VA 23228; telephone (800) 674-2900; e-mail hrgalaxymax@vcu.edu. Suggestions are always welcome as we continue to improve our service to our employees.

NOTES

1. The students used information from the following companies and sources: Dominion Co., www.dominion.com; Virginia Power; Phillip Morris; Virginia Retirement System, www.state.va.us/vrs/vrs-home-htm; Henrico County, Virginia, www.co.henrico.va.us.; MinnesotaLife.com; ambest.com; Federal Reserve Board; Stanley Corp.; Ethyl Corp.; www.Aetna.com; www.trigon.com; CIGNA, www.cigna.com; and more.

2. This case does not provide a long-term-care coverage plan. Most of the retirement plans offered by the hypothetical employers of these projects are not realistic in terms of the amounts and variety. The students are requested to provide a defined benefit plan, a defined contribution plan, and a 401(k) plan in order to experience the workings of these plans. The students did not offer a complete cafeteria plan—only a flexible spending account.

3. The work of the following students is reflected in this case: Donna Biddick, Lavonnia Bragg, Katrina Brand, Heather Cartes, Robert Cloud, Maria Conway, Thomas Dabney Clay, Lillian Dunlevy, Daniel Fleming, Shannon Fowlkes, Caroline Garrett, Barbara Guill, Steven Hall, Georgette Harris, Shirelle Harris, Tyron Hinton, Tiffany Jefferson, Tennille McCarter, Pamela Nicholson, Hiren Patel, Susan Shaban, Carolyn Shelburne, Gaurav Shrestha, Stephanie Soucy, Christopher Speight, Cassandra Townsend, Geoff Watkins, and Tresha White, from Fall 2002. Also included is the work of Margaret Maslak and Shelisa Artis from Fall 2000.

4. A qualifying event is a marriage or divorce, adoption of a child, death of a covered dependent, a change in status or eligibility of a dependent, and so forth.

Non-Traditional Insurance Programs: The New Generation

PREFACE

Case 3, unlike Cases 1 and 2, is designed for risk management students who are interested in the more complex coverages designed for large businesses. It is provided here to enhance Chapter 3 and the material provided in the textbook relating to commercial coverages. This case is from the Academy of Insurance Education. It is written by Phyllis S. Myers, Ph.D., and Etti G. Baranoff, Ph.D. and edited by Gail A. Grollman. Formerly a video education program of the National Association of Insurance Brokers. Copyright: The Council of Insurance Agents and Brokers.[1]

INTRODUCTION

Alternative risk financing (sometimes referred to as alternative risk transfer) are risk funding arrangements that typically apply to losses that are above the primary self-insurance retentions or losses above the primary insurance layer. Because of the complexities in designing these programs, they are solving the problems of large clients and merit substantial premiums.

Alternative risk transfer is an evolving area of risk finance where programs often are tailored for the individual company. Insurers have been expanding their offerings and creativity in designing methods of financing corporate risk. This new generation of financing risk is increasingly becoming the mainstream as more experience is gained by insurers, brokers, and risk managers.

An analogy between alternative medicine and alternative risk financing is made to demonstrate the importance of such insurance programs. The evolution of alternative risk transfer holds a striking parallel to that of alternative medicine. Individuals and the medical community began turning to alternative medicine when conventional methods failed. Alternative risk transfer is not much different. Risk managers were looking for alternatives when the conventional insurance markets failed them. When availability and affordability issues occurred in the insurance markets,[2] risk managers resorted to higher retention levels and creative methods of risk financing. In this process, corporations' risk tolerance levels increased, as did the expertise and comfort level of risk managers in managing risk. Consequently, they did not rush back into the market when it softened. Many of today's risk managers are protecting themselves from being at the mercy of the insurance industry. The current[3] (1997) long period of softness also has put the buyers in the drivers' seats and the buyers have been demanding products that align more closely with their company's needs. Alternative risk financing was created to heal availability and affordability problems. It also has been adopted to improve cash flows and effectively handle all risks in the organization. As in alternative medicine, the new methods are seen as viable options for the improved (financial) health of the organization.

Risk managers began taking and maintaining long-term control of the process. They have been looking for cost, accounting, and tax efficiencies. So, in addition to using the captives and risk retention groups discussed in Chapters 3 and 5, they have been establishing customized finite, multi-year, multi-line integrated risk programs; and they have been insuring risks that previously were once considered uninsurable. In this case, we first delve into explaining all these new generation products before working on the LOCO case presented later. The explanation of each program includes examples from real companies.

NEW GENERATION PRODUCTS

"New generation" risk financing programs have emerged in response to the needs of large and complex organizations. These new generation products blend with an orchestrated structure of self-insurance, captives, conventional insurance, and excess limits for selected individual lines. These more sophisticated methods of financing risk are being driven by a new breed of strategic-thinking risk managers who have an increased knowledge of risk management theory. They come to the table with a good understanding of their companies' exposures and financial resources to handle risk. They are seeking risk handling solutions that will improve efficiency, be cost-effective and stabilize earnings.

Increasingly, today's risk managers are practicing a holistic approach to risk management in which all of the corporation's risks—business, financial, and operational—are being assessed (as noted in Chapter 3). This concept, sometimes referred to as *integrated risk management,* is a coordinated approach to identifying, measuring and monitoring diverse and multiple risks that requires effective and rapid response to changing circumstances.[4] Non-traditional risk transfer programs combined with traditional coverages are being used to meet the needs of this holistic and strategic risk management approach.[5] Two of the non-traditional transfer programs available to risk managers that are covered in this case are integrated risk and finite insurance.

INTEGRATED RISK PROGRAMS

The discussion of integrated risk programs includes responses to the following questions:

1. What attracts corporations to the new integrated program?
2. What is the response of the insurance industry and the brokerage community?
3. How do you determine the coverages to include in an integrated program?
4. What limits are appropriate?
5. How do deductibles operate?
6. Why do you need a reinstatement provision?
7. What are the overall advantages of the integrated risk concept?

What Attracts Corporations to the New Integrated Programs?

The traditional approach of a tower of mono-line coverages, each with a separate policy limit, has not been meeting the needs and operations of many corporations. Companies have been looking to integrated programs that combine lines of coverages in one aggregate policy—generally for a multi-year term. These integrated programs also go by names such as concentric risk and basket aggregates. The features that are attracting corporations to these programs include:

- Less administration time and cost
- Less time and cost for negotiations with brokers and underwriters
- Elimination of the need to build a tower of coverages
- One loss triggers just one policy
- Elimination of gaps in coverage—seamless coverage
- Elimination of the need to buy separate limits for each type of coverage

Judy Lindenmayer's[6] program for FMR (Fidelity Investments) was one of the earliest integrated programs. She referred to it as concentric risk. She explained how she lowered her cost through the use of an aggregate limit. Under traditional coverage, an insured may be purchasing limits that are fifty million dollars per year, but it is unlikely that there would be a major loss every year and thus, the full limit would not be used. Therefore, there is a waste of large limits in many of the years while the insured keeps paying for them. The solution to the redundancy and the extra cost is "the integrated program, with one aggregate limit over the three-year period. You buy one fifty million dollar limit." Obviously, this is going to cost the insured less money. Judy claimed that cost reductions could be as much as thirty or forty percent.

Norwest, a bank with assets of $71.4 billion and 43,000 staff in 3,000 locations (in 1997) across the United States, Canada, Caribbean, Central and South America, and Asia, was another company that could provide an example of what attracts corporations to the new concept. Until 1994, Norwest had traditional coverages. Each class of risk had an individual limit of self-insurance, a layer of commercial insurance and an excess coverage. There were many risks that were not covered by insurance because of lack of availability.[7]

K. C. Kidder, Norwest's risk manager, established a new integrated risk financing program for simplicity and efficiency. In addition, she opted for the multi-year integrated approach. Kidder's other objectives for the major restructuring include:[8]

- Provide aggregate retentions applicable to all risks
- Develop a long-term relationship with the insurer
- Stabilize price and coverage
- Provide catastrophe protection
- Reduce third-party costs significantly
- Use the company's captive insurer
- Maximize cash flow and investment yields
- Include previously uninsured risks.

Coca-Cola was another major company that was motivated to use an integrated program.[9] Allison O'Sullivan, Coca-Cola's director of risk management, was looking for a program that would:

- Provide long-term stability
- Recognize the company's financial ability to retain risk
- Create value through attaining the lowest sustainable cost
- Increase administrative efficiencies
- Provide relevant coverage enhancements
- Strengthen market relationships
- Enhance options for hard-to-insure business risks worldwide

Another attractive integrated product of limited use is the multi-trigger contract. A multi-trigger contract is one in which claims are triggered by the occurrence of more than one event happening within the same time period. The time period is defined in the contract and could be a calendar year, fiscal year, season, or even a day. In a single trigger policy, a claim is based on the occurrence of any one covered loss, such as an earthquake or a fire. In the multi-trigger contract, a claim can be made only if two or more covered incidents occur within that defined contract period. This coverage costs less than individual coverages since the probability of the two (or more) losses happening within the contract time period is lower than the probability of a single loss occurring. In the multi-trigger policy, the insurer recognizes this lower probability in the pricing of the product. Thus, it would cost more to buy the earthquake insurance on a stand alone basis than it

would cost to buy earthquake insurance contingent on some other event that is taking place within that contract time period, such as a shift in foreign exchange or a shift in the cost of a key raw material to the client. Insureds who are concerned only with two very bad losses happening at the same time are those who are interested in a multi-trigger program.

What Is the Response of the Insurance Industry and the Brokerage Community?

Market conditions are contributing to insurers' responsiveness to risk managers. The insurance industry and brokerage community have created a new concept of bundling risks into one basket, under one limit, for multiple years. David May of J&H Marsh and McLennan[10] reported that "many insurance markets have lined up behind this new approach, offering close to $1 billion in capacity."[11] The industry provides large capacity for these types of programs. Two observations of their use are: (1) the corporations that use them are large with substantial financial strength and (2) the multi-year term of the programs promote long-term relationships.

The U.S., European, and Bermuda markets all have been actively participating in various program combinations. XL and CIGNA were among the first players when they teamed up to combine property and casualty lines of coverage. The market demanded broader coverage and the two insurers, in a very short period of time, have expanded their offerings. Other active players have been Swiss Re with its "BETA" program and in the U.S. market, AIG, Chubb, and Liberty Mutual.

Most of this capacity is not dependent on reinsurance. Some insurers offer "one stop shopping," while in other cases the structure uses a number of insurers. Coca-Cola's program, for example, was provided ultimately by several carriers.

How Do You Determine What Coverages to Include in an Integrated Program? What Limits Are Appropriate?

Integrated programs may include different combinations of coverages and may be designed for different lengths of time and different limits. Insurers provide many choices in their offerings. Programs are put together based upon each corporation's own risk profile. These products are individualized and require intensive study to respond to the client's needs.

The typical corporations looking into these types of programs are Fortune 200 corporations—companies needing $100 million to $200 million in coverage, or more.[12] These are corporations that have much larger and complex risks and need to work with a few carriers.

Judy Lindenmayer at Fidelity Investments explained the process of determining which coverages to combine:

- Review loss history
- Consider predictability of losses
- Review annual cost of coverage and coverage amount by line
- Consider risk tolerance level
- Select an aggregate limit that exceeds expected annual losses for all coverages

FMR had two separate integrated programs, as shown in Figure C3.1.[13] FMR's program for its mutual funds combines the government mandated fidelity bonds and E&O liability insurance. FMR took a very conservative approach with a separate program to protect its mutual funds clients from employees' dishonesty or mistakes. For the other part of the company, the corporate side, the coverage included consolidated financial institutions bond coverage which protects the employee benefits plans and against employees' dishonesty. The other coverages were D&O, stockbrokers E&O, Corporate E&O, E&O liability for charitable gifts, partnership liability, and electronic and computer crime. The corporate program was designed to respond to the risk management needs of the corporate side which was "on the cutting edge on a lot of things" and therefore less conservative than the mutual funds' concentric program.

Integrated programs include coverages such as D&O, fiduciary liability, crime, E&O, and employment practices liability.[14] Examples of the coverages that may be included in an integrated program under one aggregate limit are:

- Property
- Business interruption
- General, products, and automobile liabilities
- Workers compensation
- Marine liabilities and cargo
- Crime
- D&O liability
- E&O liability

For specific companies it may also include:

- Products recall
- Products tampering
- Political risks
- Environmental liabilities

Both Coca-Cola's and Norwest's programs combined a very broad array of coverages. Coca-Cola's program combines over 30 different risks in one contract. Although not doing so in 1997, Allison O'Sullivan, then Director of Risk Management for Coca-Cola, said that she was opened to the idea of blending financial risks, such as interest-rate and currency-exchange fluctuations. Norwest's program had a layer of true integrated insurance with an aggregate of $100 million limit over a five year period. It combined the following coverages in its program:

- Aircraft liability (non-owned)
- Automobile liability
- D&O (corporate reimbursement)
- Employers' liability
- Fiduciary liability
- Foreign liability
- Foreign property
- General liability
- Mail and transit
- Mortgagee E&O
- Professional liability
- Property

FIGURE C3.1   Integrated Risk Programs

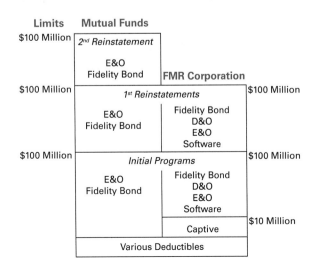

- Repossessed property
- Safe deposit
- Workers' compensation

Understanding the loss history of each line of coverage is very important to selecting the appropriate limits. The aggregate limit must be adequate to cover losses of all combined lines for the entire multi-year period.

How Do Deductibles Operate?

Programs may be structured with one aggregated deductible for the term of the policy or separate per-occurrence deductibles. Norwest's integrated program had a $25 million aggregate retention over a five-year term. They had another five-year aggregate retention that was covered by its Vermont-based captive, Superior Guaranty Insurance Company. Above their retention, they had a finite risk layer (explained in the next section of this case) of $50 million. Fifty percent of this layer was covered by the captive. The other 50 percent was covered by American International Group (AIG).

The FMR aggregate programs also are structured over retentions. As discussed previously, FMR had two separate programs. The mutual funds program had multiple deductibles and the captive was not used.[15] For the corporate concentric program, FMR's captive, Fidvest. Ltd., wrote up to $10 million in aggregate limits, as shown in Figure C3.1. Fidvest's retention included most of the risks except for the trustees' E&O. The captive retained only $5 million of this risk.

The decision of the appropriate retention levels forces the risk manager to look at risks and risk tolerance.

Why Do You Need a Reinstatement Provision?

As noted previously, selecting the limit amount that will cover all included losses over the entire multi-year period is an estimate based upon a number of factors. But that estimate can prove to be wrong. The insured could blow through its entire aggregate limit before the end of the term. For that reason, it is important to include one or more reinstatement provisions. Negotiating a reinstatement provision on the front end is critical in order to provide:

- Additional limits if the initial limits are exhausted
- Guarantee of coverage when needed
- Coverage at the right price

The FMR program contained reinstatement provisions in the event its aggregated limits were exhausted. Figure C3.1 illustrates that FMR had one reinstatement on the corporate program and an option to purchase two additional reinstatements for the funds' program.

What Are the Overall Advantages of the Integrated Risk Concept for Insureds?

The integrated risk programs are reported to produce in excess of 25 percent savings. This savings results from:

- Large premium decreases as a result of utilizing fewer carriers
- Flexibility of mixing the most appropriate risks, i.e., customized plans
- Comprehensive coverage
- More efficient operation of the captives and retentions
- Reduced administration and greater efficiency regarding renewals

The risk manager does not need to shop the market every year and prepare for renewals. The worry about the volatility of the traditional, cyclical insurance market is also reduced. These programs are expected to increase in prevalence. They have been combined with other new generation products, such as finite risk, which is discussed next.

FINITE RISK PROGRAMS

Finite risk programs are a method of financing risk assumption that had its origins in arrangements between insurers and reinsurers. Premiums paid by the corporation to finance potential losses are placed in an experience fund which is held by the insurer. The insured is paying for its own losses through a systematic payment plan over time. Thus, it is not subjected to the earnings volatility that can occur through self-insuring. If loss experience is favorable, the insured shares in the underwriting profit and investment income that accrues on its premiums. The programs recognize the individual risk transfer needs of each corporation. Consequently, each contract is unique. Generally, finite programs have the following characteristics in common:

- Multi-year term—at least three years but may be five or even ten years

- Overall aggregate limit—often one limit applies, thus all losses of any type and line will be paid until they reach the aggregate limit

- Experience fund is established for the insured's losses—monies are paid into the fund and held by the insurer over the time period

- Interest earned on funds—a negotiated interest is earned on the funds that the insured has on deposit with the insurer

- Element of risk transfer—often includes some traditional risk transfer for the program to be

- Recognized as insurance by the IRS

- Designed for each insured individually using manuscripted policy forms

Differences Between Finite Protection and Traditional Insurance

The key differences between the finite risk program and traditional insurance coverage is that the funds paid to the insurer:

- Earn interest that is credited to the insured
- Are refundable to the insured

An Example of How the Program Can Be Structured

Figure C3.2 shows an example of how a program operates. The insured, in this example, has implemented a three-year program with a $100 million aggregate coverage limit for the entire period, with annual premium payments of $20 million. Thus, the insured has promised to pay $60 million over the three-year period as denoted by the cross hatching on the graph. Actual risk transfer, i.e., the conventional insurance layer of the finite program, exists between the $60 million that the insured pays in and the $100 million limit. Thus, there is $40 million in risk transfer. This risk transfer layer is shown in the darker part of the graph.

At the end of the three-year period, the deposits may be returned to the insured with interest, less any losses. As will be discussed later, a return of funds will constitute a taxable event and the insured may choose to roll the funds over to the next term.

What If Losses Exceed the Funds Paid to Date?

What if the insured has losses that exceed the funds that it has paid in to date? In the example in Figure C3.2, the insured has paid in $20 million in the first year. But what if losses exceed $20 million in the first year? This is the timing risk that the insurer takes—the risk that losses will exceed the insured's deposit—in which case, the insurer has to pay for them prior to having received the funds from the insured. The graph shows the timing risk in white. It is the difference between the insured's accumulated payments into the fund (shown as cross hatching in the graph) and the total amount the insured promises to pay into the fund over the entire time period (in this example, $60 million over a three-year period.) The timing layer is similar to a line of credit for the insured. The insured must still pay the insurer for the losses that were paid out in advance or "loaned" to the insured.

The FMR Corporation structured its finite program around its integrated risk program. Figure C3.3 displays how FMR's finite program fits around the two integrated programs described previously. The finite program is outlined with dotted lines. An important part of its program was the inclusion of risks that are traditionally uninsurable. If a loss occurs under the finite program that is also covered by its underlying integrated coverage, the finite acts as a layer above the integrated limit. Thus, the finite risk protection is pierced when the integrated limit is exhausted—no deductible is incurred under the finite program. If, however, a loss occurs under the finite

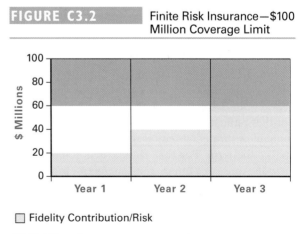

FIGURE C3.2   Finite Risk Insurance—$100 Million Coverage Limit

☐ Fidelity Contribution/Risk

■ Risk Transfer

☐ Insurer Timing/Interest Risk

FIGURE C3.3   Finite Risk Insurance—$100 Million Coverage Limit

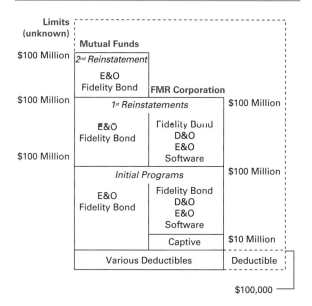

program that is not covered by the integrated program, a $100,000 aggregate deductible applies. Such losses are paid if and when aggregate losses under the finite program reach $100,000.

Finite programs can fit into a corporation's risk financing structure in other ways, as well. It can be used to fund primary losses. It also can be used in intermediate layers to stabilize infrequent, but periodic losses.[16]

An Example of How the Experience Fund Operates

Now, let us review an example of how the experience fund works. Table C3.1 displays a chart of an experience fund with annual deposits of $20 million for a three-year term. Assume an annual interest rate of 6 percent is credited quarterly to the fund. Further, assume that the interest accrues on a tax-free basis—as would be the case if the fund is placed with an offshore insurer where investment income is not subject to taxation. In this example, the insured incurs a $5 million loss in year 2. At the end of the term, the insured's balance is $62,120,260. The funds may be returned to the insured or rolled over to another contract term.

Pricing

Pricing of the product will vary. There can be an additional premium to pay for the risk transfer and timing

risk elements. Alternatively, the insurer's risk can be paid for by the spread between the interest it expects to earn on the funds and the interest credited to the insured.

Suitability of Finite Risk

Finite programs typically are used by large corporations with one or more of the following characteristics:

- High retention levels
- Unique or difficult to insure risks
- Risks where adequate limits are not available
- Ability to make large cash outlays

Advantages of a Finite Risk Program

Finite risk programs offer a number of benefits to corporations:

- Improves balance sheet—by including risks for which non-insurance reserves had been established, it allows the company to remove these reserves from its balance sheet.
- Reduces volatility in earnings—instead of paying unpredictable losses out of current earnings, the insured is paying equal payments to the insurer to cover losses and if losses exceed the payments, the insurer pays

TABLE C3.1   FMR's Finite Risk Program

Date	Credit/Debit to Fund	Fund Balance Beginning of Period	Interest Earned
Jan. 1, 1997	$ 20,000,000	$ 20,000,000	
Mar. 31, 1997		20,300,000	$ 300,000
June 30, 1997		20,604,500	304,500
Sep. 30,1997		20,913,568	309,068
Dec. 31, 1997		21,227,271	313,704
Jan. 1,1998	20,000,000	41,227,271	
Mar. 31, 1998		41,845,680	618,409
Mar. 31, 1998	(5,000,000)	36,845,680	
June 30, 1998		37,398,365	552,685
Sep. 30,1998		37,959,340	560,975
Dec. 31, 1998		38,528,730	569,390
Jan. 1,1999	20,000,000	58,528,730	
Mar. 31, 1999		59,406,661	877,931
June 30, 1999		60,297,761	891,100
Sep. 30,1999		61,202,227	904,466
Dec. 31, 1999		62,120,260	918,033

them and the insured can work out an arrangement to pay them back up to the agreed upon amount that should be paid into the fund.

- Allows for profit sharing if loss experience is favorable—the insured earns interest on the payments that it pays to the insurer. In addition, these payments can be structured to be tax deductible whereas reserves on the balance sheet are not deductible until losses are paid.

- Helps secure insurance for uninsurable risks—since the losses are paid by the insured, a program can be structured without limitations on what types of risk can be included.

- Accesses new capacity for catastrophic risks—finite programs can be structured so they are layered over a very large retention level, a captive or other insurance program, such as integrated risk programs or conventional insurance.

Determining the Risks to Include in a Finite Program

Finite risk programs can be structured to include any type of risk contingent upon approval by the company's auditors.[17] They are touted as a means of financing traditionally uninsurable risks. Thus, a corporation looks at its own risk profile to determine the appropriate risks to include in the program. A corporation can do this in one or more of the following ways:

- Examine the balance sheet for reserves—reserves are established for risks on which there is no insurance cover. The size of these reserves reflects the potential impact of the risk.

- Examine insurance policies for existing exclusions—this exercise will reveal important risks that currently are uninsured.

- Ask senior management what keeps them awake at night—in addition to potentially identifying previously unidentified risks, the process reveals the firm's tolerance for risk by determining what is important to management.

Potential Disadvantages of a Finite Risk Program

Finite risk programs are becoming increasingly popular. But, they are not without disadvantages:

- Tax and accounting questions—Accounting and tax rules say that there must be more than timing and interest rate risk for the insurer in order for insured's payments to be tax deductible. The tax code requires that the finite financing arrangement involve real underwriting risk transfer with a reasonable expectation of loss. Transactions that do not meet tax and accounting rules regarding risk transfer will be treated as deposits. The main requirement is that the insurer (or reinsurer) must stand to realize a significant loss from the transaction. Judy mentions a general "rule of thumb" that has developed whereby 10–15 percent of the estimated exposure should be transferred to the insurer, and the risk so transferred, must have a 10–20 percent chance of loss. Actuaries, however, caution against specifying probability thresholds because they do not allow for the differences in frequency and severity of various exposures.[18] Evaluation of the risk transfer element is a complex process that requires a complete understanding of the transaction—the details of which are beyond the scope of this study.

- The premiums should not be construed as a deposit for accounting purposes. The risk transfer element must be verified by outside auditors. It is permissible to have the tax and accounting for the finite program be on two different bases. However, doing so may draw the attention of income tax auditors.

- Any monies that are returned to the insured at the end of the period will constitute taxable income. To avoid a taxable event, the insured can roll the funds over to the next term.

- Time-consuming and complex to develop—although finite programs can save considerable time once they are in place, they can take up to a year to develop.

- Frictional costs may be greater than perceived benefits—these costs are estimated to range from 5 to 10 percent. A fee is paid to the insurer and a federal excise tax will apply to premiums paid for programs that are domiciled offshore.

- Opportunity cost of committed funds—the programs entail large outlays of cash each year of the term. These large outlays and the fact that it ties up the funds can overshadow the net cost efficiencies that might have been obtained. Generally, these cash outlays will require the involvement of the company's CFO or other senior management. Often, the cash outlays are the obstacle to obtaining senior management approval of the program.

QUESTIONS FOR REVIEW OF THE INTEGRATED RISK AND FINITE RISK PROGRAMS

What attracts corporations to the new integrated products?

Suggested answer: Corporations are attracted to integrated risk products because they:

- Require less administrative time and cost;
- Require less time and cost for negotiations with brokers and underwriters;
- Eliminate the need to build a tower of separate coverages;
- Simplify claim handling since a loss triggers only one policy;
- Eliminate gaps in coverage and provide seamless coverage; and
- Eliminate the need to buy separate limits for each type of coverage.

What is the "timing risk" in a finite risk program?

Suggested answer: The insurer is taking the timing risk. The timing risk is the probability that losses may exceed the amount the insured has paid into the experience fund thus far. For example if you paid $20 million dollars for the first year of the finite risk program and in that year you had a $40 million dollar loss, the insurer would pay out $40 million. The timing risk is that the insurer had to pay $20 million more than what the insured had paid in thus far. It is merely a timing risk—as opposed to real risk transfer—because the insured has to pay back the additional $20 million that the insurer paid out.

What are the potential disadvantages of a finite risk program?

Suggested answer: The potential disadvantages of a finite risk program include:

- Tax and accounting questions regarding deductibility of premiums
- Time-consuming and complex to develop
- Frictional costs may be greater than perceived benefits
- The opportunity cost of committed funds

Explain how to determine what coverages to include in a multi-year integrated program and the appropriate limits to select.

Suggested answer: A thorough analysis of a company's loss history is a must. This helps to determine what types of risks to include and what amount losses should be over the multi-year period. The predictability of losses is an important factor in determining which risks to include. It is important that the corporation does not exhaust its entire limit early. Very unpredictable losses are difficult to estimate and thus, not a good candidate for inclusion in an integrated program.

It is said that traditionally uninsurable risks are insurable under finite risk programs. Explain why this is possible.

Suggested answer: Finite programs entail a large amount of retention. The insurer's risk is above that large retention. Hence, it is willing to include risks that have traditionally been uninsurable.

LOCO CORPORATION CASE STUDY: PART 1

The hypothetical LOCO Corporation was created to help you apply the concepts learned above. Please read its description, then answer the discussion questions that follow.

Background Information

Since its formation in 1945, LOCO Corporation has been a leader in the investment banking field. Its largest and best known subsidiary is Loyalty Investment, an investment advisory and management company for a family of 100 funds. Through a network of 32 principal offices in 22 countries, LOCO and its subsidiary, Loyalty Investment, offer a complete range of financial services, including on-line trading and research assistance to corporations, institutions, and individuals throughout the world. LOCO, through another subsidiary, Loyalty Brokerage Group, engages in sales and trading on a discounted fee basis. It uses the most advanced technologies available in the market. Approximately 50 percent of trades (for both the direct funds and through the brokerage firm) are handled online, another 40 percent over the telephone, and 10 percent in person at sales offices around the world.

LOCO also provides financial underwriting services and advice to corporations and governments across the five continents regarding their capital structures. Its products and services include corporate finance, real estate, project finance and leasing, debt and equity capital markets, mergers and acquisitions, and restructuring.

Under Loyalty Investment are three subsidiaries:

- The Loyalty Brokerage Group (formerly the Kendu Financial Group acquired in 1994)—a stock brokerage firm that handles $4 billion annually in trades for retail and institutional clients on a discounted fee basis.

- The Loyalty Financial Services Group—insurance, estate planning and investment advisory organization for high net worth individuals operating only in the United States and United Kingdom. The non-support staff are licensed to sell insurance and securities.

- Loyalware—financial services software producer

LOCO has offices in Europe, the Middle East, the Far East, South Africa, Australia, South America, and is expanding into Russia and China. LOCO's financial highlights are shown below. They provide information on LOCO's size, liquidity, and debt positions in 1995 and 1996. Although LOCO has been enjoying increased revenues, LOCO's profit margins have decreased from 1995 to 1996. Return on equity has remained stagnant for the last two years. LOCO's Financial highlights can be seen in Table C3.2.

Recently, Dan Button, director of Risk Management, was appointed director of Global Risk Management—a newly created position to reflect the integration of domestic and international risk management operations. LOCO has a separate operating officer both for its domestic operations and its international operations. Most likely, the separation of operations was the reason that the risk management operations were handled separately as well. Dan and his CFO, Elaine Matthews were very instrumental in effecting a change. They knew that economies of scale could be realized by consolidating the risk management function on a global basis. Elaine believes in the holistic approach to risk management and involves Dan in the

TABLE C3.2	LOCO's Financial Highlights	
For the Years Ended September 30 (in Millions)	**1996**	**1995**
Cash and Marketable Securities	$ 73,259	$ 93,325
Real Estate	$ 45,464	$ 35,217
Other Assets	$ 20,000	$ 18,000
Total Assets	$138,723	$146,542
Liabilities	$115,050	$116,046
Reserves for Losses	$ 300	$ 250
Long-Term Borrowing	$ 9,114	$ 8,891
Stockholders' Equity	$ 23,259	$ 21,355
Total Liabilities and Equity	$138,723	$146,542
Net Revenue	$ 4,356	$ 3,480
Net Income	$ 696	$ 634
Net Profit Margin (Net Income ÷ Net Revenue)	15.98%	18.2%
Return on Equity (Net Income ÷ Stockholder's Equity)	2.99%	2.97%
Shares Outstanding	173,924,100	163,239,829
Number of Employees	14,987	14,321

management of all the risks facing the corporation, be they financial, business, or event-type risks that were traditionally under the authority of the risk manager.

LOCO has a rather large amount of reserves on its balance sheet. A considerable portion of the reserves are attributable to the expected E&O losses that were assumed from Kendu Financial Group when it was acquired in 1994. Another big chunk of the reserve amount is attributable to self-insured workers' compensation losses. LOCO has self-insured its domestic and international workers' compensation risk since the early 1980s. Even though claims were handled by a third-party administrator, two individuals on Dan's staff have devoted their full-time work to workers' compensation issues. With the current soft market conditions. Dan decided to insure the risk. He secured Foreign Voluntary Workers' Compensation coverage for U.S. workers abroad and for foreign nationals, as well as workers' compensation for the domestic employees. The company has built up fairly significant loss obligations from self-insuring.

LOCO's business has been changing rapidly over the last several years. It has become more global, more dependent upon technology, and more diversified in its operations. This changing risk environment along with the corporation's cost-cutting efforts, has compelled Dan to embark on a comprehensive assessment of his risk management department and the corporate risk profile.

First Group of Questions for Discussion and Answers Based on the Information in Chapter 3

Assume you are LOCO's major broker and assisting Dan in identifying the risks that LOCO faces (use the risk mapping concept of Chapter 3).

Suggested answer: The risks of LOCO Corporation include:

- Failure to perform and other liability claims against officers, directors, trustees, stockbrokers, and other employees
- Employee dishonesty, including risks associated with rogue trading
- Electronic and computer crime
- Employment practices liability, including risks associated with employee benefit plans
- Property, including losses associated with natural disaster risks
- Business interruption from physical damage and from systems failure
- General liability
- Professional liability
- Automobile liability
- Workers' compensation for U.S. workers domestically and abroad, foreign nationals abroad, and repatriation expenses associated with injured U.S. workers abroad
- Political risks in non-U.S. countries
- Interest-rate and currency-exchange risk
- Fiduciary liability
- Software property rights

Note: You may be able to think of others.

Take each risk identified above and discuss whether you expect aggregate frequency and severity of losses to be low, medium, or high.

Suggested answer: The expected frequency and severity of each of LOCO's risks are:

- Failure to perform and other liability claims against officers, directors, trustees, stockbrokers, and other employees: low frequency/medium to high severity
- Employee dishonesty/rogue trading: low frequency/medium to high severity (Similar reasoning for electronic and computer crime. With appropriate technology, procedures, and safeguards, losses should be few.

However, if a loss does occur, it could be substantial.)

- Electronic and computer crime: low frequency/high severity (This will be a function of LOCO's technology and safeguards that are in place. LOCO has the most advanced technology so we might assume that expected frequency should be low. However, if a loss does occur, it could be substantial.)
- Employment practices liability: low to medium frequency/medium to high severity (LOCO has a large number of employees and they are spread out globally. The frequency of risk will depend upon the risk management's coordination with the human resources people in providing some level of centralized control over human resource practices around the world, among other things. Like any liability risk, however, if a loss occurs, it has the potential of being a high severity.)
- Property: medium frequency/medium severity (Natural disaster risks pose a high severity.)
- Business interruption by any cause: low to medium frequency/medium to high severity (The level of LOCO's risk is dependent upon its business contingency plans and its technological systems.)
- General liability: low frequency/medium severity.
- Professional liability: low frequency/medium severity (LOCO's professional liability would be limited to the professionals that it has on staff, such as attorneys and accountants. It is not expected that these individuals would be giving advice directly or indirectly to persons outside of LOCO.)
- Automobile liability: low to medium frequency/medium severity (This would be a function of the number of employees driving corporate-owned or leased vehicles or otherwise using a vehicle, for corporate purposes.)
- Workers compensation: medium to high frequency/medium severity (This will be a function of LOCO's loss control efforts in place.)
- Political risks: low to medium frequency/high severity (LOCO is in some rather volatile locations and the likelihood of a loss associated with political risk is larger in those areas.)

- Interest-rate and currency-exchange risk: high frequency/medium to high severity (Exchange risk is frequent unless hedging controls are put into place.)

- Fiduciary liability: low to medium frequency/high severity (LOCO is in a fiduciary capacity in much of its operations, thus we have assessed the potential for fiduciary related claims as low to medium frequency.)

- Software property rights: high frequency/medium severity (Software producers have a high potential for property rights claims. This risk can be two ways—offensive, e.g., others that are infringing upon LOCO's property rights and defensive, e.g., defending claims against LOCO's alleged infringement upon the property rights of others.).

Draw a risk map graph and place your estimates from Question (2) in the appropriate quadrant. For each risk, indicate what risk handling method is suggested by your estimates.

Suggested answer: see Figure C3.4

- Failure to perform and other liability claims against officers, directors, trustees, stockbrokers and other employees: low frequency/medium to high severity: *insurance*

- Electronic and computer crime: low frequency/high severity: *insurance*

- Employee dishonesty/rogue trading: low frequency/medium to high severity: *insurance*

- Employment practices liability: low to medium frequency/medium to high severity: *insurance*

- Property: medium frequency/medium severity (natural disaster risks pose a high severity): *loss control efforts are called for along with*

retention: insurance or other risk transfer methods for property catastrophic risks

- Business interruption by any cause: low to medium frequency/medium to high severity: *insurance*

- General liability: low frequency/medium severity: *insurance*

- Professional liability: low frequency/medium severity: *insurance*

- Automobile liability: low to medium frequency/medium severity: *insurance with loss control to help reduce the frequency*

- Workers' compensation: medium to high frequency/medium severity: *loss control and retention*

- Political risks: low to medium frequency/high severity: *insurance in the less volatile areas; possibly avoidance in the more volatile areas or LOCO may choose loss control methods and retention so it can continue operations in those locales*

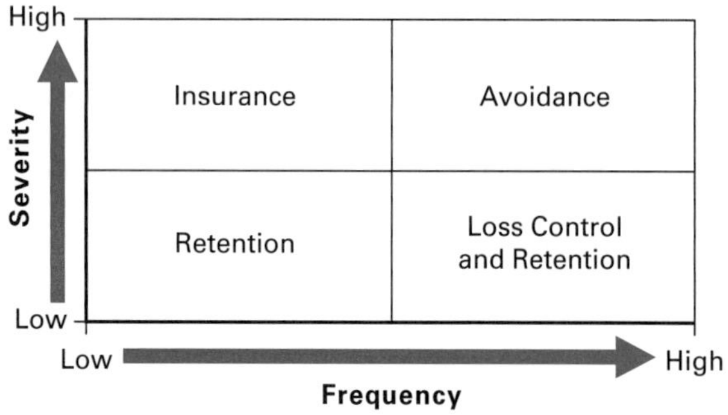

The risks that fall in the "avoidance" quadrant are not always available at any price.

- Interest-rate and currency-exchange risk—high frequency/medium to high severity: *loss control and retention; avoidance is not a viable option*

- Fiduciary liability—low to medium frequency/high severity: *loss control and retention and insurance at the high levels where there would be less frequency*

- Software property rights—high frequency/medium severity: *loss control and retention; avoidance is not a viable option unless LOCO does not want to be in the software business*

The soft market of the period in this example makes insurance an attractive risk handling method in many cases. This is the reason, for example, that LOCO has chosen to insure its worker compensation losses. The level of retention will be a function of the insured's capacity. We have chosen insurance for the liability risks—even where a "medium severity" is indicated because there is the potential for a loss of high severity. Insurance generally is used for liability risks because it is a low frequency exposure at the high amounts. Also, as noted above, often more than one risk handling method is appropriate. This is particularly true with regard to loss control methods. Loss control methods

FIGURE C3.4   Risk Management Matrix

can be employed when either insuring or retaining a risk. Important to note is the fact that risk management behavior is not as discrete as implied by the matrix of risk management. The tools are interchangeable and are often used simultaneously.

LOCO CORPORATION CASE STUDY: PART 2

Background Information

Following again are some of the actions taken by Dan's team:

- Restructured of all coverages to save money on administration and to provide stream-lined and sufficient coverages for all the risk faced by LOCO and its subsidiaries
- Found ways to take the 1991 losses of the Gulf war off the balance sheet and insure risks that previously were uninsured.

Second Group of Questions for Discussion and Answers Based on the Innovative Programs Featured Here

The current consolidation and diversification in the industry has resulted in an across-the-board corporate mandate to cut costs. Dan, like other department heads, is under pressure to increase efficiency. Dan wants to investigate the feasibility of an integrated risk management approach. What advantages would an integrated program have for LOCO? What characteristics about LOCO lend itself to an integrated program?

Suggested answer: An integrated program holds the promise of less administrative time and cost. This results from having seamless coverage of many risks in one policy—eliminating the additional administration of working with multiple policies. Also, savings result from having one overall policy limit. If LOCO obtains a multi-year contract, as most integrated programs are, it will enjoy further administrative time and cost savings by having fewer renewals. Duplication of coverages will be eliminated and gaps of needed coverages will be less likely.

LOCO is a global corporation that has had disjointed risk financing programs in the past since international operations were handled separately from domestic operations. Thus, the company should be able to realize considerable savings by integrating their program across geographical borders using fewer carriers.

In addition, LOCO's various business operations, while diversified, are related. LOCO has a blurring of operational lines. This is typical of many firms in the financial services industry. LOCO can combine its common risks for all of its subsidiaries into one integrated program. For example, an important exposure for LOCO and all of its subsidiaries is Errors and Omissions (E&O).

LOCO's E&O losses can stem from various sources: such as from an agent advising a client on estate planning, from a broker helping a mutual fund client, or from LOCO employees developing and selling software. Other important exposures are those related to employee dishonesty. If LOCO is like many other financial institutions, it probably has a tower of separate fidelity bond contracts. It would be beneficial for LOCO to cover all of these E&O and fidelity bond exposures under one contract. Related to this is the potential for other losses to customers and the funds' stockholders for which LOCO can be sued, such as electronic related malfunctions or crime. Coverage also is needed for corporate indemnification of directors and officers and for individual indemnification of directors and officers when corporate indemnification is prohibited. Affordable and available coverage *of personal* indemnification has been difficult to obtain. All of these exposures are ones that have been combined in integrated risk programs by a number of other major global corporations.

Another important characteristic about LOCO is that it is heavily dependent on the proper functioning of its electronic equipment and its information systems and not very dependent on a physical plant. Traditional insurance coverages focus on loss that occurs as a result of physical damage. An example of such risks is business interruption coverage. For example, traditional coverage for business interruption generally excludes coverage for losses caused solely by software or hardware system failure. Business interruption as a result of such failure is just as devastating to LOCO as business interruption that results from physical damage. An integrated risk program could be arranged to cover LOCO for such a loss regardless of the cause.

LOCO's good loss history is another compelling reason for it to consider an integrated program with a single policy limit. It has been paying for separate policies with separate limits that have not been needed. LOCO can purchase a single limit with one or more reinstatements of limits that will be priced less than a tower of individual coverage limits.

In addition to its good loss history, LOCO is well capitalized and thus, should be able to design a program that is mutually acceptable to it and a strong carrier. Dan should work with his broker(s) and carrier(s) on a program that meets the changing and diversified needs of LOCO. An integrated program can give LOCO the flexibility not present in traditional insurance product design.

Briefly explain what a finite risk program is. Why might such a program be appropriate for LOCO?

Suggested answer: A finite program is a method of financing a corporation's retained risks through an insurer that enables the corporation to smooth out its cash flows and improve its balance sheet. It does this by paying predetermined equal payments to a fund held by the insurer. When losses occur, they are paid for out of the fund. If it is combined with significant risk transfer, the monies paid to the insurer can be tax deductible for the corporation.

It appears that LOCO has the capacity to retain large amounts of risk and it can use risk transfer at high amounts. Thus, LOCO is a good candidate for a finite risk program. It also can bring in uninsurable risks. Adding uninsurable risks will enable LOCO to reduce the annual fluctuations in earnings and/or cash flows caused by uninsured losses. LOCO also has the large amounts of cash needed to put into the fund on a periodic basis. Finally, it appears that Dan has the support needed from higher management to initiate such a program. Convincing top management is not an uncommon obstacle to establishing a finite risk program.

BIBLIOGRAPHY

Aldred, Carolyn, "Alternative Financing of Primary Interest to Risk Managers: Expected to Become More Familiar With Non-Traditional Products," *Business Insurance* 3 September 1997.

Banham, Russ, "When Insurance Really Is A Total Risk Package," *Global Finance* February 1997: 11–12.

Doherty, Neil A., "Corporate Insurance: Competition from Capital Markets and Financial Institutions," *Assurances* April 1997: 63–94.

Helbting, Carolyn P., Georg Fallegger and Donna Hill. *Rethinking Risk Financing* (Zurich: Swiss Reinsurance Company, 1996).

Herrick, R. C. "Exploring the Efficient Frontier," *Risk Management* August 1997: 23–25.

Koral, Edward S., "A Tug of War Accounting Rules and Finite Risk Programs," *Risk Management* November 1995: 45–47.

Lenckus, Dave, "FMR Corp.," *Business Insurance* April 14, 1997: 98.

Lenckus, Dave, "Reinsurance Program Strives to Find the Right Blend of Risks," *Business Insurance* 14 April 1997: 100.

Lenckus, Dave, "Concentric Risk Programs Means Big Saving: Innovative Programs to Save FMR Time, Money," *Business Insurance* 14 April 1997: 98.

May, David G., "All-In-One Insurance," *Financial Executive* 13 no. 3 (1997): 41–43.

May, David G., "Integrated Risk; Reaching Toward Risk Management Heaven," *Viewpoint Quarterly,* Marsh & McLennan Companies, Winter 1996.

May, David G., "The Real Thing," *Financial Executive* 13 no. 3 (1997): 42.

Mello, John P. Jr., "Paradise, or Pipe Dream?" *CFO: the Magazine for Chief Financial Officers* 13 no. 2 (1997): 73–75.

Myers, Gregory K., "Alternative Risk Financing in the Traditional Insurance Marketplace," *The John Liner Review* Fall 1996 10 no. 3 (fall 1996): 6–16.

Nottingham, Lucy, "Integrated Risk Management," *The Canadian Business Review* 23 no. 2 (Summer 1996): 26–28.

Teach, Edward, "Microsoft's Universe of Risk," *CFO* March 1997: 68–72.

"What is Risk Transfer in Reinsurance? Comments on Financial Accounting Standard 113," *Contingencies* September/October 1997: 50–53.

NOTES

1. The Council of Insurance Agents and Brokers assumed all NAIB copyrights when the two organizations merged. The Council gave permission to use the material. The Council of Insurance Agents and Brokers is located in Washington, DC. This case is based on the video education series created for continuing education of brokers in 1996 and 1997. Five video education modules were created. The material used in this case is from video number 5. Some modifications to the original material were necessary when translating to print.

2. Recall the explanation of the underwriting cycles described in Chapter 5 of the text. Also, remember that this case was prepared in 1996–1997 during the end tail of a long soft market condition.

3. Remember that at the time of writing, post September 11, the markets have been very hard. This case is illustrative of the importance of the new generation risk financing products regardless of market conditions.

4. Nottingham, Lucy, "Integrated Risk Management." *The Canadian Business Review* 23 no. 2 (Summer 1996): p. 26.

5. Aldred, Carolyn, "Alternative Financing of Primary Interest: Risk Managers Expected to Become More Familiar with Non-Traditional Products," *Business Insurance* 3 September 1997.

6. Judy Lindenmayer was one of the experts contributing to the creation of this video education segment.

7. http://www2.emap.com/grmn/archive/issue/mar96/96mar29.htm

8. Ibid

9. May, David G., "The Real Thing," *Financial Executive* 13 no. 3 (1997): 42.

10. In 2002, the company name is only the Marsh part. During the period of the case, many brokerage houses merged. The large mergers and the decrease in the number of brokerage houses prompted the consolidation of the brokers an agents organizations into the Council of Insurance Agents and Brokers.

11. May, David G., "All-In-One Insurance," *Financial Executive* 13 no. 3 (1997): 41.

12. Mello, John P Jr., "Paradise, or Pipe Dream?" *CFO: The Magazine for Chief Financial Officers* 13 no. 2 (1997): 73.

13. Lenckus, Dave, "Concentric Risk Programs Means Big Saving - Innovative Programs to Save FMR Time, Money" *Business Insurance* 14 April 1997: 98.

14. http://www.marshmac.com/comment/irsk.htm—examples are provided in the Appendix. May, David G., "The Real Thing," *Financial Executive* 13 no. 3 (1997): 42.

15. Lenckus, Dave, "Reinsurance Program Strives to Find the Right Blend of Risks," *Business Insurance* 14 April 1997: 100.

16. Gregory K. Myers, "Alternative Risk Financing in the Traditional Insurance Marketplace," *The John Liner Review* 10 no. 3 (fall 1996): 13.

17. Types of risks included in the program may be restricted by the corporation's external auditors

18. "What is 'Risk Transfer' in Reinsurance? Comments on Financial Accounting Standard 113," *Contingencies* September/October 1997: 50–53. (Based on a report of the American Academy of Actuaries Committee on Property and Liability Issues.)

Financial Risk Management for Hometown Bank

PREFACE

Case 4, like Case 3, is designed for advanced studies of risk management. Here, the focus is on financial risk management of a bank using the tools and instruments that were introduced in Chapter 3. The case of the hypothetical bank was created by Denise Togger[1], a graduate finance student who also assisted in the development and writing of Chapter 3. The work was part of an independent study course in advanced risk management tools. The case featured here can be used as a template for advanced risk management projects.

INTRODUCTION

Risk management is certainly on every CEO's radar screens these days. Risk-related issues regularly make the headlines. Companies historically were classified into industry categories, usually according to what they produced or what service they provided. Today, companies can be classified in terms of the key risks that they manage. For example, a bank makes money by charging borrowers interest on loans made from their balance sheet; banks are in the business of credit risk management.[2] If this one form of risk to a bank is managed ineffectively and charges are made against bad loans, shareholder punishment is swift and stock prices plunge. Just such actions are the current concern of John Allen, CEO of Hometown Bank. Mr. Allen is addressing company-wide, long-range plans to incorporate risk management techniques to maximize his bank's financial performance and shareholder value.

HISTORY

In the early years of U.S. banking history, banks seemed to have the easiest job in the corporate world. All a bank manager had to do was receive deposits in the form of checking, savings, and deposit accounts (bank liabilities), and provide mortgage and other lending services (bank assets). Throughout the twentieth century, the banking industry prospered. For most of the post-World War II era the upward-sloping yield curve meant that interest rates on traditional thirty-year residential mortgage loans exceeded rates on shorter-term savings and time deposits.[3] The positive net margin between the two rates accounted for banks' prosperity. All of this ended abruptly when the Federal Reserve changed its monetary policy in October 1979 to one of targeting bank reserves instead of interest rates. A historical perspective of interest rates is provided in Figures C4.1 and C4.2 (note the scale on the Y-axis).

Figures C4.1 and C4.2 graphically present interest rate risk exposure faced by banks. The noticeable change is the absolute pickup in interest rate volatility from 1979 forward. As Figure C4.2 shows, three-month T-bill interest rates rose higher than 16 percent in the early 1980s. Yet many banks' assets were locked into low-interest, long-term loans, mostly thirty-year mortgages. The financial crisis that followed the rapid rise in interest rates (on both short- and long-term liabilities) was catastrophic in proportion; many banks failed by positioning their loan portfolios incorrectly for the change in interest rates. Locked-in long-term mortgage loan rates provided insufficient cash inflows to meet

FIGURE C4.1   30-Year Treasury Rates

Source: www.economagic.com; Economagic includes the original data sources: U.S. Government, Federal Reserve Board of Governors historical monthly interest rate series.

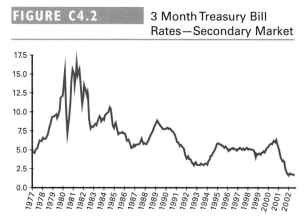

FIGURE C4.2   3 Month Treasury Bill Rates—Secondary Market

Source: www.economagic.com; Economagic includes the original data source: U.S. Government, Federal Reserve Board of Governors historical monthly interest rate series.

the higher cash outflows required on deposits. Those that survived had to make major changes in their risk management style. Later we will introduce how a specific bank, Hometown Bank, manages its interest rate exposure using derivatives.

"Modern banks employ credit-scoring techniques to ensure that they are making good lending decisions, use analytical models to monitor the performance of their portfolio of loans, and implement financial instruments to transfer out those credit risks they are not comfortable with."[4] Bankers learned a costly lesson in the 1980s by not being adequately prepared for a changing interest rate environment. Risk management must be enterprise-wide and inclusive of all components of risk. Hometown Bank is a surviving bank, with lofty goals for the future. The current focus for CEO John Allen has three components:

1. Review the primary elements of Hometown's financial risks:
   - Interest rate risk—those risks associated with changes in interest rates
   - Market risk—risk of loss associated with changes in market price or value
   - Credit risk—risk of loss through customer default

2. Review Hometown's non-financial, or operational, risks: those risks associated with the operating processes or systems in running a bank

3. Monitor the success of risk mitigation techniques the bank employs

HOMETOWN BANK

Hometown Bancorp was formed in 1985 as a financial holding company headquartered in Richmond, Virginia. Its only subsidiary is Hometown Bank, which was chartered in 1950 with the opening of its first branch in downtown Richmond. Hometown has experienced a steady growth of core assets: deposits, money market instruments, and marketable security investments. Figure C4.3 shows Hometown's investment policy and lists allowable securities for their investment securities account.

Asset growth has occurred both internally and externally with the acquisition of community banks and branches in Hometown's market. Market domain expanded to include the capital region (the city of Richmond and surrounding counties), the Tidewater region, the Shenandoah Valley region, and the northern Virginia markets. In March 2002 Hometown Bank opened its twenty-fifth branch in Virginia Beach, Virginia. With total assets of $785 million (as of December 2001), Hometown ranks as the eighth largest commercial bank in the state of Virginia. The network of branches offers a wide range of lending and deposit services to business, government, and consumer clients. The use of these deposits funds both the loan and investment portfolio of the bank. Principal sources of revenue are interest and fees on loans and investments and maintenance fees for servicing deposit accounts. Principal expenses include interest paid on deposits and other borrowings and operating expenses. Corporate goals are to achieve superior performance

FIGURE C4.3 — Hometown Bancorp Investment Policy, December 31, 2001

The securities portfolio is managed by the President and Treasurer of the Bank. Investment management is handled in accordance with the investment policy, which is approved annually by the board of directors. To assist in the management process, each investment security shall be classified as "held-for-maturity" or "available-for-sale." The investment policy covers investment strategies, approved securities dealers, and authorized investments. The following securities have been approved as investments:

- U.S. Treasury Securities
- Agency Securities
- Municipal Notes and Bonds
- Corporate Notes and Bonds
- GNMA, FNMA, and FHLMC mortgage-backed securities (MBS)
- Collateralized Mortgage Obligations (CMOs)
- Interest Rate Swaps
- Interest Rate Caps

All securities must be investment grade quality and carry a minimum rating of no less than single-A by Moody's or Standard & Poor's.

TABLE C4.1 — Hometown Bancorp and Subsidiaries Financial Statements (in thousands)

Consolidated Balance Sheet	2001	2000	1999
Interest-earning assets			
Money market investments	$ 62,800	$ 49,600	$ 39,100
Investment securities	65,500	51,700	40,800
Loans	649,300	513,000	405,000
Allowance for loan losses	(11,300)	(7,600)	(6,000)
Premises, furniture, & equipment	14,900	11,700	10,000
Other real estate	3,800	3,000	2,500
Total assets	$785,000	$621,400	$491,400
Interest-bearing liabilities			
Deposits	$467,500	$369,300	$292,000
Other short term borrowings	123,000	97,000	76,700
Non-interest borrowings	117,000	92,400	73,000
Long-term debt	12,900	10,000	8,200
Total liabilities	$720,400	$568,700	$449,900
Shareholders' equity	64,600	$ 52,700	41,500
Total liabilities and shareholders equity	$785,000	$621,400	$491,400

Consolidated Income Statement	2001	2000	1999
Interest income	$ 55,000	$ 44,000	$ 34,700
Interest expense	(27,500)	(21,100)	(18,300)
Net interest income	$ 27,500	$ 22,900	$ 16,400
Provision for loan losses	(4,400)	(3,400)	(2,700)
Net interest income after provision	$ 23,100	$ 19,500	$ 13,700
Non-interest income	4,400	2,800	1,900
Operating expenses	(16,900)	(14,300)	(10,100)
Income before taxes	$ 10,600	$ 8,000	$ 5,500
Taxes	(3,600)	(2,700)	(1,100)
Net Income	$ 7,000	$ 5,300	$ 4,400

and profitability, to gain strategic market share, and to provide superior client service. Hometown has achieved its fifth consecutive year of record earnings. Table C4.1 shows Hometown's consolidated financial statements from 1999 to 2001.

THE CHALLENGES OF MANAGING FINANCIAL RISK

The challenge that faces all corporations is identifying their most important risks. Allen has identified the following broad risk categories that Hometown Bank faces:

- **Interest rate risk** associated with asset-liability management
- **Market risk** associated with trading activities and investment securities portfolio management; that is, the risk of loss/gain in the value of bank assets due to changes in market prices
- **Credit risk** associated with lending activities, including the risk of customer default on repayment

- **Operational risk** associated with running Hometown Bank and the operating processes and systems that support the bank's day-to-day activities

Each risk component will be addressed to formulate a composite risk management framework.

Interest Rate Risk

A primary financial objective of Hometown Bank is to grow its assets. Net worth, also known as shareholder value, is defined: Shareholders' Equity = Total Assets −

Total Liabilities. Thus when assets grow more than liabilities, shareholder value also increases. Hometown Bank's assets, as noted on its consolidated balance sheet in Table C4.1, primarily consist of loans; at year-end 2001, $649.3 million of Hometown's $785 million total assets were in the form of loans. (See Table C4.2 for loan portfolio composition). Hometown obtains funding for these loans from its deposit base. Note that for Hometown Bank, as for all banks, deposit accounts are recorded as liabilities. Hometown Bank has an outstanding obligation to its deposit customers to give the money back. For Hometown, deposits make up $467.5 million, or 65 percent, of total outstanding liabilities. The mismatch between deposits and loans is the time element of each. Hometown's main asset category, retail mortgage loans, have long-term maturities, while its main liabilities are demand deposits and short-term CDs, which have immediate or short-term maturities.

Hometown's net cash outflows represent payments of interest on deposits. Because of the deposits' short-term maturities, these interest payments are subject to frequent changes. Demand depositors' interest rates can change frequently, even daily, to reflect current interest rates. Short-term CDs are also subject to changes in current interest rates because the interest rate paid to customers changes at each maturity date to reflect the current market. If bank customers are not happy with the new rate offered by the bank, they may choose not to reinvest their CD. Interest rate risk for Hometown Bank arises from its business of lending long-term, with locked-in interest rates, while growing their loan portfolio with short-term borrowings like CDs, with fluctuating interest rates. This risk has increased dramatically because of the increase in interest rate volatility. During the period of January 2001 through October 2002, three-month treasury bills traded in a range from 6.5 percent to 1.54 percent. (Refer to Figure C4.2.) During periods of inverted yield curves (where longer-term investments have lower interest rates than short-term investments), a bank's traditional strategy of providing long-term loans using deposits is a money-losing strategy. Note the normal yield curve and inverted yield curve in Figure C4.4.

FIGURE C4.4   Yield Curves

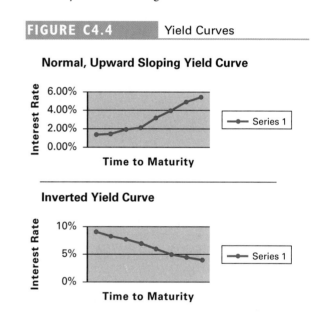

Normal, Upward Sloping Yield Curve

Inverted Yield Curve

TABLE C4.2   Loan Portfolio Composition, Hometown Bancorp (in Thousands)

	2001 Amount	%	2000 Amount	%	1999 Amount	%
Construction and Land Development						
Residential	$ 32,465	5%	$ 30,780	6%	$ 28,350	7%
Commercial	32,465	5	25,650	5	20,250	5
Other	12,986	2	20,520	4	16,200	4
Mortgage						
Residential	331,143	51	241,110	47	182,250	45
Commercial	110,381	17	82,080	16	81,000	20
Commercial and Industrial	32,465	5	41,040	8	24,300	6
Consumer	97,395	15	71,820	14	52,650	13
Total Loans Receivable	$ 649,300	100%	$ 513,000	100%	$405,000	100%

TABLE C4.3			Swap Cash Flow		

Hometown Bank	Pays 5 percent rate to	SwissBank
SwissBank	Pays LIBOR to	Hometown Bank

Swap Example for Hometown Bank

End of Year	LIBOR	Fixed Rate	Interest Obligation of Hometown Bank	Interest Obligation of SwissBank	Net Cash Payment to Hometown
1	2.50%	3%	$100,000,000 × .03 = $3,000,000	$100,000,000 × .025 = $3,000,000	$(500,000)
2	3.00%	3%	$100,000,000 × .03 = $3,000,000	$100,000,000 × .03 = $3,000,000	0
3	4.00%	3%	$100,000,000 × .03 = $3,000,000	$100,000,000 × .04 = $4,000,000	1,000,000
4	4.50%	3%	$100,000,000 × .03 = $3,000,000	$100,000,000 × .045 = $4,500,000	1,500,000
...					
10	5.50%	3%	$100,000 × .03 = $3,000,000	$100,000,000 × .055 = $5,500,000	2,500,000

When interest rates are inverted, cash outflows associated with interest payments to depositors will exceed cash inflows from borrowers, such as mortgage holders. For example, a home buyer with a thirty-year mortgage loan at 6 percent on $100,000 will continue to make principal and interest payments to Hometown at $597.65 per month. Interest cash flow received by Hometown is calculated at the 6 percent stated rate on the $100,000 loan. If short-term interest rates move higher, for example to 10 percent, Hometown will have interest cash outflows at 10 percent with interest cash inflows at only 6 percent. How will Hometown Bank deal with this type of interest rate risk?

Swaps as a Tool

An interest rate swap is an agreement between two parties to exchange cash flows at specified future times. Interest rate swaps are used by banks primarily to convert floating-rate liabilities (remember, customers will demand current market interest rates on their deposits—these are the floating rates) into fixed-rate liabilities. Exchanging variable cash flows for fixed cash flows is called a "plain vanilla" swap. Hometown can use a swap as a tool to reduce interest rate risk.

U.S. Banks		European Banks	
Assets	Liabilities	Assets	Liabilities
Fixed rate loans	Floating rate deposits	Floating rate loans	Fixed rate deposits
Hometown Bank Average Rates			
7.25%	2.5%		

Risk: If interest rates go up, interest paid on deposits could exceed interest received on loans; a loss

Risk: If interest rates go down, interest received on loans could be less than interest paid on deposits; a loss

European banks are the opposite of U.S. banks. European bank customers demand floating rate loans tied to LIBOR (London Interbank Offer Rate); their loans are primarily variable rate and their deposit base is fixed-rate time deposits. If two banks, one U.S. and one European, can agree to an exchange of their liabilities, the result is:

U.S. Banks		European Banks	
Assets	Liabilities	Assets	Liabilities
Fixed	Fixed	Floating	Floating

The swap creates a match of interest-rate-sensitive cash inflows and outflows: fixed rate assets and liabilities for the U.S. bank, and floating rate assets and liabilities for the European bank. The following steps show how Hometown Bank employs the financial instrument of a swap with SwissBank for $100 million of their mortgage loans as a risk management tool.

In our simplified example in Table C4.3, Hometown agrees to swap with SwissBank cash flows equal to an agreed-upon fixed rate of 3 percent on $100 million, a portion of their total assets. The term is set for ten years. At the same time SwissBank agrees to pay Hometown cash flows equal to LIBOR an indexed short-term floating rate of interest on the same $100 million. Remember, the contract is an agreement to exchange, or swap, interest payments only. The amount is determined by the desired amount of assets the two parties wish to hedge against interest rate risk. They agree to do this because, as explained above, it better aligns each bank's risk. They agree to swap to minimize interest-rate risk exposure. For Hometown Bank, when interest rates rise, the dollars they receive on the swap increases. This creates a gain on the swap that offsets the loss or supplements the smaller margins available to the bank because of interest rate moves. Keep in mind that the interest margin may have been profitable at the time of the original transaction; however, higher interest rates have increased cash outflows of interest paid to depositors.

In our example, we show what happens if interest rates increase. Over the sample four years shown in Table C4.3, short-term interest rates move up from 2.50 percent to 4.50 percent. If Hometown Bank was not hedged with the interest rate swap, their interest expenses would be increasing as their deposit base would be requiring higher interest cash outflows. With the swap, Hometown Bank can offset the higher cash outflows on their liabilities (higher interest payments to depositors) with the excess cash payments received on the swap. The swap mitigates the risk of increasing interest rates. Why, you might ask, would SwissBank agrees to the swap? Remember, SwissBank has floating rate loans as the majority of their asset base. As interest rates rise, their cash inflows increase. This offsets their increasing cash flows promised to Hometown Bank. The risk of loss for SwissBank comes into play when interest rates decline. If interest rates were to decline below the fixed rate of 3 percent, SwissBank would be the benefactor of the swap.

Market Risk

Market risk is the change in market value of bank assets and liabilities resulting from changing market conditions. For example, as interest rates increase, the loans Hometown Bank made at low, fixed-rates become less valuable to the bank. The total market values of their assets decline as the market value of the loans lose value. If the loans are traded in the secondary market, there would be an actual loss recorded for Hometown. Other bank assets and liabilities are at risk as well to changing market prices. Hometown accepts equity positions as collateral against loans that are subject to changing equity prices. As equity prices fall, the collateral against the loan is less valuable. If the price decline is precipitous, the loan could become undercollateralized and not provide enough protection to Hometown Bank in case of customer default. Other examples of market risk are activities of the bank in foreign exchange services. This subjects them to currency exchange rate risk. Also included is commodity price risk associated with lending in the agricultural industry.

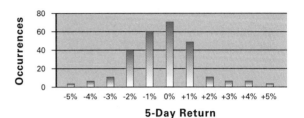

FIGURE C4.5 Hometown Bank Probability Distribution of Daily Price Movement of the Investment Securities Portfolio

Measuring Value at Risk

Sample Data

Date	Portfolio Value	% Change From Beginning Value
12-31-01	$65,500,000	0
1-02-02	$64,300,000	-1.83%
1-03-02	$64,900,000	-0.16%
1-04-02	$64,100,200	-2.14%
1-07-02	$63,900,900	-2.44%
1-08-02	$64,500,000	-1.52%

How does a bank manage the market risks it faces? Value at risk, or **VaR,** modeling has become the standard risk measurement tool in the banking industry to assess market risk exposure. VaR is defined as the worst-case scenario of loss that could occur for a company subject to a specific set of risks (interest rates, equity prices, exchange rates, and commodity prices). For a given level of confidence (using the statistical measure of standard deviation), over a specified time horizon, VaR can be used to measure risks in any single security (either a specific investment represented in their investment securities or loan from a specific customer) or an entire portfolio, as long as there is sufficient historical data. VaR asks the question "What is the worst loss that could occur?"[5]

Hometown Bank has a total of $65.5 million in investment securities. Typically these securities are held by banks until the money is needed by bank customers as loans. Hometown has an investment policy that lists their approved securities for investment. See policy dated December 31, 2001 in Figure C4.3. Because the portfolio consists of interest rate sensitive securities, as interest rates rise the value of the securities declines.[6] Mr. Allen is interested in estimating the value at risk. To illustrate the computation of VaR, a historical database can be used to track the value of the different bonds held by Hometown Bank as investment securities. How many times over a given time period—one year, in our example—did Hometown experience negative price movement on their investments? To simplify the example, we will assume the entire portfolio is invested in two year U.S. Treasury notes. A year of historical data would create approximately 250 price movement data points for the portfolio.[7] Of those 250 results, how frequently did the portfolio value decrease five per cent or more from the beginning value? What was the frequency of times the portfolio of U.S. Treasury notes increased in value more than five percent? Hometown Bank can now construct a probability distribution of returns by recording observations of portfolio performance.

The frequency distribution curve of price movement for the portfolio is charted in Figure C4.5. From that data, Hometown can measure a portfolio's VaR for a five-day period and determine the probability of a loss in magnitude greater than five percent. VaR describes the probability of potential loss in value of the U.S. Treasury notes that relates to market price risk.

Allen is concerned with a situation where the losses incurred would be more than 5 percent of the overall value. That situation appeared to occur not more than 1 percent of the time in any five-day period (1 percent out of 250 occurrences using a 95 percent confidence level). The choice of the confidence interval depends on how sure Allen wants to be of the possibility of the occurrence of a greater than 5 percent loss. The confidence level is determined by the number of standard deviations away from the mean. It answers the question, does the bank want a 95 percent or 99 percent confidence level of measuring potential price movement to the upside/downside?

Hometown presents the results of the VaR model of its $65.5 million portfolio as follows: We are 95 percent confident that the portfolio will experience a decline of no more than $65,500,000 times 1 percent, or $655,000 over 5 days.

The risk can now be communicated with the statement: Under normal market conditions, the most the investment security portfolio can lose in value over a five-day period is about $655,000 at the 95 percent confidence level.[8]

There is much debate about VaR weaknesses. "In short, VaR models do not provide an accurate measure of the losses that occur in extreme events. You simply cannot depict the full texture and range of your market risks with VaR alone."[9]

CREDIT RISK

Credit risk refers to the risk that a borrower will default on interest or principal payments. It may stem from a customer's unwillingness or inability to pay. For banks and most other credit institutions, credit risk is considered to be the form of risk that can most significantly diminish earnings and financial strength.

Credit risk management for traditional lending is fairly straightforward. Hometown Bank, as well as other lenders, credit-score their clients to better quantify their potential for default. The essential elements of credit risk management are to determine exposures enterprise-wide and apply default/recovery considerations.

Hometown Bank for the year 2001 has set aside an allowance of loan losses totaling $11,300,000. These are considered reserves for possible loan losses due to client default (see Table C4.1). The allowance has increased from $7,600,000 in 2000, almost 50 percent, because of an increase in loans as well as a slowing economy. This is necessary because of the overall industry experience of increasing non-current loans as a percentage of total bank loans (see Figure C4.6). Because of the bank's long operating history, Allen relies on past experience and payment histories to determine current allowances for potential loan losses. Hometown's credit risk and loan underwriting policy is as follows:

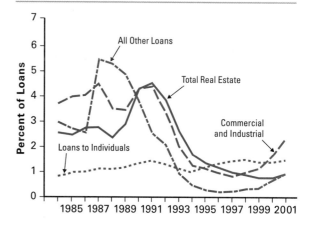

FIGURE C4.6 Non-Current Loans as a Percentage of All Bank Loans

Source: FDIC Quarterly Banking Profile, 31 December 2001. The FDIC Quarterly Banking Profile is available in hard copy format. Web access is also available; FDIC www.FDIC.gov, and specifically to the FDIC Quarterly Banking Profile; www.2.fdic.gov/qbp/2001dec/qbp.pdf

- Evaluate borrower ability to repay—their creditworthiness.
- Evaluate the value of underlying collateral.
- All credit committee members must approve loans greater than $1 million.
- No more than $10 million is lent to any one borrower.
- Track payment history of all loans.
- Status loans and reserve accordingly:
  - 0 percent reserve for standard, current loans
  - 15 percent reserve for substandard loans
  - 50 percent reserve for doubtful loans (more than 90 days past due); categorized as non-current loans
  - 100 percent reserve for uncollectible loans

In addition to historical experience, evaluation of allowance for loan losses includes growth and composition of loan portfolio, industry diversification, and general economic conditions.

OPERATIONAL RISK

Operational risks are those that relate to the ongoing day-to-day business activities of the organization. Operations are a vital part of a bank's activities, and they require high levels of technical support to deliver information and analysis to their traders, brokers, and lenders. Many of the largest publicly known losses to financial institutions suffered in the 90s are directly attributed to the failure of operational risk management.[10]

Beyond operations risk, other major categories of nonfinancial risk include regulatory, legal, and event risk.[11] Their inclusion here is to reinforce the full scope of an enterprise risk management strategy. Operational risk is mitigated most frequently through training and education to reduce frequency and size of possible losses as well as the use of insurance products.

OBJECTIVE OF ENTERPRISE RISK MANAGEMENT IN BANKS

Consolidated risk management allows firms to allocate capital efficiently. It is the job of Allen to determine that Hometown Bank is allocating its limited resources to maximize efficiency and firm value. Only effective holistic risk management processes that connect both the financial and non-financial risk elements optimize the bank's value.

NOTES

1. Written by Denise Togger; printed with permission of the author. Denise Williams Togger earned her Bachelor of Science degree in economics in 1991 and her Master of Science in finance in 2002 from Virginia Commonwealth University. In fulfilling the MS degree requirements she completed an independent study in finance focusing on enterprise risk management tools. Text and case material presented draws from curriculum, research, and her 18 years experience in the investment securities industry. Most recently Denise served as a member of the risk management committee of BB&T Capital Markets as Senior Vice President and fixed-income preferred trader. BB&T Capital Markets is the capital markets division of BB&T Corporation, the nation's 14th largest financial holding company.
2. Sumit Paul-Choudhury, "Real Options," *Risk Management Magazine* September 2001: pp 37–41.
3. Anthony Saunders, Chapter 1 in *Financial Institutions Management: A Modern Perspective,* 3rd ed. (New York: McGraw-Hill Higher Education, 2000).
4. Sumit Paul-Choudhury, p. 38.
5. James T. Gleason, *The Management Imperative in Finance Risk* (Princeton, New Jersey: Bloomberg Press, 2000), Chapter 12.
6. Valuation of bonds is covered in general finance text. Bond value = present value of coupons + present value of face value of bond.
7. The number 250 comes from a rough estimate of the number of days securities can be traded in the open market during any given year. Fifty-two weeks at 5 days per week yields 260 weekdays, and there are roughly 10 holidays throughout the year for which the market is closed.
8. Philippe Jorion, *Value at Risk: The New Benchmark for Managing Financial Risk,* 2nd Ed. (New York: McGraw Hill, 2001) Chapter 1.
9. Gleason, Chapter 12.
10. John Conley, "Running Down Rogue Traders", *Risk Management* 48 no. 1 (2001): 19.
11. Gleason, Chapter 1.

APPENDIX A

HOMEOWNERS 3 – SPECIAL FORM

AGREEMENT

We will provide the insurance described in this policy in return for the premium and compliance with all applicable provisions of this policy.

DEFINITIONS

A. In this policy, "you" and "your" refer to the "named insured" shown in the Declarations and the spouse if a resident of the same household. "We", "us" and "our" refer to the Company providing this insurance.

B. In addition, certain words and phrases are defined as follows:

1. "Aircraft Liability", "Hovercraft Liability", "Motor Vehicle Liability" and "Watercraft Liability", subject to the provisions in **b.** below, mean the following:

   a. Liability for "bodily injury" or "property damage" arising out of the:

      (1) Ownership of such vehicle or craft by an "insured";

      (2) Maintenance, occupancy, operation, use, loading or unloading of such vehicle or craft by any person;

      (3) Entrustment of such vehicle or craft by an "insured" to any person;

      (4) Failure to supervise or negligent supervision of any person involving such vehicle or craft by an "insured"; or

      (5) Vicarious liability, whether or not imposed by law, for the actions of a child or minor involving such vehicle or craft.

   b. For the purpose of this definition:

      (1) Aircraft means any contrivance used or designed for flight except model or hobby aircraft not used or designed to carry people or cargo;

      (2) Hovercraft means a self-propelled motorized ground effect vehicle and includes, but is not limited to, flarecraft and air cushion vehicles;

      (3) Watercraft means a craft principally designed to be propelled on or in water by wind, engine power or electric motor; and

      (4) Motor vehicle means a "motor vehicle" as defined in **7.** below.

2. "Bodily injury" means bodily harm, sickness or disease, including required care, loss of services and death that results.

3. "Business" means:

   a. A trade, profession or occupation engaged in on a full-time, part-time or occasional basis; or

   b. Any other activity engaged in for money or other compensation, except the following:

      (1) One or more activities, not described in **(2)** through **(4)** below, for which no "insured" receives more than $2,000 in total compensation for the 12 months before the beginning of the policy period;

      (2) Volunteer activities for which no money is received other than payment for expenses incurred to perform the activity;

      (3) Providing home day care services for which no compensation is received, other than the mutual exchange of such services; or

      (4) The rendering of home day care services to a relative of an "insured".

4. "Employee" means an employee of an "insured", or an employee leased to an "insured" by a labor leasing firm under an agreement between an "insured" and the labor leasing firm, whose duties are other than those performed by a "residence employee".

5. "Insured" means:

   a. You and residents of your household who are:

      (1) Your relatives; or

      (2) Other persons under the age of 21 and in the care of any person named above;

   b. A student enrolled in school full time, as defined by the school, who was a resident of your household before moving out to attend school, provided the student is under the age of:

      (1) 24 and your relative; or

      (2) 21 and in your care or the care of a person described in **a.(1)** above; or

c. Under Section **II**:

(1) With respect to animals or watercraft to which this policy applies, any person or organization legally responsible for these animals or watercraft which are owned by you or any person included in **a.** or **b.** above. "Insured" does not mean a person or organization using or having custody of these animals or watercraft in the course of any "business" or without consent of the owner; or

(2) With respect to a "motor vehicle" to which this policy applies:

(a) Persons while engaged in your employ or that of any person included in **a.** or **b.** above; or

(b) Other persons using the vehicle on an "insured location" with your consent.

Under both Sections **I** and **II,** when the word an immediately precedes the word "insured", the words an "insured" together mean one or more "insureds".

6. "Insured location" means:

a. The "residence premises";

b. The part of other premises, other structures and grounds used by you as a residence; and

(1) Which is shown in the Declarations; or

(2) Which is acquired by you during the policy period for your use as a residence;

c. Any premises used by you in connection with a premises described in **a.** and **b.** above;

d. Any part of a premises:

(1) Not owned by an "insured"; and

(2) Where an "insured" is temporarily residing;

e. Vacant land, other than farm land, owned by or rented to an "insured";

f. Land owned by or rented to an "insured" on which a one, two, three or four family dwelling is being built as a residence for an "insured";

g. Individual or family cemetery plots or burial vaults of an "insured"; or

h. Any part of a premises occasionally rented to an "insured" for other than "business" use.

7. "Motor vehicle" means:

a. A self-propelled land or amphibious vehicle; or

b. Any trailer or semitrailer which is being carried on, towed by or hitched for towing by a vehicle described in **a.** above.

8. "Occurrence" means an accident, including continuous or repeated exposure to substantially the same general harmful conditions, which results, during the policy period, in:

a. "Bodily injury"; or

b. "Property damage".

9. "Property damage" means physical injury to, destruction of, or loss of use of tangible property.

10. "Residence employee" means:

a. An employee of an "insured", or an employee leased to an "insured" by a labor leasing firm, under an agreement between an "insured" and the labor leasing firm, whose duties are related to the maintenance or use of the "residence premises", including household or domestic services; or

b. One who performs similar duties elsewhere not related to the "business" of an "insured".

A "residence employee" does not include a temporary employee who is furnished to an "insured" to substitute for a permanent "residence employee" on leave or to meet seasonal or short-term workload conditions.

11. "Residence premises" means:

a. The one family dwelling where you reside;

b. The two, three or four family dwelling where you reside in at least one of the family units; or

c. That part of any other building where you reside;

and which is shown as the "residence premises" in the Declarations.

"Residence premises" also includes other structures and grounds at that location.

DEDUCTIBLE

Unless otherwise noted in this policy, the following deductible provision applies:

Subject to the policy limits that apply, we will pay only that part of the total of all loss payable under Section I that exceeds the deductible amount shown in the Declarations.

SECTION I – PROPERTY COVERAGES

A. Coverage A – Dwelling

1. We cover:

   a. The dwelling on the "residence premises" shown in the Declarations, including structures attached to the dwelling; and

   b. Materials and supplies located on or next to the "residence premises" used to construct, alter or repair the dwelling or other structures on the "residence premises".

2. We do not cover land, including land on which the dwelling is located.

B. Coverage B – Other Structures

1. We cover other structures on the "residence premises" set apart from the dwelling by clear space. This includes structures connected to the dwelling by only a fence, utility line, or similar connection.

2. We do not cover:

   a. Land, including land on which the other structures are located;

   b. Other structures rented or held for rental to any person not a tenant of the dwelling, unless used solely as a private garage;

   c. Other structures from which any "business" is conducted; or

   d. Other structures used to store "business" property. However, we do cover a structure that contains "business" property solely owned by an "insured" or a tenant of the dwelling provided that "business" property does not include gaseous or liquid fuel, other than fuel in a permanently installed fuel tank of a vehicle or craft parked or stored in the structure.

3. The limit of liability for this coverage will not be more than 10% of the limit of liability that applies to Coverage **A.** Use of this coverage does not reduce the Coverage **A** limit of liability.

C. Coverage C – Personal Property

1. **Covered Property**

   We cover personal property owned or used by an "insured" while it is anywhere in the world. After a loss and at your request, we will cover personal property owned by:

   a. Others while the property is on the part of the "residence premises" occupied by an "insured"; or

   b. A guest or a "residence employee", while the property is in any residence occupied by an "insured".

2. **Limit For Property At Other Residences**

   Our limit of liability for personal property usually located at an "insured's" residence, other than the "residence premises", is 10% of the limit of liability for Coverage **C,** or $1,000, whichever is greater. However, this limitation does not apply to personal property:

   a. Moved from the "residence premises" because it is being repaired, renovated or rebuilt and is not fit to live in or store property in; or

   b. In a newly acquired principal residence for 30 days from the time you begin to move the property there.

3. **Special Limits Of Liability**

   The special limit for each category shown below is the total limit for each loss for all property in that category. These special limits do not increase the Coverage **C** limit of liability.

   a. $200 on money, bank notes, bullion, gold other than goldware, silver other than silverware, platinum other than platinumware, coins, medals, scrip, stored value cards and smart cards.

   b. $1,500 on securities, accounts, deeds, evidences of debt, letters of credit, notes other than bank notes, manuscripts, personal records, passports, tickets and stamps. This dollar limit applies to these categories regardless of the medium (such as paper or computer software) on which the material exists.

   This limit includes the cost to research, replace or restore the information from the lost or damaged material.

c. $1,500 on watercraft of all types, including their trailers, furnishings, equipment and outboard engines or motors.

d. $1,500 on trailers or semitrailers not used with watercraft of all types.

e. $1,500 for loss by theft of jewelry, watches, furs, precious and semiprecious stones.

f. $2,500 for loss by theft of firearms and related equipment.

g. $2,500 for loss by theft of silverware, silver-plated ware, goldware, gold-plated ware, platinumware, platinum-plated ware and pewterware. This includes flatware, hollowware, tea sets, trays and trophies made of or including silver, gold or pewter.

h. $2,500 on property, on the "residence premises", used primarily for "business" purposes.

i. $500 on property, away from the "residence premises", used primarily for "business" purposes. However, this limit does not apply to loss to electronic apparatus and other property described in Categories **j.** and **k.** below.

j. $1,500 on electronic apparatus and accessories, while in or upon a "motor vehicle", but only if the apparatus is equipped to be operated by power from the "motor vehicle's" electrical system while still capable of being operated by other power sources.

Accessories include antennas, tapes, wires, records, discs or other media that can be used with any apparatus described in this Category **j.**

k. $1,500 on electronic apparatus and accessories used primarily for "business" while away from the "residence premises" and not in or upon a "motor vehicle". The apparatus must be equipped to be operated by power from the "motor vehicle's" electrical system while still capable of being operated by other power sources.

Accessories include antennas, tapes, wires, records, discs or other media that can be used with any apparatus described in this Category **k.**

4. Property Not Covered

We do not cover:

a. Articles separately described and specifically insured, regardless of the limit for which they are insured, in this or other insurance;

b. Animals, birds or fish;

c. "Motor vehicles".

 (1) This includes:

  (a) Their accessories, equipment and parts; or

  (b) Electronic apparatus and accessories designed to be operated solely by power from the electrical system of the "motor vehicle". Accessories include antennas, tapes, wires, records, discs or other media that can be used with any apparatus described above.

  The exclusion of property described in **(a)** and **(b)** above applies only while such property is in or upon the "motor vehicle".

 (2) We do cover "motor vehicles" not required to be registered for use on public roads or property which are:

  (a) Used solely to service an "insured's" residence; or

  (b) Designed to assist the handicapped;

d. Aircraft meaning any contrivance used or designed for flight including any parts whether or not attached to the aircraft.

 We do cover model or hobby aircraft not used or designed to carry people or cargo;

e. Hovercraft and parts. Hovercraft means a self-propelled motorized ground effect vehicle and includes, but is not limited to, flarecraft and air cushion vehicles;

f. Property of roomers, boarders and other tenants, except property of roomers and boarders related to an "insured";

g. Property in an apartment regularly rented or held for rental to others by an "insured", except as provided in **E.10.** Landlord's Furnishings under Section **I** – Property Coverages;

h. Property rented or held for rental to others off the "residence premises";

i. "Business" data, including such data stored in:

 (1) Books of account, drawings or other paper records; or

 (2) Computers and related equipment.

 We do cover the cost of blank recording or storage media, and of prerecorded computer programs available on the retail market;

 HO 00 03 10 00

j. Credit cards, electronic fund transfer cards or access devices used solely for deposit, withdrawal or transfer of funds except as provided in **E.6.** Credit Card, Electronic Fund Transfer Card Or Access Device, Forgery And Counterfeit Money under Section I – Property Coverages; or

k. Water or steam.

D. Coverage D – Loss Of Use

The limit of liability for Coverage **D** is the total limit for the coverages in **1.** Additional Living Expense, **2.** Fair Rental Value and **3.** Civil Authority Prohibits Use below.

1. Additional Living Expense

If a loss covered under Section I makes that part of the "residence premises" where you reside not fit to live in, we cover any necessary increase in living expenses incurred by you so that your household can maintain its normal standard of living.

Payment will be for the shortest time required to repair or replace the damage or, if you permanently relocate, the shortest time required for your household to settle elsewhere.

2. Fair Rental Value

If a loss covered under Section I makes that part of the "residence premises" rented to others or held for rental by you not fit to live in, we cover the fair rental value of such premises less any expenses that do not continue while it is not fit to live in.

Payment will be for the shortest time required to repair or replace such premises.

3. Civil Authority Prohibits Use

If a civil authority prohibits you from use of the "residence premises" as a result of direct damage to neighboring premises by a Peril Insured Against, we cover the loss as provided in **1.** Additional Living Expense and **2.** Fair Rental Value above for no more than two weeks.

4. Loss Or Expense Not Covered

We do not cover loss or expense due to cancellation of a lease or agreement.

The periods of time under **1.** Additional Living Expense, **2.** Fair Rental Value and **3.** Civil Authority Prohibits Use above are not limited by expiration of this policy.

E. Additional Coverages

1. Debris Removal

a. We will pay your reasonable expense for the removal of:

(1) Debris of covered property if a Peril Insured Against that applies to the damaged property causes the loss; or

(2) Ash, dust or particles from a volcanic eruption that has caused direct loss to a building or property contained in a building.

This expense is included in the limit of liability that applies to the damaged property. If the amount to be paid for the actual damage to the property plus the debris removal expense is more than the limit of liability for the damaged property, an additional 5% of that limit is available for such expense.

b. We will also pay your reasonable expense, up to $1,000, for the removal from the "residence premises" of:

(1) Your tree(s) felled by the peril of Windstorm or Hail or Weight of Ice, Snow or Sleet; or

(2) A neighbor's tree(s) felled by a Peril Insured Against under Coverage **C**;

provided the tree(s):

(3) Damage(s) a covered structure; or

(4) Does not damage a covered structure, but:

(a) Block(s) a driveway on the "residence premises" which prevent(s) a "motor vehicle", that is registered for use on public roads or property, from entering or leaving the "residence premises"; or

(b) Block(s) a ramp or other fixture designed to assist a handicapped person to enter or leave the dwelling building.

The $1,000 limit is the most we will pay in any one loss regardless of the number of fallen trees. No more than $500 of this limit will be paid for the removal of any one tree.

This coverage is additional insurance.

2. Reasonable Repairs

a. We will pay the reasonable cost incurred by you for the necessary measures taken solely to protect covered property that is damaged by a Peril Insured Against from further damage.

b. If the measures taken involve repair to other damaged property, we will only pay if that property is covered under this policy and the damage is caused by a Peril Insured Against. This coverage does not:

(1) Increase the limit of liability that applies to the covered property; or

(2) Relieve you of your duties, in case of a loss to covered property, described in **B.4.** under Section I – Conditions.

3. Trees, Shrubs And Other Plants

We cover trees, shrubs, plants or lawns, on the "residence premises", for loss caused by the following Perils Insured Against:

a. Fire or Lightning;

b. Explosion;

c. Riot or Civil Commotion;

d. Aircraft;

e. Vehicles not owned or operated by a resident of the "residence premises";

f. Vandalism or Malicious Mischief; or

g. Theft.

We will pay up to 5% of the limit of liability that applies to the dwelling for all trees, shrubs, plants or lawns. No more than $500 of this limit will be paid for any one tree, shrub or plant. We do not cover property grown for "business" purposes.

This coverage is additional insurance.

4. Fire Department Service Charge

We will pay up to $500 for your liability assumed by contract or agreement for fire department charges incurred when the fire department is called to save or protect covered property from a Peril Insured Against. We do not cover fire department service charges if the property is located within the limits of the city, municipality or protection district furnishing the fire department response.

This coverage is additional insurance. No deductible applies to this coverage.

5. Property Removed

We insure covered property against direct loss from any cause while being removed from a premises endangered by a Peril Insured Against and for no more than 30 days while removed.

This coverage does not change the limit of liability that applies to the property being removed.

6. Credit Card, Electronic Fund Transfer Card Or Access Device, Forgery And Counterfeit Money

a. We will pay up to $500 for:

(1) The legal obligation of an "insured" to pay because of the theft or unauthorized use of credit cards issued to or registered in an "insured's" name;

(2) Loss resulting from theft or unauthorized use of an electronic fund transfer card or access device used for deposit, withdrawal or transfer of funds, issued to or registered in an "insured's" name;

(3) Loss to an "insured" caused by forgery or alteration of any check or negotiable instrument; and

(4) Loss to an "insured" through acceptance in good faith of counterfeit United States or Canadian paper currency.

All loss resulting from a series of acts committed by any one person or in which any one person is concerned or implicated is considered to be one loss.

This coverage is additional insurance. No deductible applies to this coverage.

b. We do not cover:

(1) Use of a credit card, electronic fund transfer card or access device:

(a) By a resident of your household;

(b) By a person who has been entrusted with either type of card or access device; or

(c) If an "insured" has not complied with all terms and conditions under which the cards are issued or the devices accessed; or

(2) Loss arising out of "business" use or dishonesty of an "insured".

c. If the coverage in **a.** above applies, the following defense provisions also apply:

(1) We may investigate and settle any claim or suit that we decide is appropriate. Our duty to defend a claim or suit ends when the amount we pay for the loss equals our limit of liability.

(2) If a suit is brought against an "insured" for liability under **a.(1)** or **(2)** above, we will provide a defense at our expense by counsel of our choice.

(3) We have the option to defend at our expense an "insured" or an "insured's" bank against any suit for the enforcement of payment under **a.(3)** above.

7. Loss Assessment

a. We will pay up to $1,000 for your share of loss assessment charged during the policy period against you, as owner or tenant of the "residence premises", by a corporation or association of property owners. The assessment must be made as a result of direct loss to property, owned by all members collectively, of the type that would be covered by this policy if owned by you, caused by a Peril Insured Against under Coverage **A**, other than:

(1) Earthquake; or

(2) Land shock waves or tremors before, during or after a volcanic eruption.

The limit of $1,000 is the most we will pay with respect to any one loss, regardless of the number of assessments. We will only apply one deductible, per unit, to the total amount of any one loss to the property described above, regardless of the number of assessments.

b. We do not cover assessments charged against you or a corporation or association of property owners by any governmental body.

c. Paragraph **P.** Policy Period under Section **I** – Conditions does not apply to this coverage.

This coverage is additional insurance.

8. Collapse

a. With respect to this Additional Coverage:

(1) Collapse means an abrupt falling down or caving in of a building or any part of a building with the result that the building or part of the building cannot be occupied for its current intended purpose.

(2) A building or any part of a building that is in danger of falling down or caving in is not considered to be in a state of collapse.

(3) A part of a building that is standing is not considered to be in a state of collapse even if it has separated from another part of the building.

(4) A building or any part of a building that is standing is not considered to be in a state of collapse even if it shows evidence of cracking, bulging, sagging, bending, leaning, settling, shrinkage or expansion.

b. We insure for direct physical loss to covered property involving collapse of a building or any part of a building if the collapse was caused by one or more of the following:

(1) The Perils Insured Against named under Coverage **C**;

(2) Decay that is hidden from view, unless the presence of such decay is known to an "insured" prior to collapse;

(3) Insect or vermin damage that is hidden from view, unless the presence of such damage is known to an "insured" prior to collapse;

(4) Weight of contents, equipment, animals or people;

(5) Weight of rain which collects on a roof; or

(6) Use of defective material or methods in construction, remodeling or renovation if the collapse occurs during the course of the construction, remodeling or renovation.

c. Loss to an awning, fence, patio, deck, pavement, swimming pool, underground pipe, flue, drain, cesspool, septic tank, foundation, retaining wall, bulkhead, pier, wharf or dock is not included under **b.(2)** through **(6)** above, unless the loss is a direct result of the collapse of a building or any part of a building.

d. This coverage does not increase the limit of liability that applies to the damaged covered property.

9. Glass Or Safety Glazing Material

a. We cover:

(1) The breakage of glass or safety glazing material which is part of a covered building, storm door or storm window;

(2) The breakage of glass or safety glazing material which is part of a covered building, storm door or storm window when caused directly by earth movement; and

(3) The direct physical loss to covered property caused solely by the pieces, fragments or splinters of broken glass or safety glazing material which is part of a building, storm door or storm window.

b. This coverage does not include loss:

   (1) To covered property which results because the glass or safety glazing material has been broken, except as provided in **a.(3)** above; or

   (2) On the "residence premises" if the dwelling has been vacant for more than 60 consecutive days immediately before the loss, except when the breakage results directly from earth movement as provided in **a.(2)** above. A dwelling being constructed is not considered vacant.

c. This coverage does not increase the limit of liability that applies to the damaged property.

10. Landlord's Furnishings

We will pay up to $2,500 for your appliances, carpeting and other household furnishings, in each apartment on the "residence premises" regularly rented or held for rental to others by an "insured", for loss caused by a Peril Insured Against in Coverage **C,** other than Theft.

This limit is the most we will pay in any one loss regardless of the number of appliances, carpeting or other household furnishings involved in the loss.

This coverage does not increase the limit of liability applying to the damaged property.

11. Ordinance Or Law

a. You may use up to 10% of the limit of liability that applies to Coverage **A** for the increased costs you incur due to the enforcement of any ordinance or law which requires or regulates:

   (1) The construction, demolition, remodeling, renovation or repair of that part of a covered building or other structure damaged by a Peril Insured Against;

   (2) The demolition and reconstruction of the undamaged part of a covered building or other structure, when that building or other structure must be totally demolished because of damage by a Peril Insured Against to another part of that covered building or other structure; or

   (3) The remodeling, removal or replacement of the portion of the undamaged part of a covered building or other structure necessary to complete the remodeling, repair or replacement of that part of the covered building or other structure damaged by a Peril Insured Against.

b. You may use all or part of this ordinance or law coverage to pay for the increased costs you incur to remove debris resulting from the construction, demolition, remodeling, renovation, repair or replacement of property as stated in **a.** above.

c. We do not cover:

   (1) The loss in value to any covered building or other structure due to the requirements of any ordinance or law; or

   (2) The costs to comply with any ordinance or law which requires any "insured" or others to test for, monitor, clean up, remove, contain, treat, detoxify or neutralize, or in any way respond to, or assess the effects of, pollutants in or on any covered building or other structure.

   Pollutants means any solid, liquid, gaseous or thermal irritant or contaminant, including smoke, vapor, soot, fumes, acids, alkalis, chemicals and waste. Waste includes materials to be recycled, reconditioned or reclaimed.

This coverage is additional insurance.

12. Grave Markers

We will pay up to $5,000 for grave markers, including mausoleums, on or away from the "residence premises" for loss caused by a Peril Insured Against under Coverage **C.**

This coverage does not increase the limits of liability that apply to the damaged covered property.

SECTION I – PERILS INSURED AGAINST

A. Coverage A – Dwelling And Coverage B – Other Structures

1. We insure against risk of direct physical loss to property described in Coverages **A** and **B.**

2. We do not insure, however, for loss:

   a. Excluded under Section I – Exclusions;

   b. Involving collapse, except as provided in **E.8.** Collapse under Section I – Property Coverages; or

   c. Caused by:

      (1) Freezing of a plumbing, heating, air conditioning or automatic fire protective sprinkler system or of a household appliance, or by discharge, leakage or overflow from within the system or appliance caused by freezing. This provision does not apply if you have used reasonable care to:

         (a) Maintain heat in the building; or

(b) Shut off the water supply and drain all systems and appliances of water.

However, if the building is protected by an automatic fire protective sprinkler system, you must use reasonable care to continue the water supply and maintain heat in the building for coverage to apply.

For purposes of this provision a plumbing system or household appliance does not include a sump, sump pump or related equipment or a roof drain, gutter, downspout or similar fixtures or equipment;

(2) Freezing, thawing, pressure or weight of water or ice, whether driven by wind or not, to a:

(a) Fence, pavement, patio or swimming pool;

(b) Footing, foundation, bulkhead, wall, or any other structure or device that supports all or part of a building, or other structure;

(c) Retaining wall or bulkhead that does not support all or part of a building or other structure; or

(d) Pier, wharf or dock;

(3) Theft in or to a dwelling under construction, or of materials and supplies for use in the construction until the dwelling is finished and occupied;

(4) Vandalism and malicious mischief, and any ensuing loss caused by any intentional and wrongful act committed in the course of the vandalism or malicious mischief, if the dwelling has been vacant for more than 60 consecutive days immediately before the loss. A dwelling being constructed is not considered vacant;

(5) Mold, fungus or wet rot. However, we do insure for loss caused by mold, fungus or wet rot that is hidden within the walls or ceilings or beneath the floors or above the ceilings of a structure if such loss results from the accidental discharge or overflow of water or steam from within:

(a) A plumbing, heating, air conditioning or automatic fire protective sprinkler system, or a household appliance, on the "residence premises"; or

(b) A storm drain, or water, steam or sewer pipes, off the "residence premises".

For purposes of this provision, a plumbing system or household appliance does not include a sump, sump pump or related equipment or a roof drain, gutter, downspout or similar fixtures or equipment; or

(6) Any of the following:

(a) Wear and tear, marring, deterioration;

(b) Mechanical breakdown, latent defect, inherent vice, or any quality in property that causes it to damage or destroy itself;

(c) Smog, rust or other corrosion, or dry rot;

(d) Smoke from agricultural smudging or industrial operations;

(e) Discharge, dispersal, seepage, migration, release or escape of pollutants unless the discharge, dispersal, seepage, migration, release or escape is itself caused by a Peril Insured Against named under Coverage **C**.

Pollutants means any solid, liquid, gaseous or thermal irritant or contaminant, including smoke, vapor, soot, fumes, acids, alkalis, chemicals and waste. Waste includes materials to be recycled, reconditioned or reclaimed;

(f) Settling, shrinking, bulging or expansion, including resultant cracking, of bulkheads, pavements, patios, footings, foundations, walls, floors, roofs or ceilings;

(g) Birds, vermin, rodents, or insects; or

(h) Animals owned or kept by an "insured".

Exception To c.(6)

Unless the loss is otherwise excluded, we cover loss to property covered under Coverage **A** or **B** resulting from an accidental discharge or overflow of water or steam from within a:

(i) Storm drain, or water, steam or sewer pipe, off the "residence premises"; or

(ii) Plumbing, heating, air conditioning or automatic fire protective sprinkler system or household appliance on the "residence premises". This includes the cost to tear out and replace any part of a building, or other structure, on the "residence premises", but only when necessary to repair the system or appliance. However, such tear out and replacement coverage only applies to other structures if the water or steam causes actual damage to a building on the "residence premises".

We do not cover loss to the system or appliance from which this water or steam escaped.

For purposes of this provision, a plumbing system or household appliance does not include a sump, sump pump or related equipment or a roof drain, gutter, down spout or similar fixtures or equipment.

Section I – Exclusion **A.3.** Water Damage, Paragraphs **a.** and **c.** that apply to surface water and water below the surface of the ground do not apply to loss by water covered under **c.(5)** and **(6)** above.

Under **2.b.** and **c.** above, any ensuing loss to property described in Coverages **A** and **B** not precluded by any other provision in this policy is covered.

B. Coverage C – Personal Property

We insure for direct physical loss to the property described in Coverage **C** caused by any of the following perils unless the loss is excluded in Section I – Exclusions.

1. Fire Or Lightning

2. Windstorm Or Hail

This peril includes loss to watercraft of all types and their trailers, furnishings, equipment, and outboard engines or motors, only while inside a fully enclosed building.

This peril does not include loss to the property contained in a building caused by rain, snow, sleet, sand or dust unless the direct force of wind or hail damages the building causing an opening in a roof or wall and the rain, snow, sleet, sand or dust enters through this opening.

3. Explosion

4. Riot Or Civil Commotion

5. Aircraft

This peril includes self-propelled missiles and spacecraft.

6. Vehicles

7. Smoke

This peril means sudden and accidental damage from smoke, including the emission or puffback of smoke, soot, fumes or vapors from a boiler, furnace or related equipment.

This peril does not include loss caused by smoke from agricultural smudging or industrial operations.

8. Vandalism Or Malicious Mischief

9. Theft

a. This peril includes attempted theft and loss of property from a known place when it is likely that the property has been stolen.

b. This peril does not include loss caused by theft:

(1) Committed by an "insured";

(2) In or to a dwelling under construction, or of materials and supplies for use in the construction until the dwelling is finished and occupied;

(3) From that part of a "residence premises" rented by an "insured" to someone other than another "insured"; or

(4) That occurs off the "residence premises" of:

(a) Trailers, semitrailers and campers;

(b) Watercraft of all types, and their furnishings, equipment and outboard engines or motors; or

(c) Property while at any other residence owned by, rented to, or occupied by an "insured", except while an "insured" is temporarily living there. Property of an "insured" who is a student is covered while at the residence the student occupies to attend school as long as the student has been there at any time during the 60 days immediately before the loss.

10. Falling Objects

This peril does not include loss to property contained in a building unless the roof or an outside wall of the building is first damaged by a falling object. Damage to the falling object itself is not included.

11. Weight Of Ice, Snow Or Sleet

This peril means weight of ice, snow or sleet which causes damage to property contained in a building.

12. Accidental Discharge Or Overflow Of Water Or Steam

a. This peril means accidental discharge or overflow of water or steam from within a plumbing, heating, air conditioning or automatic fire protective sprinkler system or from within a household appliance.

b. This peril does not include loss:

(1) To the system or appliance from which the water or steam escaped;

(2) Caused by or resulting from freezing except as provided in Peril Insured Against **14.** Freezing;

(3) On the "residence premises" caused by accidental discharge or overflow which occurs off the "residence premises"; or

(4) Caused by mold, fungus or wet rot unless hidden within the walls or ceilings or beneath the floors or above the ceilings of a structure.

c. In this peril, a plumbing system or household appliance does not include a sump, sump pump or related equipment or a roof drain, gutter, downspout or similar fixtures or equipment.

d. Section I – Exclusion **A.3.** Water Damage, Paragraphs **a.** and **c.** that apply to surface water and water below the surface of the ground do not apply to loss by water covered under this peril.

13. Sudden And Accidental Tearing Apart, Cracking, Burning Or Bulging

This peril means sudden and accidental tearing apart, cracking, burning or bulging of a steam or hot water heating system, an air conditioning or automatic fire protective sprinkler system, or an appliance for heating water.

We do not cover loss caused by or resulting from freezing under this peril.

14. Freezing

a. This peril means freezing of a plumbing, heating, air conditioning or automatic fire protective sprinkler system or of a household appliance but only if you have used reasonable care to:

(1) Maintain heat in the building; or

(2) Shut off the water supply and drain all systems and appliances of water.

However, if the building is protected by an automatic fire protective sprinkler system, you must use reasonable care to continue the water supply and maintain heat in the building for coverage to apply.

b. In this peril, a plumbing system or household appliance does not include a sump, sump pump or related equipment or a roof drain, gutter, downspout or similar fixtures or equipment.

15. Sudden And Accidental Damage From Artificially Generated Electrical Current

This peril does not include loss to tubes, transistors, electronic components or circuitry that are a part of appliances, fixtures, computers, home entertainment units or other types of electronic apparatus.

16. Volcanic Eruption

This peril does not include loss caused by earthquake, land shock waves or tremors.

SECTION I – EXCLUSIONS

A. We do not insure for loss caused directly or indirectly by any of the following. Such loss is excluded regardless of any other cause or event contributing concurrently or in any sequence to the loss. These exclusions apply whether or not the loss event results in widespread damage or affects a substantial area.

1. Ordinance Or Law

Ordinance Or Law means any ordinance or law:

a. Requiring or regulating the construction, demolition, remodeling, renovation or repair of property, including removal of any resulting debris. This Exclusion **A.1.a.** does not apply to the amount of coverage that may be provided for in **E.11.** Ordinance Or Law under Section I – Property Coverages;

b. The requirements of which result in a loss in value to property; or

c. Requiring any "insured" or others to test for, monitor, clean up, remove, contain, treat, detoxify or neutralize, or in any way respond to, or assess the effects of, pollutants.

Pollutants means any solid, liquid, gaseous or thermal irritant or contaminant, including smoke, vapor, soot, fumes, acids, alkalis, chemicals and waste. Waste includes materials to be recycled, reconditioned or reclaimed.

This Exclusion **A.1.** applies whether or not the property has been physically damaged.

2. Earth Movement

Earth Movement means:

a. Earthquake, including land shock waves or tremors before, during or after a volcanic eruption;

b. Landslide, mudslide or mudflow;

c. Subsidence or sinkhole; or

d. Any other earth movement including earth sinking, rising or shifting;

caused by or resulting from human or animal forces or any act of nature unless direct loss by fire or explosion ensues and then we will pay only for the ensuing loss.

This Exclusion **A.2.** does not apply to loss by theft.

3. **Water Damage**

Water Damage means:

a. Flood, surface water, waves, tidal water, overflow of a body of water, or spray from any of these, whether or not driven by wind;

b. Water or water-borne material which backs up through sewers or drains or which overflows or is discharged from a sump, sump pump or related equipment; or

c. Water or water-borne material below the surface of the ground, including water which exerts pressure on or seeps or leaks through a building, sidewalk, driveway, foundation, swimming pool or other structure;

caused by or resulting from human or animal forces or any act of nature.

Direct loss by fire, explosion or theft resulting from water damage is covered.

4. **Power Failure**

Power Failure means the failure of power or other utility service if the failure takes place off the "residence premises". But if the failure results in a loss, from a Peril Insured Against on the "residence premises", we will pay for the loss caused by that peril.

5. **Neglect**

Neglect means neglect of an "insured" to use all reasonable means to save and preserve property at and after the time of a loss.

6. **War**

War includes the following and any consequence of any of the following:

a. Undeclared war, civil war, insurrection, rebellion or revolution;

b. Warlike act by a military force or military personnel; or

c. Destruction, seizure or use for a military purpose.

Discharge of a nuclear weapon will be deemed a warlike act even if accidental.

7. **Nuclear Hazard**

This Exclusion **A.7.** pertains to Nuclear Hazard to the extent set forth in **M.** Nuclear Hazard Clause under Section I – Conditions.

8. **Intentional Loss**

Intentional Loss means any loss arising out of any act an "insured" commits or conspires to commit with the intent to cause a loss.

In the event of such loss, no "insured" is entitled to coverage, even "insureds" who did not commit or conspire to commit the act causing the loss.

9. **Governmental Action**

Governmental Action means the destruction, confiscation or seizure of property described in Coverage **A, B** or **C** by order of any governmental or public authority.

This exclusion does not apply to such acts ordered by any governmental or public authority that are taken at the time of a fire to prevent its spread, if the loss caused by fire would be covered under this policy.

B. We do not insure for loss to property described in Coverages **A** and **B** caused by any of the following. However, any ensuing loss to property described in Coverages **A** and **B** not precluded by any other provision in this policy is covered.

1. Weather conditions. However, this exclusion only applies if weather conditions contribute in any way with a cause or event excluded in **A.** above to produce the loss.

2. Acts or decisions, including the failure to act or decide, of any person, group, organization or governmental body.

3. Faulty, inadequate or defective:

a. Planning, zoning, development, surveying, siting;

b. Design, specifications, workmanship, repair, construction, renovation, remodeling, grading, compaction;

c. Materials used in repair, construction, renovation or remodeling; or

d. Maintenance;

of part or all of any property whether on or off the "residence premises".

SECTION I – CONDITIONS

A. Insurable Interest And Limit Of Liability

Even if more than one person has an insurable interest in the property covered, we will not be liable in any one loss:

1. To an "insured" for more than the amount of such "insured's" interest at the time of loss; or

2. For more than the applicable limit of liability.

B. Duties After Loss

In case of a loss to covered property, we have no duty to provide coverage under this policy if the failure to comply with the following duties is prejudicial to us. These duties must be performed either by you, an "insured" seeking coverage, or a representative of either:

1. Give prompt notice to us or our agent;

2. Notify the police in case of loss by theft;

3. Notify the credit card or electronic fund transfer card or access device company in case of loss as provided for in **E.6.** Credit Card, Electronic Fund Transfer Card Or Access Device, Forgery And Counterfeit Money under Section I – Property Coverages;

4. Protect the property from further damage. If repairs to the property are required, you must:

   a. Make reasonable and necessary repairs to protect the property; and

   b. Keep an accurate record of repair expenses;

5. Cooperate with us in the investigation of a claim;

6. Prepare an inventory of damaged personal property showing the quantity, description, actual cash value and amount of loss. Attach all bills, receipts and related documents that justify the figures in the inventory;

7. As often as we reasonably require:

   a. Show the damaged property;

   b. Provide us with records and documents we request and permit us to make copies; and

   c. Submit to examination under oath, while not in the presence of another "insured", and sign the same;

8. Send to us, within 60 days after our request, your signed, sworn proof of loss which sets forth, to the best of your knowledge and belief:

   a. The time and cause of loss;

   b. The interests of all "insureds" and all others in the property involved and all liens on the property;

   c. Other insurance which may cover the loss;

   d. Changes in title or occupancy of the property during the term of the policy;

   e. Specifications of damaged buildings and detailed repair estimates;

   f. The inventory of damaged personal property described in **6.** above;

   g. Receipts for additional living expenses incurred and records that support the fair rental value loss; and

   h. Evidence or affidavit that supports a claim under **E.6.** Credit Card, Electronic Fund Transfer Card Or Access Device, Forgery And Counterfeit Money under Section I – Property Coverages, stating the amount and cause of loss.

C. Loss Settlement

In this Condition **C.**, the terms "cost to repair or replace" and "replacement cost" do not include the increased costs incurred to comply with the enforcement of any ordinance or law, except to the extent that coverage for these increased costs is provided in **E.11.** Ordinance Or Law under Section I – Property Coverages. Covered property losses are settled as follows:

1. Property of the following types:

   a. Personal property;

   b. Awnings, carpeting, household appliances, outdoor antennas and outdoor equipment, whether or not attached to buildings;

   c. Structures that are not buildings; and

   d. Grave markers, including mausoleums;

   at actual cash value at the time of loss but not more than the amount required to repair or replace.

2. Buildings covered under Coverage **A** or **B** at replacement cost without deduction for depreciation, subject to the following:

   a. If, at the time of loss, the amount of insurance in this policy on the damaged building is 80% or more of the full replacement cost of the building immediately before the loss, we will pay the cost to repair or replace, after application of any deductible and without deduction for depreciation, but not more than the least of the following amounts:

      (1) The limit of liability under this policy that applies to the building;

      (2) The replacement cost of that part of the building damaged with material of like kind and quality and for like use; or

      (3) The necessary amount actually spent to repair or replace the damaged building.

If the building is rebuilt at a new premises, the cost described in **(2)** above is limited to the cost which would have been incurred if the building had been built at the original premises.

b. If, at the time of loss, the amount of insurance in this policy on the damaged building is less than 80% of the full replacement cost of the building immediately before the loss, we will pay the greater of the following amounts, but not more than the limit of liability under this policy that applies to the building:

(1) The actual cash value of that part of the building damaged; or

(2) That proportion of the cost to repair or replace, after application of any deductible and without deduction for depreciation, that part of the building damaged, which the total amount of insurance in this policy on the damaged building bears to 80% of the replacement cost of the building.

c. To determine the amount of insurance required to equal 80% of the full replacement cost of the building immediately before the loss, do not include the value of:

(1) Excavations, footings, foundations, piers, or any other structures or devices that support all or part of the building, which are below the undersurface of the lowest basement floor;

(2) Those supports described in **(1)** above which are below the surface of the ground inside the foundation walls, if there is no basement; and

(3) Underground flues, pipes, wiring and drains.

d. We will pay no more than the actual cash value of the damage until actual repair or replacement is complete. Once actual repair or replacement is complete, we will settle the loss as noted in **2.a.** and **b.** above.

However, if the cost to repair or replace the damage is both:

(1) Less than 5% of the amount of insurance in this policy on the building; and

(2) Less than $2,500;

we will settle the loss as noted in **2.a.** and **b.** above whether or not actual repair or replacement is complete.

e. You may disregard the replacement cost loss settlement provisions and make claim under this policy for loss to buildings on an actual cash value basis. You may then make claim for any additional liability according to the provisions of this Condition **C. Loss Settlement**, provided you notify us of your intent to do so within 180 days after the date of loss.

D. Loss To A Pair Or Set

In case of loss to a pair or set we may elect to:

1. Repair or replace any part to restore the pair or set to its value before the loss; or

2. Pay the difference between actual cash value of the property before and after the loss.

E. Appraisal

If you and we fail to agree on the amount of loss, either may demand an appraisal of the loss. In this event, each party will choose a competent and impartial appraiser within 20 days after receiving a written request from the other. The two appraisers will choose an umpire. If they cannot agree upon an umpire within 15 days, you or we may request that the choice be made by a judge of a court of record in the state where the "residence premises" is located. The appraisers will separately set the amount of loss. If the appraisers submit a written report of an agreement to us, the amount agreed upon will be the amount of loss. If they fail to agree, they will submit their differences to the umpire. A decision agreed to by any two will set the amount of loss.

Each party will:

1. Pay its own appraiser; and

2. Bear the other expenses of the appraisal and umpire equally.

F. Other Insurance And Service Agreement

If a loss covered by this policy is also covered by:

1. Other insurance, we will pay only the proportion of the loss that the limit of liability that applies under this policy bears to the total amount of insurance covering the loss; or

2. A service agreement, this insurance is excess over any amounts payable under any such agreement. Service agreement means a service plan, property restoration plan, home warranty or other similar service warranty agreement, even if it is characterized as insurance.

G. Suit Against Us

No action can be brought against us unless there has been full compliance with all of the terms under Section **I** of this policy and the action is started within two years after the date of loss.

Copyright, Insurance Services Office, Inc., 1999　　HO 00 03 10 00

H. Our Option

If we give you written notice within 30 days after we receive your signed, sworn proof of loss, we may repair or replace any part of the damaged property with material or property of like kind and quality.

I. Loss Payment

We will adjust all losses with you. We will pay you unless some other person is named in the policy or is legally entitled to receive payment. Loss will be payable 60 days after we receive your proof of loss and:

1. Reach an agreement with you;
2. There is an entry of a final judgment; or
3. There is a filing of an appraisal award with us.

J. Abandonment Of Property

We need not accept any property abandoned by an "insured".

K. Mortgage Clause

1. If a mortgagee is named in this policy, any loss payable under Coverage **A** or **B** will be paid to the mortgagee and you, as interests appear. If more than one mortgagee is named, the order of payment will be the same as the order of precedence of the mortgages.

2. If we deny your claim, that denial will not apply to a valid claim of the mortgagee, if the mortgagee:
   a. Notifies us of any change in ownership, occupancy or substantial change in risk of which the mortgagee is aware;
   b. Pays any premium due under this policy on demand if you have neglected to pay the premium; and
   c. Submits a signed, sworn statement of loss within 60 days after receiving notice from us of your failure to do so. Paragraphs **E.** Appraisal, **G.** Suit Against Us and **I.** Loss Payment under Section I – Conditions also apply to the mortgagee.

3. If we decide to cancel or not to renew this policy, the mortgagee will be notified at least 10 days before the date cancellation or nonrenewal takes effect.

4. If we pay the mortgagee for any loss and deny payment to you:
   a. We are subrogated to all the rights of the mortgagee granted under the mortgage on the property; or
   b. At our option, we may pay to the mortgagee the whole principal on the mortgage plus any accrued interest. In this event, we will receive a full assignment and transfer of the mortgage and all securities held as collateral to the mortgage debt.

5. Subrogation will not impair the right of the mortgagee to recover the full amount of the mortgagee's claim.

L. No Benefit To Bailee

We will not recognize any assignment or grant any coverage that benefits a person or organization holding, storing or moving property for a fee regardless of any other provision of this policy.

M. Nuclear Hazard Clause

1. "Nuclear Hazard" means any nuclear reaction, radiation, or radioactive contamination, all whether controlled or uncontrolled or however caused, or any consequence of any of these.

2. Loss caused by the nuclear hazard will not be considered loss caused by fire, explosion, or smoke, whether these perils are specifically named in or otherwise included within the Perils Insured Against.

3. This policy does not apply under Section I to loss caused directly or indirectly by nuclear hazard, except that direct loss by fire resulting from the nuclear hazard is covered.

N. Recovered Property

If you or we recover any property for which we have made payment under this policy, you or we will notify the other of the recovery. At your option, the property will be returned to or retained by you or it will become our property. If the recovered property is returned to or retained by you, the loss payment will be adjusted based on the amount you received for the recovered property.

O. Volcanic Eruption Period

One or more volcanic eruptions that occur within a 72 hour period will be considered as one volcanic eruption.

P. Policy Period

This policy applies only to loss which occurs during the policy period.

Q. Concealment Or Fraud

We provide coverage to no "insureds" under this policy if, whether before or after a loss, an "insured" has:

1. Intentionally concealed or misrepresented any material fact or circumstance;

2. Engaged in fraudulent conduct; or

3. Made false statements;

relating to this insurance.

R. Loss Payable Clause

If the Declarations show a loss payee for certain listed insured personal property, the definition of "insured" is changed to include that loss payee with respect to that property.

If we decide to cancel or not renew this policy, that loss payee will be notified in writing.

SECTION II – LIABILITY COVERAGES

A. Coverage E – Personal Liability

If a claim is made or a suit is brought against an "insured" for damages because of "bodily injury" or "property damage" caused by an "occurrence" to which this coverage applies, we will:

1. Pay up to our limit of liability for the damages for which an "insured" is legally liable. Damages include prejudgment interest awarded against an "insured"; and

2. Provide a defense at our expense by counsel of our choice, even if the suit is groundless, false or fraudulent. We may investigate and settle any claim or suit that we decide is appropriate. Our duty to settle or defend ends when our limit of liability for the "occurrence" has been exhausted by payment of a judgment or settlement.

B. Coverage F – Medical Payments To Others

We will pay the necessary medical expenses that are incurred or medically ascertained within three years from the date of an accident causing "bodily injury". Medical expenses means reasonable charges for medical, surgical, x-ray, dental, ambulance, hospital, professional nursing, prosthetic devices and funeral services. This coverage does not apply to you or regular residents of your household except "residence employees". As to others, this coverage applies only:

1. To a person on the "insured location" with the permission of an "insured"; or

2. To a person off the "insured location", if the "bodily injury":

   a. Arises out of a condition on the "insured location" or the ways immediately adjoining;

   b. Is caused by the activities of an "insured";

   c. Is caused by a "residence employee" in the course of the "residence employee's" employment by an "insured"; or

   d. Is caused by an animal owned by or in the care of an "insured".

SECTION II – EXCLUSIONS

A. "Motor Vehicle Liability"

1. Coverages **E** and **F** do not apply to any "motor vehicle liability" if, at the time and place of an "occurrence", the involved "motor vehicle":

   a. Is registered for use on public roads or property;

   b. Is not registered for use on public roads or property, but such registration is required by a law, or regulation issued by a government agency, for it to be used at the place of the "occurrence"; or

   c. Is being:

      (1) Operated in, or practicing for, any prearranged or organized race, speed contest or other competition;

      (2) Rented to others;

      (3) Used to carry persons or cargo for a charge; or

      (4) Used for any "business" purpose except for a motorized golf cart while on a golfing facility.

2. If Exclusion **A.1.** does not apply, there is still no coverage for "motor vehicle liability" unless the "motor vehicle" is:

   a. In dead storage on an "insured location";

   b. Used solely to service an "insured's" residence;

   c. Designed to assist the handicapped and, at the time of an "occurrence", it is:

      (1) Being used to assist a handicapped person; or

      (2) Parked on an "insured location";

   d. Designed for recreational use off public roads and:

      (1) Not owned by an "insured"; or

      (2) Owned by an "insured" provided the "occurrence" takes place on an "insured location" as defined in Definitions **B. 6.a., b., d., e.** or **h.**; or

   e. A motorized golf cart that is owned by an "insured", designed to carry up to 4 persons, not built or modified after manufacture to exceed a speed of 25 miles per hour on level ground and, at the time of an "occurrence", is within the legal boundaries of:

      (1) A golfing facility and is parked or stored there, or being used by an "insured" to:

         (a) Play the game of golf or for other recreational or leisure activity allowed by the facility;

(b) Travel to or from an area where "motor vehicles" or golf carts are parked or stored; or

(c) Cross public roads at designated points to access other parts of the golfing facility; or

(2) A private residential community, including its public roads upon which a motorized golf cart can legally travel, which is subject to the authority of a property owners association and contains an "insured's" residence.

B. "Watercraft Liability"

1. Coverages **E** and **F** do not apply to any "watercraft liability" if, at the time of an "occurrence", the involved watercraft is being:

a. Operated in, or practicing for, any prearranged or organized race, speed contest or other competition. This exclusion does not apply to a sailing vessel or a predicted log cruise;

b. Rented to others;

c. Used to carry persons or cargo for a charge; or

d. Used for any "business" purpose.

2. If Exclusion **B.1.** does not apply, there is still no coverage for "watercraft liability" unless, at the time of the "occurrence", the watercraft:

a. Is stored;

b. Is a sailing vessel, with or without auxiliary power, that is:

(1) Less than 26 feet in overall length; or

(2) 26 feet or more in overall length and not owned by or rented to an "insured"; or

c. Is not a sailing vessel and is powered by:

(1) An inboard or inboard-outdrive engine or motor, including those that power a water jet pump, of:

(a) 50 horsepower or less and not owned by an "insured"; or

(b) More than 50 horsepower and not owned by or rented to an "insured"; or

(2) One or more outboard engines or motors with:

(a) 25 total horsepower or less;

(b) More than 25 horsepower if the outboard engine or motor is not owned by an "insured";

(c) More than 25 horsepower if the outboard engine or motor is owned by an "insured" who acquired it during the policy period; or

(d) More than 25 horsepower if the outboard engine or motor is owned by an "insured" who acquired it before the policy period, but only if:

(i) You declare them at policy inception; or

(ii) Your intent to insure them is reported to us in writing within 45 days after you acquire them.

The coverages in **(c)** and **(d)** above apply for the policy period.

Horsepower means the maximum power rating assigned to the engine or motor by the manufacturer.

C. "Aircraft Liability"

This policy does not cover "aircraft liability".

D. "Hovercraft Liability"

This policy does not cover "hovercraft liability".

E. Coverage E – Personal Liability And Coverage F – Medical Payments To Others

Coverages **E** and **F** do not apply to the following:

1. Expected Or Intended Injury

"Bodily injury" or "property damage" which is expected or intended by an "insured" even if the resulting "bodily injury" or "property damage":

a. Is of a different kind, quality or degree than initially expected or intended; or

b. Is sustained by a different person, entity, real or personal property, than initially expected or intended.

However, this Exclusion **E.1.** does not apply to "bodily injury" resulting from the use of reasonable force by an "insured" to protect persons or property;

2. "Business"

a. "Bodily injury" or "property damage" arising out of or in connection with a "business" conducted from an "insured location" or engaged in by an "insured", whether or not the "business" is owned or operated by an "insured" or employs an "insured".

This Exclusion **E.2.** applies but is not limited to an act or omission, regardless of its nature or circumstance, involving a service or duty rendered, promised, owed, or implied to be provided because of the nature of the "business".

b. This Exclusion **E.2.** does not apply to:

(1) The rental or holding for rental of an "insured location";

(a) On an occasional basis if used only as a residence;

(b) In part for use only as a residence, unless a single family unit is intended for use by the occupying family to lodge more than two roomers or boarders; or

(c) In part, as an office, school, studio or private garage; and

(2) An "insured" under the age of 21 years involved in a part-timo or occasional, self-employed "business" with no employees;

3. Professional Services

"Bodily injury" or "property damage" arising out of the rendering of or failure to render professional services;

4. "Insured's" Premises Not An "Insured Location"

"Bodily injury" or "property damage" arising out of a premises:

a. Owned by an "insured";

b. Rented to an "insured"; or

c. Rented to others by an "insured";

that is not an "insured location";

5. War

"Bodily injury" or "property damage" caused directly or indirectly by war, including the following and any consequence of any of the following:

a. Undeclared war, civil war, insurrection, rebellion or revolution;

b. Warlike act by a military force or military personnel; or

c. Destruction, seizure or use for a military purpose.

Discharge of a nuclear weapon will be deemed a warlike act even if accidental;

6. Communicable Disease

"Bodily injury" or "property damage" which arises out of the transmission of a communicable disease by an "insured";

7. Sexual Molestation, Corporal Punishment Or Physical Or Mental Abuse

"Bodily injury" or "property damage" arising out of sexual molestation, corporal punishment or physical or mental abuse; or

8. Controlled Substance

"Bodily injury" or "property damage" arising out of the use, sale, manufacture, delivery, transfer or possession by any person of a Controlled Substance as defined by the Federal Food and Drug Law at 21 U.S.C.A. Sections 811 and 812. Controlled Substances include but are not limited to cocaine, LSD, marijuana and all narcotic drugs. However, this exclusion does not apply to the legitimate use of prescription drugs by a person following the orders of a licensed physician.

Exclusions **A.** "Motor Vehicle Liability", **B.** "Watercraft Liability", **C.** "Aircraft Liability", **D.** "Hovercraft Liability" and **E.4.** "Insured's" Premises Not An "Insured Location" do not apply to "bodily injury" to a "residence employee" arising out of and in the course of the "residence employee's" employment by an "insured".

F. Coverage E – Personal Liability

Coverage **E** does not apply to:

1. Liability:

a. For any loss assessment charged against you as a member of an association, corporation or community of property owners, except as provided in **D.** Loss Assessment under Section II – Additional Coverages;

b. Under any contract or agreement entered into by an "insured". However, this exclusion does not apply to written contracts:

(1) That directly relate to the ownership, maintenance or use of an "insured location"; or

(2) Where the liability of others is assumed by you prior to an "occurrence";

unless excluded in **a.** above or elsewhere in this policy;

2. "Property damage" to property owned by an "insured". This includes costs or expenses incurred by an "insured" or others to repair, replace, enhance, restore or maintain such property to prevent injury to a person or damage to property of others, whether on or away from an "insured location";

3. "Property damage" to property rented to, occupied or used by or in the care of an "insured". This exclusion does not apply to "property damage" caused by fire, smoke or explosion;

4. "Bodily injury" to any person eligible to receive any benefits voluntarily provided or required to be provided by an "insured" under any:

a. Workers' compensation law;

b. Non-occupational disability law; or

c. Occupational disease law;

5. "Bodily injury" or "property damage" for which an "insured" under this policy:

    a. Is also an insured under a nuclear energy liability policy issued by the:

        (1) Nuclear Energy Liability Insurance Association;

        (2) Mutual Atomic Energy Liability Underwriters;

        (3) Nuclear Insurance Association of Canada;

        or any of their successors; or

    b. Would be an insured under such a policy but for the exhaustion of its limit of liability; or

6. "Bodily injury" to you or an "insured" as defined under Definitions **5.a.** or **b.**

    This exclusion also applies to any claim made or suit brought against you or an "insured":

    a. To repay; or

    b. Share damages with;

    another person who may be obligated to pay damages because of "bodily injury" to an "insured".

G. Coverage F – Medical Payments To Others

Coverage **F** does not apply to "bodily injury":

1. To a "residence employee" if the "bodily injury":

    a. Occurs off the "insured location"; and

    b. Does not arise out of or in the course of the "residence employee's" employment by an "insured";

2. To any person eligible to receive benefits voluntarily provided or required to be provided under any:

    a. Workers' compensation law;

    b. Non-occupational disability law; or

    c. Occupational disease law;

3. From any:

    a. Nuclear reaction;

    b. Nuclear radiation; or

    c. Radioactive contamination;

    all whether controlled or uncontrolled or however caused; or

    d. Any consequence of any of these; or

4. To any person, other than a "residence employee" of an "insured", regularly residing on any part of the "insured location".

SECTION II – ADDITIONAL COVERAGES

We cover the following in addition to the limits of liability:

A. Claim Expenses

We pay:

1. Expenses we incur and costs taxed against an "insured" in any suit we defend;

2. Premiums on bonds required in a suit we defend, but not for bond amounts more than the Coverage **E** limit of liability. We need not apply for or furnish any bond;

3. Reasonable expenses incurred by an "insured" at our request, including actual loss of earnings (but not loss of other income) up to $250 per day, for assisting us in the investigation or defense of a claim or suit; and

4. Interest on the entire judgment which accrues after entry of the judgment and before we pay or tender, or deposit in court that part of the judgment which does not exceed the limit of liability that applies.

B. First Aid Expenses

We will pay expenses for first aid to others incurred by an "insured" for "bodily injury" covered under this policy. We will not pay for first aid to an "insured".

C. Damage To Property Of Others

1. We will pay, at replacement cost, up to $1,000 per "occurrence" for "property damage" to property of others caused by an "insured".

2. We will not pay for "property damage":

    a. To the extent of any amount recoverable under Section **I**;

    b. Caused intentionally by an "insured" who is 13 years of age or older;

    c. To property owned by an "insured";

    d. To property owned by or rented to a tenant of an "insured" or a resident in your household; or

    e. Arising out of:

        (1) A "business" engaged in by an "insured";

        (2) Any act or omission in connection with a premises owned, rented or controlled by an "insured", other than the "insured location"; or

        (3) The ownership, maintenance, occupancy, operation, use, loading or unloading of aircraft, hovercraft, watercraft or "motor vehicles".

This exclusion **e.(3)** does not apply to a "motor vehicle" that:

    (a) Is designed for recreational use off public roads;

    (b) Is not owned by an "insured"; and

    (c) At the time of the "occurrence", is not required by law, or regulation issued by a government agency, to have been registered for it to be used on public roads or property.

D. Loss Assessment

1. We will pay up to $1,000 for your share of loss assessment charged against you, as owner or tenant of the "residence premises", during the policy period by a corporation or association of property owners, when the assessment is made as a result of:

    a. "Bodily injury" or "property damage" not excluded from coverage under Section **II** – Exclusions; or

    b. Liability for an act of a director, officer or trustee in the capacity as a director, officer or trustee, provided such person:

        (1) Is elected by the members of a corporation or association of property owners; and

        (2) Serves without deriving any income from the exercise of duties which are solely on behalf of a corporation or association of property owners.

2. Paragraph **I.** Policy Period under Section **II** – Conditions does not apply to this Loss Assessment Coverage.

3. Regardless of the number of assessments, the limit of $1,000 is the most we will pay for loss arising out of:

    a. One accident, including continuous or repeated exposure to substantially the same general harmful condition; or

    b. A covered act of a director, officer or trustee. An act involving more than one director, officer or trustee is considered to be a single act.

4. We do not cover assessments charged against you or a corporation or association of property owners by any governmental body.

SECTION II – CONDITIONS

A. Limit Of Liability

Our total liability under Coverage **E** for all damages resulting from any one "occurrence" will not be more than the Coverage **E** limit of liability shown in the Declarations. This limit is the same regardless of the number of "insureds", claims made or persons injured. All "bodily injury" and "property damage" resulting from any one accident or from continuous or repeated exposure to substantially the same general harmful conditions shall be considered to be the result of one "occurrence".

Our total liability under Coverage **F** for all medical expense payable for "bodily injury" to one person as the result of one accident will not be more than the Coverage **F** limit of liability shown in the Declarations.

B. Severability Of Insurance

This insurance applies separately to each "insured". This condition will not increase our limit of liability for any one "occurrence".

C. Duties After "Occurrence"

In case of an "occurrence", you or another "insured" will perform the following duties that apply. We have no duty to provide coverage under this policy if your failure to comply with the following duties is prejudicial to us. You will help us by seeing that these duties are performed:

1. Give written notice to us or our agent as soon as is practical, which sets forth:

    a. The identity of the policy and the "named insured" shown in the Declarations;

    b. Reasonably available information on the time, place and circumstances of the "occurrence"; and

    c. Names and addresses of any claimants and witnesses;

2. Cooperate with us in the investigation, settlement or defense of any claim or suit;

3. Promptly forward to us every notice, demand, summons or other process relating to the "occurrence";

4. At our request, help us:

    a. To make settlement;

    b. To enforce any right of contribution or indemnity against any person or organization who may be liable to an "insured";

c. With the conduct of suits and attend hearings and trials; and

d. To secure and give evidence and obtain the attendance of witnesses;

5. With respect to **C.** Damage To Property Of Others under Section **II** – Additional Coverages, submit to us within 60 days after the loss, a sworn statement of loss and show the damaged property, if in an "insured's" control;

6. No "insured" shall, except at such "insured's" own cost, voluntarily make payment, assume obligation or incur expense other than for first aid to others at the time of the "bodily injury".

D. Duties Of An Injured Person – Coverage F – Medical Payments To Others

1. The injured person or someone acting for the injured person will:

a. Give us written proof of claim, under oath if required, as soon as is practical; and

b. Authorize us to obtain copies of medical reports and records.

2. The injured person will submit to a physical exam by a doctor of our choice when and as often as we reasonably require.

E. Payment Of Claim – Coverage F – Medical Payments To Others

Payment under this coverage is not an admission of liability by an "insured" or us.

F. Suit Against Us

1. No action can be brought against us unless there has been full compliance with all of the terms under this Section **II**.

2. No one will have the right to join us as a party to any action against an "insured".

3. Also, no action with respect to Coverage **E** can be brought against us until the obligation of such "insured" has been determined by final judgment or agreement signed by us.

G. Bankruptcy Of An "Insured"

Bankruptcy or insolvency of an "insured" will not relieve us of our obligations under this policy.

H. Other Insurance

This insurance is excess over other valid and collectible insurance except insurance written specifically to cover as excess over the limits of liability that apply in this policy.

I. Policy Period

This policy applies only to "bodily injury" or "property damage" which occurs during the policy period.

J. Concealment Or Fraud

We do not provide coverage to an "insured" who, whether before or after a loss, has:

1. Intentionally concealed or misrepresented any material fact or circumstance;

2. Engaged in fraudulent conduct; or

3. Made false statements;

relating to this insurance.

SECTIONS I AND II – CONDITIONS

A. Liberalization Clause

If we make a change which broadens coverage under this edition of our policy without additional premium charge, that change will automatically apply to your insurance as of the date we implement the change in your state, provided that this implementation date falls within 60 days prior to or during the policy period stated in the Declarations.

This Liberalization Clause does not apply to changes implemented with a general program revision that includes both broadenings and restrictions in coverage, whether that general program revision is implemented through introduction of:

1. A subsequent edition of this policy; or

2. An amendatory endorsement.

B. Waiver Or Change Of Policy Provisions

A waiver or change of a provision of this policy must be in writing by us to be valid. Our request for an appraisal or examination will not waive any of our rights.

C. Cancellation

1. You may cancel this policy at any time by returning it to us or by letting us know in writing of the date cancellation is to take effect.

2. We may cancel this policy only for the reasons stated below by letting you know in writing of the date cancellation takes effect. This cancellation notice may be delivered to you, or mailed to you at your mailing address shown in the Declarations. Proof of mailing will be sufficient proof of notice.

a. When you have not paid the premium, we may cancel at any time by letting you know at least 10 days before the date cancellation takes effect.

b. When this policy has been in effect for less than 60 days and is not a renewal with us, we may cancel for any reason by letting you know at least 10 days before the date cancellation takes effect.

c. When this policy has been in effect for 60 days or more, or at any time if it is a renewal with us, we may cancel:

(1) If there has been a material misrepresentation of fact which if known to us would have caused us not to issue the policy; or

(2) If the risk has changed substantially since the policy was issued.

This can be done by letting you know at least 30 days before the date cancellation takes effect.

d. When this policy is written for a period of more than one year, we may cancel for any reason at anniversary by letting you know at least 30 days before the date cancellation takes effect.

3. When this policy is canceled, the premium for the period from the date of cancellation to the expiration date will be refunded pro rata.

4. If the return premium is not refunded with the notice of cancellation or when this policy is returned to us, we will refund it within a reasonable time after the date cancellation takes effect.

D. Nonrenewal

We may elect not to renew this policy. We may do so by delivering to you, or mailing to you at your mailing address shown in the Declarations, written notice at least 30 days before the expiration date of this policy. Proof of mailing will be sufficient proof of notice.

E. Assignment

Assignment of this policy will not be valid unless we give our written consent.

F. Subrogation

An "insured" may waive in writing before a loss all rights of recovery against any person. If not waived, we may require an assignment of rights of recovery for a loss to the extent that payment is made by us.

If an assignment is sought, an "insured" must sign and deliver all related papers and cooperate with us.

Subrogation does not apply to Coverage **F** or Paragraph **C.** Damage To Property Of Others under Section **II** – Additional Coverages.

G. Death

If any person named in the Declarations or the spouse, if a resident of the same household, dies, the following apply:

1. We insure the legal representative of the deceased but only with respect to the premises and property of the deceased covered under the policy at the time of death; and

2. "Insured" includes:

a. An "insured" who is a member of your household at the time of your death, but only while a resident of the "residence premises"; and

b. With respect to your property, the person having proper temporary custody of the property until appointment and qualification of a legal representative.

POLICY NUMBER:

HOMEOWNERS
HO 04 27 04 02

THIS ENDORSEMENT CHANGES THE POLICY. PLEASE READ IT CAREFULLY.

LIMITED FUNGI, WET OR DRY ROT, OR BACTERIA COVERAGE

FOR USE WITH FORMS HO 00 03 AND HO 00 05

SCHEDULE*

These limits of liability apply to the total of all loss or costs payable under this endorsement, regardless of the number of "occurrences", the number of claims-made, or the number of locations insured under this endorsement and listed in this Schedule.		
1.	Section I – Property Coverage Limit Of Liability for the Additional Coverage "Fungi", Wet Or Dry Rot, Or Bacteria	$
2.	Section II – Coverage **E** Aggregate Sublimit of Liability for "Fungi", Wet Or Dry Rot, Or Bacteria	$
*Entries may be left blank if shown elsewhere in this policy for this coverage.		

DEFINITIONS

The following definition is added:

"**Fungi**"

a. "Fungi" means any type or form of fungus, including mold or mildew, and any mycotoxins, spores, scents or by-products produced or released by fungi.

b. Under Section II, this does not include any fungi that are, are on, or are contained in, a good or product intended for consumption.

SECTION I – PROPERTY COVERAGES

E. Additional Coverages

Paragraph **10.k.(2)(d)** is deleted in Form **HO 00 05** only.

The following Additional Coverage is added:

13. "**Fungi**", **Wet Or Dry Rot, Or Bacteria**

a. The amount shown in the Schedule above is the most we will pay for:

(1) The total of all loss payable under Section I – Property Coverages caused by "fungi", wet or dry rot, or bacteria;

(2) The cost to remove "fungi", wet or dry rot, or bacteria from property covered under Section I – Property Coverages;

(3) The cost to tear out and replace any part of the building or other covered property as needed to gain access to the "fungi", wet or dry rot, or bacteria; and

(4) The cost of testing of air or property to confirm the absence, presence or level of "fungi", wet or dry rot, or bacteria whether performed prior to, during or after removal, repair, restoration or replacement. The cost of such testing will be provided only to the extent that there is a reason to believe that there is the presence of "fungi", wet or dry rot, or bacteria.

b. The coverage described in **13.a.** only applies when such loss or costs are a result of a Peril Insured Against that occurs during the policy period and only if all reasonable means were used to save and preserve the property from further damage at and after the time the Peril Insured Against occurred.

c. The amount shown in the Schedule for this coverage is the most we will pay for the total of all loss or costs payable under this Additional Coverage regardless of the:

(1) Number of locations insured under this endorsement; or

(2) Number of claims-made.

d. If there is covered loss or damage to covered property, not caused, in whole or in part, by "fungi", wet or dry rot, or bacteria, loss payment will not be limited by the terms of this Additional Coverage, except to the extent that "fungi", wet or dry rot, or bacteria causes an increase in the loss. Any such increase in the loss will be subject to the terms of this Additional Coverage.

This coverage does not increase the limit of liability applying to the damaged covered property.

SECTION I – PERILS INSURED AGAINST

In Form **HO 00 03:**

A. Coverage A – Dwelling And Coverage B – Other Structures

Paragraph **2.c.(5)** is deleted and replaced by the following:

(5) Caused by constant or repeated seepage or leakage of water or the presence or condensation of humidity, moisture or vapor, over a period of weeks, months or years unless such seepage or leakage of water or the presence or condensation of humidity, moisture or vapor and the resulting damage is unknown to all "insureds" and is hidden within the walls or ceilings or beneath the floors or above the ceilings of a structure.

Paragraph **2.c.(6)(c)** is deleted and replaced by the following:

(c) Smog, rust or other corrosion;

B. Coverage C – Personal Property

12. Accidental Discharge Or Overflow Of Water Or Steam

Paragraph **b.(4)** is deleted and replaced by the following:

(4) Caused by constant or repeated seepage or leakage of water or the presence or condensation of humidity, moisture or vapor, over a period of weeks, months or years unless such seepage or leakage of water or the presence or condensation of humidity, moisture or vapor and the resulting damage is unknown to all "insureds" and is hidden within the walls or ceilings or beneath the floors or above the ceilings of a structure.

In Form **HO 00 05:**

A. Under Coverages **A, B** and **C:**

Paragraph **2.d.** is deleted and replaced by the following:

d. Caused by constant or repeated seepage or leakage of water or the presence or condensation of humidity, moisture or vapor, over a period of weeks, months or years unless such seepage or leakage of water or the presence or condensation of humidity, moisture or vapor and the resulting damage is unknown to all "insureds" and is hidden within the walls or ceilings or beneath the floors or above the ceilings of a structure.

Paragraph **2.e.(3)** is deleted and replaced by the following:

(3) Smog, rust or other corrosion;

SECTION I – EXCLUSIONS

Exclusion **A.10.** is added.

10. "Fungi", Wet Or Dry Rot, Or Bacteria

"Fungi", Wet Or Dry Rot, Or Bacteria meaning the presence, growth, proliferation, spread or any activity of "fungi", wet or dry rot, or bacteria.

This exclusion does not apply:

a. When "fungi", wet or dry rot, or bacteria results from fire or lightning; or

b. To the extent coverage is provided for in the "Fungi", Wet Or Dry Rot, Or Bacteria Additional Coverage under Section I – Property Coverages with respect to loss caused by a Peril Insured Against other than fire or lightning.

Direct loss by a Peril Insured Against resulting from "fungi", wet or dry rot, or bacteria is covered.

SECTION I – CONDITIONS

Condition **P. Policy Period** is deleted and replaced by the following:

P. Policy Period

This policy applies to loss or costs which occur during the policy period.

SECTION II – CONDITIONS

Condition **A. Limit Of Liability** is deleted and replaced by the following:

A. Limit Of Liability

Our total liability under Coverage **E** for all damages resulting from any one "occurrence" will not be more than the Coverage **E** limit of liability shown in the Declarations. This limit is the same regardless of the number of "insureds", claims-made or persons injured. All "bodily injury" and "property damage" resulting from any one accident or from continuous or repeated exposure to substantially the same general harmful conditions will be considered to be the result of one "occurrence".

Our total liability under Coverage **F** for all medical expense payable for "bodily injury" to one person as the result of one accident will not be more than the Coverage **F** limit of liability shown in the Declarations.

However, our total liability under Coverage **E** for the total of all damages arising directly or indirectly, in whole or in part, out of the actual, alleged or threatened inhalation of, ingestion of, contact with, exposure to, existence of, or presence of any "fungi", wet or dry rot, or bacteria will not be more than the Section **II** – Coverage **E** Aggregate Sublimit of Liability for "Fungi", Wet Or Dry Rot, Or Bacteria. That sublimit is the amount shown in the Schedule. This is the most we will pay regardless of the:

1. Number of locations insured under the policy to which this endorsement is attached;

2. Number of persons injured;

3. Number of persons whose property is damaged;

4. Number of "insureds"; or

5. Number of "occurrences" or claims-made.

This sublimit is within, but does not increase, the Coverage **E** limit of liability. It applies separately to each consecutive annual period and to any remaining period of less than 12 months, starting with the beginning of the policy period shown in the Declarations.

With respect to damages arising out of "fungi", wet or dry rot, or bacteria described in **A.** Limit Of Liability of this endorsement, Condition **B. Severability Of Insurance** is deleted and replaced by the following:

B. Severability Of Insurance

This insurance applies separately to each "insured" except with respect to the Aggregate Sublimit of Liability described in this endorsement under Section **II** – Conditions, **A.** Limit Of Liability. This condition will not increase the limit of liability for this coverage.

All other provisions of the policy apply.

APPENDIX B

PERSONAL AUTO POLICY

AGREEMENT

In return for payment of the premium and subject to all the terms of this policy, we agree with you as follows:

DEFINITIONS

A. Throughout this policy, "you" and "your" refer to:

   1. The "named insured" shown in the Declarations; and

   2. The spouse if a resident of the same household.

If the spouse ceases to be a resident of the same household during the policy period or prior to the inception of this policy, the spouse will be considered "you" and "your" under this policy but only until the earlier of:

   1. The end of 90 days following the spouse's change of residency;

   2. The effective date of another policy listing the spouse as a named insured; or

   3. The end of the policy period.

B. "We", "us" and "our" refer to the Company providing this insurance.

C. For purposes of this policy, a private passenger type auto, pickup or van shall be deemed to be owned by a person if leased:

   1. Under a written agreement to that person; and

   2. For a continuous period of at least 6 months.

Other words and phrases are defined. They are in quotation marks when used.

D. "Bodily injury" means bodily harm, sickness or disease, including death that results.

E. "Business" includes trade, profession or occupation.

F. "Family member" means a person related to you by blood, marriage or adoption who is a resident of your household. This includes a ward or foster child.

G. "Occupying" means in, upon, getting in, on, out or off.

H. "Property damage" means physical injury to, destruction of or loss of use of tangible property.

I. "Trailer" means a vehicle designed to be pulled by a:

   1. Private passenger auto; or

   2. Pickup or van.

It also means a farm wagon or farm implement while towed by a vehicle listed in **1.** or **2.** above.

J. "Your covered auto" means:

   1. Any vehicle shown in the Declarations.

   2. A "newly acquired auto".

   3. Any "trailer" you own.

   4. Any auto or "trailer" you do not own while used as a temporary substitute for any other vehicle described in this definition which is out of normal use because of its:

    a. Breakdown;

    b. Repair;

    c. Servicing;

    d. Loss; or

    e. Destruction.

   This Provision **(J.4.)** does not apply to Coverage For Damage To Your Auto.

K. "Newly acquired auto":

   1. "Newly acquired auto" means any of the following types of vehicles you become the owner of during the policy period:

    a. A private passenger auto; or

    b. A pickup or van, for which no other insurance policy provides coverage, that:

     (1) Has a Gross Vehicle Weight of less than 10,000 lbs.; and

     (2) Is not used for the delivery or transportation of goods and materials unless such use is:

      (a) Incidental to your "business" of installing, maintaining or repairing furnishings or equipment; or

      (b) For farming or ranching.

   2. Coverage for a "newly acquired auto" is provided as described below. If you ask us to insure a "newly acquired auto" after a specified time period described below has elapsed, any coverage we provide for a "newly acquired auto" will begin at the time you request the coverage.

    a. For any coverage provided in this policy except Coverage For Damage To Your Auto, a "newly acquired auto" will have the broadest coverage we now provide for any vehicle shown in the Declarations. Coverage begins on the date you become the owner. However, for this coverage to apply to a "newly acquired auto" which is in addition to any vehicle shown in the Declarations, you must ask us to insure it within 14 days after you become the owner.

If a "newly acquired auto" replaces a vehicle shown in the Declarations, coverage is provided for this vehicle without your having to ask us to insure it.

b. Collision Coverage for a "newly acquired auto" begins on the date you become the owner. However, for this coverage to apply, you must ask us to insure it within:

(1) 14 days after you become the owner if the Declarations indicate that Collision Coverage applies to at least one auto. In this case, the "newly acquired auto" will have the broadest coverage we now provide for any auto shown in the Declarations.

(2) Four days after you become the owner if the Declarations do not indicate that Collision Coverage applies to at least one auto. If you comply with the 4 day requirement and a loss occurred before you asked us to insure the "newly acquired auto", a Collision deductible of $500 will apply.

c. Other Than Collision Coverage for a "newly acquired auto" begins on the date you become the owner. However, for this coverage to apply, you must ask us to insure it within:

(1) 14 days after you become the owner if the Declarations indicate that Other Than Collision Coverage applies to at least one auto. In this case, the "newly acquired auto" will have the broadest coverage we now provide for any auto shown in the Declarations.

(2) Four days after you become the owner if the Declarations do not indicate that Other Than Collision Coverage applies to at least one auto. If you comply with the 4 day requirement and a loss occurred before you asked us to insure the "newly acquired auto", an Other Than Collision deductible of $500 will apply.

PART A – LIABILITY COVERAGE

INSURING AGREEMENT

A. We will pay damages for "bodily injury" or "property damage" for which any "insured" becomes legally responsible because of an auto accident. Damages include prejudgment interest awarded against the "insured". We will settle or defend, as we consider appropriate, any claim or suit asking for these damages. In addition to our limit of liability, we will pay all defense costs we incur. Our duty to settle or defend ends when our limit of liability for this coverage has been exhausted by payment of judgments or settlements. We have no duty to defend any suit or settle any claim for "bodily injury" or "property damage" not covered under this policy.

B. "Insured" as used in this Part means:

1. You or any "family member" for the ownership, maintenance or use of any auto or "trailer".

2. Any person using "your covered auto".

3. For "your covered auto", any person or organization but only with respect to legal responsibility for acts or omissions of a person for whom coverage is afforded under this Part.

4. For any auto or "trailer", other than "your covered auto", any other person or organization but only with respect to legal responsibility for acts or omissions of you or any "family member" for whom coverage is afforded under this Part. This Provision **(B.4.)** applies only if the person or organization does not own or hire the auto or "trailer".

SUPPLEMENTARY PAYMENTS

In addition to our limit of liability, we will pay on behalf of an "insured":

1. Up to $250 for the cost of bail bonds required because of an accident, including related traffic law violations. The accident must result in "bodily injury" or "property damage" covered under this policy.

2. Premiums on appeal bonds and bonds to release attachments in any suit we defend.

3. Interest accruing after a judgment is entered in any suit we defend. Our duty to pay interest ends when we offer to pay that part of the judgment which does not exceed our limit of liability for this coverage.

4. Up to $200 a day for loss of earnings, but not other income, because of attendance at hearings or trials at our request.

5. Other reasonable expenses incurred at our request.

EXCLUSIONS

A. We do not provide Liability Coverage for any "insured":

1. Who intentionally causes "bodily injury" or "property damage".

2. For "property damage" to property owned or being transported by that "insured".

3. For "property damage" to property:
   a. Rented to;
   b. Used by; or
   c. In the care of;
   that "insured".

   This Exclusion (A.3.) does not apply to "property damage" to a residence or private garage.

4. For "bodily injury" to an employee of that "insured" during the course of employment. This Exclusion (A.4.) does not apply to "bodily injury" to a domestic employee unless workers' compensation benefits are required or available for that domestic employee.

5. For that "insured's" liability arising out of the ownership or operation of a vehicle while it is being used as a public or livery conveyance. This Exclusion (A.5.) does not apply to a share-the-expense car pool.

6. While employed or otherwise engaged in the "business" of:
   a. Selling;
   b. Repairing;
   c. Servicing;
   d. Storing; or
   e. Parking;

   vehicles designed for use mainly on public highways. This includes road testing and delivery. This Exclusion (A.6.) does not apply to the ownership, maintenance or use of "your covered auto" by:
   a. You;
   b. Any "family member"; or
   c. Any partner, agent or employee of you or any "family member".

7. Maintaining or using any vehicle while that "insured" is employed or otherwise engaged in any "business" (other than farming or ranching) not described in Exclusion A.6.

   This Exclusion (A.7.) does not apply to the maintenance or use of a:
   a. Private passenger auto;
   b. Pickup or van; or
   c. "Trailer" used with a vehicle described in a. or b. above.

8. Using a vehicle without a reasonable belief that that "insured" is entitled to do so. This Exclusion (A.8.) does not apply to a "family member" using "your covered auto" which is owned by you.

9. For "bodily injury" or "property damage" for which that "insured":
   a. Is an insured under a nuclear energy liability policy; or
   b. Would be an insured under a nuclear energy liability policy but for its termination upon exhaustion of its limit of liability.

   A nuclear energy liability policy is a policy issued by any of the following or their successors:
   a. Nuclear Energy Liability Insurance Association;
   b. Mutual Atomic Energy Liability Underwriters; or
   c. Nuclear Insurance Association of Canada.

B. We do not provide Liability Coverage for the ownership, maintenance or use of:

1. Any vehicle which:
   a. Has fewer than four wheels; or
   b. Is designed mainly for use off public roads.

   This Exclusion (B.1.) does not apply:
   a. While such vehicle is being used by an "insured" in a medical emergency;
   b. To any "trailer"; or
   c. To any non-owned golf cart.

2. Any vehicle, other than "your covered auto", which is:
   a. Owned by you; or
   b. Furnished or available for your regular use.

3. Any vehicle, other than "your covered auto", which is:
   a. Owned by any "family member"; or
   b. Furnished or available for the regular use of any "family member".

   However, this Exclusion (B.3.) does not apply to you while you are maintaining or "occupying" any vehicle which is:
   a. Owned by a "family member"; or
   b. Furnished or available for the regular use of a "family member".

4. Any vehicle, located inside a facility designed for racing, for the purpose of:
   a. Competing in; or
   b. Practicing or preparing for;

   any prearranged or organized racing or speed contest.

LIMIT OF LIABILITY

A. The limit of liability shown in the Declarations for each person for Bodily Injury Liability is our maximum limit of liability for all damages, including damages for care, loss of services or death, arising out of "bodily injury" sustained by any one person in any one auto accident. Subject to this limit for each person, the limit of liability shown in the Declarations for each accident for Bodily Injury Liability is our maximum limit of liability for all damages for "bodily injury" resulting from any one auto accident.

The limit of liability shown in the Declarations for each accident for Property Damage Liability is our maximum limit of liability for all "property damage" resulting from any one auto accident.

This is the most we will pay regardless of the number of:

1. "Insureds";

2. Claims made;

3. Vehicles or premiums shown in the Declarations; or

4. Vehicles involved in the auto accident.

B. No one will be entitled to receive duplicate payments for the same elements of loss under this coverage and:

1. Part **B** or Part **C** of this policy; or

2. Any Underinsured Motorists Coverage provided by this policy.

OUT OF STATE COVERAGE

If an auto accident to which this policy applies occurs in any state or province other than the one in which "your covered auto" is principally garaged, we will interpret your policy for that accident as follows:

A. If the state or province has:

1. A financial responsibility or similar law specifying limits of liability for "bodily injury" or "property damage" higher than the limit shown in the Declarations, your policy will provide the higher specified limit.

2. A compulsory insurance or similar law requiring a nonresident to maintain insurance whenever the nonresident uses a vehicle in that state or province, your policy will provide at least the required minimum amounts and types of coverage.

B. No one will be entitled to duplicate payments for the same elements of loss.

FINANCIAL RESPONSIBILITY

When this policy is certified as future proof of financial responsibility, this policy shall comply with the law to the extent required.

OTHER INSURANCE

If there is other applicable liability insurance we will pay only our share of the loss. Our share is the proportion that our limit of liability bears to the total of all applicable limits. However, any insurance we provide for a vehicle you do not own shall be excess over any other collectible insurance.

PART B – MEDICAL PAYMENTS COVERAGE

INSURING AGREEMENT

A. We will pay reasonable expenses incurred for necessary medical and funeral services because of "bodily injury":

1. Caused by accident; and

2. Sustained by an "insured".

We will pay only those expenses incurred for services rendered within 3 years from the date of the accident.

B. "Insured" as used in this Part means:

1. You or any "family member":

a. While "occupying"; or

b. As a pedestrian when struck by;

a motor vehicle designed for use mainly on public roads or a trailer of any type.

2. Any other person while "occupying" "your covered auto".

EXCLUSIONS

We do not provide Medical Payments Coverage for any "insured" for "bodily injury":

1. Sustained while "occupying" any motorized vehicle having fewer than four wheels.

2. Sustained while "occupying" "your covered auto" when it is being used as a public or livery conveyance. This Exclusion **(2.)** does not apply to a share-the-expense car pool.

3. Sustained while "occupying" any vehicle located for use as a residence or premises.

4. Occurring during the course of employment if workers' compensation benefits are required or available for the "bodily injury".

5. Sustained while "occupying", or when struck by, any vehicle (other than "your covered auto") which is:

a. Owned by you; or

b. Furnished or available for your regular use.

6. Sustained while "occupying", or when struck by, any vehicle (other than "your covered auto") which is:

a. Owned by any "family member"; or

b. Furnished or available for the regular use of any "family member".

However, this Exclusion **(6.)** does not apply to you.

7. Sustained while "occupying" a vehicle without a reasonable belief that that "insured" is entitled to do so. This Exclusion **(7.)** does not apply to a "family member" using "your covered auto" which is owned by you.

8. Sustained while "occupying" a vehicle when it is being used in the "business" of an "insured". This Exclusion **(8.)** does not apply to "bodily injury" sustained while "occupying" a:

    a. Private passenger auto;

    b. Pickup or van that you own; or

    c. "Trailer" used with a vehicle described in **a.** or **b.** above.

9. Caused by or as a consequence of:

    a. Discharge of a nuclear weapon (even if accidental);

    b. War (declared or undeclared);

    c. Civil war;

    d. Insurrection; or

    e. Rebellion or revolution.

10. From or as a consequence of the following, whether controlled or uncontrolled or however caused:

    a. Nuclear reaction;

    b. Radiation; or

    c. Radioactive contamination.

11. Sustained while "occupying" any vehicle located inside a facility designed for racing, for the purpose of:

    a. Competing in; or

    b. Practicing or preparing for;

    any prearranged or organized racing or speed contest.

LIMIT OF LIABILITY

A. The limit of liability shown in the Declarations for this coverage is our maximum limit of liability for each person injured in any one accident. This is the most we will pay regardless of the number of:

1. "Insureds";

2. Claims made;

3. Vehicles or premiums shown in the Declarations; or

4. Vehicles involved in the accident.

B. No one will be entitled to receive duplicate payments for the same elements of loss under this coverage and:

1. Part **A** or Part **C** of this policy; or

2. Any Underinsured Motorists Coverage provided by this policy.

OTHER INSURANCE

If there is other applicable auto medical payments insurance we will pay only our share of the loss. Our share is the proportion that our limit of liability bears to the total of all applicable limits. However, any insurance we provide with respect to a vehicle you do not own shall be excess over any other collectible auto insurance providing payments for medical or funeral expenses.

PART C – UNINSURED MOTORISTS COVERAGE

INSURING AGREEMENT

A. We will pay compensatory damages which an "insured" is legally entitled to recover from the owner or operator of an "uninsured motor vehicle" because of "bodily injury":

1. Sustained by an "insured"; and

2. Caused by an accident.

The owner's or operator's liability for these damages must arise out of the ownership, maintenance or use of the "uninsured motor vehicle".

Any judgment for damages arising out of a suit brought without our written consent is not binding on us.

B. "Insured" as used in this Part means:

1. You or any "family member".

2. Any other person "occupying" "your covered auto".

3. Any person for damages that person is entitled to recover because of "bodily injury" to which this coverage applies sustained by a person described in **1.** or **2.** above.

C. "Uninsured motor vehicle" means a land motor vehicle or trailer of any type:

1. To which no bodily injury liability bond or policy applies at the time of the accident.

2. To which a bodily injury liability bond or policy applies at the time of the accident. In this case its limit for bodily injury liability must be less than the minimum limit for bodily injury liability specified by the financial responsibility law of the state in which "your covered auto" is principally garaged.

---

3. Which is a hit-and-run vehicle whose operator or owner cannot be identified and which hits:

    a. You or any "family member";

    b. A vehicle which you or any "family member" are "occupying"; or

    c. "Your covered auto".

4. To which a bodily injury liability bond or policy applies at the time of the accident but the bonding or insuring company:

    a. Denies coverage; or

    b. Is or becomes insolvent.

However, "uninsured motor vehicle" does not include any vehicle or equipment:

1. Owned by or furnished or available for the regular use of you or any "family member".

2. Owned or operated by a self-insurer under any applicable motor vehicle law, except a self-insurer which is or becomes insolvent.

3. Owned by any governmental unit or agency.

4. Operated on rails or crawler treads.

5. Designed mainly for use off public roads while not on public roads.

6. While located for use as a residence or premises.

EXCLUSIONS

A. We do not provide Uninsured Motorists Coverage for "bodily injury" sustained:

1. By an "insured" while "occupying", or when struck by, any motor vehicle owned by that "insured" which is not insured for this coverage under this policy. This includes a trailer of any type used with that vehicle.

2. By any "family member" while "occupying", or when struck by, any motor vehicle you own which is insured for this coverage on a primary basis under any other policy.

B. We do not provide Uninsured Motorists Coverage for "bodily injury" sustained by any "insured":

1. If that "insured" or the legal representative settles the "bodily injury" claim without our consent.

2. While "occupying" "your covered auto" when it is being used as a public or livery conveyance. This Exclusion (**B.2.**) does not apply to a share-the-expense car pool.

3. Using a vehicle without a reasonable belief that that "insured" is entitled to do so. This Exclusion (**B.3.**) does not apply to a "family member" using "your covered auto" which is owned by you.

C. This coverage shall not apply directly or indirectly to benefit any insurer or self-insurer under any of the following or similar law:

1. Workers' compensation law; or

2. Disability benefits law.

D. We do not provide Uninsured Motorists Coverage for punitive or exemplary damages.

LIMIT OF LIABILITY

A. The limit of liability shown in the Declarations for each person for Uninsured Motorists Coverage is our maximum limit of liability for all damages, including damages for care, loss of services or death, arising out of "bodily injury" sustained by any one person in any one accident. Subject to this limit for each person, the limit of liability shown in the Declarations for each accident for Uninsured Motorists Coverage is our maximum limit of liability for all damages for "bodily injury" resulting from any one accident.

This is the most we will pay regardless of the number of:

1. "Insureds";

2. Claims made;

3. Vehicles or premiums shown in the Declarations; or

4. Vehicles involved in the accident.

B. No one will be entitled to receive duplicate payments for the same elements of loss under this coverage and:

1. Part **A.** or Part **B.** of this policy; or

2. Any Underinsured Motorists Coverage provided by this policy.

C. We will not make a duplicate payment under this coverage for any element of loss for which payment has been made by or on behalf of persons or organizations who may be legally responsible.

D. We will not pay for any element of loss if a person is entitled to receive payment for the same element of loss under any of the following or similar law:

1. Workers' compensation law; or

2. Disability benefits law.

OTHER INSURANCE

If there is other applicable insurance available under one or more policies or provisions of coverage that is similar to the insurance provided under this Part of the policy:

1. Any recovery for damages under all such policies or provisions of coverage may equal but not exceed the highest applicable limit for any one vehicle under any insurance providing coverage on either a primary or excess basis.

2. Any insurance we provide with respect to a vehicle you do not own shall be excess over any collectible insurance providing such coverage on a primary basis.

3. If the coverage under this policy is provided:

   a. On a primary basis, we will pay only our share of the loss that must be paid under insurance providing coverage on a primary basis. Our share is the proportion that our limit of liability bears to the total of all applicable limits of liability for coverage provided on a primary basis.

   b. On an excess basis, we will pay only our share of the loss that must be paid under insurance providing coverage on an excess basis. Our share is the proportion that our limit of liability bears to the total of all applicable limits of liability for coverage provided on an excess basis.

ARBITRATION

A. If we and an "insured" do not agree:

   1. Whether that "insured" is legally entitled to recover damages; or

   2. As to the amount of damages which are recoverable by that "insured";

   from the owner or operator of an "uninsured motor vehicle", then the matter may be arbitrated. However, disputes concerning coverage under this Part may not be arbitrated.

Both parties must agree to arbitration. If so agreed, each party will select an arbitrator. The two arbitrators will select a third. If they cannot agree within 30 days, either may request that selection be made by a judge of a court having jurisdiction.

B. Each party will:

   1. Pay the expenses it incurs; and

   2. Bear the expenses of the third arbitrator equally.

C. Unless both parties agree otherwise, arbitration will take place in the county in which the "insured" lives. Local rules of law as to procedure and evidence will apply. A decision agreed to by two of the arbitrators will be binding as to:

   1. Whether the "insured" is legally entitled to recover damages; and

   2. The amount of damages. This applies only if the amount does not exceed the minimum limit for bodily injury liability specified by the financial responsibility law of the state in which "your covered auto" is principally garaged. If the amount exceeds that limit, either party may demand the right to a trial. This demand must be made within 60 days of the arbitrators' decision. If this demand is not made, the amount of damages agreed to by the arbitrators will be binding.

PART D – COVERAGE FOR DAMAGE TO YOUR AUTO

INSURING AGREEMENT

A. We will pay for direct and accidental loss to "your covered auto" or any "non-owned auto", including their equipment, minus any applicable deductible shown in the Declarations. If loss to more than one "your covered auto" or "non-owned auto" results from the same "collision", only the highest applicable deductible will apply. We will pay for loss to "your covered auto" caused by:

   1. Other than "collision" only if the Declarations indicate that Other Than Collision Coverage is provided for that auto.

   2. "Collision" only if the Declarations indicate that Collision Coverage is provided for that auto.

   If there is a loss to a "non-owned auto", we will provide the broadest coverage applicable to any "your covered auto" shown in the Declarations.

B. "Collision" means the upset of "your covered auto" or a "non-owned auto" or their impact with another vehicle or object.

   Loss caused by the following is considered other than "collision":

   1. Missiles or falling objects;

   2. Fire;

   3. Theft or larceny;

   4. Explosion or earthquake;

   5. Windstorm;

   6. Hail, water or flood;

   7. Malicious mischief or vandalism;

   8. Riot or civil commotion;

   9. Contact with bird or animal; or

   10. Breakage of glass.

   If breakage of glass is caused by a "collision", you may elect to have it considered a loss caused by "collision".

C. "Non-owned auto" means:

   1. Any private passenger auto, pickup, van or "trailer" not owned by or furnished or available for the regular use of you or any "family member" while in the custody of or being operated by you or any "family member"; or

   2. Any auto or "trailer" you do not own while used as a temporary substitute for "your covered auto" which is out of normal use because of its:

      a. Breakdown;

      b. Repair;

      c. Servicing;

      d. Loss; or

      e. Destruction.

TRANSPORTATION EXPENSES

A. In addition, we will pay, without application of a deductible, up to a maximum of $600 for:

1. Temporary transportation expenses not exceeding $20 per day incurred by you in the event of a loss to "your covered auto". We will pay for such expenses if the loss is caused by:

a. Other than "collision" only if the Declarations indicate that Other Than Collision Coverage is provided for that auto.

b. "Collision" only if the Declarations indicate that Collision Coverage is provided for that auto.

2. Expenses for which you become legally responsible in the event of loss to a "non-owned auto". We will pay for such expenses if the loss is caused by:

a. Other than "collision" only if the Declarations indicate that Other Than Collision Coverage is provided for any "your covered auto".

b. "Collision" only if the Declarations indicate that Collision Coverage is provided for any "your covered auto".

However, the most we will pay for any expenses for loss of use is $20 per day.

B. If the loss is caused by:

1. A total theft of "your covered auto" or a "non-owned auto", we will pay only expenses incurred during the period:

a. Beginning 48 hours after the theft; and

b. Ending when "your covered auto" or the "non-owned auto" is returned to use or we pay for its loss.

2. Other than theft of a "your covered auto" or a "non-owned auto", we will pay only expenses beginning when the auto is withdrawn from use for more than 24 hours.

C. Our payment will be limited to that period of time reasonably required to repair or replace the "your covered auto" or the "non-owned auto".

EXCLUSIONS

We will not pay for:

1. Loss to "your covered auto" or any "non-owned auto" which occurs while it is being used as a public or livery conveyance. This Exclusion (**1.**) does not apply to a share-the-expense car pool.

2. Damage due and confined to:

a. Wear and tear;

b. Freezing;

c. Mechanical or electrical breakdown or failure; or

d. Road damage to tires.

This Exclusion (**2.**) does not apply if the damage results from the total theft of "your covered auto" or any "non-owned auto".

3. Loss due to or as a consequence of:

a. Radioactive contamination;

b. Discharge of any nuclear weapon (even if accidental);

c. War (declared or undeclared);

d. Civil war;

e. Insurrection; or

f. Rebellion or revolution.

4. Loss to any electronic equipment designed for the reproduction of sound and any accessories used with such equipment. This includes but is not limited to:

a. Radios and stereos;

b. Tape decks; or

c. Compact disc players.

This Exclusion (**4.**) does not apply to equipment designed solely for the reproduction of sound and accessories used with such equipment, provided:

a. The equipment is permanently installed in "your covered auto" or any "non-owned auto"; or

b. The equipment is:

(1) Removable from a housing unit which is permanently installed in the auto;

(2) Designed to be solely operated by use of the power from the auto's electrical system; and

(3) In or upon "your covered auto" or any "non-owned auto" at the time of loss.

5. Loss to any electronic equipment that receives or transmits audio, visual or data signals and any accessories used with such equipment. This includes but is not limited to:

a. Citizens band radios;

b. Telephones;

c. Two-way mobile radios;

d. Scanning monitor receivers;

e. Television monitor receivers;

f. Video cassette recorders;

g. Audio cassette recorders; or

h. Personal computers.

This Exclusion (**5.**) does not apply to:

a. Any electronic equipment that is necessary for the normal operation of the auto or the monitoring of the auto's operating systems; or

Copyright, Insurance Services Office, Inc., 1997   **PP 00 01 06 98**

b. A permanently installed telephone designed to be operated by use of the power from the auto's electrical system and any accessories used with the telephone.

6. Loss to tapes, records, discs or other media used with equipment described in Exclusions **4.** and **5.**

7. A total loss to "your covered auto" or any "non-owned auto" due to destruction or confiscation by governmental or civil authorities.

This Exclusion (**7.**) does not apply to the interests of Loss Payees in "your covered auto".

8. Loss to:

   a. A "trailer", camper body, or motor home, which is not shown in the Declarations; or

   b. Facilities or equipment used with such "trailer", camper body or motor home. Facilities or equipment include but are not limited to:

      (1) Cooking, dining, plumbing or refrigeration facilities;

      (2) Awnings or cabanas; or

      (3) Any other facilities or equipment used with a "trailer", camper body, or motor home.

   This Exclusion (**8.**) does not apply to a:

   a. "Trailer", and its facilities or equipment, which you do not own; or

   b. "Trailer", camper body, or the facilities or equipment in or attached to the "trailer" or camper body, which you:

      (1) Acquire during the policy period; and

      (2) Ask us to insure within 14 days after you become the owner.

9. Loss to any "non-owned auto" when used by you or any "family member" without a reasonable belief that you or that "family member" are entitled to do so.

10. Loss to equipment designed or used for the detection or location of radar or laser.

11. Loss to any custom furnishings or equipment in or upon any pickup or van. Custom furnishings or equipment include but are not limited to:

    a. Special carpeting or insulation;

    b. Furniture or bars;

    c. Height-extending roofs; or

    d. Custom murals, paintings or other decals or graphics.

       This Exclusion (**11.**) does not apply to a cap, cover or bedliner in or upon any "your covered auto" which is a pickup.

12. Loss to any "non-owned auto" being maintained or used by any person while employed or otherwise engaged in the "business" of:

    a. Selling;

    b. Repairing;

    c. Servicing;

    d. Storing; or

    e. Parking;

    vehicles designed for use on public highways. This includes road testing and delivery.

13. Loss to "your covered auto" or any "non-owned auto", located inside a facility designed for racing, for the purpose of:

    a. Competing in; or

    b. Practicing or preparing for;

    any prearranged or organized racing or speed contest.

14. Loss to, or loss of use of, a "non-owned auto" rented by:

    a. You; or

    b. Any "family member";

    if a rental vehicle company is precluded from recovering such loss or loss of use, from you or that "family member", pursuant to the provisions of any applicable rental agreement or state law.

LIMIT OF LIABILITY

A. Our limit of liability for loss will be the lesser of the:

   1. Actual cash value of the stolen or damaged property; or

   2. Amount necessary to repair or replace the property with other property of like kind and quality.

   However, the most we will pay for loss to:

   1. Any "non-owned auto" which is a trailer is $500.

   2. Equipment designed solely for the reproduction of sound, including any accessories used with such equipment, which is installed in locations not used by the auto manufacturer for installation of such equipment or accessories, is $1,000.

B. An adjustment for depreciation and physical condition will be made in determining actual cash value in the event of a total loss.

C. If a repair or replacement results in better than like kind or quality, we will not pay for the amount of the betterment.

PAYMENT OF LOSS

We may pay for loss in money or repair or replace the damaged or stolen property. We may, at our expense, return any stolen property to:

1. You; or

2. The address shown in this policy.

If we return stolen property we will pay for any damage resulting from the theft. We may keep all or part of the property at an agreed or appraised value.

If we pay for loss in money, our payment will include the applicable sales tax for the damaged or stolen property.

NO BENEFIT TO BAILEE

This insurance shall not directly or indirectly benefit any carrier or other bailee for hire.

OTHER SOURCES OF RECOVERY

If other sources of recovery also cover the loss, we will pay only our share of the loss. Our share is the proportion that our limit of liability bears to the total of all applicable limits. However, any insurance we provide with respect to a "non-owned auto" shall be excess over any other collectible source of recovery including, but not limited to:

1. Any coverage provided by the owner of the "non-owned auto";

2. Any other applicable physical damage insurance;

3. Any other source of recovery applicable to the loss.

APPRAISAL

A. If we and you do not agree on the amount of loss, either may demand an appraisal of the loss. In this event, each party will select a competent appraiser. The two appraisers will select an umpire. The appraisers will state separately the actual cash value and the amount of loss. If they fail to agree, they will submit their differences to the umpire. A decision agreed to by any two will be binding. Each party will:

1. Pay its chosen appraiser; and

2. Bear the expenses of the appraisal and umpire equally.

B. We do not waive any of our rights under this policy by agreeing to an appraisal.

PART E – DUTIES AFTER AN ACCIDENT OR LOSS

We have no duty to provide coverage under this policy unless there has been full compliance with the following duties:

A. We must be notified promptly of how, when and where the accident or loss happened. Notice should also include the names and addresses of any injured persons and of any witnesses.

B. A person seeking any coverage must:

1. Cooperate with us in the investigation, settlement or defense of any claim or suit.

2. Promptly send us copies of any notices or legal papers received in connection with the accident or loss.

3. Submit, as often as we reasonably require:

   a. To physical exams by physicians we select. We will pay for these exams.

   b. To examination under oath and subscribe the same.

4. Authorize us to obtain:

   a. Medical reports; and

   b. Other pertinent records.

5. Submit a proof of loss when required by us.

C. A person seeking Uninsured Motorists Coverage must also:

1. Promptly notify the police if a hit-and-run driver is involved.

2. Promptly send us copies of the legal papers if a suit is brought.

D. A person seeking Coverage For Damage To Your Auto must also:

1. Take reasonable steps after loss to protect "your covered auto" or any "non-owned auto" and their equipment from further loss. We will pay reasonable expenses incurred to do this.

2. Promptly notify the police if "your covered auto" or any "non-owned auto" is stolen.

3. Permit us to inspect and appraise the damaged property before its repair or disposal.

PP 00 01 06 98

PART F – GENERAL PROVISIONS

BANKRUPTCY

Bankruptcy or insolvency of the "insured" shall not relieve us of any obligations under this policy.

CHANGES

A. This policy contains all the agreements between you and us. Its terms may not be changed or waived except by endorsement issued by us.

B. If there is a change to the information used to develop the policy premium, we may adjust your premium. Changes during the policy term that may result in a premium increase or decrease include, but are not limited to, changes in:

   1. The number, type or use classification of insured vehicles;

   2. Operators using insured vehicles;

   3. The place of principal garaging of insured vehicles;

   4. Coverage, deductible or limits.

If a change resulting from **A.** or **B.** requires a premium adjustment, we will make the premium adjustment in accordance with our manual rules.

C. If we make a change which broadens coverage under this edition of your policy without additional premium charge, that change will automatically apply to your policy as of the date we implement the change in your state. This Paragraph **(C.)** does not apply to changes implemented with a general program revision that includes both broadenings and restrictions in coverage, whether that general program revision is implemented through introduction of:

   1. A subsequent edition of your policy; or

   2. An Amendatory Endorsement.

FRAUD

We do not provide coverage for any "insured" who has made fraudulent statements or engaged in fraudulent conduct in connection with any accident or loss for which coverage is sought under this policy.

LEGAL ACTION AGAINST US

A. No legal action may be brought against us until there has been full compliance with all the terms of this policy. In addition, under Part **A**, no legal action may be brought against us until:

   1. We agree in writing that the "insured" has an obligation to pay; or

   2. The amount of that obligation has been finally determined by judgment after trial.

B. No person or organization has any right under this policy to bring us into any action to determine the liability of an "insured".

OUR RIGHT TO RECOVER PAYMENT

A. If we make a payment under this policy and the person to or for whom payment was made has a right to recover damages from another we shall be subrogated to that right. That person shall do:

   1. Whatever is necessary to enable us to exercise our rights; and

   2. Nothing after loss to prejudice them.

   However, our rights in this Paragraph **(A.)** do not apply under Part **D**, against any person using "your covered auto" with a reasonable belief that that person is entitled to do so.

B. If we make a payment under this policy and the person to or for whom payment is made recovers damages from another, that person shall:

   1. Hold in trust for us the proceeds of the recovery; and

   2. Reimburse us to the extent of our payment.

POLICY PERIOD AND TERRITORY

A. This policy applies only to accidents and losses which occur:

   1. During the policy period as shown in the Declarations; and

   2. Within the policy territory.

B. The policy territory is:

   1. The United States of America, its territories or possessions;

   2. Puerto Rico; or

   3. Canada.

   This policy also applies to loss to, or accidents involving, "your covered auto" while being transported between their ports.

TERMINATION

A. Cancellation

This policy may be cancelled during the policy period as follows:

   1. The named insured shown in the Declarations may cancel by:

   a. Returning this policy to us; or

   b. Giving us advance written notice of the date cancellation is to take effect.

   2. We may cancel by mailing to the named insured shown in the Declarations at the address shown in this policy:

   a. At least 10 days notice:

   (1) If cancellation is for nonpayment of premium; or

(2) If notice is mailed during the first 60 days this policy is in effect and this is not a renewal or continuation policy; or

b. At least 20 days notice in all other cases.

3. After this policy is in effect for 60 days, or if this is a renewal or continuation policy, we will cancel only:

a. For nonpayment of premium; or

b. If your driver's license or that of:

(1) Any driver who lives with you; or

(2) Any driver who customarily uses "your covered auto";

has been suspended or revoked. This must have occurred:

(1) During the policy period; or

(2) Since the last anniversary of the original effective date if the policy period is other than 1 year; or

c. If the policy was obtained through material misrepresentation.

B. Nonrenewal

If we decide not to renew or continue this policy, we will mail notice to the named insured shown in the Declarations at the address shown in this policy. Notice will be mailed at least 20 days before the end of the policy period. Subject to this notice requirement, if the policy period is:

1. Less than 6 months, we will have the right not to renew or continue this policy every 6 months, beginning 6 months after its original effective date.

2. 6 months or longer, but less than one year, we will have the right not to renew or continue this policy at the end of the policy period.

3. 1 year or longer, we will have the right not to renew or continue this policy at each anniversary of its original effective date.

C. Automatic Termination

If we offer to renew or continue and you or your representative do not accept, this policy will automatically terminate at the end of the current policy period. Failure to pay the required renewal or continuation premium when due shall mean that you have not accepted our offer.

If you obtain other insurance on "your covered auto", any similar insurance provided by this policy will terminate as to that auto on the effective date of the other insurance.

D. Other Termination Provisions

1. We may deliver any notice instead of mailing it. Proof of mailing of any notice shall be sufficient proof of notice.

2. If this policy is cancelled, you may be entitled to a premium refund. If so, we will send you the refund. The premium refund, if any, will be computed according to our manuals. However, making or offering to make the refund is not a condition of cancellation.

3. The effective date of cancellation stated in the notice shall become the end of the policy period.

TRANSFER OF YOUR INTEREST IN THIS POLICY

A. Your rights and duties under this policy may not be assigned without our written consent. However, if a named insured shown in the Declarations dies, coverage will be provided for:

1. The surviving spouse if resident in the same household at the time of death. Coverage applies to the spouse as if a named insured shown in the Declarations; and

2. The legal representative of the deceased person as if a named insured shown in the Declarations. This applies only with respect to the representative's legal responsibility to maintain or use "your covered auto".

B. Coverage will only be provided until the end of the policy period.

TWO OR MORE AUTO POLICIES

If this policy and any other auto insurance policy issued to you by us apply to the same accident, the maximum limit of our liability under all the policies shall not exceed the highest applicable limit of liability under any one policy.

   PP 00 01 06 98

APPENDIX C

ELECTRONIC COMMERCE
(E-COMMERCE)

This endorsement modifies insurance provided under the following:

COMMERCIAL PROPERTY COVERAGE PART

SCHEDULE*

Description Of Business	Location Of Business	Annual Aggregate Limit Of Insurance	Anti-Virus Waiver	Section I Deductible ($)
			☐	

* Information required to complete this Schedule, if not shown in this endorsement, will be shown in the Declarations.

A. Introduction

1. Under this endorsement, the business of e-commerce and e-commerce activity mean commerce conducted via the Internet or other computer-based interactive communications network. This includes business-to-business commerce conducted in that manner.

2. As used in this endorsement, electronic data means information, facts or computer programs stored as or on, created or used on, or transmitted to or from computer software (including systems and applications software), on hard or floppy disks, CD-ROMs, tapes, drives, cells, data processing devices or any other repositories of computer software which are used with electronically controlled equipment. The term computer programs, referred to in the foregoing description of electronic data, means a set of related electronic instructions which direct the operations and functions of a computer or device connected to it, which enable the computer or device to receive, process, store, retrieve or send data.

3. As used in this endorsement, loss or damage to electronic data means destruction or corruption of electronic data.

4. As used in this endorsement:

   a. The term employee includes a leased or temporary employee; and

   b. The term contractor, which includes an employee or any agent of the contractor, means an entity that has a written agreement with you to inspect, design, install, test, maintain, repair or replace any part of your computer system including electronic data.

5. In this endorsement, reference to your computers or your computer system means those which are owned by you or licensed or leased to you.

B. Section I – Electronic Data Coverage

1. The coverage provided under Section I of this endorsement is limited to electronic data which is owned by you or licensed or leased to you, originates and resides in computers located in the Coverage Territory, and is used in the e-commerce activity of your business described in the Schedule.

   Under Section I of this endorsement, electronic data does not include your electronic data that is licensed, leased or rented to others.

2. We will pay for the cost to replace or restore electronic data which has suffered loss or damage by a Covered Cause of Loss as described in Section III of this endorsement, subject to the valuation provisions in **B.3.** below.

© ISO Properties, Inc., 2001

3. The **Valuation** Condition is replaced by the following with respect to the coverage provided under Section I of this endorsement:

   a. Loss or damage to electronic data will be valued at the cost of restoration or replacement, including the cost of data entry, re-programming and computer consultation services. But we will not pay the cost to duplicate research that led to the development of your electronic data or any proprietary or confidential information or intellectual property in any form. To the extent that electronic data is not replaced or restored, the loss will be valued at the cost of replacement of the media on which the electronic data was stored, with blank media of substantially identical type.

   b. If you recover, from a licenser or lessor, for loss or damage to electronic data, our loss payment to you will be reduced to the extent of such recovery.

C. **Section II – Time Element Coverage**

1. **Coverage**

   We will pay for the actual loss of Business Income you sustain and/or Extra Expense you incur due to the necessary suspension (slowdown or cessation) of the e-commerce activity of your business described in the Schedule, for the applicable period of time specified in **C.2.** The suspension must be caused by:

   a. A loss covered under Section I of this endorsement; or

   b. Interruption in normal computer network service or function caused by a Covered Cause of Loss as described in Section III of this endorsement.

   Income or expense from outside the Coverage Territory, generated by or pertaining to the e-commerce activity of the business described in the Schedule, is not covered under this endorsement.

2. **Period Of Coverage**

   a. If the suspension of e-commerce activity is caused by a loss covered under Section I of this endorsement, then the period of coverage begins 24 hours after the time of such loss and ends on the earliest of:

      (1) The time when e-commerce activity is resumed;

      (2) The time when the electronic data is restored; or

      (3) 90 days after the date of the loss covered under Section I of this endorsement.

   b. If the suspension of e-commerce activity is caused solely by an interruption described in **C.1.b.** above, then the period of coverage begins 24 hours after the interruption begins. Under this endorsement, the interruption in service is deemed to begin when service to your website is interrupted. The period of coverage ends on the earliest of:

      (1) The time when your e-commerce activity is resumed;

      (2) The time when service is restored to you; or

      (3) Two weeks after the interruption began.

   c. The time periods expressed in **2.a.** and **2.b.** above (including the 24-hour waiting period) apply to the coverage under Section II of this endorsement and are not affected by any provision in any form or endorsement relating to or modifying business income coverage.

3. **Business Income**

   a. Business Income means the:

      (1) Net Income (Net Profit or Loss before income taxes) that would have been earned or incurred; and

      (2) Continuing normal operating expenses incurred, included payroll.

   b. The amount of Business Income loss will be determined based on consideration of the following, **b.(1)** through **b.(4)**. However, the amount of loss will be reduced to the extent that the reduction in the volume of business from the affected e-commerce activity is offset by an increase in the volume of business from other channels of commerce.

      (1) The Net Income of the business of e-commerce before the loss or damage or interruption in service or function occurred;

      (2) The likely Net Income of the business of e-commerce if no loss or damage or interruption in service had occurred, but not including any Net Income that would likely have been earned as a result of an increase in the volume of business due to favorable business conditions caused by the impact of the Covered Cause of Loss on customers or on other businesses;

(3) The operating expenses, including payroll, necessary to resume e-commerce activity with the same quality of service that existed before the loss or damage or interruption in service or function; and

(4) Other relevant sources of information, including your financial records and accounting procedures, bills, invoices and other vouchers, and deeds, liens and contracts.

4. **Extra Expense**

a. Extra Expense means necessary expenses you incur:

(1) During the period of coverage set forth in **C.2.** of this endorsement, that you would not have incurred if there had been no loss or damage or interruption in service or function, subject to **(2)** below;

(2) To avoid or minimize the suspension of e-commerce activity.

b. The amount of Extra Expense will be determined based on:

(1) Necessary expenses that exceed the normal operating expenses that would have been incurred in the course of e-commerce activity during the period of coverage if no loss or damage or interruption in service or function had occurred. We will deduct from the total of such expenses the salvage value that remains of any property bought for temporary use during the period of coverage, once e-commerce activity is resumed; and

(2) Necessary expenses that reduce the Business Income loss that otherwise would have been incurred during the period of coverage.

5. **Resumption Of E-Commerce Activity**

a. We will reduce the amount of your Business Income loss to the extent that you can resume e-commerce activity, in whole or in part, by using damaged or undamaged equipment or electronic data at the described premises or elsewhere.

b. We will reduce the amount of your Extra Expense loss to the extent that you can return e-commerce activity to normal and discontinue Extra Expense.

c. If you do not resume e-commerce activity, or do not do so as quickly as possible, we will pay based on the length of time it would have taken to resume such activity as quickly as possible.

D. **Section III – Causes Of Loss**

1. The provisions of this endorsement do not supersede or in any way affect the application of the Exclusion Of Certain Computer-Related Losses if such exclusion is endorsed to or otherwise made part of the Commercial Property Coverage Part. The exclusion addresses the inability of a computer system to correctly recognize, process, distinguish, interpret or accept one or more dates or times.

2. The Causes Of Loss – Special Form, by means of exclusions and limitations stated therein and all modifications stated in **D.2.** through **D.4.** of this endorsement, provides the Covered Causes of Loss applicable to Section **I** and Section **II** of this endorsement.

a. The Utility Services Exclusion does not apply with respect to power or communications supply services, provided that there is an interruption in utility service which is caused by a "specified cause of loss" as defined in the Causes Of Loss – Special Form.

b. The exclusion of artificially generated electrical current, including electrical arcing, does not apply.

c. The exclusion of mechanical breakdown does not apply with respect to the breakdown of your computers and their related equipment, but this exception is limited to the effect of such mechanical breakdown on electronic data.

d. The following exclusions are added. We will not pay for loss or damage caused by or resulting from:

(1) A virus, malicious code or similar instruction introduced into or enacted on a computer system (including electronic data) or a network to which it is connected, designed to damage or destroy any part of the system or disrupt its normal operation. But this exclusion does not apply if your e-commerce activity is conducted via a computer system that is equipped with virus-scanning or anti-virus software, or if the Anti-Virus Waiver is indicated as applicable in the Schedule. When this exclusion does not apply, then coverage also extends to shut-down of the computer system if the shut-down is undertaken in response to the detection of a virus or other incident by virus-scanning software, to mitigate or avoid attack, infiltration or infection of the system;

(2) Unauthorized viewing, copying or use of electronic data (or any proprietary or confidential information or intellectual property in any form) by any person, even if such activity is characterized as theft;

(3) Errors or omissions in programming or processing electronic data;

(4) Errors or deficiency in design, installation, maintenance, repair or modification of your computer system or any computer system or network to which your system is connected or on which your system depends (including electronic data);

(5) Manipulation of your computer system, including electronic data, by an employee, volunteer worker or contractor, for the purpose of diverting electronic data or causing fraudulent or illegal transfer of any property;

(6) Interruption in normal computer function or network service or function due to insufficient capacity to process transactions or to an overload of activity on the system or network. But this exclusion does not apply if such incident is caused by a virus, malicious code or similar instruction introduced into or enacted on a computer system or network;

(7) Unexplained or indeterminable failure, malfunction or slowdown of a computer system, including electronic data and the inability to access or properly manipulate the electronic data;

(8) Complete or substantial failure, disablement or shut-down of the entire Internet, regardless of the cause.

3. The Covered Causes of Loss include removal of electronic data from your system in an act of thievery by someone other than an employee, volunteer worker or contractor. Removal means that the electronic data is no longer in your computer system. Removal does not mean viewing, copying or use of electronic data (or any proprietary or confidential information or intellectual property in any form). Coverage for removal does not include transfer of funds, securities or similar property which is designated in the Coverage Form as Property Not Covered, even if eliminated from Property Not Covered by endorsement.

4. An endorsement(s) which adds or eliminates a Covered Cause of Loss from the Causes Of Loss – Special Form also applies to coverage under this endorsement, unless such other endorsement contains a specific provision to the contrary or is made inapplicable to this endorsement via its Schedule or the Declarations.

E. Section IV – Other Provisions

1. General

The coverage under this endorsement is limited as described, and does not extend to or modify any coverage provided under any other form or endorsement in this policy.

2. Claim-Related Fees

We will not pay for costs, fees or other expenses you incur in establishing the amount of your claim.

3. Coinsurance

The Coinsurance Condition does not apply to the coverage provided under this endorsement.

4. **Limit Of Insurance – Annual Aggregate**

   The applicable Limit of Insurance shown in the Schedule is the most we will pay under this endorsement, for the total of all losses covered under Sections I and II of this endorsement and sustained in any one policy year, regardless of the number of occurrences of loss or damage or the number of premises, locations or computer systems involved. If loss payment on the first occurrence does not exhaust the applicable Limit of Insurance, then the balance of that Limit is available for subsequent loss sustained in but not after that policy year. With respect to an occurrence which begins in one policy year and continues or results in additional loss or damage in a subsequent policy year(s), all loss or damage is deemed to be sustained in the policy year in which the occurrence began.

5. **Deductible**

   The Deductible shown in the Schedule applies to loss covered under Section I of this endorsement. We will not pay for loss in any one occurrence until the amount of loss exceeds the Deductible. We will then pay the amount of loss in excess of the Deductible, subject to the available limit of the Limit of Insurance.

6. **Coverage Territory**

   With respect to the coverage provided under this endorsement, the following is added to the Coverage Territory Condition:

   A computer virus or other incident that occurs on the Internet or other computer-based interactive communications network may originate anywhere in the world. However, even if an incident that originates outside the Coverage Territory results in coverage under this endorsement, the coverage is limited to the Coverage Territory (United States of America, its territories and possessions, and Puerto Rico and Canada) in accordance with the provisions of Paragraphs **B.1.** and **C.1.** of this endorsement.

IL 09 40 01 02

THIS ENDORSEMENT CHANGES THE POLICY. PLEASE READ IT CAREFULLY.

EXCLUSION OF TERRORISM (WITH LIMITED EXCEPTION) AND EXCLUSION OF WAR AND MILITARY ACTION

This endorsement modifies insurance provided under the following:

COMMERCIAL INLAND MARINE COVERAGE PART
COMMERCIAL PROPERTY COVERAGE PART
FARM COVERAGE PART
STANDARD PROPERTY POLICY

A. The War And Military Action Exclusion is replaced by the following Exclusion. With respect to any Coverage Form to which the War And Military Action Exclusion does not apply, that Exclusion is hereby added as follows.

WAR AND MILITARY ACTION EXCLUSION

We will not pay for loss or damage caused directly or indirectly by the following. Such loss or damage is excluded regardless of any other cause or event that contributes concurrently or in any sequence to the loss.

1. War, including undeclared or civil war; or

2. Warlike action by a military force, including action in hindering or defending against an actual or expected attack, by any government, sovereign or other authority using military personnel or other agents; or

3. Insurrection, rebellion, revolution, usurped power, or action taken by governmental authority in hindering or defending against any of these.

With respect to any action that comes within the terms of this exclusion and involves nuclear reaction or radiation, or radioactive contamination, this War And Military Action Exclusion supersedes the Nuclear Hazard Exclusion.

B. Regardless of the amount of damage and losses, the Terrorism Exclusion applies to any incident of terrorism:

1. That involves the use, release or escape of nuclear materials, or that directly or indirectly results in nuclear reaction or radiation or radioactive contamination; or

2. That is carried out by means of the dispersal or application of pathogenic or poisonous biological or chemical materials; or

3. In which pathogenic or poisonous biological or chemical materials are released, and it appears that one purpose of the terrorism was to release such materials.

Except as provided in **B.1., B.2.** or **B.3.** above, the Terrorism Exclusion will only apply to an incident of terrorism in which the total of insured damage to all types of property in the United States, its territories and possessions, Puerto Rico and Canada exceeds $25,000,000. In determining whether the $25,000,000 threshold is exceeded, we will include all insured damage sustained by property of all persons and entities affected by the terrorism and business interruption losses sustained by owners or occupants of the damaged property. For the purpose of this provision, insured damage means damage that is covered by any insurance plus damage that would be covered by any insurance but for the application of any terrorism exclusions. Multiple incidents of terrorism which occur within a 72-hour period and appear to be carried out in concert or to have a related purpose or common leadership will be deemed to be one incident.

The preceding paragraph describes the threshold used to measure the magnitude of an incident of terrorism and the circumstances in which the threshold will apply, for the purpose of determining whether the Terrorism Exclusion will apply to that incident. When the Terrorism Exclusion applies to an incident of terrorism, there is no coverage under this Coverage Part or Standard Property Policy.

In the event of any incident of terrorism that is not subject to the Terrorism Exclusion, coverage does not apply to any element of loss or damage that is otherwise excluded under this Coverage Part or Standard Property Policy.

TERRORISM EXCLUSION

We will not pay for loss or damage caused directly or indirectly by terrorism, including action in hindering or defending against an actual or expected incident of terrorism. Such loss or damage is excluded regardless of any other cause or event that contributes concurrently or in any sequence to the loss.

But if terrorism results in fire, we will pay for the loss or damage caused by that fire. However, this exception for fire applies only to direct loss or damage by fire to Covered Property. Therefore, for example, the exception does not apply to insurance provided under Business Income and/or Extra Expense coverage forms or endorsements which apply to those forms, or to the Legal Liability Coverage Form or the Leasehold Interest Coverage Form.

Terrorism means activities against persons, organizations or property of any nature:

1. That involve the following or preparation for the following:
   a. Use or threat of force or violence; or
   b. Commission or threat of a dangerous act; or
   c. Commission or threat of an act that interferes with or disrupts an electronic, communication, information, or mechanical system; and

2. When one or both of the following applies:
   a. The effect is to intimidate or coerce a government or the civilian population or any segment thereof, or to disrupt any segment of the economy; or
   b. It appears that the intent is to intimidate or coerce a government, or to further political, ideological, religious, social or economic objectives or to express (or express opposition to) a philosophy or ideology.

But with respect to any such activity that also comes within the terms of the War And Military Action Exclusion, that exclusion supersedes this Terrorism Exclusion.

In the event of an incident of terrorism that involves nuclear reaction or radiation, or radioactive contamination, this Terrorism Exclusion supersedes the Nuclear Hazard Exclusion.

APPENDIX D

COMMERCIAL GENERAL LIABILITY
CG 21 67 04 02

THIS ENDORSEMENT CHANGES THE POLICY. PLEASE READ IT CAREFULLY.

FUNGI OR BACTERIA EXCLUSION

This endorsement modifies insurance provided under the following:

COMMERCIAL GENERAL LIABILITY COVERAGE PART

A. The following exclusion is added to Paragraph **2.**, Exclusions of **Section I – Coverage A – Bodily Injury And Property Damage Liability:**

2. Exclusions

This insurance does not apply to:

Fungi or Bacteria

a. "Bodily injury" or "property damage" which would not have occurred, in whole or in part, but for the actual, alleged or threatened inhalation of, ingestion of, contact with, exposure to, existence of, or presence of, any "fungi" or bacteria on or within a building or structure, including its contents, regardless of whether any other cause, event, material or product contributed concurrently or in any sequence to such injury or damage.

b. Any loss, cost or expenses arising out of the abating, testing for, monitoring, cleaning up, removing, containing, treating, detoxifying, neutralizing, remediating or disposing of, or in any way responding to, or assessing the effects of, "fungi" or bacteria, by any insured or by any other person or entity.

This exclusion does not apply to any "fungi" or bacteria that are, are on, or are contained in, a good or product intended for consumption.

B. The following exclusion is added to Paragraph **2.**, Exclusions of **Section I – Coverage B – Personal And Advertising Injury Liability:**

2. Exclusions

This insurance does not apply to:

Fungi or Bacteria

a. "Personal and advertising injury" which would not have taken place, in whole or in part, but for the actual, alleged or threatened inhalation of, ingestion of, contact with, exposure to, existence of, or presence of any "fungi" or bacteria on or within a building or structure, including its contents, regardless of whether any other cause, event, material or product contributed concurrently or in any sequence to such injury.

b. Any loss, cost or expense arising out of the abating, testing for, monitoring, cleaning up, removing, containing, treating, detoxifying, neutralizing, remediating or disposing of, or in any way responding to, or assessing the effects of, "fungi" or bacteria, by any insured or by any other person or entity.

C. The following definition is added to the **Definitions** Section:

"Fungi" means any type or form of fungus, including mold or mildew and any mycotoxins, spores, scents or byproducts produced or released by fungi.

APPENDIX E

STATE FARM LIFE INSURANCE COMPANY

HOME OFFICE: ONE STATE FARM PLAZA, BLOOMINGTON, ILLINOIS 61710-0001

INSURED	John J Doe (Male)
AGE	35
POLICY NUMBER	LF-0000-0000
POLICY DATE	January 15, 1994
BASIC PLAN AMOUNT	$15,000
TOTAL INITIAL AMOUNT	$15,000

This policy is based on the application and the payment of premiums while the Insured lives. State Farm Life Insurance Company will pay the policy proceeds to the beneficiary when due proof of the Insured's death is received.

30-Day Right to Examine the Policy. This policy may be returned within 30 days of its receipt for a refund of all premiums paid. Return may be made to State Farm Life Insurance Company or one of its agents. If returned, this policy will be void from the policy date.

Read this policy with care. This is a legal contract between the Owner and State Farm Life Insurance Company.

Secretary

President

Registrar

BASIC PLAN DESCRIPTION
Whole life insurance. Insurance is payable when the Insured dies. Premiums are payable while the Insured is alive. The basic plan is eligible for annual dividends.

CONTENTS

The Application and any Riders and Endorsements follow page 12.

POLICY IDENTIFICATION

Insured	John J Doe (Male)	Age	35
Policy Number	LF-0000-0000	Basic Plan Amount	$15,000
Policy Date	January 15, 1994	Total Initial Amount	$15,000
Issue Date	January 15, 1994	Policy Class	1

SCHEDULE OF BENEFITS

Form	Description	Initial Amount	Benefit Period Ends	Annual Premium	Premiums Payable
94000	Basic Plan (Whole Life)	$15,000	With Life	$278.85	For Life

SCHEDULE OF PREMIUMS

Beginning	For periods of:	12 months	6 months	3 months	1 month
January 15, 1994		$278.85	$146.10	$75.10	$26.90

Initial payment of $278.85 will provide coverage to January 15, 1995.

SCHEDULE OF INSURANCE AND VALUES

- Insurance Amount - On Insured	Jan 15,	End of Policy Year	Guaranteed Values		
			Cash Value Dollars	Paid up Insurance Dollars	Extended Term Ins Yrs Days
$15,000	1994				
15,000	1995	1	.00	0	0 0
15,000	1996	2	34.80	180	0 268
15,000	1997	3	196.05	915	3 254
15,000	1998	4	362.85	1,620	6 34
15,000	1999	5	535.20	2,295	8 29
15,000	2000	6	712.95	2,940	9 276
15,000	2001	7	896.25	3,555	11 52
15,000	2002	8	1,085.10	4,140	12 95
15,000	2003	9	1,279.65	4,710	13 63
15,000	2004	10	1,480.05	5,235	13 338
15,000	2005	11	1,686.30	5,745	14 198
15,000	2006	12	1,898.55	6,240	15 17
15,000	2007	13	2,117.10	6,705	15 159
15,000	2008	14	2,342.10	7,155	15 266
15,000	2009	15	2,573.40	7,590	15 343
15,000	2010	16	2,810.85	7,995	16 30
15,000	2011	17	3,054.15	8,400	16 61
15,000	2012	18	3,303.00	8,775	16 75
15,000	2013	19	3,556.95	9,120	16 74
15,000	2014	20	3,815.55	9,465	16 57
15,000	2015	21	4,068.60	9,765	16 12
15,000	2016	22	4,325.85	10,050	15 318
15,000	2017	23	4,587.45	10,320	15 248
15,000	2018	24	4,853.55	10,590	15 166
15,000	2019	25	5,124.00	10,830	15 74
15,000	2020	26	5,398.20	11,070	14 339
15,000	2021	27	5,675.55	11,295	14 235
15,000	2022	28	5,955.15	11,520	14 125
15,000	2023	29	6,236.10	11,715	14 8
15,000	2024	30	6,517.95	11,910	13 259
15,000	2025	31	6,845.40	12,090	13 141
15,000	2026	32	7,083.45	12,270	13 17
15,000	2027	33	7,367.25	12,435	12 263
15,000	2028	34	7,652.10	12,585	12 139
15,000	2029	35	7,937.10	12,735	12 8
15,000	2030	36	8,221.50	12,885	11 249
15,000	2031	37	8,503.50	13,020	11 120
15,000	2032	38	8,781.00	13,140	10 350
15,000	2033	39	9,052.35	13,260	10 226
15,000	2034	40	9,316.35	13,380	10 95
15,000	2019	Age 60	5,124.00	10,830	15 74
15,000	2021	Age 62	5,675.55	11,295	14 235
15,000	2024	Age 65	6,517.95	11,910	13 259
15,000	2029	Age 70	7,937.10	12,735	12 8

Guaranteed values at the end of any policy year presume payment of all specified premiums to the end of such policy year. The interest rate for guaranteed values and single premiums is 5% a year. The mortality tables are as follows: For extended term insurance, the 1980 CET mortality table. For other guaranteed values and single premiums, the 1980 CSO mortality table.

DEFINITIONS

We, us, and our refer to State Farm Life Insurance Company.

You and your refer to the Owner.

Application. Includes any life insurance application, medical history, questionnaire, and other documents from you or any other person proposed for insurance which are made a part of this policy.

Basic Plan Amount. The amount of insurance on the Insured provided by the Basic Plan.

Benefit Period Ends. The coverage for the benefit extends to, but does not include, the policy anniversary in the year shown on page 3 under this heading.

Dividend Credits. Any dividend accumulations or any current dividend under dividend options 1 or 3.

Dollars. Any money we pay, or which is paid to us, must be in United States dollars.

Effective Date. Coverage starts on this date.

Initial Amount. The amount of coverage on the effective date of each benefit.

Insurance Amount. The amount of life insurance provided by the Basic Plan and any rider on the dates shown on page 4. If an accidental death benefit rider is part of this policy, such benefit rider amount will be in addition to the Insurance Amount.

Officer. The president, a vice president, the secretary, or an assistant secretary of State Farm Life Insurance Company.

Payee. On the Insured's death, the benefi-ciaries shown in the application, unless changed. If you cash surrender this policy, the persons that you have named. A payee can be other than a natural person only if we agree.

Policy Class. The underwriting classification of the Basic Plan.

Policy Date. The effective date of this policy.

Policy Month, Year, or Anniversary. A policy month, year, or anniversary is measured from the policy date.

Premiums Payable. Premiums are payable until the policy anniversary in the year shown on page 3 under this heading.

Proceeds. The sum of the insurance amounts payable under
  (1) the Basic Plan,
  (2) any paid-up additions, and
  (3) any rider on the Insured
plus any dividend credits, any dividend payable at the Insured's death, and any premium paid for part of the payment period beyond the Insured's death less any loan, any accrued loan interest, and any part of a premium due.

Request. A written request signed by the person making the request. Such request must be sent to and be in a form acceptable to us.

Rider. Any benefit, other than the Basic Plan, made a part of this policy.

Total Initial Amount. The amount of life insurance on the Insured provided by the Basic Plan and any rider on the policy date. If an accidental death benefit rider is part of this policy, such benefit rider amount will be in addition to the Total Initial Amount.

OWNERSHIP PROVISIONS

Owner. The Owner is as named in the application, unless changed. You may exercise any policy provision only by request and while the Insured is alive.

Change of Owner. You may change the ownership of this policy by sending us a request while the Insured is alive. We have the right to request this policy to make the change on it. The change will take effect the date you sign the request, but the change will not affect any action we have taken before we receive the request. A change of owner does not change the beneficiary designation.

PAYMENT OF BENEFITS PROVISIONS

Beneficiary Designation. This is as shown in the application, unless you have made a change. It includes the name of the beneficiary and the order and method of payment. If you name "estate" as a beneficiary, it means the executors or administrators of the last survivor of you and all beneficiaries. If you name "children" of a person as a beneficiary, only children born to or legally adopted by that person will be included.

We may rely on an affidavit as to the ages, names, and other facts about all beneficiaries. We will incur no liability if we act on such affidavit.

Change of Beneficiary Designation. You may make a change while the Insured is alive by sending us a request. The change will take effect the date the request is signed, but the change will not affect any action we have taken before we receive the request. We have the right to request your policy to make the change on it.

Order of Payment on the Insured's Death.
When the Insured dies, we will make payment in equal shares to the primary beneficiaries living when payment is made. If a primary dies after the first payment is made, we will pay that primary's unpaid share in equal shares to the other primaries living when payment is made. If the last primary dies, we will make payment in equal shares to the successor beneficiaries living when payment is made. If a successor dies while receiving payments, we will pay that successor's unpaid share in equal shares to the other successors living when payment is made. If, at any time, no primary or successor is alive, we will make a one sum payment in equal shares to the final

beneficiaries. If, at any time, no beneficiary is living, we will make a one sum payment to you, if living when payment is made. Otherwise, we will make a one sum payment to the estate of the last survivor of you and all beneficiaries. "When payment is made" means (1) the date that a periodic payment is due or (2) the date that a request is signed for a cash withdrawal or a one sum payment. You may change this order of payment by sending us a request while the Insured is alive.

Methods of Payment. We will pay the proceeds under the Interest method unless you choose another method. If the payee is other than a natural person, we will make payment under the One Sum method.

All payment intervals are measured from the date the policy is surrendered or from the date the Insured dies. No part of any payment can be assigned before the payment is made.

After the Insured's death, anyone who has the right to make a withdrawal may change the method of payment and may name a successor to their interest. The successor payee may be their estate.

Method 1 (Interest Method). We will pay interest at the end of each monthly interval. The interest rate will be at least 3½% a year. If chosen, we will pay interest at the end of 3, 6, or 12 month intervals. Withdrawals may be made at any time, but any withdrawal must be at least $500. We will pay interest to the date of withdrawal on the amount withdrawn.

PAYMENT OF BENEFITS PROVISIONS (CONTINUED)

Method 2 (Fixed Years Method). We will make equal payments at the end of each monthly interval for a fixed number of years. These payments include interest. The guaranteed interest rate is 3½% a year. The present value of any unpaid payments may be withdrawn at any time.

FIXED YEARS TABLE

Monthly payments that $1000 will provide for the number of years chosen. Payments for years not shown will be given, if requested.

Years	Payments	Years	Payments
1	$84.90	8	$11.93
2	43.18	9	10.78
3	29.28	10	9.86
4	22.33	15	7.12
5	18.17	20	5.77
6	15.39	25	4.98
7	13.41	30	4.46

Method 3 (Life Income Method). We will make equal payments at the end of each monthly interval as long as the payee is alive. We base the amount of each payment on the payee's age and sex at the start of the first monthly interval. We may require proof of the payee's age and sex. The payee may not withdraw the present value of the payments. If the payee dies during a certain period, we will continue the payments to the end of the certain period; or the successor payee may have the present value of any remaining payments paid in one sum.

LIFE INCOME TABLE

Monthly payments for life that $1000 will provide. Payments for ages not shown will be given, if requested.

Age Last Birthday	Life		Life with 10 Years Certain	
	Male	Female	Male	Female
50	$4.50	$4.15	$4.46	$4.13
55	4.91	4.48	4.84	4.45
60	5.47	4.92	5.34	4.86
65	6.25	5.53	5.98	5.41
70	7.34	6.38	6.76	6.12
75	8.85	7.64	7.62	7.01

Method 4 (Fixed Amount Method). We will make equal payments at the end of 1, 3, 6, or 12 month intervals. We will continue payments until the amount put under this method together with compound interest has been paid. The interest rate will be at least 3½% a year. The payment interval chosen must provide a total annual payment of at least $100 for each $1000 put under

this method. The unpaid balance may be withdrawn at any time.

Method 5 (Joint Life Income Method). We will make equal payments at the end of each monthly interval as long as at least one of the two payees is alive. We will base each payment on the age and sex of both payees at the start of the first monthly interval. We may require proof of the age and sex of each payee. The payees may not withdraw the present value of any payments.

JOINT LIFE INCOME TABLE

Monthly payments that $1000 will provide as long as at least one of the two payees is alive. Payments for age combinations not shown will be given, if requested.

Age Last Birthday Male	Female			
	60	65	70	75
60	$4.45	$4.69	$4.91	$5.10
65	4.60	4.92	5.24	5.55
70	4.71	5.11	5.56	6.02
75	4.79	5.26	5.83	6.47

Method 6 (One Sum Method). We will pay the cash surrender value or the proceeds in one sum. Interest at the rate of at least 3½% a year will be paid from the date of the Insured's death to the date of payment.

Method 7 (Other Method). Payment by any other method may be made if we agree.

Minimum Payment. If any payment, except the last, under a method of payment would be less than $100 per payee, we will pay the present value of any unpaid payments in one sum.

Basis of Computation for Payments. The monthly payments shown for methods 3 and 5 are guaranteed payments based on an interest rate of 3½% a year and the 1983 Table a, projected 10 years using Projection Scale G.

Any present values will be based on the interest rate used in determining the payments for the method.

Additional Amounts Payable. Each year we may apportion and pay dividends or additional interest under any method of payment.

PREMIUM PROVISIONS

Payment of Premiums. You may pay premiums at our Home Office, a regional office, or to one of our agents. We will give you a receipt signed by one of our officers, if you request one.

The first premium is due on the policy date. All other premiums are payable on or before their due dates. A due date is the first day of each payment period. Such period may be 1, 3, 6, or 12 months, starting on the same day of the month as the policy date. If a due date does not appear in a calendar month's days, the due date will be the last day of that same month. You may change the period on any due date by paying the premium for the new period, but you cannot change the period if premiums are being waived.

Grace Period. Except for the first premium, 31 days are allowed for the payment of a premium after its due date. During this time, the policy benefits continue.

Nonpayment of Premium. If any premium has not been paid by the end of its grace period, the Accumulations to Avoid Lapse and, if chosen, the Automatic Premium Loan provisions will apply. If neither of these provisions apply, this policy will lapse as of the due date of any unpaid premium. With such lapse, coverage ceases unless continued as extended term or paid-up insurance.

Accumulations to Avoid Lapse. If any premium has not been paid by the end of its grace period, any dividend accumulations will be used to pay all or part of that premium. The unpaid balance of that premium will be due the day after the end of the partial payment period. A new grace period will be allowed for the payment of this unpaid balance.

We will send you a notice if accumulations are used to pay part of any premium. We will not use accumulations if you choose an available guaranteed values provision within 90 days after the premium due date. Your choice will take effect as of the premium due date.

Automatic Premium Loan. This provision will apply if you chose it on the application or later request it. This provision will apply if there is enough loan value to pay the unpaid premium for the current payment period and there are no dividend accumulations. Any premium or part of any premium that is not paid by the end of its grace period will be paid by policy loan. Loan interest will be charged from the due date of the unpaid premium. You may cancel this provision at any time. We must receive your request to elect or cancel this provision before the policy lapses.

Reinstatement. If you have not surrendered this policy for cash, you may apply to reinstate it within 5 years after lapse. You must give us proof of the Insured's insurability that is satisfactory to us. You must pay all unpaid premiums with compound interest from their due dates. The interest rate is 6% a year. You must repay or restore any loan at the time of lapse with compound interest, based on the loan interest rates in effect during the period of lapse, to the date of reinstatement. The amount restored cannot be greater than the loan value on the date of reinstatement. Reinstatement will take effect on the date we approve the Insured's insurability.

Premium Adjustment When the Insured Dies. If the Insured dies during a grace period, any part of a premium due will be paid from the proceeds. Any premium paid for the payment period beyond the Insured's death will be part of the proceeds.

PRINTED IN U.S.A.

DIVIDEND PROVISIONS

Annual Dividends. We may apportion and pay dividends each year. Any such dividends will be paid only at the end of the policy year. There is no right to a partial or pro rated dividend prior to the end of the policy year. Such dividends will not be paid if all premiums due have not been paid or if the Basic Plan is in force as extended term insurance.

Dividend Options. You may choose to have your dividend used under one of these options:

1. **Premium Payment.** We will apply it toward payment of a premium then due.

2. **Paid-up Additions.** We will use it to buy a paid-up life insurance addition to the Basic Plan. Additions are bought at the single premium rate for the Insured's sex and attained age at that time. We may also pay dividends on these additions. You may surrender paid-up additions for their cash value at any time. If surrendered prior to the end of the policy year, there is no right to a partial or pro rated dividend. Additions in force at the Insured's death will be part of the proceeds.

3. **Dividend Accumulation.** We will hold it at interest. We will credit interest at a rate not less than 3½% a year. Such interest will be paid only at the end of the policy year. You may withdraw accumulations at any time. If withdrawn prior to the end of the policy year, there is no right to a partial or pro rated credit of such interest. Accumulations plus interest to the Insured's death will be part of the proceeds.

4. **Cash.** We will pay it to you in cash.

If you do not choose an option or the option you choose is not available, we will use option 2. You may request to change the option. The change will apply only to dividends paid after we receive the request.

Dividend When the Insured Dies. We may pay a dividend when the Insured dies. Such dividend will be a partial or pro rated amount based on the period from the start of a policy year to the Insured's death.

GUARANTEED VALUES PROVISIONS

Guaranteed Values. The guaranteed values shown on page 4 are based on your payment of all premiums when they are due. These values are as of the end of the policy years shown. They do not include the value of any paid-up additions and will be adjusted for any dividend credits or loans on this policy. We will furnish you with any values not shown if you request them.

Cash Value. The cash value is the sum of the cash values provided by the Basic Plan and any riders. Any cash values on the Basic Plan not shown on page 4 will be calculated as specified in the Basis of Computation provision. The cash value will be based on the date to which premiums have been paid. If any amount of premium is due and not paid, the cash value for the 90 days after that due date is the same as on such due date.

If the Basic Plan has been in force for more than 90 days as extended term or paid-up insurance, the cash value is the single premium for the insurance remaining. The cash value of such insurance will not decrease during the 31 days after a policy anniversary.

Cash Surrender. You may request surrender of this policy at any time. All coverage ceases on the date we receive the request or later date if you so request it. We will pay you the cash surrender value as of the date coverage ceases. We will pay you in one sum unless you choose another method of payment. The cash surrender value of this policy is its cash value plus the cash value of any paid-up additions plus any dividend credits less any loan and accrued loan interest. We may defer paying you the cash surrender value for up to 6 months after receiving your request.

GUARANTEED VALUES PROVISIONS (CONTINUED)

Extended Term and Paid-up Insurance. If this policy lapses and there is a cash surrender value, we will continue the Basic Plan as extended term or paid-up insurance. Extended term insurance is available only if this policy is in Policy Class 1 or 2. Extended term insurance will be used at the time of lapse unless you choose to continue this policy as paid-up insurance or surrender this policy. If this policy is in Policy Class 3, paid-up insurance will be used at the time of lapse unless you surrender this policy.

You may choose to have the Basic Plan continued as extended term insurance, if the policy is not in Policy Class 3, or as paid-up insurance. To be effective on the due date of any unpaid premium, your request and the policy must be received by us within 90 days after that date.

The amount of extended term insurance will be the Basic Plan Amount plus any paid-up additions plus any dividend credits less any loan and accrued loan interest. The amount will stay level. The extended term period will be determined by applying the cash surrender value as a single premium at the Insured's age and sex on the due date of any unpaid premium. If there is more value than needed to provide extended term insurance for life, we will promptly pay you the

excess in one sum. Extended term insurance has no loan value and will receive no dividends.

The amount of paid-up insurance will be determined by applying the cash value plus the cash value of any paid-up additions less any loan and accrued loan interest as a single premium at the Insured's age and sex on the due date of any unpaid premium. The amount will stay level. Paid-up insurance has loan value and may be eligible for dividends.

Basis of Computation. The guaranteed values in this policy are at least as large as those required by law in the state where it is delivered. The insurance authority there has a statement of how these values are determined.

The guaranteed values and single premiums are based on the Insured's age last birthday and sex. It is assumed that premiums are paid continuously and claims are paid immediately. The interest rate is shown on page 4. For guaranteed values and single premiums, the mortality tables that we use are shown on page 4. The cash values for the Basic Plan not shown on page 4 are equal to the reserves which are calculated using the Commissioners Reserve Valuation Method.

POLICY LOAN PROVISIONS

Loan. You may borrow against this policy unless the Basic Plan is in force as extended term insurance. This policy is the sole security for such loan. We may defer a loan for up to 6 months after receiving your request unless the loan will be used to pay premiums on this or other policies with us.

You may borrow the loan value less any existing loan, accrued interest, and unpaid premiums. If your unpaid loan plus accrued interest exceeds the loan value, we will send you a policy termination notice. Policy termination will occur 31 days after we have mailed that notice to you and to any assignee of record. If the loan value is exceeded during the policy year and this is the

result of a change in the policy loan interest rate, policy termination will occur at the later of the end of the policy year or 31 days after mailing of the notice. At policy termination, we will then pay you any dividend accumulations.

Loan Value. The loan value is the cash value of this policy and any paid-up additions on the next premium due date discounted at the loan interest rate from the next policy anniversary to the date of the loan. If premiums are no longer payable, the loan value will be the cash value of this policy and any paid-up additions on the next policy anniversary discounted at the loan interest rate from that policy anniversary to the date of the loan.

PRINTED IN U.S.A.

POLICY LOAN PROVISIONS (CONTINUED)

Loan Interest. The loan interest rate is an adjustable rate. We determine the rate each calendar quarter. Such rate will take effect the first day of January, April, July, and October after the date we determine it. Such rate will apply to any new and existing loan under this policy.

Any change in the rate will be subject to the following:
(1) The rate will be lowered to be equal to or less than the legal maximum rate if such legal maximum is ½% or more a year lower than our rate then in effect.
(2) The rate may be increased by at least ½% a year if the legal maximum is ½% or more a year higher than our rate then in effect. Such rate cannot exceed the legal maximum.

The legal maximum interest rate is the greater of:
(1) The Moody's Corporate Bond Yield Average - Monthly Average Corporates as published by Moody's Investors Service, Inc. for the calendar month ending 2 months prior to the date the loan interest rate is to go into effect, or 15% a year, if less, or
(2) The interest rate used to calculate cash values under this policy during the period for which the loan interest rate is being determined plus 1% a year or 15% a year, if

less.

If the Moody's Corporate Bond Yield Average - Monthly Average Corporates is no longer published, the rate used in its place will be set by law or regulation of the insurance supervisory official in the jurisdiction where this policy was delivered.

We will:
(1) Notify you of the initial loan interest rate at the time a loan is made, unless it is an automatic premium loan;
(2) Notify you of the initial loan interest rate as soon as practical after an automatic premium loan is made; and
(3) Give you advance notice of any increase in the loan interest rate, if you have a loan at that time.

We charge interest each day on any loan. Interest is due at the end of each policy year or at the time the loan is repaid, if earlier. Interest is added to the loan if not paid when due.

Loan Repayment. You may repay all or part of a loan at any time before the Insured dies or the policy is surrendered. Any loan that we deducted when the Basic Plan was placed on extended term or paid-up insurance may be repaid or restored only if the Basic Plan is reinstated.

GENERAL PROVISIONS

The Contract. The policy contains the Basic Plan, any amendments, endorsements, and riders, and a copy of the application. The policy is the entire contract. We have relied on the statements in the application in issuing this policy. We reserve the right to investigate the truth and completeness of those statements. In the absence of fraud, they are representations and not warranties. Only material misstatements in the application will be used to contest this policy or deny a claim.

Only an officer has the right to change this policy. No agent has the authority to change the policy or to waive any of its terms. All endorsements, amendments, or riders must be signed by an officer to be valid.

Assignment. You may assign this policy or any interest in it. We will recognize an assignment only if it is in writing and filed with us. We are not responsible for the validity or effect of any assignment. An assignment may limit the interest of any beneficiary.

GENERAL PROVISIONS (CONTINUED)

Error in Age or Sex. If the Insured's date of birth or sex is not as stated in the application, we will adjust each benefit on the Insured to that which the premium paid would have bought at the correct age and sex. Such adjustment will be based on the premium rates in effect on the issue date of the benefit.

Incontestability. Except for nonpayment of premiums, we will not contest the Basic Plan after it has been in force during the Insured's lifetime for 2 years from the issue date of the policy. Each rider has its own incontestability provision.

Limited Death Benefit. If the Insured dies by suicide while sane or by self-destruction while insane within 2 years from the issue date of the policy, the Basic Plan Amount will not be paid. The proceeds in this case will be limited to the premiums paid on the Basic Plan less any loan, accrued loan interest, and any dividends paid on the Basic Plan. Each rider has its own limited death benefit provision.

APPENDIX F

613

STATE FARM LIFE INSURANCE COMPANY

HOME OFFICE: ONE STATE FARM PLAZA, BLOOMINGTON, ILLINOIS 61710-0001

INSURED	John J Doe
	(Male)
AGE	35
POLICY NUMBER	LF-0000-0000
POLICY DATE	January 15, 1994
INITIAL BASIC AMOUNT	$50,000

This policy is based on the application and the payment of premiums, as specified in the policy. State Farm Life Insurance Company will pay the proceeds to the beneficiary when due proof is received that the Insured died before this policy terminated. If the Insured is alive on the maturity date, the cash surrender value on the maturity date will be paid to the Owner and this policy will terminate.

30-Day Right to Examine the Policy. This policy may be returned within 30 days of its receipt for a refund of all premiums paid. Return may be made to State Farm Life Insurance Company or one of its agents. If returned, this policy will be void from the policy date.

Read this policy with care. This is a legal contract between the Owner and State Farm Life Insurance Company.

Secretary

President

Registrar

BASIC PLAN DESCRIPTION

Flexible premium adjustable life insurance. A death benefit is payable if the Insured dies before the maturity date. The cash surrender value is payable if the Insured is alive on the maturity date. Coverage may terminate prior to the maturity date. Flexible premiums are payable while the Insured is alive until the maturity date. The basic plan is eligible for annual dividends.

CONTENTS

The Application and any Riders and Endorsements follow page 14.

POLICY IDENTIFICATION

Insured	John J Doe (Male)		Age	35
Policy Number	LF-0000-0000		Initial Basic Amount	$50,000
Policy Date	January 15, 1994			
Issue Date	January 15, 1994			

SCHEDULE OF BENEFITS

Universal Life Basic Plan:
   Death Benefit Option 1 (Basic Amount includes the account value)
   Basic Amount (Standard rate class - male non-tobacco): $50,000

SCHEDULE OF PREMIUMS

The initial premium is $456.00.
Planned premiums are included in the schedule shown below. The payment period for the planned premiums is 12 months starting on January 15, 1995.
A premium expense charge of 5% is deducted from each premium paid.

| Beginning: | Total Premiums
For Policy Year |
| January 15, 1994 | $ 456.00 |

MONTHLY DEDUCTIONS

The deduction date is the 15th of each month.

Maximum monthly cost of insurance rates are shown on page 4. The cost of insurance is deductible while the policy is in force.
The monthly expense charge is $5.00.

NOTE: Insurance may terminate if premiums paid are not sufficient to continue the insurance.

SCHEDULE OF SURRENDER CHARGES

Beginning Policy Year	Policy Month	Surrender Charge	Beginning Policy Year	Policy Month	Surrender Charge
1	1	$ 21.50	2	1	$258.00
1	2	43.00	3	1	258.00
1	3	64.50	4	1	225.75
1	4	86.00	5	1	193.50
1	5	107.50	6	1	161.25
1	6	129.00	7	1	129.00
1	7	150.50	8	1	96.75
1	8	172.00	9	1	64.50
1	9	193.50	10	1	32.25
1	10	215.00	11	1	0.00
1	11	236.50			
1	12	258.00			

COST OF INSURANCE RATES AND MONTHLY CHARGES

Maximum Monthly Cost of Insurance Rates
Per $1000

(Standard rate class - male non-tobacco)

Age	Rate	Age	Rate	Age	Rate	Age	Rate
35	.1810	51	.6381	67	2.6886	83	11.9024
36	.1935	52	.6968	68	2.9344	84	13.0775
37	.2077	53	.7640	69	3.2063	85	14.3247
38	.2236	54	.8380	70	3.5147	86	15.6263
39	.2420	55	.9180	71	3.8670	87	16.9762
40	.2629	56	1.0030	72	4.2723	88	18.3754
41	.2854	57	1.0932	73	4.7329	89	19.8343
42	.3097	58	1.1894	74	5.2401	90	21.3788
43	.3365	59	1.2942	75	5.7847	91	23.0518
44	.3649	60	1.4109	76	6.3595	92	24.9371
45	.3950	61	1.5430	77	6.9577	93	27.2442
46	.4277	62	1.6923	78	7.5852	94	30.4453
47	.4620	63	1.8597	79	8.2619	95	35.4922
48	.4989	64	2.0454	80	9.0119	96	44.5151
49	.5399	65	2.2459	81	9.8582	97	62.8314
50	.5852	66	2.4605	82	10.8223	98	73.0824
						99 & over	83.3333

DEFINITIONS

We, us, and **our** refer to State Farm Life Insurance Company.

You and **your** refer to the Owner.

Application. Includes any life insurance application, any application for change in the policy, medical history, questionnaire, and other documents from you or any other person proposed for insurance which are made a part of this policy.

Basic Amount. The Initial Basic Amount plus any increases less any decreases.

Basic Amount Mininum. On or after the policy anniversary when the Insured is age 55, the Basic Amount cannot be less than $25,000. Otherwise, the Basic Amount cannot be less than $50,000.

Benefit Period Ends. For any rider, the policy anniversary in the year shown under this heading on page 3 is the date the rider terminates.

Deduction Date. The policy date and each monthly anniversary of the policy date.

Dollars. Any money we pay, or which is paid to us, must be in United States dollars.

Effective Date. Coverage starts on this date.

Initial Basic Amount. The amount of coverage on the Insured provided by the Basic Plan on the policy date.

Insurance Amount. The amount of coverage on the effective date of each rider shown on page 3.

Maturity Date. The policy anniversary when the Insured is age 100.

Monthly Charge Deductible. A monthly charge for any rider is deducted as part of the monthly deduction until the policy anniversary in the year shown on page 3.

Officer. The president, a vice president, the secretary, or an assistant secretary of State Farm Life Insurance Company.

Payee. On the Insured's death, the beneficiaries shown in the application, unless changed. If you cash surrender this policy or this policy matures, the persons that you have named. A payee can be other than a natural person only if we agree.

Planned Premium. The premium amount that you have chosen. This amount is shown on page 3 for the payment period that you have chosen.

Policy Date. The effective date of this policy.

Policy Month, Year, or Anniversary. A policy month, year, or anniversary is measured from the policy date.

Proceeds. The amounts payable on the death of the Insured.

Rate Class. The underwriting class of the person insured. A rate class will be determined for the Initial Basic Amount and each increase in the Basic Amount.

Request. A written request signed by the person making the request. Such request must be sent to and be in a form acceptable to us.

Rider. Any benefit, other than the Basic Plan, made a part of this policy.

OWNERSHIP PROVISIONS

Owner. The Owner is as named in the application, unless changed. You may exercise any policy provision only by request and while the Insured is alive.

Change of Owner. You may change the ownership of this policy by sending us a request while the Insured is alive. We have the right to request this policy to make the change on it. The change will take effect the date you sign the request, but the change will not affect any action we have taken before we receive the request. A change of owner does not change the beneficiary designation.

DEATH BENEFIT AND DEATH BENEFIT OPTIONS PROVISIONS

Death Benefit. The amount of death benefit is an amount of insurance based on the death benefit option plus any insurance amounts payable under any riders on the Insured and the part of the cost of insurance for the part of the policy month beyond the Insured's death less any loan, accrued loan interest, and, if the Insured dies during the grace period, the monthly deductions from the start of the grace period.

Death Benefit Options. There are two death benefit options. If you do not choose an option, we will use option 2. The account value on the date of death is used in determining the amount of insurance.

Option 1. The amount of insurance will be the greater of (1) the Basic Amount plus 95% of any premium received since the last deduction date plus interest earned on that amount of premium or (2) a percentage of the account value. Such percentage is based on the Insured's age at the start of the current policy year.

Option 2. The amount of insurance will be the greater of (1) the Basic Amount plus the account value or (2) a percentage of the account value. Such percentage is based on the Insured's age at the start of the current policy year.

Percentage of Account Value Table			
Age	Percentage	Age	Percentage
0-40	250%	61	128%
41	243%	62	126%
42	236%	63	124%
43	229%	64	122%
44	222%	65	120%
45	215%	66	119%
46	209%	67	118%
47	203%	68	117%
48	197%	69	116%
49	191%	70	115%
50	185%	71	113%
51	178%	72	111%
52	171%	73	109%
53	164%	74	107%
54	157%	75-90	105%
55	150%	91	104%
56	146%	92	103%
57	142%	93	102%
58	138%	94	101%
59	134%	95 & up	100%
60	130%		

Change in Basic Amount. You may request a change in the Basic Amount once each policy year. The minimum amount of change is $25,000 for an increase and $10,000 for a decrease. For any change in Basic Amount, we will send you a revised page 3 to be placed with this policy.

If you request an increase, an application must be completed, evidence of insurability satisfactory to us must be furnished, and there must be enough cash surrender value to make a monthly deduction which includes the cost of insurance for the increase. No increases will be allowed after the policy anniversary when the Insured is age 80. The revised page 3 will show the amount of the increase and its effective date.

If you request a decrease, the Basic Amount remaining after the decrease cannot be less than the Basic Amount Minimum. We reserve the right to not accept a request for a decrease in the Basic Amount if such decrease could result in this policy being disqualified as a life insurance contract under any section of the United States Internal Revenue Code, as amended from time to time. Any decrease will first be used to reduce the most recent increase. Then, the next most recent increases will be reduced. Finally, the Initial Basic Amount will be reduced. The revised page 3 will show the amount of decrease and its effective date. The decrease will take effect on the date we receive the request.

Change of Death Benefit Option. You may request a change of death benefit option once each policy year. For a change in death benefit option, we will send you a revised page 3 to be placed with this policy. The revised page will show the effective date of the change.

If the change is to option 1, the Basic Amount will be increased by the account value on the effective date of the increase. We reserve the right to not accept a request for a change to option 1 if such change could result in this policy being disqualified as a life insurance contract under any section of the United States Internal Revenue Code, as amended from time to time.

If the change is to option 2, the Basic Amount will be decreased by the account value on the effective date of the decrease.

PAYMENT OF BENEFITS PROVISIONS

Beneficiary Designation. This is as shown in the application, unless you have made a change. It includes the name of the beneficiary and the order and method of payment. If you name "estate" as a beneficiary, it means the executors or administrators of the last survivor of you and all beneficiaries. If you name "children" of a person as a beneficiary, only children born to or legally adopted by that person will be included.

We may rely on an affidavit as to the ages, names, and other facts about all beneficiaries. We will incur no liability if we act on such affidavit.

Change of Beneficiary Designation. You may make a change while the Insured is alive by sending us a request. The change will take effect the date the request is signed, but the change will not affect any action we have taken before we receive the request. We have the right to request your policy to make the change on it.

Order of Payment on the Insured's Death. When the Insured dies, we will make payment in equal shares to the primary beneficiaries living when payment is made. If a primary dies after the first payment is made, we will pay that primary's unpaid share in equal shares to the other primaries living when payment is made. If the last primary dies, we will make payment in equal shares to the successor beneficiaries living when payment is made. If a successor dies while receiving payments, we will pay that successor's unpaid share in equal shares to the other successors living when payment is made. If, at any time, no primary or successor is alive, we will make a one sum payment in equal shares to the final beneficiaries. If, at any time, no beneficiary is living, we will make a one sum payment to you, if living when payment is made. Otherwise, we will make a one sum payment to the estate of the last survivor of you and all beneficiaries. "When payment is made" means (1) the date that a periodic payment is due or (2) the date that a request is signed for a cash withdrawal or a one sum payment. You may change this order of payment by sending us a request while the In-

sured is alive.

Methods of Payment. We will pay the proceeds under the Interest method unless you choose another method. If the payee is other than a natural person, we will make payment under the One Sum method.

All payment intervals are measured from the date the policy is surrendered or from the date the Insured dies. No part of any payment can be assigned before the payment is made.

After the Insured's death, anyone who has the right to make a withdrawal may change the method of payment and may name a successor to their interest. The successor payee may be their estate.

Method 1 (Interest Method). We will pay interest at the end of each monthly interval. The interest rate will be at least 3½% a year. If chosen, we will pay interest at the end of 3, 6, or 12 month intervals. Withdrawals may be made at any time, but any withdrawal must be at least $500. We will pay interest to the date of withdrawal on the amount withdrawn.

Method 2 (Fixed Years Method). We will make equal payments at the end of each monthly interval for a fixed number of years. These payments include interest. The guaranteed interest rate is 3½% a year. The present value of any unpaid payments may be withdrawn at any time.

FIXED YEARS TABLE
Monthly payments that $1000 will provide for the number of years chosen. Payments for years not shown will be given, if requested.

Years	Payments	Years	Payments
1	$84.90	8	$11.93
2	43.18	9	10.78
3	29.28	10	9.86
4	22.33	15	7.12
5	18.17	20	5.77
6	15.39	25	4.98
7	13.41	30	4.46

PAYMENT OF BENEFITS PROVISIONS (CONTINUED)

Method 3 (Life Income Method). We will make equal payments at the end of each monthly interval as long as the payee is alive. We base the amount of each payment on the payee's age and sex at the start of the first monthly interval. We may require proof of the payee's age and sex. The payee may not withdraw the present value of the payments. If the payee dies during a certain period, we will continue the payments to the end of the certain period; or the successor payee may have the present value of any remaining payments paid in one sum.

LIFE INCOME TABLE
Monthly payments for life that $1000 will provide. Payments for ages not shown will be given, if requested.

Age Last Birthday	Life		Life with 10 Years Certain	
	Male	Female	Male	Female
50	$4.50	$4.15	$4.46	$4.13
55	4.91	4.48	4.84	4.45
60	5.47	4.92	5.34	4.86
65	6.25	5.53	5.98	5.41
70	7.34	6.38	6.76	6.12
75	8.85	7.64	7.62	7.01

Method 4(Fixed Amount Method). We will make equal payments at the end of 1, 3, 6, or 12 month intervals. We will continue payments until the amount put under this method together with compound interest has been paid. The interest rate will be at least 3½% a year. The payment interval chosen must provide a total annual payment of at least $100 for each $1000 put under this method. The unpaid balance may be withdrawn at any time.

Method 5 (Joint Life Income Method). We will make equal payments at the end of each monthly interval as long as at least one of the two payees is alive. We will base each payment on the age and sex of both payees at the start of the first monthly interval. We may require proof of the age and sex of each payee. The payees may not withdraw the present value of any payments.

JOINT LIFE INCOME TABLE
Monthly payments that $1000 will provide as long as at least one of the two payees is alive. Payments for age combinations not shown will be given, if requested.

Age Last Birthday Male	Female			
	60	65	70	75
60	$4.45	$4.69	$4.91	$5.10
65	4.60	4.92	5.24	5.55
70	4.71	5.11	5.56	6.02
75	4.79	5.26	5.83	6.47

Method 6 (One Sum Method). We will pay the cash surrender value or the proceeds in one sum. Interest at the rate of at least 3½% a year will be paid from the date of the Insured's death to the date of payment.

Method 7 (Other Method). Payment by any other method may be made if we agree.

Minimum Payment. If any payment, except the last, under a method of payment would be less than $100 per payee, we will pay the present value of any unpaid payments in one sum.

Basis of Computation for Payments. The monthly payments shown for methods 3 and 5 are guaranteed payments based on an interest rate of 3½% a year and the 1983 Table a, projected 10 years using Projection Scale G.

Any present values will be based on the interest rate used in determining the payments for the method.

Additional Amounts Payable. Each year we may apportion and pay dividends or additional interest under any method of payment.

PREMIUM PROVISIONS

Payment of Premiums.   You may pay premiums at our Home Office, a regional office, or to one of our agents. We will give you a receipt signed by one of our officers, if you request one.

The initial premium is shown on page 3 and is due on the policy date. All other premiums may be paid in any amount and at any time if:
(1)   the amount is at least $25 and
(2)   in a policy year, the total premiums, excluding the initial premium, do not exceed without our consent, the total Planned Premiums for a policy year.

Premium Limitations.   We reserve the right to refund any premium paid if such premium amount would be in excess of the guideline premium limitation as defined by Section 7702, Internal Revenue Code of 1988 (or as later amended). No expense charge will be deducted from the refunded premium.

Grace Period.   If, on any deduction date, the cash surrender value is not enough to cover the monthly deduction, the policy will stay in force until the end of the grace period. The grace period is 61 days and starts on that deduction date. We will mail a notice at least 31 days prior to the end of the grace period to you and to any assignee of record. A premium large enough to cover the monthly deductions for the grace period and any increase in the surrender charges must be paid before the end of the grace period; otherwise, this policy will lapse and terminate without value.

Reinstatement.   If the policy is terminated at the end of the grace period, you may apply to reinstate it within 5 years after lapse. You must give us proof of the Insured's insurability that is satisfactory to us. You must pay premiums (1) to keep the policy in force for 2 months and (2) to pay the monthly deductions for the grace period. Reinstatement will take effect on the date we approve the application for reinstatement.

GUARANTEED VALUES PROVISIONS

Account Value.   The account value on the policy date is 95% of the initial premium less the monthly deduction for the first policy month.

The account value on any deduction date after the policy date is the account value on the prior deduction date:
(1)   plus 95% of any premiums received since the prior deduction date,
(2)   less the deduction for the cost of insurance for any increase in Basic Amount and the monthly charges for any riders that became effective since the prior deduction date,
(3)   less any withdrawals since the prior deduction date,
(4)   less the current monthly deduction,
(5)   plus any dividend paid and added to the account value on the current deduction date, and
(6)   plus any interest accrued since the prior deduction date.

The account value on any other date is the account value on the prior deduction date:
(1)   plus 95% of any premiums received since the prior deduction date,
(2)   less the deduction for the cost of insurance for any increase in Basic Amount and the monthly charges for any riders that became effective since the prior deduction date,
(3)   less any withdrawals since the prior deduction date, and
(4)   plus any interest accrued since the prior deduction date.

Monthly Deduction.   This deduction is made each month, whether or not premiums are paid, as long as the cash surrender value is enough to cover that monthly deduction. Each deduction includes:
(1)   the cost of insurance,
(2)   the monthly charges for any riders, and
(3)   the monthly expense charge.

GUARANTEED VALUES PROVISIONS (CONTINUED)

Cost of Insurance. This cost is calculated each month. The cost is determined separately for the Initial Basic Amount and each increase in Basic Amount.

The cost of insurance is the monthly cost of insurance times the difference between (1) and (2), where:
  (1) is the amount of insurance on the deduction date at the start of the month divided by 1.0032737, and
  (2) is the account value on the deduction date at the start of the month before the cost of insurance and the monthly charge for any waiver of monthly deduction benefit rider are deducted.

Until the account value exceeds the Initial Basic Amount, the account value is part of the Initial Basic Amount. Once the account value exceeds that amount, if there have been any increases in Basic Amount, the excess will be part of the increases in order in which the increases occurred.

Monthly Cost of Insurance Rates. These rates for each policy year are based on the Insured's age on the policy anniversary, sex, and applicable rate class. A rate class will be determined for the Initial Basic Amount and for each increase. The rates shown on page 4 are the maximum monthly cost of insurance rates for the Initial Basic Amount. Maximum monthly cost of insurance rates will be provided for each increase in the Basic Amount. We can charge rates lower than those shown. Such rates can be adjusted for projected changes in mortality but cannot exceed the maximum monthly cost of insurance rates. Such adjustments cannot be made more than once a calendar year.

Interest. An interest rate of at least 4% a year will be applied to the account value. The rate applied to the amount of account value up to the amount of any loan may differ from the rate

applied to the account value in excess of the amount of any loan. We will determine these rates at least once a year.

Cash Surrender Value. You may request surrender of this policy at any time. This policy will terminate on the date we receive the request or later date if you so request it. We will pay you the cash surrender value as of the date coverage ceases plus the monthly deduction for the part of the policy month beyond that date. We will pay you in one sum unless you choose another method of payment. The cash surrender value of this policy is its account value less any surrender charge and any loan and accrued loan interest. The cash surrender value on the maturity date will be the account value on that date less any loan and accrued loan interest. The cash surrender value will not be less than zero. If this policy is surrendered within 31 days after a policy anniversary, the cash surrender value will not decrease within that period except for any loans or withdrawals. We may defer paying you the cash surrender value for up to 6 months after receiving your request.

Withdrawals. You may request to withdraw part of the account value while this policy is in force. No more than 4 withdrawals can be made in any policy year. Any withdrawal must be at least $500 and must be less than the cash surrender value. We may defer paying you a withdrawal for up to 6 months unless the withdrawal is to pay premiums on other policies with us.

If death benefit option 1 is in effect, then the Basic Amount will be reduced by the withdrawal, effective with the date of the withdrawal; however, no withdrawal can be made which will reduce the Basic Amount to less than $25,000. The reduction will be made as if a decrease in the Basic Amount had been requested.

624 APPENDIX F

PRINTED IN U.S.A.

```
┌─────────────────────────────────────────────────────┐
│     GUARANTEED VALUES PROVISIONS (CONTINUED)          │
└─────────────────────────────────────────────────────┘
```

Surrender Charge. The schedule of surrender charges is shown on page 4. For each increase in Basic Amount, additional surrender charges will apply. A revised page 4 will show a revised schedule of surrender charges which includes those additional charges.

Upon reinstatement, the surrender charges will be adjusted for any surrender charge deducted at the time of lapse. A revised page 4 will show a schedule of the adjusted surrender charges.

A schedule of surrender charges is determined separately for the Initial Basic Amount and for each increase in Basic Amount. A schedule is determined using a Base Surrender Charge and covers 120 policy months following the policy date or the effective date of an increase in Basic Amount. For the Initial Basic Amount, use the surrender charge at the Insured's age on the policy date. For each increase in Basic Amount, use the surrender charge at the Insured's age on the policy anniversary on or first preceding the effective date of that increase. Take that surrender charge times the Initial Basic Amount, or the amount of the increase, if applicable, divided by 1,000. Then, divide that result by 12 to determine the surrender charge that will apply for that amount of insurance for the first policy month after its effective date. The surrender charge increases by that amount for each of the next 11 policy months. The surrender charge then remains level for the next 24 policy months. The surrender charge decreases after 36 policy months and then decreases by that same amount after each successive 12 policy months. The amount of each decrease is equal to the surrender charge in effect at the end of 36 policy months divided by 8.

Basis of Computation. The guaranteed values in this policy are at least as large as those required by law in the state where it is delivered based on the Commissioners 1980 Standard Ordinary Mortality Table with an interest rate of 4% a year. The insurance authority there has a statement of how these values are determined.

The guaranteed values and maximum cost of insurance rates are based on the Insured's age last birthday and sex. The interest rate is 4% a year. The Commissioners 1980 Standard Ordinary Mortality Table is used. Modifications are made for rate classes other than standard.

BASE SURRENDER CHARGE
The base surrender charge is for each $1,000 of Initial Basic Amount or amount of increase in Basic Amount.

Age	Base Surrender Charge	Age	Base Surrender Charge
0-19	$ 1.20	45	$9.72
20	1.32	46	10.32
21	1.44	47	10.80
22	1.56	48	11.40
23	1.80	49	11.88
24	2.04	50	12.72
25	2.40	51	13.44
26	2.64	52	14.04
27	2.88	53	14.88
28	3.12	54	15.36
29	3.36	55	16.02
30	3.60	56	16.20
31	3.84	57	16.68
32	4.20	58	17.16
33	4.68	59	17.40
34	4.68	60	18.00
35	5.16	61	18.36
38	5.40	62	18.48
37	5.64	63	18.60
38	6.36	64	18.60
39	6.72	65	19.40
40	7.38	66	19.56
41	7.44	67	19.80
42	8.16	68	20.40
43	8.76	69	20.64
44	9.12	70-80	21.00

POLICY LOAN PROVISIONS

Loan. You may borrow against this policy. This policy is the sole security for such loan. We may defer a loan for up to 6 months after receiving your request unless the loan will be used to pay premiums on other policies with us.

You may borrow the loan value less any existing loan and accrued interest and monthly deductions for the next 2 months. If your unpaid loan plus accrued interest exceeds the loan value on the monthly deduction date, the Grace Period provision will apply.

Loan Value. The loan value is the account value of this policy less the surrender charge.

Loan Interest. Interest accrues and is payable each day at a rate of 8% a year. Any interest not paid is added to the loan on each policy anniversary.

Loan Repayment. You may repay all or part of a loan at any time before the Insured dies or the policy is surrendered or terminated.

GENERAL PROVISIONS

The Contract. The policy contains the Basic Plan, any amendments, endorsements, and riders, and a copy of the application. A copy of any application for a change to this policy will be sent to you to be placed with the policy. Such applications become part of this policy. The policy is the entire contract. We have relied on the statements in the application in issuing this policy. We reserve the right to investigate the truth and completeness of those statements. In the absence of fraud, they are representations and not warranties. Only material misstatements in the application will be used to contest this policy or deny a claim.

Only an officer has the right to change this policy. No agent has the authority to change the policy or to waive any of its terms. All endorsements, amendments, and riders must be signed by an officer to be valid.

Annual Report. Each year, we will send you a report. This report will show:
  (1) the account value, the cash surrender value, any loan and accrued loan interest, and the amount of the death benefit as of the date of the report and
  (2) any premiums paid, any deductions made, and any withdrawals made since the last report.

Projection of Benefits and Values. You may request a projection of death benefits, account

values, and cash surrender values. We may charge a reasonable fee not to exceed $25 for providing this projection.

Annual Dividends. We do not expect to pay dividends on this policy; however, we may apportion and pay dividends each year. Any such dividends will be paid only at the end of the policy year. There is no right to a partial or pro rated dividend prior to the end of the policy year.

Dividend Options. You may choose to have your dividend used under one of these options:

  1. **Cash.** We will pay it to you in cash.

  2. **Addition to Account Value.** We will add it to the account value at the end of the policy year.

If you do not choose an option or the option you choose is not available, we will use option 2. You may request to change the option. The change will apply only to dividends paid after we receive the request.

Assignment. You may assign this policy or any interest in it. We will recognize an assignment only if it is in writing and filed with us. We are not responsible for the validity or effect of any assignment. An assignment may limit the interest of any beneficiary.

GENERAL PROVISIONS (CONTINUED)

Error in Age or Sex. If the Insured's date of birth or sex is not as stated in the application, we will adjust each benefit on the Insured to the benefit payable had the Insured's age and sex been stated correctly. Such adjustment will be based on the ratio of the correct monthly deduction for the most recent deduction date for that benefit to the monthly deduction that was made. For the Basic Plan, the adjustment is made to the amount of insurance less the account value.

Incontestability. We will not contest the Basic Plan after it has been in force during the Insured's lifetime for 2 years from the issue date of the policy. We will not contest any increase in Basic Amount or reinstatement after it has been in force during the lifetime of the Insured for 2 years from the effective date of the increase in Basic Amount or reinstatement. We will not contest an increase due to a change to Death Benefit Option 1. Any contest of any increase in Basic Amount or reinstatement will be limited to material misstatements contained in the application for such increase or reinstatement.

Each rider has its own incontestability provision.

Limited Death Benefit. If the Insured dies by suicide while sane or by self-destruction while insane within 2 years from the issue date of the policy, the Basic Amount will not be paid. The proceeds in this case will be limited to the premiums paid on the Basic Plan less any loan, accrued loan interest, any withdrawals from the account value, and any dividends paid on the Basic Plan.

Any increase in Basic Amount or amount reinstated will not be paid if the Insured's death results from suicide while sane or self-destruction while insane within 2 years from the effective date of such increase or reinstatement. The proceeds of the increase will be limited to the monthly deductions for the increase. This does not apply to an increase due to a change to Death Benefit Option 1. The proceeds of a reinstated policy will be limited to the premiums paid on the Basic Plan since reinstatement less any loan, accrued loan interest, any withdrawals from the account value, and any dividends paid on the Basic Plan.

Each rider has its own limited death benefit provision.

INDEX